Holiday Law

WITHDRAWN

HOLIDAY LAW

By

DAVID GRANT,
*Vantage Insurance Visiting Professor of Travel Law
at Leeds Metropolitan University,
Emeritus Professor, Northumbria University,
Editor, Travel Law Quarterly*

&

STEPHEN MASON M.A., (CANTAB.),
*Partner in Travlaw LLP, Solicitors,
Holder of Higher Courts (Civil Proceedings)
Qualification*

SWEET & MAXWELL

 THOMSON REUTERS

Published in 2012 by Sweet & Maxwell,
100 Avenue Road, London NW3 3PF
part of Thomson Reuters (Professional) UK Limited
(Registered in England and Wales, Company No 1679046.
Registered Office and address for service:
Aldgate House, 33 Aldgate High Street, London EC3N 1DL)

First edition 1995
Second edition 1998
Third edition 2003
Fourth edition 2007
Fifth edition 2012

Typest by YHT Ltd, London
Printed in Great Britain by CPI Group (UK) Ltd, Croydon, CR0 4YY

For further information on our products and services, visit
www.sweetandmaxwell.co.uk

No natural forests were destroyed to make this product;
only farmed timber was used and replanted

A CIP catalogue record
for this book is available
from the British Library

ISBN 978–0–414–04612–2

Thomson Reuters and the Thomson Reuters logo are trademarks of
Thomson Reuters.
Sweet & Maxwell ® is a registered trademark of Thomson Reuters
(Professional) UK Limited.

Preface

Welcome to the fifth edition of Holiday Law. Seventeen years have elapsed since the first edition in 1995, and obviously the whole world has changed since those far off days when the Package Travel Regulations were still a novelty. But what is much more startling is the pace of change since our last edition, a mere five years ago. This book represents a major rewrite since last time. A small selection of what's new, and the chapters where they are substantially dealt with, would include: the introduction of flight-plus by the 2012 ATOL Regulations (Ch.12); the repeal and replacement of old favourites the Trade Descriptions Act and Consumer Protection Act (Chs 17 and 18); very important case law such as *Milner v Carnival* on damages (Ch.10), *Parker v Tui*, *Moore v Hotelplan* and *Harrison v Jagged Globe* on excursions (Ch.5), and the Travel Republic cases plus *Titshall v Qwerty* on that perennial favourite, what is a package? (Ch.2) The *Medhotels* case impacts on the very basis of agency arrangements in the travel industry (Ch.11), whilst *Gouldbourn v Balkan* progresses the debate about the applicability of "local standards" (Ch.5). The ECJ has been very busy explaining the workings of the Denied Boarding Regulation in the *Wallentin-Hermann* and the *Sturgeon* cases, to name but two (Ch.13). And on top of that, the Ministry of Justice has been pressing for the introduction of the Jackson reforms, which will have a major impact on the conduct of injury and illness claims against the travel industry, when introduced, supposedly in April 2013 (Ch.15).

All this has happened against a background of world events which keeps the travel industry in the headlines, from the closure of air space by an unpronounceable Icelandic volcano to the sinking of the Costa Concordia, via civil unrest in Egypt and much else besides; and of a world in which people use mobile phone apps to research and book travel, as much as they do brochures.

There is one dog which has failed to bark in the night (or indeed at any time!), however; in the Preface to our 2007 edition we said "the EU is working to revise the Package Travel Directive ... although the slow speed at which the EU moves leaves us a little anxious as to whether this will be completed in time for our fifth edition!". Well, we got that bit right, if nothing else. (Compare the appeal court in the *Travel Republic* case, one of whose reasons in May 2010 for not referring the case to the ECJ was that there was soon to be a new Directive!) The latest estimate is that it will be 2015 before we see a new Directive in force.

The authors dedicate this book to their families, who continue to support and inspire them.

Foreword

Since the first edition of *Holiday Law* was published in 1995, there have been significant developments in this whole area of law. Each new edition brings with it a series of new cases and other developments, which shows the fluidity and dynamic pace of change in the jurisprudence affecting the travel industry. Considering that the industry is itself changing rapidly, this is no real surprise.

However, the challenge for any book of this nature is to attempt both to capture the changes, and make them comprehensible for the average reader—whether they be the student trying to grapple with the intricacies of the subject matter for the first time, or the old hand who has been dealing with the subject for many years.

It is no small credit to the authors, David Grant and Stephen Mason, that they manage successfully to meet that challenge. Their long and collective experience, in trying to explain this subject clearly, whether to students or to Court of Appeal Judges has undoubtedly helped enormously in achieving that objective. As a result, this fifth edition is every bit as compelling and essential reading as that first edition was in 1995.

The developments since the last edition include significant decisions by the Court of Appeal and European Court of Justice on key aspects of holiday law, and publication will coincide with a whole new regime of financial protection regulation in the UK, but sadly not, as yet, any of the much needed changes to the Package Travel Directive to reflect the changes in the market place.

The only way to understand clearly the whole picture is by works such as these, and I am sure that this fifth edition will be as well received as all its predecessors, and will form an essential part of the library of all those interested or involved in travel law at any level.

Andy Cooper
Director of Government and External Affairs
Thomas Cook Group

Acknowledgements

The authors and publishers would like to thank the following for permission to reproduce materials from publications in which they have copyright.

Code of Conduct of ABTA The Travel Association. Reproduced with the permission of ABTA.

While every care has been taken to establish and acknowledge copyright, and contact the copyright owners, the publishers tender their apologies for any accidental infringement. They would be pleased to come to a suitable arrangement with the rightful owners in each case.

Acknowledgments

Contents

CONTENTS

CONTENTS

CONTENTS

Table of Cases

TABLE OF CASES

TABLE OF CASES

TABLE OF CASES

TABLE OF CASES

TABLE OF CASES

TABLE OF CASES

TABLE OF CASES

TABLE OF CASES

TABLE OF CASES

TABLE OF CASES

Table of Statutes

Table of Statutory Instruments

Table of Treaties

Table of European Legislation

TABLE OF EUROPEAN LEGISLATION

Introduction

Previous editions of this book were devoted almost exclusively to the law relating to package holiday contracts. The reason for this was that the majority of people in this country chose to go abroad on holiday in that way. But this situation has changed radically. In recent years the sales of package holidays has first stagnated and is now slowly declining, but, thanks to the advent of the internet and the rise of the no frills airlines, the number of independent travellers has increased exponentially. Just how radically the holiday market has changed is illustrated by the tables on pp.4 and 5 which show figures compiled by the Civil Aviation Authority and the International Passenger Survey demonstrating the relative decline in package holidaymakers and the consequential loss in overall consumer protection and insolvency protection—in particular due to the decline of the Air Travel Organisers' Licensing scheme (ATOL). As a consequence, the focus of this book has also changed. While we still devote a major part of the book to an examination of package holidays, more emphasis is placed this time on the rights of the independent traveller. We will look in particular at carriage by air where Regulation (EC) 261/2004 has had a big impact and is continuing to cause controversy, and also to the purchasing of accommodation abroad. Thus, throughout the book there will be references not only to package travel contracts but also more generally to travel contracts—a term which encompasses not simply package holiday contracts but also any other travel related contract: with airlines, cruise lines, ferries, accommodation providers, etc.

In due course we shall be examining these contracts in some detail but before we do that it is necessary to do two other things. First, we will explain the scheme of the book, and secondly, we will endeavour to place travel contracts in context. The first is easily done. The second involves an examination of the travel industry and a look at some of the agencies that regulate the industry. It also involves a brief look at what can be broadly called the English legal system—to provide a general background into which to fit the specific rules relating to travel contracts.

THE SCHEME OF THE BOOK

After this introductory chapter, the book falls conveniently into a number of sections. First, to give it due prominence, we look at the definition of a package holiday. Secondly, we look at the law of contract in relation to package holidays in particular, but also in relation to other travel contracts in general. The approach we have taken here is to adopt the conventional scheme used in most major works on contract: How is a contract made? What is in it? Who is a party to it? What can go wrong? How can it be brought to an end? What are the remedies for breach of the contract? In adopting this scheme, however, we have chosen to give prominence only to those aspects of contract law that we believe are of practical relevance or of particular importance to travel contracts. So, for instance, purists may notice that we devote very little space to an examination of the rules relating to consideration and none to assignment. It is not that we have overlooked these topics it is simply that we do not think that they are of sufficient practical importance to devote space to them in a book of this kind.

Thirdly, we look at several important aspects of travel law that do not fit neatly into a contract law/criminal law classification but which are essential for a complete picture of the law in this area. In this part of the book we look at the legal position of travel agents; the protection offered consumers through the bonding and security system established by the Package Travel Regulations; a brief look at the practical aspects of litigation in travel cases; an examination of those aspects of air and sea law of particular interest to holidaymakers; an examination of accommodation contracts made over the internet; and finally, of interest to those increasing numbers of independent travellers who have no tour operator to sue, how to pursue an action against a foreign supplier.

Finally, we spend time looking at the regulation of travel contracts by the criminal law. This is a form of regulation which has grown considerably in recent years. In previous editions we devoted considerable space looking at both the Trade Descriptions Act 1968 and the Consumer Protection Act 1987 but both these pieces of legislation have now been superseded by the Consumer Protection from Unfair Trading Regulations 2008, so we have a new chapter on those Regulations which are of general application but clearly apply to the travel industry as well. In addition, the Package Travel Regulations also created criminal offences applying specifically to package holidays. Both pieces of legislation have a major impact on the way travel services are marketed and sold. No one with an interest in travel law can afford to be ignorant of this legislation.

THE TRAVEL INDUSTRY

The Size and Structure of the Industry

The Size of the Holiday Market

In 2010, UK residents made just under 55 million visits abroad, of which 36 million were holiday visits. Out of this figure of 36 million, inclusive tours accounted for 14 million, or 39 per cent of the total number of holiday visits (down 7 per cent as a proportion over the decade since 2000). Air inclusive tours accounted for 11.5 million and 32 per cent respectively. Figures like these clearly demonstrate the present healthy state of the "outgoing" holiday industry and the extent to which, even today, it is still dominated by the package holiday. However, all the recent growth has been in independent travel rather than package travel.

The reasons why the inclusive tour in general and the air inclusive tour in particular reached such a position of pre-eminence are complex, but they can be attributed to a number of factors. These include the fact that the components of a "typical" British holiday abroad—sea, sun and sand—are most readily available only at those destinations which are most easily accessible by air.

INTRODUCTION

Other factors include the continuing technical advances in aeroplane design which have combined to increase capacity and reduce costs; the convenience of buying a ready-packaged holiday rather than putting it together oneself (although this is of declining importance); the gradual relaxation of the regulations governing airlines and charter flights; a corresponding relaxation in currency regulations and passport formalities; and action by successive governments and by the industry itself to protect the position of holidaymakers caught out by the financial collapse of a tour operator. *Jarvis* (p.4) mentions the importance of the credit card and the increased use of air-conditioning as other factors promoting the growth of travel. Nor should the success of the tour operators in promoting themselves and their products be forgotten. The names of such companies as TUI (including Thomson and First Choice), Thomas Cook (including MyTravel and Airtours), Cosmos and Kuoni are every bit as familiar and reassuring to consumers as other well known high street brands. In common with other successful consumer-oriented companies, they produce standard products at attractive prices, thereby setting the standards for the rest of the industry. In so doing, they have acquired the trust and confidence of the public upon which their growth and success has been based.

It should also be borne in mind that since the war higher levels of disposable income have contributed to a socio-economic climate where average and below average income earners not only have the earning capacity to purchase an annual holiday abroad, but have come to regard it as a product to be enjoyed as a matter of course—not as a luxury. It is simply another aspect of consumption to be ranked alongside a smartphone, a tablet computer and a 3D television, although during economic hard times it has become conventional wisdom that a holiday is one of the last items consumers will dispense with.

Although there is an understandable tendency to think of the package holiday as being two weeks sitting by a hotel swimming pool in Majorca eating chips with paella and drinking cheap Bacardi there is in fact a remarkable diversity of packages available. The mass summer market, concentrating mainly on the Mediterranean basin, may correspond to the caricature above, but tour operators rely heavily on other markets for a proportion of their income. Not surprisingly, one of the major alternatives to the summer sun paradigm is merely a variation on the same theme—namely the winter sun programmes offered by most large operators. Combined with the skiing packages also offered, these holidays contribute to overheads during the thinner winter months.

Still in the mass market are those holidays which appeal to particular age groups, e.g. holidays offered by "Club 18–30" or Saga. Long haul holidays to the Far East, Africa, Australia and Florida have now become commonplace. Cruising is also a type of holiday that is increasingly popular, casting off its rather staid reputation and appealing to a younger age group.

Smaller operators tend to be specialists, catering for the portion of the market that is unprofitable for large scale operators—often offering tailor-made holidays to more exotic and out of the way destinations. It is in this segment of the market that the theme holidays and special interest holidays are to be found—concentrating mainly on sport and adventure but also encompassing a bewildering variety of hobbies and interests, from astronomy to yoga, and taking in arts festivals, carnivals, history and literature along the way. A significant part of the market outside the mainstream is school travel, which has its own specialist

Table 1. Visits abroad by UK residents.

Year	All visits	Holidays	ITs	Air ITs
1980	17.5	11.7	6.2	4.8
1981	19.0	13.1	6.8	5.1
1982	20.6	14.2	7.7	5.8
1983	20.9	14.5	8.0	5.7
1984	22.0	15.3	9.0	6.9
1985	21.6	14.8	8.5	6.4
1986	24.9	17.8	10.6	8.3
1987	27.4	19.7	11.9	9.7
1988	28.8	20.7	12.6	10.3
1989	30.8	21.7	12.5	10.0
1990	31.2	21.3	11.4	8.8
1991	30.5	20.6	10.6	7.9
1993	35.8	24.3	13.3	10.6
1994	39.9	27.3	15.1	12.2
1995	41.9	28.1	15.3	12.2
1996	43.1	27.4	14.1	11.5
1997	45.9	29.1	15.4	12.2
1998	50.8	32.3	17.4	13.8
1999	53.9	35	19	15
2000	56.7	36.6	20	16.4
2001	58.2	38.7	20.6	16.9
2002	59.4	39.9	20.6	16.7
2003	61.4	41.2	19.5	16.4
2004	64.2	42.9	19.8	16.5
2005	66.4	44.2	19	16
2006	69.5	45.2	18.9	15.6
2007	69.5	45.4	18.7	15.5
2008	69	45.5	17.9	14.7
2009	58.6	38.5	14.5	11.9
2010	54.9	36.1	14	11.5

Source: ONS International Passenger Survey; CAA.

operators—although they are not immune from the problems suffered by other tour operators as evidenced by the insolvency of Skiing Europe in 2011.

Many of the factors which have led to the growth of the package holiday industry have also fuelled the growth in independent travel, but two factors in particular—the advent of the internet and the arrival of the "no frills" airlines—have really driven this growth. Travel search engines enabling users to discover the vast array of options available and to seek out the best prices have revolutionised travel in the 21st century. Now it is perfectly possible for the tourist to sit at home with his or her PC and book not only the flights but also the accommodation, and pay for it all by credit card without stirring from their chair. It can be confidently predicted that this trend towards more independent

INTRODUCTION

Table 2. Number of holidaymakers who travel by air who are protected against insolvency by the ATOL scheme.

Year	Holiday	Visiting friends or Relatives	All leisure	ATOL protected	ATOL share of All leisure
1997	19,937	4,094	24,031	23,491	98%
1998	22,945	4,449	27,394	25,043	91%
1999	25,282	4,974	30,256	26,359	87%
2000	27,901	5,643	33,544	28,016	84%
2001	29,842	6,046	35,888	29,083	81%
2002	30,472	6,293	36,765	27,908	76%
2003	32,644	6,939	39,583	27,578	70%
2004	34,363	8,179	42,542	28,144	66%
2005	36,001	9,113	45,114	27,218	60%
2006	37,007	10,245	47,252	25,741	54%
2007	36,877	10,402	47,279	23,276	49%
2008	36,740	10,678	47,418	21,850	46%
2009	30,458	9,592	40,050	19,638	49%

Source: ONS International Passenger Survey; CAA.

travel at the expense of package travel will probably accelerate rapidly in the next few years, and there is a danger that the package holiday, with all the protections it brings, will become an endangered species. The reason for this is that conventional tour operators, again thanks to the internet, will be able to sell travel arrangements that do not amount to packages much more easily than previously and are incentivised to do so by the costs and liabilities associated with the package travel legal regime. Movement is not, however, all in one direction—many internet travel agencies such as Expedia and Travelocity do offer packages over the internet and the airline easyJet has just announced its intention to sell packages, and "flight-plus" will be added to consumer protection (see Ch.12).

Tour Operators and Travel Agents

In the pre-internet days of "bricks and mortar" travel companies it was possible to draw a reasonably clear distinction between tour operators and travel agents. Tour operators were companies that put together package holidays, published a hard copy brochure and sold their products to consumers—either through a travel agency or direct to the public. The legal distinction was that tour operators did business as principals selling their product by means of a contract with the consumer, whereas travel agents sold the product of others and had no contractual relationship with the consumer for the sale of the travel product (although there might be other contractual and tortious relationships—see Ch.11). This legal distinction remains, and is of crucial importance, but with the advent of the internet we find that travel companies cannot be so easily categorised as either tour operators or travel agents—principals or agents. All the major players can be seen as acting as both tour operator and travel agent depending upon the circumstances. So, as indicated above, it is possible to visit the Expedia website and find that packages put together by other companies are being sold, alongside single travel products such as flights and accommodation. In these instances the company is acting as agent for other suppliers, but there is also the facility for the consumer to put together their own "holiday" where Expedia accept liability as "organisers" of "packages".

Despite this blurring of the distinction, one rough and ready way of determining which companies are the leading tour operators is to look at the figures published by the CAA for the number of passengers carried by the leading ATOL licence holders. These figures reflect both the number of air package holidays that are sold and also the number of "flight-only" sales which are covered by the ATOL scheme. The latest figures available can be found in Table 3.

Table 3. Passengers carried by the leading ATOL licence holders.

Rank	Licence Holder	ATOL Number	Passengers Licensed
1	TUI UK Ltd	2524	4,361,203
2	Thomas Cook Tour Operations Ltd	1179	4,037,900
3	Gold Medal Travel Group PLC	2916	684,050
4	Expedia, Inc	5788	489,021
5	Thomas Cook Retail Ltd	0020	433,533
6	Virgin Holidays Ltd	2358	399,529
7	Travelworld Vacations Ltd	4108	399,500
8	Trailfinders Ltd	1458	367,732
9	Avro PLC	1939	350,001
10	Cosmos Holidays plc	2275	300,001
11	The Airline Seat Company Ltd	3971	257,216
12	LM Travel Services Ltd	3970	226,963
13	Jet2Holidays Ltd	9618	217,047
14	Carnival PLC	6294	207,083
15	Co-op Group Travel 1 Ltd	6613	206,500
16	Flight Centre (UK) Ltd	4267	198,600
17	Southall Travel Ltd	5553	190,000
18	The Mileage Company Ltd	4562	174,956
19	Acromas Holidays Ltd	0308	174,412
20	The Global Travel Group Ltd	3973	172,398

From these figures, it can be seen that the market is dominated by TUI and Thomas Cook, who have several hundred brands between them, including Thomson, First Choice, Airtours, Neilson, Sunworld, Hayes and Jarvis, Club 18–30, Citalia, Crystal and Simply Travel. These two companies, together with the other eight companies making up the top 10 ATOL holders, account for over 60 per cent of ATOL passengers. These are the mass market operators whose brochures are to be found in virtually every travel agency in the country, and whose brands are every bit as familiar as Heinz, Ford, Coca-Cola and Persil. At the other end of the scale are the "independent" tour operators, who exist by selling only a few thousand holidays a year. Indeed, there are some independents who make a comfortable living on the basis of selling only a few hundred holidays a year. Whereas most larger operators belong to ABTA and, in general, sell their holidays through travel agencies, the independent operators often do not belong to any trade association and sell their holidays direct to the public.

In much the same way as a handful of companies dominate the tour operating market, travel high street retailing demonstrates similar levels of concentration. Of the major travel agencies, TUI have almost 1,000 branches, and Thomas Cook have 800, but their merger with the Co-operative gives them over 1,300 branches. In addition to these major chains which are vertically linked to tour operators, there are consortia of independent travel agents, such as Worldchoice with almost 800 outlets, and Advantage also with 800 outlets (*Mintel*, Travel Agents—UK, December 2010).

At the other end of the travel agency market are the independents—one or two agency companies—which exist not by competing with the vertically integrated companies on price, but by offering a more personal service with tailor-made travel arrangements that the larger companies find too inconvenient to deal with.

There used to be a medium-sized category falling somewhere in-between the vertically integrated companies and the independents, but these chains of regional travel agencies are now an endangered species and have virtually ceased to exist. The few remaining examples include Dawson & Sanderson and Hays Travel, both based in the North-East.

A relatively new phenomenon is the growth of home-based agencies—such as Travel Counsellors, with over 700 agents in the UK operating from home—able to sell both individual travel products and dynamically packaged holidays. Hays Travel also has a home worker section.

Vertical Integration in the Package Travel Industry

Since the last edition of this book in 2007, there have been two large scale mergers in the travel industry. The four largest travel companies are now two. Thomson, part of the TUI group, merged with First Choice, and Thomas merged with MyTravel (formerly Airtours). Each of these groups own their own airlines and chains of travel agents as well as a number of bed wholesalers or "bed-banks". In the past, increasing integration provoked charges of anti-competitive practices (see *Holiday Which?* January 1996, p.13) and the matter was referred to the Monopolies and Mergers Commission (MMC) which reported in 1997 (Cm. 3813). The MMC did not find any major market distortions caused by vertical integration and the recommendations it made did not fundamentally affect the structure of the industry. (See "The Monopolies and Mergers Commission Report on Foreign Package Holidays" Sarah Mercer [1998] I.T.L.J. 6 for a brief account on the report.) The most obvious result of the investigation was The Foreign Package Holidays (Tour Operators and Travel Agents) Order 2001 (SI 2001/2581) which regulates the use of insurance as an inducement in the sale of holidays and outlaws attempts by tour operators to insist on "most favoured customer" status with travel agents.

The Airline Industry

Figures from the CAA show that in 2010 there were 209 million terminal passengers at UK airports. This is down from a figure of 216 million in 2009 and is indicative of the downturn in the economy (Source: CAA, Aviation Trends).

The industry can be divided into three broad categories. First, there are the full service, traditional scheduled airlines providing both short haul and long haul routes. This category includes UK registered airlines, British Airways, Virgin Atlantic and British Midland. However, now that European air transport has been de-regulated it also includes KLM/Air France as a significant presence flying from many UK airports using its hub airports in Amsterdam and Paris as stepping off points for longer journeys. Secondly, there are the "no frills" airlines which include easyJet and Ryanair as well as Flybe and Jet2. The essence of these carriers is that they provide cheap flights on a point to point basis with none of the frills that the full service airlines offer, such as interlining, meals, business class seats, etc. Finally, there are the charter airlines catering for the clients of tour operators on package holidays or those who want "flight-only" to holiday destinations. They include Thomsonfly (formerly Britannia), First Choice Airways and Thomas Cook Airlines. Monarch Airlines, traditionally a charter airline, has recently announced a change of direction to become a scheduled airline. As far as independent travellers are concerned, one of the few distinguishing features between the various types of airline, other than quality, is that charter airlines have tended to sell their flights through their tour operating arms and are thus covered by an ATOL, whereas scheduled airlines tend to sell their flights directly to the public and do not need an ATOL. Even this, however, is changing, as Thomas Cook and TUI have recently decided that sales of flights direct to the public will not be covered by an ATOL.

Contractual Relationships Within the Travel Industry

The Package Holiday Contract

The focus of this book is the legal relationship that exists between the traveller and the travel suppliers—including airlines and hotels but, in particular, the package holiday contract between the consumer and the tour operator. However, in order to properly understand this latter relationship it is useful to have a picture of the network of contracts and relationships that lie behind or alongside this main contract and which are responsible for creating many of the problems that bedevil the relationship between tour operator and consumer.

Positioned at the centre of the complex of contracts with a pivotal role is the tour operator. Not only does the tour operator contract with the consumer, but also with the suppliers of the elements that go to make up the package—the hotelkeepers, the airlines and the transfer companies and ground operators. (Although known as "suppliers", this is a term which serves only to deceive. In reality they are no more than what would be known as subcontractors in other industries.) It is this role of assembler of other contractors' products that commercially is so convenient to the consumer, but legally has proved so inconvenient. On the one hand, historically at least, it has permitted the tour operator to reduce his liability on the grounds that defects in the package were not his fault

INTRODUCTION

but the fault of an independent contractor (see *Wall v Silver Wing Surface Arrangements* Unreported 1981, which is looked at in detail later; cf. Grant & Urbanowicz "Tour Operators, Package Holiday Contracts and Strict Liability" [2001] J.B.L. 253.) On the other hand, it has created a barrier to the consumer effectively suing the supplier in his own right. If the only contract that the consumer has is with the tour operator, then to bring an action against a supplier, say for serious quality defects at an hotel or even for personal injury, will mean bringing an action in tort rather than contract—in a foreign jurisdiction. This is not a prospect that appeals to many consumers, and even if such an action is pursued the chances of success are limited (see M.A. Jones "Tour Operators and the Unfair Contract Terms Act" [1983] *Gazette* 2964; but see also Ch.8 on Privity and the new Contracts (Rights of Third Parties) Act 1999 and Ch.19).

It would be a mistake, however, to think that the disadvantages of the package holiday contract are all one-way. It is certainly the case that as the lot of the consumer has been improved by the Package Travel Regulations the tour operator can be found complaining that he is "piggy-in-the-middle", caught between consumers on the one hand with strong legally protected rights, and commercially stronger suppliers on the other hand (airlines in particular) which impose terms on them that leave them having to foot the bill when things go wrong. For instance, in the charter agreement between the airline and the tour operator, the airline may reserve the right to change timings and schedules and the tour operator may be left with no recourse against the airline while at the same time having to pay substantial compensation to consumers for flight changes. (See Briggs "Tour Operators and Airlines—Between a Rock and a Hard Place" [1994] T.L.J. 44.) Hotel safety is another issue that causes concern to tour operators. In cases of hotel fires, swimming pool drownings, food poisoning and other injuries which occur abroad, the tour operator is liable to the consumer under the Package Travel Regulations for the defaults of their suppliers. However, the domestic safety legislation that these suppliers are subject to may not impose particularly stringent standards—leaving the tour operator to carry the can (see *Wilson v Best Travel* [1993] 1 All E.R. 353; and Lakin "Hotel Safety: Can Things Only Get Better?" [2002] I.T.L.J. 189). It is partly for this reason that the major tour operators are "unbundling" their packages so that they can avoid these liabilities. It was also one of the drivers behind the litigation between ABTA and the CAA and Travel Republic over the definition of a package which many envisaged would enmesh not just tour operators but also travel agents in its liability and bonding regimes (see Ch.2 for an account of this). This fear was not realised, but the new "flight-plus" regime goes some way to increasing the liability of travel agents.

The Travel Agency Relationship

In Ch.11, we grapple with the problem of the precise legal status of the travel agent, but here it is only necessary to point out that when he acts as agent for the tour operator, then he clearly has the capacity to influence (and not always benignly) the content of the contract between the consumer and the tour operator. When not acting as agent for the tour operator, he may either be acting as agent for the consumer or, if he has no contractual relationship with the consumer, he may be liable to him in tort for any misstatements that he makes.

As indicated above, the travel agent may, on occasion, be regarded as a tour operator if he puts packages together. Plans by the CAA to extend ATOL protection to "flight-plus" arrangements will have the effect of pulling many of the arrangements made by travel agents into the insolvency protection scheme offered by ATOL (see Ch.12 on Insolvency and Security).

The Airline/Passenger Relationship

When the traveller contracts directly with the airline this relationship is governed partly by the law of contract and partly by international convention. In the event of personal injury or death, delay to passengers or baggage or loss or damage to baggage, the relationship is governed by the Montreal Convention. Apart from that, the law of contract applies. However, these rules are now supplemented by European legislation, Regulation (EC) 261/2004 Establishing Common Rules on Compensation and Assistance to Passengers in the Event of Denied Boarding and of Cancellation or Long Delay of Flights, which, as its name suggests, is designed to give rights to passengers who suffer long delays or cancellation or who are denied boarding. This legislation has proved very unpopular with airlines, particularly after the problems caused by the eruption of the Eyjafjallajökull volcano in Iceland, and has been the subject of a number of cases in the ECJ. All this is examined in some detail in Ch.13 on Air and Sea Travel.

Additionally, there is the situation where consumers buy "flight-only" arrangements on charter airlines from tour operators or on scheduled airlines through what are known as "consolidators". In each of these situations the arrangements are covered by the ATOL scheme because the seats are not being bought directly from the airline—so the consumer will have the benefit of financial protection. However this gives rise to a more complex legal relationship between the parties. We believe that there will be a *contractual* relationship between the consumer and the tour operator/consolidator (who deal with each other as principals) for the provision of the flight and a *statutory* relationship between the consumer and the airline based upon the provisions of the Montreal Convention. Thus the consumer can sue the tour operator/consolidator for breach of contract and the airline for breach of the Montreal Convention. This was tested in the County Court in *Blumer v Gold Medal* [2008] C.L.Y. 650 in a case where the airline was bankrupt but the ticket had been supplied by a consolidator. The consumer was awarded damages against the consolidator for deficiencies in the flight.

The Hotel/Guest Relationship

Where the guest is accommodated at an hotel booked for him/her as part of a package there is no direct contractual relationship between the guest and the hotel and, therefore, in the event of dispute between the hotel and the guest, any action must be brought in tort rather than contract—although of course the guest will be able to sue the tour operator under the Package Travel Regulations for any defect in the package contract.

However, for guests who book their foreign hotels direct, invariably over the internet, they may have a contract direct with the hotel, which, in theory at least, entitles them to sue the hotel for any defects in the accommodation. We say "in theory" because there are difficult problems of jurisdiction and choice of law to be overcome before it becomes practical to bring an action. We also say the guest "may" have a contract with the hotel because often these contracts are made via bed wholesalers or bedbanks who may be acting merely as agents or maybe as principals in their own rights. Again, these issues are dealt with in full later in Ch.14.

The Business Environment

Many of the problems arising from package holidays can be laid at the feet of the unstable environment in which travel companies have to operate. A number of features can be identified that make up this difficult environment. First, there is the problem of fluctuating exchange rates which often result in the imposition of unwelcome surcharges and which can radically affect the marketing of certain destinations. One only has to look at the popularity of a destination such as Florida and measure it against the pound/dollar exchange rate to see the effects currency fluctuations can have. Secondly, there are the problems associated with political unrest and terrorism. Destinations such as former Yugoslavia, China, Sri Lanka, South Africa, Indonesia, North Africa, the Middle East and many others have all been afflicted by political problems that have had a detrimental effect on their tourism industry. Fuel prices, which are affected by both the first two factors, are another important element in the environment that travel companies inhabit. Finally, there is the weather itself. Severe weather conditions, either at home or at the holiday destination, can seriously disrupt the best planned schedules. (See Hannigan "Reservations Cancelled" [1980] *Annals of Tourism Research* VII(3), 366, for a fuller account of the tour operating environment.)

Trade Associations and Regulatory Bodies

ABTA

It is not possible to have a complete grasp of package holiday law in this country without understanding the role of the Association of British Travel Agents (ABTA; *www.abta.com*). ABTA is the trade association which, confusingly, represents both travel agents and tour operators. Although formed in the 1950s it grew to prominence in the 1960s thanks largely to the introduction of "stabiliser". Stabiliser is, or was, a clause in ABTA's articles of association, introduced in 1966, that provided that ABTA tour operators could only sell their products through ABTA travel agencies and that ABTA travel agencies could only sell ABTA tour operators' products.

Stabiliser created a cartel within the travel industry. The effect of this was quite simple. Membership of the cartel was a licence to trade whereas exclusion from membership amounted to commercial suicide. However, the reasons behind stabiliser were more complex than simply establishing a cartel. Although prior to stabiliser ABTA enforced financial controls on members and had established a rescue fund for the clients of failed members it could not of course enforce higher standards on the industry as a whole and there continued to be regular failures of companies who were not members of ABTA—which did nothing to create confidence in the industry as a whole. ABTA was sufficiently large already that by creating stabiliser it meant that virtually all travel companies had to join or risk extinction. This in turn meant that standards could be properly enforced because the ultimate sanction, exclusion from membership, was not a consequence that travel companies could seriously contemplate.

Stabiliser was the subject of an action before the Restrictive Practices Court brought by the Office of Fair Trading (*Re Association of British Travel Agents Ltd's Agreement* [1984] I.C.R. 12) on the grounds that it contravened the Restrictive Trade Practices Act 1976. Although ABTA was a cartel the court refused to declare stabiliser to be contrary to the public interest. They arrived at this decision on the grounds that the removal of stabiliser would "deny to the public specific and substantial benefits" (s.19(1)(b)). In other words, the financial safeguards that ABTA provided to the public at that time made the existence of stabiliser reasonable.

Subsequently, ABTA voluntarily abolished stabiliser. The reason was that the Package Travel Regulations created an environment where consumers are entitled to such a high level of protection under the general law that it was no longer necessary for ABTA to maintain a cartel to protect the consumer interest. If ABTA had not moved to abolish stabiliser in October 1993 the Office of Fair Trading would almost certainly have instituted fresh proceedings against it—this time with a greater chance of success.

Since the abolition of stabiliser, ABTA has remained largely intact. Companies which remain outside ABTA include Expedia and Travel Counsellors, but one large online travel agency which has joined is Travel Republic. Whether it continues in its present form as both a trade association and a regulator of trading standards remains to be seen. Despite doubts expressed in the second edition of this book about its continuing existence in the long term as a trade association representing both tour operators and travel agents, it has continued successfully in this role and the regulatory side of its affairs commands general acceptance (but see *R. (on the application of Sunspell) v ABTA* [2001] A.C.D. 16 for a challenge to its authority).

Until very recently, what set ABTA apart as a trade association was the level of financial protection it offered to consumers over and above what the law required and the existence of its Code of Conduct which also offered the public significant benefits beyond what the law provided for. However, the financial protection has now been reduced so that consumers will get no more than the Package Travel Regulations require and the Code of Conduct has also been watered down to the extent that it no longer qualifies as one of the OFT's Approved Codes of Practice—although it still contains many provisions of benefit to consumers.

The Code of Conduct regulates the conduct of travel agents and tour operators both between themselves and, more importantly for our purposes, between themselves and their clients. We shall look at it in more detail at various points in the book but for the present it is sufficient to say that its importance stems from the fact that it confers upon the consumer rights which he or she is not necessarily entitled to at common law. It does this by requiring tour operators to insert into their contract with the consumer certain mandatory terms. These terms cover many of the most important features of the package holiday contract— cancellation, major changes, surcharges, force majeure, liability, etc. The Code (See Appendix 3) is revised at regular intervals, the latest revision being in 2009 and the degree of protection which it affords has varied considerably over time.

Certainly, the version which was in existence between 1990 and 1993 was much in advance of the existing law but since then the passage of the Package Travel Regulations has reduced its impact.

Other Trade Associations

Apart from ABTA, there are a variety of other trade associations in the travel industry. Probably the most important is the Federation of Tour Operators (FTO; *www.fto.co.uk*). It was an organisation that operated independently from ABTA, but in 2008 the two organisations merged, although the FTO has retained a separate identity within ABTA. Membership is by invitation only and consists chiefly of the larger tour operators. It has a strong health and safety remit and it lobbies on behalf of the industry. One of its chief functions is in connection with the bonding of its members. Where a package does not include a flight, the FTO sets the level of bonding required by members and, if necessary in the event of a member's insolvency, it will call the bond and administer it in favour of the consumers affected as a result of the insolvency.

AITO (*www.aito.co.uk*), the Association of Independent Tour Operators, is a trade association representing independent tour operators—small and medium-sized operators, many of whom are not members of ABTA and who mostly sell their holidays directly to the public. Although small, it is increasing in size and has an influential voice. It too exercises a bonding function on behalf of members.

The Travel Trust Association (*www.traveltrust.co.uk*) has about 370 members who offer protection to consumers by means of a trust fund (see Ch.12).

Coach tour operators are represented by the Confederation of Passenger Transport (CPT; *www.cpt-uk.org/cpt*) who have their own bonding scheme— Bonded Coach Holidays (BCH; *www.bondedcoachholidays.co.uk*). Cruise operators are brought together by the Passenger Shipping Association (PSA; *www.psa-psara.org*) which also has a bonding scheme for non-licensable activities. Travel agents have a number of associations to which they may belong, including the long established Guild of Travel Management Companies, formerly the Guild of Business Travel Agents (GTMC, *www.gtmc.org*), and the industry has many other specialist groupings, of which ABTOF, the Association of British Tour Operators to France, is perhaps the best known (*www.holidayfrance.org.uk*).

The Civil Aviation Authority

The chief responsibility of the CAA is the economic and safety regulation of civil aviation in the UK. As far as travel law is concerned, its chief importance is that it operates the ATOL system. Every tour operator who sells package holidays by air must have an ATOL—an air travel organiser's licence—and it is the CAA that administers the system. Broadly speaking, an applicant for an ATOL must be able to satisfy the CAA as to its financial stability and it must collect an APC (ATOL Protection Contribution, currently set at £2.50) from every passenger they carry. The APC is paid to the Air Travel Trust which reimburses passengers if their tour operator goes bankrupt. In addition, some operators must take out a bond which can be called and used to protect its consumers in the event of its insolvency. Package holidays covered by an ATOL are known as "licensable" activities—to distinguish them from non-licensable activities which are not covered by the CAA regime. Under the Package Travel Regulations, a company that has an ATOL is regarded as satisfying the requirements under the Regulations as to the protection of consumers in the event of insolvency for holidays which include an air travel component.

The ATOL system has undergone a number of major revisions in its time. In the mid-1990s the Civil Aviation (Air Travel Organisers' Licensing) Regulations 1995 (SI 1995/1054) brought flight consolidators within the ATOL Regulations and tightened up the financial scrutiny of ATOL holders. It also saw the introduction of directors' personal guarantees to help counter abuse of the system by individuals repeatedly setting up travel companies which then became insolvent. (See H. Simpson "Recent Developments on the ATOL Regulations" [1997] I.T.L.J. 113 for a discussion of those changes.) In August 2002, the CAA issued a consultation document on the issue of "split contracts" (see Ch.2) with a view to extending the ATOL system to fill the loopholes which exist in the bonding system caused by the fact that the ATOL system and the Package Travel Regulations do not provide complete protection against insolvency. (See also Simpson "Financial Protection for Scheduled Airline Passengers" [2002] I.T.L.J. 15.) Following this consultation, amendments were made to the ATOL Regulations which were designed to align the Regulations more closely with the Package Travel Regulations with the aim of eliminating or reducing the problem of "split contracting". These amendments were followed in turn by the publication of Guidance Notes. These proved so controversial that ABTA brought judicial review proceedings against the CAA which, after an appeal to the Court of Appeal (*ABTA v CAA* [2006] EWCA Civ 1299), resulted in the Guidance Notes having to be withdrawn. Further litigation in the case of *CAA v Travel Republic Ltd* [2010] EWHC 1151 has gone some way to clarifying the interpretation of the Regulations. (See Ch.2 for a full discussion of both these judgments.)

Despite the fact that for most of its history the ATOL scheme has been regarded as an unmitigated success, reimbursing or repatriating many hundreds of thousands of holidaymakers affected by tour operator insolvencies, the importance of the scheme has diminished as fewer passengers have come under its protective umbrella—due, as already indicated, to the rise of no frills airlines, the internet and independent, non-packaged, travel. Another issue with the scheme is that the fund created by the scheme to cover the insolvencies, the Air Travel Trust, is heavily overdrawn, and after the collapse of the XL company in 2008, the CAA had to increase contributions to the fund from £1.00 per head to £2.50 per head to cover the losses to the fund. This shortfall, coupled with the reduction in coverage, has prompted the Department for Transport and the CAA to propose a major extension of the scheme to cover not only package holidays but also "flight-plus" products where travel agents sell arrangements that appear to the consumer to be much the same as packages. (See: Civil Aviation Authority: ATOL Reform Briefing [2011] T.L.Q. 18; Kolatsis "ATOL Reform – Is it Enough" [2011] T.L.Q. 86.) These developments are discussed fully in Ch.12 on Insolvency and Security.

Other Regulatory Bodies

The Office of Fair Trading (OFT; *www.oft.gov.uk*) was first established by the Fair Trading Act 1973 but now derives its powers from the Enterprise Act 2002. It has a wide responsibility for the promotion of consumer protection as well as wide ranging responsibilities in the field of competition law. It was in this latter capacity that it instituted action against ABTA under the Restrictive Trade Practices Act. The OFT also has the power to undertake initial investigations into monopolies and to make references to the Competition Commission (formerly the MMC) when it is felt necessary. It was in the exercise of this power that the issue of vertical integration in the travel industry was referred to the MMC in November 1996. Another duty of the OFT, to be found in s.8 of the Enterprise Act, is the promotion of good consumer practice. One way in which this can be achieved is to encourage and approve the use of "consumer codes". In 2006, the ABTA Code of Practice became an OFT approved code, but shortly afterwards this accreditation was withdrawn following the issue of the September 2006 version of the code. The OFT considered that the amendments would "not protect consumers' deposits and prepayments to the same extent as the existing OFT approved Code".

The OFT is also charged with policing the Unfair Terms in Consumer Contracts Regulations, a task which it has undertaken enthusiastically in relation to unfair terms in package holiday contracts. In October 2002, it compelled all the major tour operators to make significant changes to their standard terms and conditions, and this was followed up in 2004 with the publication of extensive guidance on unfair contract terms for tour operators ("Guidance on Unfair Terms in Package Holiday Contracts", March 2004, OFT 668).

However, at the time of going to press, uncertainty exists as to the future of the OFT. The government has announced that its competition jurisdiction will be merged with the Competition Commission to form a new Competition and Markets Authority and that its consumer functions will be devolved to Trading Standards Departments. However Consumer Focus (*www.consumerfocus.org.uk*), the statutory body promoting consumer rights, has expressed concern about whether the consumer protection functions can be adequately performed by Trading Standards Departments. In particular, they are worried about:

- Lack of will/ability to pick up the big (sometimes risky) national cases or to facilitate and pay for services working together; as councils choose to focus scarce resources on local matters.

- Enforcement deserts, where there is effectively no Trading Standards function of any consequence, or areas with tiny teams lacking the scale and skills to make a difference. In these places, consumers will be unprotected and rogue traders may flourish.

- Lack of effective national dissemination and co-ordination of information and evidence which will leave unaddressed gaps in consumer protection enforcement.

Trading Standards Departments, sometimes also known as Weights and Measures Departments or Consumer Protection Departments, are charged with enforcing a wide range of consumer protection legislation of which that affecting the travel industry is a very small part. Of particular relevance to the industry are two pieces of legislation—the Package Travel Regulations 1992 and the Consumer Protection from Unfair Trading Regulations 2008. They confer upon Trading Standards Officers wide powers to investigate and prosecute complaints arising under the legislation with corresponding powers of search and seizure and the power to interview suspects. All this legislation is dealt with in detail in later chapters.

The English Legal System

Introduction

In this section we hope to do three things. First, to explain to you the sources of English law; secondly, to explain the difference between civil and criminal law; and thirdly, to give you a brief description of the court system. To put it more simply, we will tell you where our laws come from, what kinds of laws we have and where you will end up if you infringe them.

Sources of law

Very broadly speaking, we have two sources of law—legislation and case law. Legislation is law made by Parliament and is the collective name for what are also known as Acts of Parliament or statutes. Case law is law made by the courts and is also known as the common law or judicial precedent.

Legislation

An Act of Parliament, or a statute, is a law which has been passed by Parliament after being subjected to a rigorous scrutiny by both the House of Commons and the House of Lords (often after an equally rigorous consultation process outside Parliament). This process includes a formal introduction into one House by means of a *first reading*, of what is then known as a *bill*. Then there is a full scale debate on the merits of the bill during the *second reading*. After the second reading the bill goes through the *committee stage* where it is looked at in some detail—often clause by clause. Finally, it is returned to the floor of the House where, after a *report stage*, it receives its *third reading*. Then the bill is sent to the other House where it undergoes a similar process. If it survives all this it then receives the *royal assent* and becomes law.

Parliament only has time to deal with about 70 or 80 new statutes a year and most of these deal with social, environmental and economic matters. Examples of statutes passed in recent years that don't fall into these categories but have had a direct bearing on the regulation of the travel industry include the Unfair Contract Terms Act 1977 and the Civil Aviation Act 1982.

INTRODUCTION

Delegated Legislation

Apart from Acts of Parliament, another very important form of legislation is *delegated legislation.* For a variety of reasons, including lack of time, lack of technical expertise or the need for speed, Parliament often delegates the making of legislation to an inferior body—usually a minister but sometimes a local authority. Many former nationalised industries, such as British Rail, had limited powers to make by-laws which are a form of delegated legislation. Much law is therefore made without full Parliamentary consideration.

The manner in which this is usually done is for Parliament to pass an enabling Act—which is an Act of Parliament which contains a power enabling a minister, or whoever, to make delegated legislation. One example of delegated legislation with which most in the travel industry should be familiar is the Civil Aviation (Air Travel Organisers' Licensing) Regulations, otherwise known as the ATOL Regulations.

These were first enacted in 1972 and amended on a number of occasions. They were repealed and re-enacted in 1995 as the Civil Aviation (Air Travel Organisers' Licensing) Regulations 1995 (SI 1995/1054). These Regulations provide that tour operators who offer air-inclusive package holidays must be licensed and bonded by the CAA. They were amended again in 2012 to bring "flight-plus" arrangements within the scheme. The minister responsible for bringing them into force is the Secretary of State for Transport and the Act of Parliament which gives him this power is the Civil Aviation Act 1982.

The most important example of delegated legislation relevant to the travel industry is of course the Package Travel, Package Holidays and Package Tours Regulations 1992 (SI 1992/3288). In this instance, the enabling Act is the European Communities Act 1972. This Act was passed when the UK joined the EEC and provides that European legislation can be enacted in the UK by means of delegated legislation. This was how the EC Directive on Package Travel, Package Holidays and Package Tours 1990 became part of English law.

European Legislation

Increasingly, much of our law comes from Brussels rather than Westminster and it is necessary therefore to give a brief explanation of the types of legislation that we are subject to as members of the European Union.

First of all there are the treaties—the European Community Treaty (the Treaty of Rome), the Single European Act, the Treaty on European Union (the Maastricht Treaty), the Treaty of Amsterdam, the Treaty of Nice and the Treaty of Lisbon. These are all *primary* sources of European law and are *directly applicable* in the UK by virtue of the European Communities Act 1972, s.2(2). This means that they create rights in English law without the necessity for legislation by Parliament.

Secondary sources of European law include *Directives* and *Regulations* (not to be confused with the Regulations mentioned earlier which are forms of delegated legislation made by our own Parliament). In general, Directives are not directly applicable in the UK unless Parliament gives effect to them by statute or delegated legislation. As explained above, this is how the Package Travel Regulations came into being. Regulations, on the other hand, are directly applicable.

Occasionally, Directives are regarded as being directly applicable without

Parliament having implemented it by means of domestic legislation. This is only possible once the deadline for implementation of the Directive has elapsed. Moreover, only those provisions in a Directive which are sufficiently clear, precise and unconditional could be so regarded. Additionally, Directives can be regarded as directly applicable, and be relied upon as if they were national legislation in the national courts, only in cases involving disputes between citizens and State authorities. For example, Directive 87/102 on consumer credit was due to be implemented in 1990. However, Spain had not done so when Cristina Blázquez Rivero booked herself a holiday through El Corte Inglés (ECI), a Spanish travel agency. She had to obtain a loan via a company that had an exclusive right to provide loans to ECI's customers. The holiday proved to be very disappointing and Ms Blázquez Rivero stopped repayments on the loan. When an action was brought against her in the Spanish courts, she purported to rely upon certain provisions in the Directive. However, she was unable to do so: although the deadline for implementation had passed, and the provisions on which she was relying were clear, the case did not involve a dispute between a citizen and a State authority (*El Corte Inglés SA v Blázquez Rivero* C–192/94).

However, when this happens, people such as Ms Blázquez Rivero can claim compensation from the defaulting Member State instead. Thus, it is now quite clear that if the UK had not complied with its European obligations by bringing Directive 90/314, the Package Travel Directive, into force by December 31, 1992, any clear, precise and unconditional provisions in it would nevertheless have been directly applicable in the UK—but only in disputes between citizens and the government of the UK. However, any UK citizen who had been adversely affected by the failure of the UK government to bring the EC Directive into force could have sued the government for the losses caused by the failure.

Thus, if a tour operator had become insolvent before the government had implemented the requirements about security then the consumers harmed by this failure could claim compensation from the Government. The reason we can say this with such certainty is that this is just the situation that arose in Germany in 1993. A major German tour operator became bankrupt before the German government had implemented the Directive, and German consumers commenced an action against their government to recover their money lost in the insolvency. The case of *Dillenkofer v Germany* (C-178/94) eventually reached the European Court of Justice which decided that the German Government should compensate the consumers for their loss which had been caused by the Government's failure to implement the Directive by the required deadline (See H.A. O'Connor "Advance Deposits and the Package Travel Directive: The Final Judgment" [1997] I.T.L.J. 54).

Note that the Directive is directly applicable against the state—known as *vertical* applicability—but it does not create rights as between individuals—*horizontal* applicability.

Another example of a Regulation of significant relevance to the travel industry is Regulation 261/2004 establishing common rules on compensation and assistance to passengers in the event of denied boarding and of cancellation or long delay of flights. We look at this in some detail in Ch.13 on Air and Sea Travel.

INTRODUCTION

Case Law

A large part of our law is not to be found in statutes at all. It can be found instead in case law—decisions made by the judges in individual cases which create *precedents* which are then *followed* by other judges. At one time our criminal law, tort law and contract law consisted almost entirely of case law and it still remains important today.

English law has developed a system of *binding precedent* (otherwise known as *stare decisis*)—which means that once a court has decided a case then the rule or principle that it establishes is binding in later cases. The rule that the case establishes is also known by a fancy Latin name—the *ratio decidendi*—the reasons for the decision. The judge in a subsequent case has no choice in the matter, he *must* follow the previous *ratio* no matter how much he disagrees with it. The reason for this is to establish consistency in the law. If a judge could decide a case according to whatever principles he chose then it would be difficult for anyone to know where they stood in any particular situation. They would not be able to order their affairs in accordance with what they believed the law to be. For instance, there was confusion for a short time before the law was settled on the issue of whether or not it amounted to contributory negligence not to wear a seatbelt in a car. Some High Court judges (whose decisions are not binding on other High Court judges) believed that failure to wear a seatbelt amounted to contributory negligence whereas other High Court judges took a different view. It required an appeal to the Court of Appeal before the matter was settled and a rule established that had to be followed by all High Court judges.

The disadvantage of such a system of binding precedent is that it creates a rigid system with no flexibility, and as a consequence, the law is unable to grow or adapt to changing circumstances and unjust decisions are perpetuated. This is to overstate the position, however, because the system in practice does possess sufficient flexibility to overcome the problems of excessive rigidity.

This is achieved in a number of ways. First, it is possible for a court higher up in the hierarchy of courts to *overrule* a previous decision of a lower court. For instance, the Court of Appeal can overrule decisions of the High Court, and the Supreme Court can overrule decisions of the Court of Appeal. (A case is *overruled* when a court in a *later* case decides that the *ratio* of the first case is wrong. A case is *reversed* when a court to which *that* case is appealed decides that the decision of the lower court was wrong.) Note that it is higher courts that bind lower courts, not vice versa. A High Court decision binds the County Court but it does not work the other way round.

Secondly, a subsequent court can *distinguish* the decision of a previous court and refuse to follow it. To distinguish a previous case is not to disagree with the principle or rule that it lays down but simply to say that the facts are sufficiently different to justify coming to a decision which is not based on that principle. For instance, the case of *Jarvis v Swans Tours* [1973] 1 All E.R. 71 establishes that in holiday cases a claimant is entitled to damages for distress and disappointment. But how far does this principle extend? The House of Lords, in *Farley v Skinner* [2001] 3 W.L.R. 899, decided that it extended to situations where only *part* of the purpose of the contract was to provide peace of mind or freedom from distress. So what about a "flight-only" contract to a holiday destination? Does this come within *Jarvis* and *Farley* or does it fall outside? It would be possible for a judge, if he so wished, to distinguish the facts of such a case from either *Jarvis* or *Farley*—giving him the freedom to decide the case as he saw fit. This would not require him to ignore or overrule these decisions—merely to say that the factual situation he is dealing with does not fit comfortably within the principles established by those cases and therefore need not be followed. An indication of how the courts might approach this issue is to be found in *Lucas v Avro* [1994] C.L.Y. 1444. (See also *Brunton v Cosmosair* [2003] C.L.Y. 232; cf. "Case Note: *Marshall & Dixon v KLM*" [2002] I.T.L.J. 63; Sharon & Marco "Delayed Flight – Cause for Compensation on Grounds of Mental Anguish" [2011] T.L.Q. 98.)

Finally, it is possible, if all else fails, for legislation to be passed to overrule inconvenient or unjust precedents. This is effectively what the Package Travel Regulations have done to large parts of the common law relating to package holidays. For instance, the decision in *Wall v Silver Wing Surface Arrangements* Unreported 1981, a High Court decision which was followed in a number of County Court cases, laid down that a tour operator was not liable to clients who were injured on holiday by the negligence of the hotel they were booked into. Now, reg.15 of the Package Travel Regulations effectively provides that a tour operator is responsible for the negligence of suppliers (but see the much fuller discussion in Ch.5).

Civil and Criminal Law

Broadly speaking, the criminal law is concerned with offences that are regarded as being sufficiently serious or anti-social that when they occur the state should intervene to maintain order or to protect citizens who may be unable or unwilling to protect themselves. This intervention will usually take the form of an individual being *prosecuted* by the state in a criminal court and if the *defendant* is found *guilty* then *punishment* such as a fine or imprisonment will be imposed. This clearly applies to "traditional" crimes such as murder, manslaughter, arson, rape, theft, etc. but the criminal courts also deal with large numbers of "regulatory" offences such as parking on double yellow lines or dropping litter or failing to label the contents of processed food properly. These are not criminal offences in the traditional sense but in order to regulate a complex modern society it has been necessary to classify such activities as criminal and to impose criminal penalties simply in order to ensure that traffic flows freely, that our streets are not unbearably filthy and that we are properly informed as to what we are eating.

Into this latter category falls the Consumer Protection from Unfair Trading Regulations 2008 which, like its predecessors, the Trade Descriptions Act 1968 and the Consumer Protection Act 1987, will impact heavily on the travel industry—and many of the provisions in the Package Travel Regulations relating to the provision of information. Lord Scarman said of the Trade Descriptions Act:

"it is not a truly criminal statute. Its purpose is not the enforcement of the criminal law but the maintenance of trading standards. Trading standards, not criminal behaviour are its concern." (*Wings v Ellis* [1985] A.C. 272).

INTRODUCTION

The civil law, on the other hand, is largely concerned with disputes between individuals. In this book we are largely concerned with that branch of civil law known as contract law, but occasionally we also mention the law of torts. In these two branches of civil law the dispute will often resolve itself into a situation where a *claimant* (formerly referred to as a *plaintiff*), i.e. the person with the grievance, is *suing* a *defendant* in a civil court. If the defendant is found *liable* then the court will endeavour to find a *remedy*—usually financial compensation called *damages* but occasionally an *injunction* or an award of *specific performance*.

Often the same set of facts can give rise to both criminal and civil liability. For instance if a tour operator describes a hotel in a misleading fashion, e.g. by stating that the hotel has a children's swimming pool when it doesn't, this may give rise to a criminal prosecution under the provisions of the CPR 2008 or reg.5 of the Package Travel Regulations. It may also give rise to a civil action for breach of contract or misrepresentation. If the misrepresentation was deliberate then this amounts to the tort of deceit. The tour operator may end up paying both a hefty fine for the criminal offence and substantial damages for the civil liability.

The Court System

General Features

Should you be unfortunate enough to engage in litigation—an activity that has not contributed notably to the happiness of mankind—you will inevitably encounter the court system. Certain features characterise the system. First, as a general proposition, the courts can be divided into civil courts and criminal courts—although their functions do overlap on occasions. Secondly, there are courts of trial (or first instance) and courts of appeal—but again there are overlaps—some courts have both first instance and appellate functions. Thirdly, just as there is a hierarchy of courts so there is a hierarchy of judges. In the lower courts the judges are less experienced, sometimes part-time and, in the magistrates' court in particular, have no formal legal qualifications. At the other end of the scale, judges in the Supreme Court are full-time and extremely experienced—ranking in quality alongside any final court of appeal in the world.

Finally, the whole system is complicated by the fact that on matters of European legislation the Supreme Court, our highest domestic court, is no longer our highest court. Disputes involving a European element now may be referred to the European Court of Justice in Luxembourg for decisions on the interpretation of European legislation.

We will now look briefly at the important features of each court taking the criminal courts first.

Criminal Courts

The Magistrates' Court

Jurisdiction Magistrates' courts are the workhorses of the criminal court system. Situated in every town (often several of them in the larger conurbations) and open for business every day of the week, they deal predominantly with what can be termed "petty crime" although their jurisdiction is very wide indeed—including not only crime but also a wide range of family matters and a miscellaneous jurisdiction that includes liquor licensing and the recovery of certain debts such as gas, electricity and council tax.

Apart from proceedings dealing with children and young offenders in a special youth court the criminal jurisdiction of the magistrates can be broadly divided into two types of proceedings—*summary proceedings* and *committal proceedings*. In summary proceedings the court acts as a trial court and will *try* all *summary* offences and many *indictable* offences. A summary offence is one where the defendant has no right to a jury trial in the Crown Court and must be dealt with by the Magistrates' Court. Indictable offences are ones where the defendant does have such a right to trial by jury but may, in certain cases, waive that right and choose to be tried by the magistrates. Some indictable offences are so serious, e.g. murder, manslaughter, rape, etc. that they can only be tried in the Crown Court but many are said to be *triable either way*, i.e. they can be tried either by the magistrates or in the Crown Court depending on their gravity. For instance, a small theft may not warrant a full jury trial but a large bank robbery would. All the offences under the Package Travel Regulations 1992 dealt with in later chapters are offences triable either way. In 2005, Ryanair were charged with offences under the Consumer Protection Act 1987 (now repealed) for giving misleading price indications and chose, somewhat unusually, to have the case heard by a jury in Chelmsford Crown Court.

As well as trying offenders, the Magistrates' Court also deals with offenders who are to be tried in the Crown Court by means of a "sending for trial" hearing where defendants are given notice of the evidence against them; the offences for which they are to be tried and where they are to be tried. This procedure was introduced by the Criminal Justice Act 2003 and replaced the more cumbersome committal procedure.

Personnel The jurisdiction of the Magistrates' Court is usually exercised by a bench of three lay magistrates (although two are sufficient) or one professional magistrate with legal training known as a District Judge (Magistrates' Court), formerly known as a stipendiary magistrate—usually only found in larger cities. The lay magistrates have no formal legal training and apart from attending training courses and agreeing to devote a minimum amount of time to the task every year they are entirely without legal qualification or experience. Their main qualification for the job is being upstanding members of the local community. For this reason they rely heavily on the legally trained court clerk whose function it is to advise them on the law. There are no juries in the Magistrates' Court.

Powers The powers of the Magistrates' Court include the ability to impose a prison sentence of up to 12 months and to fine a defendant by reference to the standard scales which go up to £5,000, although some statutes permit fines of more than this. Where a defendant has been convicted of an indictable offence and it turns out that the offence was more serious than originally thought, the magistrates can commit the defendant for sentence in the Crown Court if they think the defendant deserves a greater punishment than they are able to mete out.

Appeals A defendant may appeal against *conviction* or simply against *sentence* to the Crown Court. Both the defendant and the prosecutor can appeal on a *point of law* to the *Divisional Court*. This latter process is known as an appeal by way of *case stated*. The Divisional Court is the Queen's Bench Divisional Court which is a branch of the High Court. In limited circumstances the prosecution can appeal against sentence.

As far as the travel industry is concerned, it is offences against the Package Travel Regulations 1992 and the Consumer Protection from Unfair Trading Regulations 2008 that are most likely to bring them before the Magistrates' Court. Offences under this legislation are offences triable either way, but in practice they tend to be dealt with summarily by the magistrates rather than on indictment in the Crown Court.

The Crown Court

The main function of the Crown Court is to try indictable offences. It hears appeals against conviction and against sentence from the Magistrates' Court. It also hears those "either way" offences where the defendant or the court chose to have it heard in the Crown Court. Judges who sit in the Crown Court can be, in order of seniority, High Court judges, circuit judges, district judges or recorders. They are all legally qualified and cases are assigned to them according to the seriousness of the offence, so for instance High Court judges will hear the most serious cases—murder, manslaughter, rape, etc.—and circuit judges, district judges and recorders will hear the less serious cases. High Court judges, circuit judges and district judges are full-time judges but recorders are only part-time judges appointed for specific periods. Magistrates also sit in the Crown Court but only with other judges, on appeals.

If the defendant pleads guilty to an offence the court will proceed to sentence him without the aid of a jury, but where the defendant pleads not guilty to a charge there will be a full trial with a jury. It is the function of the jury to decide on the facts of the case whether the defendant is guilty and for the judge to advise them on the law. It is no longer necessary for the jury to reach a unanimous verdict; it is possible for the jury to reach a decision on the basis of a majority verdict of not less than 10:2.

A defendant may make an appeal against conviction to the Court of Appeal Criminal Division but leave to appeal must be granted by the Court of Appeal or the trial judge.

If the defendant has already appealed from the Magistrates' Court to the Crown Court then an appeal by way of case stated on a point of law can be made to the Divisional Court.

The Divisional Court

The Queen's Bench Division (QBD) is a branch of the High Court—a civil court—but two High Court judges of the QBD, or a High Court judge and a Court of Appeal judge, can act as an appeal court to hear appeals by way of case stated from the Magistrates' Court and the Crown Court on points of law only. The appeal is based on documents only accompanied by legal argument from counsel but no witnesses are heard. Many travel cases involving criminal appeals have been heard in the Divisional Court including *Thomson Tour Operations v Birch* (1999) 163 J.P. 465; *Airtours v Shipley* (1994) 158 J.P. 835 and *Hotel Plan v Tameside MBC* [2001] EWHC Admin 154. Despite this, surprisingly few appeals proceed down this simple and effective route.

There is a further right of appeal from the Divisional Court to the Supreme Court, but only if the case involves a point of law of general public importance and either the Divisional Court or the Supreme Court gives leave to appeal.

The Court of Appeal Criminal Division

The Court of Appeal hears criminal appeals against conviction and sentence where the defendant has been tried on indictment in the Crown Court. Appeals are usually heard by three *Lords Justices of Appeal*—although two is sufficient. The president of the Court of Appeal Criminal Division is the *Lord Chief Justice*, also known as the *President of the Courts of England and Wales.*

A further appeal is possible to the Supreme Court but again, only if a point of law of general public importance is involved and either the Court of Appeal or the Supreme Court gives leave to appeal.

The Supreme Court

Parliament is made up of two legislative chambers—the House of Commons and the House of Lords. Until 2009, the House of Lords Appellate Committee, which was our final court of appeal, was part of the House of Lords, but since then it has been renamed the Supreme Court and is independent of the House of Lords and has separate premises in the old Middlesex Guildhall in Westminster.

Like the Court of Appeal it hears both criminal and civil appeals. Acting as a final court of appeal in criminal matters it hears appeals on points of law of general public importance from both the Divisional Court and the Court of Appeal Criminal Division. Very few criminal appeals actually reach the Supreme Court—only about 10 are heard each year. One important travel case which did reach the Supreme Court (then the House of Lords) was *Wings Ltd v Ellis* [1985] A.C. 272 which concerned the interpretation of s.14 of the Trade Descriptions Act 1968.

The head of the Supreme Court is the *President* and he has a *Deputy-President* and 10 *Justices* to assist him. Five justices usually hear an appeal but in important cases a full court of seven might be assembled. The Justices are all appointed on the basis of their judicial ability—unlike in the past when any member of the peerage was entitled to be a member of the House of Lords.

Civil Courts

The County Court

There are over 200 County Courts in England and Wales presided over by Circuit Judges or District Judges (formerly called Registrars). They have a very wide jurisdiction over most civil matters and in most respects the County Court has the same jurisdiction as the High Court. What distinguishes the two is that the High Court deals with those cases which involve more money or which are of greater complexity. So for instance, in civil disputes involving a breach of contract or the commission of a tort, the County Court has jurisdiction over claims for any amount; but in practice, as a general rule, those claims involving over £50,000 will be heard in the High Court. However, cases involving amounts in excess of this are frequently heard in the County Court if the issues involved are relatively straightforward. The nature and value of holiday claims are such that most of them will be heard in the County Court rather than the High Court.

One important aspect of the work of the County Court is what is popularly known as the Small Claims Court. This is where claims for £5,000 or less (£1,000 for personal injury claims) are referred to a small claims trial by the District Judge. The procedure is informal and legal costs are not recoverable by either party. Many holiday claims are dealt with by this procedure. We look at it in much more detail in Ch.15.

In civil courts, juries have been almost completely dispensed with and it is very rare indeed to find a jury in a County Court. On the rare occasions where a jury is used it consists of eight members.

Either party who is dissatisfied with the result of the action may appeal from the Circuit Judge to a High Court judge (fast track cases) or to the Court of Appeal Civil Division (multi-track cases). There are limitations on the right of appeal. Permission to appeal must be given. Appeals from the decision of a District Judge at a trial (small claims or fast track) or an interlocutory point are made to a Circuit Judge in the same County Court. Permission is again required. Appeals can only be made if the original decision was wrong, or unjust because of serious procedural or other irregularity.

The High Court

The High Court sits mainly in London but also has regular sittings in the provinces. It is divided into three divisions—the Queen's Bench Division, the Chancery Division and the aptly named Family Division. The Queen's Bench Division is the busiest of the three. It hears contract and tort cases and also has specialist courts within the division—the Commercial Court and the Admiralty Court. Most holiday cases which are heard by the High Court will be dealt with in the Queen's Bench Division. The president of the Queen's Bench Division is the *Lord Chief Justice*; the Family Division is led by the President of the Family Division; and the head of the Chancery Division is the Chancellor of the High Court.

A single High Court judge (known also as a *puisne* judge) will try disputes, usually without the assistance of a jury. The only civil cases today that employ a jury on a regular basis are cases against the police and cases in defamation, but even in defamation cases they can be dispensed with.

The main difference in practice between the jurisdiction of the High Court and the County Court is that the High Court deals with cases of greater complexity; cases involving larger sums of money; and cases where the remedy required cannot be granted by the County Court. It also has an appeal jurisdiction which the County Court does not have. Each of the divisions of the High Court can sit as a Divisional Court where two judges hear appeals. We have already seen that the Queen's Bench Divisional Court hears criminal appeals from the Magistrates' Court and the Crown Court. There are also Family Divisional Courts and Chancery Divisional Courts.

Appeals against the decision of the High Court are made to the Court of

Appeal Civil Division. On rare occasions in special circumstances an appeal can be made direct to the House of Lords which "leapfrogs" the Court of Appeal.

Court of Appeal Civil Division

The Court of Appeal Civil Division hears appeals from the High Court and the County Court. As in the Criminal Division, appeals are usually heard by three judges—Lords Justices of Appeal. The president of the Civil Division is the *Master of the Rolls*. Appeals from the Civil Division lie to the House of Lords if permission is given. There is no requirement that the appeal is on a point of law of general public importance but permission to appeal is unlikely to be given if it is not.

Supreme Court

Much of what was said about the Supreme Court in its capacity as the final court of appeal in criminal cases applies to its function as a court of appeal in civil cases. The main practical difference is that the bulk of its time is spent on civil rather than criminal appeals and that it is possible for it to consider appeals on the facts as well as the law in civil cases.

European Court of Justice

For most purposes, the Supreme Court is the final court of appeal in the UK, but for disputes which involve an element of European Union law the European Court of Justice (the ECJ; *www.curia.eu.int*) has an important function. The ECJ sits in Luxembourg and has 27 judges (and eight Advocates-General who assist the court) drawn from the member states.

The jurisdiction of the court includes hearing disputes between member states; deciding whether member states have fulfilled their obligations under European law; and to determine whether European institutions such as the Council and the Commission have acted illegally. It also has a power under art.267 of the Treaty on the Functioning of the European Union to give preliminary rulings, in cases referred to it by domestic courts, on the interpretation of European legislation. What this means in practice is that if, say, the Divisional Court was faced with a dispute over the meaning of part of the Package Travel Regulations and whether the Regulations properly reflected the meaning of the EC Directive on Package Travel, the Divisional Court could refer the matter to the ECJ. While this was done the case in the Divisional Court would be adjourned until the ECJ gave a ruling on the meaning of the disputed provision. Then the Divisional Court would decide the case in the light of the interpretation provided by the ECJ. Thus, the actual decision is made by the English court but only after the ECJ has provided guidance. In the *Dillenkofer* case referred to earlier this was the procedure followed by the German court before which the German consumers brought their case. The German court adjourned the case while the point of law was decided by the ECJ. Apart from the *Dillenkofer* case there have been a number of other cases referred to the ECJ on the interpretation of the Package Travel Directive, including *AFS Intercultural Programs Finland ry v Kuluttaja-virasto* (C-237/97), *Rechberger v Republic of Austria* (C-140/97), *Verein fur Konsumenteninformation v Osterreichische Kreditversicherungs AG* (C-364/96)

INTRODUCTION

and: *Club-Tour, Viagens e Turismo Sa v Alberto Carlos Lobo Goncalves Garrido* (C-400/00). More recently, the Denied Boarding Regulations (261/2004) have been the subject of litigation in the ECJ (see *Sturgeon v Condor* (C-402/07); *Bock v Air France* (C-432/07) and *Wallentin-Hermann v Alitalia* (C-549/07)).

Under art.267 the position is that only the final court of appeal in the domestic system *must* refer a matter of interpretation to the ECJ. Courts lower in the hierarchy have a discretion whether or not to make a reference. In fact, courts at all levels of our system have made references. The decision when to do so depends upon a number of factors including convenience, cost, the difficulty of the point of law, the existing state of the law and whether or not the reference will settle the matter. Interestingly, the Divisional Court in the case of *CAA v Travel Republic* chose not to make a reference on the grounds that by the time the case was heard the law would probably have changed—which would have undermined the fact that the case was brought as a test case to clarify the existing law (Elias L.J. at para.66). In so doing, the judge showed greater faith than many in the ability of the European Commission to come up with a reform of the Package Travel Directive any time soon. The Department for Transport has, however, moved more quickly and has enacted rules for "flight-plus" arrangements that will go some way to mitigating the problems of consumer protection revealed by the case.

CHAPTER TWO
Package Travel Regulations: Definitions

INTRODUCTION

Until 1993 there was virtually no statutory control of package holidays. The relationship between tour operators and clients was left almost entirely to the common law. However, in 1990 the Council of the European Communities (the EC) adopted a Directive—The Package Travel, Package Holidays and Package Tours Directive (90/314) which had to be implemented by EC members by December 31, 1992. As a consequence the British Parliament passed the snappily entitled Package Travel, Package Holidays and Package Tours Regulations (SI 1992/3288) at the end of 1992. For most purposes it brought the Directive into effect from December 23, 1992.

As an aside, it is interesting to note that despite the fact that these Regulations originate in Europe this is not something that you would necessarily realise from reading English case law on the subject. In almost 20 years since its passage only three cases we know of have referred to the Directive—albeit important ones: *Hone v Going Places* [2001] EWCA Civ 947; *The Association of British Travel Agents Ltd v Civil Aviation Authority* [2006] EWCA Civ 1299 and *Civil Aviation Authority v Travel Republic Ltd* [2010] EWHC 1151 (Admin). Certainly there is no reference to the EC Treaty and the consumer protection provisions contained in art.153 which commit the Community to ensuring "a high level of consumer protection". It is a tribute to the insularity of English law that even in these three cases there was no real desire on the part of anyone involved to refer the issue in the case to the ECJ when it cried out for such a reference.

Nevertheless, even with this reluctance to permit a European hand on the steering wheel, it is hard to overestimate the effect that these Regulations have had on the travel industry. The provisions in the Regulations created a completely new statutory framework within which tour operators must work. Important new civil liabilities were imposed and there are a battery of new criminal offences. Additionally, a new system of consumer protection was created to protect clients against the insolvency of tour operators. However, having said that it is important to realise that despite their undoubted significance the Regulations are not comprehensive—they do not set out to regulate every aspect of the package holiday contract. Large parts of the contract still remain a matter for the common law. For instance, the calculation of damages is one aspect of contract that is largely untouched by the Regulations. Damages are still determined by decisions based on the case of *Jarvis v Swans Tours Ltd* [1973] 1 All E.R. 71; [1973] Q.B. 233. Even here, however, there is increasing European influence—see *Leitner v TUI Deutschland GmbH & Co KG* (C-168/00).

What has happened is that a large number of additional rules have been created which operate alongside the ordinary law of contract and impact upon it to a greater or lesser extent. Thus, on the one hand, the rules on offer and acceptance have not been changed, but an operator has to be much more alert to the rules because a number of Regulations require him to provide information to clients before the contract is made—on pain of committing a criminal offence (reg.7) or of running the risk that a client can withdraw from the contract (reg.9). By contrast, the existing law on privity of contract is greatly changed because the Regulations provide that persons other than the immediate parties to the contract acquire rights under it and can sue.

Those two examples are relatively straightforward but this is not always the case. Take frustration of contract for instance. Nothing in the Regulations specifically excludes the rules on frustration of contract or the Law Reform (Frustrated Contracts) Act 1943 so we must assume that they continue to apply to package holiday contracts. However, the Regulations do introduce a new concept to package holidays—the concept of *force majeure*. *Force majeure* resembles frustration of contract in many ways but there are significant differences—not only in its application but also in the consequences that flow from it. The result is not entirely clear but in our view the effect of the *force majeure* rules is to render the rules on frustration of contract largely redundant.

Because of this close inter-relationship between the Regulations and the existing law the Regulations will not be treated as a separate topic. Instead, the provisions will be integrated into the appropriate sections of the book, along with the law relevant to independent travellers, wherever they are relevant. However, it is important that certain issues arising from the Regulations are dealt with at the outset because they are necessary for a full understanding of what comes later. In particular, the scope of the Regulations and some of the more important definitions will be dealt with now rather than later. A brief overview will also be given at this stage so that you can grasp the full import of the Regulations at an early stage.

Although, as indicated in Ch.1, package travel is diminishing in significance in relative terms, a clear understanding of the definitions in this chapter is even more important than previously because so many so-called independent travellers stand to lose the protection of the Regulations. It is imperative to be able to draw a clear line between package travel and independent travel so that proper advice can be given and appropriate rights enforced. However, readers will soon discover that this is a counsel of perfection—changes in business practice and a retreat by judges into fact-specific decisions has left that line as obscure as ever.

SCOPE OF THE REGULATIONS

One purpose of the Directive on Package Travel was to regulate conventional package holidays—two weeks of sun, sea and sand in the Mediterranean basin and other similar arrangements. On this everyone is agreed but unfortunately (or fortunately depending upon your perspective), the scope of the definition of a "package" in reg.2 is so wide that it goes far beyond conventional package holidays. Much of what it takes in, in addition to conventional packages, is uncontroversial, e.g. coach trips to London involving overnight accommodation and perhaps a show; or special weekends offered by hotels and guest houses—murder and mystery weekends, etc. Beyond that, however, there are an amazing variety of travel and holiday arrangements over which fierce arguments rage—do they or don't they come within the definition of package, e.g. overnight ferry trips to the Continent; business travel; holiday camps and caravan sites; "tailor-made" packages put together by travel agents; sleeper accommodation on the railways; "bareboat" charters; holidays provided by local authority social services departments for their pensioners; activity holidays provided by schools or local education authorities; "reproductive tourism" for childless couples (*The Independent*, May 18, 2002, p.11); "face-lift safaris" for those wanting a package including cosmetic surgery (*The Independent*, July 1, 2001, p.5; *The Guardian*, August 20, 2005); and a huge and increasing range of medical tourism packages (see Kogut "Medical Tourism: When Money Talks Individuals Fly" [2011] T.L.Q. 35). Both the Department for Trade and Industry (DTI), the government department originally responsible for guiding the legislation through Parliament, and ABTA, the main trade association, issued guidelines on the scope of the Regulations and they disagreed fundamentally on the extent of the definition. LACORS (formerly LACOTS), the Local Authorities Co-ordinators of Regulatory Services Standards, also issued guidance notes on some of the more difficult aspects of the Regulations. Of much more significance than these commentaries are decisions of the European Court of Justice: *AFS Intercultural Programs Finland Ry* (C-237/97); *Rechberger v Austria* (C-140/97) and *Club Tour Viagens e Turismo SA v Alberto Carlos Lobo Goncalves Garrido* (C-400/00) in which the Court gave its views on what constituted a package. We will give our own views on the above examples in due course. The European Commission has also issued a number of consultation documents on the implementation and reform of the Directive, including the definition of "package", which can be found on the Europa website.

The problem that the broadness of the definition causes is that a set of rules designed for one purpose may have to be applied to a set of circumstances for which they were not designed. Operators selling non-conventional packages will find themselves square pegs in round holes.

This section is concerned with examining the scope of the definitions in the Regulations with a view to determining what falls within the Regulations and is subject to its regime, in particular the rules relating to bonding and liability, and what falls outside and remains regulated solely by the common law. The burdens imposed by the Regulations have caused many operators to examine ways of avoiding the Regulations and it appears that the internet has provided them with such a possibility. As a consequence, as already indicated, the traditional package holiday is beginning to decline in popularity as operators "unpackage" their holidays.

The Regulations are of course based upon the Package Travel Directive, a piece of European legislation, and the EU Commission has been working on possible reforms of the Directive since at least 2007. The latest news from the Commission is that they hope to come forward with new proposals some time in 2012.

The Definition of Package

The Regulations define package in the following manner:

"2(1) 'Package' means the pre-arranged combination of at least two of the following components when sold or offered for sale at an inclusive price and when the service covers a period of more than twenty-four hours or includes overnight accommodation:

(a) transport;
(b) accommodation;
(c) other tourist services not ancillary to transport or accommodation and accounting for a significant proportion of the package,

and

(i) the submission of separate accounts for different components shall not cause the arrangements to be other than a package;
(ii) the fact that a combination is arranged at the request of the consumer and in accordance with his specific instructions (whether modified or not) shall not of itself cause it to be treated as other than pre-arranged;"

The elements of the definition pose a number of problems of interpretation and each will be looked at in turn. Throughout this examination, however, it should be borne in mind that for there to be a package all the elements of the definition must be satisfied, not just some, although in particular cases it is usually just one or two of the elements that are in issue. This is particularly true of the *ABTA v CAA* case and the *CAA v Travel Republic* case, both of which largely turned upon the interpretation of "inclusive price". It should also be noted that until quite recently "traditional" tour operators, i.e. those that published brochures and sold their holidays predominantly through high street travel agencies fitted quite comfortably within the definition and were willing to admit to it. As with most laws, the difficulties arise at the margins and in those situations where perhaps it was not intended that the Regulations would apply.

"pre-arranged combination"

It is important to note that the phrase "pre-arranged combination" which is discussed here is almost inextricably linked with the phrase "inclusive price" which is discussed in the next section. Cases such as *ABTA v CAA* and *CAA v Travel Republic* touch upon both these aspects of the definition and readers are advised to study both sections before arriving at any conclusions on what is the law in this area.

The words "pre-arranged combination" cover a standard brochured package, i.e. an "off the shelf" package, and therefore conventional tour operators will clearly be encompassed within this part of the definition. The question arises however as whether it covers "tailor-made" packages put together by travel agents, or indeed by tour operators? Does pre-arranged mean pre-arranged *before the client enters a travel agency* or does it mean that all the components of the package are in place *before the contract is concluded*? It could also mean put together *before the client travels*? If it is either of the latter two then a travel agent or tour operator who puts ad hoc travel and accommodation components together for clients could become liable for the proper performance of the whole arrangement. Not only will the travel agent/tour operator incur liability for the whole package but it will also mean that he is subject to the bonding and information regime.

This was a question that caused considerable difficulty for travel agents but two cases have endeavoured to make the position clearer. The first of these cases is *Club Tour Viagens e Turismo v Garrido* (C-400/00). The facts of the case were that the defendant booked a holiday through a travel agency in Portugal. The holiday consisted of accommodation at an all-inclusive resort operated by Club Med in Greece plus flights from Portugal. It was the travel agent who combined the flights (from a different supplier) with the all-inclusive resort. While on holiday the resort became infested with thousands of wasps which prevented the defendant from enjoying his stay. Despite his complaints, neither the travel agency nor Club Med could provide suitable alternative accommodation. On his return the defendant refused to pay for the holiday and the travel agent sued him. The domestic court in Portugal referred the case to the European Court of Justice for a ruling on two issues. The first of these was whether arrangements put together by a travel agent at the request of, and according to the specifications of, a consumer or defined group of consumers fell within the definition of a package. The second was whether the term "pre-arranged combination" could be interpreted as meaning a package put together at the time when the contract was concluded. In a brief but robust judgment the European Court of Justice held that both questions should be answered in the affirmative. On the first issue the court said that there was nothing in the definition which prevented such arrangements from being a package; and on the second issue it said that, given the answer to the first question, then it necessarily followed that the arrangements were pre-arranged if they consisted of elements chosen by the consumer before the contract was concluded. Note that the travel agent was suing for non-payment—i.e. breach of contract, therefore it was impossible for them to argue that there was no contract.

The second case is the case of *ABTA v CAA* referred to above. The facts of the case were that the CAA had issued guidance to the travel industry on what constituted a package. (Guidance Note 26. See [2005] I.T.L.J. 71 for the text of this Note which has now been withdrawn.) The reason they did this was because, as administrators of the ATOL system, they wanted tour operators and travel agents to know just where they stood when it came to whether or not an ATOL licence was required. The ATOL system is a part fulfilment of the UK government's obligation to ensure that "organisers" of "packages" can provide sufficient evidence of financial security in the event of their insolvency. To do this the government incorporated the definition of package from the Package Travel Directive into the ATOL Regulations. However, the advice offered in the CAA's Guidance Note was considered by the travel industry to be too broad and they challenged it in the High Court by means of judicial review. What the industry was concerned about was the extension of the definition of package to encompass travel agents who as part of their normal activities put together ad hoc travel arrangements which would be caught within the CAA's definition of a package—resulting in the need for travel agents to bond these activities, and, as a side effect, creating liability for all the components of this "package". This case will be examined in much more detail below but one of the issues raised in it was the meaning of "pre-arranged". The Court of Appeal's decision was very much in accordance with the *Club Tour* decision. This is what the Court had to say about the *Club Tour* decision:

"The requirement that the components of the package must be sold or offered for sale as a 'pre-arranged combination' is met not only where the components are put together by the organiser without input from the customer (typically, the brochure holiday) but also where the components are put together by the organiser in accordance with the specifications of the individual customer (or consumer) or group of customers (typically, the 'customised' holiday)—*Club-Tour, Viagens e Turismo SA v Alberto Carlos Lobo Gonçalves Garrido* (Case C-400/00) [2002] ECR I-4051. And the requirement is satisfied not only in cases where the components have been put together and offered for sale by the organiser in advance of any contact with the individual customer but also in cases 'where the combination of tourist services is the result of the wishes expressed by the customer up to the moment when the parties reach an agreement and conclude the contract'—*ibid*, paragraph [19]. It can be seen, of course, that the principle is expressly stated, as proviso (ii), in the definition of 'package' in ... the Package Travel Regulations ... That proviso did not appear in the Directive, which was the text which the Court of Justice was required to consider in the *Garrido* case." (Chadwick L.J. at para.20)

It is worthwhile mentioning as an aside that the recommendation made in the European Commission consultation document (SEC (1999) 1800 final) was that:

" ... the word 'pre-arranged' seems to be artificial, of unclear meaning and effect and could be eliminated." (p.8)

As Chadwick L.J. said, the approach taken by the ECJ in the *Club Tour* case was foreshadowed in our own legislation by the proviso to reg.2(1)(c) which states:

"(ii) the fact that a combination is arranged at the request of the consumer and in accordance with his specific instructions (whether modified or not) shall not of itself cause it to be treated as other than pre-arranged."

This gives the impression that a tailor-made package is within the definition of package, but closer examination reveals that this is not so. It is merely stating that there is nothing in the definition of a package that *prevents* a tailor-made package from being a package. It does *not* say that a combination that is put together at the request of the consumer *is* a package. However, in conjunction with the *Club Tour* case, there is clearly nothing in the UK legislation to prevent a similar approach being taken by the UK courts and this is what the Court of Appeal seems to have accepted.

The consequences of this for travel agents can be far-reaching. If, as the case suggests, most travel agents who put tailor-made packages together could be within the scope of the Directive then they will have to comply with all the requirements of the Directive. In practical terms this means that they must comply with the information regime; they must be bonded; and they must accept liability for all the components of the package—including all the defaults of the hotels they book for clients in whatever far off place clients choose to go to. (Note again, however, that this extension of liability is subject to what is said below in the section on "inclusive price" in the *ABTA v CAA* and *CAA v Travel Republic* cases.)

Although the *Club Tour* and *ABTA v CAA* cases go a long way to clarifying one of the more contentious parts of the law, there are nevertheless some types of arrangement which either fall outside the definition or where the answer is not so clear cut. One type of arrangement which falls outside the definition are excursions or other arrangements which are purchased in resort or after the package has been sold. *Gallagher v Airtours Holidays Ltd* [2001] C.L.Y. 4280 is a simple example of such a case. The claimant had purchased a skiing holiday from the defendants and then, while on the transfer bus to the resort, had purchased a "ski-pack". She was injured due to the alleged negligence of the skiing tutor whose services were included in the ski-pack. It was held, amongst other things, that there was no liability under the Package Travel Regulations because the ski-pack was not part of the "pre-arranged combination" that made up the package. (See also *Sheppard v Crystal Holidays Ltd* [1997] C.L.Y. 3858.) There is nothing, however, to prevent a tour operator voluntarily accepting liability for excursions which do not form part of a pre-arranged combination. *Waters v Thomson* [2000] 8 C.L. 106 is such a case; where the tour operator did accept liability but was found not liable on the facts. (See also M. Chapman "Excursions: Tour Operators and the Negligence of Local Suppliers" [2002] I.T.L.J. 123; and M. Chapman "Holidays, Excursions, Trips, Tours, Promotions Packages? A Voyage Around Regulation 2(1) of The Package Travel Regulations 1992" [2004] I.T.L.J. 129; and for recent case law, *Moore v Hotelplan* [2010] EWHC Civ 276 in Ch.5.)

More difficult are those arrangements which are referred to as "contract splitting". Another term used in this context is "dynamic packaging". Neither is a term of art and often they are used interchangeably. (Whichever term is used the essence is that it is something done by travel agents which may or may not result in a "package" as defined.) Very broadly what it means is that one party, either the travel agent or tour operator, sells the consumer the elements of what could be a package, most commonly flights and hotel accommodation, but denies that it makes up a package on the grounds that the consumer is not making one contract, with the travel agent or tour operator, but two contracts—with the suppliers of the transport and accommodation. The rationale behind this is apparently that the travel agent/tour operator is not a principal, making a contract in his own right but only an agent making a contract on behalf of others—the suppliers. While this is a perfectly legitimate claim, and can actually be seen as enhancing the rights of the consumer by giving him direct rights against the supplier that he might not otherwise have, it does not necessarily mean that the travel agent/tour operator is outside the scope of the Regulations. Liability is imposed on "organisers" not "principals" and the term "organiser" cuts across the conventional categories of principal and agent. It is possible to be an agent but also an "organiser" and therefore have liabilities under the Regulations. What is important in this context is whether the organiser has put together a package which amounts to a "pre-arranged combination". (But see the decision of Goldring J. in the High Court in *ABTA v CAA* on this point, quoted below at p.61.)

At one end of the scale, where the elements of the package are contained in a brochure, and where the consumer can "pick and mix" from a wide offering of transport and accommodation, any statement to the effect that this is not a package because the consumer is merely entering into separate contracts with different suppliers is unlikely to succeed. The travel agent/tour operator who put the brochure together will be regarded as selling a pre-arranged combination every bit as much as the travel agent in the *Club Tour* case, if not more so.

At the other end of the scale much more difficult issues are raised by those internet sites which offer the consumer the facility to book both flights and accommodation, e.g. Ryanair, easyJet, Opodo, lastminute.com, Expedia. Some of these sites enable the consumer to place their purchases in a "basket" and pay for them with one payment at the end of the transaction. Subject to what is said below about what is meant by an "inclusive price" these appear to fit within the definition of a package. And some of these are happy to acknowledge that what they are selling are packages. However, others give rise to much more difficulty. After booking the flight the consumer is invited to book a hotel as well and on taking up the invitation a separate site opens up from which the hotel can be booked. When the consumer has completed the booking he will have two contracts with two suppliers represented by two separate debits on his credit card. Does this amount to a "pre-arranged combination" sold by an "organiser"?

The immediate problem facing the consumer is that the arrangements he has made appear to be separate arrangements with two separate suppliers rather than a combination. This is probably no accident; the separation of the elements may be just what the website host sets out to achieve—in all probability it has been done deliberately so as to avoid creating a package. In commercial terms it produces two benefits that we referred to earlier—there will be no need to incur the cost of bonding the arrangements, nor will liability for the defaults of the suppliers have to be taken on.

What is the difference, it can be argued, between this situation, where the airline, as a convenience to the consumer, provides a link from his website to the site of a separate trader altogether, and the situation where the consumer logs off one site and then proceeds to the other site himself. Where the consumer makes his way independently to the sites could this be regarded as a "pre-arranged combination"? Is it not more akin to the situation where the consumer, using less technologically advanced methods, telephones the airline and books tickets and then, in a separate call, books his hotel room? No one would call this latter arrangement a package so why should the former be one simply because the number of clicks required is fewer?

On the other hand, what is the difference between what these sites can do for the consumer and what a travel agent can do? If I go into a travel agency as an independent traveller the agent can log on to a CRS or a viewdata system and book my flights and then log on to another system and book my hotel rooms—probably accessing the same inventory in the same way as the internet host site. If, according to the *Club Tour* case this would be a package when put together by the travel agent, why would it not be a package when put together by the company hosting the internet site? The travel agent hosts the CRSs in physical premises on the high street whereas the internet operator hosts them in cyberspace but it is essentially the same process.

Another way of looking at it would be to ask what is the purpose of such sites, which permit a consumer to book both flights and accommodation at the same time? And, also, what are the commercial relationships between the host and the other suppliers on the site? A further question might be to ask how the arrangements are viewed by the consumer.

The answer to the first question is that the host, for good commercial reasons, wants to be able to offer the consumer more. Purchasing services over the internet can be a frustrating business and the convenience of buying all one's travel needs via one site is very attractive to the consumer. Putting it another way, it means that the host can offer "one-stop shopping" for the consumer—permitting him to buy what is to all intents a package.

Looking at the second question, it may very well be the case that the host is making money not only on his own product but may also profit from sales made by the other suppliers with links from his site. If this were the case it becomes more difficult to distinguish the conventional travel agent from the internet host in that they both perform similar functions and are rewarded in much the same way. All that the links between the websites do is to make more transparent a process that already takes place in a travel agency.

Viewed from the consumer's perspective, if he gives any thought to the transaction, he may very well consider that by the time he logs off the site he has purchased a combination of elements that could constitute a package. Again, the transparency of the transaction may be an issue. If it is not clear to the consumer that he is leaving the host's website and entering that of another supplier's it could be argued that the host could be seen to be putting a combination together. The more "seamless" the transition is between the sites the more likely this argument is to succeed. Where the transition is clearly flagged up and there are clear indications that the consumer has ceased to deal with one company and is now dealing with another then the argument becomes harder to sustain. But how different is this from the travel agent who says "I have booked you a flight with BA and you now have a contract with them for a transatlantic flight, and now I am going to book you a Marriott hotel in New York using another CRS and when I have finished you will also have a separate contract with them"?

Some of these problems seem to have been tackled in the "ATOL Reform Consultation Document" issued by the Department for Transport in June 2011 (available at *http://www.dft.gov.uk/consultations/dft-2011-17/*). The proposals aim to bring "flight-plus" arrangements within the ATOL Regulations. A "flight-plus" arrangement is where a "flight-plus arranger" makes available a flight plus either car hire or accommodation. If the request for these arrangements is made within a period of 24 hours then the arranger will be caught by the new regulations and they will have to obtain an ATOL licence and their consumers will be protected against insolvency. By insolvency the proposals mean not only the insolvency of the flight-plus arrangers but also their suppliers—with the consequence that if the arranger remains solvent but their supplier(s) don't the arranger will have to replace the components—or offer a refund. This has the effect of creating "quasi packages" where the arranger will have a similar liability to reg.14 of the PTR but not the liability found under reg.15 (see Ch.10 on Remedies and Ch.5 on Liability for a more extensive discussion of these liabilities and Ch.12 for an explanation of the ATOL rules on insolvency).

The definition of "flight-plus arranger" in the new ATOL regulations is wide enough to also take in "click throughs", but because of limitations on the power of the DfT and the CAA to legislate on the regulation of airlines this extension of liability does not go so far as to regulate click throughs by airlines, who remain exempt from the ATOL scheme—unless of course they are actually selling packages. In early 2012 the Government indicated an intention to tackle this loophole eventually.

"inclusive price"

This element of the definition has taken on increased significance following the *ABTA* case. The case, in both the High Court and the Court of Appeal, examined a number of possible interpretations. For instance, it might be possible to interpret the word restrictively as meaning only those prices where the price is a global price for the whole package and where the individual components of the package are not priced or costed out: in other words, where the price of the individual elements is disguised from the client. The argument would be that where a tailor-made package has been put together and the elements are itemised on the invoice before being totalled up the final price would not be an inclusive price. But this raises the problem of conventional packages where certain elements can be priced separately, e.g. airport supplements and meal supplements.

If such a distinction could be made then this might be one way of taking tailor-made packages out of the Regulations. However, there are limitations on this approach because the Regulation clearly states that:

> "the submission of separate accounts for different components shall not cause the arrangements to be other than a package." (reg.2(1)(c)(i))

This reflects the provisions of the Directive (art.2(1)) which states:

> "The separate billing of various components of the same package shall not absolve the organizer or retailer from the obligations under this Directive".

Clearly, that prevents an operator from breaking up an acknowledged package and submitting separate invoices and claiming it is not a package because it is not sold at an inclusive price. But does it prevent a travel agent from separately itemising on one bill the different components of a tailor-made package and arguing that it is not a package as defined in the Regulations, on the grounds that he is not selling it at an inclusive price? To go one stage further, does it prevent the same agent submitting more than one invoice for the tailor-made package and arguing that this is quite legitimate because it is not a package?

Looked at this way, the travel agent is deploying two arguments to buttress his case. First he is saying that this is not a package because it is not a "pre-arranged combination". Then he consolidates that view by issuing an itemised invoice or more than one invoice to reflect the fact that these are separate components not sold at an inclusive price.

The trouble with this approach is that it creates the impression of being a sham. Far from being an effective means of evading the Regulations it would probably have the counter-productive effect of alienating those judges who encountered it. So it will be difficult for a travel agent to convince a court that it is not selling holidays at an inclusive price but to avoid such a conclusion we would suggest that probably the only safe way of not selling at an inclusive price is to demonstrate that the consumer booked components on separate occasions. Even then, however, there are dangers, as the DTI pointed out:

> "... someone wanting to book a package holiday could be sold accommodation and told to return later to arrange and purchase the necessary transport. This

would create separate bills for each element, but such an artificial arrangement would not mean that a package had not been sold." (*Looking into the Package Travel Regulations*, p.7, note 14, DTI, 1994, URN 94/645. Note that this version of the DTI guidance appears to have been withdrawn.)

It was issues such as these that were at the heart of the *ABTA* case. The Court of Appeal had to tackle head on the issue of what was meant by "inclusive price". The underlying issue, as expressed in a letter from ABTA to the CAA (see para.53), was that ABTA did not want travel agents to incur the burdens of the package travel regime if all they were doing was what they had traditionally done for consumers:

"It is important to note that travel agents putting together flight seats and accommodation etc. at the request of a client at the time a booking is made, without any advertising of the possibility of combining the elements in question are simply carrying on the normal business of a travel agent. This is distinct in most cases from agents who are selling split contract packages, which are advertised as such and/or involve some pre-planning by the agent as to the possibility of the elements being combined. This is obviously a complex and often grey area *but normal travel agency business should not be caught*." (Emphasis added)

It is worthwhile quoting at length from the judgment of Chadwick L.J. to show how he tackles the issue. He begins by showing how the concept of "a pre-arranged combination" is inextricably linked with "inclusive price":

" ... The requirement that the components be sold or offered for sale 'at an inclusive price' must be read in conjunction with the requirement that the components be sold or offered for sale as a pre-arranged combination. The price is the price of the combination." (para.24)

He then goes on to explain what he understands by an inclusive price:

"25. In many cases—indeed, I suspect, in the majority of cases—the price of the combination will not be the aggregate of the prices for which the components within the combination would have been sold or offered for sale if each component had been sold or offered for sale as a separate service outside the combination. That may be because some of the components (for example, the services of the organiser's local representative) would not be available as a separate service outside the combination. Or it may be because some of the components can be provided more cheaply if provided in conjunction with other components—the hotel may provide a courtesy airport transfer service. Or it may be that, in order to sell the package, the organiser will price attractively: the organiser will offer the package of services at a price which is below the aggregate of the prices which would be charged if the components had been sold separately. In those cases there is unlikely to be difficulty in reaching the conclusion, on the facts, that the components (including flight accommodation) are being sold as a pre-arranged combination and at an inclusive price. The same could be said of cases—which, I suspect, are likely to be rare indeed—in which the price of the combination exceeds the aggregate of the prices for which the components would have been sold or offered for sale separately.

26. The more difficult cases are those in which the price for the whole is equal to the aggregate of the prices for which the components would have been sold or offered for sale separately. The principle is, perhaps, easier to state than to apply in practice. If the components are offered for sale as a pre-arranged combination—albeit that the components are not combined (and, perhaps, not all identified) until 'the moment when the parties reach an agreement and conclude the contract' (to adopt the language of the Court of Justice in the *Garrido* case)—then the price for the combination will be "an inclusive price" notwithstanding that it may have been calculated, arithmetically, by aggregating the prices of the components: that is to say, notwithstanding that the price for the combination is the aggregate of the prices for which each component would have been sold or offered for sale if it had been sold or offered for sale as a separate service outside the combination. The factual question to be resolved—on a case by case basis—is whether the services are being sold or offered for sale as components of a combination; or whether they are being sold or offered for sale separately, but at the same time.

27. The point may be illustrated by examples. Suppose a customer, in London, who wishes to spend a week at a named hotel in, say, Rome. He asks his travel agent what the trip will cost him. The agent ascertains that the cost of the return flight will be £X, the cost of accommodation will be £Y and the cost of the airport transfers will be £Z. Without disclosing the individual cost of each service, the agent offers the customer flights, accommodation and transfers at a price of £(X+Y+Z). The customer accepts without further inquiry. In that case there would be little doubt—as it seems to me—that the services were sold as a pre-arranged combination and at an inclusive price.

28. Now suppose that the agent has informed the customer that the cost of flights will be £X, the cost of accommodation will be £Y and the cost of transfers will be £Z; and has explained to the customer that he can purchase any one or more of those services, as he chooses, without any need to purchase the others. He has explained, in effect, that the customer can choose to purchase the other services elsewhere; or to make other arrangements. In that case—as it seems to me—there would be little doubt that the services are not offered for sale as a pre-arranged combination and at an inclusive price.

29. What, then, if the customer chooses, and contracts for, one of those services. It is plain that that service would not be sold as a pre-arranged combination: it is not sold in combination with any other service. And it is plain that that position would not alter, if having paid for one of those services, the customer subsequently decides to take, and contracts for, another of the services. Nor would the position alter if, after paying for the second service, the customer later decides to take, and contracts for, the third service. And it would make no difference if, having entered into three separate contracts and received three separate invoices, the customer were to pay the three invoices

with a single cheque. The position would be the same. There would have been no sale of a pre-arranged combination of components at a single inclusive price. Rather, there would have been three separate sales of independent services, the aggregate of the prices payable for the three separate services being satisfied by a single payment.

30. Nothing in the preceding paragraph is inconsistent with proviso (i) to the definition of 'package' in the Package Travel Regulations ... ('the submission of separate accounts for different components shall not cause the arrangements to be other than a package') or with the proviso to the definition in the Directive ('The separate billing of various components of the same package shall not absolve the organiser or retailer from the obligations under this Directive'). As the judge explained at paragraph [158] of his judgment, if the arrangements would otherwise be a 'package'—because the services are sold or offered for sale as components of a pre-arranged combination and at an inclusive price— the substance of the arrangements is not altered by invoicing the components separately. But, if the arrangements would not otherwise be a 'package'—because the services are, in fact, sold or offered for sale separately—separate billing merely reflects the substance of the arrangements. The most that could be said is that composite billing might be evidence (in the particular case) that the services had been sold as a package.

31. Returning to the second of the examples which I have set out, difficult questions of fact are likely to arise if the customer chooses and contracts for two or more of the services on the same occasion. The principle is not in doubt. If the services are sold or offered for sale as components of a combination, there is a package: if they are sold or offered for sale separately but at the same time, there is no package. The question whether they are sold as components of a combination—or separately but at the same time—is a question of fact. That question may not be easy to resolve in the particular case."

Before we examine this in more detail, it is instructive to see what was said in the High Court about the meaning of "inclusive price" because the approach taken by the Court of Appeal is different. In the High Court, Goldring J. Said:

"97. This [the meaning of 'inclusive price'] is at the heart of Mr. Haddon-Cave's submissions [counsel for ABTA]. His submission comes to this. An inclusive price is a single, comprehensive or overall price. It is more than a total or aggregate price. 'Inclusive' connotes something extra. It is analogous to the distinction between the sale in the supermarket of 'three for the price of two,' as opposed to the bill produced at the checkout. The bill is simply an arithmetical total of different and separate purchases. An 'inclusive price' imports an element of things tied or linked together in a financial sense. If it is a package, one element cannot be removed. The buyer has the choice of taking or leaving it. A sale at an inclusive price does not mean, submits Mr. Haddon-Cave, that the individual components cannot be identified, or made up in different ways; for example, with different choices of hotels or flights or whatever.

...

98. Third, the words 'inclusive price' should be given their ordinary and natural meaning. The ordinary and natural meaning of the word 'inclusive' connotes *more than a mere arithmetical total of the component parts of a price*. If the substance of a transaction is the sale by the travel agent of separate and discrete components of (for example) a holiday, with no one part being connected with or dependent upon any other part (other than that they are sold together), to call the resulting price 'inclusive' is in my view to stretch the ordinary and natural meaning of that word. It is in reality no more an 'inclusive price' than is the total price of goods at the check out of a supermarket. For the sale of a package at an inclusive price the relationship between the component parts of that package must be such as to mean that the consumer is buying and paying for them as a whole: that the sale or offer for sale of one component part is in some way connected with or dependent on the sale or offer for sale of the others." (Emphasis added. Cf. the Court of Appeal decision)

In para.45 of the judgment, Chadwick L.J. raises the issue of whether the subjective intention of the consumer makes a difference as to whether a package is being sold. He says:

" ... the fact that the customer *thinks* [emphasis added] he is buying two or more separate services at the same time rather than a combination of services at an inclusive price—(or *vice versa*)—may be a powerful evidential pointer to the true nature of the transaction."

So what can we say about what the Court of Appeal believes is meant by "inclusive price"?

First, although in many cases an "inclusive price" will not be the same as a "total price" it is nevertheless *possible* for a total price, i.e. a simple arithmetic total of the various elements of the combination, to amount to an inclusive price.

Secondly, it is possible that the "pre-arranged combination" and the "inclusive price" may only be identified at the moment the contract is concluded.

Thirdly, consistent with the Directive, separate billing of the components will not be sufficient to demonstrate there is not a package if in fact there is one.

Fourthly, where the consumer chooses from a menu of different components in circumstances where it has been explained that he can purchase any one or more of the services, which he can take or leave as he sees fit, and where the price will always be an arithmetical total, there is a greater chance that this may not be a package. The impression given, however, is that the court favours the non-package alternative in this scenario. The explanation must be compellingly communicated, however; and the imposition of an opaque service charge might tip a court towards finding that there is a package—*Titshall v Qwerty Travel Ltd* [2011] EWCA Civ 1569.

Fifthly, the supermarket analogy used by Goldring J. in the High Court turns out to be over-simplistic, although it does have the merit of accessibility (but see the *Titshall* case on this point).

Sixthly, the state of mind of the consumer *may* have a bearing on whether the consumer has purchased a package or not.

Seventhly, some components such as the services of a representative, are not available separately, which make it unlikely that it is being sold otherwise than as part of a pre-arranged combination sold at an inclusive price.

Finally, and most importantly, whether there is an inclusive price will turn upon whether there is a pre-arranged combination and this, in turn, will depend upon whether the components are bought as a combination or whether they are offered for sale *separately but at the same time*. On this issue, Chadwick L.J. said that "difficult questions of fact are likely to arise" and that the question "may not be easy to resolve in the particular case."

If we put these findings to the test, what answers do we come to? Let us imagine, for the sake of argument, that a consumer enters a travel agency with the idea of booking a city break to Barcelona—a typical transaction that travel agents encounter every day of the week. She only knows roughly when she wants to go, which airline she wishes to fly with and where she wants to stay—but she is happy to be guided by the travel agent on all these things. But she does know that before she leaves the agency it is her intention to book both a flight *and* accommodation because she does not want the one without the other. The travel agent is only too willing to help her and when he discovers that what she wants cannot be purchased "off the shelf" as a package from a conventional tour operator he offers her a wide choice of scheduled flights and accommodation from a variety of sources to suit her needs. Let us also say that he offers various "permutations" (to endeavour to use a neutral word), e.g. different classes of hotel; different hotel locations; different flight times; different airports, etc, each with different prices, until she finds one that suits her. If, after she has made her final choice, she has both a flight and a hotel, does this amount to a package? Or to borrow from the words of Chadwick L.J., did she buy the components as a combination or were they sold separately but at the same time? We venture to suggest, although somewhat tentatively, that in *this* example, despite what his lordship had to say in para.28, it is the former rather than the latter. When she entered the agency she intended to purchase a combination; she informed the travel agent that she wanted both a flight and accommodation; and, at the end of the transaction she had secured what she wanted—a combination of the two. But would this kind of arrangement be regarded as a package if bought over the internet?

Following the ABTA case, the Civil Aviation Authority, in an attempt to clarify the law, in particular in relation to travel arrangements made over the internet, brought a prosecution, which was regarded as a test case, against an internet travel agent, Travel Republic Ltd—*CAA v Travel Republic Ltd* [2010] EWHC 1151 (Admin). The essence of the case was that, contrary to the ATOL Regulations (Civil Aviation (Air Travel Organisers' Licensing) Regulations 1995, as amended), Travel Republic were selling packages without holding an ATOL licence and thus putting their consumers at risk if they became insolvent.

The case was heard first in the Magistrates' Court by a District Judge. He was faced with 20 informations charging Travel Republic with breaches of the Regulations. Most of the charges related to arrangements booked over the internet (although it was possible to book over the phone) and most of these involved the consumers choosing the "Tailor Made Holidays" option on Travel

Republic's website. The judge looked exhaustively at the booking process which permitted the consumer to choose from a wide range of flights, then from a wide range of accommodation and then offered the possibility of an airport transfer. Once the consumer had made his selection he was invited to complete and pay for his booking. Once the booking was made, the consumer would receive emails confirming each of the elements of the booking. Of particular significance in the process was that at various stages Travel Republic informed the consumer that he was not buying a package and that Travel Republic were only agents and not principals.

After quoting extensively from the *ABTA v CAA* case (much the same passages are quoted above), which of course he was bound by, the judge concluded that in accordance with para.28 of Chadwick L.J.'s judgment in that case that Travel Republic had:

" ... adequately explained to the consumers in this case that they could purchase any one or more of the services on offer as they might wish, without the need to purchase any other." (para.47)

He went on to say:

"[48] In my judgment the prosecution has failed to discharge the burden of proving that TRL did anything other than sell or offer to sell components of holidays separately, but at the same time. I am not satisfied, beyond reasonable doubt, that TRL made available to any of the customers named in the charges, flight accommodation which constituted a component of a package holiday."

The CAA appealed the case to the Divisional Court. The question before the Divisional Court in the appeal was not whether Travel Republic was selling packages but whether the judge was entitled to find, in the light of the evidence before him, that Travel Republic had not made the arrangements available as components of a package. The Divisional Court could only find against Travel Republic if " ... there was no evidence to sustain the decision or that it was otherwise a perverse conclusion on the evidence, i.e. one no reasonable judge could have reached" (para.51). The Divisional Court upheld the decision of the District Judge on the basis that he had applied the law (in the *ABTA* case) correctly to the facts and had come to a reasonable decision. It was perfectly acceptable for the judge to rely upon the words of Chadwick L.J. in para.28 of the *ABTA* case (quoted above) that such arrangements were not sold as components of a package. The judge was entitled to prefer the statements in para.28 of the *ABTA* case to the less assertive statement in para.31.

In a passage which incorporates the Court's view of the subjective nature of the transaction, Elias L.J. had this to say:

"49. It is clear from paragraph 45 of Chadwick LJ's judgment that the subjective perception of the customer is not conclusive as to the nature of the transaction. I accept, as did Chadwick LJ, that the distinction between cases caught by the regulation and those falling outside it can on the particular facts be a fine one; to that extent each transaction is fact sensitive. So the regulation will almost certainly bite in a case where the customer specifically tells the agent that he wishes to buy a holiday and the component services are either offered or suggested to him as part of a proposed single holiday package. The combination is then put together by the agent for the customer. Whilst that may well have happened on occasions with this agent, particularly where holidays were booked by telephone, that is not the typical situation which we are required to address in this test case.

50. Essentially we are dealing with a situation where the customer chooses his or her own combination of services from a wide range of options, in circumstances where TRL does not know whether a customer will select only a single service or a combination. The customer is putting together his own combination for himself. Of course, TRL will wish to sell as many services as it can, and it will know that the majority—and perhaps an overwhelming majority—of its customers are seeking to combine the services to make a holiday. Their website recognises that fact when it advertises that holiday packages are available. But, in my judgment, that does not necessarily mean that they are selling the services or otherwise making them available at the point of sale as component elements of a pre-arranged combination."

On the subjective nature of the issue the District Judge in the Magistrates' Court provided an interesting analogy. Endeavouring to illustrate that the subjective approach is not necessarily determinative at para.31 he says:

"Say someone wants to buy a cow. He approaches a farmer who removes a horse from his field. On the side of the horse someone has painted the letters 'C-O-W'. Assume both the farmer and the purchaser believe that what is being sold and purchased is a cow. The transaction is concluded. It doesn't matter what they think, the purchaser has bought a horse not a cow."

When deciding what weight to put on the *Travel Republic* case it is important to note that the Divisional Court in the case was bound by the decision in the *ABTA* case which was decided in the Court of Appeal so there is no surprise in the fact that they chose not to be critical of the *ABTA* decision—in reality they had no choice but to accept the reasoning in that case.

Secondly, it was only a decision on the facts. In the words of Elias L.J.:

"I accept, as did Chadwick LJ, that the distinction between cases caught by the regulation and those falling outside it can on the particular facts be a fine one; to that extent each transaction is fact sensitive." (para.49)

Thirdly, however, it has to be recognised that it is entrenching the view that travel components can be purchased separately but at the same time. There may be scope for a well-informed consumer when dealing directly with a travel agent on the high street to say that what they want is a "package" and a court would agree, but a carefully constructed website such as in the *Travel Republic* case offers little hope for that kind of interpretation.

Where Are We Now?

Following the *Travel Republic* case the law seemed to be favouring those travel agents who do business over the internet and sell their products on a "separate but at the same time" model. By doing so they escape both the PTR and the ATOL scheme and as a consequence offer none of the protection to consumers under that legislation and they benefit from the lower costs this entails. This gives them a price advantage over more conventional ways of selling holiday products while at the same time offering the consumer more flexibility and a more convenient way of purchasing travel.

However the new "flight-plus" rules have effectively reversed much of the *Travel Republic* case and have imposed liabilities on travel agents that come some way towards package travel liabilities. It will be interesting to see how the travel industry will react to the new law and whether they will find ways of evading the new rules. If so, it may not be long before the EU legislates on the matter and it is anticipated that any new legislation will also bring internet agents within the package travel fold again.

In the meantime, it is still the case that both the *ABTA* and *Travel Republic* decisions turned on their facts, and some travel agents may yet find themselves in danger of a decision on the facts which places them on the other side of the line, as occurred in the *Titshall* case. (See Saggerson "The One Thing Needful" [2006] I.T.L.J. 183 for some trenchant views on the tendency in English cases to deliver fact-specific decisions. See also Chapman "What does the *ABTA* Judgment Mean for Internet Sales?" [2006] I.T.L.J. 85 and Chapman "Packages, The Sale of Separate Components and the Administrative Court" [2010] T.L.Q. 199.)

Another Aspect of Inclusive Price

The *Rechberger* case (C-140/97) referred to in Ch.1 focuses on a different aspect of "inclusive price". The facts were that the claimants had won a prize offered by a daily newspaper. As regular subscribers they were offered the opportunity of a holiday abroad on very advantageous terms. If they travelled alone all they had to pay was an airport departure tax and a single room supplement—flights and accommodation being otherwise free. If they travelled with a companion who paid the full price all the subscribers had to pay was the airport tax. The newspaper left the organisation of the holidays to a tour operator. Unfortunately, the offer proved to be far more successful than the tour operator had anticipated, and this caused logistical and financial difficulties which forced it into bankruptcy. The claimants, who had all paid in full, had all had their holidays cancelled and lost their money. The reason for this was twofold. First, the Austrian government had not implemented the provisions in the Directive relating to insolvency in accordance with the deadline laid down in the Directive; secondly, when they did implement it, the provisions were not adequate to protect consumers as the bank guarantees required by the Austrian legislation were not enough to cover the losses incurred by the consumers. Thus, some of the claimants were suing the Austrian government for non-implementation of the Directive and others for improper or inadequate implementation—depending on whether they had booked their holidays before or after the implementation date.

One of the issues in dispute at domestic level was whether or not those consumers who travelled alone fell within the scope of the Directive. In those circumstances, the National Court decided to stay proceedings and refer the following questions to the Court for a preliminary ruling:

(1) Does the protective purpose of art.7 of Council Directive 90/314/EEC of June 13, 1990 on package travel, package holidays and package tours also extend to trips for which, on the basis of the contract, the principal contractor has to pay:

   (a) if he travels alone, apart from airport security tax (departure tax), only a single-room supplement, or
   (b) if he is accompanied by one or more persons paying the full price, only the airport security tax (departure tax)

and nothing in respect of the flight and accommodation in a room with two or more beds?

The court held that this was a pre-arranged combination of at least two elements and that even though what the consumers paid for the package did not correspond to its value, or even to one component, it was nevertheless a package. To put it another way, the price was inclusive even if the price didn't cover everything that the consumer obtained.

Note that when excursions are bought in resort from tour operators, as previously discussed, it would be difficult to regard these as being purchased as part of an inclusive price.

"two of the following"

There was a time when if you looked carefully at the small print of a "flight-only" contract you would see that, at the insistence of some foreign governments, the contract also included accommodation (not uncommonly a tent in a field a hundred miles from the airport) which, in practice, was never used. Fortunately, this practice is almost unheard of today but it raised the interesting question of whether travel companies who offered such products were covered by the Regulations. Technically it appears that they would have been.

In the ECJ case, *easyCar (UK) Ltd v Office of Fair Trading* (C-336/03) the Court was asked to decide whether the term "transport services" used in the Distance Selling Directive (97/7/EC) included car hire. If so, it meant that car hire firms were exempt from the cancellation provisions of the Directive, i.e. consumers could not cancel the car hire contract after it had been made, unlike contracts for other services where they could. The decision, which was that car hire was a transport service, may very well have a bearing on the interpretation of the Package Travel Directive. If car hire is regarded as a transport service for the purposes of the Distance Selling Directive could it be similarly regarded for the purposes of the Package Travel Directive? More specifically, could a "fly-drive" package consisting of flights and car hire only, fall outside the scope of the Package Travel Directive on the basis that the consumer is only receiving two transport services? On the face of it this would appear to be the case. (See McDonald "Distance Contracts Directive and Tourist Bookings: *easyCar v OFT*" [2005] I.T.L.J. 192 for a discussion of this case.) However, if the Government's "flight-plus" proposals become law then these arrangements will at least be covered by the ATOL legislation. But, note that if the consumer booked rail travel to the continent and then picked up a car at his/her destination they would still be faced with the question of whether it was a transport and transport arrangement.

"accommodation"

Hotels, dormitories, caravans, chalets and tents—and probably even timeshare exchanges—would all fall within the meaning of accommodation and would form one element of a package, but there are marginal forms of accommodation which will cause difficulty. For instance, what about a berth on a North Sea ferry or a sleeper on an overnight train? If accommodation is to be equated with sleeping accommodation and if, as is generally the case, extra is paid for this "accommodation", then it would be hard to deny that it fell within the definition. The difficulty is that first, the perception of such arrangements is that the main purpose of such contracts is the transport element and the accommodation is entirely incidental to it. Secondly, although this is not a fatal argument, such arrangements are often not regarded or even purchased as a holiday or for leisure purposes. People do not regard them as "package holidays".

The answer to the first argument is that there is no requirement in the definition that the accommodation makes up a *significant* element of the package—merely that the package includes accommodation. Secondly, it should be borne in mind that the Regulations are not concerned exclusively with holidays. They are directed at a wider concept—tourism—which takes in not simply leisure travel but also business travel and other forms of tourism (although on this issue see the *AFS Finland* case below). This might be sufficient to account for the berth on the ferry and the sleeping compartment on the train but what about a couchette on the ferry or the reclining seats in the first class sections on planes that can be turned into beds? Given that all transport requires the provision of accommodation in the widest sense, there has to be a line drawn between what is purely accommodation for the purposes of travel—seats—and accommodation which goes beyond this—berths and sleeping compartments.

The Trading Standards Institute (formerly the Institute of Trading Standards Administration) has indicated its view that accommodation incidental to travel to a destination and where the consumer is not participating in a holiday does not create a package. This view can be typified as the "instinctive" or "common sense" approach. Would the man on the Clapham omnibus agree that a passenger who booked a sleeping compartment on the overnight train from Aberdeen to London had purchased a package? Of course not. While not denying that such an approach has its merits, it is nevertheless hard to square with the precise words of the definition and it ignores the view that tourism encompasses more than simply holidays and leisure travel. The DTI guidelines endorse the TSI view:

> "For 'accommodation' to be an element in the creation of a package, it needs to represent more than a facility which is ancillary to other aspects of an arrangement. [It would regard, for example, a berth on a cross-channel ferry or sleeping accommodation on an overnight train as a facility. But a cabin on a cruise ship would, in the opinion of the Department, create a package because

the consumer is being accommodated whilst being taken on a pre-arranged itinerary ...]" ("The Package Travel Regulations. Question and Answer Guidance for Organisers and Retailers" DTI, September 2005, URN 05/1694. Note that the text in the square brackets appeared in the 1994 guidance)

Interestingly, those companies which run overnight North Sea ferry crossings from England to continental Europe are increasingly emphasising the luxury and comfort of their ships and the nature of the onboard experience. No longer are they simply ferries, they are now "cruise ferries". ("On board our cruise ferries you'll enjoy award-winning service and top-class facilities" *www.brittany-ferries.co.uk*, July 2011.) Recently, the ECJ in the case of *Peter Pammer v Reederei Karl Schlüter GmbH & Co KG* (C-585/08) came very close to deciding that a cruise was a "package" in so many words. What it did decide was that for the purposes of Council Regulation (EC) 44/2001 on jurisdiction, a voyage by freighter "is a contract of transport which, for an inclusive price, provides for a combination of travel and accommodation" thus triggering the Regulation in favour of the consumer.

In the *AFS Finland* case referred to earlier, the facts were that AFS was an organisation whose object was to promote international co-operation and exchanges between various cultures. To that end, like its sister organisations in other countries, it organised exchange programmes for students aged between 16 and 18 years of age. To organise these activities, AFS relied on the support of various donors and foundations as well as on the work of volunteers. It also received aid from the Finnish State in order to finance its activities. AFS sent students abroad twice a year, usually for a period of 6 to 11 months. The students attended schools in the host country and lodged with families which put them up free of charge. AFS selected the students and placed them with suitable families selected on the basis of interviews. AFS arranged the students' transport to the host country by scheduled flights and, as a rule, the host family collected the student at the arrival point. Before departure the students had to prepare themselves by following courses on conditions abroad. Ten per cent of the cost of the journey was paid when the student was admitted to the exchange programme, that is to say normally about 10 months before departure. The balance was then paid before the beginning of the visit, in three instalments. On departure, the student received a pre-paid return air ticket. Part of AFS's fees went into a reserve fund which ensured, amongst other things, that the student could be transported home in circumstances where the return ticket issued to them could not be used for some reason.

A number of issues arose from the case but the one of particular relevance here is whether or not the stay with the host family could be regarded as "accommodation" within the meaning of art.2(1)(b) of the Directive (the equivalent of reg.2(1) of the Regulations). The court considered that the fact that the accommodation was free, that it was not in a hotel or similar accommodation and that it was for a long period of time were not reasons in themselves for saying that the stay with the family was not "accommodation" as defined. However, they went on to say that:

"their combined effect is such that 'hosting' which possesses all those characteristics cannot be described as accommodation within the meaning of the Directive."

There is little or no reasoning in support of this view, but taken in the context of the whole case the Court seems to be saying that this is not the kind of accommodation that the Directive was intended to cover because it is not "holiday" or "tourist" accommodation. This is a somewhat restrictive view of the scope of the Directive, one which we will return to when we look at the meaning of "other tourist services" below. Interestingly, the Advocate-General's opinion in the *AFS* case, which the court chose not to follow, was unequivocal on the question of accommodation. He said:

> "The definition of 'accommodation', in its turn, clearly covers any kind of accommodation, whether it be in a hotel, with a family, in a hostel, or wherever. The duration of the accommodation is of no importance in the scheme of the Directive, which, in this regard, does no more than lay down a minimum limit: the whole service offered to the consumer must last not less than 24 hours or must at least include overnight accommodation. By the same logic, the fact that the student is received into the family with which he boards as if he were a child of the family, is also of no consequence."

"transport"

In general, there should be little difficulty with this part of the definition. There may, however, be doubts over such things as cycling holidays or fly-drive holidays. With the former can it be said that transport is an element of the package when it is the client who actually transports himself from A to B? Does transport mean that the client *is transported* from A to B or can it also encompass a situation where a *means of transport* is provided and the client accomplishes the journey himself? In the cycling holiday example it may not matter because even if the cycle does not qualify as transport it will amount to another "tourist service" and still form one element of a package, assuming accommodation is also provided.

On the other hand, in a fly-drive holiday, if the drive element *is* regarded as transport there is no package, but if it can be classified as another tourist service there is a package. A court may very well say that fly-drive "feels" like a package, that car hire is a tourist service, and therefore the consumer has the protection of the Regulations. In practice, the distinction may not matter thanks to the tendency of many tour operators using the same set of terms and conditions to cover fly-drive holidays as well as conventional packages and thereby conferring on their fly-drive consumers the same rights as their other clients.

It may very well be that the *easyCar* case referred to above is determinative of the issue, i.e. car hire is a transport service therefore fly-drive contracts are not packages.

Keppel-Palmer v Exus Travel [2003] EWHC 3529 (QB) was a case which concerned a Millennium holiday in Barbados. The claimants hired a villa for $140,000 for a month and with the villa came a transfer in a limousine from the airport to the villa. One of the many questions that the court had to answer was whether or not the provision of the limousine transfer meant that the claimant had purchased a package consisting of accommodation and transport services. The High Court judge answered the question in the negative for a number of reasons. First, that there was no evidence that the limousine had been used.

Secondly, even if it had it was so insignificant a part of the contract that it could be disregarded as *de minimis*. This was "a question of fact and degree" according to Gage J. Thirdly, as the limousine had not been charged to the claimant it had not been "sold or offered for sale" and therefore it was not within reg.2. Although the decision feels right, each of these reasons could be challenged on technical grounds. First, it is not necessary to use the components of the package for the component to be part of a package. For instance, I may purchase a package, one of the benefits of which is the services of the tour operator's representative. Whether or not I need his or her services they are nevertheless one of the components of the package. Secondly, there is nothing in the regulation to the effect that the transport has can be discounted because it is *de minimis*; in contrast to the issue of "other tourist services" which have to comprise a "significant" part of the package. In this case the limousine transfer was to take 45 minutes, hardly, we would suggest, *de minimis*. Thirdly, so long as the transfer is packaged together with the villa, it does not have to be paid for—as decided in the *Rechberger* case. There was actually a finding which makes these arguments a little irrelevant, which was that the limousine transfer was not part of a combination anyway—it was thrown in free at a later stage. (See Saggerson "One Man's Mansion is Another Woman's Monstrosity" [2003] I.T.L.J. 185.) One area where this may be of significance is when an airport hotel offers a free shuttle bus service to the airport. It may be "free"; it may not be used by everyone; and for some it may be "*de minimis*" but for others it may be the very reason they chose that particular hotel. The DTI, however, are of the opinion that this will not count:

"**Question 9: Apart from providing accommodation all I do is collect people from the local railway station. Is this transport for the purpose of the Regulations?**
Answer: Where guests have arranged their own transport by air, rail, etc., the provision of free transport to take hotel guests from the local airport or railway station to the hotel is unlikely to be a transport component which goes to create a package. This would probably be considered a facility offered by the hotel." (URN 06/1640)

If a free limousine transfer is not "transport" for the purposes of the Regulations, what about a free "mule transfer"? Visitors to the Kasbah du Toubkal in Morocco, situated at the top of a mountain, are offered the option of walking up the hill or riding up by mule (see *www.kasbahdutoubkal.com*).

"other tourist services not ancillary to transport or accommodation"

What is a *tourist* service? Is there a class of services which are exclusive to tourists? Can a service be distinguished from a facility? When is the service ancillary to transport or accommodation and when is it not? Are meals at a hotel ancillary to the accommodation? All these words cause difficulty and have provoked some of the greatest disagreements about the scope of the Regulations.

"*other*" The question implicitly raised by this word is: "Other than what?" And the answer must be "other than transport and accommodation". In other words, if the service consists of transport or accommodation then it cannot be another tourist service. The Regulations are drawing a distinction between services which are transport and accommodation and other services. This may very well be the solution to the problem raised above about fly-drive and cycling holidays. Car hire and cycle hire are undoubtedly services but they are transport services and therefore should be classified as transport and not as other tourist services. (See now *easyCar v OFT* (C-336/03).)

"tourist" If a tourist is regarded as simply someone who travels for pleasure, a holidaymaker in other words, then the ambit of the Regulations is much reduced. The DTI's opinion, as expressed in their 1994 guidance notes on the Regulations, takes such a limited view:

"For example, a conference which included the provision of accommodation would not be a package just because of this, as a conference is not a tourist service. In the opinion of the Department, education is not a tourist service, provided it is undertaken with a view to obtaining a recognised qualification."

It is interesting to see that the Department have softened their line on this. In the first issue of their guidelines they took a much stronger line:

"Examples of services which are not tourist services are: educational services, business services, conference services etc."

In the *AFS Finland* case the ECJ specifically addressed the question of whether the arrangement of the student visits amounted to "other tourist services". Their answer, albeit brief, was quite categorical. On the issue of the selection of a school they said:

"In this connection, it should first be observed that selection of a school by the organiser of the package cannot in itself be regarded as a tourist service within the meaning of Article 2(1)(c) of the Directive. The specific purpose of such a service, offered to the students taking part in international student exchanges, is the education of the participants."

And on the issue of selecting a host family they said:

"Next, the service constituted by the selection of a family to host a student during his stay is in any event an ancillary service within the meaning of Article 2(1)(c) of the Directive and is therefore not covered by the concept of other tourist services."

Thus, they are not prepared to extend the meaning of tourist beyond someone who travels for pleasure or leisure—which is consistent with the overall philosophy that they applied to the Directive.

However, any respectable definition of tourist goes much further than "someone who travels for pleasure" (see Robinson "Who is a tourist? Issues arising from the Package Travel Regulations" [1995] T.L.J. 77 for definitions of tourist and tourism). People who travel on business and for educational purposes, or as pilgrims (the original tourists), would all qualify as tourists. Thus, a business conference which included hotel accommodation as well as business sessions would constitute a package. More surprisingly, an Open University summer school, if purchased as a single transaction, would also be a package. Perhaps the surprise would not be so great if it was accepted that participants in such activities could all be legitimately classified as tourists—every bit as much as the lager lout in Benidorm or the participants in a hen party in Dublin or Tallinn or Newcastle. Of course, many educational or business trips include both transport and accommodation and their status as packages is therefore beyond doubt. However, if educational and business services were not tourist services then there is a potential paradox. If the consumer buys only accommodation and an educational or business service then no package exists and there is no recourse against the organiser for defaults in the services under the PTR. However, if transport were added to the arrangements then this would constitute a package and the defaults in the non-tourist services would fall within the PTR.

Again, the Advocate-General in the AFS case was at odds with the stance eventually taken by the court. On the issue of tourist he had this to say:

"20. The purposes of the Directive, its wording and the preparatory work leading up to it disclose nothing to suggest that its scope is limited *exclusively* to tourist services. Since the Directive is a measure for the harmonisation of national laws which has as its main objective the protection of the weaker party to the travel contract, it is clear that all package services sold within the territory of the Community are subject to those requirements of consumer protection which justify the application of the protective provisions referred to in the Directive. As for the wording of the Directive itself, it is clear even from its title that it applies to package travel, package holidays and package tours, and this plainly means that there are types of travel included within the Directive's scope of application which are not undertaken for the purpose of holidays in the strict sense. Article 2(4) of the Directive, which contains a definition of 'consumer', also militates in favour of a broad interpretation of the scope of the Directive. As observed by the Finnish Government, that provision does no more than state that 'consumer' means the person who takes or agrees to take the package, as defined in Article 2, without laying down any requirements with respect to the purposes of the travel, and indeed this is quite different from what one finds in certain other directives aimed at protecting the consumer in which the concept of 'consumer' is expressly limited to 'any natural person who acts for purposes other than those of his professional business'.

21. Moreover, even if one were to concede that the Directive meant only to deal with services in the nature of Tourism, I do not think that this justifies, in any event, the conclusion proposed by the plaintiff in the main proceedings and by the United Kingdom Government. The problem would immediately arise of defining the concept of tourism, the answer to which appears to be anything but clear-cut. It is manifestly not equivalent to that of holidays. There can, of course, be cultural tourism, environmental tourism and so on. Moreover, a single journey may appear in the eyes of the person undertaking it as a holiday or as a form of cultural enrichment, for example. It would therefore seem quite arbitrary to define tourist services by reference to the purpose of the package

travel. Consequently, there would be no justification for limiting the protection which the Directive aims to provide to all consumers of package services only to those cases where services are offered to holiday travellers.

22. The scope of the Directive application cannot, therefore, be defined by reference to the purpose of the travel. There is nothing, either in the wording of the Directive or related to its objectives, that can be prayed in aid, to support the conclusion that only 'recreational' travel is protected under the substantive rules of the Directive and that travel for other purposes (business, conferences, family visits, study, to name but a few) is by definition excluded and therefore not subject to the consumer-protection provisions contained in the Directive. Quite apart from the obvious difficulties of identifying the intentions of those who enter into package-travel agreements, the need to prevent the risk, mentioned earlier, of the protection which the Directive aims to provide being evaded militates in favour of not ascribing any importance to the purposes for which the travel is undertaken."

"Services" This is also a word that has provoked discussion. In its 1994 guidelines the DTI (now DBIS) suggested that a distinction can be drawn between "services" and "facilities". They say:

"There is an important distinction between a service and a facility. Where a facility is available to all, and is provided with one other element of either transport or accommodation, then no package is created. However, where the facility is restricted to only a few who book or pay in advance then it becomes a tourist service and may create a package. As examples: access to fishing rights on a local river would *normally* be a service whereas the provision of a swimming pool at a hotel would be a facility. So the provision of a facility does not automatically amount to a tourist service." (p.8, note 26, emphasis added)

In the 2006 guidance (Question and Answer Guidance for Organisers and Retailers, November 2006, URN 06/1640) the treatment is much briefer:

"**Question 9: Would putting on special Christmas entertainment for the guests in my hotel mean I am selling a package?**
Answer: If the entertainment would be available to everybody who stayed at the hotel it would be regarded as a facility for all guests and not a tourist service."

Doubtless such a distinction can be made, but is it a real one? The DTI itself was sufficiently unsure of its own original example to qualify it with the word "normally", although its attitude seems to have hardened. If a hotel were asked what services it offered, would the answer be different to the one it would have given if it had been asked what facilities it offered? Even if certain things could be classified as facilities—the swimming pool, the golf course, the tennis courts, the health centre—they might all have services connected to them—the pool attendant, the golf professional, the tennis coach, the masseuse, etc, making a nonsense of the distinction. The effect of such a distinction is of course to obscure further a piece of legislation which is already riddled with such difficulties. It is interesting that ABTA have also issued guidelines, and on this point they too are unhappy with the distinction between services and facilities. They say that they "are not certain that the DTI are clear on the difference between a facility and a service." Saggerson is equally dismissive of the DTI approach (4th edn, pp.40–41).

"Ancillary": subsidiary, subservient, subordinate, supplementary or auxiliary. Unfortunately, none of these fine words helps to overcome the problem of deciding when a service will be ancillary or not. The problem arises most acutely with the range of services offered by hotels. Are the swimming pool, the golf course, the tennis courts, the health centre, ancillary to the hotel? Some guidance can be derived by looking at what ancillary does not mean—distinct, independent, autonomous. Are these services sufficiently distinct to make them a separate part of the package or are they so fully integrated into the accommodation that they can be regarded as one and the same thing? If, when the consumer books the accommodation, all these other services are automatically available without extra charge or without being promoted or marketed as a special feature then perhaps they can be regarded as ancillary to the accommodation. Saggerson suggests the following services at a hotel would be ancillary services: chambermaid and laundry services; concierge facilities; room service; security (4th edn, p.42). Normal service of hotel meals would also fall into this category. However, if the consumer has to pay extra for the services or if a special feature is made of them, e.g. a "cordon bleu" weekend, then the converse applies. Holiday villages are a case in point. Apart from accommodation they offer a range of services—water parks, funfairs, mini-golf, baby-sitting, bars, restaurants, dancing, cabaret, etc. On the one hand, all these services could be regarded as ancillary to the accommodation in that they all come as part of the price, they are available to all, they are situated in close proximity to the accommodation, etc. On the other hand, they form such a large proportion of the price and they figure so prominently as the reason for choosing this particular kind of holiday that they cannot legitimately be regarded as ancillary to the accommodation. The reality is that in many of these villages the accommodation is sometimes so basic that it is not the other services that are ancillary to the accommodation but rather the converse.

It is probably already evident that this part of the definition will have most impact upon the hotel sector. One only has to turn to the small ads in the Sunday papers to see this. There it is possible to find all kinds of short breaks offered by hotels and guest houses with a multitude of added extras—"cordon bleu" cookery weekends (as distinct from normal meals), drama weekends, mystery weekends, gliding weekends, slimming weekends, holidays for the lovesick (see *www.liebeskummer.de*) and even divorce weekends! Virtually all of these would fall into the category of package holidays because the services they offer are not ancillary to the accommodation. As will be discussed in more detail later, this will make the hoteliers not only liable for their own acts but also for the acts of their suppliers. In the case of a gliding weekend that goes wrong this liability could be substantial.

But, note that rail and coach operators who organise trips to rock concerts, musicals or similar events would not be affected to the same degree as hoteliers because they would not be caught by the Regulations unless the trip lasted for more than 24 hours or there was overnight accommodation. Likewise, a flight to a major European football match which included match tickets but where the whole of the arrangements took less than 24 hours would also not be caught.

And it would also be the case that unless sleeping accommodation or car hire were also included it would not be caught by the "flight-plus" provisions brought into effect in 2012 (see Ch.12).

"significant proportion of the package" This requirement should pose few problems. Significant can be measured in a number of ways—by the proportion of the price, by the proportion of time spent on it or perhaps, in cases where it costs little and is over quickly, by the importance attached to it. Tour operators often feel that however insignificant the service they fail to provide, consumers will always claim that it was the main reason for choosing this particular package. Experience suggests that courts will normally side with the consumer unless they lack credibility. In the *AFS Finland* case the court held that the preparation of the documentation and the preparatory courses for the students could not be regarded as a significant proportion of the package.

One issue which arises in this context is the status of holiday insurance. Is it "another tourist service" or not? It is our view that either it is not a "tourist service", or that in any event it is ancillary to the other components of the package.

There was a case referred to the ECJ which it was hoped would settle some of these matters. In *Toni Georgiev Semerdzhiev v Del-Pi-Krasimira Mancheva* (C-32/10), one of the questions posed to the Court was "How is the term 'other tourist services' in Article 2(1)(c) of Directive 90/314/EEC to be interpreted, and does that term cover the organiser's obligation to insure the consumer?" However, the ECJ held for some reason that it did not have jurisdiction so we will have to wait for another case to decide the matter.

"sold or offered for sale"

The purchase of a package holiday is generally a commercial transaction and when the organiser provides the holiday in exchange for the consumer's money this can accurately be labelled as a "sale". However, there are some packages, where even though money changes hands, it has been suggested that there is not a sale. This is what the DTI had to say:

> **"Question 2: I am just putting together a holiday for members of my social club. Am I caught?**
> Answer: The Regulations apply to selling and offering for sale. If the members of the social group have agreed to share the cost of a package they have decided to organise themselves, and they have merely appointed you to organise the details, then you are unlikely to be selling or offering for sale the package—even though a surplus may be retained by the organisation to be disposed of as the members may decide." (URN 06/1640)

The 1994 advice, now superceded, added this to the example above:

> "Similarly, packages organised as part of a course of education (for example a geology field trip) are unlikely to be sold in the normal sense of the word and will probably therefore not fall within the scope of the Regulations."

While recognising that the first example may demonstrate the validity of this argument, the second example is not so straightforward. The pupil or the student who purchased the field trip from his school or college might very well argue that they were "sold" a package. They would certainly see it as a commercial transaction and if anything went wrong they would regard themselves as having a contract with the provider whom they could sue if necessary—especially if the existence of a contract with the provider (i.e. the school or college) insulated the actual supplier from contractual liability. Note, however, that under the Contracts (Rights of Third Parties) Act 1999 the members of the party might have a direct action against the suppliers.

Even the first example is not clear cut. If the member of the organisation regarded the package as being put together at arm's length as a commercial transaction by the organisation from whom he then purchased it, then again it might be regarded as having been "sold" to him. LACORS discussed just this problem in one of their advice sheets. They were asked to advise on whether or not packages put together by a National Trust Members' Centre was "sold" to members. Their initial comment was that it would depend upon the exact make-up and constitution of the organisation involved but in the case in point they concluded that the packages were "sold"—largely because the packages were also made available to non-members.

Furthermore, the very existence of reg.21 (trust accounts for packages which are not organised as part of a business) suggests that many of these types of arrangements were intended to be caught as packages. See also the case of *Keppel-Palmer v Exus Travel* referred to earlier, on the issue of whether the limousine transfer was "sold or offered for sale".

Upon Whom is Liability Imposed?

The Regulations impose liability on "the organiser", upon the "retailer" and upon "the other party to the contract". These terms will be examined in turn.

Organiser

> "2(1) 'Organiser' means a person who, otherwise than occasionally, organises packages and sells or offers them for sale, whether directly or through a retailer."

The test here is how frequently the organiser arranges packages, not, as in other consumer protection legislation, whether the organiser acts in the course of a business. The definition will clearly catch conventional tour operators but there is a fear that some organisations who organise trips might be caught by this definition even though they act in a non-professional non-profit making capacity. For instance, what about the local authority which through its social services department organises holidays for pensioners on a regular basis? Also, organisations such as the Salvation Army which arranges holidays for its members? Schools which organise a number of trips a year for pupils run the risk also of being caught by the Regulations—but not of course if they sold a ready-packaged trip from a tour operator rather than putting together the coach, accommodation, etc, themselves.

The chief significance is that it will catch most travel agents in its net. If "tailor-made packages" are regarded as "pre-arranged" and "sold at an inclusive price" then it will be very rare indeed that a travel agent can say that he does not "otherwise than occasionally" put a package together. In this context it is important to note that the term organiser cuts across the more conventional terms of principal and agent. To be an organiser it is not necessary to be a principal and by the same token an agent is not precluded from being an organiser simply because he is an agent. The criterion is whether a person "organises" a package, not whether they act as principal. Thus a travel agent, who acts as no more than an agent, would still be an organiser if he *organised* a package. For instance if a client asked an agent, without being too specific about precisely what he wanted, to book flights and accommodation for a trip to New York and the agent did just this, in other words he *organised* a package, he would be an organiser. This presupposes that the agent exercised some skill and expertise in the matter, some organisational skills. If, however, the consumer's instructions were extremely precise, e.g. particular flights and a particular hotel, then the agent might just escape classification as an organiser. If it couldn't be said that he actually organised anything, merely passively followed instructions, his function might not be that of an organiser. But even this is dubious. At the end of the day the agent may not have had a very high-level input but nevertheless he did sufficient for it to be said in ordinary everyday English that he had organised the package, albeit on someone else's very specific instructions—after all, he had *some* skills which the consumer chose to use. Whether this analysis applies to online travel agents after the *Travel Republic* case is a moot point.

Taking the matter one step further, it is conceivable that a travel agent who sold a conventional package, say a Thomas Cook or a TUI package, to a consumer and as part of the same transaction arranged for transport to the airport or hotel to be added to it would be an organiser of a package. The agent would be organiser for the whole package in addition to his more limited responsibilities as retailer of the conventional package (see the *Club Tour* case on this point). Meanwhile, Thomas Cook or TUI would also be liable as organiser for the conventional package. This is yet another controversial area awaiting a court decision. However, according to guidance published by the DfT and the CAA on the new "flight-plus" rules such an arrangement would fall within a flight-plus arrangement in any event.

In the case of *Hone v Going Places* [2001] EWCA Civ 947 a retailer was found liable for packages it sold via teletext because they had held themselves out as principals. They were only travel agents but had created the impression that they were tour operators.

Returning to the issue of "contract splitting": Can the company hosting the internet site be regarded as an "organiser"? The answer is just as obscure as with those other parts of the definition of a package we have already examined—"pre-arranged combination" and "inclusive price" but it is quite conceivable that a company which provides the infrastructure from which a package could be put together could be regarded as having "organised" that package. Certainly, they have invested heavily in the technology which enables the arrangements to be made and the outcome is one which they desire.

The chief significance of being labelled an organiser is that it is generally believed that the liabilities are much greater that those of a retailer. The organiser is responsible for the performance of the whole package but the retailer's liabilities are much more narrowly defined. There are also additional criminal offences for organisers to fall foul of.

Retailers

"2(1) 'Retailer' means the person who sells or offers for sale the package put together by the organiser."

The definition clearly covers the activities of travel agents. Under the Directive, member states had the option of imposing liability on either organisers or retailers or both for failures in the package itself. It is generally believed that the Regulations do not impose such extensive liabilities on retailers but they do make them subject to the provision of information regime (reg.5 and possibly also regs 7 and 8) and they incur civil liability under reg.4 for providing misleading descriptive matter. There is, however, an argument, which will be explored shortly, that the retailer's liability is concurrent with the organiser's in most respects. If so, this represents an unwelcome extension of liability for travel agents (see the comments in *Hone v Going Places* on this issue which appear to adopt our view) but by the same token a considerable degree of extra protection for consumers.

As previously stated, a travel agent who puts a package together and sells it in his own name, acting as principal, falls within the definition of organiser rather than retailer and is subject to the more stringent liabilities in the Regulations. Similarly, the agent who packages extra elements with a conventional package is likely to be classified as an organiser rather than a retailer.

It would appear that newspapers which offer reader holidays could also be classified as organisers rather than retailers. Despite the fact that they may have sub-contracted virtually the whole package to a tour operator it could nevertheless be said that they were the organisers of the holiday. They might escape liability by making it clear that they were only agents selling the packages of others but often that is not the way such packages are marketed. The newspaper will commonly use phrases such as "come with us on our Rhine cruise", or "our choice of hotel" or even "we have organised". Meanwhile the "real" tour operator is featured in a minor role. In determining whether the newspaper is an organiser a court will look carefully at the wording of the advertisements and also at how, and to whom, the money is payable by the consumer. Even if the newspaper escapes liability as an organiser it will still be classified as a retailer.

The essence of the *Travel Republic* case was that Travel Republic were only acting as agents, but *if* they had been regarded as selling packages then it would follow from this that they were organisers of those packages—in which case they would be both agent and organiser.

The Other Party to the Contract

"The other party to the contract" is not a term to be found in the Directive itself. It is a term coined by the DTI draftsman to encompass those situations where the Directive invited member states (some of which have very differently constituted tourist industries) to impose liability on either the organiser or the retailer or both. It is defined in reg.2(1):

" 'the other party to the contract' means the party, other than the consumer, to the contract, that is, the organiser or the retailer, or both, as the case may be."

Taking up the invitation in the Directive, the Regulations sometimes impose liability solely on the organiser (e.g. regs 12, 13 and 14), sometimes on the retailer alone (e.g. reg.5(2)) but sometimes on "the other party to the contract" (e.g. regs 7, 8, 9, 10 and 15). The problem that arises is that it is not immediately clear precisely when "the other party to the contract" is intended to mean just the organiser or just the retailer or both.

Take reg.7, for instance. It states that the other party to the contract shall provide the consumer with certain information before the contract is concluded. The information concerns passport and visa requirements, health formalities and the protection available to the consumer in the event of insolvency. This is information which the organiser could supply quite readily but it is also information which the retailer could supply, and as a matter of practice does so routinely. Is, therefore, the retailer to be liable as well?

Take also reg.15, which imposes liability on the other party to the contract for the proper performance of the contract. In other words, civil liability is imposed for defects in the package. Prior to the passage of the Regulations this was a liability which only affected tour operators. If the meaning of "other party to the contract" is extended to cover retailers as well as organisers in this Regulation it would impose a massive extension of liability on travel agents. But does it?

"as the case may be"

One clue in the definition is that the retailer will be liable "as the case may be". This effectively leaves the question wide open. Presumably, the answer can be found by looking not only at the context in which the definition is employed in the Regulations but also at wider considerations such as the commercial context and the legislative history, i.e. the Directive itself.

Looking first at the Directive for guidance, three points need to be made. First, the Directive is designed to be a consumer protection measure as well as a harmonising measure. Secondly, a number of Articles in the Directive, as indicated earlier, permit member states to impose liability on the organiser and/or the retailer (see arts 4 and 5 in particular). Thirdly, art.7 permits member states to adopt or return more stringent measures to protect the consumer. But, as with the Regulations, there is no clear guidance on when liability should attach solely to the organiser and when to the retailer as well. The most that can be said is that although member states are free to choose there is a bias towards extending the protection of consumers rather than restricting it.

One explanation given for leaving the choice open for member states is that commercial practice varies from state to state and governments should be free to impose liability on tour operators or travel agents or both—whichever they felt was most appropriate. Applying that kind of reasoning to a UK context it could be argued that it would be more appropriate to impose liability on tour operators rather than travel agents. The justification for this is that tour operators put the package together and market it; they are in a position to influence and monitor its quality; and they are in direct contractual relationship with the consumer. The travel agent on the other hand, so the argument goes, is only an intermediary who has no direct control over the quality of the package and who has no contractual relationship with the consumer.

This is a seductive argument but it does not necessarily correspond to commercial reality even in the traditional market. Increasingly, the larger chains of travel agencies are using their commercial power to dictate to operators not only the terms on which their brochures will be racked but also to insist on proper quality control. In other words travel agencies have as much influence on what the consumer buys and the quality of what he buys as many tour operators and should therefore be prepared to accept some of the responsibility. It is also the case that the large chains of travel agents are vertically integrated with the major operators, and while legally this means they are distinct entities, commercially they work together closely. It is not too outrageous, therefore, to suggest that the law should reflect their common commercial purpose.

"the contract"

What is perhaps more to the point is that it is arguable that the travel agent does not have a contract with the consumer for the sale of the package. Therefore, if he is not in fact a party to the contract he should not be classified as "the other party to the contract". There is a simple logic to this which is attractive but it breaks down in the face of the definition of "contract" in the Regulations. It has been given an extended meaning in reg.2(1):

> " 'contract' means the agreement linking the consumer to the organiser or the retailer, or to both, as the case may be."

The significant point here is that a "contract" is not defined in the same way a contract in English law would be defined. It is a much looser definition. It is merely an agreement which *links* the consumer to the organiser or retailer. An agreement *linking* parties in this way is not a term of art known to English law. In ordinary everyday English to link simply means to connect or join. Using the word in this way it is perfectly possible for a package holiday contract to link the consumer to both the organiser/operator (with whom he has a contract) and the retailer/agent (with whom he does not have a contract). The link is a commercial link rather than a legal one but it is nevertheless a link.

Thus, it is perfectly possible for the "other party to the contract" to mean someone who is not in fact a party to any contract with the consumer. The definitions of "contract" and "the other party to the contract" are just a means of extending liability where appropriate—or "as the case may be" to use the words in the Regulations.

It is not beyond the bounds of possibility that even under the same Regulation the liability could vary depending on the facts of the case. For instance, under reg.15 one court might take the view that if a small travel agency sells a major tour operator's package then only the tour operator should be liable. Conversely, if one of the multiple travel agencies sold a small tour operator's package another court might decide that the travel agent should be liable as well as the tour operator—or maybe only the travel agent.

Little help is derived by looking at the Parliamentary debates which considered the Regulations. In the House of Commons the minister responsible for leading the debate said, in the only direct reference to this matter, "Regulation 15 is important and makes the organiser, *or possibly in certain circumstances the retailer*, strictly liable for the performance of the contract." (December 10, 1992, emphasis added.) In the Lords the same form of words was adopted: "Regulation 15 makes the organiser, *or possibly in certain circumstance the retailer*, strictly liable for the performance of the contract" (December 17, 1992, emphasis added). There is a suggestion in the House of Commons debate that the minister was simply saying that the retailer would be liable when he acted as organiser not simply in his capacity as retailer but the matter remains ambiguous. (See the comments of the Court of Appeal in *Hone v Going Places* on this passage.)

Thus, a major area of doubt remains as to how far the liability of a retailer extends and no consistent principles can be discerned as to how to resolve this problem. However, it is suggested that, in particular, reg.15 and the Regulations dealing with insolvency were not intended to include retailers within their scope. The reason for this is not simply because it would represent such an immense extension of liability for travel agents, nor because it cuts across established business and legal practice, but mainly because it would be so unexpected. The basis on which all sides to the debate have proceeded is that in this country the main burden of the liability would be carried by the tour operator rather than the travel agent. To extend that liability would be contrary to everyone's expectations. There is, if you like, an underlying presumption which is not articulated in the Regulations but forms the basis on which they are to be interpreted that the liability of travel agents is not to be extended beyond the provision of information. The authors do not pretend that this is a satisfactory means of interpreting the Regulations but in the circumstances this "instinctive" approach best reflects the intention of the legislation. As a "flight-plus arranger", however, travel agents would have to accept liability for the insolvency of their suppliers although this would fall short of full PTR liability.

One day a court will be called upon to decide this point. A likely scenario is this: a consumer has had a disastrous holiday but before the matter can be settled the organiser goes into liquidation. The consumer's only recourse is against the retailer. Once again the judge will be under intense emotional pressure to find for the consumer. Time will tell. (See *Minhas v Imperial Travel* [2003] I.T.L.J. 69 for a small claims court decision on just this point.)

On this issue, Goldring J. had some interesting things to say in his High Court decision in the *ABTA* case. He was asked by the claimants to declare that the rules in English law on contract and agency applied to package contracts. If this was so, it was argued by the claimants, this would have meant that a travel agent who, acting as an agent, sold discrete components from travel supplier principals to a consumer but had no contract with a consumer himself would not have a contract for a package with the consumer. Goldring J.'s answer to this is:

"161. Eighth, the PTR do not exclude the application of the English law of contract. There is continual reference to 'the' contract and 'the other party to the contract:' see paragraphs 2, 6(3), 7(1), 8(1) and 9(1). In my view, whether the agreement links the consumer to the organiser or retailer or both depends upon the application of the English law of contract, in particular the law of agency. So too do decisions as to whether the organiser or retailer or both are parties to the contract or whether under Regulation 15, the organiser or retailer or both are liable under it. If by application of the English law of contract the retailer is liable under the contract between him and the consumer, he cannot escape his liability by blaming the lack of proper performance of the obligations under it on someone else. For, additionally, he is responsible for the proper performance by others who may supply services under the contract. Equally under Regulation 16 the retailer must provide sufficient evidence of security. In short, that there may be such an additional obligation upon the retailer does not mean that the normal English law of contract has no relevance. It means that in the case of the sale of a package, the retailer cannot escape liability by pointing to someone else's failure: that he must provide sufficient bonding to give that obligation value."

If there is such a contract then the Regulations impose further burdens upon the agent—liability for the acts of his suppliers and an obligation to comply with the bonding regime. This issue was not addressed by the Court of Appeal, leaving the status of this passage unclear. It is possible to argue that the decision of the Court of Appeal to the effect that there was a package if the travel agent put together discrete components from separate suppliers, overruled the High Court decision on this matter, i.e. there could be a package even if the travel agent were not a principal.

In Whose Favour is the Liability Imposed?

The Regulations impose civil liability on the organiser, and, in the light of what has just been said, perhaps the retailer, in favour of "consumers":
"Consumer" is given an extended meaning in the Regulations:

"2(2) 'consumer' means the person who takes or agrees to take the package ('the principal contractor') and elsewhere in these Regulations 'consumer' means, as the context requires, the principal contractor, any person on whose behalf the principal contractor agrees to purchase the package ('the other beneficiaries') or any person to whom the principal contractor or any of the other beneficiaries transfers the package ('the transferee')."

English Common Law

Before we look in detail at the definition it is necessary to point out that in English law, until quite recently, only a party to a contract was entitled to take the benefit of it. A person named in a contract but not party to it (a third party beneficiary) had no rights to sue on the contract. With the advent of the Contracts (Rights of Third Parties) Act 1999 that position has changed radically and there will be many instances now where a third party beneficiary can enforce rights under a contract between two other parties. In package holiday cases, however, there was case law, which preceded the new Act, on the extent to which members of a client's family who were named on the booking form but who might not have been a party to the contract were entitled to the benefits of the contract—see *Jackson v Horizon* [1975] 3 All E.R. 92 and *Woodar v Wimpey* [1980] 1 All E.R. 571. The problem also extended to members of a party where one person had made the booking on behalf of others. In one unreported case a woman bought a holiday for her cleaning lady which went wrong. The court awarded only nominal damages to the purchaser of the holiday because *she* had suffered no damage. The cleaning lady, who had suffered the damage, was not a party to the contract and had no rights under it.

By making what amounted to a revolutionary change to a long established rule of English law the definition of "consumer" in the Regulations went some way to eliminating those problems before they were tackled more generally by the new Act. However, the Regulations go further than the new Act by providing that if a consumer transfers his booking to another person, as he is sometimes entitled to do now under reg.10, the transferee stands in the same position as the original consumer.

The Definition

Regulation 2(2) identifies three types of consumer:

- the principal contractor;
- the other beneficiaries; and
- the transferee.

As a broad proposition it could be said that the legislation was intended to cover three types of person:

- a person who buys the package, but may or may not go on it;
- a person who goes on the package, but is paid for by another; and
- a person who acquires a package indirectly from one of the other types of consumer but not directly from the organiser.

Looked at this way anyone who either pays for a package or who goes on a package will get the protection of the Regulations. However, as with the other definitions the wording is a little clumsy and could lead to technical difficulties. The three types of consumer need examining carefully.

The Principal Contractor

The principal contractor is defined as a person who "takes or agrees to take the package". The problem here is the word "takes". It can have at least two meanings. First, it could mean the person who actually goes on the package, or secondly it could mean the person who agrees to purchase the package. At first glance the former meaning appears to fit the word best. To *take* a package holiday usually means to go on a package holiday. However, to adopt this first meaning in preference to the second raises the problem of what is meant by the two other definitions—other beneficiaries and transferees. If anyone who goes on a package is a principal contractor then the two other definitions appear redundant. Why is it felt necessary to define "other beneficiaries" and "transferee" if, as appears the case, "principal contractor" encompasses them both?

There is also the problem that if a principal contractor is a person who takes a package, in the first sense, then where does that place the person who purchases a package for another but does not go on the package himself? For instance, what about a company that purchases a package for an employee. The employee is protected by the Regulations but the company is not. This may not matter in most circumstances because when there is a failure in the performance of the contract the employee, as consumer, will have the right to sue, but there may be circumstances where the employee is unable or disinclined to sue and therefore the organiser will not be answerable to the employer—who paid for the package but is unable to obtain redress. This may very well have the effect of removing most purchasers of business travel (and perhaps even their employees) from direct access to the provisions of the Regulations. (It must be remembered, however, that the employer may still have rights at common law, although these might not be as extensive as under the Regulations.)

To attribute the second meaning to the word "takes", i.e. a principal contractor is someone who purchases a package, would broaden the definition sufficiently to bring in the person who purchased the package but may not have gone on it. This would satisfy the spirit of the legislation although not fitting entirely comfortably with the language employed. It would also accord with the use of the word "contractor" in the definition. To be labelled a contractor implies that the person taking the package has a contract with the organiser. If that is the case then it would also fit better with the definitions that follow.

Other Beneficiaries

If a principal contractor is someone who "takes" a package then why do we need a definition of another beneficiary? What does this second definition of consumer add to the first? If it is not to be redundant then the implication is that the definition of principal contractor is more restricted than simply anyone who goes on a package. It confirms the suggestion above that to be a principal contractor a person has to have a contract with the organiser. By thus narrowing the definition of principal contractor "other beneficiary" can then take on a meaning that is not redundant, i.e. a person for whom a package is purchased by someone else—the principal contractor. They are the third party beneficiaries who would not normally have a right of action under English law.

One important point to note here is that the other beneficiary is defined in terms of a principal contractor. There cannot be another beneficiary *unless* there is *also* a principal contractor. Thus, where there is no principal contractor there can be no other beneficiary. So if a person cannot be defined as a principal contractor because he does not "take" a package then any person for whom he buys a package will have no rights under the Regulations.

This hinges upon the acceptance of the first interpretation of the word "take" as meaning "going on the package". If the second meaning is accepted, i.e. a person who has a contract for a package, whether or not they go on it, then the problem ceases to exist. As long as a person has his holiday purchased for him by a person who had a contract with the organiser then they will be another beneficiary. On the whole this seems a more sensible approach to take as it will extend the protection of the Regulations rather than diminish it. But then there remains the mystery that a principal contractor is a person who "takes" a package whereas the other beneficiary is a person on whose behalf the principal contractor "purchases" a package. Why, if the second interpretation is to be preferred, are two different words used to mean the same thing? If they were intended to have the same meaning why was not the same word used?

Some clue may be found in the preamble to the Directive which states:

"Whereas the consumer should have the benefit of the protection introduced by this Directive irrespective of whether he is a direct contracting party, a transferee or a member of a group on whose behalf another person has concluded a contract in respect of a package."

The language used in the preamble takes a much broader approach than that found in reg.2(2) (which reflects exactly the wording of art.2.4 of the Directive) and if a purposive interpretation is adopted then the second interpretation of "takes" is entirely consistent with the intent of the preamble.

One large category of "other beneficiary" will be school children on packages organised by specialist tour operators or schools. As consumers they will be subject not only to the benefits under the contract but also the obligations, for instance not to be disruptive. But to what extent can these obligations be enforced on very young children? Often the contract spells out that the penalty for such disruptive behaviour is the termination of the contract but this is not necessarily the outcome that one would want to impose on a young child. The practical solution is to make the party leader/teacher responsible for the conduct of the party and to frame the contract in such a way that decisions on termination and the cost of repatriation fall on the school rather than the tour operator.

Transferees

Under reg.10 it is possible, in certain limited circumstances, for a consumer to transfer his booking to another person—a transferee. A transferee is defined as being a person to whom a principal contractor or another beneficiary transfers the package. The transferee then acquires the same legal rights as any other consumer. Again the problem arises that there cannot be a transferee unless there is first a principal contractor or another beneficiary. If a person acquires a package from a person who does not fall into one of those two categories he does not become a transferee and hence acquires no rights under the Regulations.

Variations on a Theme

Proceeding on the basis that the first interpretation is the preferred one, it remains the case that care must be taken to identify just who is a consumer in any particular set of circumstances. Take a conventional package holiday for instance. The tour operator will be the organiser and the consumers will be the persons who go on the holiday. The chances are that there will be one principal contractor and several other beneficiaries. The principal contractor will be the person who agrees to take the package and the other beneficiaries will be the members of his family on whose behalf he purchases the package.

If the tour operator sells the package to a group of adults rather than to a family the position is that everyone named on the booking form is a principal contractor in his own right. This is despite the fact that the wording on the booking form may state that the person who signs it is signing it "on behalf of" everyone else. All this means is that he is acting as their agent and they have given him the authority to make a contract on their behalf. They are just as much a principal as the person signing the booking form.

These are relatively straightforward examples. There are much more complicated ones. Take for instance the case of an Indian ground operator who puts together a package consisting of hotels, bus tours and internal transfers and then sells this to an English tour operator. The English operator then adds international flights to it and sells the whole package through a brochure. The Indian ground operator is an organiser and when he sells his package to the English operator the English operator becomes a consumer. When the English operator then adds on the extra flights and sells it to English tourists he becomes an organiser in his own right and his clients are consumers. However, these clients are not only consumers of the English tour operator's package they are also consumers of the Indian ground operator's package. In the latter circumstances they are other beneficiaries because the English tour operator bought the package on their behalf. Thus the clients will acquire rights against not only the English operator in respect of the whole package but also direct rights against the Indian ground operator in respect of the Indian part of the package. This would be important if the English organiser became insolvent.

Contracts (Rights of Third Parties) Act 1999

Since the Package Travel Regulations were passed, conferring specific rights on consumers of package holidays, the government has passed legislation of a more general nature—the Contracts (Rights of Third Parties) Act 1999—which does for all third party beneficiaries what the PTR has already done for package holidaymakers. To all intents and purposes this has the effect of duplicating the protection already conferred by the PTR.

Its main provision is:

"Right of third party to enforce contractual term

1(1) Subject to the provisions of this Act, a person who is not a party to a contract (a "third party") may in his own right enforce a term of the contract if—

(a) the contract expressly provides that he may, or
(b) subject to subsection (2), the term purports to confer a benefit on him.

(2) Subsection (1)(b) does not apply if on a proper construction of the contract it appears that the parties did not intend the term to be enforceable by the third party.

(3) The third party must be expressly identified in the contract by name, as a member of a class or as answering a particular description but need not be in existence when the contract is entered into.

(4) This section does not confer a right on a third party to enforce a term of a contract otherwise than subject to and in accordance with any other relevant terms of the contract.

(5) For the purpose of exercising his right to enforce a term of the contract, there shall be available to the third party any remedy that would have been

available to him in an action for breach of contract if he had been a party to the contract (and the rules relating to damages, injunctions, specific performance and other relief shall apply accordingly).

(6) Where a term of a contract excludes or limits liability in relation to any matter references in this Act to the third party enforcing the term shall be construed as references to his availing himself of the exclusion or limitation."

It is clear from this that all the persons on a booking form, subject to express words to the contrary, would be able to claim the benefit of the legislation just as they can under the PTR. (See also Ch.8 on Privity.)

Jurisdiction

Regulation 3 provides:

"3(1) These Regulations apply to packages sold or offered for sale in the territory of the United Kingdom."

Thus, they would cover:

- purely domestic packages, e.g. packages sold in Britain for a holiday confined entirely to Britain;

- purely EU packages, e.g. package holidays to Spain sold in Britain;

- packages sold in Britain for destinations outside the EU, e.g. packages to the Caribbean or Thailand starting from London;

- packages with no EC connection at all except that they are sold here, e.g. an American company which advertises packages confined solely to the US.

In one respect, the Regulations are narrower than the Directive. The Directive states that it covers packages "sold or offered for sale in the territory of the Community" (art.1) whereas the Regulations only cover packages "sold or offered for sale in the territory of the United Kingdom". This means, for instance, that a tour operator established in the UK who sells packages to the UK but only sells them in Holland would not be covered by the Regulations. This is clearly a contravention of the Directive and if put to the test would surely be overruled (see the *Dillenkofer* case).

An issue connected with this is the question of what is meant by selling or offering for sale packages *in* the UK? What if, for instance, a potential client phones up a hotel in the Channel Islands, which is not in the EU, and is informed that not only can the hotel accommodate the client but they can also organise a package for him consisting of flights from his nearest airport, transfers to the hotel, the accommodation and a variety of excursions. Is this a package sold *in* the UK? If the answer to the question depends upon where the contract is made the answer will vary according to how the rules of offer and acceptance are applied to the negotiations. Thus, in some circumstances, the client will be protected by the Regulations and in others will not, depending upon who had the final say. Alternatively, a broader meaning can be attributed to the word "in".

There is a case in criminal law, *Smith v Hughes* [1960] 1 W.L.R. 830; [1960] 2 All E.R. 859, where a woman was accused of soliciting *in* the street. The facts were that she stood at a window and tapped on the pane to attract men in the street below. By a series of gestures she would invite them in and negotiate the price. It was held that she was guilty of soliciting in the street. On appeal it was stated:

"Everybody knows that this was an Act intended to clean up the streets, to enable people to walk along the streets without being molested or solicited by common prostitutes. Viewed in that way, it can matter little whether the prostitute is soliciting while in the street or is standing in a doorway or on a balcony, or at a window, or whether the window is shut or open or half open; in each case her solicitation is projected to and addressed to somebody walking in the street."

While not for a moment wishing to imply that selling holidays is the same as selling sex, it is nevertheless the case that a similar line of reasoning can be adopted. If the purpose of the Regulations is to protect UK consumers in respect of packages which they buy while resident in the UK then the interpretation to adopt is to say that the package was sold over the phone to a consumer *in* the UK. This is a perfectly acceptable interpretation and it should not make any difference that, for technical reasons, the contract was made in the Channel Islands rather than Leeds or Newcastle. Similar issues arise in the context of contracts made over the internet or by email.

Readers should also take note of what is said in Ch.14 on jurisdictional issues and in particular the cases of *Peter Pammer v Reederei Karl Schlüter GmbH & Co KG* (C-585/08) and *Hotel Alpenhof GesmbH v Oliver Heller* (C-144/09). These cases discuss the situation where a company in one country has a website which is "directed" to consumers in other countries and whether this gives the courts in the consumer's country jurisdiction over the product sold.

An Overview

Before moving on to the detailed treatment of package holiday contracts it will be useful for readers to have an overview of the full extent of the Regulations. Despite the wide scope of the Regulations it is possible to distinguish particular themes or topics and these will be examined briefly in turn. Full treatment of these issues appears later in the relevant sections of the book.

Provision of Information

There is a heavy emphasis in the Regulations on the provision of essential information. In a contract where the consumer cannot see or sample the product before he buys it this enables him to make a more rational choice initially and, if he is subsequently disappointed, it gives him a yardstick by which to measure the performance of the tour operator and to assess whether the tour operator is in breach of contract. It should also mean that there are fewer complaints because consumers will be able to make a more informed choice if the information is accurate, and are therefore less likely to be disappointed.

Regulation 4 imposes civil liability on both organisers and retailers for supplying misleading information. This is a new form of statutory civil liability which resembles both an action for misrepresentation and breach of contract. If a brochure is made available to consumers, reg.5 requires certain information to be included in the brochure and failure to provide it in a legible, comprehensible and accurate manner amounts to a criminal offence by the organiser, and in some circumstances, the retailer. Regulation 6 reinforces reg.5 by elevating *all the particulars* in the brochure into implied warranties, i.e. minor terms of the contract.

Regulation 7 provides that information on subjects such as visa and health requirement be given to consumers before the contract is concluded and failure to do so is also a criminal offence. Yet another criminal offence is committed if, in breach of reg.8, the other party to the contract fails to provide information on insurance, contact names and addresses and on intermediate stops and accommodation during the journey.

Finally, reg.9 requires all the terms of the contract to be communicated to the consumer before the contract is concluded, if possible, and in all cases it must be reduced to writing and a copy supplied to the consumer. The penalty for failure to do so is that the consumer can cancel the package.

Changes and Cancellation

A package holiday is a complex product which is designed and marketed many months, if not years, in advance of performance. It is not uncommon therefore for circumstances to change in the meantime and for operators to have to make alterations to the holiday or even to cancel it altogether. There are several Regulations which deal with these possibilities. The important thing to note about them is that not only do they label such changes as breach of contract by the operator for which compensation is payable, i.e. a financial remedy for the consumer, they also provide a range of other remedies, i.e. the offer of an alternative holiday; or a requirement that the operator do something practical to put things right; or a right to be brought home early in some circumstances.

Regulation 12 provides that if the organiser makes a significant alteration to a package the consumer is entitled to withdraw from the package or to accept a rider to the contract specifying the alterations made and the impact on the price. If the consumer does withdraw or the organiser cancels the package the consumer is entitled to be offered an alternative package or a refund of his money. Compensation is also payable except in certain limited circumstances. If after departure a significant proportion of the services is not provided then the organiser is under a duty to make alternative arrangements and if it is not possible to do this the consumer has a right to be taken back to his point of departure.

CHAPTER TWO

Liability

At common law it was generally, but not universally, accepted, that a tour operator's liability was fault based (see *Wall v Silver Wing Surface Arrangements* Unreported 1981. See also *Wong Mee Wan v Kwan Kin Travel Services* [1995] 4 All E.R. 745. Regulation 15 changes all this by introducing a qualified form of strict liability. Subject to certain broad exceptions an organiser is made strictly liable for the "proper performance" of the obligations under the contract irrespective of whether the failures are due to his own actions or those of his suppliers (subcontractors). The liability is further reduced by provisions which permit the organiser to exclude or limit his liability in certain circumstances. These include circumstances where international carriage is involved or where there is no personal injury.

Protection in the Event of Insolvency

There are extensive provisions in the Regulations intended to protect consumers if the tour operator with whom they are dealing becomes insolvent either before they travel or while they are abroad. To protect consumers' prepayments organisers must adopt one of the options set out in regs 17–21. These include bonding, insurance or the establishment of a trust fund. Additionally, organisers must be able to demonstrate that in the event of the insolvency occurring while consumers are abroad they will be repatriated.

Other Provisions

Apart from the themes just identified there are a number of miscellaneous matters dealt with by the Regulations. Regulation 10 permits a consumer to transfer his booking to another in certain limited circumstances. Regulation 11 preserves the right of an organiser to surcharge consumers but severely circumscribes the circumstances in which this can be done. Regulations 13 permits an organiser to cancel a package for lack of minimum numbers so long as this was expressly stated in the contract and the organiser adheres to the deadlines set out in the contract.

Offer and Acceptance: Do We Have a Contract?

INTRODUCTION

This chapter is concerned with establishing precisely *when* and *how* a contract comes into existence between a travel company and a consumer. The importance of establishing this is threefold.

First, so that both the travel company and the consumer know precisely when they become legally bound to each other. In other words, they know that from that moment they have legal rights and obligations under the contract. So on the one hand, the travel company will know that it will be able to demand payment under the terms of the contract, but it will also have to deliver the services it has promised. On the other hand, the consumer knows that s/he is legally bound to pay for the holiday but s/he has the right to receive the services s/he has paid for.

Secondly, knowing how and when the contract is made enables the travel company to establish procedures so that the contract is made on *its* terms and conditions. For instance, tour operators' payment clauses often provide for surcharges, and cancellation clauses provide for the payment of cancellation charges; airlines have sophisticated sets of terms and conditions often running to many pages and providing for every eventuality; and hotels are not averse to burying "resort charges" and "service charges" deep within their terms and conditions. None of these provisions would be terms of the contract unless the travel company took steps to ensure they were there.

Thirdly, as far as package travel is concerned, reg.9 of the Package Travel Regulations provides that the terms of the contract must be communicated to the consumer *before* the contract is concluded. The price for failing to do so is that the consumer may be able to withdraw from the contract without penalty.

The consequences of not knowing the theory and practice of making a contract should be self-evident. First, a travel company may invest considerable time and effort in a consumer only to end up with no contract at the end of the day. Secondly, and maybe even worse, the travel company may end up with a contract with the consumer but the contract may not include all the carefully drafted terms and conditions in the company's standard form contract (see *Blumer & Grant v Gold Medal Travel Group Plc* [2008] C.L.Y. 650). Thirdly, in package contracts, even if a contract appears to be concluded it may be repudiated if the consumer was not informed in advance of all the terms. All three eventualities could be costly to the travel companies and, in extreme cases, subject them to the even more costly uncertainties of litigation.

CHAPTER THREE

What is a Contract?

For our purposes, a contract can be defined as *a legally binding agreement*. Essentially, there are two elements to this definition. First, there is the requirement that the agreement between the parties is one which is intended to have *legally enforceable consequences*. In other words, the parties envisage that as a last resort, if the contract was broken, they could sue the other party and the courts would enforce the contract—usually by awarding damages. Some agreements of a social or domestic nature, such as an invitation to dinner, are not legally binding but commercial agreements such as those between travel companies and consumers are presumed to be legally enforceable. It would be hard to envisage circumstances where a travel contract would not be enforced by the courts.

Secondly, there must actually be an *agreement*. If the parties have not come to an agreement then there will be no contract. Most of what follows is concerned with the mechanisms by which agreement is reached, but put at its simplest, a tour operator will have a contract if the consumer signifies that he is quite happy to pay £560 per person half board for two weeks in the Hotel Excelsior in the resort of his choice for the first two weeks in August departing from Leeds. Conversely, there will not be a contract if the consumer is perfectly happy with all the arrangements except the departure airport—he is not willing to purchase the holiday if he cannot secure a departure from Newcastle but unfortunately the operator does not have a Newcastle departure on the date the consumer requires.

Other Requirements

Apart from the need for an agreement and for the parties to that agreement to intend that it be legally binding, there are other requirements for a valid contract. These are that the parties both provide *consideration*; that they both have the legal *capacity* to make a contract; and that the contract is in the right *form*. The first two of these requirements can be dealt with quite briefly because, although they are important in many types of contract, they are of only minor practical importance in travel contracts. The requirement that the contract be in the right form is more important and will be given full treatment.

Consideration

The requirement that both parties provide consideration before the contract is binding means that each must provide the other with something of value. In a package holiday contract the consideration by the consumer would be the payment for the holiday and the consideration by the tour operator would be the provision of the holiday itself. Likewise, in a flight contract the consideration by the passenger is the promise to pay and the consideration by the airline is the promise to provide the flight. The consideration need not actually be exchanged for the contract to be binding; it is sufficient that each party has *promised* to provide the consideration in exchange for the other's promise. In general, no widespread difficulties are likely to arise over the provision of consideration in travel contracts, although there may be marginal cases where it is relevant. In the past, problems have arisen most often where one person has given a holiday as a gift to another, with the result that the recipient of the gift cannot enforce the contract because they have provided no consideration. This problem has largely been overcome in package holiday contracts by the wide definition of consumer found in reg.2 (see Ch.2) and in other contracts by the Contracts (Rights of Third Parties) Act 1999 (see Ch.8).

Capacity

The parties to a contract must be legally capable of making the contract. Minors, i.e. persons under 18, are the largest single group of people that do not have full capacity to make contracts. Given the number of minors that take holidays there is theoretical potential for difficulties to arise, but in practice this rarely occurs and does not justify more than the briefest of mentions.

Form

Although there are very good reasons for putting all but the simplest contracts into writing, most contracts are perfectly valid even if they are only oral. However, there are a minority of contracts that must be reduced to writing, or at least some of the terms must be put in writing. Contracts for the sale of land and contracts of hire purchase fall into this category. Prior to 1992, there was no such requirement for package holiday contracts and it was possible, although not advisable, to make one without putting it into writing. All that changed when the Regulations were introduced. Regulation 9 requires that consumers be given a written copy of all the terms of the contract—in most cases before the contract is made. This was a major development for both tour operators and consumers and we will deal fully with the impact of it in this chapter. For contracts made over the internet, the Electronic Commerce (EC Directive) Regulations 2002 (SI 2002/2013) also provide for certain formalities (see Ch.14).

How is Agreement Reached?

To establish whether a contract exists or not a lawyer would break down the process of arriving at an agreement into two elements—*offer and acceptance*. For there to be an agreement, one party must make an offer to the other party which the other one accepts.

An offer can be defined as a statement by one party of the terms he is *prepared to be bound by* if his offer is accepted. In other words, the offeror (as he is known) is *prepared to commit himself* to the terms of his offer.

An acceptance is the *unqualified agreement* to the terms of the offer. In other words, the offeree, having received the terms of the offer, is equally prepared to commit himself and does so simply by agreeing, without any strings attached, to what the offeror proposes.

In terms of a package holiday contract, or simply a contract for a flight, what this boils down to is that if a consumer, after long discussions with his travel agent about all the details of a holiday, finally says "Yes, I would like to buy that particular holiday" or "Yes, I would like to buy that flight" this will amount to an offer, and if the operator or the airline responds by saying "Yes I am prepared to sell it to you" this will amount to an acceptance and from that moment a contract exists.

Two things should be noted about this example. First, the parties themselves did not use the words "offer" or "acceptance". In real life people do not go around talking like lawyers and expressing themselves in the formal language of the law. Ordinary people use words and phrases like "buy" and "sell" and "Do you want it?" and "Yes I'll have it", rather than "I am offering to sell you a holiday" and "I am prepared to accept your offer of a holiday". This does not prevent what they say from being an offer or an acceptance so long as it can be categorised as one or the other. The important thing is not whether the words are formal but whether the words show that the parties are prepared to legally bind themselves.

The second thing to note is that in the example the offeror was the consumer who was making an *offer to buy* the holiday or the flight. The offeree (also called the acceptor in this case) was the tour operator or the airline which was accepting the offer by saying that he was *prepared to sell*. These are not fixed categories. If the facts had been slightly different then it could have been the operator or the airline which was making an *offer to sell* and the consumer who was the acceptor, saying he was *prepared to buy*.

Invitations to Treat

It is only in the very simplest of contractual situations that the process of arriving at an agreement consists only of an offer followed by an acceptance. In most cases there are preliminary discussions and negotiations before the parties begin making legally binding statements. When one party wants to indicate that he is prepared to enter into negotiations or prepared to commence negotiations with the other party he will often make, what is called by lawyers, an *invitation to treat*. An invitation to treat, as its name suggests, is an indication by one party that they are prepared to receive offers from the other. They are inviting the other party to make the first move. Legally speaking, they are saying that they are prepared to enter into the bargaining process but they are not yet prepared to commit themselves to a formal offer.

In many cases the distinction between an invitation to treat and an offer is quite clear cut. For instance, there is a world of difference between saying "I'm thinking of selling my car. Would you be interested in buying it?" and "If you give me £4,000 right now you can have my car." The first statement merely invites the other party to enter into negotiations; the latter is a firm offer which can be accepted by a simple yes.

However, the distinction is not always so clear, and it is not uncommon for someone to think that he has been made an offer which he has accepted when in fact it was only an invitation to treat that the other party had made. The difference of course is crucial. In the former case a contract would have been concluded whereas in the latter it would not. One of the most famous cases in English law, *Carlill v Carbolic Smoke Ball Co* [1893] 1 Q.B. 256, turned on just this point.

The defendants, who were manufacturers of smoke balls, placed an advertisement in a newspaper stating that if the public purchased their smoke balls and used them as directed this would protect them from flu. If, despite the use of the smoke balls, a purchaser contracted flu the company was prepared to pay them £100 reward. As an indication of their sincerity in the matter they had deposited £1,000 with a bank to meet any claims that might be made. Mrs Carlill had purchased one of the balls from a retailer, a chemist, and used it in the prescribed manner but had nevertheless caught flu. She claimed her reward but the Smoke Ball company refused to pay. One of the defendant's arguments for rejecting liability was that the advertisement was only an invitation to treat not an offer. In such circumstances, the defendant argued, there could be no contract because even if Mrs Carlill's purchase and use of the ball could be interpreted as an offer to enter into a contract with the defendant on the terms set out in the advertisement, the defendant had not accepted her offer. Mrs Carlill's contention was that the advertisement constituted an offer which she had accepted by using the ball in the manner prescribed. In upholding Mrs Carlill's view Bowen L.J. said of the advertisement:

> "It is an offer to become liable to anyone who, before it is retracted, performs the condition on the faith of the advertisement. It is not like cases in which you offer to negotiate, or you issue advertisements that you have got a stock of books to sell, or houses to let, in which case there is no offer to be bound by any contract. Such advertisements are offers to negotiate—offers to receive offers—offers to chaffer, as, I think, some learned judge in one of the cases has said. If this is an offer to be bound, then it is a contract the moment the person fulfils the condition. That seems to me to be sense".

If you doubt the relevance of this case, where the facts are far removed from the travel industry, you need look no further than the case of *Bowerman and Wallace v Association of British Travel Agents Ltd* [1996] C.L.C. 451 (CA). The facts of the case were that the claimants had booked a skiing holiday with Adventure Express, an ABTA tour operator, specialising in skiing holidays for school children. Adventure Express became insolvent shortly before the claimants were due to go on holiday. In accordance with the ABTA scheme set up to protect holidaymakers against the risk of insolvency, ABTA refunded the claimants the money they had paid for their holiday. The claimants, in turn, assigned their right to this money to Skibound, another ski tour operator, which arranged another holiday for them. The problem was, however, that ABTA did not refund the whole of the holiday price. They deducted a small sum to cover the insurance premiums that were part of the price of the holiday. The claimants contended that ABTA should not have deducted this sum—they should have refunded the whole cost of the holiday. The basis of this contention was that a notice published by ABTA, entitled "Notice describing ABTA's scheme of protection against the financial failure of ABTA members", which ABTA required to be displayed prominently at the premises of all travel agents and tour operators who were members of ABTA, constituted a contractual promise by ABTA to refund customers of failed ABTA tour operators *in full*. To put it more simply, the claimants said that the notice was an offer by ABTA to members of the public that if they booked with an ABTA tour operator then ABTA would ensure that *all* their money was safe. (The extent of this protection has since been watered down by ABTA.)

The Court of Appeal, by a two to one majority, held that the notice was a contractual document containing the promise contended for by the claimants, despite the fact that it contained "a remarkable variety of tone and language" (Waite L.J.).

Waite L.J. approached the interpretation of the document in this fashion:

"Before analysing the detail in that Notice, it may be helpful to stand aside and look for a moment at the attributes which need to be given to the ordinary member of the public as he or she steps down from the omnibus, enter the travel agency in which the Notice is displayed, and reads it. Such a reader would be aware of the vulnerability of agents and operators in a highly competitive market where failures are not uncommon, and of the disappointment and financial loss which members of the public have experienced in the past as a result of sudden cancellations following financial collapse. The reader would appreciate, too, that ABTA is not a charity or a friendly society, but (as its full name makes clear) an association, for the purposes of trade, of persons and firms carrying on the business of travel agent. He or she would, further, be aware that it is in the interests of such an association to win business for its constituent members by inspiring public confidence. There should also be imputed to the reader common knowledge that those who wish to disclaim legal liability for public representations frequently say so—in large print or in small. Finally it is to be assumed that such a person would read the whole notice—neither cursorily nor with pedantic analysis of every nuance of its wording, but with the ordinary care to be expected of the average customer who is applying money they could not easily afford to lose in buying a holiday which it would be a serious disappointment to forego."

Hobhouse L.J., dealing with how the notice should be interpreted, quoted from the judgment of Bowen L.J. in *Carlill*:

"It was intended to be issued to the public and to be read by the public. How would an ordinary person reading this document construe it?"

His answer to the question was:

"In my judgment this document is intended to be read and would reasonably be read by a member of the public as containing an offer of a promise which the customer is entitled to accept by choosing to do business with an ABTA member. A member of the public would not analyse his situation in legal terms but would clearly understand that this notice would only apply to him if he should choose to do business with an ABTA member and he would also understand that if he did so he would be entitled to hold ABTA to what he understood ABTA to be promising in this document. In my judgment it satisfies the criteria for a unilateral contract and contains promises which are sufficiently clear to be capable of legal enforcement. The principles established in the *Carbolic Smoke Ball* case apply. The plaintiffs are entitled to enforce the right of reimbursement given to them in paragraph 5."

Objective Interpretations

It is worth noting that in *Carlill* the Court of Appeal's interpretation of the advertisement, and in *Bowerman* the interpretation of the notice, was an objective one. They did not ask whether the defendant really intended the document to be an offer or an invitation to treat but whether, objectively, from a disinterested outsider's point of view the words used could be interpreted as conveying the impression that they were willing to be bound or not. In the circumstances, the language used in both documents taken in context led the court to conclude that an offer was being made. This was probably quite contrary to the subjective intention of the defendants who probably thought, in the *Carlill* case, they had merely indulged in some harmless advertising which would not be binding upon them, and in the *Bowerman* case, that they had retained the discretion to refuse payment when they thought it appropriate.

This objective approach to interpretation is reflected in the words of Blackburn J. in *Smith v Hughes* (1871) L.R. 6 Q.B. 597:

> "If, whatever a man's intention may be, he so conducts himself that a reasonable man would believe that he was assenting to the terms proposed by the other party, and that other party upon that belief enters into the contract with him, the man thus conducting himself would be equally bound as if he had intended to agree to the other party's terms."

Legal Status of the Brochure

Travel companies publicise their holidays in a number of ways including newspaper advertising, TV advertising and, increasingly, the internet, but probably even now one of the most important and widespread mediums is the brochure. The question arises as to the legal status of "offers" made in brochures to "sell" holidays to consumers. Are they offers or only invitations to treat? If they are offers then, just like the Carbolic Smoke Ball Co, tour operators may end up with contracts they did not intend to make. If they are invitations to treat then there can be no contract until the tour operator accepts the consumer's offer to buy the holiday.

It can be said with some certainty that, in the vast majority of cases, such statements are only invitations to treat not offers. The reasons for this are practical. If, for the sake of argument, an operator issues a brochure with special low lead-in prices for early bookers he may be faced with a position where demand outstrips supply many times. If a court interpreted the brochure as meaning that the tour operator was "offering" such holidays for sale then every consumer who came forward and "accepted" the offer before it was withdrawn would have a contract with the tour operator. In these circumstances the operator could end up with 1,000 contracts but only 500 available holidays and no way of making up the difference. The logic of the situation would be that the operator would be in breach of 500 contracts!

A number of cases suggest that a court would be very unlikely to take this line. Where products have been advertised in newspapers or a price list has been circulated the courts have held that no offer was made, only an invitation to treat. In *Grainger & Son v Gough* [1896] A.C. 325 Lord Herschell said:

"The transmission of a price list does not amount to an offer to supply an unlimited quantity of the wine described at the price named, so that as soon as an order is given there is a binding contract to supply that quantity. If it were so the merchant might find himself involved in any number of contractual obligations to supply wine of a particular description which he would be unable to carry out, his stock of wine of that description being necessarily limited."

A court took a similar line in the case of *Partridge v Crittenden* [1968] 1 W.L.R. 1204 where an advertisement was placed in a periodical, *Cage and Aviary Birds*, which stated:

"Quality British ABCR Bramblefinch cocks, Bramblefinch hens, 25s each."

It was argued that the advertisement amounted to an offer to sell the birds. However, Lord Parker C.J. said:

"I think that when one is dealing with advertisements and circulars, there is business sense in their being construed as invitations to treat and not offers for sale. It seems to me that not only is that the law, but common sense supports it."

There is a world of difference between a holiday and a crate of wine or a bramblefinch hen, but legally speaking, a brochure, a price list and an advertisement can all be analysed the same way. Invariably, they are invitations to treat rather than offers, simply because the product being sold is not available in unlimited quantities. As the judges indicated it would be unrealistic and impractical to categorise them otherwise.

The advertisement in the *Carlill* case was of course an offer but that is simply the exception that proves the rule. The words used in that case were such that they could be interpreted as an offer. It would be possible for a tour operator to phrase his brochure copy or his advertising in such a way that it could be interpreted as an offer. For instance, if a major operator which sold hundreds of thousands of holidays a year whipped up public interest just prior to the launch of their summer sun brochure by advertising that when the brochure was published the first 100 consumers could purchase any holiday in the brochure for only £10 per head, this could easily be equated with the advertisement in *Carlill's* case. It would be a brave operator who argued otherwise.

Stating in the brochure that all holidays are "subject to availability" is a two-edged sword. On the one hand, it clearly prevents the operator being saddled with a contract after he has sold out of a particular package, but by the same token it may very well imply that if the holidays are available the operator is committed to selling them. In most cases that would not be a problem, but there may be circumstances where the operator wants to have the option of refusing a consumer—whether the holidays are available or not.

OFFER AND ACCEPTANCE: DO WE HAVE A CONTRACT?

Typical Situations

Travel companies contract with their consumers in a number of ways. Some use online computer systems and consumers can conclude a booking in a few minutes in a travel agency. Even today there are companies, who also use travel agents as intermediaries, which still use the telephone, fax or correspondence to make the contract although this is increasingly rare. Correspondence, the internet and email are also methods chosen by those who deal direct with the public. For last minute bookings the telephone (coupled with the use of credit cards) is often used. As indicated earlier, the internet, whether coupled with email or not, is an increasingly important way of doing business for all travel companies. The principles of offer and acceptance apply to them all but precisely *who* makes the offer and the acceptance and *when* the contract is concluded varies according to the circumstances. It is proposed to examine some of the most commonly occurring booking procedures and analyse what goes on in terms of offer and acceptance.

Internet Bookings

Travel companies, particularly airlines and hotels, have found that the internet is an invaluable means of marketing and selling their products. However, internet sales are regulated in a way that other forms of contracting are not. Directive 2000/31/EC, the Directive on Electronic Commerce, which was transposed into UK law by the Electronic Commerce (EC Directive) Regulations 2002 (SI 2002/2013), contains some rudimentary rules which impact upon the process of offer and acceptance over the internet. Before we look at these rules, however, it is useful to examine how a contract might be made over the internet.

In many ways, it resembles the way in which a contract is concluded by viewdata, described below, except that the consumer navigates his way through the screens without the assistance of a travel agent (although travel agencies do make bookings for consumers over the internet). Essentially, what happens is that the consumer will visit a travel-related internet site and, having reached a stage where he has selected what he wants, he will be prompted to commit himself to the travel company by clicking on the appropriate part of the screen. As with viewdata bookings this can be analysed, at a very basic level, as an *offer by the travel company to sell* the selected products, and an *acceptance by the consumer* of what is on offer. But in practice, the situation is often very different because the process usually involves some sort of confirmation or acknowledgement by the travel company that the order has been received/accepted— suggesting that it is the consumer who is *offering to buy* and the travel company which is *accepting the offer*. Often, this will be reinforced by the terms and conditions of the travel company which have been incorporated into the contracting process as the consumer proceeds through the various screens. For internet bookings this will be very simple for the operator to achieve. All he has to do is to compel the consumer to "click through" a page on which the terms and conditions are displayed or referred to or "tick" a box to accept he is bound by them.

What then do the Electronic Commerce Regulations have to say that is relevant to this process? Regulation 9(1) provides that where a contract is to be concluded by electronic means, a service provider (in our case a travel company selling over the internet) shall:

"prior to an order being placed by the recipient of a service [the consumer] provide to that recipient in a clear, comprehensible and unambiguous manner the information set out in (a) below—

(a) the different technical steps to follow to conclude the contract".

And reg.9(3) requires that:

"Where the service provider provides terms and conditions applicable to the contract to the recipient, the service provider shall make them available to him in a way that allows him to store and reproduce them."

According to reg.11(1), if a consumer places an "order" by electronic means the travel company must acknowledge receipt of the order to the recipient of the service without undue delay and by electronic means. Furthermore, reg.11(2) states that:

"the order and the acknowledgement of receipt will be deemed to be received when the parties to whom they are addressed are able to access them".

The meaning of "order" is amplified in reg.12:

"12. Except in relation to regulation 9(1)(c) and regulation 11(1)(b) where 'order' shall be the contractual offer, 'order' may be but need not be the contractual offer for the purposes of regulations 9 and 11."

So what is the practical impact of this? First, we should note that the Regulations are not prescriptive. They do not require service providers to contract in a particular way, they leave them free to adopt any process they wish so long as they inform the consumer. However, because travel companies do have to set out the technical steps by which a contract is concluded they should at least have given some thought to the contracting process. This, coupled with the requirement that if they do have terms and conditions, which invariably they do, they have to make them available to the consumer in a form in which they can be stored and reproduced will make it almost inevitable that somewhere on the site it will say *when* the contract is concluded. Given that it lies within the control of the travel company to dictate the time at which the contract is concluded it would be wise of them to take advantage of the opportunity.

But what is advisable and what happens in practice are two different things. It is entirely conceivable that some travel companies either do not set out the contracting process or do so in a manner which is defective or ambiguous, in which case the answer would have to be determined by recourse to first principles. The problem, as with the post, is that the contract is made at a distance and the question arises, as it does with fax and telex, as to whether the communication by the travel company acknowledging the order of the consumer, or indeed the order by the consumer (if it could be construed as an acceptance) should take effect on dispatch or receipt. Some assistance can be found in the wording of reg.11(2), quoted above, which suggests that it is a receipt rule.

The same issue has been litigated on a number of previous occasions in relation to contracts made by telex. In *Brinkibon Ltd v Stahag Stahl und Stahlwarenhandels-Gesellschaft mBH* [1983] A.C. 34 Lord Wilberforce said that there could be no hard and fast rule in such cases:

"Since 1955 the use of telex communication has been greatly expanded, and there are many variants on it. The senders and recipients may not be the principals to the contemplated contract. They may be servants or agents with limited authority. The message may not reach, or be intended to reach, the designated recipient immediately: messages may be sent out of office hours, or at night, with the intention, or upon the assumption, that they will be read at a later time. There may be some error or default at the recipient's end which prevents receipt at the time contemplated and believed in by the sender. The message may have been sent and/or received through machines operated by third persons and many other variations may occur. No universal rule can cover all such cases: they must be resolved by reference to the intentions of the parties, by sound business practice and in some cases by a judgment where the risks should lie."

It is probably the case that the same kind of pragmatic approach will be adopted in relation to internet contracts where the travel company has not made it clear in its terms and conditions what the position is.

A case decided in Singapore *Chwee Kin Keong v Digilandmall.com* [2004] 2 S.L.R. 594 (affirmed [2005] S.G.C.A. 2) is one of the few cases to examine the practicalities of contracting by internet. The case involved a pricing error on its website by the defendant company. Instead of advertising digital printers at over $3,800 each the company mistakenly priced them at only $66. The claimants realised this almost immediately and ordered several hundred of the printers, intending to sell them on quickly at a large profit. When the defendant discovered the mistake they refused to honour the contracts and the claimants sued them for breach of contract. The case itself turned on whether the claimants, whose claim failed, knew that a mistake had been made but the judge took the opportunity to pass a few remarks about internet contracting. He had this to say on basic principles:

"91. There is no real conundrum as to whether contractual principles apply to Internet contracts. Basic principles of contract law continue to prevail in contracts made on the Internet. However, not all principles will or can apply in the same manner that they apply to traditional paper-based and oral contracts. It is important not to force into a Procrustean bed principles that have to be modified or discarded when considering novel aspects of the Internet."

And on website displays he had this to say:

"93. Website advertisement is in principle no different from a billboard outside a shop or an advertisement in a newspaper or periodical. The reach of and potential response(s) to such an advertisement are however radically different.

Placing an advertisement on the Internet is essentially advertising or holding out to the world at large. A viewer from any part of the world may want to enter into a contract to purchase a product as advertised. Websites often provide a service where online purchases may be made. In effect the Internet conveniently integrates into a single screen traditional advertising, catalogues, shop displays/windows and physical shopping."

The problem with such advertisements, as with conventional advertisements and shop displays, is that it is possible, depending on the language used, for the display to be seen as an offer rather than an invitation to treat and:

"As with any normal contract, Internet merchants have to be cautious how they present an advertisement, since this determines whether the advertisement will be construed as an invitation to treat or a unilateral contract. Loose language may result in inadvertently establishing contractual liability to a much wider range of purchasers than resources permit."

A distinction is drawn between contracts concluded by email and those involving interactive websites. As far as the former is concerned, he looks briefly at the relative merits of a "recipient" rule or the "postal rule" (see below) but does not offer a view on which should prevail. As for the latter, he favours the recipient rule as the default rule, i.e. a contract is formed at the point that the acceptance is received. The rationale for this is that when dealing with interactive websites the communication is virtually instantaneous. However this carries with it a warning:

"Application of such a rule may however result in contracts being formed outside the jurisdiction if not properly drafted. Web merchants ought to ensure that they either contract out of the receipt rule or expressly insert salient terms within the contract to deal with issues such as a choice of law, jurisdiction and other essential terms relating to the passing of risk and payment. Failure to do so could also result in calamitous repercussions. Merchants may find their contracts formed in foreign jurisdictions and therefore subject to foreign laws." (See the ECJ cases *Peter Pammer v Reederei Karl Schlüter GmbH & Co KG* (C-585/08) and *Hotel Alpenhof GesmbH v Oliver Heller* (C-144/09) on jurisdiction and dealing over the internet which are discussed in Ch.14.)

This would seem to apply equally to travel companies and, as we shall see later when examining online contracts for accommodation, it appears that many travel companies have not thought through their terms and conditions and adapted them for an internet environment.

Online Booking Systems Using VDU's in Travel Agencies

Even today, many contracts for package holidays made through a travel agent involve the use of "viewdata", a relatively primitive interactive system that predates the internet by some years and which is overdue for replacement. The typical scenario here is that the consumer, having examined an operator's brochure, or having a vague idea of the kind of holiday he wants, enters the travel agency with a view to booking a holiday. The travel clerk will bring up on the VDU the details of holidays that the consumer might be interested in. Eventually, the consumer will refine his choice until the screen contains details of a holiday that he wants. All it takes at this stage is for the consumer to say yes and for the travel clerk to convey this information to the tour operator by pressing the correct button on the keyboard, and there will be a contract.

In terms of offer and acceptance the analysis here is that the brochure, if one was used, constitutes an invitation to treat. The consumer entering the travel agency and asking for details of holidays is indicating that he is interested in a holiday, although, clearly, he is not prepared to commit himself at this stage. Any interest he shows at this stage falls far short of making an offer to buy a holiday. Until the choice is narrowed down to precisely what the consumer wants no offer is made. Once the holiday the consumer wants is displayed on the screen this can be interpreted as an *offer to sell the holiday* by the tour operator. When the consumer indicates to the travel agent that he is happy with the choice and the appropriate button can be pressed this amounts to *an acceptance by the consumer to buy the holiday offered*. The contract is made once the button is pressed.

The display on the screen is an offer rather than an invitation to treat because the circumstances show that the stage in the bargaining has been reached where one party, in this case the tour operator, is prepared to commit himself. There are no problems with availability because otherwise the holiday would not be displayed on the screen and there is nothing else to indicate any qualification to what is being offered on the screen.

Viewed like this the outcome seems to be precisely what the operator wants. He has succeeded in tying the consumer down to a contract. At this stage he can look forward to collecting his money as it falls due. *But on what terms?* If the travel clerk has done her job properly the consumer will have signed the booking form in the operator's brochure *before* the button was pushed (or at the very least made aware that the contract is subject to terms and conditions). This ensures that the contract is made on the operator's terms and all the small print at the back of the brochure has been incorporated into the contract. The case of *L'Estrange v Graucob* [1934] 2 K.B. 394 decided that once a person has *signed* a document they are bound by its terms even though they have not read them.

The analysis of the process of agreement is not affected by the presence of the booking form. The tour operator is effectively saying that he is prepared to sell the holiday displayed on the screen on the terms in the brochure. The acceptance is made by the consumer signing the booking form and indicating to the travel clerk to press the button. Both the offer and the acceptance have two elements. The offer consists of what is on the screen combined with what is in the booking form. The acceptance is not complete until the booking form has been signed and the button has been pressed.

But what if the travel clerk fails to obtain the signature on the booking form? The position here would almost certainly be that there *is* a contract but *not* on the terms and conditions contained in the brochure. The information displayed on the screen is quite sufficient to form the basis of a contract. It contains everything the consumer needs to know—dates, price, hotel, mealplan, airport, departure times, etc. Once the button has been pressed a contract exists despite the omission of the operator's terms and conditions. (In the past a failure by the travel clerk might have resulted in the operator being unable to limit his liability under the Warsaw Convention—at a potential cost of millions of pounds—see Ch.6 on Exclusion of Liability.) The travel clerk may very well have contravened the tour operator's booking procedures but that will not affect the validity of the contract. That is a private matter between the travel agency and the tour operator.

If the travel clerk obtained the consumer's signature and deposit *immediately after* the button was pressed this would *probably* not disadvantage the operator. So long as the signature was obtained at roughly the same time as the pressing of the button it could be viewed as part of a single process of offer and acceptance. In *Williams v Thomson Tour Operations Ltd* Unreported 1997, Gloucester County Court, the claimant booked a fly-drive holiday over the telephone via a travel agent; the agent then told the claimant to come down to his shop that day to sign the booking form. It was held that the claimant was bound by her signature to the terms of the contract, including requirements set out in the brochure to pay extras for the hire car. The basis of the decision was that the telephone call and the signing of the booking form were all part of the same transaction (the first edition of this book was cited in argument on this point).

If the travel clerk informed the consumer before the button was pressed that a signature on the terms and conditions was required but for some reason omitted to obtain the signature, the operator would *probably* still not be disadvantaged. The significance of the signature is that it provides *proof* that the consumer has had the terms and conditions drawn to their attention and has agreed that they form part of the contract. If the consumer has had the terms and conditions drawn to their attention and it is clear that the contract is being made on the basis of those terms and conditions, then the fact that there is no signature does not alter the basic legal position. The problem that arises is that with no signature there is no proof that the consumer has agreed to what is on the booking form and therefore if a dispute arises later, how is the operator to establish that the consumer knew about the booking terms? The travel clerk is unlikely to be able to provide convincing evidence simply because she will be unable to remember one transaction amongst hundreds. So although in principle the lack of a signature in these circumstances is not fatal, in practice, the operator, without a signed document, will be hard pressed to make his terms stick.

There are a number of what are called "ticket cases" involving cruise lines and ferries which illustrate the importance of getting booking procedures right to ensure that the operator's terms and conditions are properly incorporated in the contract.

One of these is *Hollingworth v Southern Ferries Ltd (The "Eagle")* [1977] 2 Lloyd's Rep. 70. The claimant had been injured on the defendant's ship due to the defendant's negligence. Their defence was that there was a clause in the contract which exempted them from liability. The facts were that the contract had been made on the claimant's behalf by a friend who was acting as her agent. He had acquired a brochure from a travel agency and then gone back some time later and made a firm booking for the two of them. The booking was made over the phone in the travel agent's office and a booking form was not signed. Nor were the booking conditions in the brochure drawn to the attention of the consumer at the time of booking, nor indeed was it brought home to the consumer that the booking was made subject to the booking conditions. There was certainly an exclusion clause on the ticket which the claimant was given prior to departure but that was long after the contract had been made. It was held that the exclusion clause *had not been incorporated* in the contract and therefore the defendants were not protected by it. The fact that there were conditions in the brochure which the claimant's friend had seen was not good enough. The judge said:

"I do not consider that merely seeing a statement of this kind in a brochure makes that statement in effect of the same import as would be the case if one were shown that document at the time when one was making the contract; the statement in the brochure merely gives an intending passenger advance notice of the terms which he may expect to find when he enters into the contract."

Effectively, he was saying that insufficient action had been taken to bring the conditions to the notice of the claimant so that they were brought home to the claimant *at the time the contract was made.*

He also went on to say that even if he was wrong on this point the conditions in the brochure would still be of no help to the defendants. The brochure did not print the terms and conditions in their entirety, it merely said that the voyage was subject to terms and conditions which could be inspected at the defendant's offices in Southampton. In some cases that might be sufficient, but in the present case the conditions were so sweeping in nature it was not enough to print a general notice like this. It did not bring home to the claimant the nature of the particular clause which exempted liability.

A contrasting case is *Budd v Peninsular and Oriental Steam Navigation Co* [1969] 2 Lloyd's Rep. 262. In that case, the claimant was injured due to the admitted negligence of the defendants. However, in this case when the claimant had entered into the contract at the premises of the defendant's agents the agents had made sure she signed the declaration on the booking form. It stated:

"and I understand that all accommodation is offered and fares are quoted subject to the Regulations and Conditions of Carriage as printed on the Passage Ticket of the Line concerned."

One of the conditions on the ticket, which was legible and reasonably comprehensible to the average person, exempted the defendants from liability. The judge said:

"The law of this country is plain. If you choose to put your signature to a document in which it is made plain that the obligations of the party with whom you are contracting is contained in certain conditions, then you are bound by those conditions."

The claimant therefore failed in her action. The difference between the cases is simply that in the former proper procedures were not followed, whereas in the latter they were. For a further example of the consequences of failing to follow a proper booking procedure the case of *Fosbroke-Hobbes v Airwork Ltd* [1937] 1 All E.R. 108 discussed in Ch.6 on Exclusion of Liability is instructive. (Note that since 1977 when the Unfair Contract Terms Act was passed exemption clauses which attempt to exclude liability for personal injury caused by negligence are no longer valid.)

If, however, the terms and conditions signed by the consumer at the same time as the button is pressed expressly state that the contract is not concluded until, for instance, confirmation is sent (or received) by the consumer then the analysis may be different. Here the tour operator is reserving to himself the opportunity of *accepting or rejecting the offer made by the consumer* to buy the holiday. The conclusion of the contract is being postponed until the tour operator decides he wishes to make the contract—by posting the confirmation, i.e. the acceptance. Given the automated nature of the contracting process in these circumstances and the unlikelihood of any human intervention at such a late stage, it is a little puzzling why a tour operator would wish to do this. All it seems to accomplish is to give the consumer an opportunity to reconsider and perhaps withdraw their offer before the tour operator has had a chance to accept. (For withdrawal of offers, see below.) For a practical example of how this might work against the tour operator see "The Problem Page" [1994] T.L.J. 26. See also *Saggerson*, 4th edn, p.245 on this issue.

As indicated at the beginning of this section, travel agents also offer consumers the opportunity of contracting with travel companies over the internet. Here the analysis is much the same as with Viewdata systems. One advantage seems to be that the internet booking offers more in the way of information to the consumer if they choose to access it—including photographs and videos of the hotels and resorts on offer. Such information is of course a two-edged sword for the travel companies. On the one hand, it permits consumers to make a much more informed choice, hopefully leading to a satisfactory holiday. On the other hand, if the information turns out to be wrong or misleading it is easier to bring an action.

Dealing Direct with the Public Using Correspondence

Although fast diminishing in importance, it is still possible to contract for travel services by post. A typical scenario here would be that the consumer acquires a brochure, fills in the booking form, posts it off to a tour operator who then confirms the booking by sending a letter of confirmation to the consumer. The analysis in this situation would be that the brochure constitutes an invitation to treat. The operator is saying that he has holidays that he wishes to sell and is inviting the public to make an offer to buy them. By filling in the booking form the consumer makes such an offer and the operator accepts this offer by despatching the confirmation of booking letter. Under this system the operator has the last word. He is in a position to accept or reject the consumer's offer which he will do according to whether the holiday is available or not.

As far as incorporation of the terms and conditions is concerned, this is achieved by requiring the consumer to sign a booking form containing a declaration that he agrees to take the holiday on the terms spelt out in the brochure. If, for some reason, the declaration is not signed, the operator, to protect himself, should send the form back and insist that it is signed. To send a letter of confirmation without first obtaining the signature is to create an avoidable risk.

One problem that arises when dealing with correspondence is that there is necessarily a delay between when the letter of acceptance is posted and when it arrives. Sometimes, as over the Christmas period, that delay can be substantial and in rare circumstances the letter can go missing altogether. The question that this poses is *when* is the contract concluded? When the letter is posted or when it arrives?

The tour operator in fact has control over this situation should he care to take advantage of it. It is open to the operator to provide in the brochure and the booking conditions that acceptance will take effect from the moment the letter of confirmation is despatched. Thus, he can be secure in the knowledge that once the letter is posted a contract exists. He is not left at the mercy of the Post Office. The consumer of course *is* at the mercy of the Post Office. He is left in a state of uncertainty as to whether he has a contract or not until the letter of confirmation arrives, but that is the risk he takes when he contracts on terms and conditions drafted by someone else.

However, even without express words in the terms and conditions providing that the acceptance takes effect on posting, the rule of the common law, known as the postal rule, provides that in the absence of circumstances to the contrary, when the post is the accepted means of communication, the acceptance takes effect when it is posted, *even if it never arrives* (*Household Fire and Carriage Accident Co v Grant* (1879) L.R. 4 Ex. D. 216). This rule, which is entirely arbitrary, is an exception to the general rule that in contract the acceptance does not take effect until it has been communicated to the offeror. In other words, there is no contract until both parties know about it. It substitutes a *dispatch* rule for the normal *receipt* rule. Because it is an exception the courts will not apply it if it leads to absurd or inconvenient results. (Note that in the *Carlill* case the claimant did not communicate her acceptance of the offer to the advertisers when she bought the smoke ball and started using it. In the circumstances it was held that the defendants had waived their right to have the acceptance communicated.)

Just as the operator can expressly provide for what the booking procedure will be when using the post, so too can the consumer. Consider the following facts: a consumer, immediately prior to Christmas, wishes to book a holiday for early in the New Year. Being aware of the difficulties with postal communication at that time of year he phones up in advance to enquire about availability. The operator tells him that a holiday is still available but that no bookings can be taken over the phone, nor will an option be held. The consumer responds by saying that he will post the booking immediately but in the circumstances he would appreciate a response within the week.

In these circumstances there would be grounds for saying, in the absence of express words on the booking form, that the acceptance would only take effect when communicated to the consumer and if it arrived outside the time limit laid down by the consumer it would be too late. The offer was only open for a certain length of time. After that time it is no longer open to be accepted. The consumer clearly did not want to be left hanging around not knowing whether he has a contract or not. He specified a time limit, after which he would be free to go elsewhere. The operator cannot fall back on the postal rule and argue that there was a contract as soon as the letter was posted. In these circumstances it will be the operator who runs the risk of the delays in the post over Christmas, not the consumer.

CHAPTER THREE

Last Minute, Direct-sell, Telephone Bookings

It is increasingly the case that consumers can book holidays or flights over the phone, using a credit card for payment, and perhaps never sign a booking form. The dangers here for the operator are obvious. He may sell the holiday but not on his terms (see G. Ridler "The Dangers of Telephone Booking" [2006] I.T.L.J. p.13; cf. *Gow v TUI* [2006] C.L.Y. 1993).

Suppose, for instance, that a consumer sees a last minute bargain advertised on TV using teletext (which is now available on digital TV platforms). He can ring up the operator concerned, obtain full details over the phone, pay by credit card and pick up the tickets and accommodation details at the airport. The advertisement on Teletext is only an invitation to treat and many advertisements make this plain by stating that they are "subject to availability". The initial enquiry by the consumer will not be an offer simply because the screen does not give enough detail on which to base a firm offer. The offer is probably made by the sales staff describing the holiday and stating that it is available if the consumer wants it. The acceptance is made by the consumer agreeing to take the holiday and giving details of his name and address and his credit card number. Unless the sales staff indicate to the consumer that there are conditions attached to the booking the contract will consist solely of the details described over the phone. Sending written confirmation of the booking later with conditions attached will not change the situation. Conditions added later are not effective. It is not possible for one party to unilaterally insert terms into the contract which the other party did not know of or agree to (see, for instance, *Olley v Marlborough Court Hotel Ltd* [1949] 1 K.B. 532 discussed in Ch.6 on Exclusion of Liability).

Note that if the sales staff had indicated that there were conditions attached to the booking then even though the consumer had not read them they would nevertheless still form part of the contract. It is not necessary for the consumer to have read them, merely to have had them drawn to his attention. Once he knows of their existence he is bound by them if he goes ahead and makes the contract. But in these circumstances there remains a practical problem. It frequently happens that a travel clerk asserts that attention was drawn to the conditions but the consumer equally assertively denies that this was done. The courts often find in favour of the consumer's version of events—often with serious consequences for the operator. There is really no 100 per cent substitute for a signed booking form, although one that goes some of the way to solving the problem might be the use of tape recordings of bookings.

Forsdyke v Panorama Holiday Group Ltd [2002] C.L.Y. 2321 is an example of a last minute booking where the consumer made clear his particular wishes, i.e. a heated swimming pool, at the time of booking, and the tour operator was held to be in breach when this was not supplied.

The Impact of Regulation 9 of the Package Travel Regulations

Up to now we have seen that the penalty the tour operator pays for failing to incorporate his terms and conditions in the contract is simply that he will not be able to rely upon them. This may be a problem but it is not fatal to the existence of the contract. However, reg.9 changes all that. It provides not only that certain information must be incorporated in the contract but also, if practicable, that it must be put in writing and communicated to the consumer *before* the contract is made. In all cases, a written copy must be supplied to the consumer. Failure to comply gives the consumer the right to cancel.

Regulation 9 states:

"9(1) The other party to the contract shall ensure that—

(a) depending on the nature of the package being purchased, the contract contains at least the elements specified in schedule 2 to these regulations;
(b) subject to paragraph (2) below, all the terms of the contract are set out in writing or such other form as is comprehensible and accessible to the consumer and are communicated to the consumer before the contract is made; and
(c) a written copy of these terms is supplied to the consumer.

(2) Paragraph (1) (b) above does not apply when the interval between the time when the consumer approaches the other party to the contract with a view to entering into a contract and the time of departure under the proposed contract is so short that it is impracticable to comply with the sub-paragraph.

(3) It is an implied condition of the contract that the other party to the contract complies with the provisions of paragraph (1)."

Regulation 9(1)(b) which requires the information to be provided *before the contract is made* should be read in conjunction with reg.9(1)(a) which requires the information to be *in the contract*. For conventional tour operators this should not pose a problem. According to reg.5 and Sch.1 (see Ch.16), a tour operator who publishes a brochure must ensure that the brochure contains certain information. This information is similar, but not identical, to the information required by Sch.2. On the face of it, therefore, the brochure can be used to kill two birds with one stone. Regulation 9(1)(b) can be satisfied by putting the information in the brochure; reg.9(1)(a) is satisfied by ensuring that when the booking form is signed the consumer agrees that the relevant information from the brochure is incorporated in the contract. But care will have to be taken to communicate some of the requirements of Sch.2 to the consumer at the appropriate time because the information may not be found in the brochure. Paragraph 2, for instance, (means, characteristics and categories of transport to be used and the dates, times and points of departure and return) has no direct equivalent in Sch.1. Nor has para.8 (name and address of the organiser, the retailer and, where appropriate, the insurer) or para.11 (special requirements).

The alternative is to produce another standard form contract at the time of contracting, or even to produce a tailor-made or individualised contract at that time. Provision of the information on a confirmation invoice or a computer print out *after* the contract has been made will not be permissible given the requirement in reg.9(1)(b) that the information be provided *before the contract is concluded*.

Last Minute Bookings

An exception to this is to be found in reg.9(2) in the case of "last minute" bookings. If it is not practicable to comply then the tour operator does not have to supply the information "in writing or such other form" before the contract is made. However, given the fact that much if not all the information might be already available in a brochure, and given the speed of modern communications, it will probably be the exception rather than the rule that this requirement will be waived for conventional tour operators selling holidays from brochures via travel agents.

The real difficulty will be for operators who sell their holidays using telephone credit card sales where the contract is concluded over the phone and where written communication before the contract is made is difficult, if not impossible. Given that the Regulation states that the contract should be set out in writing *or such other form as is comprehensible and accessible*, then it would be legitimate to provide the information over the phone. The problem, of course, would be the length of time required to provide it. Schedule 2 is not short and several valuable minutes could be consumed just repeating routine information—and then there are the other terms such as exclusion clauses, limitation clauses, cancellation charges, etc. The Regulation will be broken if either the information is provided *after* the contract has been made or if the information is not *communicated* at all.

It is, of course, possible to incorporate terms by reference, i.e. by informing the consumer that the contract is subject to terms and conditions without actually spelling out precisely what they are. This is what most transport companies do. On their tickets they state that the ticket is "subject to conditions" (see Ch.6 on Exclusion of Liability for more on this). Thus, the very least the telesales operator must do to be able to rely on his small print is to inform the consumer over the phone that the contract contains terms and conditions other than the basic details of price, date, destination, etc. But the question arises as to whether or not the tour operator has done sufficient to comply with reg.9(1)(b) by merely referring to the small print rather than reading it all out? By using this shorthand method, has the operator communicated all the terms in a *form* which is accessible? Although a respectable argument could be made out for saying that such a shorthand form was an appropriate form in the circumstances, one has to remember that this is a consumer protection measure and therefore any interpretation that permits less than the full terms of the contract to be communicated is not to be encouraged.

So if reading out all the terms over the phone is impracticable, what else is possible? Could the operator be expected to say to the consumer that the contract will not be concluded until the information has been posted or faxed to him? Where time is not of pressing importance this would be entirely reasonable. It would merely place the telesales operator in the same position as other direct sell operators who advertise in papers or other print media and use the post to communicate. However, the nature of telesales is that a large part of the market is "late sales" where it is in the interests of both parties to be able to conclude the contract over the phone. Neither party wishes to lose the sale by having to postpone the conclusion of the contract until the terms have been communicated in full in writing. The reality is that if the consumer were told that he couldn't make the contract there and then he would simply put the phone down and then ring another operator who would be more obliging.

The problem is where to draw the line between "last minute" sales where the operator cannot be expected to comply fully with reg.9(1)(b) and other sales where compliance is not a problem. A previous edition of the DTI guidelines suggested that as a matter of "good practice" the dividing line is the one suggested by trade bodies, i.e. last minute bookings are those taken within 14 days of departure.

Even if the telesales operator satisfies reg.9(1)(a) and (b) by providing the information orally or is not required to provide the information in full because it is a last minute booking reg.9(1)(c) still requires them to put all the terms of the contract in writing afterwards. It requires that *a written copy of these terms is supplied to the consumer* although no time limit is placed on this requirement. Presumably a court would imply a term to the effect that the written contract be supplied within a reasonable time after the conclusion of the contract and if the operator did not comply then they would be in breach of reg.9.

Mention was made earlier of internet bookings. Given the nature of the technology it is difficult to see how an internet travel company could ever take advantage of the last minute rule—simply because it is so easy for them to comply with the Regulation.

The Penalty for Non-compliance

The penalty for not complying with reg.9 is to be found in reg.9(3). It states that it is an implied *condition* that the operator will comply with the Regulation. Breach of an implied condition gives the consumer the right to withdraw from the contract. Effectively, this means that if a tour operator fails even marginally to comply with the Regulation the consumer will have the right to withdraw. Regulation 9(1)(a) requires *at least* the elements listed in the Schedule to be contained in the contract and reg.9(1)(b) requires that *all the terms* of the contract are set out in writing.

This places a premium on getting the paperwork right and at the right time. What the tour operator does not want is large numbers of consumers being able to cancel merely because the details were not provided at the right time. Making sure the brochure is as comprehensive as possible is one way. Making sure that agents are aware of their responsibilities is another.

On the face of it the penalty for non-compliance is severe. The operator stands the risk of losing the contract altogether. In practice, however, the penalty is probably more apparent than real. It depends upon first, the consumer knowing that he has the right to withdraw, and secondly, the consumer being prepared to exercise that right. It is doubtful how many consumers are aware of this right and, even when they are, it depends on whether they have sufficient confidence to exercise it. They need the confidence to do so because, in most cases, their money will already be in the hands of the tour operator and they risk losing everything if their decision is wrong. It is unfortunately the case that most telesales operators could probably ignore the provisions of reg.9 because the sanction is not likely to be effective.

In *Foster v Dial A Flight Ltd* Unreported 1998, Altrincham County Court, the claimant argued that the tour operator had failed to comply with reg.9 and sued for breach of condition and the return of his money. The issue went unresolved, however, because the court held that the arrangements purchased by the claimant did not amount to a package and therefore the Regulations did not apply. Given the more recent decisions of the ECJ and the Court of Appeal in the *Club Tour* and *ABTA* cases it may be that if the facts of *Foster* occurred again the consumer would be more successful.

Even where last minute bookings are not an issue, a tour operator who fails to comply with reg.9 might escape the full impact of the sanction. There is authority to the effect that a victim of a breach of condition may lose the right to withdraw from the contract in circumstances where the common law doctrine of affirmation applies. If the consumer, knowing that a breach of condition has occurred, chooses to affirm the contract then the right to repudiate is lost. Thus, if the consumer knew that by not supplying all the terms of the contract in writing in advance the tour operator was in breach of reg.9 and yet still chose to continue with the contract, e.g. by paying the balance when it fell due, the consumer would lose the right to repudiate for breach of condition (see the Law Commission Working Paper No. 85 paras 261–263 and *Chitty on Contracts*, para.24–002 for further discussion of this point).

However *Akehurst v Thomson Holidays Ltd and Britannia Airways Ltd* Unreported May 6, 2003, Cardiff CC suggests that reg.9 may have more bite to it than suspected. The claimants were Thomson Holiday clients who had been injured or suffered psychological damage when the Britannia plane that was flying them to Spain crashed at Gerona Airport. One of the issues in the case was whether Thomson Holidays had protected themselves against liability by incorporating Britannia's terms and conditions into the contract between Thomson and their clients. On the facts of the case Thomson had not done so—yet another example of bad drafting—but the judge spoke at some length on whether reg.9 could assist the clients:

"The purpose of these Regulations, and in particular Regulation 9, is to protect the consumer. All the terms of the contract must be brought reasonably and fairly to his notice, particularly where terms are onerous or exclude or limit liability. I agree with the claimants that the object is to avoid the manifestly unjust situation in which a consumer is said to be bound by terms to which had had no idea that he had 'agreed'. I agree of course that the terms of The Charter and Britannia's Conditions of Carriage were all set out in writing. I also agree that the terms of The Charter were provided to the consumer before the contract was made by inclusion in the Brochure. I do not agree that all the terms were communicated to the consumer before the contract was made. Firstly, it is not sufficient communication to tell the consumer that he can ask the travel agent booking his holiday to get him 'a copy of any condition that apply to your journey if he/she had not already got them'. Thomson's obligation was to ensure ('shall ensure') that all the terms of the contract set out in writing were communicated to the consumer before the contract was made. That obligation was not discharged by attempting to place the onus on the consumer to ask the travel agent to get him a copy of 'any' conditions (not even 'the' conditions) that applied to his journey. Secondly, it was not clearly set out in writing or in any other form comprehensible and accessible to the consumer that it was a term of the contract the benefits conveyed by clause 6 and 7 were being substantially cut down by the air carrier's Condition of Carriage which in turn incorporated the Warsaw Convention. The consumer was not told that 'any' (hence unspecified) conditions that applied (which were not communicated to him but which the travel agent might have and, if he did not, would obtain if asked) applied not only between himself and the carrier but also between himself and Thomson, even though Thomson was not the carrier and not a party to the air carrier's contract."

Thomson endeavoured to argue that even though reg.9 had been broken by an inadequate communication of the terms of the contract this wrong did not affect the substance of the contract. The judge rejected this.

> "What this means, it seems to me, is that Thomson can ignore Regulations put in place to protect consumers in an industry in which it is a leading operator. It can fail to ensure, as it is required to do, that all the terms of the contract are set out in writing and communicated to the consumer before the contract is made, fail to supply a written copy of the terms to the consumer and then rely against the consumer upon terms which it has failed to communicate and supply in writing to him. The Regulations are of no avail to the consumer. I cannot accept this. In my view, Thomson certainly is seeking to take advantage of its own wrong. It is seeking to hold the consumer to an alleged term of which he was unaware because it, Thomson, failed to communicate the term to him when it was under and express statutory obligation to do so."

The essence of this judgment seems to be that where the tour operator endeavours to incorporate their terms by reference then, even though at common law they might succeed, the tour operator cannot rely upon them if it is in breach of reg.9.

Note that if the tour operator has not drawn the attention of the consumer to the terms and conditions of the contract *at all* before the contract was concluded, then on the basis of the principles already discussed they do not form part of the contract and therefore the tour operator is not in breach of reg.9. So, for instance, for telephone bookings, as long as the basic details of the contract have been agreed orally over the phone the tour operator may have a perfectly valid contract but he runs the risk of not being able to enforce any of the terms and conditions he may subsequently send to the consumer.

The Other Party to the Contract

Regulation 9 imposes the liability upon "the other party to the contract", i.e. the "organiser or the retailer, or both, as the case may be". At first glance one is tempted to say that this seems irrelevant. If the information was not provided does it matter who didn't provide the information? However, closer examination suggests that it may have a practical effect. Where a consumer is buying a holiday at the last minute from a travel agent on the high street, perhaps with less than 24 hours to go before departure, it might be perfectly justifiable for the tour operator to claim that he could not supply all the information in writing to the consumer. The travel agent on the other hand may be in a position to do so, and failure to comply would result, at least in theory, in the consumer being able to cancel.

Offers, Withdrawal of Offer and Counter-offers

The process of bargaining described above is a little misleading as it gives the impression that the parties proceed from one stage to the next—invitation to treat, followed by offer, followed by acceptance—in a relatively straightforward manner. But life is more complicated than that. Often the bargaining process is much more complicated.

Take, for instance, the VDU booking. Imagine that at the height of the booking season consumers have entered a travel agency and with the assistance of the travel clerk have chosen a holiday. They then ask for just a couple of minutes to deliberate. While this is happening the holiday they chose disappears from the screen because it is now fully booked. When the couple make up their minds to take the holiday it is no longer available. Legally speaking what has happened is that although the operator made them an offer that offer was *withdrawn before it was accepted*. In such circumstances there is no contract. The consumers will have to start all over again. The logic of the situation is that if there is no offer on the table there is nothing to be accepted and the parties will have no contract. Frustratingly, this is often the case with internet bookings. The availability of flights or the price of a particular flight change with remarkable speed as anyone will attest who has spent any time researching the best price on the internet only to return to a site to discover the offer has already disappeared.

This is just a specific example of the general rule that a party can withdraw his offer at any time before acceptance (*Offord v Davies* (1862) C.B.N.S. 748) and there will be no contract (subject to what is said below about options).

What would be the position if a consumer filled in the booking form for a direct sell operator and despatched it (with deposit) and then immediately afterwards wrote again saying that he is "reconsidering" the hotel he had chosen and would it be possible to upgrade to a higher grade hotel? After receiving both letters the operator writes back explaining that an upgrade is not possible and confirms the original booking. Is there a contract? There is clearly an original offer to buy by the consumer which has ultimately been accepted by the operator but what is the effect of the intervening enquiry by the consumer? Is it a withdrawal of his original offer? If so, then any attempted acceptance by the operator is to no avail, there is no longer an offer to accept. But what if the second letter is not a withdrawal, merely a request for something different if it can be arranged, but which still leaves the original offer open if the request cannot be satisfied. In this case the operator might successfully argue that he has a contract. It would be a question of what *objective* interpretation a court would place upon the second letter.

It is not unknown in the travel industry for consumers to haggle over the price. Take the consumer who rings up a hotel and asks what the weekend rate for a family room is. He is told that it is £120 per night for a couple. This includes bed, breakfast and evening meal and accommodation in a room which will sleep two adults and two children but the children will have to pay for meals as taken. Knowing that this is the low season for hotels the consumer manages to bargain the price down to £100 but is still not satisfied and says that unless the children can be accommodated in a separate room he will not make a booking. The reservations clerk has no further discretion in the matter and asks the consumer to hang on a moment while he consults the manager.

OFFER AND ACCEPTANCE: DO WE HAVE A CONTRACT?

The manager is horrified that the clerk has even considered such a booking because there is a conference booked into the hotel that weekend and almost all the rooms are taken already and the rest can certainly be sold off at full price. The clerk informs the consumer that there is no way they can accommodate the children in a separate room. The consumer then backs down and says that he will take the family room for £100 but the clerk informs him that if he wants the room he will have to pay the regular weekend rate. Is there a contract? Probably not.

What has happened here is that the hotel has made an offer to sell the room for £100 per night. The offer was not accepted by the consumer. The consumer went so far as to say that he would not have the room at that price and proposed a different arrangement altogether. This amounts to a counter-offer and the legal effect of a counter-offer is to destroy the original offer. The counter-offer was not accepted by the hotel and therefore the consumer attempted to accept the original offer by the hotel, but this no longer existed. In effect the consumer was making another new offer and this in turn was rejected by the hotel.

One of the leading cases on this point is *Hyde v Wrench* (1840) 49 All E.R. 132. The facts were that the defendant wrote to the claimant on June 6, offering to sell his farm for £1,000. The claimant responded immediately by making an offer of £950 which the defendant refused on June 27. On June 29, the claimant wrote and "accepted" the offer of June 6. On the question of whether there was a contract, Lord Langdale, the Master of the Rolls, said:

> "Under the circumstances stated I think there exists no valid binding contract between the parties for the purchase of the property. The defendant offered to sell it for £1000 and if that had been at once unconditionally accepted, there would undoubtedly have been a perfect binding contract; instead of that, the plaintiff made an offer of his own, to purchase the property for £950, *and he thereby rejected the offer previously made by the defendant.* I think that it was not afterwards competent for him to revive the proposal of the defendant, by tendering an acceptance of it; and that, therefore, there exists no obligation of any sort between the parties" (Emphasis added)

The important thing to note here is that the response by the claimant amounted to a *rejection* of the original offer. A different response may have kept the original offer open as in the case of *Stevenson v McLean* (1880) 5 Q.B.D. 346. In that case the facts were that in the course of negotiating the sale of a quantity of iron the defendant wrote to the claimants on Saturday saying: "I would now sell for 40s net cash, open till Monday." On Monday the claimants telegraphed back: "Please wire whether you would accept forty for delivery over two months, or if not, longest limit you would give." After receiving this telegram the defendants sold the iron to a third party and telegraphed the claimants to this effect at 13.25pm. The telegram did not arrive until 13.46pm. In the meantime, having received no reply to their original enquiry the claimants had telegraphed the defendant at 13.34pm accepting the original offer outright.

It was held that the enquiry by the claimants as to the terms on which they could purchase the iron was no more than that, just an enquiry. In the words of Lush J.:

"Here there is no counter proposal. The words are, 'Please wire whether you would accept forty for delivery over two months, or, if not, the longest limit you would give.' There is nothing specific by way of offer or rejection, but a mere inquiry, which should have been answered and not treated as a rejection of the offer."

It was decided, therefore, that there was an offer which had been accepted by the claimants and therefore the defendant was in breach of contract.

Note that although the defendant had telegraphed the withdrawal of his offer *before* he had received the acceptance, the withdrawal did not take effect until it arrived. This is in accordance with the rule laid down in the case of *Byrne v Van Tienhoven* (1880) 5 C.P.D. 344 to the effect that a revocation of an offer must be communicated before it takes effect.

If we apply *Stevenson v Mclean* to the example used above of the haggling over the hotel room, we can see that if the consumer had been less assertive in his negotiations he might at least have acquired the room for £100. If he had framed his request for a separate room for the children as an enquiry rather than a rejection of the hotel's offer there would still have been an offer on the table for him to accept.

Options

Although this has become uncommon, some travel companies permit consumers to hold options. An option is simply a willingness to hold an offer open for a specified period of time. With a VDU booking system it allows the consumer a period of consideration and consultation before having to make a final decision. With a manual system, the travel company may grant an option following a telephone enquiry which will allow the consumer time to fill in the booking form and post it off.

So long as the offer is still open it can be accepted by the consumer but it will lapse at the end of the specified period and the consumer will have nothing to accept. The only problem that arises with options is whether or not the offer can be withdrawn before the time limit has expired and the answer to this is quite straightforward. It was settled in the case of *Routledge v Grant* (1828) 130 All E.R. 920. As with any other offer an option can be withdrawn at any time before it has been accepted so long as the withdrawal is communicated to the other party. The only exception to this, which is unlikely to be found in a travel industry context, is when one party *pays* the other party for an option. In these circumstances the offer must be kept open until the option expires.

Some online travel agents and tour operators permit consumers to place travel products in a "basket" and then come back to them at a later stage. Such practices have to be examined on a case by case basis but it is unlikely that these would amount to true options because there is often an express disclaimer that the products will be available when the consumer returns.

Certainty

Before it can be said that a contract has been concluded the terms of the contract must be *certain*. If the terms of the purported contract are uncertain or incomplete or vague the parties cannot be said to have truly agreed; their "agreement" is defective and will lead to difficulties. For instance, to take a simple example, a consumer may ring up a travel company's call centre and "agree" to purchase a holiday—four adults in "four star self catering accommodation" in Nice, with airport transfers for 14 nights from August 1, for £800 per person departing from Gatwick Airport on Flight XY1234 at 6am. Clearly, there is "agreement" on all these details but if the company sends a confirmation letter indicating that the "four star accommodation" they were selling was a "four star" caravan on a campsite—when the consumer expected a four star hotel—then a legitimate argument could be made for saying that the term "four star accommodation" was sufficiently vague and uncertain to demonstrate that no real agreement had been reached.

In the case of *Scammell (G) & Nephews v Ouston* [1941] AC 251 the parties "agreed" that a van would be bought on "hire purchase" terms. The House of Lords held that the term was too vague to be unenforceable. Hire purchase could take so many different forms that the term could not be defined with any certainty, and it was not for the courts to define the terms but for the parties.

However, the courts will not be too astute to hold that a term is too vague to be enforced, not wishing a party to escape from an otherwise firm agreement by pointing at some term which they say is uncertain. This was the situation in a recent travel related case, *Durham Tees Valley Airport Ltd v Bmibaby Ltd* [2010] EWCA Civ 485. The airline had agreed to base two aircraft at Durham Tees Valley Airport for a period of at least 10 years. In return they had been given financial incentives which the airport would recoup over the 10-year period by virtue of the increased passenger numbers passing through the airport. The airline found that basing aircraft at DTV was a loss-making enterprise and withdrew from the "agreement". When sued by DTV they pleaded that the agreement was too vague to be enforceable because it did not specify how many flights, if any, the airline was to fly. The Court of Appeal rejected this argument. They said:

"59. The question for the judge faced with an allegation of breach of contract would be whether BMIB was, in a real and genuine sense, flying its aircraft. Token flights or a complete absence of any flights (which is this case) clearly would not amount to operating the aircraft. Subject to this, the question of how many times and to where are matters for the airline's discretion."

On that basis the airline were in breach of contract and compelled to pay damages.

CHAPTER FOUR
Contents of the Contract

INTRODUCTION AND OVERVIEW

As part of the bargaining process before a contract is concluded the two parties will make a variety of statements to each other, either orally or in writing. Some of these statements may end up as part of the contract and some may not. Those which end up as part of the contract may vary in importance. This chapter is concerned with how to classify these statements. It is important to be able to do this because the rights of the parties clearly depend upon whether a statement is part of the contract or not, and if it is, the relative importance to be attached to it.

This introductory section gives a brief overview of the classification process. The rest of this chapter and Chs 5 and 6 amplify what is said here.

Terms, Representations and Mere Puffs

The task of classification is complicated by the fact that English law distinguishes between three different types of statement. First, there are those statements which end up as *terms of the contract*, which, if broken, give the victim a straightforward action for *breach of contract*. These are the things which the other party has *promised* you will get. In a package holiday context it will be a term of the contract, for instance, that it is a four star hotel, that the clients will get a balcony and private facilities, that there are three pools and two bars, that it has a children's club, etc. Generally, these are all statements which are printed in the brochure and are what the operator has *contracted* to provide. In a contract with an airline there will be departure and arrival times, departure and arrival airports, class of travel, meal plan, etc, all of which are also terms of the contract. Beware the small print in these contracts, however, where many of the airlines endeavour to diminish their liability for such terms (subject to the rules on exclusion clauses discussed in Ch.6) and there is also a statutory overlay provided by the Montreal Convention (see Ch.13).

Secondly, there are statements which *induce* the other party to enter into the contract but do not become terms of the contract. These are known as *representations* and if they are *false* they give rise to an action for *misrepresentation*. An action for misrepresentation is not as straightforward as an action for breach of contract and the remedies available may be inadequate, although case law suggests that in certain circumstances they may be superior (See *Royscot Trust Ltd v Rogerson* [1991] 3 All E.R. 294 and Ch.7). Often, it is difficult to distinguish between a term and a representation but, for example, it would *probably* only be a representation if an operator, having described the hotel, then went on to describe the resort as having a "wide range of shops". The operator is contracting to provide a hotel with particular facilities but then, in order to

98

encourage the client to enter into the contract, he makes other statements which will influence the client's decision but which do not form part of the contract. If the resort turns out not to have a wide range of shops the client can sue for misrepresentation but not for breach of contract. The rules on misrepresentation can be found in Ch.7 on misrepresentation. See, however, *Jones v Sunworld Ltd* [2003] EWHC 591 where it was held that the lagoon described in the holiday brochure was a term of the contract, just as much as the accommodation, and therefore the tour operator had to ensure that that part of the package was delivered with reasonable care and skill (para.27).

Thirdly, there are statements which have no legal force at all. These are known as "puffs" or "mere puffs". A victim of such a statement has no redress at all. In a holiday case, *Hoffman v Intasun* Unreported 1990, High Court, the claimant tried to make out that because of the extravagantly worded statements made at the beginning of a "Club 18–30" brochure the defendants, Intasun, had *contracted* that they owed her an especially high standard of care. The judge rejected this approach. He decided that the statements had no contractual effect at all. This is what he said:

> "I am asked to say that because of the advertising—what lawyers call puff—in the early part of the brochure, the Defendants were undertaking to give an especially high standard of care. That is an argument that I reject. Puff is puff, and if that is what lawyers call it, lay people have their own expressions for it which are perhaps less flattering. Everybody knows that travel agents [sic] set out to create an atmosphere on paper of a wonderful holiday and marvellous value for money. It cannot possibly be said that a visitor to the Tyrol can sue the travel company for breach of contract if he fails to have any respiratory defect in regarding the breathtaking views of the mountains there—and so on. I look for example at how the Club reps are described on page 8 of the brochure. Mr Eccles [counsel for Intasun] in his opening drew my attention to it specifically saying that the reps were the life and soul of the party, hard working, good timing, trouble shooting, guitar playing, beach partying, smooth operators. I do not know if Miss Gail Tarburn [the Intasun rep] can even play the guitar and I am certain that it could not form any part of a breach of contract if she cannot."

Much of the advertising that goes into the front of brochures falls into this category—statements that make the holiday sound good but do not amount to specific contractual promises. Open most brochures at the beginning and you are bound to find examples—"picturesque villages set amidst glorious scenery"—"quality hotels"—"the number one choice for families"—"the holiday of a lifetime"—"the most beautiful locations around the Mediterranean"—"hand-picked accommodation"—"a luxury cruise around the glittering Caribbean" and so on. In *Griffiths v Waymark* Unreported 1993, Slough County Ct (but see [1994] T.L.J. 122) the judge regarded the phrase "ever-friendly hotel" as not amounting to a legal representation.

Thus, not only do terms have to be distinguished from representations, they both have to be distinguished from mere puffs.

Conditions, Warranties and Innominate Terms

Terms can be classified into either *conditions* or *warranties*. A condition is a major term of the contract which, if broken, provides the victim of the breach with not only a right to damages but also the right, if they wish, to terminate the contract altogether. A warranty, on the other hand, only gives rise to an action for damages. There is no right to terminate the contract for what is regarded as a breach of a minor term of the contract. There is also an intermediate form of term—called an *innominate* term—which cannot immediately be classified as either a condition or a warranty. Its classification depends upon the nature and severity of the breach.

Express and Implied Terms

Terms can be further classified into *express* terms and *implied* terms. An express term, as its name suggests, is one which is expressed in some way—in writing or orally or even, in the case of brochures, pictorially. An implied term is one where the term is not expressed but can nevertheless be implied into the contract. Terms can be implied in a number of ways: by statute (e.g. the requirement that goods be of satisfactory quality implied by s.14 of the Sale of Goods Act 1979); by custom; or by the courts—in which case they can be implied either *in fact* or *in law*. These terms will be explained in due course. However, there is one travel law case, decided before the Package Travel Regulations were passed, *Wall v Silver Wing Surface Arrangements* Unreported 1981, which revolved around the issue of implied terms, and which illustrates the problem vividly. A party of holidaymakers were injured in a hotel fire in Tenerife. They had been unable to escape down the fire escape because the hotel owners had padlocked the gate at the bottom. In the contract between the clients and the tour operators nothing was expressly stated about safety at the hotel but the clients alleged that there was an implied term in the contract that they would be reasonably safe in using the hotel for the purposes for which they had been invited to be there. Ultimately, the court held that there was no such term but it had to make a difficult choice between protecting the interests of the clients by implying a term relating to their safety and the interests of the tour operator by not extending their liability to all the components of the package. This case is placed in context in Chs 5 and 6.

The Package Travel Regulations and the Classification of Terms

The classification of terms in a package holiday contract is no longer simply a matter for the common law. It is heavily affected by the Package Travel Regulations.

For instance, reg.6 states that all the *particulars* in the brochure (whatever that means) are implied warranties. On the face of it this has two major effects. First, it potentially upgrades just about every statement in the brochure to at least a term of the contract—representations and puffs alike. Secondly, it appears to classify all statements as minor terms of the contract.

As far as this second effect is concerned closer examination of the Regulations shows that this is not entirely so. For instance, reg.9 explicitly states that it is an implied *condition* that certain information must be supplied to the consumer before the contract is made. In addition, there are other regulations which have the same effect. Regulation 12 permits a consumer to withdraw from the contract if significant alterations have been made to the contract before departure, and reg.14 effectively gives the consumer the right to terminate a contract if, after departure, a significant proportion of the services cannot be provided.

Regulation 4

Regulation 4 creates a new right of action against organisers or retailers who supply misleading descriptive matter to consumers. This new right of action is a statutory action rather than a contractual action and therefore it cuts across the categories already discussed. Insofar as it only gives a right to damages rather than a right to terminate the contract, it resembles an action for breach of warranty. However, it is available against the retailer as well as the organiser even though the consumer may not have a contract with the retailer. It also covers *any misleading information*, which again extends the action further than any contractual action.

Exclusion Clauses

One very important type of term, which will be looked at in a subsequent chapter, is the exclusion clause—also known as an exemption clause or an exception clause. These are clauses where one party to the contract endeavours to escape liability for breach of contract by inserting a clause into the contract excluding his liability. There is a considerable body of law on this subject which includes the Unfair Contract Terms Act 1977, the Unfair Terms in Consumer Contracts Regulations 1999, provisions in the Package Travel Regulations 1992 relating to specifically to package holidays, and also significant case law at common law. All this will be examined in detail in Ch.6.

DISTINGUISHING TERMS FROM OTHER STATEMENTS

Whether a statement is a term of a contract or not is a matter of intention to be determined by the court. As with offer and acceptance the intention is determined objectively rather than subjectively. As might be expected, there are no precise rules for distinguishing terms from other statements but there are some indicators which have been developed by the courts.

The Importance of the Statement

If it can be shown that one party was most unlikely to have made the contract except on the basis of the statement it is likely to be a term of the contract. In the case of *Bannerman v White* (1861) 10 C.B. N.S. 844 an intending buyer of hops asked the seller whether sulphur had been used in their cultivation because if it had then he was not interested in them. The seller assured him that it had not. It was held that this was a term of the contract. (See also *Pritchard v Cook and Red Ltd* Unreported June 4, 1998, cited in Poole, 10th edn, p.208.)

One can imagine a situation where, say, a disabled client rings up a hotel asks whether it has wheelchair access because if it hasn't then he is not interested. If the hotel responds that it has this would be a breach of contract if wheelchair access was not possible.

Was the Statement Verified?

Two contrasting cases illustrate this point. In *Ecay v Godfrey* (1947) 80 Ll. L. Rep. 286 the seller of a boat stated that the boat was sound but advised the buyer to have it surveyed. In other words, he was saying that he could not verify the condition of the boat and was not contracting on the basis that it was sound. It was held that the condition of the boat was not a term of the contract.

In *Schawel v Reade* [1913] 2 I.R. 64 the purchaser of a horse was about to examine it when the seller told him not to bother looking at it. He said: "You need not look for anything; the horse is perfectly sound. If there was anything the matter with the horse I should tell you." It was held that the statement was a term of the contract.

Again, one can imagine a client enquiring of an operator whether it can be confirmed that the water sports mentioned as being available at the hotel will actually be available at the beginning of the season and the operator responding by saying that they always have in the past but it would be better if the client checked with the hotel before booking. These circumstances are similar to *Ecay v Godfrey* and it would probably be the case that it would not be a term of the contract that water sports would be available.

Alternatively, if the operator confirmed in unequivocal terms that the water sports would be available because they had contracted with the hotel for them then it would almost certainly be a term of the contract.

There is an interesting relationship with reg.9 in these cases. If a client obtains an express oral promise that the facilities he is interested in exist then these become terms of the contract. Under reg.9 these should be reduced to writing before the contract is concluded. Failure to do so gives the client the right to withdraw (see Ch.3). However, it is very likely, given the circumstances, that the interchange will not be reduced to writing. This opens up the possibility that the consumer may be able to withdraw from the contract—in theory at least. The procedure adopted by many tour operators of including a term in their contracts stating that they are not prepared to guarantee "special requests" would go some way to averting this problem—but such a term may fall foul of the Unfair Terms in Consumer Contracts Regulations 1999.

Did One Party Have Special Knowledge?

In *Oscar Chess Ltd v Williams* [1957] 1 All E.R. 325 a private individual sold his car to a garage on the basis of a statement in the log book (which had been forged by a previous owner) that the car was a 1948 model whereas in fact it was much older. It was held that the garage were specialists and as such were in at least as good a position as the seller to know whether the statement was true or not and that therefore the age of the car was only a representation not a term.

The case of *Dick Bentley Productions Ltd v Harold Smith (Motors) Ltd* [1965] 1 W.L.R. 623 can be contrasted with the *Oscar Chess* case. In that case a dealer sold a Bentley car, saying that the car had only travelled 20,000 miles since having a new engine fitted when in fact it had travelled nearly 100,000 miles. It was held that the statement was a term of the contract. The seller in this case was clearly in a better position than the buyer to know the truth of the statement.

Where a long haul tour operator prints in the brochure the average temperatures to be expected in some exotic island in a remote part of the Indian Ocean or where an operator gives the distance from the hotel to the beach a court might say that given the relative knowledge and expertise of the tour operator such statements would be terms rather than representations.

When Was the Statement Made?

In *Routledge v McKay* [1954] 1 All E.R. 855 the seller of a motorcycle stated, on October 23, during preliminary negotiations, that it was a 1942 model when in fact it was a 1930 model. A week later on October 30, the motorcycle was sold and the terms of the contract were reduced to writing. The contract made no mention of the age of the motorcycle. It was held that *at the time the statement was made* it was not intended that it would have contractual force. The omission from the written contract, although not fatal in itself, merely reinforced the view that the statement was not intended as a term. The clear time interval between the making of the statement and the final contract assisted the court in coming to the decision.

In *Inntrepreneur Pub Co v East Crown Ltd* [2000] 2 Lloyds Rep. 611 Lightman J. said that there was a "prima facie assumption that the written contract includes all the terms the parties wanted to be binding between them" and that "the longer the interval" between the making of the statement and the conclusion of the contract "the greater the presumption must be that the parties did not intend the statement to have contractual effect".

It is possible to illustrate this point using the facts of a travel law case. *Kemp v Intasun* [1987] 2 F.T.L.R. 234 is *not* a case on misrepresentation but it demonstrates the significance of an interval between the stages of negotiation and the importance of bringing significant matters to the attention of the other party *at the time the contract is made*. In the *Kemp* case the claimant's wife had entered a branch of Thomas Cook and made preliminary enquiries about holidays. She mentioned in passing that her husband was not with her because he was ill. She said that he was suffering from an asthmatic and bronchial attack. It was not until almost four weeks later that she returned the booking form and concluded the contract. On the first night of their holiday, because of overbooking, the Kemps were accommodated in a substandard room. The dirt and dust in the room brought on an asthma attack and the first week of their holiday was ruined as a result. It was held that the casual remark to the travel agent about Mr Kemp's asthma made at an early stage of the negotiations was insufficient to create contractual obligations for Intasun. They were not liable for problems to

Mr Kemp's health which they could not foresee and which had not been drawn to their attention.

It would have been different altogether if Mrs Kemp had specifically drawn the asthma attacks to the attention of Intasun at the time the contract was made in such a way as to make it clear that Intasun were accepting a booking from a person with health problems.

Clearly, the passage of time between first mentioning the illness and the ultimate conclusion of the contract resulted in the statement having no contractual effect at all. It would be the same with an action for misrepresentation.

These cases and guidelines illustrate the difficulty of distinguishing between terms and other statements. At the margins the distinction is often very difficult indeed to make and can be regarded as more of an art than a science.

If the claimant is fortunate then the statement will have been categorised as a term and there will be a straightforward action for breach of contract, but if it is not a term there is the further difficulty of distinguishing between statements which are representations and those which are mere puffs.

DISTINGUISHING BETWEEN REPRESENTATIONS AND PUFFS

A representation is a statement of fact made by one party to the contract to the other which induces the other to enter into the contract but which does not form part of the contract itself. A misrepresentation is merely a false representation.

From this definition it can be seen that there are two conditions that a statement must satisfy before it can be classified as a representation. First, it must be a statement of fact, therefore statements of opinion or statements as to the future or future intention do not qualify. Secondly, the statement must actually induce the contract. If the statement has no effect upon the other party it will not amount to a representation. Additionally, the statement must be material. In other words the statement must be of some significance to the reasonable person before it can give rise to an action for misrepresentation.

There Must be a Statement of Fact

To be a misrepresentation the statement must be one of fact. This branch of the law protects the victim from statements which are false but not against opinions which turn out to be wrong or predictions as to the future which are not realised. However, what amounts to a statement of fact has been given a fairly extended meaning in the law of misrepresentation as can be seen from the following cases.

In *Edgington v Fitzmaurice* (1885) L.R. 29 Ch. D. 459 the directors of a company stated in a prospectus that they wanted to raise money to improve buildings and extend the business. In fact, they were going to pay off existing debts with the money. On the face of it this was not a statement of existing fact but a statement of future intention. However, Bowen L.J. said:

"The state of a man's mind is as much a fact as the state of his digestion. It is true that it is very difficult to prove what the state of a man's mind at a particular time is, but if it can be ascertained it is as much a fact as anything else. A misrepresentation as to the state of a man's mind is, therefore, a mis-statement of fact."

On that basis there was a finding of misrepresentation.

In the case of *Smith v Land and House Property Corp* (1885) L.R. 28 Ch. D. 7 the owner of a hotel put it up for sale saying that at present it was let to "Mr Frederick Fleck (a most desirable tenant) at a rental of £400 per annum for an unexpired term of 27 years, thus offering a first class investment." In fact, Mr Fleck was two quarters behind with the rent. Again, the statement that Fleck was a desirable tenant appears only to be a statement of opinion and therefore not actionable, but the court nevertheless held in favour of the buyer. Bowen L.J. said:

"if the facts are not equally known to both sides, then a statement of opinion by the one who knows the facts best makes very often a statement of material fact, *for he impliedly states that he knows facts which justify his opinion.*" (Emphasis added)

In *Esso Petroleum Ltd v Mardon* [1976] Q.B. 801 the claimants had represented to a garage owner that his garage would sell 200,000 gallons of petrol a year. In fact, sales never reached more than 78,000 gallons. The business went bankrupt and the claimants sought to repossess the garage. It was held that the claimants had made a statement of fact in relation to their prediction as to future sales—that they had exercised reasonable care and skill in arriving at the figure—which in fact they had not.

In contrast is the case of *Bisset v Wilkinson* [1927] A.C. 177 (which was distinguished in the *Esso* case) where the seller of land, which had never been used for sheep-farming, made a statement to the purchaser to the effect that he estimated that it would carry 2,000 sheep. This turned out not to be possible. Both parties knew that the land had not been used for sheep-farming previously. It was held that the statement was simply an honest statement of opinion and the purchaser had no action for misrepresentation.

In applying these cases to package holiday contracts one thinks immediately of those brochures where the operator has a section on each resort or hotel where he states what in "Our Opinion" the delights of the resort are. Take the following example for instance:

"On a peaceful stretch of Kalutara Beach, the Mermaid is a small hotel with a friendly atmosphere, the gardens stretch to the seashore enabling you to relax in the shade of the tall palm trees." (Tradewinds 3 Star Collection brochure published June 1997)

Clearly, this passage is designed to encourage the client to choose that particular hotel but the statements in it probably fall short of being terms of the contract (but see reg.6). What then would be the position if the hotel had 500 rooms (as opposed to 72), there were no palm trees to shelter under and no one talked to clients for the duration of the holiday? The statement about the palm trees is a statement of fact which, because it is false, is an actionable misrepresentation. On the other hand, the statement that the hotel is "friendly" is no more than a statement of opinion and so long as the clients cannot prove that the tour operator did not actually hold that opinion there is nothing that can be done about it. "Small" is much more difficult but probably falls into the category of opinion rather than fact—unless again the tour operator can be shown not to actually hold that opinion. If the hotel did indeed have 500 rooms that might be a conclusion that a court could come to.

Brochures often contain a statement that a particular resort is "lively". This is obviously inserted to make the resort appeal to younger people. On the face of it it is only a statement of opinion but if the clients arrived to find the resort inhabited entirely by clients of Saga could they justifiably complain? If the statement was solely a statement of opinion nothing could be done—it would be mere puff. However, there is a strong argument for saying that *implied* in the statement is a statement of fact, i.e. that the tour operator has facts at his disposal that give rise to his opinion that the resort is lively. The statement implies that there are plenty of bars and nightclubs in the resort and that it is filled with young people.

In such circumstances, the clients would have a case based on the principle of *Smith v Land and House Property Corp.*

In *Spice Girls Ltd v Aprilia World Service BV* [2000] E.M.L.R. 478 the claimants had entered into an agreement to sponsor a tour of the defendant pop group. The group participated in promotional activities at a time that they knew that before the end of the tour one of its members would be leaving. It was held that this was a misrepresentation by conduct that the group did not know and had no reasonable grounds to believe that any member of the group would be leaving before the tour was over.

The Statement Must Induce the Contract

The statement will have no legal effect if the person to whom it was made did not in fact rely upon it. This point is simply illustrated by the case of *Smith v Chadwick* (1884) L.R. 9 App. Cas. 187. The claimant in that case bought shares in a company on the basis of a prospectus issued by the company. The prospectus included a statement that a certain person, Grieve, was on the board of the company. Subsequently the claimant sought to bring an action for misrepresentation because in fact Grieve was not on the board of the company. The claim was dismissed on the grounds that the claimant had never heard of Grieve and the fact that he was supposed to be on the board had not influenced his decision to purchase the shares.

It is not necessary for the representation to be the only reason for entering the contract. As long as it is one of the reasons then it can form the basis of an action. This was the position in *Edgington v Fitzmaurice*. The claimant had invested in debentures in the company not only because of the statement that the company would use the money to expand the business but also because he thought that his loan would be secured on the company's assets. It was held that even though the statement as to the uses to which the money would be put was not his only reason for investing he could nevertheless bring an action on the basis of it.

If a brochure states, for instance, that a wide variety of water sports are available in resort, whereas in fact they are not, this would not amount to a misrepresentation if the claimant was a 70-year-old asthmatic who had no intention of going water-skiing. It may have been a false statement but it was not one of the reasons that particular client chose the holiday. The position would be similar if a brochure which featured both self-catering and hotel holidays falsely stated that there were nearby supermarkets. Clients who were on hotel holidays would probably not be able to show that the existence of a supermarket influenced their decision. On the other hand the self-catering clients would probably have a good case.

If a hotel advertised itself on the internet and made available a wide range of images of the hotel and its surroundings, perhaps showing misleading pictures of its location, then potentially this could give rise to an action for misrepresentation. However, if the guest did not access these images before making the booking they could not complain of misrepresentation later as they had not influenced the guest's decision. Note, however, that should these statements be regarded as terms of the contract then an action would lie for breach of contract. (On this point see the discussion of regs 4 and 6 of the PTR.)

The Statement Must be Material

The false statement must be of sufficient significance that it would affect the judgment of a reasonable man in deciding whether to enter into the contract or not. If it is not material then it does not matter whether the other party has relied on it or not. For instance, it may be the case that a brochure features an outdated picture of an hotel and the windows have shutters painted in a glorious shade of red which the client thinks is just perfect and books the hotel on the basis of the red shutters. On arrival the shutters are discovered to have been painted blue and have been so for the previous three seasons. There may have been a false statement of fact which in fact induced the contract but it is hardly material and the claim is likely to be turned down.

Omissions

The general rule is that remaining silent does not amount to misrepresentation. Usually, there must be a positive statement of fact before an action can be brought. Occasionally, however, an omission to say something may amount to a misrepresentation. For instance, in the case of *Dimmock v Hallett* (1866) L.R. 2 Ch. App. 21 the defendant stated, quite correctly, that all the farms on the estate he was selling were let. However, this was only a half truth. What he omitted to say was that all the tenants had given notice to quit. It was held that this amounted to misrepresentation. If a tour operator was asked about the beaches at a resort and replied that there was a mile and a half of black sand in front of the hotel he might be guilty of a misrepresentation if he omitted to say that the sand was black because of an oil spill rather than because this was a volcanic island.

CHAPTER FOUR

CONDITIONS, WARRANTIES AND INNOMINATE TERMS

In some contracts the terms can be classified as either conditions or warranties in advance. This can be achieved in a number of ways. For instance, there are statutes, such as the Sale of Goods Act 1979, where some of the terms in a sale of goods contracts are classified by the statute into conditions and warranties. Section 14, for example, makes it an implied condition that where goods are sold in the course of a business they will be of satisfactory quality.

This approach can be seen in the Package Travel Regulations. Regulation 9, for instance, states that if the tour operator does not give a written copy of *all* the terms of the contract to the consumer this amounts to a breach of condition. Regulation 6 states that all the particulars in the brochure are warranties.

Apart from the statutory examples just mentioned, the parties themselves are generally free to classify the terms of the contract into conditions or warranties depending upon the importance they wish to attach to them. The courts have also been prepared to classify terms as either conditions or warranties.

The effect of this prior classification means that if a breach occurs then the parties know immediately where they stand. Either it is a breach of condition and one party can terminate the contract at his option as well as claiming damages, or it is only a breach of warranty, in which case the contract must continue but damages must be paid.

This has the advantage of certainty but occasionally causes injustice where, for instance, there is a minor breach of a condition but the victim of the breach decides to exercise his right to terminate the contract—a drastic step in view of the minor infringement. This is what happened in the case of *Arcos Ltd v EA Ronaasen & Co* [1933] A.C. 470. In that case, the buyer ordered a quantity of wooden staves for making barrels. Each of the staves had to be half an inch thick. When they arrived only five per cent were the right thickness but the rest were no more than 9/16 of an inch—which made them perfectly usable even though they did not meet the specification exactly. Under the Sale of Goods Act, s.13 it is an implied *condition* that goods must correspond to their description. The buyer was therefore able to reject the goods for what amounted to a mere technicality.

There is a possibility that such a state of affairs could arise under reg.9. If a tour operator omits a very minor detail from the written copy of the contract then he will be in breach of condition. For example, he may omit some of the hotel facilities that are required to be detailed under Sch.2 of the Regulations. These facilities may be of no importance to the consumer but their omission from the written contract gives the consumer the right to cancel—a drastic remedy for a minor oversight that has no real significance.

To combat the very rigid approach of classifying terms as either conditions or warranties the courts have developed a third category of terms. These are known as *innominate* terms. An innominate term is one which cannot be pre-classified as either a condition or a warranty. The remedy available will depend upon the severity of the breach. For instance, in the case of *Hong Kong Fir Shipping Co Ltd v Kawasaki Kisen Kaisha Ltd* [1962] 1 All E.R. 474 the charterer of a ship wanted to terminate the contract because the ship was "unseaworthy". The charterer said that this was a condition of the contract which automatically gave him the right to terminate. The Court of Appeal said that "unseaworthiness" covered a multitude of sins—from minor problems to very serious ones. According to Upjohn L.J. the ship would be unseaworthy:

"if a nail is missing from one of the timbers of a wooden vessel, or if proper medical supplies or two anchors are not on board at the time of sailing."

It would be wrong for the charterer to be able to repudiate the contract for such trivial defects. The term relating to seaworthiness was therefore only an innominate term and could only be classified as a condition or a warranty once the extent of the breach became clear. The advantage of this approach is that it provides flexibility, i.e. a term is not rigidly classified until it is known how serious the breach is. On the other hand it does result in uncertainty—the parties do not know in advance what their rights are and may have to make difficult judgments as to when the breach is serious enough to warrant terminating the contract. If they decide wrongly they might find themselves in breach of condition.

In the case of *The Mihalis Angelos* [1970] 3 All E.R. 125 the Court of Appeal was faced with the problem of classifying the term "expected ready to load" in a shipping contract. A ship which was "expected ready to load" on July 1, had not been ready and the charterers said that this amounted to a breach of condition which entitled them to repudiate the contract—even though it had caused them no loss. Despite the absence of damage the court did classify it as a condition. With time clauses like this in commercial contracts it was important that the parties could predict with some certainty what the consequences of a breach would be and the courts should interpret such clauses consistently—even if in some cases the remedy was out of all proportion to the loss.

The question arises as to how the terms in a package holiday contract are classified—which ones are conditions, which ones are warranties and are there any innominate terms? Or to put it in more practical terms—for which breaches can the consumer repudiate the contract?

The answer is that, at first glance, a very large proportion of them appear to be only warranties, giving the consumer no right to repudiate. The reason for this is that, as we have just seen, reg.6 states that all the particulars in the brochure are implied warranties. (See "All at Sea: Regulation 14 of The Package Travel Regulations And 'Appropriate Compensation' ", M. Chapman [2002] I.T.L.J. 7 for an application of reg.6 to a brochure.) Given that most of the terms of the contract will be found in the brochure, largely because of the combined requirements of reg.5 and Sch.1, you could be forgiven for concluding that just about everything in the contract is only a warranty. However, you would be mistaken in this belief because reg.6 has to be read in conjunction with other Regulations, in particular reg.12.

Regulation 12, which is dealt with in more detail in Ch.10, provides that where an organiser is constrained before departure to "alter significantly an essential term of the contract" then the consumer has the right not only to accept the change subject to a rider specifying the impact on the price but also to *withdraw* from the contract. This *appears* to create a term which is a condition but on closer examination the position is less clear.

The regulation actually describes the term as an *implied* term. It does not classify the term one way or the other. This suggests that it might be either a condition or a warranty depending upon the circumstances, i.e. it is more akin to an innominate term. In practice, this is how it will work out. The consumer has two hurdles to overcome before he can withdraw. First, he must show that there is a change to an *essential* term but then he must show that the alteration is a *significant* alteration. If he can show that there is such an alteration he can withdraw—but not otherwise. Thus, if he can show a major change this will be treated as a breach of condition but if it is only a minor change it will be treated as simply a breach of warranty.

Regulation 14 is similar. It creates implied terms to the effect that the organiser must make *suitable* alternative arrangements if a *significant* proportion of the services cannot be provided after departure. Failure to do this gives the consumer the right to be taken home. Thus, depending upon the severity of the breach, the consumer can terminate the contract and come home or must remain on holiday and be content with damages.

The practical effect of all this is that the consumer will have a right to terminate for serious breaches but will have the difficult task of judging when it is sufficiently serious to do so.

In a hotel contract it seems self-evident that it will be a condition of the contract that guest rooms will have a bed. On the other hand, it will probably only be a breach of warranty if the promised mini-bar or flat-screen TV is missing. Failure to provide high-speed internet access is more debatable; much more like an innominate term. For the business traveller this is an essential service, probably justifying them in checking-out, but for the leisure traveller it is much less important and the damage caused much less significant. But, even in this latter example, one can imagine that the leisure traveller has chosen a particular hotel at the remote airport they are flying out of after their holiday so that they can check-in online and so avoid the ruinous costs of checking-in at the airport imposed by the so-called "low-cost" airlines. Costs which may very well exceed the price of the hotel room.

Express and Implied Terms

Express Terms

An express term, as indicated earlier, is a term which has actually been expressed, either orally or in writing, or perhaps even in the form of a photograph or diagram. As far as packages are concerned, reg.9 requires an organiser to reduce *all* the terms to writing. Thus, in theory all the terms of the contract will be express terms. Therefore, the only problems that should arise will concern the interpretation of the express terms in the written contract. For instance what does "private pool" mean? Does it mean that the clients will have exclusive use of the pool or that the pool is not overlooked or that it will be shared but only by a few families but not the general public? If a garden is described as "private" does it comply with its description if occupants are shielded from public view by a high hedge but is severely affected by the noise coming from the four lane highway on the other side of the hedge? What appliances does a "self-catering apartment" have to include—a microwave as well as a cooker; a dishwasher as well as a washing machine; a freezer as well as a fridge? If a dog owner chooses a self-catering cottage because it has an "enclosed" garden can they complain when the fence enclosing the garden is not "dog proof"? In practice, however, despite the existence of reg.9, there will be many package holiday cases where there will also be additional express terms in the form of oral statements and many cases where there will also be implied terms, and of course reg.9 does not apply to other travel contracts. It is important, therefore, to know the circumstances where the courts will imply terms into a contract.

Implied Terms

In English law, terms can be implied into a contract in three ways: by custom, by statute or by the courts. Terms implied by custom are not relevant to travel contracts but statutory and judicial implied terms are. Note that this section is concerned with giving a broad overview of *how* and *why* the courts imply terms *in general* whereas Ch.5, which covers much of the same ground, is more concerned with how the law has been applied *specifically* in a travel contract context.

Terms Implied by Statute

Package holiday contracts contain terms implied by the Package Travel Regulations. Regulation 12, for instance, implies a term into package holiday contracts that if the tour operator makes significant changes to essential terms of the contract then the consumer has the right to withdraw from the contract. Regulation 13 implies a term into the contract about the remedies available to the consumer following such a withdrawal and reg.14 implies a term about the consumer's rights in the event of the tour operator being able to perform the contract as promised. All these terms are dealt with in greater detail in Ch.10.

Another statutory implied term sometimes referred to in holiday cases, and is of wider application than simply package holidays, is s.13 of the Supply of Goods and Services Act 1982 to the effect that:

> "In a contract for the supply of a service where the supplier is acting in the course of a business, there is an implied term that the supplier will carry out the service with reasonable care and skill."

In both *Wilson v Best Travel* [1993] 1 All E.R. 353 and *Wong Mee Wan v Kwan Kin Travel Services Ltd* [1995] 4 All E.R. 745, which were both cases involving the implication of terms, the court discussed the effect of s.13, and both were decided without the benefit of the Package Travel Regulations.

Terms Implied by the Courts

These fall into two types: they can be implied *in fact*, i.e. based upon the presumed intention of the parties, or they can be implied *in law* irrespective of the presumed intention of the parties.

The test for whether a term can be implied in fact is known as the "officious bystander" test (*Shirlaw v Southern Foundries Ltd* [1939] 2 K.B. 206). In attempting to find the presumed intention of the parties the courts use a mythical third party, the officious bystander, who intervenes during the making of the contract and asks whether the parties intended the disputed term to be a term of the contract, and if he is testily suppressed by both parties with a common "oh, of course" then this is sufficient to establish the term as part of the contract. On the other hand, if the parties disagreed fundamentally about the existence of the term when questioned about it then a court would conclude that the term could not be implied in fact.

When terms are implied in law the basis of implication is that the courts consider that it is desirable that in certain types of contract the law should impose duties on the parties irrespective of their presumed intention. In the words of one leading textbook:

"In all these cases the court is really deciding what should be the content of a paradigm contract of hire, of employment, etc. The process of decision is quite independent of the parties except that they are normally free, by using express words, to exclude the terms which would otherwise be implied. So the court is in effect imposing on the parties a term which is reasonable in the circumstances." (Cheshire, Fifoot & Furmston, *Law of Contract*, 15th edn, p.181)

The operation of these two rules can be seen in the case of *Wall v Silver Wing Surface Arrangements* Unreported 1981.

The facts of the case were that Mr and Mrs Wall and Mr and Mrs Smith and their son David booked a 14-day holiday with Enterprise Holidays at the Martina Apart Hotel in Puerto de la Cruz in Tenerife. They had rooms on the third floor. One night a fire broke out at the hotel. The claimants could not use the lift to escape from their rooms so they tried to use the fire escape, which was made out of concrete and ran down the side of the hotel. Unfortunately, for reasons which did not emerge from the case, the hotel management had padlocked the gate at the bottom of the fire escape and it could not be used. The party therefore returned to their rooms and made a makeshift rope out of sheets. In using the rope, three of the party fell and were injured; one very seriously.

The hotel had been inspected regularly by a representative of Enterprise who had noted that it had an excellent fire escape. He had used it himself late one night and not found it obstructed. There was no suggestion in the case that Enterprise had failed to take reasonable care. They were not at fault and the Judge said as much.

In the absence of any negligence on behalf of the tour operator the claimants pleaded their case on the basis of an implied term in the contract that they "would be reasonably safe in using the hotel for the purpose for which they were invited to be there".

When the Judge applied the officious bystander test the conclusion he reached was that:

"if an officious bystander had suggested either to the tour operator or, I think, to most customers, that the tour operator would be liable for any default on the part of any of these people [hotel keepers, airlines, taxi proprietors, etc.] both would, to put it mildly, have been astonished."

The judge also decided not to imply a term in law. His decision relied heavily upon the judgment of Lord Wilberforce in the case of *Liverpool City Council v Irwin* [1977] A.C. 239. This House of Lords case decided that as a matter of law a term could be implied in a contract for a tenancy in a high-rise block of flats that the landlords (the council) should be under an obligation in respect of the common areas to exercise reasonable care to keep the means of access in reasonable repair. The term was implied on the basis that it was a "necessity". In the words of Lord Wilberforce:

"In my opinion such obligation (in respect of the common areas), should be read into the contract as the nature of the contract implicitly required, no more, no less; a test in other words of necessity."

Applying this line of argument the judge in the *Wall* case said that in his view there must be:

"a requirement that there be some form of necessity before the court will impose upon the parties obligations which they have not expressly entered into. In my judgment the relationship of customer and tour operator is not one of the type as would justify the courts in imposing obligations upon the parties as a matter of general law."

Although views may differ about the correctness of the decision in *Wall* (see Grant "Tour Operators' Liability for Hoteliers' Negligence" *Trading Law*, 6(2), 1988, p.44) the judgment is to be applauded for the clarity of its approach to implied terms—dealing both with terms implied in fact and terms implied in law in a manner which exposes the issues plainly and clearly.

Two other travel cases involving implied terms are *Wilson v Best Travel* [1993] 1 All E.R. 353 and *Wong Mee Wan v Kwan Kin Travel Services* [1995] 4 All E.R. 745. (See also the extensive discussion of *Hone v Going Places* [2001] EWCA Civ 947 in Ch.5.) The former is an English case decided on facts which occurred before the passage of the Package Travel Regulations, but as we shall see in Ch.5 there is nothing in the Regulations which requires that the case would be decided differently today. The latter is a Hong Kong case decided by the Privy Council on common law grounds, as the Regulations are not applicable in Hong Kong.

The facts in the *Wilson* case were that the claimant, who had bought a package holiday from the defendants, had fallen through a glass patio door at the accommodation where he was staying. The glass in the door complied with Greek but not British standards. The issue at stake was what liability would be imposed on the tour operator in respect of the quality of the glass in the patio door. There was no express term in the contract about the quality of the glass and therefore the court had to imply a term. The judge rejected a term that the hotel would be reasonably safe, basing his decision on the judgment in *Wall*. The conclusion he came to was that the tour operator was under a duty, based upon s.13 of the Supply of Goods and Services Act 1982, to exercise reasonable care in respect of the glass. What this amounted to was that as long as the glass complied with local standards and those standards were not so low as to cause a reasonable holidaymaker to decline to take a holiday at the hotel in question then the duty was satisfied.

The judge said:

"What is the duty of a tour operator in a situation such as this? Must he refrain from sending holidaymakers to any hotel whose characteristics, in so far as safety is concerned, fail to satisfy the standards which apply in this country? I do not believe that his obligations in respect of the safety of his clients can extend this far. Save where uniform international regulations apply, there are bound to be differences in the safety standards applied in respect of the many hazards of modern life between one country and another. All civilised countries attempt to cater for these hazards by imposing mandatory regulations. The duty of care of a tour operator is likely to extend to checking that local safety regulations are complied with. Provided that they are, I do not consider that the tour operator owes a duty to boycott a hotel because of the absence of some safety feature which would be found in an English hotel unless the absence of such a feature might lead a reasonable holidaymaker to decline to take a holiday at the hotel in question. On the facts of this case I do not consider that the degree of danger posed by the absence of safety glass in the doors of the Vanninarchis Beach Hotel called for any action on the part of the defendants pursuant to their duty to exercise reasonable care to ensure the safety of their clients.

It is perhaps significant that Mr Norris did not expand on what action the defendants would have taken. It was not suggested that they had a duty to warn clients of this characteristic or that such warning would have prevented the accident in this case. What was, I think, implicit in the plaintiff's case was that the defendants should not have permitted the Vanninarchis Beach Hotel to feature in their brochure. If that contention were valid, it would, on the evidence of Mr Vanninarchis, apply to many, if not the majority, of the other hotels, pensions and villas featured in the defendants' brochure and no doubt the brochures of the other tour operators who send their clients to Greece."

The facts of *Wong Mee Wan* were that the claimant's daughter had purchased a package holiday from the first defendants, who were a Hong Kong company. The holiday consisted of a tour of mainland China and included both accommodation and transport. The highlight of the tour was a visit to a lake in China which also involved a lake crossing. The first defendants had subcontracted the performance of the tour to the second defendants. When the claimant's daughter reached the lake with her party they were not able to make the crossing by ferry as originally planned. Instead, the second defendants arranged for the third defendants to convey the party across by speedboat. To transport the whole party across the lake involved making three return journeys. On the third journey, due to the negligence of the boat driver, the boat collided with a junk and sank. The claimant's daughter was drowned.

The Privy Council held the first defendants liable for the death. The approach they took is found in this passage from Lord Slynn's judgment:

"The issue is thus whether in *this particular contract* the first defendant undertook no more than that it would arrange for services to be provided by others as its agent (where the law would imply a term into the contract that it would use reasonable care and skill in selecting those other persons) or whether it itself undertook to supply the services when, subject to any exemption clause, there would be implied into the contract a term that it would as supplier carry out the services with reasonable case and skill." (Emphasis added)

After a careful analysis of the contract in this case their Lordships concluded that:

"Taking the contract as a whole their Lordships consider that the first defendant here *undertook to provide and not merely to arrange* all the services included in the programme, even if some activities were to be carried out by others. The first defendant's obligation under the contract that the services would be provided with reasonable skill and care remains even if some of the services were to be rendered by others, and even if tortious liability may exist on the part of those others." (Emphasis added)

What weighed particularly heavily in favour of liability was the wording of the brochure which emphasised the role of the first defendants at the expense of the second and third defendants. Throughout the brochure and the itinerary there were statements to the effect that "we"—the first defendants—were responsible for the provision of the various elements of the package:

"Throughout the detailed itinerary it is always 'we' who will do things—board the bus, go for lunch, live in the hotel. Their Lordships do not think that 'we' is to be read simply as referring to the customers—*i.e.* in an attempt to lay the foundations for a friendly atmosphere on the tour. 'We' includes the company offering the tour and integrates the company into each stage of the tour. At Zhu Hai it is 'our staff' who will handle the customs formalities for you. There is nothing to indicate that 'the tourist guide' who is accompanying the group to the Village is other than an employee of the first defendant and in para 7 it is the 'escorts of our company' who may request a member to leave the tour."

On the question of the status of *Wall v Silver Wing* their Lordships had this to say:

"In their Lordships' view it was an implied term of the contract that those services would be carried out with reasonable skill and care. That term does not mean, to use the words of Hodgson J in *Wall v Silver Wing Surface Arrangements Ltd* that the first defendant undertook an obligation to ensure 'the safety of all the components of the package'. The plaintiff's claim does not amount to an implied term that her daughter would be reasonably safe. It is a term simply that reasonable skill and care would be used in rendering the services to be provided under the contract. *The trip across the lake was clearly not carried out with reasonable skill and care in that no steps were taken to see that the driver of the speedboat was of reasonable competence and experience and the first defendant is liable for such breach of contract as found by the trial judge.*" (Emphasis added. Note the confusion here in the reasoning)

"if the tour operator agrees that services will be supplied, whether by him or others on his behalf, to imply a term that those services will be carried out with

115

reasonable skill and care is not imposing on the tour operator a burden which is 'intolerable' as the Court of Appeal thought. Nor is it wholly unreasonable, as Hodgson J thought in *Wall v Silver Wing Surface Arrangements Ltd*."

Note that although the defendants were made liable for the defaults of one of their subcontractors this was because they had assumed this more extensive liability by the wording of their brochure. Less extravagant prose would probably have saved them from liability. Note also that the court was not required, as in *Wall* and *Wilson*, to decide upon a term of strict liability—that the consumer would be reasonably safe. It is not clear whether the Privy Council would have been prepared to go that far if asked to do so. See the section below for the competing arguments for and against strict liability.

Both the "officious bystander" test and its close cousin the "business efficacy" test have stood the test of time when it comes to implying terms into a contract but more recently Lord Hoffmann in *Att-Gen of Belize v Belize Telecom Ltd* [2009] UKPC 10 has suggested a more straightforward test. He said that it was simply a matter of interpretation of the contract and that the central issue was whether the implication "would spell out in express words what the instrument, read against the relevant background, would reasonably be understood to mean." Whether this test will supplant the others remains to be seen but it is already being cited in later cases.

Express and Implied Terms and the Level of Liability

As we have just seen, the obligations contained in the package holiday contract will be a mixture of both express and implied terms. However, with both express and implied terms difficult questions arise not only about their interpretation and existence but, more importantly, about the level of liability (or the standard of duty) that they impose. This can be illustrated by the use of a simple example. Let us say that the brochure states expressly that the hotel has a swimming pool. By virtue of reg.6 this is undoubtedly a term of the contract. If the consumer arrives and finds no pool then is the tour operator liable? One's instinctive reaction is to say yes. They have promised a pool and there isn't one. One is inclined to argue that not only is the term a warranty, i.e. a minor term of the contract (reg.6), but also that the tour operator *warrants* that it will be there—in the sense that he guarantees that it will be there. Arguments advanced by the tour operator that he had contracted with the hotel for the provision of the pool and was only informed by the hotelier at the last minute that it had been turned into a sunken garden would fall on deaf ears. This is a strict liability obligation. (See *Cook v Spanish Holiday Tours* [1959] 103 S.J. 873.)

However, if we were to take a variation on this theme then the answer may not be quite so apparent. Let us say that although the pool did exist, it was entirely inadequate for the numbers wishing to use it—in other words it was not fit for its purpose. Again, one's instinctive reaction is to say that the tour operator is liable. But what if the reason for its inadequacy was that during the close season the hotelier had built a large new wing onto the hotel with the result that the pool was simply overwhelmed with guests wanting to use the pool? Can the tour operator's express promise that a pool will be *provided* be extended to include an implied obligation that it will be *fit for its purpose*—even in circumstances where the operator is not at fault? Probably yes.

Finally, take a third variation. Let us say that a pool is provided and that it is of adequate size but because of a failure in the chlorination system it becomes contaminated with life-threatening micro organisms and clients suffer death and illness as a result. Is the tour operator liable? If this was not the fault of the tour operator then, according to the *Wall* case, there will be no liability and even according to *Wong Mee Wan* there will be no liability so long as the tour operator worded his brochure in such a way that it diminished his liability to that of a mere arranger.

Coincidentally, a variation on this illustration was adopted in *Hone v Going Places* by Longmore L.J.:

"If the brochure or advertisement, on which the consumer relies, promises a swimming-pool, it will be a term of the contract that a swimming-pool will be provided. But, in the absence of express wording, there would not be an absolute obligation, for example, to ensure that the holiday-maker catches no infection while swimming in the swimming-pool. The obligation assumed will be that reasonable skill and care will be taken to ensure that the pool is free from infection."

This leaves a situation where the courts now say that the question of the *existence* of the pool and perhaps its *fitness for purpose* are strict liability obligations but when it comes to issues of *safety* then the obligations are fault based. Why this distinction? Why is it that strict liability, a higher burden, is imposed in respect of the provision and adequacy of the pool but a lesser obligation in respect of the safety—which is surely more important? To put it more bluntly why does the tour operator warrant the existence of the pool but not its safety?

To this question there is no easy answer, and certainly Longmore L.J. did not explore it in *Hone*. According to Collins (*The Law of Contract*, 1st edn, 1986, p.165):

"In the absence of statutory guidance, the courts must decide whether or not a party is strictly liable for any defect in performance, and if not, what standard of care should have been expected from him.

In tackling this issue, the courts avoid the enunciation of general principles. They consider each contract in its social context and the particular facts of the case."

Other commentators confirm this pragmatic approach adopted by the English courts (see J.W. Carter, *Breach of Contract*, 1984, p.22; P.S. Atiyah, *An Introduction to the Law of Contract*, 1995, p.214). This makes it difficult to predict how a court would view the implication of a term in a novel situation where, as in most holiday cases, there was until recently no body of case law to offer guidance—where, not to put too fine a point upon it, the courts are making the law rather than applying it.

If we accept this then we also have to accept that the decision to imply a term or not is a policy decision, i.e. the courts are deciding what the law *should* be as opposed to what it *is*. Support for this view can be found in the case law. In his decision in the *Wall* case, Hodgson J., relied heavily on the judgment of Lord Wilberforce in the House of Lords case *Liverpool City Council v Irwin* [1977] A.C. 239. In that case, Lord Wilberforce hinted that "wider considerations" may be taken into account when implying a term—by which he meant policy considerations.

Looking at the existing case law we can see some of the emerging policy reasons. In *Wall* itself the judge felt that it would be "unreasonable" to impose strict liability on a tour operator to guarantee the safety of the accommodation in a package holiday, particularly as the holidaymaker would have direct rights against the suppliers of the services which failed. In *Wilson*, the judge considered that to impose a duty on tour operators not to send consumers to hotels which did not comply with the same safety standards as British hotels was too onerous. Implicit in his judgment was that this would be impracticable. To impose such a standard would result in most accommodation in places such as Cyprus being removed from brochures altogether. In *Wong Mee Wan* the Privy Council felt that it was not "wholly unreasonable as Hodgson J thought in [Wall]" to imply a term that the services promised in a package holiday contract would be carried out with reasonable care and skill even though carried out by others. However, underlying the *Wong* decision is the clear suspicion that if the brochure in that case had not been so extravagantly worded then the tour operator would have escaped liability. The decision appears based on the reasoning that the defendants had taken on or assumed liability for the whole of the package and that if they hadn't volunteered so much then they may not have been found liable.

Despite the weight of case law being in favour of fault liability rather than strict (see Ch.5 and, in particular, the discussion of *Hone v Going Places*) there are powerful arguments the other way. They find voice in the writing of two American commentators. In the following passage, taken from a cogently written article on the legal status of travel agents, Wohlmuth discusses the liability of travel agents to their clients when the services booked on their behalf (hotels, airlines, etc) have proved defective. The reasons he gives for imposing liability on travel agents seem equally applicable to tour operators:

"In particular courts in the future may ask whether there is any less reason to hold the travel agent liable for faulty accommodations than to hold a retailer liable for imperfections in goods sold to the consumer in the original sealed container. The parallel between these two cases is obvious. Just as the travel agent cannot adequately control the quality of performance of the hotel or carrier, so the retailer cannot adequately protect himself against imperfections in goods sold to the consumer in the original sealed container. Many of the justifications for finding the latter liable appear applicable to the former. Just as the stocking by a retailer of goods on his shelf, even though in the original sealed package, is some indication to the consumer that the retailer stands behind them, so the booking of reservations by the travel agent at a particular hotel or on a particular carrier is some indication that he stands behind the performance of that hotel or carrier. Just as the accessibility of the retailer to suit by the consumer makes good sense from a policy standpoint because of jurisdictional problems in suing the manufacturer, so making the travel agent available to suit by the client makes good policy sense in terms of the difficulties inherent in obtaining jurisdiction over the carrier or hotel. Finally, both the retailer and the travel agent have ultimate recourse against the person whose 'product' they sell, and he, after all, is the one best able to bear the risk of loss by passing it on to the consumer through higher prices." ("The Liability of Travel Agents: A Study in the Selection of Appropriate Legal Principles" [1966] T.L.Q. 29)

Dickerson makes the same point:

"Although the courts have been willing to find a duty to deliver specific travel services, such a duty has not yet been extended to the provision of 'safe transportation' or 'safe accommodations'. There is no justification nor rationale for so holding, however, since travelers have a right to expect the delivery of travel services which do not cause physical injuries. In such cases the courts may refer to the responsible party as an independent contractor whose tortious conduct should not be shifted to the tour operator-principal. In many of these cases however, the responsible party is out of the jurisdiction of local courts and unavailable to satisfy access to any recovery even though the tour operator made a profit on the transaction. The inequity of these cases is surely obvious and it is likely that future cases will, indeed, find tour operators liable for the misconduct of suppliers resulting in physical injuries." (*Travel Law*, 5–62, 5–63)

From these two pieces a number of countervailing policy reasons can be identified: considerations of consumer protection; the ability to pass liability up the chain of supply to the person ultimately responsible; considerations of loss spreading and identifying who is best placed to bear the risk; access to courts within the local jurisdiction; making a trader responsible for the services he sells; and, as with the arguments deployed by the other side, considerations of what is "just" and "reasonable".

Given the present weight of case law in favour of fault liability, it would be incorrect at present to suggest that a tour operator is under a general duty of strict liability to clients, but it would be possible to construct a respectable argument, deploying the policy reasons just mentioned, to show that a tour operator *should* be under such a liability. (See Grant & Urbanowicz "Tour Operators, Package Holiday Contracts and Strict Liability" [2001] J.B.L. 253 for a longer discussion of these issues.)

One travel case which involved a discussion of the level of liability is *Akehurst v Thomson Holidays Ltd & Britannia Airlines* Unreported May 6, 2003, Cardiff CC (but see J. Rees "Getting From Warsaw To Gerona: A Tour Operator's Liability" [2004] I.T.L.J. 7). Strictly speaking this was not a case on implied terms but on the interpretation of express terms, but it helps to point up the consequences of regarding a term as one of fault liability rather than strict liability. The facts of the case were that the claimants were clients of Thomson Holidays on a package holiday to Spain. The plane which was carrying them to Spain crashed at Gerona Airport and several passengers suffered physical injuries and others suffered psychological injuries. The airline admitted liability for the former but denied liability for the latter on the grounds that they were protected by the Warsaw Convention which only covered "bodily injury" not mental injury. The clients with psychological injuries sued Thomson on the grounds that under reg.15 of the Package Travel Regulations they were liable for the defaults of their suppliers (see Ch.5 for a fuller discussion of reg.15). One of the issues in the case was whether a term in their contract with Thomson imposed strict liability. The relevant term was as follows:

"6. Our responsibility for your holiday.

We are responsible for making sure that each part of the holiday you book with us is provided *to a reasonable standard* and as described in this brochure or in any amendments to it. If any part of your holiday is not provided as described and this spoils your holiday, we will pay you appropriate compensation.
We have taken all reasonable care to make sure that all the services which make up the holidays advertised in this brochure are provided by efficient, safe and reputable businesses and that they follow the local and national laws and regulations of the country where they are provided" (Emphasis added).

The judge summed up the issue this way:

"The question for me in the present case is whether Thomson did assume an absolute obligation by virtue of the terms of The Charter in respect of the Flight."

After a careful examination of the contract he came to the conclusion that:

"In my view, an objective bystander would understand 'a flight provided to a reasonable standard' to mean that the aircraft would be of a size and type, with equipment and fittings, reasonable appropriate to the nature and length of the journey and the type and cost of the holiday; maintained with reasonable care; and operated by properly trained and competent staff who would exercise reasonable care in the performing their duties.
I agree that the phrase used ['to a reasonable standard'] clearly refers to the required standard, a reasonable standard, i.e. a standard achieved by the exercise of reasonable skill and care.
Reading the clause as a whole leads to the construction that if Britannia did use all reasonable skill and care in the conduct of the Flight, the Flight was provided to a reasonable standard, albeit that it crash landed."

With all due respect to the judge, the interpretation he arrives at in this last sentence is hard to accept. It really does seem to do damage to the English language to say that "provided to a reasonable standard" means the same as "to exercise reasonable care and skill to provide a service of a reasonable standard". Ironically, however, in a supplementary judgment, it was held that another passage in the terms and conditions did impose strict liability on Thomson for personal injury arising out of travel by air for sums up to £85,000 and, beyond that, unlimited sums so long as it could not be proved that the airline took all measures to avoid the injury. As a consequence, there was no reason to challenge the reasoning above.

Regulation 9

According to reg.9 all the terms of a package holiday contract must be reduced to writing before the contract is concluded. But what if the tour operator does not do this? (And cases such as *Wall v Silver Wing* and *Wilson v Best Travel* suggest that this may very well happen.) Does this mean that any term which has not been reduced to writing will not be a term of the contract? Does it mean the end of the implied term in package holiday contracts?

The answer to this must be no. The fact that the tour operator has not reduced all the terms to writing will not mean that statements not in the written contract will not be part of the contract. All it will mean is that the tour operator will be in breach of reg.9. A court would still accept that there could be other express and implied terms which the tour operator had omitted from the contract for some reason—either through poor contracting procedures or lack of foresight. The logical consequence of this, however, is that once an implied term is found to exist a client automatically has the right to rescind for breach of reg.9, even though by definition an implied term is never reduced to writing! (See also Ch.3 for the remarks about the *Akehurst* case and reg.9.)

REGULATION 4

As indicated in the introduction to this chapter, reg.4 creates a statutory right to compensation for the consumer that cuts across the traditional boundaries of the common law. It imposes civil liability on both organisers and retailers if they supply misleading information. It states:

"4(1) No organiser or retailer shall supply to a consumer any descriptive matter concerning a package, the price of a package or any other conditions applying to the contract which contains any misleading information.

4(2) If an organiser or retailer is in breach of paragraph (1) he shall be liable to compensate the consumer for any loss which the consumer suffers in consequence."

The liability that this imposes is very extensive, going in many cases beyond normal contractual liability. It will be examined in more detail in Ch.5 on liability.

REGULATION 6

Regulation 6 provides:

"6(1) the particulars in the brochure (whether or not they are required by regulation 5(1) above to be included in the brochure) shall constitute implied warranties for the purposes of any contract to which the particulars relate."

This is a little puzzling. First, what is meant by the word "particular", which is not a term of art known to English law? Secondly, and more fundamentally, what does reg.6 add to the existing common law?

In trying to ascertain the answer to the first question some assistance can be obtained by tracing the derivation of the provision. Article 3.2 of the Directive states:

"When a brochure is made available to the consumer, it shall indicate in a legible, comprehensible and accurate manner both the price and adequate information concerning:

(a) the destination and the means, characteristics and categories of transport used;

(b) the type of accommodation, its location, category or degree of comfort and its main features, its approval and tourist classification under the rules of the host Member State concerned;

(c) the meal plan;

(d) the itinerary;

(e) general information on passport and visa requirements for nationals of the Member State or States concerned and health formalities required for the journey and the stay;

(f) either the monetary amount or the percentage of the price which is to be paid on account, and the timetable for payment of the balance;

(g) whether a minimum number of persons is required for the package to take place and, if so, the deadline for informing the consumer in the event of cancellation.

The particulars contained in the brochure are binding on the organizer or retailer".

The first part of art.3.2 is enacted in UK law by reg.5, which makes it a criminal offence not to provide the listed information in a comprehensible, legible and accurate form (see Ch.16). It is from the second part of art.3.2 that reg.6 is derived, i.e. that the particulars in the brochure are legally binding. It is possible to say with some certainty therefore that "particulars" relate to those statements in the brochure which are listed in art.3.2. Thus, if there is a statement about the number of meals, or the classification of the hotel or the places the bus tour visits these are all contractual warranties, which, if broken, give rise to an action for damages.

However, reg.6 goes further than art.3.2 by stating that any of the particulars in the brochure, whether required by reg.5(1) (i.e. art.3.2) to be included or not are to be regarded as warranties. This might cover holidays where the brochure states that the holidays are exclusively for couples or singles; or that the guides have particular qualifications; or that the temperature will be within a particular range. All these are factual statements, going beyond art.3.2, but perfectly capable of giving rise to contractual liability and should cause no difficulty. More problematic, however, are photographs. If a photograph shows a hotel with windsurfing equipment drawn up on the beach in front of it does this mean that consumers will be able to sample windsurfing at that hotel, and if so, for the whole season or only part of it? Does the picture *promise* the opportunity to go windsurfing? Suitably crafted text to go with the photograph may go some of the way to resolve the problem but certainly tour operators should examine their photographs carefully to ensure they do not give the wrong message to the consumer.

It may not simply be what the photograph shows that could cause a problem but what it omits. What if there is a photograph of a picturesque hotel beside the Mosel in Germany showing all the rooms with balconies facing onto the river accompanied by text that all rooms have river views. However, part of the top half of the picture has been cropped and what have been omitted are the top floor rooms which do not have balconies. Consumers might be understandably upset if they were put into an upper floor room without a balcony. The picture suggests that they will get a balcony. But is it a "particular" in the brochure that all the rooms have balconies if what gives rise to that belief is the photograph rather than the text? The dictionary definition of a "particular" is that it means "a distinct or minute part; a single point; a single instance; item; detail" (Chambers). Certainly, the photograph contains "details" about the hotel and therefore is probably within the scope of reg.6. (On the question of photographs see Saggerson, 4th edn, pp.94–95.)

Although photographs could be interpreted as containing factual information that amount to particulars and therefore covered by reg.6 where does this take us in terms of the second question: What impact, if any, does reg.6 have on the existing common law? It seems perfectly possible to arrive at the conclusion that the photographs of the windsurfing and the balconies are capable of being interpreted as terms of the contract without the necessity of invoking reg.6. In answer to that question there are at least two possibilities as to the effect of reg.6.

First, its purpose may be to settle that the statements in the brochure capable of being terms are *only* warranties, not conditions (unless stated otherwise). In other words it is solely to categorise terms that already exist, not to create contractual liability for statements that are not terms at common law. Thus its effect would not be to extend liability to statements which are not terms. The second approach is to say that Regulation 6 might be going further and is saying that some statements, described as "particulars", are to be regarded as terms even though at common law they might not be.

If it is possible to find a situation where the brochure contains "particulars" that would not normally amount to terms of the contract then perhaps there is a case for saying that reg.6 extends the law beyond its present limits. For instance, if we look at the kind of purple prose found in *Hoffman v Intasun* quoted earlier could this be categorised as "particulars" and therefore become legally binding on the tour operator. The answer, we venture to suggest, is no. However if we look at statements that might only amount to representations or puffs at common law then the answer might be different. What about all-inclusive resorts described as "elegant and sophisticated" (supported by pictures of men and women in formal evening wear) that, contrary to expectations, are largely patronised by groups of drunken youths? Such statements, while probably not amounting to terms at common law, might give rise to liability under reg.6.

Note also that reg.6 provides that if the brochure contains an express statement that changes may be made in the particulars before a contract is concluded, and such changes are clearly communicated to the consumer before a contract is concluded, then those particulars are not binding on the organiser. However once a contract is concluded reg.6 further provides that particulars are binding unless the consumer consents to a variation.

SURCHARGES

One term which is frequently found in a package holiday contract is a surcharge clause. We have chosen to deal with it here rather than elsewhere largely because it does not fit neatly into any particular category.

Surcharging is a practice which has caused a great deal of controversy over the years. No one likes to have to pay extra at the last minute and this feeling of grievance is often exacerbated by a suspicion, not completely unfounded, that tour operators, certainly in the past, have included an element of profit in the surcharges. More recently, the worst excesses of surcharging seem to have been largely eliminated by low inflation and ABTA's surcharging policy. Nevertheless, the issue was considered so important that there are specific provisions in the Regulations to govern it. We also examine the provisions in the 2009 ABTA Code of Conduct on surcharges.

Regulation 11

Regulation 11 preserves the right of the tour operator to surcharge but restricts the circumstances in which this can be done. It provides:

"11(1) Any term in a contract to the effect that the prices laid down in the contract may be revised shall be void and of no effect unless the contract provides for the possibility of upward or downward revision and satisfies the conditions laid down in paragraph (2) below.

(2) The conditions mentioned in paragraph (1) are that—

(a) the contract states precisely how the revised price is to be calculated;
(b) the contract provides that price revisions are to be made solely to allow for the following variations in:—

   (i) transportation costs, including the cost of fuel,
   (ii) dues, taxes or fees chargeable for services such as landing taxes or embarkation or disembarkation fees at ports and airports, or
   (iii) the exchange rates applied to the particular package; and

(c) the contract provides that—

   (i) no price increase may be made in a specified period which may not be less than 30 days before the departure date stipulated; and
   (ii) as against an individual consumer liable under the contract, no price increase may be made in respect of variations which would produce an increase of less than 2%, or such greater percentage as the contract may specify, ('non-eligible variations') and that the non-eligible variations shall be left out of account in the calculation."

This reflects the existing common law position which permits price variation clauses so long as they are built into the contract. The difference is that the Regulation circumscribes the items which can be surcharged. It permits surcharging for variations in transport costs, exchange rates and taxes but not for hotel costs. It requires the first two per cent of any price increase be absorbed by the operator. There is no corresponding provision that the consumer be given the right to cancel if surcharges reach more than a particular amount but this is provided for in reg.12 which permits the consumer to cancel for "significant changes" to essential terms. Price is specifically referred to as an essential term. Just how large the increase has to be before it is regarded as significant is left open.

The statutory provisions, unlike the provisions in previous versions of the ABTA Code (now repealed) there is no notification and monitoring system to ensure that tour operators do not indulge in profiteering. An attempt to overcome this problem is reflected in reg.11(2)(a) where it is provided that the manner in which any price revision is made must be stated *precisely* in the contract. The greater the precision the less likely it is that a tour operator will be able to include an element of pure profit in his surcharges.

According to reg.11(1), any price rise will be of no effect if it does not comply with the Regulation. Additionally, there may be criminal liability under the Consumer Protection from Unfair Trading Regulations 2008 if the means of calculating the price increase is misleading.

In previous editions we said that some Trading Standards Departments have interpreted reg.11 as meaning that if the contract does not provide for *both* an upward *and* a downward revision then the term is void. In other words, if the tour operator is prepared to raise prices for currency fluctuations that move against him he must also be prepared to reduce them if the fluctuation is in the consumer's favour.

Such an interpretation depends upon interpreting the word "or" in reg.11(1) as meaning "and", i.e. "upward *or* downward revision" could be interpreted as meaning "upward *and* downward revision", i.e. the "or" is conjunctive rather than disjunctive. Such an interpretation is not beyond the bounds of probability. For instance, in the following sentence the word "or" can be interpreted as meaning "and": "It is possible to travel from Newcastle to London via Leeds or York or Manchester." But is this a proper interpretation in the circumstances? Use of the word "or" *usually* means one or the other but not both. Given that it was open to the draftsman to use the word "and" so as to make the position clearer, and given also that the commercial context is that price revision clauses have always been used to put prices up rather than down, it is reasonable to conclude that the Regulation does not require tour operators to allow for downward revisions. However, it seems that for all practical purposes this view is unlikely to prevail. In its "Guidance on unfair terms in package holiday contracts" (OFT 668, March 2004) the OFT states that it is:

"firmly of the view that terms providing for price revisions are void under the PTRs unless they provide for both upward and downward revision."

It is dubious whether the following wording, used by a cruise line member of ABTA would comply with the OFT guidance:

"A significant decrease in the cost of providing the cruise holiday may be passed on to you at the discretion of [the tour operator]"

Prior to that, in October 2002, the OFT had exercised its powers under the Unfair Terms in Consumer Contracts Regulations 1999 to require all four of the major tour operators: Thomson, MyTravel, Thomas Cook and First Choice to make changes to their standard terms and conditions. The surcharge clauses had to be changed so that if the operators wished to impose surcharges for rises in costs they also had to offer consumers a reduction if there was a reduction in cost.

There is some ambiguity about reg.11(2)(b)(ii) which states that a surcharge can be levied for:

"dues, taxes or fees chargeable for services such as landing taxes or embarkation or disembarkation fees at ports and airports".

Are the words "dues" and "taxes" qualified by what follows—"chargeable for services such as" or do they stand alone. In other words, can a tour operator levy a surcharge for any rise in taxes or dues or can he only levy it if the tax is raised for services such as landing taxes, etc? In the first edition of this book we inclined to the latter view, and indeed can still see some justification for such an interpretation, but on balance we now prefer the former. To interpret it otherwise would put tour operators at the mercy of changes in taxes which did not relate to the services listed in reg.11(2)(b)(ii), such as the imposition of APD and its subsequent increase.

Following the events of September 11, 2001, a number of airlines increased their level of security and passed the increase on to tour operators. Some tour operators, who had already set the price of their holidays and sold them at that price, endeavoured to pass the increase on to consumers by levying a surcharge under their surcharge clause. It is an open question whether they could bring such charges within the rubric of reg.11(2)(b)(ii); but the typical charge (£7 per person), combined with the requirement to absorb the first two per cent of price rises, made this fairly academic. Industry attempts to lobby the government to suspend the two per cent requirement fell on deaf ears, as it did again when APD was suddenly increased on February 1, 2007.

Under the Code

The ABTA Code has a separate section devoted to the imposition of surcharges on packages. In essence, the Code simply requires ABTA members to comply with reg.11 before surcharges can be imposed. However, it supplements the Regulations by providing for a "light touch" monitoring and enforcement system. Before ABTA members can impose surcharges ABTA must be notified and tour operators must provide evidence justifying the surcharges. An administrative fee of £1 is permitted by the ABTA Code. Tour operators which surcharge can be found on the ABTA website.

Under the previous version of the Code there were some discrepancies between the Regulations and the Code, ostensibly permitting members to surcharge for more items than actually provided for under the Regulations. The danger of this course was that an attempt to surcharge for items which are not permitted may result in not being able to surcharge even for those items which are permitted. Regulation 11 provides that price revision terms in a contract will be void unless the contract satisfies certain conditions. One of those conditions is that price revisions can be *solely* for the variations listed in reg.11(2)(b). Thus, if a tour operator attempts to surcharge for increases in hotel costs, not only will he not be able to do so, he will not be able to surcharge for legitimate items such as currency fluctuations and transport costs. The changes in the Code have now eliminated this possibility.

A further aspect of the Code is that ABTA also requires members to include in their brochures and websites one of two mandatory clauses set out in the Code. The first of these clauses is a no surcharge guarantee clause and the second provides a range of items which the tour operator may surcharge for.

Non-package Surcharges

Although surcharges are tightly controlled for packages under the Package Travel Regulations, there is no such control, beyond the common law, for non-package travel contracts where the contract provides for surcharges. One industry that has taken full advantage of this is the airline industry. Following the rises in fuel prices in recent years it is quite common to find airlines imposing "fuel surcharges" on top of their regular fares. Unlike tour operators' surcharges which are imposed *after* the contract has been made and often come as a nasty surprise on the final invoice, airline surcharges are generally prospective in effect, i.e. they are imposed before or at the time of booking and passengers are aware of them at the time the contract is made. As such they are not true price revision clauses— they are just part of the price that the passenger has to pay.

If this is the case it raises the question of why the airlines don't simply consolidate the surcharge within the overall price. The answer seems to be that it allows the airlines, particularly on internet booking sites, to advertise a low "headline price" to attract passengers and then add the surcharge in later, when perhaps the decision to purchase has already been made and inertia carries the passenger through to the final page. It is all part of that sad phenomenon known as "confusion pricing" where consumers are misled as to the true price of the goods and services they are purchasing.

While there may be no penalty for this in contract law (although such policies may fall foul of the UTCCR), there may be pitfalls as far as the criminal law is concerned. The Consumer Protection from Unfair Trading Regulations 2008 make it illegal to mislead consumers about prices—which includes giving a misleading indication as to how a price is calculated (see Ch.17).

THE E-COMMERCE DIRECTIVE

The Directive on Electronic Commerce (2000/31/EC) came into force in June 2000 and was required to be transposed into the domestic law of Member States by January 17, 2002. In the UK this was done by the Electronic Commerce (EC

Directive) Regulations 2002 (SI 2002/2013) which came into force in August and October 2002.

Broadly speaking, the Directive applies to "information society services", that is "any service normally provided for remuneration, at a distance, by means of electronic equipment for the processing (including digital compression) and storage of data, and at the individual request of a recipient of a service". The reason for discussing it at this point is that it sets out certain procedural and informational requirements that must be satisfied when entering into an internet contract. We have already touched upon this in Ch.3 on Offer and Acceptance but it is worth repeating this information here for the sake of completeness.

Contract Formalities

Article 5 provides that the following general information must be provided:

"1. In addition to other information requirements established by Community law, Member States shall ensure that the service provider shall render easily, directly and permanently accessible to the recipients of the service and competent authorities, at least the following information:

(a) the name of the service provider;
(b) the geographic address at which the service provider is established;
(c) the details of the service provider, including his electronic mail address, which allow him to be contacted rapidly and communicated with in a direct and effective manner;
(d) where the service provider is registered in a trade or similar public register, the trade register in which the service provider is entered and his registration number, or equivalent means of identification in that register;
(e) where the activity is subject to an authorisation scheme, the particulars of the relevant supervisory authority".

Article 10 regulates the information to be provided when entering into a contract:

"1. In addition to other information requirements established by Community law, Member States shall ensure, except when otherwise agreed by parties who are not consumers, that at least the following information is given by the service provider clearly, comprehensibly and unambiguously and prior to the order being placed by the recipient of the service:

(a) the different technical steps to follow to conclude the contract;
(b) whether or not the concluded contract will be filed by the service provider and whether it will be accessible;
(c) the technical means for identifying and correcting input errors prior to the placing of the order;
(d) the languages offered for the conclusion of the contract.

2. Member States shall ensure that, except when otherwise agreed by parties who are not consumers, the service provider indicates any relevant codes of conduct to which he subscribes and information on how those codes can be consulted electronically.

CONTENTS OF THE CONTRACT

3. Contract terms and general conditions provided to the recipient must be made available in a way that allows him to store and reproduce them.

4. Paragraphs 1 and 2 shall not apply to contracts concluded exclusively by exchange of electronic mail or by equivalent individual communications."

Article 11 also provides for certain formalities in the making of the contract:

"1. Member States shall ensure, except when otherwise agreed by parties who are not consumers, that in cases where the recipient of the service places his order through technological means, the following principles apply:

— the service provider has to acknowledge the receipt of the recipient's order without undue delay and by electronic means,
— the order and the acknowledgement of receipt are deemed to be received when the parties to whom they are addressed are able to access them.

2. Member States shall ensure that, except when otherwise agreed by parties who are not consumers, the service provider makes available to the recipient of the service appropriate, effective and accessible technical means allowing him to identify and correct input errors, prior to the placing of the order.

3. Paragraph 1, first indent, and paragraph 2 shall not apply to contracts concluded exclusively by exchange of electronic mail or by equivalent individual communications."

Taken together these provisions ensure that the consumer knows:

- Who s/he is contracting with.
- Where the service provider is established.
- How the service provider can be contacted.
- How a contract is concluded.
- How input errors can be identified and corrected before the contract is concluded.
- In what languages the contract can be concluded.
- What the terms and conditions of the contract are.
- That a contract has been concluded because of the provision relating to the acknowledgement of orders.

Note that some of these requirements do not apply where the contract is concluded exclusively by email.

The Directive applies of course not just to foreign transactions, but also to British ones, e.g. electronic booking of an English hotel. Failure to comply is a criminal offence, mirroring the approach of the Package Travel Regulations which require certain information to be provided by tour operators and making it a criminal offence if they do not comply. However, the E-Commerce Regulations have a wider scope than simply packages; they cover all kinds of e-commerce and would therefore apply not just to tour operators who contracted over the internet but also to hotels, airlines, bedbanks, timeshare companies, ferry companies, etc.

Liability

Throughout this book, we place emphasis on how liability varies depending on whether a product being sold is a package or not. Sometimes (e.g. Security, Ch.12), the difference is very great; at other times (e.g. Unfair Contract Terms, Ch.6) the difference can be insignificant. But in this chapter, which deals with the liability of the travel company to the consumer, the difference is stark indeed. First of all we will examine the rather undeveloped field of liability for non-packages; and then the law relating to liability for packages. The latter will be the longer section, simply because the law has had the chance to develop. We end with a related topic: supplier contracts. Although these are not consumer contracts they must nevertheless take into account the travel company's liability to the consumer otherwise the company may find themselves "piggy in the middle"—liable to the consumer but with no redress against the foreign supplier.

LIABILITY FOR NON-PACKAGES

It is a statement of the obvious, but important nonetheless, to say this: whereas there is one distinct piece of law (the Package Travel Regulations) which (together with the case law which has grown around it) contains the legal position for packages, there is no equivalent provision to which one can point which regulates the law relating to non-packages. There are not, as it were, any Non-Package Travel Regulations. Therefore, one has to study a wide range of different bits of law to extract parts which may assist consumers, or may clarify the responsibility of travel companies.

Looking at the matter from the consumer's perspective, the core question is this: what sort of creature is the consumer dealing with? The possibilities are:

- The actual supplier of the service itself, e.g. an airline or hotelier.

- A company which sets itself up as acting merely as an agent for the supplier.

- A company which is acting as a principal, and therefore contracting with the consumer to provide the service; but exactly what service, and above all, on what terms?

- A company that sets itself up as acting as agent for the consumer.

- A company that is selling a flight-plus (see Ch.12).

It will be absolutely crucial to study the terms of the contract to establish the nature of the transaction. Many traditional tour operators sell non-package elements (e.g. accommodation-only) using the same booking conditions as they do for packages, and therefore reflecting the more consumer-friendly regime of the PTRs. Further, it is worth remembering that a trader who claims to be "only an agent", a middle man between the consumer and supplier who accepts no legal responsibility on himself whatever, carries the burden of showing that he has made that quite clear to the consumer. As is said in *Chitty on Contracts* (para.31.082, 30th edn) he must "show that by the law of agency he is held to have expressly or impliedly negatived his personal liability". Whether someone is an agent is a question of fact which will depend upon all the circumstances in which the travel arrangements were made. It is interesting to note that in late 2006 following a tragic accident in Corfu where members of a family died after being overcome by fumes from the gas installation in their accommodation, "accommodation-only" providers felt pressurised by the market into abandoning an agency status and accepting liability as a principal. Some commercial pressures work the other way however—only a true agent can avoid paying VAT under the Tour Operators Margin Scheme (TOMS)—see the VAT Tribunal cases of *International Life Leisure Ltd v Commissioners for HM Revenue and Customs* Unreported March 14, 2006 and *Secret Hotels2 v Commissioners for Revenue and Customs* [2011] UKUT 308 (TCC). See more on the agency aspects of all this in Ch.11 on Agency.

Liability

Before we turn to deal with the position of non-package traders who are principals, it is worth setting out the other sections of this book which may well be relevant to establishing the rights and duties of the parties in non-package cases:

- As stated, more about the position of agents is set out in Ch.11.

- Flight-plus is dealt with in Ch.12

- See Chs 3 and 4 for the making of the contract and the terms of the contract.

- See Ch.6 on Unfair Contract Terms, and Ch.7 on Misrepresentation.

- The section on the Contracts (Rights of Third Parties) Act 1999 in Ch.8, and the topic of *force majeure* in Ch.9 will be relevant.

- The section on damages in Ch.10 is applicable to non-packages.

- The rights of consumers as against airlines and sea carriers are set out in Ch.13. The Denied Boarding Regulations, and its new equivalents for sea, rail and land transport are particularly important to the non-package traveller.

- Finally, the matters in Ch.14 will often (unfortunately for the consumer) be relevant in establishing whether he has the right to sue in his home country, and if not what to do, and what the applicable law will be.

However, it has to be recognised that no matter how many different sources of law are available, the position of the consumer of a non-package is nothing like as well protected, as is that of his brother who buys a package.

The Non-package Principal

The most common type of contract where the consumer may have this relationship is likely to be with either a company which provides tailor-made arrangements or "dynamic packages", which has managed to sell the arrangements in such a way as to avoid selling a package within the 1992 Regulations, as explained in the *ABTA v CAA* case (see Ch.2); or an accommodation-only provider who is not an agent. Where the arrangements amount to a flight-plus (whether sold as a principal or as an agent), there may be financial protection in the event of failure, but as we shall see in Ch.12, no liability is imposed in the ATOL Regulations for quality, descriptions or health and safety.

What is the liability, at common law, that a trader has for its independent subcontractors?

The basic answer is that the liability depends on the terms of the contract—express or implied. One particular problem that commonly arises is where the principal has subcontracted part of the performance to independent subcontractors. This was the issue which arose in two contrasting cases—*Wall v Silver Wing* and the *Wong Mee Wan* case both referred to in Ch.4.

Wall v Silver Wing, decided by the High Court in 1981, is important because, although it is no longer law in the field of packages because of the provisions of the 1992 Regulations, it is submitted that it continues to have relevance and demonstrates the law for non-packages. This case does not appear to have been formally reported, but transcripts exist and the case is referred to in the reported cases dealt with below of *Wilson v Best* and *Wong Mee Wan*. In *Wall*, the holidaymakers had booked a package holiday to Tenerife. They were staying in a modern hotel. A fire broke out one night. The four claimants attempted to exit the hotel by the fire door, only to find it locked. (This had apparently been done by a security guard because of problems with local troublemakers.) The claimants returned to their room and endeavoured to exit the hotel by means of climbing down a series of sheets which they had tied together. Not surprisingly, during this risky enterprise, two of them fell and were seriously injured. They sued the defendant tour operator (which traded as Enterprise Holidays). The case came before Hodgson J., as he then was. He said:

"Tour operators who provide so called package holiday are a comparatively recent and very welcome arrival on the holiday scene. The tour operator puts together a number of holiday which are then included in this brochure for that year. The brochure typically contains—as did the brochure in this case—a booking form. Each holiday offered includes for a fixed sum travel arrangements, hotel accommodation, and usually some provision for a representative at the holiday resort to see that the customers of the tour operator are being looked after and obtaining that which they bargained for. The tour operator, by making block bookings on aeroplanes and at hotels, can offer its customers holidays which are far cheaper than could be obtained by individual reservations. In the normal way it is perfectly well known that the tour operator neither owns, occupies or controls the hotels which are included in his brochure, any more than he has any control over the airlines which fly his customers, the airports whence and whither they fly and the land transport which conveys then from airport to hotel. It is of course also true that the customer

133

makes no contract himself with the hotel, airline, taxi or coach proprietor. It is clear, I think, that the agreement contained in the booking form and brochure is perfectly efficacious in a business sense, standing on its own. It needs no additional terms to make it work and, if injury is caused by the default of the hotel owners and occupiers, the airline, the airport controllers as well as the taxi proprietor, the customer will have whatever remedy the relevant law allows.

It is also I think clear, despite the heroic efforts by [counsel for the claimant] to persuade me to the contrary, that if an officious bystander had suggested either to the tour operator or, I think, to most customers that the tour operator would be liable for any default on the part of any of these people both would, to put it mildly, have been astonished".

The judge concluded that the tour operator had a duty to make a reasonable choice of subcontractor and to inspect the hotel. In this case the hotel had a perfectly satisfactory fire escape which was open at the time it was inspected by Enterprise. Therefore, the defendants were held not liable for the injuries suffered.

The reasoning in *Wall v Silver Wing* was adopted in a number of County Court decisions including *Gibbons v Intasun Holidays* [1988] C.L.Y. 168; *Kaye v Intasun Holidays* [1987] C.L.Y. 1150; *Toubi v Intasun Holidays* [1988] C.L.Y. 1060 and *Usher v Intasun Holidays* [1987] C.L.Y. 418. *Wilson v Best Travel* [1993] 1 All E.R. 353, a High Court case decided on common law principles, decided that the tour operator was not simply under a duty to take reasonable care (as in *Wall*) but arguably had a duty to see that care was taken, in that the judge required tour operators to consider the safety of hotels, and exclude from their brochures any hotel in which a holidaymaker could not stay in reasonable safety. But this is a long way short of making the travel company responsible for day-to-day mishaps in the hotel, such as the cleaner leaving a marble floor wet without any warning sign to alert guests. And it is, we suggest, this unsatisfactory regime which still represents the law as far as non-package travel arrangements are concerned. (It should be pointed out, however, that the decisions were not all one-way. There were notable exceptions including *Tucker v OTA* [1986] C.L.Y. 383 and a much overlooked Court of Appeal decision *Cook v Spanish Holiday Tours* (1959) 103 S.J. 873, both of which imposed strict liability on tour operators.)

But most recent decisions support our conclusion. In *Murphy v Thomas Cook* Unreported April 9, 2009, Keighley County Court, the claimant had booked accommodation-only. They suffered illness whilst staying there. The claimant argued that the defendant must accept some responsibility, because it took upon itself the hygiene auditing of the property. But the court held that, whilst the defendant was a principal to the contract, its only liability would arise if they had made a poor choice of accommodation, which had not happened. The case of *Moir and Fraser v Thomas Cook Tour Operations Ltd* Unreported October 13, 2010, Newcastle County Court, took this a stage further, because the claimants had booked a package holiday, but the hotel element had been booked on a room only basis. However, there was a restaurant at the hotel, and indeed the Thomas Cook brochure had mentioned it, and said that a discount was available to its customers in the restaurant. The claimants contracted food poisoning from food in the restaurant. Because food was not one of the "obligations under the contract" as per reg.15, the judge held that the only basis for liability would arise if Thomas Cook had had no business to promote the restaurant, if, for example, it had notoriously poor standards. But the lapse in hygiene in this case was only a one off, and therefore Thomas Cook themselves had not been negligent and were not liable.

Although the cases appear to conflict, the approach in each is consistent, i.e. what does the contract say and what does it mean? (And see below for the approach to this of the Privy Council in the *Wong Mee Wan* case.) In this context, the Supply of Goods and Services Act 1982 imposes an implied term to exercise reasonable care and skill in the supply of their services, but the question, as ever, is what are the services? Merely the arrangement of the holiday components, or the actual performance of the services contracted for?

Strict and Fault Liability

Before we examine package travel and reg.15 in detail it will be worthwhile explaining again the difference between obligations imposing fault liability and those imposing strict liability.

Fault liability is where a court will only hold a party to be in breach of contract if it can be shown that they were at fault in some way. For instance, in the case of *Wall v Silver Wing* Unreported 1981, which we discussed above, the tour operator was found not liable for the injuries to their clients because they were not at fault. The hotelkeeper was at fault but the tour operator was not liable for the faults of others, as the law stood in 1981. Strict liability, on the other hand, is where a party will be held to be in breach of contract even though they are not at fault. For instance, under s.14 of the Sale of Goods Act 1979 a seller of goods is under a strict obligation to ensure that the goods he sells are of satisfactory quality and it is no defence to say that it was not his fault. As long as the buyer can show that the goods are defective in some way then the seller is liable. This means that in many instances a perfectly innocent retailer must compensate consumers for defects caused by the manufacturer of the goods—defects which the retailer didn't know about and which he might not have been able to detect even if he had looked for them.

The example given by Longmore L.J. in *Hone v Going Places* quoted in Ch.4 about the swimming pool is worth quoting again as a good illustration of the difference:

"If the brochure or advertisement, on which the consumer relies, promises a swimming-pool, it will be a term of the contract that a swimming-pool will be provided. But, in the absence of express wording, there would not be an absolute obligation, for example, to ensure that the holiday-maker catches no infection while swimming in the swimming-pool. The obligation assumed will be that reasonable skill and care will be taken to ensure that the pool is free from infection."

The reason why it is important to distinguish between strict and fault liability is that this has been the major battleground between consumers and tour operators over the years. Tour operators have argued that they are only subject to fault liability whereas consumers have contended that strict liability should prevail. (See Saggerson [2001] I.T.L.J. 159.)

LIABILITY FOR PACKAGES

At first, the law moved in a direction which was favourable to the package holiday tour operators. As we have seen, the early leading authority was *Wall v Silver Wing*, decided by the High Court in 1981, and described above. Then along came the PTRs, in 1992.

The Scope of Regulation 15

Regulation 15 provides:

> "15(1) The other party to the contract is liable to the consumer for the proper performance of the obligations under the contract, irrespective of whether such obligations are to be performed by that other party or by other suppliers of services but this shall not affect any remedy or right of action which that other party may have against those other suppliers of services.
>
> (2) The other party to the contract is liable to the consumer for any damage caused to him by the failure to perform the contract or the improper performance of the contract unless the failure or the improper performance is due neither to any fault of that other party nor to that of another supplier of services, because—
>
> (a) the failures which occur in the performance of the contract are attributable to the consumer;
>
> (b) such failures are attributable to a third party unconnected with the provision of the services contracted for, and are unforeseeable or unavoidable; or
>
> (c) such failures are due to—
>
>   (i) unusual and unforeseeable circumstances beyond the control of the party by whom this exception is pleaded, the consequences of which could not have been avoided even if all due care had been exercised; or
>
>   (ii) an event which the other party to the contract or the supplier of services, even with all due care, could not foresee or forestall.
>
> (3) In the case of damage arising from the non-performance or improper performance of the services involved in the package, the contract may provide for compensation to be limited in accordance with the international conventions which govern such services.
>
> (4) In the case of damage other than personal injury resulting from the non-performance or improper performance of the services involved in the package, the contract may include a term limiting the amount of compensation which will be paid to the consumer, provided that the limitation is not unreasonable.

(5) Without prejudice to paragraph (3) and paragraph (4) above, liability under paragraphs (1) and (2) above cannot be excluded by any contractual term.

(6) The terms set out in paragraphs (7) and (8) below are implied in every contract.

(7) In the circumstances described in paragraph (2) (b) and (c) of this regulation, the other party to the contract will give prompt assistance to a consumer in difficulty.

(8) If the consumer complains about a defect in the performance of the contract, the other party to the contract, or his local representative, if there is one, will make prompt efforts to find appropriate solutions.

(9) The contract must clearly and explicitly oblige the consumer to communicate at the earliest opportunity, in writing or any other appropriate form, to the supplier of the services concerned and to the other party to the contract any failure which he perceives at the place where the services concerned are supplied."

In very broad terms reg.15 does a number of things. First, reg.15(1) provides that a tour operator shall properly perform the obligations under the contract and shall be liable for breach of those obligations irrespective of who had to perform those obligations—the tour operator or his subcontractors such as transport or hotel companies. Secondly, reg.15(2) provides that in cases where neither the tour operator nor his suppliers are at fault there is no liability. Thirdly, regs.15(3)–(5) govern the use of exclusion and limitation clauses in package holiday contracts. Fourthly, regs.15(6)–(8) require the tour operator to offer assistance to consumers in difficulty. Finally, reg.15(9) deals with making complaints. In this section we are concerned with regs 15(1) and 15(2). Rendering assistance is also dealt with in a later section of this chapter. Exclusion clauses are discussed in the next chapter and reg.15(9) is examined in the section on mitigation of loss in Ch.10.

There was general agreement after the passage of the Package Travel Regulation that all had changed and that by virtue of reg.15 of the Package Travel Regulations tour operators are now under a form of qualified strict liability—by which we mean that their liability has been extended beyond fault liability but falls some way short of full strict liability. (For a short bibliography of how the commentators greeted this change see previous editions of this book.) The next section of the book is devoted to demonstrating the extent of this liability.

Regulation 15(1)—Proper Performance of the Obligations Under the Contract

Regulation 15(1) does two, related, things. First, it states that a tour operator must properly perform the obligations under the contract and secondly, makes it clear that if the obligation is broken by virtue of some default by a "supplier" the tour operator is nevertheless still liable to the consumer. How the courts have interpreted this we shall examine shortly.

"Supplier" is not a term of art but would certainly encompass direct subcontractors such as transport companies and hoteliers and perhaps also sub-

subcontractors such as independent contractors hired by the immediate sub-contractors to perform part of the services making up the contract—courtesy bus providers, tennis coaches, entertainers, etc. But how far does the term in fact extend? Saggerson in "Trumpeting the cause of shocking suppliers" [2005] I.T.L.J. 63, suggests that "English lawyers and judges are profoundly anchored to concepts of fault ... somehow it *just doesn't feel right* to the English Judicial mind that a hotel and/or a tour operator should be held responsible for the short-comings of the local electricity board or [the mahout at an elephant sanctuary]" (though he regrets this judicial conservatism). In a case ongoing as we go to press, a claimant is suing a tour operator in these circumstances: she changed planes at Dubai airport, and whilst at the airport transfer lounge she visited the toilets. She there found an already opened water bottle, left abandoned and with some liquid in it, which she chose to drink, but the contents turned out to be cleaning fluid. Assuming the airport were negligent, will a court regard this as being the act of a supplier, rendering the tour operator liable, notwithstanding the remoteness and lack of control? Saggerson may well turn out to be correct as to the judicial approach.

The Regulation expressly reserves the right of the tour operator to sue "suppliers" directly or join them as Pt 20 (Additional) defendants in any action brought against the tour operator by a consumer (assuming there is such a right). Of course, the consumer may also have a claim against the supplier. This may not be a right which is much exercised. In practice, it would entail a consumer suing a foreign company in a foreign court in the local equivalent of the law of tort—not a prospect which the average holidaymaker would relish—indeed the very problem reg.15 is intended to answer for consumers. It probably explains why in the *Wall* case the claimants chose to sue their tour operator in an English court rather than embark upon litigation in Spain against the hotel (Jones "Tour Operators and the Unfair Contract Terms Act" [1983] Gazette 2964. See also Ch.8 on Privity and the Contracts (Rights of Third Parties) Act 1999). More recently, the European Small Claims Procedure may have slightly alleviated the burden for consumers facing this prospect—see Ch.14.

Regulation 15(2)—Qualified Strict Liability

After ascertaining what the tour operator's obligations are under the contract it is necessary (at least in cases of strict liability (e.g. where there has been a breach of an express promise that a specific facility will be available at the hotel—see the passage on *Hone v Going Places* below) to look carefully at reg.15(2) which contains a number of sweeping qualifications to the tour operator's liability. However, the extent of those qualifications is not immediately apparent. Regulation 15(2) states that the tour operator will be liable:

"unless such failure to perform or improper performance is attributable neither to *any* fault of theirs nor to that of another supplier of services, *because—*" (Emphasis added)

It then goes on to specify the situations in which the organiser will not be liable. Are the words quoted above general words providing that the organiser will never be liable if there is no fault on his behalf or the suppliers' behalf, and the categories which follow merely examples of situations of no fault and the list is not exhaustive? Or are the categories a closed list and if a situation arises where there is improper performance which is not the fault of the organiser or the supplier and yet is not provided for in the list then the operator is still liable.

The use of the word "because" suggests the latter, i.e. the interpretation to be placed upon it is that the organiser will not be liable if the failure is not his fault *for the following reasons only*, suggesting that if it is not for the following reasons then the operator remains liable.

On the other hand, the use of the word "any" suggests that if there is *no* fault on the operator's behalf or by the supplier then the operator is not liable and the list is merely illustrative of the situations where the operator escapes liability.

If, in fact, the list encompasses every situation where there is failure of performance and yet the operator is not at fault then the problem may be a little academic. To answer this requires an examination of the four relevant provisions.

The first is where the failure is attributable to the consumer. It is difficult to see why it was felt necessary to include this. On simple principles of causation a tour operator would not normally be held liable for damage caused to the consumer if the consumer was the author of his own downfall. One reported case that would fall into this category is *Hartley v Intasun* [1987] C.L.Y. 1149. The claimant in that case arrived at the airport a day late. Intasun put him on the next available plane and he arrived in the resort to find that his room had been re-let and he had to accept inferior accommodation. On his return he sued for breach of contract. It was held that his failure to turn up at the airport on time amounted to a cancellation of the contract and therefore the defendants were under no obligation to do anything for him. They should not be penalised for doing their best to patch up some kind of holiday for him.

The second exception is where the failure is attributable to a third party unconnected with the provision of the services *and* was unforeseeable or unavoidable. Thus, if the hotel swimming pool was unusable for a number of days because vandals had broken into the hotel grounds and put dye in the water then certainly this would have been due to third parties unconnected with the provision of the services, but would it be unforeseeable or unavoidable? If it had happened before on a regular basis and if it could have been avoided by more stringent security it might be the case that the operator would still be liable.

What if a tour operator books a party into a downtown Miami hotel in an area frequented by drug addicts and a child in the party is injured when she steps on a hypodermic needle in the grounds of the hotel? Such an injury may have been caused by a third party unconnected with the provision of the services, but could it be said to be unforeseeable or unavoidable? But there again, has there been a failure of performance of contractual obligations? Perhaps so, if the hotelier knew of the risk but failed to do anything about it.

If the dye had been put in the pool by a recently dismissed employee would this be a "third party unconnected" with the provision of the service? In English law an employer is usually vicariously liable for the wrongful actions of his employees if they are committed in the course of their employment, even if they are carrying out that employment in a way contrary to instructions. Depending on the facts, however, such an act of vandalism could be regarded as outside the course of employment.

The third exception to strict liability is where there is a *force majeure* event. *Force majeure* is examined in detail in Ch.9 and therefore only a brief explanation is necessary here. For the exception to apply the failure must be due to *unusual and unforeseeable circumstances beyond the control of the organiser, the consequences of which could not have been avoided even if all due care had been exercised.*

The requirements are cumulative and therefore will be difficult for an operator to satisfy. How many things that go wrong with a package are unusual *and* unforeseeable *and* beyond the control of the operator *and* he could not have avoided them by the exercise of reasonable care? Apart from acts of God such as earthquakes and hurricanes (and even then, there is a question whether, for example, hurricanes are unforeseeable in the Caribbean in September), and sudden outbreaks of war or civil unrest, e.g. *Charlson v Mark Warner* (a case about snow) (see Ch.9 on *Force Majeure*) it appears that this exception will not be available to the organiser—but see the surprising decision in *Hibbs v Thomas Cook* [1999] C.L.Y. 3829 where a mechanical failure of a ferry was held to be *force majeure*.

The fourth exception is where the failure is due to an event which the operator or the supplier could not have foreseen or forestalled even with all due care.

Unlike the third exception this provision will have the effect of drastically narrowing the operator's liability. It would cover things such as air traffic controllers' strikes which, if not unforeseeable, are unavoidable. Waiters' strikes might fall within this exception as well. Hurricanes also, even if foreseeable, are unavoidable. Whether it would cover technical breakdown of aircraft is more debatable. Are such events foreseeable or avoidable? (See [1997] I.T.L.J. 117 on charter airline delays.) One County Court case, *Bedeschi & Holt v Travel Promotions Ltd* Unreported January, 1998, Central London County Court, demonstrates how significant this exception can be. The claimants had suffered from vomiting and diarrhoea attributable to the food and drink they consumed on the defendant's Nile cruise boat. On the basis of expert evidence that standards of hygiene in Egypt were such that the risk of infection could not be eliminated the court held that the claimants' illness might have been foreseeable but could not have been forestalled. (Following *Hone v Going Places*, below, however, the judge would not now have needed to look at the exception, as the claimant could not prove improper performance; see also Shafi "Bugs on the Nile" [2006] I.T.L.J. 142, which suggests that the judge in *Bedeschi* was not presented with a true picture of hygiene in Egypt.) Two contrasting cases are *Hayes v Airtours* [2001] 2 C.L. 436 (hurricane not an event which could be forestalled, or even predicted) and *Bensusan v Airtours* (original decision at [2001] C.L.Y. 432, but overturned on appeal Unreported August 8, 2001). In the latter case, discussed below, the judge held that a cumulative series of minor reasons for delay could be regarded as one "event", which in the circumstances was preventable. Judge Edwards said:

"In my judgment the word 'event' comprises a chain or series of separate events as well as each separate event itself. Each one of a number of events may be separately foreseeable or forestallable but their combination may not."

Development of the Law to Date

As we have said, the initial view of the effect of the Regulations was this: that now, for the first time, tour operators were strictly liable for the proper performance of the holiday. If a consumer is on the holiday, using the hotel provided, and is injured (e.g. by a glass door) or made ill (for example, by the food), then the tour operator will be liable. He cannot escape by blaming his suppliers, however creditably that supplier had performed in the past. The only way in which the tour operator could escape liability was by demonstrating that he came within one of the exceptions to reg.15(2), set out above, for example by showing than an accident on a transfer coach was caused by a third party driver, or by showing a *force majeure* event.

The high point of this line of thinking is illustrated by the case *Jordan v Thomson Holidays Limited*, a decision of a district judge at Bristol County Court reported at [1999] C.L.Y. 3828. It is not, in fact, a personal injury case. What happened was this: some days into their holiday the Jordans returned to their apartment to find workmen repairing a burst pipe in one bedroom. As a result of the burst pipe, the Jordans suffered a flood and had to move apartments twice. They claimed compensation.

The district judge held that to escape liability, Thomson would have to rely on reg.15(2)(c), an occurrence which was unusual and unforeseeable. It was held that pipes can and often do burst without warning and the burden of proof was on Thomson that it came within reg.15(2)(c). They could not discharge that burden and accordingly were held liable for the spoilt holiday.

The Privy Council Weighs In

The decision which at first blush appeared to support the above line of thinking was the Privy Council decision in *Wong Mee Wan v Kwan Kin Travel Services Ltd* [1995] 4 All E.R. 745. This was an appeal from the Hong Kong Court of Appeal and therefore, obviously, not subject to any European directives. The first defendant was a Hong Kong tour operator. It is a tragic case. What happened was this: Miss Yee contracted to take a package tour in China. There was a party of 24. They left Hong Kong first by ferry and then by coach. They were accompanied by a tour leader employed by Kwan Kin. There was a delay at the border. Once in China they were accompanied by a tour guide from a Chinese tour company. The coach took them to the guest house where they were to spend the first night. The tour guide told them that they should leave their luggage quickly as, because of the delays, they were late to visit the ethnic village at the lake. When they got to the pier at the lake they were told by the guide that the coach and ferry had already gone and there was no alternative for the group but to cross the lake in a speed boat. Since the speed boat took only eight persons, three trips were involved each taking 15 minutes. After two trips, the speed boat employee refused to do the third. A volunteer from the boat company was found to drive the boat. It seems that the boat went very fast, perhaps racing another speed boat, and hit a fishing junk. The occupants were thrown into the water and two, including Miss Yee, were drowned. The Hong Kong Court of Appeal had held, in respect of the defendant, that:

"It must have been clear to all members of the tours that it could not provide all those services itself but would delegate to other companies in China its duty to provide the bulk of them. It would in my view impose an intolerable burden if the firm which put the tour package together was to be held liable for the negligence of a transport operator in another country".

The Privy Council disagreed. They concluded that:

"The first defendants obligation under the contract that the services would be provided with reasonable skill and care remains even if some of the services were to be rendered by others.

In their Lordships' view it was an implied term of the contract that those services would be carried out with reasonable skill and care. That term does not mean that the first defendant undertook an obligation to ensure 'the safety of all the components of the package'. The plaintiff's claim does not amount to an implied term that her daughter would be reasonably safe. It is a term simply that reasonable skill and care would be used in rendering the services provided under the contract."

Unfortunately, for those seeking clarity in this area of law, this apparently helpful definition in the judgment of Lord Slynn is undermined in two ways. First of all, immediately after the above quoted passage, he muddies the waters by adding:

"the trip across the lake was clearly not carried out with reasonable skill and care in that no steps were taken to see that the driver of the speed boat was of reasonable competence and experience and the First defendant is liable for such breach of contract."

Surely, on the test which the judge had laid out, one would have expected him to say: "the trip across the lake was clearly not carried out with reasonable skill and care in that the driver of the speed boat drove recklessly"; instead, by making the breach of contract refer to the question of monitoring the quality of the driver, the judge appears to take us straight back to the test in *Wall v Silver Wing* (a decision with which, by the way, Lord Slynn appeared to disagree).

A second problem is this: Lord Slynn starts his analysis by referring to the contractual terms, namely the promises in the brochure, including: "we will firstly gather ... we will board the deluxe double jet hydrofoil ... our staff will handle the customs formalities for you ... we will board the deluxe coach ... we will visit the rustic and beautiful holiday village" and so on and so on with repeated use of the word "we". Lord Slynn says:

" 'we' includes the company offering the tour and integrates the company into each stage of the tour taking the contract as a whole their Lordships consider that the First defendant here undertook to provide and not merely to arrange all the services included in the programme, even if some activities were to be carried out by others."

One gets the clear impression that if the tour operator had not so clearly taken obligations on themselves with the word "we", the decision might have been different. Consequently, this case has generally been regarded as turning on its own facts and has been cited but rarely applied in subsequent holiday cases.

Hone v Going Places

The current law was settled by a Court of Appeal decision, *Hone v Going Places Leisure Travel Limited* [2001] EWCA Civ 947. The facts were rather unusual. First of all, Going Places is or was a travel agent (now part of the Thomas Cook group), and not a tour operator. This was an issue in the original High Court trial, where the judge concluded that they had held themselves out as a tour operator and were therefore potentially liable on the contract. This issue was not revisited in the Court of Appeal. (See Ch.11 on Travel Agents.)

Turning to the more important issue, the claimant and his family were on their way home by aeroplane from a holiday in Turkey. Shortly after takeoff there was a bomb scare on board and the pilot decided to divert to Istanbul. The passengers were instructed to prepare for an emergency landing and then for a crash landing, after which, the passengers would have to descend from the aeroplane by emergency chute. When the claimant was at the top of the chute he noticed a large lady, who had also been on holiday, at the bottom of the chute. In the course of his descent, Mr Hone realised that she was stuck at the bottom of the chute and unable to move away. He opened his legs wide enough to avoid striking her back but collided with her. His fiancée followed him down the chute and struck his back with her shoes, causing a spinal injury which was exacerbated when he tried to assist the large lady to stand up.

Mr Hone sued the defendant relying entirely on reg.15 of the Package Travel Regulations. The Court of Appeal were called upon to decide two points: whether reg.15 imposed strict liability; and whether the onus of proving fault was with the claimant, rather than on the defendant to disprove fault. It is worth setting out the submissions that were made by Counsel for Mr Hone, as set out in para.10 of the judgment:

"1. That on their true construction, the 1992 Regulations imposed absolute or strict liability on the other party, subject to the defences, the onus for proving which was on that other party [Note this is the argument we saw above accepted in the *Jordan* case].

2. The requirement in reg.15 for 'improper performance' was met because the expectation was for safe carriage, and if injury was sustained during carriage, there was improper performance.

3. That the intention of the PTR's was to achieve a comparable result with the Warsaw [now Montreal] Convention, which imposed strict liability for death or injury, subject to limits.

4. That if the burden was on the claimant to prove improper performance in the sense of fault, the existence of the fault based exceptions was otiose and made no sense."

Longmore L.J. said:

"The starting point must in my view be the contract which Mr Hone made with the defendant in the absence of any contrary intention, the normal implication will be that the service contracted for will be rendered with reasonable skill and care. Of course, absolute obligations may be assumed. If the brochure or advertisement on which the consumer relies promises a swimming pool, it will be a term of the contract that a swimming pool will be provided. But in the absence of express wording, there would not be an absolute obligation for example to ensure that the holidaymaker catches no infection while swimming in the swimming pool. The obligation assumed will be that reasonable skill and care will be taken to ensure that the pool is free from infection."

He went on:

"Going Places is liable for 'the proper performance of the obligations under the Contract'. But Regulation 15(1) says nothing about *the content of that performance*" (Emphasis added).

"Regulation 15(2) provides for [the tour operator] to be liable for any damage caused to the consumer by failure to perform the contract or by the improper performance of the contract. The present case is not a case of failure to perform. It can only be a case of improper performance. It is only possible to determine whether it is a case of improper performance by reference to the terms of the contract which is being performed. *To my mind, Regulation 15(2) does not give the answer to the question, 'what is improper performance?' rather, it is a requirement of the application of Regulation 15(2) that there should be improper performance* (Emphasis added). That can only be determined by reference to the terms of the contract I would not, for my part, accept that the existence of the fault based exceptions in Regulation 15(2) makes it otiose or nonsensical for the claimant to have to prove fault in an appropriate case. The exceptions will, in any event, come into play if the other party to the contract assumes obligations which are themselves not fault-based."

Longmore L.J. also emphasised that the burden of proof is on the claimant to prove the fault; in this case, the claimant would have needed expert evidence as to how the evacuation of an aeroplane should have been done, in order to succeed, but he had no such evidence. In restating the classic common law position in relation to the burden of proof, Longmore L.J. was echoing what had been said by the same court in the previous year in *C (A Child) v Thomson Tour Operations Ltd* (see below), in which Swinton Thomas L.J. said :

"this is not a case in which, in my view, it is appropriate to say that the hotel or the tour operator is liable for this accident without proof of negligence. In order to succeed, the claimant must prove that the hotel management was negligent either in relation to the maintenance of the lift or in relation to the safety procedures."

Hone gives the lie to the simplistic formulation that the effect of the PTR's is this: that if the supplier is liable, then the tour operator is liable under reg.15. In *Hone* the *airline* was liable by virtue of the strict liability regime in the (then) Warsaw Convention. However, Longmore L.J. expressly rejected the idea that strict liability similarly applied to the tour operator, because of the use of the words "improper performance" in reg.15. This begs the question of why Mr Hone did not bring an (unanswerable) claim against the carrier.

In summary, therefore, a claimant must go through the following process:

- He must establish the terms of the contract.

- Unless they impose strict liability, there will only be fault-based obligations.

- The burden of proof is on the claimant to prove that fault.

Nothing in reg.15(2) switches the burden of proof in such circumstances. Indeed, in fault liability cases, the exceptions in reg.15 will always be irrelevant. Either the claimant can prove fault, in which case, of course, it is impossible for the defendant to prove lack of fault; or the claimant cannot prove fault, the case fails, and the exceptions never come into play. The exceptions will therefore rarely, if ever, come into play in personal injury cases; such claims routinely arise out of situations on which the brochure or website is silent. There will never be express terms, e.g. that the cleaner will put up a warning sign after washing a marble floor, or that the tiles around a pool are of non-slip material, or that the raw and cooked meats are kept separately in the kitchen. Longmore L.J.'s implied term will always therefore be the basis of any claim, i.e. reasonable care and skill being used.

For further commentary on *Hone* see Saggerson [2001] I.T.L.J. 159.

Strict Liability Terms

Hone v Going Places is a case where the court held that liability was fault based and the burden of proof was on the claimant to prove fault. By way of contrast *Bensusan v Airtours* mentioned above is a case where the judge decided that the duty on Airtours to fly the claimants to Jamaica in time to join their cruise was an obligation of strict liability. It therefore fell upon Airtours to prove that one of the statutory defences applied, in this case that the delays could not have been foreseen or forestalled with all due care. This they failed to do. Presumably there was felt to be an express promise regarding meeting the cruise; as per the swimming pool example in *Hone*, above. If you promise a pool, there must be a pool; it will avail you nought to say that you used reasonable skill and care to try and get a swimming pool; but the defendant can try and discharge the burden of proving one of the defences in reg.15(2).

The terms of the contract are therefore now king. (See also further support for this view in the case of *Williams v Travel Promotions Ltd, The Times*, March 9, 1998 (CA) where the Court of Appeal adopted the approach later found in *Hone*.) It seems clear that once the obligations under the contract have been established, the tour operator cannot escape liability for those obligations by blaming his subcontractors. The following question could, however, be asked: what is to stop a tour operator from defining his obligations in the contract, using the formula from *Wall v Silver Wing*? In other words, a tour operator would say that its obligations under the contract extend only to making a good choice of subcontractor and (perhaps) monitoring its performance. Any defect in performance by the subcontractor is not then a breach of the operator's contracted obligation to make a good choice, and as the subcontractor had no part in discharging the "good choice" obligation, reg.15 is circumvented. All we can say is that courts are likely to strive for a method of rejecting such an attempt to restrict liability, although this type of philosophy seems to underpin the decision of Reading County Court in *Grahame v JMC Holidays Ltd* [2002] C.L.Y. 2324 whereby JMC were found not liable for aircraft delay because they had used reasonable skill and care in selecting the airline.

Wilson v Best Travel and the Standard of Care

So we see that the test, especially in injury/illness claims, will be whether reasonable skill and care was used. But how does one measure what constitutes reasonable care in the context of a foreign hotel (or coach, ski school, etc)? Does one apply British standards or the local standards where the hotel is situated?

For many years, the leading case has been *Wilson v Best Travel Ltd*, decided in April 1991 but not reported until [1993] 1 All E.R. 353. It is a classic glass door case. On the first morning of their holiday on the Greek island of Kos, the claimant's party were in a hotel bedroom. The claimant tripped and fell against the glass patio door. The door shattered and the claimant fell through it sustaining lacerations from the broken glass to shoulder, elbow, hand and in particular to the right leg. "The gravity of the consequences was attributable to the fact that the glass fragmented into fragments of razor edged sharpness."

Phillips J. (as he then was) held:

"I am satisfied, having read their brochure, that the service provided by the defendants included the inspection of the properties offered in their brochure.

In my judgment one of the characteristics of accommodation that the defendants owed the duty to consider when inspecting properties included in their brochure was safety. The defendants owe their customers, including the plaintiff, a duty to exercise reasonable care to exclude from the accommodation offered any hotel whose characteristics were such that guests could not spend their time there in reasonable safety. I believe that this case is about the standard to be applied in assessing reasonable safety."

Five millimetre annealed glass of the type used in this hotel was common in Greece. British Standards require the use of safety glass in doors and large panels, although (at least in 1991) these were not mandatory by law, but "it is nonetheless the practice in England to comply with the relevant standards".

As we have previously seen the judge went on to say:

"What is the duty of a tour operator in a situation such as this? Must he refrain from sending holidaymakers to any hotel whose characteristics, in so far as safety is concerned, fail to satisfy the standards which apply in this country? I do not believe that his obligations in respect of the safety of his clients can extend this far. Save where uniform international regulations apply, there are bound to be differences in the safety standards applied in respect of the many hazards of modern life between one country and another. All civilised countries attempt to cater for these hazards by imposing mandatory regulations. The duty of care of a tour operator is likely to extend to checking that local safety regulations are complied with. Provided that they are, I do not consider that the tour operator owes a duty to boycott a hotel because of the absence of some safety feature which would be found in an English hotel unless the absence of such a feature might lead a reasonable holiday maker to decline to take a holiday at the hotel in question."

Thus, it can be seen that local safety standards apply unless:

- There are contrary international regulations; or
- The absence of the safety feature would lead a reasonable holiday maker to decline to go. A glass door did not come within this exception. It must follow from the judgment that the judge is saying that, had the claimant been told about the glass in advance, she would still have been happy to take the holiday. One can, however, imagine how the parents of a toddler might decline a holiday in an upstairs bedroom with a balcony whose railings were wide enough for the child to slip through, notwithstanding any argument that such a balcony complied with local safety standards (it follows from the judgment that Philips J. accepts that had Mrs Wilson been told about the type of glass in her Greek hotel in advance, she would not reasonably have cancelled her holiday); or
- There are express provisions in the contract to the contrary.

Over the years since *Wilson v Best Travel* was decided, there has been much debate as to whether it was correctly decided, whether it would survive a challenge in a suitable case to the Court of Appeal; in particular whether the Package Travel Regulations 1992, not in force at the time of *Wilson v Best Travel*, would change the outcome. These questions have now been answered, although not without the occasional wobble along the way!

The Wilson principle was tested in the Court of Appeal in the case of *C (A Child) v Thomson Holidays Ltd*, *The Times*, October 20, 2000. This case arose out of an accident suffered by a 10-year-old child with the glass lift door of his hotel in Majorca. The lift had an outer door which was hinged and an inner sliding door which closed automatically when the outer door had been closed. The claimant and his sisters went into the lift and neither of the doors shut. It appears that the outer door had for some reason jammed before it reached its proper resting place in the door frame. The claimant put his right hand round the door and pulled it towards him. The door then shut quickly and caught his right middle finger as a result of which he sustained a serious injury to it.

By the contract terms, Thomson agreed that they would be liable for injuries caused by the negligence of their suppliers, in this case the hotel.

The court had before it documentation which showed that in accordance with Spanish law, the lifts at the hotel were examined on a monthly basis by engineers. There was evidence that the lifts were working satisfactorily prior to and after the accident and there were no regulations in Spain which required safety signs to be posted in a lift or the requirement that there should be an emergency alarm or emergency procedure in the lift if the door did not close or the lift became stuck. There is such a requirement in English law. The lift did not comply with those regulations but complied with Spanish legislation.

> "Accordingly [the trial judge] arrived at the conclusion that negligence had not been established against the hotel owners or managers and in consequence it was not established against the tour operator."

The claimant, a litigant in person, challenged this decision in the Court of Appeal on a variety of grounds which included "that the onus of proving that the accident did not result from the negligence of the hotel or Thomson was upon them and not on the claimant" and "that the judge was in error in not applying the British Standards to this particular lift."

The Court of Appeal rejected both of these submissions. As we have already seen, Swinton Thomas L.J., on the first point, said:

> "this is not a case in which, in my view, it is appropriate to say that the hotel or the tour operator is liable for this accident without proof of negligence. In order to succeed, the claimant must prove that the hotel management was negligent either in relation to the maintenance of the lift or in relation to the safety procedures."

On the second point, that British Standards should apply, he said:

> "that is not a correct approach to a case such as this where an accident occurred in a foreign country. The law of this country is applied to the case as to the establishing of negligence, but there is no requirement that a hotel for example in Majorca is obliged to comply with British Safety Standards" (Cf. case of *Barlow v TUI* described below)

and he approved *Wilson v Best Travel*.

Although this answered many of the outstanding questions, it left one: because the case proceeded on the basis of Thomson's booking conditions, the Package Travel Regulations were never mentioned. Do they make a difference? This question, as we shall see, has been answered "no".

Wilson v Best Travel—The Story Continues

Claimants remain unhappy with *Wilson v Best Travel* and there have been interesting attempts to get around it. One example at county court level is the case of *Barlow v TUI (UK) Ltd* Unreported October 4, 2005, Liverpool County Court. The claimant was injured when some automatically closing sliding doors leading from the foyer of the hotel in Benidorm malfunctioned, closing rapidly on the claimant trapping her and causing her to fall. There had been no previous similar incidents although it happened again a few days later. The doors complied with all Spanish safety and technical standards. However, the claimant relied on ss.25 and 26 of the consumer law of the Spanish Civil Code. This, it was said, imposed "quasi strict liability" on the hotel. The judge, however, held this approach to be incorrect. He said that:

> "Spanish laws, rules, Regulation etc set a standard to be obtained in terms of compliance, in terms of the performance of the service, but it is the law of England and not the law of Spain which applies in determining the issue of liability in the case of this kind if Spanish technical practices and standards had been complied with, then in my Judgment it is irrelevant that nevertheless a Spanish Court would have found liability on the basis of some principle going beyond such compliance and amounting to 'quasi strict liability'."

And the judge relied upon the passages from *C (A Child) v Thomson Holidays* and *Hone v Going Places* already set out above—indeed, it may be felt that this passage explains rather clearly what Swinton Thomas L.J. intended in the second passage we have cited from his judgment.

It was the same Judge who a month later heard the case of *Hilton v Mytravel* Unreported November 1, 2005, Manchester County Court. Here, the claimant was injured slipping on liquid spilt on a restaurant floor. The Judge disallowed all of the claimant's costs of obtaining Spanish legal expert evidence about the Spanish Civil Code and Consumer Law on the grounds that such evidence was irrelevant and immaterial to the issues in the case—there being no Spanish technical standard breach of which had been alleged. The Judge concluded that reliance on the Spanish Consumer Law, in which the burden of proof was reversed and standard of care one of "all due diligence" was misplaced. The reasons were similar to those in *Barlow*. However, the claimant won anyway, applying English principles, on the basis of *Ward v Tesco Stores* (see below).

The principle was further explored and developed by the case of *Holden v First Choice Holidays and Flights Ltd* Unreported May 22, 2006, QBD, Winchester. An accident had occurred at a hotel in Tunisia on some steps leading to the hotel restaurant, as a result (it was found) of the spillage of some colourless odourless liquid. The trial judge had found First Choice liable. He felt able to infer that Tunisian standards, on which he had heard no evidence, must be very high, because of the excellent medical treatment the claimant had received after the accident; they must, therefore, require that a hotel employee check the steps every time someone used the steps while carrying a container of liquid.

On appeal, Goldring J. (as he then was) overturned the judgment. Among his interesting findings were:

- The claimant carries the burden of proof, and that includes proving the local safety, etc standards. It is not for the defendant to prove anything.

- The judge cannot infer the standards, absent such evidence.

- Any alleged distinction between alleged failures of equipment or the fabric of the building, and alleged failings in systems, was irrelevant.

- The fact that a particular hotel or company aspires to standards higher than local law requires is irrelevant (unless they have been incorporated in the contract). Goldring J. said: "It is no substitute for evidence of what *is* local custom and what may *be* the local regulations".

See Prager "Have claimants been shown the red card?" [2006] I.T.L.J. 131. Following *Holden*, a number of claims failed for lack of expert evidence on standards, e.g. *Taylor v Sunstar Leisure* Unreported 2007, Liverpool Country Court—claimant fell on pathway made slippery by garden sprinklers.

The next significant exploration of the extent of and limits to the principle was the case of *Evans v Kosmar Villa Holiday Plc* [2007] EWCA Civ 1003. The claimant was catastrophically injured when he dived into the shallow end of the hotel swimming pool at the hotel in Corfu which he had booked as part of his package holiday with the defendant company. The trial judge had found that there was negligence in that signage about depths and "no diving", additional to those already displayed, would have prevented the accident. In reaching his decision, he was no doubt swayed by the fine impression made by the claimant in evidence, and by his contrasting finding that Kosmar's witnesses (reps, etc) had "conspired together to deceive" the court in their evidence. As Richards L.J. said on appeal, this feature was "deeply troubling" but "none of this can affect the legal analysis".

Richards L.J. made the following findings:

1. He confirmed that the passage set out above from *Wilson v Best Travel* remains good law following the introduction of the Package Travel Regulations 1992, saying that such a claim would now be " ... put differently, since the tour operator is directly liable under those Regulations for improper performance of the contract by the hotel ... the focus can be on the exercise of reasonable care in the operation of the hotel itself rather than in the selection of the hotel and the offer of accommodation at it. But I do not think that this affects the principle laid down as to the standard to be applied to a hotel abroad, namely that the hotel is required to comply with local safety regulations rather than with British safety standards".

2. He did, however, go on to say that it was possible to pursue the claim on other bases. "What was said in *Wilson v Best Travel Ltd* did not purport to be an exhaustive statement of the duty of care, and it does not seem to me that compliance with local safety regulations is necessarily sufficient to fulfil that duty". (For commentary see below.)

3. The bases pleaded by the claimant were (i) a breach of local regulations (of which there was no evidence), (ii) a breach of the minimum reasonable standards recommended by the Federation of Tour Operators in the "Suggestions for swimming pool safety" section of its health and safety handbook, (iii) a breach of the duty to use reasonable care and skill in the provision of the swimming pool, where it was known that young people used the pool at all hours of the day and night, often after drinking alcohol.

4. Richards L.J. dealt with the FTO point as follows, "In my view the handbook is referred to correctly as guidance. It is advisory in character and has no legal force. It does not lay down standards with which Kosmar is required to comply". (Although *Holden v First Choice* is not cited in the judgment, this is consistent with what Goldring J. found there about the effect of any standards which may be higher than the locally required ones.)

5. As to pleaded ground (iii), Richards L.J. found that on the facts of this
    case, no "duty to guard the claimant against the risk of his diving into the
    pool and injuring himself" arose. "That was an obvious risk, of which he
    was well aware". Since there was no duty to warn, it followed that
    questions of the adequacy of signage became irrelevant. He also added,
    obiter, that even had there been a breach of duty, it would not have been
    causative of the accident.

These findings may be unexceptional in themselves, particularly in the light of
Tomlinson (see below), but the obiter statements about *Wilson v Best Travel* set
out at our para.2 above have provoked much interesting discussion. The tenor of
the comments is favourable to claimants, of course. What exactly do they mean?
In what circumstances might there be liability notwithstanding compliance with
local regulations? And do those circumstances differ in any way from the caveats
entered by Philips J. himself in *Wilson*, as set out in the passage quoted above
with commentary—e.g. that there would still be liability in circumstances where
"a reasonable holiday maker [might] decline to take a holiday at the hotel in
question" (or perhaps where the standards were those of a country which was not
a "civilised" one, to use Philips J.'s word)?

See Prager and Mason "Regulation 15 of the Package Travel regulations.
Where are we now? Where are we going?" [2008] I.T.L.J. 149, for a discussion of
these issues.

It is instructive to see how the courts have dealt with what Richards L.J. said,
in subsequent cases. *Drabble v Sunstar Leisure* Unreported February 27, 2008,
was a classic glass partition case, similar to *Wilson*. In the trial at Oldham
County Court, the claimant submitted that, if there were no breach of local
standards, there was still liability based on the Richards L.J. dictum and/or the
"reasonable holiday maker" test from *Wilson*. There were also factual issues as
to whether the partition had warning stickers on it or not.

The trial judge said that, absent any clarification from Richards L.J. as to the
circumstances in which a claimant could succeed despite compliance with local
standards, he would assume that such a result was limited to "exceptional or
unusual" circumstances, which this was not. In refusing permission to appeal,
Keane L.J. made no comment, favourable or otherwise, about what the judge had
said on this point, but dealt with it in this way, saying "quite frankly, given the
failure to prove the absence of a warning sticker, there is no realistic prospect of
establishing such a breach of duty". This disposed of the "reasonable holiday
maker" test as well.

Of significance is the Court of Appeal decision in *Gouldbourn v Balkan
Holidays Ltd* [2010] EWCA Civ 372. First of all, this is a leading case on local
standards that is not about a hotel, but about skiing tuition, and whether it
negligently led to the claimant injuring herself because she was placed on a slope
that was too difficult for her abilities. The trial judge at Birmingham had found
that the experts called by both parties were experts on Western European ski
tuition standards, but not on the standards in Bulgaria, where the accident took
place. The trial judge said of the tutor: "it may be that he fell below those
standards, but that is not something I can properly infer from the evidence I have
heard".

In the Court of Appeal, the claimant argued that there was a uniform international regulation (which is one of the exceptions to the local standards test as listed in *Wilson*), namely, the Federation Internationale de Ski ("FIS") Rules as set out in their handbook. Leveson L.J. agreed with Balkan that, at most, the FIS rules set up a general duty of care, but "the implementation of that duty, namely how a particular country goes about ensuring it, is a question of local standards". He noted that the FIS rules "equally make it clear that 'skiing like all sports entails risk' ".

The most interesting points arising out of *Gouldbourn* are these:

1. Leveson L.J. cites *Holden*, which, as stated, was not cited in *Evans*, and says, in support of his own approach to the *Gouldbourn* evidence, that the case "has been taken to entrench the need for evidence of local standards".

2. As to the observation of Richards L.J. in *Evans* about the rule in *Wilson*, Leveson L.J. said: "It is a mistake to construe the judgment of Phillips J as if it were a statute: see the observation of Richards LJ in *Evans v Kosmar* ... to the effect that the case did not purport to be an exhaustive statement of the duty of care. Nevertheless it does identify a very important signpost to the correct approach to cases of this nature, which will inevitably impact on the way in which organisations from different countries provide services to UK tourists. To require such organisations to adopt a different standard of care for different tourists is quite impracticable. What might be required for American tourists may well be different to that required by a French or Western European tourist, itself different to that required by a Japanese tourist. Neither do I consider that the [Package Travel] Regulations impose a duty on English tour operators to require a standard of care to be judged by UK criteria or necessarily western European criteria."

So, to summarise where we are now, everyone now pays lip service to the observation of Richards L.J. in *Evans*, but no one can provide an illustration of when it might apply.

Whilst this is good news for defendants, four notes of caution need to be sounded. Firstly, one argument they have tried to run has been rejected. Compliance must be with the actual local regulations; therefore, the fact that the local authority—or whoever—had signed off the hotel as compliant, when it was not, will not afford a defence—see *Singh v Libra*, and *Healy v Cosmosair*, below.

Secondly, the fact that local standards might actually be *higher* than UK ones may create unpleasant surprises for tour operators. In *Eldridge v TUI UK Ltd* Unreported January 14, 2011, Birmingham County Court, the claimants were 57 consumers, most of whom suffered cryptosporidium as a result of swimming in the pool at a hotel in Majorca. (See below for more about illness claims.) The judge was H.H. Judge Worcester, who was also the original trial judge in *Gouldbourn*. In defining what were the "obligations under the contract" as per reg.15 of the PTR's, the judge noted that TUI's booking conditions provided:

"We are responsible for making sure that each part of the holiday you book with us is provided to a reasonable standard ... we have taken all reasonable care to make sure that all the services which make up the holidays ... are provided by efficient and reputable businesses who should follow the local and national laws and regulations of the country where they are provided ..."

It was found (with expert evidence) that the relevant Spanish Decree stipulated for hotel pools that the standard for fresh water (inter alia) was "Absence of pathogenic parasites, algae or larvae".

The judge found that the effect of the booking conditions, combined with the absolute requirement in Spain that the water be free of parasites, meant that TUI were under an absolute or strict liability; even if no one was to blame for the cryptosporidium getting into the water, TUI were still rendered liable for the mere fact that it was present.

Thirdly, in road traffic accident cases our courts seem willing to impose their own view of negligent driving standards—see *McGeough v Thomson Holidays Ltd* [2007] EWCA Civ 1509.

Fourthly, the cases do seem to have a gap which is potentially unfair to claimants. What if a claimant proves that in a "civilised" country there is no regulation which governs the alleged negligent act? Will our courts then be willing to look at how the foreign court would approach the standard of care, or does that come too close to applying foreign law? We await with interest a decision on this point. For an extended discussion of this difficult point see Saggerson, 4th edn, pp.184–188.

The lesson for tour operators is not to assume that raising a local standards defence will always make life easier; and that booking conditions need constant revision to ensure that the "obligations under the contract" are defined as fault liability in such a case. If they had been, *Ellridge* could have followed the same path as *Hone*, in which, it will be remembered, the Court held that although the airline operated under a strict liability regime, the tour operator did not. (It *could* have followed that path, as we say; but in fact it would not have, as the judge held obiter that, in case he was wrong on the primary point, the hotel was negligent anyway in their management of the pool!)

Beware Tunnel Vision

It is easy to fall into the trap of thinking that travel/holiday law exists in a bubble, proceeding on its own sweet way. But of course that is not the case. Non-travel related developments are an important influence too. Examples which must be kept in mind are:

- The House of Lords decision in *Tomlinson v Congleton BC* [2003] UKHL 47. This case changed the "mood music" of leisure claims, with its emphasis on the freedom of the individual to pursue leisure activities, even those with some risk attached; and an attack on "dull and grey safety regimes" which are, astonishingly, described as evil. A young man had dived into shallow water in a country park, and suffered severe injury; Lord Hoffmann said: "Any premises can be said to be dangerous to someone who chooses to use them for some dangerous activity. The risk arose out of what he chose to do and not out of the state of the premises." This case was followed by the Court of Appeal decision in *Keown v*

Coventry Healthcare NHS Trust [2006] EWCA 39; the defendant knew that children used their premises as a play area. An 11-year-old boy climbed a fire escape in the grounds and fell from it, from about 30 feet up. The trial judge found for the claimant saying that the Trust knew of the children playing, and of the risk. They should have taken steps to protect children, which would not have been expensive. The Court of Appeal, relying on *Tomlinson*, reversed this. Did it make any difference that the claimant was a child? Longmore L.J. said that it was "a question of fact and degree"; a toddler in a derelict house might be one thing; but "it would not be right to ignore a child's choice to indulge in a dangerous activity". An 11-year-old who climbed in this way appreciated the risk of falling, and that what he was doing was dangerous. Further, the judge was horrified that the Trust had now put up a perimeter fence, and a guard was on duty to turn away children. "The hospital ground is becoming a bit like a fortress. The amenity ... which children had of harmlessly playing in the grounds has now been lost. It is not reasonable to expect that this should happen to avoid the occasional injury, however sad". (Note these cases were decided under the Occupiers' Liability Acts; while these Acts do not apply to overseas premises, it has been held that the reasonable skill and care test in holiday cases amounts to the same basis of liability as that in the Acts, when looking at premises—see the *Isle and Dean* case referred to below).

- The relevance of *Tomlinson* (and indeed of *Isle and Dean*) is confirmed by Richards L.J. in *Evans*. He said "the core reasoning in *Tomlinson's* case ... was that people should accept responsibility for the risks they choose to run and that there should be no duty to protect them from obvious risks" (see judgment paras 39–40).

- For a holiday case which followed a similar logic to *Keown*, see *Labourn v Thomas Cook Tour Operations Ltd* Unreported January 30, 2008, Leeds County Court, in which an 11-year-old girl, having gone the long and safe way round the hotel grounds to retrieve a ball which had become stuck on a cliff ledge, then decided to speed the return by climbing down the sheer cliff face with the inevitable consequence. Held: A child of that age could appreciate the danger/risk, and there was no negligence by the tour operator.

- The follow up to this was s.1 of the Compensation Act 2006. This provides:

"A court considering a claim in negligence or breach of statutory duty may, in determining whether the defendant should have taken particular steps to meet a standard of care (whether by taking precautions against a risk or otherwise) have regard to whether a requirement to take those steps might—

(a) prevent a desirable activity from being undertaken at all, to a particular extent or in a particular way, or
(b) discourage persons from undertaking functions in connection with a desirable activity".

There has been much debate about the meaning of "desirable activities" but they can certainly be argued to include holidays, and excursions and activities offered while on holiday. (There may also be an issue as to whether a claim for negligent breach of contract is included in "a claim for negligence"; in our view it probably is.). But it has to be said that we are unaware of any holiday or travel case in which the Compensation Act has influenced the decision.

- Although we have seen that the claimant carries the burden of proof (the C *(A Child)*, *Hone* and *Holden* cases referred to above), it must always be remembered that such burden only arises if, in a case where the facts alleged are consistent with negligence, the defendant had discharged the "evidential burden" of supplying some evidence consistent with absence of negligence. In *Ward v Tesco Stores Ltd* [1976] 1 All E.R. 219, the claimant was unable to prove how long the yoghurt, on which she had slipped, had been on the floor. Tesco said therefore that she could not discharge the burden of proof; but the Court of Appeal held that, as Tesco had provided no real evidence consistent with their lack of negligence, the burden of proof did not arise. It was on this basis that the claimant won the case of *Hilton v Mytravel*, above. So defendants cannot merely sit back and do nothing, relying on the burden of proof being on the claimant. The point was raised by the claimant in *Drabble*, referred to above, but Keane L.J. said that in *Ward v Tesco*, it was the fact of the presence of the spillage which called for explanation, not the accident. In *Drabble*, the presence of the glass did not call for explanation. And now the Court of Appeal has cast further restrictions on when the principle in *Ward* will apply.

- In *Hufton v Somerset CC* [2011] EWCA Civ 789, the claimant was injured when she slipped on water on the floor of school premises. Jackson L.J. (in rejecting the claimant's appeal) distinguished *Ward* on the ground that the defendant had a system in place to avoid such accidents, and whilst they had failed to follow it 100 per cent, they had operated it such as to avoid any accidents in the previous six years. Unlike in *Ward*, there were not frequent risks of slippages calling for special attention. For a case going the other way see *Dawkins v Carnival Plc* [2011] EWCA Civ 1237 where spillages were held to be likely in a cruise ship restaurant, and the defendant called no evidence.

Specific Issues

Dangerous Destinations

From terrorist attacks to street crime, political unrest, and outbreaks of illness; what is the liability of a tour operator when such events affect a destination?

In one case, Torquay County Court decided that where illness is known by the tour operator to be prevalent in a resort there is a duty to warn customers—*Davey v Cosmos Air Holidays* [1989] C.L.Y. 2561. In *Beales v Airtours* Unreported 1996, CA, the claimants had booked a holiday whereby they chose to go to the Algarve but the precise location of the resort and hotel were left to the tour operator. Whilst in the resort of Vilamoura the claimant and his wife were mugged. They sued the tour operator for sending them to a dangerous destination. It was held by the Court of Appeal (on an application for permission to appeal) that the claimants had no case. Saville L.J. said:

> "To my mind the starting point of the claim advanced by Mr Beales must be that Vilamoura was at the material time a resort in the Algarve marked out as one of special danger to holiday-makers from the activities of street robbers. The reason for this is that it is Mr and Mrs Beales themselves who chose to go to a resort in the Algarve, leaving only the specific choice of resort to the tour operators. Having themselves chosen that part of the world for their holidays, it seems to me, really as a matter of common sense as much as a matter of law, that Mr and Mrs Beales could hardly complain of the state of affairs in resorts in the Algarve generally. Thus, apart from anything else, it seems to me that Mr Beales, to have any chance of success, has to demonstrate that Vilamoura, as opposed to resorts in the Algarve generally, fell into a special category of danger to holiday-makers of such a marked kind that either the tour operator should have refrained from sending holiday-makers to that resort at all or at least should have given more than the general warnings that they did give to holiday-makers and to Mr and Mrs Beales." (See [1996] T.L.J. 167 for a short commentary on this case)

This can be seen as a case where the tour operator was held not liable for the actions of a third party. Pushing the logic of the case to its extremes it appears that a tour operator can never be liable for sending a client to a dangerous destination *which the client has chosen*. However, in our view tour operators cannot afford to be complacent—a slightly different set of facts could very well produce a different result. Indeed, it does not seem that tour operators themselves believe this to represent the extent of their legal duties; they follow Foreign Office advice and will stop holidays to a destination which the foreign Office declares "off-limits" (as, for example, happened following a terrorist attack in Bali). The 2009 ABTA Code (para.2H) requires members to advise customers of the availability of advice on the FCO website.

Nonetheless, one sees the *Beales* principle applied in cases such as *Robinson v Balkan Holidays* Unreported 2006, Southport County Court, where a complaint that a Black Sea resort was spoiled by the large numbers of prostitutes plying for trade was dismissed; the claimants chose to go there and that was what the area was like.

A variation on the theme was the case of *Jones v Sunworld Ltd* [2003] EWHC 591. This involved a holiday to one of the Maldive islands; the hotel was the only feature on the island, on clearly delineated grounds. Beyond that was the lagoon, which guests frequently walked round, splashing through the surf. When Mr Jones drowned because the sea bed suddenly shelved down, and he fell below the water, the question arose: can a tour operator be liable for events beyond the boundaries of the hotel? Field J. said:

> "In my opinion it would be wholly artificial to draw a line in the sand along the water's edge and say that the landward area was within the resort and hence within the package but the lagoon, marked off as it was from the open sea by the house reef, was not part of the resort and was therefore outside the package. It does not follow from this finding that the defendant was obliged to assess the safety of the lagoon in the same manner as it assessed (and was

156

obliged to assess) the safety of the buildings and paved areas on the island which could relatively easily be inspected for such things as fire safety and other risks to physical harm. Given the nature and size of the lagoon, I do not think that the defendant was under an obligation to survey it to discover features that might have a bearing on its safety. Instead, I find that the defendant was obliged to undertake a visual inspection of the lagoon, to enquire of the resort's management if they were aware of any particular features of the lagoon that might have a bearing on safety and to inspect the records kept by the resort of any accidents reported to have occurred in the lagoon. There is no evidence that the defendant carried out any of these steps."

Thus, it can be seen that there is an obligation on the tour operator to make inspection, albeit at a lower level than that required for hotel, etc, premises.

Contributory Negligence

Whilst it can be said that individual cases are fact sensitive, nonetheless, there are enough cases to enable us to distinguish trends.

In *Brannan v Airtours Plc, The Times*, February 1, 1999, Airtours had organised an entertainment evening. They pointed out to customers the overhead fans. The claimant was hemmed into a corner and, having been plied with alcohol all evening, needed to go to the toilet. He climbed onto the table and was injured by the fan. Airtours had put him in this difficult position where injury was foreseeable; on the other hand, the danger was patent, not hidden, and warning had been given. Not surprisingly, perhaps, the Court of Appeal decided that Airtours were liable but reduced the damages by 50 per cent because of the contributory negligence of the claimant.

Contrast this with *Williams v First Choice* [2001] C.L.Y. 4282 a plate smashing evening which resulted in injury to the claimant. Here it was held that the defendants had taken all necessary precautions to warn customers about their behaviour, and to avoid the risks.

In *Logue v Flying Colours* [2001] C.L.Y. 4281, a case similar on its facts to *Wilson v Best Travel*, the defendant was found not liable for the injuries caused when the claimant went through a glass patio door; but the judge commented that had he found the defendant liable, he would have reduced the claimant's damages by 75 per cent for contributory negligence as he was considerably affected by alcohol.

In *Isle and Dean v Thomson Holidays Limited* Unreported 2000, QBD, the claimants, also to some extent inebriated, were looking for somewhere to relieve themselves late at night and fell down an insufficiently guarded cliff. The defendants were held liable, but with 60 per cent contributory negligence by the claimants, who had been at the hotel for two weeks and knew the layout of it. (It is interesting to speculate whether the case would still have the same result today, following the case of *Tomlinson v Congleton BC* described above.)

Similar considerations led to a reduction of 33 per cent against a claimant who slipped on a marble ramp on the tenth day of his holiday. The anti-slip tape on the marble was missing, but the claimant was aware of the hazard (*Shore v First Choice* Unreported, 2002, Bristol County Court.

In *Moore v Hotelplan Ltd (t/a Inghams Travel)* (see the section on excursions below), the primary cause of the claimant's loss of control of the snowmobile was found to be defective tuition; but a 30 per cent contributory negligence finding was made because the claimant did not use the brake, when she could have done so.

And in *Evans v Kosmar*, above, Richards L.J. held that had he found liability against Kosmar, he would have made a finding of 50 per cent contributory negligence.

Another case where a 50 per cent contribution was found was *Hurst v Thomson Holidays Ltd* [2004] C.L.Y. 1879; this arose out of a pool game called "the biggest splash" (the sophisticated readership of this book will not require an explanation of the rules of such a game!). Thomson were found liable because insufficient explanation of the risks and proper procedures was given to participants; but the claimant should have acted more sensibly herself.

However, a claimant attending a line dancing class could be expected to be concentrating on learning these new skills rather than looking out for drink spillages on the floor, so there was no finding of contributory negligence in *Cook v First Choice Holidays* Unreported October 22, 2003. (Note this case is criticised, but on other points, in *Holden v First Choice*, above.)

Children and Parents

Unfortunately, accidents on holiday sometimes befall children. The duty of care of a tour operator towards children is that of the reasonable parent, particularly where children are participating in organised "children's club" activities. Where a parent has authorised participation by the child in an activity, there is therefore unlikely to be liability on the tour operator if injury to the child results (unless, of course, there was a defect in the delivery of the activity, e.g. the hotel had failed to maintain playground equipment properly in a way which may not have been obvious to the parent).

Thus, in one unreported case at Liverpool County Court, Thomson Holidays were found not liable to a child who fell and was injured whilst dancing the "hokey cokey", with which the daily children's mini disco always ended. The parents had watched their child on a number of previous occasions, knew exactly what was involved, and had approved it.

A case which vividly and tragically illustrates the circumstances in which the tour operator is liable, the parents are liable, or maybe both are liable to a child, is *R. (A Child) v Iberotravel Ltd* [2001] C.L.Y. 4453. The family consisted of Mr and Mrs Roberts, their son Kevin (the claimant) aged six, and other sons aged nine and one. They arrived at their Spanish hotel late one night. The next day the family visited the pool. Kevin could not swim. He did not have his arm bands. Kevin was in the pool in the company of his nine-year-old brother, and his parents were elsewhere. It was the first day of the holiday. What exactly happened is not known, but two teenage girls pulled Kevin's body from the water and a doctor eventually arrived and resuscitated him; but not in time to prevent serious brain damage. Kevin sued the tour operator Iberotravel. The damages in this case were very substantial, well into seven figures. The Judge decided that liability depended upon two separate questions and each would attract an equal half share of the damages:

1. Why did Kevin get into difficulty?

2. Why was he not rescued sooner?

On the first point the Judge held the tour operator liable because the pool shelved too steeply and it had insufficient warnings about depth, suitability for children, etc. The parents had been made Pt 20 defendants. The Judge (Gibbs J.) said:

" ... the fact remains that Kevin was permitted into the pool unaccompanied, save for his nine-year-old brother. If the pool was unsafe for use by a child who could not swim, it was not in my judgment a reasonably sufficient safeguard to leave him with a child of nine, even one who could swim. Kevin's parents had used armbands for him previously. If he was to be left, even temporarily unattended, then the use of armbands though not a complete safeguard would have been a reasonable and sensible precaution. The reasonableness of the parent's actions has to be seen in a context that the depth and dimensions of the pool were completely unknown to them. It was a foreign country. It was their first visit to it. I regret that I am driven to the conclusion that to allow Kevin into the pool in those circumstances did fall short of the reasonable standard of care to be accepted of them".

In respect of how Kevin got into difficulty, the Judge held that the tour operator was 50 per cent to blame and the parents were 50 per cent to blame.

In respect of the failure to rescue Kevin more quickly, the Judge held, following *Wilson v Best Travel*, that the tour operator was 100 per cent to blame; because in breach of Spanish regulations there was no lifeguard on duty.

Similarly, in *Murphy v JMC Holidays* Unreported 2003, Ashford County Court, parents were found 50 per cent liable on a Pt 20 claim where their four-year-old son fell from a window while eating breakfast with them. The tour operator was liable for creating the danger, the parents for not looking after their child.

Fifty per cent is always a likely result in such cases; if the duty of a tour operator is that of the reasonable parent, and at the same time the actual parent is present, their responsibility might well be seen to be at the same level.

A case which pushed these issues a bit further was *McNeil v Thomas Cook* Unreported 2006, Birmingham County Court. A child had been cheeky and disrespectful to a poolside entertainer, who was "in drag"; the child repeatedly fired his "super-soaker" pistol at the entertainer, and the antique accordion which he carried. The entertainer forcibly dragged the boy from the pool causing bruises and PTSD. The tour operator was liable, and the parents again made the subject of a 50 per cent contribution order; this time, not for failure to supervise, but for failing to discipline, and indeed "egging on" their son in his mischief.

Defective Furniture

For a typical case of a collapsing sun lounger or plastic chair, see *McRae v Thomson Holidays Ltd* [2001] C.L.Y. 4291. The *Hone* principle was applied: did the hotel act with reasonable skill and care in maintaining the chair, or should they have spotted the defects? In this case Thomson were found not liable. *Griffin v My Travel* [2009] NIQB 98, a Northern Ireland High Court case, criticised for its approach to the local standards argument, nevertheless imposed liability for a collapsing bed in a Greek hotel.

Illness

Illness contracted while on holiday tends to fall into three broad categories:

- Legionnaires disease: applying the *Hone* principle, we believe that these claims will often go well for the claimants. As we understand it, a hotel run with reasonable skill and care should not have legionella bacteria in its water supply/air-conditioning and the claimant should have little difficulty proving this.

- Food poisoning: a large outbreak of food poisoning in a hotel, with many people affected, and not duplicated in the rest of the resort, is again suggestive of liability on the part of the hotel and, therefore, the tour operator. It is likely that there has been some lack of reasonable care and skill in preparation or handling of food. Individual one off cases are more of a problem. Where only one person in the hotel suffers food poisoning, e.g. salmonella, it is suggested that the source of the illness may be elsewhere and the tour operator not liable; alternatively, that there has been no sufficient lack of care and skill. Certainly, issues of credibility are raised.

- Cryptosporidiosis: In the UK this illness is most commonly associated with water supplies; in a holiday context, the swimming pool is a common culprit. Because of the way in which the organisms enter the water (faecal accident), such infection can be contracted from the best run pool. However, a poorly run pool, particularly with a poor filtration system, can make matters a lot worse. See *Eldridge v TUI*, 2011, above, for a case where TUI were found liable even without proof of negligence in a cryptosporidium case.

The largest group action against the holiday industry (the *Torremolinos Beach Club Group*) raised issues of liability for Norovirus, which as its name suggests is a virus, not a bacterium or other organism. For the costs implications of such huge group actions, see Mason "If the cap fits" [2005] I.T.L.J. 177. (See also Shafi "Bugs on the Nile" [2006] I.T.L.J. 142.)

In all cases of illness, attention needs to be paid to the incubation periods when considering the issue of causation.

Causation

Curiously, causation provides a hurdle which claimants in holiday cases seem to have difficulty overcoming; in other words, even if they can show that the defendant is in breach of duty, can they show that the breach actually caused the accident?

One case that went in favour of the claimant raised this question: can a statement in a brochure that a hotel is suitable for families be, in law, the cause of a mother falling downstairs whilst, with her husband, carrying a child's buggy, when it turned out that there was no lift access to the restaurant? There was no defect in the stairs. In *Mawdsley v Cosmosair Plc* [2002] EWCA 587, it was held that the tour operator was liable. (For the facts and a fuller discussion see below.)

Note this case was brought under reg.4 as well as in negligent misrepresentation and breach of contract—see below for more detail about this case.

More conventional cases on causation are *Singh v Libra Holidays* [2003] EWHC 276 (QB) where a drunken consumer was injured in an insufficiently marked pool and *Jones v Sunworld* above. Although the defendant in *Jones* had failed to inspect the lagoon area, this did not cause the accident because the shelving sea bed was an unsurprising feature which adults did not need to be warned of. Another swimming pool accident where the claim failed for reasons of causation is *Healy v Cosmosair Plc* [2005] EWHC 1657 (QB). It was true that there was insufficient non-slip material around the pool to comply with local regulations, but this was not the cause of the accident. As we have seen, *Evans v Kosmar* followed a similar pattern on the subsidiary issue of causation.

Indeed, the Court of Appeal has emphasised that causation is a hurdle which must be overcome in personal injury claims—*Clough v First Choice* [2006] EWCA Civ 15. The absence of non-slip paint by a pool created an increased risk but the trial judge held this had not caused or materially contributed to the accident. It was a conclusion which, said the Court of Appeal, he had been entitled to reach.

Excursions

This is a topic on which the courts have been busy of late. Of course, if an excursion is sold as part of a package at an inclusive price, then there is no difficulty in establishing the basis of liability, i.e. in accordance with reg.15 PTR, discussed above. But what if the excursion is sold separately, at a "welcome meeting" or similar, by the rep?

Such excursions do not form part of a package and therefore a consumer acquires no rights under the Regulations in respect of the excursion. Older examples of the consequences of this, for instance, are the case of *Sheppard v Crystal Holidays Ltd* [1997] C.L.Y. 3858, in which the tour operator was found not liable for injuries sustained on holiday due to the negligence of a ski instructor who had been employed by the claimant while in the resort—even though the services has been purchased through the operator's representative. See also the case of *Gallagher v Airtours Holidays Ltd* [2001] C.L.Y. 4280, another skiing accident case. There are difficult questions of the basis of liability; was the tour operator's representative acting as agent for the excursion company in selling the excursion at the welcome meeting? Or is the excursion company agent for the tour operator? Can the tour operator be made liable for negligent misstatements under the principle of *Hedley Byrne v Heller* [1964] A.C. 465? Was the consumer even aware that the excursion was being provided by someone else, or did the tour operator hold out the trip as their own? Much turns on the precise wording of any written or oral terms or representations. See *Patrick v Cosmosair* Unreported March 5, 2001, Manchester County Court discussed in Chapman "Excursions, Tour Operators and the Negligence of Local Suppliers" [2002] I.T.L.J. 123. (See also Fahrenhorst "Case Notes from Germany: Liability of Tour Operators for Excursions Purchased While Abroad" [2006] I.T.L.J. 153.)

What is said about excursions by a tour operator in their booking conditions is important. In *Brook v Direct Holidays* Unreported January 18, 2004, Bradford

CHAPTER FIVE

County Court, the defendant in its booking conditions accepted liability for problems with excursions, although the claim in fact failed because the mountain path down which the claimant had to walk was no different from what one would expect to find. There was no requirement on the defendant to provide a handrail!

The first sign of a hardening in attitude by the Courts towards tour operator excursion liability, and another case in which the precise words mattered a great deal, was the High Court Case of *Moran v First Choice Holidays and Flights Ltd* [2005] EWHC 2478. The claimant purchased a quad bike excursion from the rep at a welcome meeting. The brakes were defective and injury was suffered. In fact, the excursion was offered by a local company in the Dominican Republic. The First Choice welcome pack said "First Choice offer an exciting selection of trips to suit everybody, all our excursions are fully insured and regularly checked to ensure they meet our safety standards". The booking form included the words "there are several pirate companies operating excursions in the Dom Rep. These companies are not used by British tour operators because they do not reach the quality safety and hygiene standards that we as your tour operator demand. We can't accept any responsibility for illness injury or death caused as a result of participating in a pirate excursion". The receipt issued by the rep was on the note paper of a local agency (not the company who ran the quad bike tour however). The Judge (Miss N. Davies QC sitting as a Deputy Judge of the Queens Bench Division) found for the claimant:

"I am satisfied that in respect of the quad bike excursion First Choice did not disclose that it was acting for its pleaded agent, namely Dominican Quad Bike Adventure. It is unsurprising that provided with this documentation the claimant and her husband believed that First Choice was supplying the excursion and with it the relevant safety checks and insurance."

The next issue which arose was this: even if the rep does sell only as agent, and therefore there is no contract, can the tour operator possibly be liable in tort instead?

This was a question which arose in the case of *Parker v TUI UK Ltd* [2009] EWCA Civ 1261. Mrs Parker and her family had booked a holiday in Austria with TUI. Although the internet brochure had mentioned that tobogganing was available at the resort, this was not part of the pre-arranged package so the Package Travel etc Regulations 1992 did not apply. The party approached the rep and were able to book the tobogganing through her, paying by credit card. The supplier of the event was called ACZ. Their bus took people to the toboggan run and they handed out tickets which could be exchanged for a toboggan and a gondola ride. Four TUI reps also attended the run and spread themselves out amongst the 70 guests which included people travelling with other tour operators. The actual toboggan run passed off without incident. About 100 metres before the red light which marked the end of the run came a right hand bend after which the ground flattened out. There was then a slight slope, and then a snow bank with, beyond it, a drop onto a ski piste. Then the road went around a left hand bend quite steeply downhill towards the cable car station. There was a wide expanse of field on either side of this lower road. There was an exit into the car park on the right. At the bottom of this steep slope some straw bales had been

162

placed. The accident happened because Mrs Parker and her passenger had remounted their toboggan and come down the lower road too fast. Trying to avoid the buildings they careered into the straw bales which were hard and frozen. The decision to ride down was partly because they found it difficult to walk on the slippery road down. They could not explain why they did not walk down the side of the road where there was deeper snow, easier to walk on. Other members of their party had done that. There was no TUI rep present at this particular point.

The trial judge held that there was no contract between the claimant and TUI, who had only acted as intermediaries to bring Mrs Parker into a contract with ACZ. There had been no negligence.

The claimant appealed on the ground that the judge had ignored evidence by TUI's resort manager that TUI ran the event under the umbrella of Crystal/Thomson, and that there was negligence because the road had not been gritted and there was no rep in the area to assist or warn.

In the Court of Appeal, Longmore L.J. said it was difficult to say whether there was a contract or not.

"The rep certainly took the money but it must have been clear that it was not TUI who was going to provide the toboggan or the gondola ride. It must also have been clear that those services were going to be provided by a local operator even though the identity of that operator may not have been made clear until the ticket was issued on the bus".

The precise evidence of the resort manager had been,

"even though ACZ were the agents, did the organising for us, we still ran the event under the umbrella of Crystal/Thomson, yes, and we had extremely strict guidelines".

Longmore L.J. said:

"That is very relevant to the question of assumption of responsibility for the purpose of finding a duty of care that is to my mind equivocal in relation to contract. There was evidence from Mrs Owen that the ticket given on the bus had the name of ACZ on the top and in the light of that the Judge was, in my view, entitled to conclude that ACZ gave out the tickets and was the supplier of the service and was the counterparty to the contract [with Mrs Parker]".

But, said the Judge, it was irrelevant whether there was a contract or not, because there was a duty of care.

"Had there been a contract, the only relevant term would be an implied term that TUI would exercise due diligence; whether they did exercise such due diligence is of course the key question in this case".

TUI's barrister argued that there was no duty of care and, as Longmore L.J. put it, that they could "leave their customers to the tender mercies of the elements and the icy terrain at night without a qualm. The Judge did not accept that;

neither did the tour representatives at the time, since they took it on themselves to accompany the run in the way I have described. Their own recognition of their responsibility ... is enough to persuade me that TUI accepted responsibility to their customers and owed them a duty of care in tort".

On the facts, the Judge found that there was no negligence. He said

"it comes down to the question whether someone should have positioned themselves at the corner as well as (or instead of) at the end of the run. The purpose of thus positioning such a person would only have been to repeat the warning, already given, not to remount the toboggan and to point out the obvious fact that it was more feasible to tread in the snow at the edge of the road rather than on the road itself. I cannot bring myself to hold that it is the duty of the tour operator dealing with rational adults on a winter holiday to repeat simple warnings already given with clarity or to point out obvious dangers of ice on the road and the relative safety of snow at its side. So to hold would only encourage potential claimants to believe that whenever an injury occurs someone must be to blame. That is not what the law of negligence is about".

As is often the case, it is the obiter comments which cause difficulty, rather than the actual decision, which was clear enough. On reading the judgment we are left wondering:

(a) What is meant by liability for "due diligence"? Does that mean liability for any mistake which the supplier might make? Or the lesser liability of checking out the supplier to ensure they are reputable and run a safe excursion? The phrase normally suggests the latter, e.g. in trading standards type cases. But the position is far from clear.

(b) What would have happened if no reps had attended the excursion at all? Would TUI have been found liable or would that merely have been proof that they did not owe a duty of care? Either are possible interpretations of the judgment; which is the correct one though? And how can decisions be made by tour operators against a background of such uncertainty? We would venture to suggest that it comes down again to the wording of the actual paperwork, what is said at point of sale, and all the surrounding circumstances.

See also *Harrison v Jagged Globe* Unreported April 17, 2011, Central London County Court, currently awaiting a Court of Appeal decision. A case which went the other way on the contract point is *Moore v Hotelplan Ltd (t/a Inghams Travel)* [2010] EWHC Civ 276 (QB), in the High Court. Mrs Moore was part of a large party who booked a snowmobile excursion from the rep. Inghams argued that the rep was acting as an agent for the snowmobile operator. However, the judge found differently. He relied on the following: the brochure description of the skiing resort had a list of attractions in the resort ranging from tobogganing to pizzerias and bars, and including snowmobiles. The information booklet sent out shortly before departure, and after the contract was made, said that the representative would try to arrange events which could include a variety of matters including snowmobiles.

"Please note that payments for these optional events will always be made with credit cards. Representatives will provide you with full details of all available excursions and resort activities. Certain activities deemed as hazardous are not organised or promoted by Inghams and as such we can take no responsibility in respect of them. Our local staff will be available to advise you on the events we can offer".

A leaflet was handed out giving a list of excursions which Inghams could organise, including "Skidoo Sensation". The leaflet said "our suppliers operate a strict cancellation policy, 24 hours cancellation notice required". They met the rep and paid her in cash. She, in turn, gave them a receipt with the Inghams logo. Members of the party gave evidence. Some described the arrangements in terms that suggested their contract was with Inghams. Others were aware that there was a supplier who was providing the snowmobiles, and talked in terms of "commission" and other agency concepts.

Upon arriving at the snowmobile garage shortly before the excursion, the party were handed by the rep a disclaimer form in Italian and English heading "declaration of liability". It was a form prepared by the actual provider of the trip, intended for his benefit. The rep told the Court:

"This is a disclaimer I had and that's the one that I used, well I didn't have the Inghams one on me at the time and so I used this one so that the guests would be aware that they had to take responsibility for their own driving".

The judge concluded that if Inghams were acting as an agent, why did they normally feel the need to use their own disclaimer? Indeed, the Inghams reps manual included a provision that "you may sell skidoo/snowmobiles only if ... you obtain the guest's signature beforehand on the disclaimer, absolving the company of third party liability".

The judge was also persuaded by an answer given by the Italian supplier himself in evidence; when asked whose customers he thought the passengers were, his or Inghams', he replies "Inghams' ".

So the judge held that Inghams contracted as principals. But on what terms?

The claimant argued that the excursion should be treated as part of the package holiday contract, and on the same terms (i.e. whereby liability for negligence of suppliers was incurred as required by reg.15 PTR). The Judge got to the same conclusion but by a different route. He found that all the above indications showed that it was Inghams who were providing the excursion. The contract was with Inghams; but it was not part of the original package. In a controversial passage, the Judge (Owen J.) said,

"The holiday contract provided the context within which the excursion contract was entered into. To view it in isolation from that contract would be wholly artificial. Given the existing contractual relationship between the parties, I am satisfied that the contract to supply the skidoo excursion was impliedly subject to the terms of the holiday contract, and in particular to the 'our liability' clause in the booking conditions ... accordingly the defendant is liable to the claimant under the terms of the excursion contract for injury and consequent losses caused by the lack of reasonable care and skill on the part of the [the snowmobile organiser]."

In other words, he implied into the excursion contract the same terms that were in the package contract. (But would the tour operator have said "oh, of course", had the officious bystander asked the parties during their negotiations whether this was what they intended? But see also the test for implied terms formulated by Lord Hoffmann in *Att-Gen of Belize v Belize Telecom Ltd* [2009] UKPC 10.)

He found that the organiser had not pointed out, during his instructions on the use of snowmobiles, the engine cut out button for use in emergencies. After 45 minutes of driving the skidoos, Mrs Moore drove too close to the vehicle in front, panicked, veered to the right, grabbed the accelerator instead of the brake, and continued to accelerate until she crashed into a parked car in the adjoining car park. It was held that Inghams were liable because, had the cut out button been pointed out, it was likely that Mrs Moore would have used it and it was likely that the vehicle would have stopped in time to avoid the catastrophic injuries suffered. (For details of the finding re contributory negligence see the section on that topic above.)

The finding that package travel-style liability should be imposed in the sale of an excursion is, it is submitted, a bold one. If such terms ought to be implied into the contract, one wonders why the Package Travel Regulations were necessary at all, if such terms merely represent the pre-existing common law.

Yet again, we would submit that the answer lies in precise wording and surrounding circumstances. The package booking conditions can, of course, endeavour to provide different conditions applicable to locally sold excursions, if that is what the tour operator desires. But there needs to be consistency throughout the process, including the way in which the trip is sold, what guidance is given to reps, and how the money is handled. (See further Mason "Alarms and Excursions" [2010] T.L.Q. 75.)

Finally, many excursions sold by tour operators' representatives in popular Mediterranean resorts amount to packages in their own right. These raise difficult questions of jurisdiction—as do excursions where it is the local supplier who has liability—which are dealt with in Ch.14. (See Prager "The Assumption of Responsibility in Holiday Cases: The Impact of *Parker v TUI* [2009] EWCA Civ 1261 on Unregulated Holidays" [2011] T.L.Q. 83 for a discussion of a case, *Harrison v Jagged Globe* (currently being appealed), which raises difficult questions of liability for local suppliers.)

The ABTA Code of Conduct

At the time of going to press, there is a 2009 Code with 2011 Guidance and 2008 Standards on Brochures and Booking Conditions. The Standards in effect merely say that members must accept the liability that is imposed by the law, including the Unfair Terms in Consumer Contracts Regulations 1999 (see Ch.6). The major consumer bonus found in the Code is para.2I, and para.7 of the Guidance, which requires an organiser to notify (and allow to transfer elsewhere) consumers where building work will seriously impair enjoyment of the holiday, regardless of whether the building work is a breach of the contractual obligations or not (e.g. if work was on neighbouring premises to the hotel); cf. *Griffiths v Flying Colours*

Holidays Ltd [1999] C.L.Y. 3820). The Standards on Brochures also require that information about noise which might cause offence (e.g. airports, discos, etc) must be given in brochures.

Rendering Assistance—(1) The Regulations

If consumers are injured or mugged on holiday or if their money and passports are stolen they are clearly going to be in some difficulty. Even if they have insurance which will cover the financial consequences of such a disaster they are nevertheless often a long way from home and the support of family and friends. They may not be able to speak the language of the country they find themselves in and they may not understand the complexities of the legal or medical systems they have to contend with. It is for reasons like this that reg.15 provides that even in situations where the tour operator is not at fault the operator must nevertheless offer assistance to consumers. This is an area where the ABTA Code of Conduct also contains provisions to protect the consumer. However, there are significant differences between the Regulations and the Code. For the sake of completeness, therefore, we will look first at the Regulations and then at the Code of Conduct.

Prompt Assistance

If there has been some failure in the contract but the organiser is not liable under reg.15(2)(b) and (c) he is nevertheless under an obligation to render prompt assistance.
Regulation 15(7) provides:

"15(7) In the circumstances described in paragraph (2)(b) and (c) of this regulation, the other party to the contract will give prompt assistance to a consumer in difficulty."

The Regulation requires that there be a *failure in the performance of the contract* before this provision is triggered—not simply a client in difficulty, as in the ABTA Code which will be examined shortly. So, for instance, if the consumer was run down by a drunk driver while coming back from the beach the organiser would be under no obligation to do anything. The accident may have been caused by a third party unconnected with the provision of the services but it did not result in "failure to perform" or "improper performance" of the contract. It would be different if vandals had wrecked the air-conditioning system of the hotel or if a transfer bus had been hit by a drunken driver. In those circumstances there would be failure of performance of the contract. The organiser would not be liable but would have to render assistance. (See *Josephs v Sunworld* [1998] C.L.Y. 3734 for a decision on this point which seems clearly wrong; see also *Coughlan v Thomson Holidays Ltd* [2001] C.L.Y. 4276 for a case where the court held that assistance should have been given more promptly.)
No financial limit is placed on this assistance and it is difficult to establish to what lengths the tour operator is obliged to go to in order to comply. Does it merely extend to the giving of advice or making appropriate telephone calls or does it go further? If more concrete help is extended, e.g. taking the client to hospital or putting them on a flight home, can the tour operator charge for this?

The answer is far from clear but some indication may be gained from an examination of reg.15(8) which is dealt with below.

Finding Appropriate Solutions

Regulation 15(8) provides:

> "15(8) If the consumer complains about a defect in the performance of the contract, the other party to the contract, or his local representative, if there is one, will make prompt efforts to find appropriate solutions."

This is the corollary to reg.15(9) which imposes a duty on the consumer to complain if he finds fault with the package. If the consumer complains then the organiser must endeavour to do something about it. The difficulty is in establishing whether it adds anything to the requirement in reg.15(7) to render "prompt assistance". The answer seems to be that reg.15(7) only covers situations where the organiser is *not liable* to the consumer whereas reg.15(8) covers all situations where the consumer has a complaint about defects in the performance of the contract—although, as Saggerson says at p.239, it must be assumed that the complaint has to be a justified one. The interesting point is that in cases of no breach of contract covered by reg.15(7) the organiser seems to be under a more onerous duty—to render "assistance"—than when there is a breach of contract where the duty is to make "efforts" to find an appropriate solution. The answer probably lies in the fact that reg.15(7) refers to consumers *in difficulty*. This suggests a more serious level of need and therefore greater efforts need to be taken to remedy the situation.

Neither reg.15(7) nor reg.15(8) imposes a limit on the efforts the organiser is required to make. One can envisage a situation where a tour operator has thousands of clients waiting at the airport because of an air traffic controllers' strike. Clearly the organiser is *obliged* to do something, either under reg.15(7) or reg.15(8). But if this means providing bed and board for them at great expense is this cost to be borne by the organiser or the consumer? Under reg.15(7) the answer would point to the consumer. If the organiser is not in breach then even though he must render assistance he may be able to claim an indemnity from the consumer for any expense should he so wish. Under reg.15(8), assuming a breach of contract, the answer may be different. Here, the Regulations are saying that as the organiser is in breach then he must mend that breach, not by the payment of damages, but in some more practical form by putting the problem right. It is important to bear in mind that in this example the consumer may very well have other remedies available to him under reg.14, discussed in Ch.10 on Remedies, and under Regulation 261/2004 on denied boarding, long delays and cancellation of flights, discussed in detail in Ch.13.

This view of reg.15(8) corresponds with the provisions of reg.14 with which it overlaps. Where there is a non-provision of services after departure, reg.14 provides that the organiser *must* make suitable alternative arrangements and may also have to pay damages. In cases therefore of *non-provision* the consumer would make his case under reg.14 whereas for *improper* provision the claim would be made under reg.15(8). It would be strange if the remedy under reg.15 were to be different than under reg.14.

In *Russell v Thomas Cook* Unreported 2006, Preston County Court, the District Judge found the defendant not liable for mosquitoes in a hotel, but still ordered them to pay the cost of the return airfares incurred by the claimants who left early because of the mosquitoes. The finding was said to be under reg.15(8) but, as there was no defect in performance of the contract by the defendant, the decision was clearly wrong; and the claimant conceded the point on appeal.

All these issues became pressing during the "volcanic ash" crisis of April 2010, and they are fully explored in Ch.13. For now, it suffices to say that where consumers are stranded overseas at the end of their holiday and unable to return home it seems that the only duties on the tour operator under reg.15 are to render "assistance". However, the duties under reg.14 may be more extensive—see Ch.10 on Remedies. What is clear, however, is that the primary duty in these circumstances falls upon carriers under Regulation 261/2004 on denied boarding, long delay and cancellation of flights. Persuading carriers of this, however, is another matter.

Rendering Assistance—(2) The ABTA Code of Conduct

The first thing to say is that the Code contains no precise equivalent of reg.15(7) or (8). Neither does the 2009 Code contain the former detailed provisions, allowing inter alia for legal expenses to be paid by the tour operator to assist a customer who wishes to sue a third party who had caused them injury, etc. What it does have is para.4E. This simply states: "Where appropriate and subject to their reasonable discretion, [ABTA Principals] shall provide prompt assistance to Clients in difficulty."

Client in Difficulty

The ABTA requirement has the merit of simplicity. It avoids all the problems we have found in regs.15(7) or (8); there does not have to be any breach of contract before this provision kicks in. If the client is "in difficulty", they are entitled to prompt assistance—albeit at the operator's discretion and where appropriate. This probably means that the assistance should not be unreasonably withheld. If the client is in a difficulty of their own making—e.g. they have assaulted someone and been arrested, or been ejected from the hotel for damaging it, or are suffering from a drugs overdose—these may justify the operator in withholding assistance. But even in these cases, many operators would help as a matter of moral, rather than legal, obligation. Most other difficulties would be covered—e.g. the consumer has been injured while crossing the road, or has had their passport stolen by a mugger, or has simply fallen ill and needs help (ranging from telling people at home, help with the authorities or sorting out insurance details). The essence of the paragraph is that the tour operator shall lend assistance to clients in circumstances where the tour operator is not contractually liable to them but nevertheless they are deserving of help.

As in reg.15, no guidance is given as to the financial value of such help as is required. It may be that where money has to be expended, this can be done on an "emergency loan" basis.

REGULATION 4

We turn now to reg.4 which creates a statutory right to compensation for the consumer that cuts across the traditional boundaries of the common law. It imposes civil liability on both tour operators and travel agents if they supply misleading information. It states:

> "4(1) No organiser or retailer shall supply to a consumer any descriptive matter concerning a package, the price of a package or any other conditions applying to the contract which contains any misleading information.
>
> (2) If an organiser or retailer is in breach of paragraph (1) he shall be liable to compensate the consumer for any loss which the consumer suffers in consequence."

The elements of the Regulation are that if:

- an organiser or a retailer
- supplies
- descriptive matter
- to a consumer
- containing misleading information
- concerning a package
- compensation will be payable for any losses suffered as a consequence."

We shall examine these elements in turn.

Organiser or Retailer

The significant point here is that the travel agent retailer as well as the tour operator could incur liability. (Remember that retailers also include newspapers or magazines selling "Readers Offers" type trips.) Not only that, but there is also the possibility that it is the agent who will be first in the firing line. If the consumer has a complaint about a misleading brochure then there is a chance that he will take it up first with his agent, who is local, rather than the operator who will usually not be as accessible. It may be that the agent can deflect complaints by blaming the operator but this may not always be possible. The Sale of Goods Act, for instance, has educated many consumers to the concept of the retailer being liable to them rather than the manufacturer. The true difficulty for the travel agent, however, is that the liability appears absolute; there is no defence. In the equivalent criminal legislation, such as the Consumer Protection from Unfair Trading Regulations 2008, there is a due diligence defence but it appears that under reg.4 once it can be shown that the travel agent did the supplying then he will be liable without fault. It is as well for travel agents that the public have as yet shown little appetite to target them instead of tour operators.

It is hard to over emphasise the effect reg.4 could have on travel agents. It creates civil liability for every detail in a tour operator's brochure that is misleading—the location, the price, the meal plan, the hotel facilities, the resort facilities, the availability of excursions, the availability of car hire, etc. The only way to combat this liability is to ensure that the agency agreements they have with operators contain indemnity clauses. Whether they do may very well be a matter of bargaining power (see Ch.11); but an indemnity will be valueless in the likely event that the consumer exercises his right to sue the retailer because the tour operator is insolvent, which is perhaps the most likely scenario in which the consumer will prefer to pursue the retailer. (See *Minhas v Imperial Travel* [2003] C.L.Y. 2043 on this point.)

Supplies

It is beyond doubt that a tour operator is the person who supplies the brochure to the consumer, even though it is distributed via an intermediary, but the question arises as to whether the travel agent is also a supplier. In the sense that he is not the originator or publisher of the brochure and is only the means by which the tour operator supplies the consumer with the brochure it could be argued that he is not the supplier—any more than a vending machine is the supplier of cigarettes or confectionery. On the other hand, the travel agent does exercise some judgment in the matter—he chooses which tour operators to deal with; he decides which brochures to rack; and he decides which brochures might appeal to the consumer. As such, he is not simply a passive conduit and therefore should bear responsibility. This was surely the intention of the Regulation.

What about the client who acquires a misleading brochure from Agent A but then books his holiday through Agent B? Although B has booked the holiday he is not liable under reg.4 because he did not supply the brochure (although ironically he may very well have dozens of other such brochures in his agency). Agent A has supplied the brochure but has not had the advantage of making a sale. Is he to be liable even though he has no connection with the contract which ultimately results? On the one hand, he has aided in the deception by racking the brochure in the first place, on the other, it seems a little harsh to penalise him when he has not profited from the transaction.

Closer examination of reg.4 may provide the answer. For liability to be imposed it must be shown that the misleading descriptive matter concerned:

"a package, the price of a package or any other conditions applying to *the contract*". (Emphasis added)

"Contract" is further defined in reg.2(1) as meaning:

"the agreement linking the consumer to the organiser or to the retailer or both, as the case may be".

Taking these together, it suggests that Agent A will escape liability because although he was a retailer who supplied a brochure he was not a retailer who supplied it in relation to a contract which linked him to the consumer and the organiser.

One way in which reg.4 is wider than an action in misrepresentation (see Ch.7) is that there seems no requirement that the information be supplied *before* the contract is concluded or that it induced the contract. It might be the case that after the contract is concluded the consumer returns to the travel agency and asks for clarification about the features of the resort where he has booked his holiday and the travel agent photocopies a page from a gazetteer for the consumer which contains misleading information. This would appear to be a contravention of the Regulation. Alternatively, the client may have booked the holiday without the benefit of a brochure, using viewdata alone, and then subsequently returns to the travel agency and acquires a misleading brochure. Traditionally, the ticket wallet supplied by the tour operator shortly before departure contains much information about the resort and the itinerary, all of which could potentially ground a claim if misleading. More complex cases might arise. Take, for example, the case of a Mediterranean cruise calling at a number of ports where particular shore excursions are possible. Let us say that when the ship docks in Malaga and passengers are given a sheet of tourist information that states, amongst other things, that the castle in Malaga—one of the excursions mentioned—is open for the duration of the ship's stay. A consumer, in reliance on this information, hires a taxi to take him to the castle only to find it closed for renovation works. He has been supplied with misleading descriptive matter and suffered in consequence. It would appear he had a good case for compensation. Whether the courts will be happy to extend liability to post-contractual matter in this way remains to be seen.

Descriptive Matter

The liability is imposed for supplying misleading descriptive *matter* not simply the supply of misleading *information*. The implication here is that it will cover written matter but not oral statements. The word "matter" suggests something tangible. It will obviously cover brochures and other brochure-like leaflets and it would most probably extend to videos of holiday destinations. It probably does not extend to window displays or window cards because the requirement is that the matter be *supplied to* the consumer and it cannot be said that such matter is supplied to the consumer. Press advertisements are a different matter. It is a moot point whether it can be said that the operator or the retailer have supplied the matter. It comes in a paper or journal supplied by a publisher or newsagent.

Now that most tour operators and travel agents have websites, there exists the possibility that reg.4 could be broken by placing misleading information on the website. But does this involve the supply of misleading descriptive *matter*? In the light of what has been said above it appears that the Regulation will only be broken when the consumer downloads the information and prints it off—simply reading it on the screen may not be enough—a rather unsatisfactory distinction. A consumer excluded in this way would have to rely on narrower rights in misrepresentation. It is interesting to compare this position with the contrasting effect of the words "directs activities to" consumers, under art.15 of EC44/2001, and recent ECJ case law thereunder. See Ch.14.

A Consumer

The extended meaning of consumer would apply here. Thus, a tour operator might find himself liable to holidaymakers with whom he did not originally have any contractual relationship, e.g. transferees and other beneficiaries—so long as it could be shown that there was a supply by the operator to these other consumers.

Containing Misleading Information

Misleading is a word which goes much further than "inaccurate" or "false". The clear indication here is that although the information may be technically correct, if it gives rise to a false impression then liability will result; the emphasis is thus on the impression reasonably created in the mind of the consumer, whereas "false" refers to matters which are more objectively measurable. Cropped photographs are an example. Technically, the photograph may be accurate in that it correctly depicts the hotel sited right on the seafront skirted by golden sands, but by failing to show the shanty town just next door it conveys a misleading impression. (This is mirrored by the criminal offence of a "misleading omission" under reg.6 of the 2008 Regulations—see Ch.17.) One adjudication by the Advertising Standards Authority concerned misleading photographs. The ASA received a complaint from a holidaymaker who had booked a holiday with Airtours from their "Golden Years" brochure. The brochure claimed "Thousands more holidays for the over 50s" on the front cover and contained photographs of groups of middle-aged and elderly people. The complainant, who found that the age of guests at her resort ranged from 10 months to 86 years, objected to the misleading impression that holidaymakers at the resorts featured would be over 50 years old. In upholding the complaint the ASA agreed that the photographs in the brochure could give readers the overall impression that the accommodation was exclusively for the over-50s. (ASA Monthly Report No.78 p.7). We hasten to add that this is not a decision under reg.4 but it shows how photographs can be misleading.

One wonders, however, at what point the courts would cease to hold the information misleading and say that it amounted to mere puff with no legal effect. For example, take a brochure which sold holidays to India and which featured a photograph of the Taj Mahal on the front cover. In front of the Taj Mahal is the reflecting pool and behind it is a red sun, low on the horizon, bathing the monument and the pool in a rosy glow. What could be more romantic? The truth, however, may be a little more prosaic. When tourists arrive they find that the rosy glow is rather more permanent than they anticipated because it is caused by the effect of viewing the sun through the acrid stifling smog that smothers the area for much of the year. This is not a sunset but a by product of an environmental disaster. But is it misleading? Technically, of course, the information is correct; it is possible to see such a sight at the Taj Mahal. It is the impression created by the photograph that is misleading—it leads consumers to believe that this is a sunset, viewable only at certain times of the day when in fact, due to the smog, it is visible all day and very disappointing because of that. But are consumers misled or is this mere puff? Presumably the test will be: what would the reasonable consumer understand by the picture and would they be misled? (See the section below on *Mawdsley v Cosmosair*, which shows how wide "misleading" can be.)

Disclaimers may also have a bearing on the question of what is misleading. Tour operators frequently state that facilities and services may not be available or may be temporarily out of order. This is a typical example:

> "All due care and diligence has been exercised in the production of this brochure. All of the information in this brochure concerning resorts, hotels and their facilities has been compiled as accurately as possible by our own staff and has been checked at the time of going to press. However there may be times when certain amenities are temporarily not available and it is possible, particularly in the low season, that a facility we have described in our brochure may have been modified or is not available. For example electrical equipment and lifts may break down and some of the shops, restaurants and night-clubs may not be in full operation. Such situations may be dictated by local circumstances, unsuitable weather conditions, necessity for maintenance or redecoration, local licensing regulations or government fuel saving legislation There may be a charge made payable locally for some facilities e.g. cots, sauna, gymnasium. tennis, squash courts, TV in rooms etc." (Direct Cruises, Summer 1998 brochure, 2nd edn) (Such a clause should be read in the context of the OFT's 2004 Guidance on Unfair Terms in package holiday contracts, which implies that such terms would be unfair in its view.)

To be effective we would suggest that a starting point would be the old Trade Descriptions case of *Norman v Bennett* [1974] 1 W.L.R. 1229 where Lord Widgery C.J. said that a disclaimer which was "as bold, precise and compelling" as the original description would be effective to negate the effect of a false odometer reading on a car. The case of *R. v Clarksons Holidays Ltd* (1973) 57 Cr. App. R. 38 might also be a useful pointer. That case, which was also a false trade descriptions case, turned upon what meaning was conveyed by a brochure picture which consisted of an artist's impression of a hotel. The court held that it was a reasonable conclusion for a jury to come to that the picture was a statement that the hotel actually existed even though there was a disclaimer in the brochure that where there was an artist's impression of an hotel it meant that the hotel had not been built yet.

One point to mention here, which helps to bring home the extent to which a consumer of package holidays is now protected, is that the same false or misleading description in a brochure could give rise to prosecutions both under the 2008 Regulations and reg.5 of the Package Travel Regulations (see Chs 16 and 17) as well as forming the basis of civil actions under reg.4, for breach of contract or for misrepresentation.

There is nothing in the Regulation which expressly provides for the situation where the information in the brochure is initially correct but subsequently becomes misleading. To supply the information after it has become misleading is clearly a breach but can a tour operator be held retrospectively liable to a consumer if the information was correct when given but later becomes misleading? We are inclined to think not. The reason being that the breach is committed when the descriptive material is *supplied* and if at that moment it is not misleading then there is no breach.

Suffers as a Consequence

The other qualification is that liability is only imposed where the consumer, as a result of the misleading information, *suffers in consequence*. For the consumer to show that as a consequence of the descriptive material he suffered loss there will have to be some evidence of cause and effect. He will have to show that he relied upon the information otherwise how can it be said that he suffered loss as a consequence?

The issues of causation, and indeed the full impact of the words "misleading", were considered by the Court of Appeal in the case of *Mawdsley v Cosmosair Plc* [2002] EWCA Civ 587. In a nutshell, this case seeks to answer the question; "Can reading a brochure cause you to fall down stairs?" (other, that is, than by walking downstairs whilst reading the brochure!)

The claim was put under reg.4, and also for negligent misrepresentation and/or breach of contract. It was agreed by the court that the words "suffered in consequence" in reg.4 did not mean anything different from the established concept of causation.

The facts are these: Mr and Mrs Mawdsley and their two children then aged three years and six months went on holiday to a hotel described as a village complex, with accommodation either in bungalows in the grounds, or in the main block. The brochure from which the claimants made their booking showed photographs of the hotel and pool area. To the rear of the hotel, viewing it from the sea, was the main building. To the front of the main building at the lower level was a substantial terrace. The terrace extended underneath the main building and also outward towards the sea. Immediately below that terrace was another terrace which in turn gave access via a single flight of steps to the pool area. The photographs showed two substantial flights of steps leading from the upper terrace to the lower terrace.

The description in the brochure rather curiously did not mention a restaurant at all, but it is clear there must have been one as the holidays were offered on an all-inclusive full-board basis. Among the facilities listed was "lift (in main building)". As it turned out, the restaurant was on the Mezzanine Terrace described above; and although there was a lift in the main building, it stopped at every floor except the Mezzanine Terrace. Thus, to access the restaurant, it was necessary to take the lift to the reception floor above the terrace and walk downstairs, or to the pool level and walk upstairs. On the fifth day of their holiday Mr and Mrs Mawdsley were walking downstairs from reception to the restaurant carrying their baby in a buggy. Mrs Mawdsley was, quoting from the Trial Judge: "holding the handle of the pushchair, which was facing downstairs. Her husband, having his back to the pushchair, was holding the foot area, a position which wives and husbands can regularly be seen to take in carrying a pushchair downstairs". Mrs Mawdsley lost her footing and slipped, suffering a back injury. There was never any allegation that the stairs were in any way defective.

As to whether the brochure was misleading, Jonathan Parker L.J. said:

"The description 'lift (in main building)' in the brochure does represent that all levels in the main building can be accessed directly by lift. ... Nor does the fact that the brochure makes no specific mention of the restaurant assist in this connection. Absent any such specific mention, a reader of the brochure would, it seems to me, naturally assume that the restaurant was situated somewhere in the main building and consequently accessible directly by lift."

The Trial Judge had further found that the fact that there was no direct access to the restaurant by lift rendered the hotel "unsuitable for parents with young children" but Jonathan Parker L.J. overruled that, saying that,

"it is unrealistic to conclude that the mere fact that access to the hotel involves negotiating stairs renders the hotel unsuitable for young children, the more so when one looks at the nature of the hotel complex as shown in the photographs in the brochure."

But, as has been seen, on the first point (lifts in main buildings), the court found there was misleading information under reg.4, as well as a misrepresentation and a breach of contract.

On the point of causation, the court was also against Cosmos. The court distinguished *Quinn v Burch Bros (Builders) Ltd* [1966] 2 Q.B. 370, a long established authority on causation in the law of contract. In *Quinn*, the claimant was a plasterer carrying out work under a subcontract. The defendants, the main contractors, in breach of contract failed to supply him with a step ladder despite his request for one. In order to complete his work in the absence of a step ladder, the claimant chose to prop a folded trestle against the wall and used it as a ladder. The foot of the trestle slipped causing the claimant to fall and suffer injuries. He claimed damages for breach of contract. Jonathan Parker L.J. said about *Quinn*:

"In that case it was truly said that the defendant's breach of contract provided no more than the opportunity for the claimant to do what he did. In the instant case there is in my judgment a sufficient causal link between the misrepresentation that the restaurant could be accessed by lift and the accident which occurred on the stairs. [T]he misrepresentation served to expose Mrs Mawdsley to the risk of suffering the very type of accident which in the event she suffered. It is not just that 'but for' the representation Mrs Mawdsley would not have been in the hotel at all; the misrepresentation related directly to the means of access to the restaurant the Judge expressly found that it was reasonable for her to descend the stairs in the way she did".

So it seems that reading a misleading description can be the cause of an accident taking place many months later. This case illustrates the wide ambit which the courts are prepared to give to reg.4 and in particular the words "misleading" and "suffers as a consequence". (Criticism of *Mawdsley* can be found at [2002] L.S.G. May 16, 35.) There is an analogy here with misrepresentation (see below). For a more conventional approach to causation readers are referred to the case of *Singh v Libra Holidays Ltd* [2003] EWHC 276 (QB), and the section entitled Causation above.

A further complication is that reg.4 covers *any loss* suffered as a consequence but does not indicate the basis of calculation of that loss, i.e. contractual or tortious. What if, for instance, the brochure stated wrongly that a hotel had a children's pool and it only had a pool suitable for adults? Clearly, damages for distress and disappointment would be recoverable in such circumstances if a consumer's young children had a miserable time as a consequence of not being able to use the adult pool. However, a scenario could be imagined where a child, in defiance of a parent's express instructions, entered the adult pool and was drowned. Is such a loss suffered as a consequence of the misleading information? A case could be made out for compensation in such circumstances. This is a problem which is in part concerned with *remoteness of damage* which is explored in more detail in Ch.10 on remedies, but also see the passage on *Mawdsley v Cosmosair*, above.

It was indicated earlier that there was no requirement that the misleading information be supplied before the contract has been concluded, but where it has been supplied afterwards problems may arise when trying to ascertain whether the consumer suffered as a consequence. For instance, what if the consumer booked a holiday without the benefit of a brochure or website description, perhaps it was a late booking and no brochure description was available, and no mention of a swimming pool was made. If, when the consumer arrives at the hotel he discovers that there is no pool, he has no right of action against the tour operator because he had not been promised a pool. However, *after* making the booking he may have asked the travel agent if the agent had any further details about the hotel and the agent might have supplied him with a photocopy of an out of date brochure which said that the hotel had a pool. Clearly this is misleading but does the consumer suffer as a consequence? In strict contractual terms probably not. If he had not paid for a pool how can he complain that he suffered as a consequence of not having one? He is not out of pocket as a consequence. But this is to view the issue as a contractual issue when this is not strictly the case. Regulation 4 creates a *statutory* right to damages and it may be possible to show losses arising from the breach of reg.4 which would not give rise to damages in contract but which might still be recoverable. For instance, as a consequence of relying on the misleading information, the consumer might have purchased swimming costumes and bathing towels and this expenditure would be wasted. This would not be recoverable as damages for breach of contract but may very well be in an action based on reg.4. More debatable in these circumstances would be recovery of damages for distress and disappointment (e.g. as a result of the heightened anticipation of enjoyment caused by reading the photocopy). While such damages are clearly recoverable in an action for breach of contract (see Ch.10 on Remedies) there is no authority for their recovery in an action for breach of statutory duty. On the other hand, the Regulation does provide for the recovery of "any loss which the consumer suffers in consequence" which may be a form of words wide enough to cover distress and disappointment.

Exclusion of Liability

Regulation 4 creates a statutory duty rather than a contractual duty, and therefore the ability of the tour operator to contract out of liability under the Regulation by the use of an exclusion clause is probably not possible. The reasons for this are twofold. First, it is a general principle of the law that if Parliament has created a duty then the parties to a contract cannot contract out of it by private bargain. Secondly, in reg.15(5), which provides for limitation of liability in certain circumstances, exclusion of liability is only permitted for breaches of regs 15(1) and (2), i.e. for breaches of the *obligations under the contract*—not for breach of reg.4.

Regulation 4 and Misrepresentation

There are clear similarities between an action under reg.4 and misrepresentation (dealt with in Ch.7), as demonstrated by *Mawdsley*. However, it should not be supposed that an action under reg.4 would be the same as an action for misrepresentation. Although the two actions would be similar in that both require the consumer to have relied upon the statement, an action under reg.4 would go further because it covers *any misleading information concerning a package*. This could be given a very wide interpretation by the courts to include, for example, resort descriptions as well as hotel descriptions. A tour operator might try to argue that the beautiful sandy beach he described as being a mile from the hotel, but which was in fact shingle, was not part of the package and therefore not covered by the Regulation (but see *Jones v Sunworld* above). An action for misrepresentation is narrower because it only covers false statements of *fact*. Statements of opinion and statements as to the future do not give rise to liability in misrepresentation but they would under reg.4. As we have seen, a misrepresentation must have induced the actual contract, whereas reg.4 can cover material supplied after the contract was made. On the other hand, an action in misrepresentation would cover oral statements whereas reg.4 probably does not (but see *Minhas v Imperial Travel* [2003] C.L.Y. 2043). And of course, the Misrepresentation Act is far wider in that it applies to all contracts (including non-packages) whereas obviously reg.4 applies to packages only.

SUPPLIER CONTRACTS—PRACTICAL ADVICE

As we have seen, reg.15 expressly preserves the right of package organisers to effect recovery against their supplier in respect of any claim brought against the organiser by a consumer. We set out advice to organisers below on the essentials which should be included in any contract with a supplier (e.g. hotel, ski school, coach company, etc). This advice is based upon many years of seeing common errors recurring. Of course it applies equally to those selling single components (e.g. a hotel) as principals.

Whom is the Contract Between?

The name of the British travel company is usually clear enough, but if you put on the name of the hotel being, for example "The Grand Hotel", who is that? Or what is that? You can't sue a building! Who owns the hotel? Is it a private individual? Or is it a company that owns or manages the hotel? Or one owning company, and one managing one? And even if you put someone's name, is that the owner or the head receptionist or what? It is very important that the contract states precisely who is the other contracting party; this is because when you want to sue them, you want to be sure who it is exactly that you are entitled to make a recovery from. Where a hotel is deliberately presented as part of a franchised chain or brand, the franchising brand owner may be liable, *Arfilli v Fleetway and Starwood Hotels* Unreported January 19, 2012, Central London County Court.

The Indemnity Clause

Most contracts do have an indemnity clause, which is good, but the problem is that quite often they don't really set out what you need the indemnity for. It is not just, for example, an indemnity for any compensation which is paid out for any breach of the specific terms of the contract. For example, the contract will often say that if there is an overbooking at the hotel then the hotel must supply alternative accommodation. It is no good just having an indemnity for this specific clause, because what you need is an indemnity for every type of compensation which you may have to pay out as the result of any fault or default on the part of the hotel, or the ski school, etc. Also, it is not just compensation, of course, but it is costs as well that need to be covered. It is the claimant's costs and your own legal costs that must be covered in an indemnity clause. And, of course, it is not just an indemnity if there is a court order, i.e. the claimant succeeds against you and gets a judgment against you for some sum of money; you need to have a right to indemnity in respect of any settlement which you reach with a claimant, because otherwise there is always the risk that you settle with a claimant and then you try and make recovery from the supplier and the supplier says "well you shouldn't have settled, why did you settle?"

The Jurisdiction Clause

We can't believe how many contracts we see with suppliers which do not have in them an English jurisdiction clause—that is, a clause saying that the contract is subject to the jurisdiction of the courts of England and Wales. If you don't have such a jurisdiction clause, you cannot make a recovery in the courts of England and Wales (although you might be able to join the hotel as a third party in the action brought against you by the claimant as long as there isn't a jurisdiction clause giving jurisdiction to some other country) but you won't be able to bring your own fresh action against the supplier in England and Wales unless you have a jurisdiction clause. So you would need, in that case, to invite the claimant to issue a court claim (even though you may wish to settle amicably with the claimant), just so that you can effect recovery. All those problems are solved if there is an effective English jurisdiction clause. (See more on this, in particular the legal niceties, in Ch.14 on Foreign Affairs.) Another point: there is a big difference between a jurisdiction clause and a law clause; if the contract says "this contract is subject to English law", that is something completely different and is not the same as English jurisdiction. It is jurisdiction that is (usually) the more important one, because otherwise, you probably won't be able to bring a claim in the English courts and may end up trying to pursue it at great expense and huge delay in a foreign court where they may not sympathise with British tour operators and may give a judgment which conflicts with the pro-consumer English judgment; the devil and the deep blue sea indeed.

Exclusion of Liability and Unfair Contract Terms

INTRODUCTION

There are a number of ways in which a travel company can reduce its liability for breach of contract. The first way is to supply a product of the right quality. It may be stating the obvious but if there is nothing wrong with the product and the client gets precisely what he contracted for, then there will be no breach of contract. It is for this reason that the consumer relations department should always have an input into the company's quality control function. Prevention is always better than cure and a consumer relations department which is solely concerned with sorting out the problems created by others will soon become demoralised. (See Grant and O'Cain "Lies, Damn Lies and Holiday Brochures" [1995] T.L.J. 4 for an example of the tensions created by marketing defective products.)

Secondly, the travel company can endeavour to reduce its liability by promising less in the first place. Prior to the 1990 revision of the ABTA Code of Conduct for Tour Operators and the passage of the Package Travel Regulations it was possible for a tour operator with a set of suitably drafted terms and conditions to escape with liability only for its own fault. In *Wall v Silver Wing* Unreported 1980, High Court, which has been discussed in some detail already in relation to implied terms, that is precisely what the tour operator succeeded in doing. In cases such as *Gibbons v Intasun Holidays* [1988] C.L.Y. 168; *Kaye v Intasun Holidays* [1987] C.L.Y. 1150; *Toubi v Intasun Holidays* [1988] C.L.Y. 1060 and *Usher v Intasun Holidays* [1987] C.L.Y. 418, tour operators also succeeded on this basis. The passage of the Package Travel Regulations and the 1990 revision of the ABTA Code of Conduct made significant changes to the liability of tour operators, but, as we have just seen in Ch.5, there remains the possibility that a travel company, by adopting a suitably drafted set of terms and conditions, may get away with restricted liability in many cases.

The third means by which a travel company can seek to reduce or limit its liability, and which forms the subject matter of this chapter, is by the use of exclusion clauses.

Exclusion of Liability

The conventional approach to exclusion clauses is to see them as terms in a contract by which one party seeks to exclude or limit or restrict his liability for a breach of contract. Viewed in this way an exclusion clause is a *defence mechanism* used by a party to a contract to protect himself when in breach of a

180

proven liability. There are other ways of viewing exclusion clauses and these will be examined later but for the moment the conventional approach will suffice.

One's first reaction to such a device is perhaps to ask how come they are acceptable. How is it that one party to a contract is permitted to break the contract and then escape liability by relying on the small print? The immediate answer to such a question is that acceptability does not come into it. It is simply a matter of making a contract with the appropriate terms in it. If one party offers to make a contract on certain terms and the other party accepts such terms then the courts will enforce the agreement they have made.

In reality, the answer to the question is much more complex. First of all, the courts, and then Parliament, recognised that in many cases the *agreement* between the parties was often more illusory than real. Exclusion clauses are typically to be found in standard form contracts drafted by a commercially stronger party and offered to a weaker party on a take it or leave it basis. There is no question of being able to negotiate over the terms and conditions (even if you could find someone to negotiate with) and the only freedom of choice available is to go to a rival who offers much the same package of terms and conditions.

Lord Reid summed up the situation in the case of *Suisse Atlantique Societe D'Armement SA v NV Rotterdamsche Kolen Centrale* [1966] 2 All E.R. 61. He said:

> "Exemption clauses differ greatly in many respects. Probably the most objectionable are found in the complex standard conditions which are now so common. In the ordinary way the customer has no time to read them, and, if he did read them he would probably not understand them. If he did understand and object to any of them, he would generally be told that he could take it or leave it. If he then went to another supplier, the result would be the same."

Given this lack of real agreement and the ability of one party to exploit their bargaining position to the detriment of the other party, the courts, without ever going so far as striking out exclusion clauses simply because they were unreasonable, developed a number of techniques to curb some of the worst excesses of exclusion clauses. Admirable though these efforts were, the common law was simply unable to cope adequately with the problems created by exclusion clauses and it became necessary to legislate against them. The Unfair Contract Terms Act 1977 (UCTA) was a major piece of legislation which made many types of exclusion clause void altogether and made most of the rest subject to a test of reasonableness.

The common law rules and those contained in UCTA apply generally to all contracts but the Package Travel Regulations contain rules about exclusion clauses which are of specific application to package holidays. In addition to these rules there are also the Unfair Terms in Consumer Contracts Regulations 1999 ("UTCCR") (SI 1999/2083) which are derived from the Directive of the same name (93/13/EEC) and which was first implemented in the UK in 1994. As the name suggests, the UTCCR apply not only to exclusion clauses but also to clauses which are unfair—a much wider concept.

All four sets of rules will now be examined in turn. Before proceeding, however, it is necessary to point out two things. First, the rules are not exclusive of each other—they can be applied concurrently. Although this chapter will examine the rules in order of historical development a party seeking to avoid an exclusion clause would usually look first to the statutory provisions and only then to the common law. In some circumstances all four sets of rules would provide assistance.

Secondly, in relation particularly to package holiday contracts, although the Package Travel Regulations do permit certain limited exclusions, it is worth indicating at the outset that there is such a battery of weapons that can now be deployed against exclusion clauses that a travel company will find cold comfort in what follows. Should evidence be required to confirm this one only has to look at the actions of the Office of Fair Trading in October 2002 when it agreed with the four largest UK tour operators and ABTA that a whole range of standard terms and conditions were unfair and would have to be re-drafted. These terms will be examined later but a number of them had been used routinely for many years and were previously regarded as unexceptional by the industry.

The Common Law

As indicated above, the attitude of the courts to exclusion clauses was somewhat ambivalent. On the one hand the courts could never bring themselves to say that exclusion clauses should be rejected simply because they were unreasonable, but on the other hand, recognising that many such clauses were unreasonable, they created a set of technical rules which could be invoked to oust them. These rules fall into two categories.

First, the clause will not be effective unless it has been *incorporated in the contract*. In other words, if the clause does not form part of the contract then it cannot be relied upon. The clause will be incorporated in the contract by the process of offer and acceptance. (See Ch.3.) Secondly, even if the clause has been incorporated in the contract, the courts will examine it very carefully and it will be equally ineffective if it does not cover the breach that occurred. This is a matter of *construction* or *interpretation* and such clauses are interpreted very strictly—*contra proferentem*—against the person proffering the clause.

Incorporation

There are three ways in which an exclusion clause can be incorporated in a contract—by signature, by notice or by a course of dealing.

Signature

The surest way of incorporating a term in a contract is to have a contractual document signed by the other party. The leading case on this point is *L'Estrange v Graucob* [1934] 2 K.B. 394. The facts of the case were that the claimant bought an automatic vending machine from the defendants. When the machine failed to work properly she sued them. It was held that they were protected by an exclusion clause in their "Sales Agreement" which she had signed when she bought the machine. Although the clause was "in regrettably small print" it was still quite legible. Scrutton L.J. said:

"When a document containing contractual terms is signed, then, in the absence of fraud, or, I will add, misrepresentation, the party signing it is bound, and it is wholly immaterial whether he has read the document or not."

It is for this reason that travel companies place so much emphasis on obtaining the client's signature on a booking form or, more likely these days, by ticking the right box during the booking process on the internet. Once it has been signed the travel company has effectively incorporated not only any exclusion clauses in the contract but all the other terms as well.

An example of a travel case where this principle worked to the advantage of the travel company is *Budd v Peninsular and Oriental Steam Navigation Co* [1969] 2 Lloyd's Rep. 262. In that case, the claimant was injured due to the admitted negligence of the defendants. However, the claimant had entered into the contract at the premises of the defendant's agents and the agents had made sure she signed the declaration on the booking form. It stated:

"and I understand that all accommodation is offered and fares are quoted subject to the Regulations and Conditions of Carriage as printed on the Passage Ticket of the Line concerned."

One of the conditions on the ticket, which was legible and reasonably comprehensible to the average person, exempted the defendants from liability. The judge said:

"The law of this country is plain. If you choose to put your signature to a document in which it is made plain that the obligations of the party with whom you are contracting is contained in certain conditions, then you are bound by those conditions".

The claimant, therefore, failed in her action. The significance of the case is that the agent followed the procedures laid down and thereby protected the interests of the shipping company. Failure by the agent would have led to the liability of P&O, who, in turn, would probably have sought an indemnity from the agent for breaching the agency agreement. (Since 1977 exemption clauses such as these which attempt to exclude liability for personal injury caused by negligence are no longer valid because of UCTA.)

Note that under the Package Travel Regulations there is increased emphasis on the provision of information to the client both before contracting and in the contract itself. One way of proving that the information has been supplied is to have a signed booking form (or its online equivalent). It is therefore the case that a signed booking form has grown rather than diminished in importance.

Notice

Many contracts are concluded using documents which are not signed but merely handed over at the time of contracting or simply displayed at the place where the contract is made. If the document contains an exclusion clause the question of whether it has been incorporated in the contract depends upon whether *reasonable notice* of it has been given to the other party.

What amounts to reasonable notice is of course a question of fact and will vary according to the circumstances. Relevant circumstances include: the kind of document containing the clause; the amount of notice given; and the type of clause.

The Document

In *Chapelton v Barry Urban DC* [1940] 1 K.B. 532 the claimant hired a deck-chair from the defendants. He was given a receipt on the back of which were printed conditions which exempted the defendants from liability for any damage caused by the chair. When he sat on the chair it collapsed and he was injured. It was held that the defendants could not rely upon the exclusion clause because the receipt was simply a document showing that the claimant had paid for the chairs. It was not a document with contractual force.

On the other hand, a document will be treated as having contractual force if the other party knows that this was the intention or it was the kind of document that usually contains contractual terms. Most tickets for travel will fall into this latter category. In fact, in this area of the law there are a body of cases collectively known as the "ticket cases" in which railway and ferry companies feature prominently and in general it can be said that such tickets are regarded as contractual documents.

Amount of Notice Required

The leading case here is *Parker v South Eastern Railway Co* (1876–77) L.R. 2 C.P.D. 416. The facts of the case were that the claimant had deposited a bag in a cloakroom at the defendant's station. He had been given a ticket on the front of which were printed the words "See back". On the back was an exclusion clause limiting liability to £10 per item. Due to the negligence of the defendant's employees the bag was lost. The claimant claimed the value of his bag, £24, but the defendants, relying on the exclusion clause, offered him only £10. In the Court of Appeal, Mellish L.J. said the test as to whether the exclusion clause was binding on the claimant was:

> "that if the person receiving the ticket did not see or know that there was any writing on the ticket, he is not bound by the conditions; that if he knew there was writing, and knew or believed that the writing contained conditions, then he is bound by the conditions; that if he knew there was writing on the ticket, but did not know or believe that the writing contained conditions, nevertheless he would be bound, if the delivering of the ticket to him in such a manner that he could see there was writing upon it, was reasonable notice that the writing contained conditions."

A case in which this line of reasoning was applied was *Thompson v London Midland & Scottish Railway Co* [1930] 1 K.B. 41. The claimant in that case had purchased an excursion ticket. On the face of the ticket were printed the words "For conditions see back", and on the back were the words "Issued subject to the conditions and regulations in the company's timetables and notices and excursion and other bills." If the claimant had purchased a company timetable (for 20 per cent of the price of the ticket!) she could have discovered that the ticket was issued subject to the condition that the defendant was not liable for any personal injury, howsoever caused. The claimant was injured when the carriage in which she was travelling pulled up just short of the platform and she slipped and fell when alighting.

It was held by the Court of Appeal that the exclusion clause protected the defendant. Lord Hanworth M.R. said:

"it appears to me that when that ticket was taken it was taken with the knowledge that the conditions applied, and that the person who took the ticket was bound by those conditions."

He also said:

"it has not ever been held that the mere circuity which has to be followed to find the actual condition prevents the passenger having notice that there was a condition."

The decision may be considered a harsh one on the facts, but nevertheless supports the principle that terms can be incorporated in such a fashion on the grounds that otherwise many contracts would become impossibly bulky documents.

Another travel case which illustrates the principle of reasonable notice is *Richardson Spence & Co Ltd v Rowntree* [1894] A.C. 217. In that case the claimant had booked a passage on the defendant's steamer and had been handed a ticket for the voyage which was folded in such a way that no writing was visible on it. It was held by the House of Lords that reasonable notice had not been given to her of the conditions on the inside, one of which excluded liability for personal injury. Applying the three questions in *Parker v South Eastern Railway* Lord Herschell said that although the claimant knew that there was writing on the ticket she did not know that they contained conditions relating to the contract of carriage and that the defendants had not done what was reasonably sufficient to bring them to her notice.

Type of Clause

Some cases seem to suggest that where the clause is particularly unusual then greater steps should be taken to draw it to the attention of the other party. For instance, in *Thornton v Shoe Lane Parking* [1971] 2 Q.B. 163 it was held that inadequate notice had been given of a clause on the back of a car parking ticket which excluded liability for personal injury. The notice might have been adequate if the clause had merely related to damage to the car. Such a clause would not have been unusual.

In *J Spurling Ltd v Bradshaw* [1956] 1 W.L.R. 461 Denning L.J. famously said:

"Some clauses I have seen would need to be printed in red ink on the face of the document with a red hand pointing to it before the notice could be held to be sufficient."

This dictum is a favourite among District Judges who hear Small Claims Track holiday claims.

Time

It should also be mentioned that the giving of reasonable notice means that the notice must be given *before* the contract is concluded. Once the contract is made the courts will not permit terms to be added retrospectively. This point is graphically illustrated by the case of *Olley v Marlborough Court Ltd* [1949] 1 K.B. 532. The claimant in that case had belongings stolen from her hotel room due to the negligence of the hotel staff. The defendant relied upon a notice on the wall of the bedroom which excluded liability in such circumstances. The Court of Appeal held that the contract had been concluded at the reception desk when the claimant had booked into the hotel and that notice of the exclusion clause came too late. It would have been a different matter if the notice had been prominently displayed at the reception desk.

Fosbroke-Hobbes v Airwork Ltd (1936) 56 Ll. L. Rep. 209 is a travel case which vividly illustrates the importance of giving notice at the right time. The claimant in the case was a member of a party who had hired an aeroplane. The aeroplane was owned by the second defendants but hired out by the first defendants. The contract, which was negotiated some days before the flight was due to take place, was between the leader of the party and the first defendant. The claimant was killed when the pilot (employed by the second defendants) negligently crashed it just after take-off. Just before take-off the leader of the party had been handed an envelope containing a "ticket". The ticket was in fact a "special charter". It contained a number of contractual terms including an exclusion clause which exempted the second defendants and their employees from liability for negligence.

It was held that as far as the first defendants were concerned they were not liable to the claimant because as he was not a party to the contract of hire he had no rights against them. (See Ch.8 on Privity of Contract for a fuller discussion of this principle.) If they had had a contract with the claimant then the exclusion clause would not have helped them because it had not been incorporated in the contract in time. Handing the "ticket" over as the aeroplane was about to taxi off was too late—long after the contract had been concluded.

The second defendants, however, were liable. The action against them appears to be in the tort of negligence rather than contract but similar principles apply to the giving of notice. Their employee, the pilot—for whom they were vicariously liable, had been negligent and the notice that they endeavoured to give, excluding their liability, was not communicated in time to the claimant. The claimant had not had time to even see the contents of the envelope before take-off, far less read and understand them and certainly not enough time to realise that he was being carried on the basis that the owner of the plane would not be liable to him in negligence.

Course of Dealing

Where the exclusion clause has not been incorporated in the contract by signature or notice it may nevertheless form part of the contract if it can be shown that there was a course of dealing between the parties. In other words, the parties had dealt with each other on previous occasions and on those previous occasions the exclusion clause had formed part of the contract. If on one occasion the term was omitted it could nevertheless be said that it was part of the contract because that was the expectation of the parties—they always dealt on the same terms.

In *Spurling v Bradshaw* the claimant had stored some goods in the defendant's warehouse but they were damaged due to the negligence of the defendant. The contract had been made over the phone and no mention of an exclusion clause had been made. However, the defendant had subsequently sent the claimant a set of his standard terms and conditions, which included an exclusion clause. The terms were the same as had been used over a long period and on many previous occasions. It was held that a course of dealing had been established and that the term had been incorporated in the contract despite the fact that on this occasion the terms had been sent retrospectively.

However, a different result was reached in *McCutcheon v David MacBrayne Ltd* [1964] 1 W.L.R. 125. In that case the claimant had shipped his car from Islay to the Scottish mainland on the defendant's ferry. The car was lost when the ship ran aground due to the negligence of the ferry captain. When the contract was made it was entirely oral. No documents were handed over except for a receipt after the money had been paid. On previous occasions however the defendant's practice had been to obtain the claimant's signature on a "risk note" which excluded liability. The defendant endeavoured to show that there was a previous course of dealing which established that on this occasion the exclusion clause was part of the contract. However, the evidence established that the previous dealings were inconsistent. On some occasions a risk note had been signed but on other occasions it had not. Therefore, the only course of dealing that could be established was that sometimes the clause was in the contract and sometimes it wasn't.

It is interesting to note that the failure in this instance was that of the booking clerk. It was his omission or carelessness that exposed his employers to a liability they had thought they had avoided. All the fine words on the risk note could not protect them if they did not ensure that proper booking procedures were followed. It serves as an object lesson for travel companies of the importance not only of proper systems but also of proper training.

Construction

Clauses Interpreted *Contra Proferentum*

Prior to 1977, the courts, as part of their general disapproval of exclusion clauses, interpreted them strictly against the party trying to rely upon them. If there were any ambiguities or omissions the courts would give the benefit of the doubt to the innocent party.

Given that one party had made certain promises in the contract which he had then broken and was then trying to escape from liability by the use of the small print then it was perfectly logical for the courts to say that unless the words excluding liability were clear and unambiguous then the liability remained intact. However, the courts often went to extremes in their interpretation of exclusion clauses and given the flexible nature of the English language it was usually possible for a particularly determined court to find an ambiguity somewhere and use this as a reason for striking out the clause.

For instance, in the case of *Houghton v Trafalgar Insurance Co Ltd* [1954] 1 Q.B. 247 a car insurance policy excluded liability if the car was carrying an excessive *load*. The car, which was only constructed to carry five people, was involved in an accident when carrying six people. It was held that the word load applied to luggage not to passengers and the insurance company was held liable. A recent Australian case, *Insight Vacations Pty Ltd v Young* [2011] HCA 16, displays the same approach. Mrs Young was touring Europe by coach and stood up to retrieve something from her bag which was stowed in the overhead luggage shelf. The coach braked suddenly; she fell backwards and suffered injury. The defendant sought to exclude liability by use of the following clause:

"Where the passenger *occupies a motorcoach seat* fitted with a safety belt, neither the Operators nor their agents or co-operating organisations will be liable for any injury, illness or death or for any damages or claims whatsoever arising from any accident or incident, if the safety belt is not being worn at the time of such accident or incident." (Emphasis added)

Although the coach company lost the case on other grounds the court said that the clause would not have protected them anyway because at the time Mrs Young was not occupying her seat.

In *Wallis Son & Wells v Pratt & Haynes* [1911] A.C. 394 liability was excluded for breach of any *warranty* in the contract (a minor term of the contract). It was held that this did not protect the defendant against breach of a *condition* (a major term of the contract). Similarly, in *Andrews Bros (Bournemouth) Ltd v Singer & Co Ltd* [1934] 1 K.B. 17 a clause limiting liability in respect of *implied* conditions and warranties did not protect against breach of *express* conditions and warranties.

The problem with this kind of approach is that every time the court strikes out a particular type of clause the legal draftsman learns from his mistakes. The next time he is called upon to draft a clause he drafts a better one eliminating the previous loophole.

One tour operating case which shows the dangers of poor or inappropriate drafting is *Spencer v Cosmos Air Holidays Ltd*, *The Times*, December 6, 1989. The claimants had been thrown out of their hotel by the management for alleged rowdy behaviour. They sued Cosmos for breach of contract on the grounds that they had not been provided with the promised accommodation. Unfortunately for Cosmos, it could not be *proved* that the girls had been rowdy because the evidence was not sufficiently strong. If it could have been proved this would have been a complete defence. However, Cosmos also tried to rely on their exclusion clause. It stated:

"Liability

We are travel and holiday organisers only. We do not control or operate any airline neither do we own or control any shipping company, coach or coach company, hotel, transport or any other facility or service mentioned in this brochure. We take care in selecting all the ingredients in your holiday, but because we only select and inspect them and have no control in the running of them, we cannot be responsible for any injury, death, loss or damage which is caused by any negligence of the management or employees of an independent contractor arising outside our normal selection and inspection process."

The Court of Appeal held that the clause simply did not cover what had happened. Farquharson L.J. said that the words "injury, death, loss or damage" were not appropriate to cover what had happened to the claimants. Mustill L.J. said that the clause would not help the defendants, not because of inapt drafting, but because:

"the clause does not even set out to exclude claims in contract for failure to provide the services comprised in the holiday."

Another, more briefly reported, travel case which deals with exclusion clauses is *Askew v Intasun North* [1980] C.L.Y. 637. There, the claimants had been told on arrival in resort that they were being allocated to a different hotel. The court held that the exclusion clause that the defendants relied upon:

"was poorly worded and difficult to interpret, and did not exclude liability in this case."

Clearly the clause was so badly drafted it offered an open invitation to the court to avoid it. Another example of drafting that caught the tour operator out is *Williams v Travel Promotions Ltd (t/a Voyages Jules Verne), The Times*, March 9, 1998. In that case, the defendants had moved the claimant from his chosen hotel to another hotel on the day before departure. They claimed to be able to do this and not offer compensation because this was a minor change as defined in their terms and conditions for which compensation was not payable. The Court of Appeal, in a masterly judgment which managed to sidestep all the major issues raised in respect of the Package Travel Regulations and the Unfair Contract Terms Act, resolved the case on a simple interpretation of the defendant's terms and conditions. They found that the terms and conditions expressly stated that minor changes could only be made if they were "necessary" and as the defendants had not proven that this was a necessary change they were in breach of contract and had to pay compensation. (For a further example of hapless drafting, although not involving an exclusion clause, see *Marsh v Thomson Tour Operators* [2000] C.L.Y. 4044, where the tour operator shot itself in the foot over the drafting of their "money back guarantee".)

Negligence

In many contracts, one party may be under both strict liability and fault liability. For instance, in *White v John Warwick & Co* [1953] 2 All E.R. 1021 the defendant hired a cycle to the claimant. The claimant was injured when the saddle tipped forward due to the negligence of the defendant. The contract excluded liability for personal injury. The defendant in these circumstances is not only liable for negligence, he is also strictly liable to the claimant for any defects in the bike—whether caused by negligence or not. The court held that the words used in the exclusion clause were sufficient to protect against the strict liability but not the fault liability—that should have been spelt out more clearly.

Main Purpose Rule

A further rule of construction developed by the courts to deal with exclusion clauses is the "main purpose rule". In other words, an exclusion clause would not assist a party in breach to alter the main purpose or substance of the contract. If a person contracts to deliver peas and instead substitutes beans an exclusion clause will not help him. What he has delivered is so different that it can be said that he is not performing the contract at all. The exclusion clause relates to the delivery of peas not beans.

One leading case on this point is in fact a travel case, *Anglo Continental Holidays v Typaldos (London)* [1967] 2 Lloyd's Rep. 61. The claimants were travel agents who had booked a party onto the defendant's ship, *Atlantica*, for a cruise to Israel. With less than two weeks to go the defendants substituted a much inferior ship, the *Angelika*, and an equally inferior itinerary. The claimants cancelled the cruise, refunded their clients' money and sued the defendants for breach of contract. The defendants relied on an exclusion clause which stated:

"Steamers, Sailing Dates, Rates and Itineraries are subject to change without prior notice".

Lord Denning M.R. said:

"In my opinion a steamship company cannot rely on a clause of this kind so as to alter the substance of the transaction. For instance, they could not say: 'We will change you from this fine modern ship to an old tramp'. Nor could they say: 'We are putting the sailing dates back a week'. Nor could they say: 'We are taking you to Piraeus instead of to Haifa'. No matter how wide the terms of the clause, the Courts will limit it and modify it to the extent necessary to enable effect to be given to the main object and intent of the contract.

Applied to this case we have to ask ourselves: Was the proposed trip by the *Anjelika* in substance a performance of the contract or was it a serious departure from it? To my mind there is only one answer. It was a radical departure."

Russell L.J. was equally clear the clause was ineffective:

"a reasonable construction must be put upon such a term, and as a matter of construction the defendants were not enabled thereby to alter the substance of the arrangement. Whether they attempted to do so must be, in a sort of package deal like this, a question of degree and perhaps to some extent of general impression. But in my view a combination of all the matters which were in fact involved in the substitution of the *Angelika* for the *Atlantica* together did constitute an alteration of the substance of the arrangement."

EXCLUSION OF LIABILITY AND UNFAIR CONTRACT TERMS

Common Law Developments Since 1977

The impression that is gained from the discussion above is that the courts have often strained the meaning of words and created excessively technical barriers in their enthusiasm to combat exclusion clauses. Such an impression would be entirely justified. However, since the advent of UCTA in 1977 the courts have taken a more restrained view on the interpretation of such clauses. Now that there is legislation to deal with unfair and unreasonable exclusion clauses the courts no longer feel the need to stretch or bend the rules to achieve a just solution. In *Ailsa Craig Fishing Co Ltd v Malvern Fishing Co Ltd* [1983] 1 All E.R. 101 Lord Wilberforce said that:

> "one must not strive to create ambiguities by strained construction. The relevant words must be given, if possible, their natural plain meaning."

In *George Mitchell (Chesterhall) Ltd v Finney Lock Seeds Ltd* [1983] 2 All E.R. 737 Lord Diplock said that recent legislation had:

> "removed from judges the temptation to resort to the device of ascribing to the words appearing in exemption clauses a tortured meaning so as to avoid giving effect to an exclusion or limitation of liability when a judge thought that in the circumstances to do so would be unfair".

Two reservations, however, need to be expressed. First, the statements made by the House of Lords in the *Ailsa Craig* and *George Mitchell* cases were made in the context of limitation clauses rather than outright exclusion clauses. In *Ailsa Craig* Lord Wilberforce said:

> "Clauses of limitation are not regarded by the courts with the same hostility as clauses of exclusion; this is because they must be related to other contractual terms, in particular to the risks to which the defending party may be exposed, the remuneration which he receives and possibly also the opportunity of the other party to insure." (p.102)

And Lord Fraser said in the same case:

> "There are authorities which lay down very strict principles to be applied when considering the effect of clauses of exclusion or of indemnity. In my opinion these principles are not applicable in their full rigour when considering the effect of conditions merely limiting liability. Such conditions will of course be read *contra proferentem* and must be clearly expressed, but there is no reason why they should be judged by the specially exacting standards which are applied to exclusion and indemnity clauses. The reason for imposing such standards on these conditions is the inherent improbability that the other party to a contract including such a condition intended to release the proferens from a liability that would otherwise fall on him. But there is no such high degree of improbability that he would agree to a limitation of the liability of the proferens especially when, as explained in condition 4(i) of the present contract, the potential losses that might be caused by the negligence of the proferens or

191

its servants are so great in proportion to the sums that can reasonably be charged for the services contracted for." (p.105)

These statements indicate that where it is felt necessary the courts will continue to interpret exclusion clauses just as strictly as previously. (See also *Williams v Travel Promotions Ltd* referred to above.)

Secondly, in *Interfoto Picture Library Ltd v Stiletto Visual Programmes Ltd* [1989] Q.B. 433 the Court of Appeal appeared to extend rather than relax the rules on incorporation. Dealing with a particularly onerous clause Dillon L.J. said:

"In the ticket cases the courts held that the common law required that reasonable steps be taken to draw the other parties' attention to the printed conditions or they would not be part of the contract. It is in my judgement a logical development of the common law into modern conditions that it should be held, as it was in *Thornton v Shoe Lane Parking Ltd* [1971] 2 Q.B. 163 that, if one condition in a set of printed conditions is particularly onerous or unusual, the party seeking to enforce it must show that that particular condition was fairly brought to the attention of the other party."

He then went on to hold that sufficient notice had not been given of this particular term. This approach, though orthodox, nevertheless represents a highly technical application of the rules on incorporation.

In the same case, Bingham L.J. took a more novel approach. He held that where a clause was unreasonable and extortionate, as in this case, it was necessary for the party relying on the clause to draw it "fairly and reasonably" to the attention of the other party. Opening his judgment he introduced the civil law notion of good faith and suggested that in civil jurisdictions the matter might be decided by holding that:

"the plaintiffs were under a duty in all fairness to draw the defendant's attention specifically to the high price payable if the transparencies were not returned in time, and to point out to the defendants the high cost of continued failure to return them."

Later he said:

"The tendency of the English authorities has, I think, been to look at the nature of the transaction in question and the character of the parties to it; to consider what notice the party alleged to be bound was given of the particular condition said to bind him; and to resolve whether in all the circumstances it is fair to hold him bound by the condition in question. This may yield a result not very different from the civil law principle of good faith, at any rate so far as the formation of the contract is concerned." (Emphasis added)

It is difficult to divine precisely the basis of the judgment but he appears to be saying that even if a term could be incorporated into a contract by the normal operation of the rules of offer and acceptance the party seeking to rely upon it would have to demonstrate good faith.

This approach suggests that, far from relaxing the rules on incorporation, the courts are quite prepared to bolster them with new concepts when they judge it appropriate.

THE UNFAIR CONTRACT TERMS ACT 1977

Preliminary Points

Contrary to what the name of the Act suggests UCTA is not aimed at *unfair* contract terms in general, that is left to the UTCCR. Its focus is much more limited. What it does do is to curb the worst kinds of *exclusion* clause. It makes some exclusion clauses void altogether and it makes others subject to a test of reasonableness.

Two particular features of the legislation can be identified. First, there is an outright ban on clauses which exclude liability for negligence which gives rise to personal injury. Secondly, there is comprehensive protection given to consumers, i.e. those who are worst placed and least able to protect themselves.

Business Liability

One restriction on the scope of the Act is that it only applies to business liability. This is defined in s.1(3):

"1(3) In the case of both contract and tort, sections 2 to 7 apply (except where the contrary is stated in section 6(4)) only to business liability, that is liability for breach of obligations or duties arising—

(a) from things done or to be done by a person in the course of a business (whether his own business or another's);

or

(b) from the occupation of premises used for business purposes of the occupier;

and references to liability are to be read accordingly."

This is of only marginal importance because private individuals who make contracts tend to do so orally rather than in writing. Exclusion clauses are usually only found in printed standard form contracts or notices produced by businesses. Thus, most exclusion clauses will be covered by the Act.

Clauses Excluding Liability For Negligence

Section 2 of the Act imposes strict limitations on the ability to be able to exclude liability for negligence.

CHAPTER SIX

Definition of Negligence

There is a comprehensive definition of negligence in s.1(1):

"1(1) For the purposes of this Part of this Act negligence means the breach—

(a) of any obligation, arising from the express or implied terms of a contract, to take reasonable care or exercise reasonable skill in the performance of the contract;

(b) of any common law duty to take reasonable care or exercise reasonable skill (but not any stricter duty);

(c) of the common duty of care imposed by the Occupiers' Liability Act 1957 or the Occupiers' Liability Act (Northern Ireland) 1957."

Essentially, what this means is that whether you negligently break a contract or negligently injure or cause loss to people on your premises or simply commit the tort of negligence this will be covered by the Act.

Negligent breach of contract is easily illustrated. This is what happened in both *Thompson v LMS* and *Richardson Spence & Co Ltd v Rowntree*. In the former, the claimant was injured due to the train pulling up short of the platform. In the latter, the claimant was injured because the chair she fell off was not suitably constructed to withstand the rolling caused by rough seas. In both cases the actions of the defendants were negligent.

The Occupiers' Liability Act 1957 imposes a duty on occupiers of premises to take reasonable care of visitors. If a client visiting a travel agency tripped and fell on a badly fitted carpet this would amount to a breach of the Act. The position would be similar if a hotel guest was injured if the bedroom ceiling collapsed due to the negligence of the hotelier. (Note that a number of recent personal injury cases have held that the Occupiers' Liability Act does not apply where the injury occurred abroad, but the principles applied are generally similar—see *Isle and Dean v Thomson* referred to in Ch.5.)

Most negligence occurs outside the context of a contract or the Occupiers Liability Act. A very common example of the tort of negligence is when one driver negligently injures another by careless driving. Most injuries at work which lead to litigation are caused by negligence and lead to an action in tort rather than contract. The definition of negligence stops short of imposing liability for the negligence of independent subcontractors.

Death and Personal Injury Caused by Negligence

Section 2(1) states:

"2(1) A person cannot by reference to any contract term or to a notice given to persons generally or to particular persons exclude or restrict his liability for death or personal injury resulting from negligence."

Thus, in any case where the defendant is proved to be negligent it will be impossible for him to exclude liability where death or personal injury has been caused.

The immediate effect of this section is to reverse the effect of cases like

Thompson v LMS. Irrespective of whether the clause had been incorporated in the contract it would be of no effect. The railway had negligently caused personal injury and no matter what it said on the ticket they would now be unable to exclude their liability. The result would be the same with *Richardson Spence & Co Ltd v Rowntree.* There would be no need to deal with the small print on the ticket at all because it would count for nought. Examples of case law subsequent to 1977, particularly involving travel cases, are hard to find but on the European Database on Case Law about Unfair Contractual Terms (CLAB) which used to be maintained by the Health and Consumer Protection Directorate of the European Commission there was an example. It referred to an unreported County Court decision from 1994 in which a client of Aspro was injured by the defective condition of the private transport provided by the holiday firm to transport her from her home to the airport (Ref: GB000028). One of the booking conditions stated:

"Liability will only be accepted if you can prove that the death, injury or illness was caused by the negligence or breach of contract of Aspro, its servants, agents, suppliers or contractors. In all cases our liability is limited to twice the price of the holiday."

The court held that this condition "in all cases" was ineffective as it breached s.2 of UCTA.

Other Loss or Damage Caused by Negligence

Section 2(2) covers loss or damage which is caused by negligence but does not result in death or personal injury. Section 2(2) states:

"2(2) In the case of other loss or damage, a person cannot so exclude or restrict his liability for negligence except in so far as the term or notice satisfies the requirement of reasonableness."

The kind of damage envisaged here would occur if, for instance, a hotel negligently left a client's room open and personal belongings were stolen as in *Olley v Marlborough Court Ltd.* If a travel agent negligently failed to notify clients of important changes to a holiday this would also be covered by s.2(2). If a tour operator's representative sends clients' luggage to the wrong hotel and it gets lost this too would be subject to s.2(2).

The major difference between s.2(1) and s.2(2) is that the former prevents the exclusion of liability altogether whereas the latter is subject to a test of reasonableness. Precisely what this means will be dealt with later but what it means in practice is that once a client can prove that his loss or damage is caused by the negligence of the other party it is up to that other party to prove that it is reasonable for him to exclude liability. Given that it will already have been determined that he has acted without reasonable care this will not be easy to establish.

CHAPTER SIX

Clauses Excluding Liability for any Breach of Contract

As explained above, a party may be under different kinds of liability, strict or fault, and the contract may try to exclude liability for both or either. Section 2 deals with negligent breaches of contract, as well as the tort of negligence and breach of the Occupiers' Liability Act, but s.3 deals with any kind of breach of contract whether it be a breach of a strict obligation or was caused by negligence.

Section 3 states:

> "3(1) This section applies as between contacting parties where one of them deals as consumer or on the other's written standard terms of business.
>
> (2) As against that party, the other cannot by reference to any contract term—
>
> > (a) when himself in breach of contract, exclude or restrict any liability of his in respect of the breach; or
> > (b) claim to be entitled—
> >
> > > (i) to render a contractual performance substantially different from that which was reasonably expected of him, or
> > > (ii) in respect of the whole or any part of his contractual obligation, to render no performance at all,
>
> except in so far as (in any of the cases mentioned above in this subsection) the contract term satisfies the requirement of reasonableness."

Broadly speaking, this section will protect a person if they can establish two things: first, that they are the victim of any one of three types of unreasonable exclusion clause; secondly, if they can establish that they fall into one of two categories—either they "deal as consumer" or they deal on the other party's "written standard terms of business". These two categories and the three types of term will now be dealt with in turn.

"Dealing As Consumer"

A client will get the benefit if he can show that he "deals as consumer". This is defined in s.12:

> "12(1) A party to a contract 'deals as consumer' in relation to another party if—
>
> > (a) he neither makes the contract in the course of a business nor holds himself out as doing so; and
> > (b) the other party does make the contract in the course of a business; and
> > (c) in the case of a contract governed by the law of sale of goods or hire-purchase, or by section 7 of this Act, the goods passing under or in pursuance of the contract are of a type ordinarily supplied for private use or consumption."

Holidays are services rather than goods and therefore s.12(1)(c) is not relevant in this context.

The service is sold by a company, which makes the contract in the course of a business, to a client who does not make it in the course of a business. In these circumstances, if the contract contained an exclusion clause the client could claim the benefit of s.3. In the case of business travel, however, the client would be making the contract in the course of a business and therefore does not qualify as a consumer. This issue of who is a consumer under this section was discussed in *R&B Customs Brokers Co Ltd v United Dominions Trust Ltd* [1988] 1 All E.R. 847 in which the court was heavily influenced by the meaning of the phrase "course of a business" as used in the old Trade Descriptions Act 1968 but this approach has been criticised (see Poole, 8th edn, p.280; Cheshire, Fifoot & Furmston, 15th edn, p.239).

Section 12(3) places the burden of proof on the tour operator or travel company in these circumstances to prove that the client is not a consumer rather than for the client to prove he is.

Note that the term "consumer" used in s.3 of UCTA has a different meaning to the same term in the Package Travel Regulations and the two should not be confused. The definition is different again in the UTCCR.

Dealing on Written Standard Terms of Business

"Written standard terms of business" is not defined in the Act but it can be taken to include the small print in a travel company's or website's brochure in which the terms and conditions are set out. They are certainly written; they are terms of business; and they are standard in the sense that these are the terms and conditions which the travel company invariably deals on. They are not subject to negotiation. They are simply presented to the client on a take it or leave it basis. They always form the basis of the contract.

Thus, any client signing a booking form (or its online equivalent) which incorporates such a standard set of conditions will qualify for the protection offered by s.3. Note that the average client will qualify for protection under both categories whereas a business traveller would only qualify in the latter category.

An early case on the meaning of "written standard terms of business" case is *McCrone v Boots Farm Sales Ltd* 1981 S.L.T. 103. This is a Scottish case and in the part of the Act that applies to Scotland a slightly different form of words is used—"standard form contract" instead of "written standard terms of business" but to all intents and purposes the meaning is the same. In *McCrone* Lord Dunpark said:

"the section is designed to prevent one party to a contract from having his contractual rights, against a party who is in breach of contract, excluded or restricted by a term or condition, which is one of a number of fixed terms or conditions invariably incorporated in contracts of the kind in question by the party in breach, and which have been incorporated in the particular contract in circumstances in which it would be unfair and unreasonable for the other party to have his rights so excluded or restricted. If the section is to achieve its purpose, the phrase 'standard form contract' cannot be confined to written contracts in which both parties use standard forms. It is in my opinion wide enough to include any contract, *whether wholly written or partly oral*, which includes a set of fixed terms or conditions which the proponer applies, without material variation, to contracts of the kind in question." (Emphasis added)

Thus, according to Lord Dunpark, the contract does not have to be wholly written, it can include oral terms just so long as there are fixed terms in it. He would also permit minor alterations to the fixed terms without them losing the characteristics of a standard form contract.

Flamar Interocean v Denmac (The Flamar Pride and the Flamar Progress) [1990] 1 Lloyd's Rep. 434 is a case involving the breach of a ship management contract. It was argued by the owners of the vessels concerned that the management contract was made on written standard terms of business and therefore UCTA applied. The judge rejected this argument. He said that although the starting point for negotiating the management contract had been the standard form contract used by one of the parties, it had been subjected to a number of individually negotiated alterations to fit the particular circumstances of the case. In these circumstances, it could no longer be said to be on written standard terms.

The issue was discussed at some length in *Chester Grosvenor Hotel Co v Alfred McAlpine Management* 56 B.L.R. 115 where Judge Stannard had this to say on the meaning of written standard terms:

"In my judgment the question is one of fact and degree. What are alleged to be standard terms may be used so infrequently in comparison with other terms that they cannot realistically be regarded as standard, or on any particular occasion may be so added to or mutilated that they must be regarded as having lost their essential identity. What is required for terms to be standard is that they should be regarded by the party which advances them as its standard terms and that it should habitually contract in those terms. If it contracts also in other terms, it must be determined in any given case, and as a matter of fact, whether this has occurred so frequently that the terms in question cannot be regarded as standard, and if on any occasion a party has substantially modified its prepared terms, it is a question of fact whether those terms have been so altered that they must be regarded as not having been employed on that occasion."

Apart from a package holiday contract itself, there are innumerable standard form contracts in the travel industry. Tour operators contract with airlines and hotels on a regular basis and invariably these will be on standard terms. Hotels themselves will have any number of supply contracts.

In such cases, the tour operator or hotel may be contracting on their own standard terms or they may be contracting on the other party's. In the case of their own they need to be aware that any exclusion clause will be subject to a test of reasonableness. On the other hand, if the terms have been imposed upon them by the other party they can take the benefit of s.3. For instance, a tour operator dealing with a charter airline is likely to be faced by a standard contract which is non-negotiable. In these circumstances, if the airline broke the contract and wished to rely upon an exclusion clause they would have to prove that it was reasonable to do so. (For more on standard terms in tour operator/airline contracts see Briggs [1994] T.L.J. 20 and 44.)

The relevance of cases like *McCrone*, *The Flamar Pride* and *The Chester*

Grosvenor Hotel and subsequent cases such as *St Albans City and DC v International Computers Ltd* [1996] 4 All E.R. 481, *Pegler Ltd v Wang (UK) Ltd* [2000] B.L.R. 218 and *Watford Electronics Ltd v Sanderson CFL Ltd* [2000] 2 All E.R. (Comm) 984, however, is that once the parties depart from the standard form contract and begin negotiating terms on an individual basis the contract ceases to be covered by s.3. The logic of this is that if the parties are able to negotiate on the terms then it is less likely that the terms will be unreasonable. It will be more likely that any exclusion clause will have been part of a genuine bargaining process.

Breach of Contract

Once a party has qualified for the protection of s.3 then he will get that protection against three kinds of exclusion clause—so long as the term cannot be shown to be reasonable. The first of these is to be found in s.3(2)(a). If a person deals as consumer or on the other's written standard terms then:

"3(2) As against that party, the other cannot by reference to any contract term—

(a) when himself in breach of contract, exclude or restrict any liability of his in respect of the breach;".

This is relatively straightforward. If a travel company has made certain promises in its contract which it fails to keep then it will be in breach of contract. Any term which purports to exclude or limit that liability will not be entirely void but will have to be justified as being reasonable. So, for instance, if the tour operator has promised the client that he will be accommodated at the four star Grand Hotel and then at the last minute substitutes the three star Rustic Hotel this will be a simple breach of contract and the company will have to prove that any exclusion clause is reasonable.

Substantially Different From What Was Reasonably Expected

Section 3(2)(b)(i) covers an entirely different kind of clause. Subject again to the test of reasonableness, it states that where one party deals as consumer or on the other's written standard terms of business then:

"3(2) As against that party, the other cannot by reference to any contract term—

(a)

(b) claim to be entitled—

(i) to render a contractual performance substantially different from that which was reasonably expected of him."

If a tour operator says that he will take you on a day trip to Lapland at Christmas and when you arrive you will be taken on a sleigh drawn by reindeer to see Santa Claus, he will be in breach of contract if he substitutes a 4x4 vehicle for the sleigh and reindeer. It is a term of the contract that you will get the sleigh ride and he has broken it. In these circumstances, s.3(2)(a) will apply if his terms and condition include an exclusion clause. (See *Guardian*, December 8, 2004, p.6, for an example of such a trip that went badly wrong. See also Mather "The Importance of an English Jurisdiction Clause" [2007] I.T.L.J. 22 for a discussion of the arbitration which followed.)

However, he might have drafted his terms and conditions in a more sophisticated manner. What they might have said is that if you cannot ride on the sleigh he has the right to substitute another kind of transport. In other words, the small print is not *excluding* his liability it is *defining* it. The tour operator is saying that when he supplies a 4x4 instead of a sleigh he is not breaking the contract, he is actually fulfilling his contractual obligations as set out in the contract. Those obligations are drafted in such a way that they impose a very low level of liability on the tour operator.

It is against this kind of clause that s.3(2)(b)(i) will protect the consumer. What it says is that even if the tour operator has managed to define his liability in such a way that it could be said that providing a 4x4 instead of a sleigh is to actually "render a contractual performance", nevertheless, if this amounts to something *substantially different* from what the client *reasonably expected* it will be subject to a test of reasonableness.

There is an argument (see Yates, *Exclusion Clauses in Contracts*, 2nd edn, p.104) which says that if the tour operator has actually managed to draft his terms and conditions in such a way that he could actually convince a court that he was entitled to substitute a 4x4 for a sleigh and not be in breach of contract then how could anyone "reasonably expect" anything else. If it is reasonable to interpret the contract as meaning that, how is it possible to say it means something else? It is difficult to argue with the strict logic of this but it assumes, of course, that the other party has actually read the contract, which many clients do not, and it also assumes that one's expectations are created solely by reading the contract.

In its *Second Report on Exclusion Clauses*, No.69, 1975, the Law Commission included a draft bill which eventually became the Unfair Contract Terms Act 1977. In the commentary accompanying the draft clause which became s.3(2)(b)(i) they said:

"In deciding what was reasonably expected under the contract the terms of the contract will not be decisive: regard will be had to all the circumstances."

They justified this view in the body of the report.

"[Definitional clauses] have been the subject of complaint on the ground that they deprive the persons against whom they are invoked of contractual rights which those person legitimately expected to enjoy. They can be so expressed that the promisee may think that the promisor is undertaking an obligation which is more valuable to the promisee than in fact it is".

"it is the likelihood (in the light of the surrounding circumstances including the way in which the contract is expressed) that the promisee might reasonably have misunderstood the extent of the promisor's obligation." (para.143)

"The flaw in the weapons that the courts now have at their disposal for dealing with cases of the sort under consideration is that they are not sufficiently flexible to deal with what appears to us to be the essential danger, namely that the relatively unsophisticated or unwary party will not realise what or how little he has been promised, although the legal scope and effect of the contract may be perfectly clear to a lawyer." (para.145)

Thus, the Law Commission is saying that although the contract can legitimately be interpreted as meaning one thing, nevertheless, it is possible to have a reasonable expectation that something different has been promised.

This can arise not only from the words of the contract itself but also from the presentation of the information in the rest of the brochure or the website or other promotional material. In the case of package holidays it is from the body of the brochure/website that a client is most likely to derive his expectations. It is here that the operator sets out his stall and gives the impression, perhaps, of being able to deliver more than he actually promises in the small print. Similarly, with web-based travel products it is the images and the colourful promotional text that provides the consumer with his expectations rather than the terms and conditions of the contract which can be clicked through without being read. In many cases, they are less accessible than in the conventional tour operator's brochure.

To qualify for protection under s.3(2)(b)(i) the performance must not only be contrary to the client's reasonable expectations, it must also be *substantially different*. This is a question of degree and there will obviously be room for argument at the margins, but to return to the sleigh ride example that would clearly be a substantial difference. If, however, dogs were substituted for reindeer then the difference is less marked—although not perhaps to a five-year-old who was expecting to see "Rudolf". Perhaps a better example would be the hotel which reserved the right to substitute twin beds for doubles, or Queen beds for King beds.

A case mentioned earlier, *Anglo Continental Holidays v Typaldos (London)*, is one which today would probably be decided using s.3(2)(b)(i). Russell L.J. said of the exclusion clause that:

"It is not an exemption clause. It is a clause under which the actual contractual liability may be defined, and not one which will excuse from the actual contractual liability."

In cases like this, the courts could take the line that even though the ship owners were not actually in breach of contract, nevertheless, they were offering a performance substantially different from that which was reasonably expected, and therefore could not rely upon the clause in the contract to protect themselves.

It is conceivable, however, on the facts of the case that a court could say that although the performance was substantially different it was still within the realms of what the claimant *in this case* could reasonably expect. Remember that this claimant was not an innocent consumer requiring the protection of the law but someone in the travel business who could perhaps be expected to know and understand the terms of the contract and, moreover, be aware that this kind of thing goes on regularly.

One common problem that arises with package holidays is that flight times are often changed substantially—frequently at the last minute—but unless the change involves more than a 12-hour time difference, compensation is not usually payable. First of all, is a change of say only 10 or 11 hours *substantially different*? Secondly, is it a performance substantially different from what was *reasonably expected*? The answer to the first question must surely be yes. A difference of almost half a day when the typical package holiday only lasts one or two weeks is a substantial difference by anyone's reckoning. On the other hand, if the change only amounted to some two or three hours the answer would almost certainly be different.

As far as the second question is concerned, it could very well be argued that such a change was to be expected—partly because the terms will say as much and partly because transport delays are a fact of life to be expected by all travellers. But whether it is reasonable to expect such substantial delays is debatable.

Of course, the answer to such clauses may be that they are not definitional clauses at all, to be dealt with under s.3(2)(b)(i), but merely traditional exclusion clauses falling under s.3(2)(a), i.e. the consumer would argue that the operator was under an obligation to depart at a particular time and failure to depart on time amounted to a simple breach of contract—which the clause dealing with delays simply excludes.

To Render No Performance at All

Section 3(2)(b)(ii) covers the situation where the tour operator is under a contractual obligation but a clause permits him to render no performance at all.

> "3(2) As against that party, the other cannot by reference to any contract term—
>
> (b) claim to be entitled—
>
> (i)
> (ii) in respect of the whole or any part of his contractual obligation, to render no performance at all,
>
> except in so far as (in any of the cases mentioned above in this subsection) the contract term satisfies the requirement of reasonableness."

This is a provision which has puzzled most commentators because it is hard to see what it adds to the existing provisions. If a term in the contract gave a party the right not to perform at all then it could be argued that there was no contract at all. If, on the other hand, it gave the right not to perform part of the contract then this would be covered by s.3(2)(b)(i). Poole (*Textbook on Contract*, 8th edn, p.285) describes it as a "red herring" and Yates (*Exclusion Clauses in Contracts*, 2nd edn, p.94) says that "It is doubtful if section 3(2)(b)(ii) adds anything but confusion".

There is one example given in Cheshire, Fifoot & Furmston's *Law of Contract* (15th edn, p.238) that would probably be covered by s.3(2)(b)(ii):

> "Suppose for instance a supplier of machine tools provided in his standard printed conditions that payment terms are 25% with order and 75% on

delivery and that he should be under no obligation to start manufacture until the initial payment is made."

Such a term would literally be within s.3(2)(b)(ii) but it is doubted whether it was intended that such situations would come within its scope.

In a package holiday context it would probably apply to those situations where a consumer turns up at the airport late, as the claimant did in *Hartley v Intasun*, and the flight has already gone. In these circumstances an operator's terms and conditions often explicitly state that the operator will be under no liability. As with the example above, it is hard to see this as an exclusion clause at all but now, by virtue of reg.15(2)(a) (failures wholly attributable to the consumer) it is entirely redundant.

Varieties of Exclusion Clause

A straightforward exclusion or limitation clause is not the only way of reducing liability. It can be done in a variety of other, more subtle, ways. To combat this s.13 provides:

"13(1) To the extent that this Part of this Act prevents the exclusion or restriction of any liability it also prevents—

(a) making the liability or its enforcement subject to restrictive or onerous conditions;
(b) excluding or restricting any right or remedy in respect of the liability, or subjecting a person to any prejudice in consequence of his pursuing any such right or remedy;
(c) excluding or restricting rules of evidence or procedure;

and (to that extent) sections 2 and 5 to 7 also prevent excluding or restricting liability by reference to terms and notices which exclude or restrict the relevant obligation or duty."

This would include, for instance, imposing very short time limits for the receipt of claims as in *RW Green Ltd v Cade Bros Farms* [1978] 1 Lloyd's Rep. 602 (see below); threatening to blacklist consumers if they complain; offering only replacements rather than full refunds; etc.

ABTA tour operators routinely provide in their terms and conditions that consumers must submit claims within 28 days of the end of the holiday. The reasonableness of such clauses is discussed shortly but it seems to have been accepted without argument that the time limit was a variety of exclusion clause.

The Test of Reasonableness

Both s.2 and s.3 impose a test of reasonableness on exclusion clauses which do not involve negligence causing death or personal injury.

A number of issues are involved with this test: who has to prove the reasonableness or unreasonableness of the clause? When is the reasonableness to be measured? How will the courts decide whether a clause is reasonable? These issues will be examined now.

The Burden of Proof

Section 11 provides:

> "11(5) It is for those claiming that a contract term or notice satisfies the requirement of reasonableness to show that it does."

Thus, it is not for the client to establish that the clause is unreasonable but for the travel company to show that it is reasonable.

When the Reasonableness is Measured

This depends upon whether the exclusion is included in a contract or not. If, as is most likely in travel cases, the exclusion is contained in a contract then s.11(1) applies.

> "11(1) In relation to a contract term, the requirement of reasonableness for the purposes of this Part of this Act is that the term shall have been a fair and reasonable one to be included having regard to the circumstances which were, or ought reasonably to have been, known to or in the contemplation of the parties when the contract was made."

This means that the courts will not take into account any events occurring after the contract was made. It is the state of mind and the circumstances existing at the time the contract was made that are relevant to the reasonableness of the clause.

In particular, the courts will not be able to take into account the extent or seriousness of the breach if that was not something which could have been foreseen by the parties.

If the claim is being made in tort rather than contract then s.11(3) applies:

> "11(3) In relation to a notice (not being a notice having contractual effect), the requirement of reasonableness under this Act is that it should be fair and reasonable to allow reliance on it, having regard to all the circumstances obtaining when the liability arose or (but for the notice) would have arisen."

Thus, in a tortious claim, the reasonableness of the notice is to be measured when the tort took place—not necessarily when the claimant was given notice of the exclusion.

In *Monarch Airlines Ltd v London Luton Airport Ltd* [1998] 1 Lloyd's Rep. 403 the claimant's aircraft was damaged by the defective state of the runway caused by the negligence of the defendant airport. The defendants had a set of standard terms and conditions which contained an exclusion clause which, on its proper construction, protected them against negligence. However, there was some doubt as to whether the clause was a contractual clause, incorporated into a contract between the two parties, or whether it was a notice which operated to exclude the defendant's liability under the Occupiers' Liability Act 1957, i.e. was the defendant's liability contractual or tortious? A further complication was the issue as to whether, if it was a contractual clause, the contract had been concluded at the beginning of the season or on the day of the accident. Unfortunately, the case does not give us the answer to these questions because it was only concerned with deciding some preliminary issues. However, the judge did say that *if* the contract was concluded at the beginning of the season then the clause was a reasonable one to include:

"Having tried to take all the circumstances of the case into account I have reached the conclusion that, if cl. 10 is considered as at say March or April, 1992, it was a fair and reasonable term to include in the terms and conditions. As already stated, it was generally accepted in the market, including the insurance market. Indeed, so far as I am aware, there has been no suggestion in the market (whether it be from the airlines, the airports or the insurers) that the clause be amended in any way. It was accepted by the plaintiff without demur. It has a clear meaning and the insurance arrangements of both parties could be made on the basis that the contract was governed by standard terms which had already been held to be reasonable in principle. It follows that, judged as at the beginning of the year in April, the terms did not fall foul of the Unfair Contract Terms Act, as issue 3 puts it. It does not, however, necessarily follow that the answer is the same if the question is posed as at the day of the accident." (Because the claimant alleged that the defendant had made an inspection which revealed the state of the runway just a few days prior to the making of the contract.)

The judge further said that if the liability was tortious, then the reasonableness of the notice would be measured at the time of the tort not the giving of the notice, i.e. if circumstances had changed between giving the notice and the tort being committed these could be taken into account.

Determining Reasonableness

There is no comprehensive definition of reasonableness in the Act but since its passage there have been a number of cases from which guidance can be obtained. Before looking at these cases, however, it is necessary to point out that the Act is not entirely silent about the reasonableness test. Section 11(4), for instance, sets out factors which are to be taken into account if the clause restricts liability to a sum of money rather than excludes liability outright. It states:

"11(4) Where by reference to a contract term or notice a person seeks to restrict liability to a specified sum of money, and the question arises (under this or any other Act) whether the term or notice satisfies the requirement of reasonableness, regard shall be had in particular (but without prejudice to subsection (2) above in the case of contract terms) to—

(a) the resources which he could expect to be available to him for the purpose of meeting the liability should it arise; and
(b) how far it was open to him to cover himself by insurance."

Many tour operators have clauses limiting their liability to specified sums of money in various circumstances. In particular, they have scales of compensation covering major changes and cancellation before departure. This is not the kind of situation where a breach of contract gives rise to a liability out of all proportion to the price of the service and, therefore, the tour operator should have the resources to meet the claims in full.

This provision is intended to cover a much different kind of situation far removed from travel cases, where, say, a client asks a surveyor to do a valuation of a property for a relatively small fee. If the surveyor overlooks a major defect and the property turns out to be worthless, then there may be insufficient resources available to meet the claim. Not only that, but the risk in relation to the remuneration is disproportionate. Is it reasonable to expect a professional to take on that kind of risk for that level of fee?

On the other hand, the second limb of s.11(4) may count against the surveyor in such circumstances. This is indeed what happened in the case of *Smith v Eric S Bush* [1990] 1 A.C. 831. The House of Lords decided that one of the reasons for an exclusion clause being unreasonable in such circumstances was the fact that insurance was available on reasonable terms to cover the surveyor's risk.

Apart from s.11(4), there is also a schedule to the Act which sets out guidelines for determining the reasonableness of an exclusion clause. These guidelines in Sch.2 relate specifically to the sale and supply of goods not to contracts for services such as holidays. However, the Act does not say that the guidelines cannot be applied to contracts for services and it is clear that the courts are adopting the guidelines in non-sale of goods cases. The reason for this is quite straightforward. Most of the guidelines are as applicable to services as they are to goods—an approach which was adopted in *Phillips Products Ltd v Hyland* [1987] 2 All E.R. 620. The guidelines provide that when assessing the reasonableness of a clause regard should be had to:

(a) the strength of the bargaining positions of the parties relative to each other, taking into account (among other things) alternative means by which the customer's requirements could have been met;

(b) whether the customer received an inducement to agree to the term, or in accepting it had an opportunity of entering into a similar contract with other persons, but without having to accept a similar term;

(c) whether the customer knew or ought reasonably to have known of the existence and extent of the term (having regard, among other things, to any custom of the trade and any previous course of dealing between the parties);

(d) where the term excludes or restricts any relevant liability if some condition is not complied with, whether it was reasonable at the time of the contract to expect that compliance with that condition would be practicable;

(e) whether the goods were manufactured, processed or adapted to the special order of the customer.

Applying these guidelines to a typical travel contract it can be seen that (a) will probably favour the client. The bargaining power is all with the travel company rather than the client.

It is difficult to see how (b) applies but Cheshire, Fifoot & Furmston (15th edn, p.242) give the example of what used to happen under the Railway and Canal Traffic Act 1854. Under that Act, carriers used to offer two tariffs to passengers, a cheap one excluding liability, and a more expensive one without exclusions. This was held to be reasonable. In *Woodman v Photo Processing* (1981) N.L.J. 933, a case decided under UCTA, a County Court judge held that it was unreasonable for a film processing company to exclude liability when accepting films to be developed. One factor which weighed heavily with the judge was that it was possible for the defendants to have offered a two tier system of liability but had failed to do so. Another factor was the difficulty of finding any company at all which did not exclude liability.

In both *Love v Arrowsmith* [1989] C.L.Y. 1187 and *Usher v Intasun Holidays* [1987] C.L.Y. 418 the court held that as the exclusion clause was one which was almost universal in package holiday contracts then this was grounds for establishing its reasonableness. Although it is possible to see the merit in this argument, i.e. if it is generally accepted it must be reasonable, it nevertheless seems to fly in the face of (b) in that the consumer is faced with the situation that no matter where he goes he will have to accept the same kind of clause.

In relation to (c), it has been pointed out by Cheshire, Fifoot & Furmston that unless the other party had reasonable notice of the term in the first place it would not even be part of the contract. They suggest that what it means is that if a party is not only aware of the term, but understands the full consequences of it, then this will point to the reasonableness of the term.

Guideline (d) applies in situations where one party says to the other that if he wishes to assert his rights then he must complain within a certain time limit. In *RW Green Ltd v Cade Bros Farm* [1978] 1 Lloyd's Rep. 602 the claimant bought seed potatoes which were not of merchantable quality. There was a term in the standard form contract which required complaints to be made within three days of receipt. The justification for this was that the goods were highly perishable and could easily deteriorate rapidly after delivery, especially if not stored properly. However, the particular defect with the potatoes was not discoverable by inspection. It was held that the time limit was unreasonable in the circumstances.

In the past, most tour operators imposed a time limit of 28 days for the receipt of complaints, after which no claims would be entertained. Two cases raised the issue of whether such a limit would be reasonable. In *Davison v Martyn Holidays* Unreported 1990, Leeds County Court, the court held that the 28 day rule was unreasonable. This was largely because it was contained in a clause which imposed other conditions relating to the complaints procedure and which, taken as a whole, was unreasonable because of the unreasonable burdens it placed upon consumers who wished to complain. In *Sargant v C.I.T.* [1994] C.L.Y. 566, however, another county court held that the 28 day rule was reasonable. The judge chose not to follow the *Davison* case on the grounds that the decision in that case was based upon a concession by counsel that the clause should stand or fall as a whole. The judge in the *Sargant* case felt that the concession should not have been made and it was possible to consider the 28 day rule in isolation from the rest of the complaints procedure. Although the decision was not based on the Package Travel Regulations, he also went on to say that the clause was reasonable in the light of reg.15(9) and Sch.2 of the Regulations which permits time limits to be placed on the making of complaints. (See now the advice issued by the OFT in "Guidance on Unfair Terms in Package Holiday Contracts", March 2004, OFT 668 para.3.40 and the discussion below on the UTCCR.)

Guideline (e) also seems to have no immediate relevance to the travel industry. However, the principle can perhaps be applied to tailor-made packages. For instance, a client may approach a travel agent and ask him to put together a specific package to some remote third world country consisting of airlines, hotels and excursion companies the travel agent has never heard of. In such circumstances it might be reasonable for the agent to say that he cannot guarantee the quality of the products he is selling.

Moving away from the guidelines, it must be remembered that whether a term is reasonable or not is largely a question of fact rather than law and, therefore, what is reasonable in the circumstances of one case may not be so in another. For instance, in *Wight v British Railways Board* [1983] C.L.Y. 424 a court held that it was reasonable for British Rail to limit their liability for loss of luggage by reference to the weight of the luggage. The reason for this was that BR had no means of knowing how valuable the contents were, whereas the owner did and could insure them. Moreover, BR's competitors used similar or less generous terms. In contrast, in the earlier case of *Waldron-Kelly v British Railways Board* [1981] C.L.Y. 303 the court held that it was unreasonable to limit the liability by weight. The claimant recovered the full value of the contents rather than the amount he was limited to by the contract.

These are both only County Court decisions of little value as precedents. They demonstrate not only how very similar circumstances can give rise to very different decisions, but also that counsel for British Rail must have learnt from their earlier set-back and prepared a new set of arguments for the later case!

Lord Bridge, in *George Mitchell Ltd v Finney Lock Seeds* [1983] 2 All E.R. 737 explained how a court should approach the application of the reasonableness test, and, in particular, how an appellate court should treat an appeal that the decision was wrong. He said:

"the court must entertain a whole range of considerations, put them in the scales on one side or the other and decide at the end of the day on which side the balance comes down. There will sometimes be room for a legitimate difference of judicial opinion as to what the answer should be, where it will be impossible to say that one view is demonstrably wrong and the other demonstrably right. It must follow, in my view, that, when asked to review such a decision on appeal, the appellate court should treat the original decision with the utmost respect and refrain from interference with it unless satisfied that it proceeded on some erroneous principle or was plainly and obviously wrong."

This is a clear warning to contracting parties that appeals on the question of reasonableness will not be entertained unless an obviously perverse decision has been reached.

Before leaving the test of reasonableness it is necessary to point out that the court will assess reasonableness in relation to the *particular contract* that is under consideration. It does not matter that the clause could be regarded as reasonable in most situations if in a particular contract it was not reasonable—bearing in mind the circumstances "which were, or ought reasonably to have been, known to in the contemplation of the parties *when the contract was made*" (s.11(1)). That was the decision in *Phillips Products Ltd v Hyland* [1987] 2 All E.R. 620.

It was mentioned earlier that if a tour operator imposed a 28 day time limit for the receipt of complaints then this might be regarded as reasonable as a general rule. This does not mean, however, that because it was generally reasonable that it would be regarded as reasonable in all cases. There will be circumstances where, for instance, clients are injured on a skiing holiday and spend weeks or months afterwards in hospital. Would it be reasonable in such a case, where injuries are not uncommon, to impose a 28 day limit on the receipt of claims arising from the incident? (But note that if the injury was caused by the negligence of the tour operator itself, liability could not be excluded at all (s.2(1) and see also reg.15(5) below on the extent to which such claims can be excluded.).)

The Package Travel Regulations

The Regulations contain not only many new obligations, but also sweeping provisions preventing tour operators from excluding liability if they break these new obligations.

Exclusion of Liability in General

Regulation 15 regulates the ability of a tour operator to exclude his liability. The three relevant paragraphs are:

"15(3) In the case of damage arising from the non-performance or improper performance of the services involved in the package, the contract may provide for compensation to be limited in accordance with the international conventions which govern such services.

15(4) In the case of damage other than personal injury resulting from the non-performance or improper performance of the services involved in the package, the contract may include a term limiting the amount of compensation which will be paid to the consumer, provided that the limitation is not unreasonable.

15(5) Without prejudice to paragraph (3) and paragraph (4) above, liability under paragraphs (1) and (2) above cannot be excluded by any contractual term."

Regulation 15(5) is of general application and will be examined now. Regulation 15(3) and (4) will be examined shortly.

The importance of reg.15(5) is that it imposes an outright prohibition (subject to reg.15(3) and (4)) on any term of a contract which excludes liability for a breach of any of the obligations under the contract. This is the approach taken by the judge in *Lathrope v Kuoni Travel Ltd* [1999] C.L.Y. 1382. Kuoni argued that an exclusion clause in their contract excluded liability for a 26-hour delay on the outbound leg of a seven day package holiday to the Bahamas. Failing that, their liability was limited to £50 per head. The court held that the exclusion clause was caught by reg.15(5) and therefore ineffective. The limitation of liability was caught by reg.15(4) and as the sum was unreasonably low it too was ineffective.

Thus, on the one hand, the Regulations impose potentially greater liability on tour operators than ever before, while on the other, they prevent the exclusion of that liability.

Note, however, that the tour operator will only need to invoke an exclusion clause if there has been a breach of contract. If there has been no breach, the existence or the effectiveness of any exclusion clause is irrelevant. A clear example of this is the case of *Wilson v Best Travel Ltd* [1993] 1 All E.R. 353 which we have already examined in relation to implied terms (see Chs 4 and 5). The issue in that case was whether or not the glass in the patio door should conform to British or Greek standards. It was held that it was sufficient that the glass complied with Greek standards and, therefore, there was no breach of contract. This was a case decided at common law before the passage of the Package Travel Regulations, but the outcome would be the same today (see *Evans v Kosmar* referred to in Ch.5). A court would decide that there had been no breach of reg.15, i.e. the tour operator had properly performed his obligations under the contract. Therefore, there would be no need for the tour operator to have to rely on any exclusion clauses in his contract with the consumer—which is just as well because they would have been ineffective. (See also Sch.2, para.3 of the Package Travel Regulations.)

We have already looked briefly at the case of *Sargant v C.I.T.* [1994] C.L.Y. 566 where a court held that a client who did not complain within 28 days of return was barred from making a claim by a term in the contract. This was upheld as being reasonable under the Unfair Contract Terms Act. However, the case could have been decided entirely differently under the Regulations if they had been applicable. *Sargant* was a case involving personal injury and therefore the blanket prohibition on exclusion clauses in reg.15(5) may catch the 28 day rule and make it ineffective in such cases (although it must be said that the combined effect of regs.15(9) and Sch.2, para.12 conflicts with this view—which, in turn, seems to conflict with the view of the OFT).

This is dependent, of course, on a 28 day limit for receipt of claims being regarded as an exclusion clause. Views may differ on this. One way of looking at such a clause is to say that it is an exclusion clause because failure to comply has the effect of denying the consumer rights he would otherwise have but for the clause. Another way is to say that there is no denial of rights at all, merely a justifiable encouragement to act on those rights in a timely fashion. In both *Sargant* and in *Davison v Martyn Holidays* the view taken by the court was that the clause was an exclusion clause. In adopting this stance the courts were guided by s.13 of UCTA, which as we have already seen regards the imposition of "restrictive or onerous conditions" as a variety of exclusion clause. The thrust of this provision however is that the imposition of such a condition is only an exclusion clause if it is *restrictive or onerous*. In other words, such conditions are not automatically to be regarded as exclusion clauses—only if the condition is too stringent. Thus, UCTA imposes a twofold test. First, is the condition restrictive or onerous?—in which case it can be regarded as an exclusion clause. Secondly, if it is an exclusion clause, is it unreasonable?

If we adopt this kind of approach to a time limit that falls to be decided under the Regulations we would have to say first whether it was restrictive or onerous.

If not, then it would not be regarded as an exclusion clause at all and the tour operator could rely on it. If it was regarded as restrictive, then it would automatically fail because it would be caught by the blanket restriction under reg.15(5). It must, however, be remembered that although it would be convenient to adopt the wording from UCTA, "restrictive or onerous", that is merely a shorthand version of the real question: is it an exclusion clause? But if that approach is adopted it is difficult to deny that a 28 day limit is *restrictive*. Since the intervention of the OFT (see below), most travel companies have watered down the effect of such clauses, so that they tell consumers something anodyne like "failure to do so may affect your rights". The authors are unaware of any recent attempts by such companies to argue at court that such a clause has the effect of excluding liability, if disobeyed by the consumer.

Limitation in Accordance with International Conventions

Regulation 15(3) permits a tour operator to limit his liability in accordance with international conventions. The Regulations do not actually specify which international conventions are being referred to. However, the preamble to the Directive does refer to the Warsaw Convention on Carriage by Air, the Berne Convention on Carriage by Rail, the Athens Convention on Carriage by Sea and the Paris Convention on the Liability of Hotelkeepers. It can be assumed, therefore, that these conventions at least will be relevant to reg.15(3) and perhaps others as well because the list contained in the preamble is not exhaustive. (Note that the Warsaw Convention has now been superseded in large parts of the world by the Montreal Convention and the limits on liability are now either much more generous, or non-existent, compared to the limits in the Warsaw Convention which were particularly parsimonious. See Ch.13 for a fuller explanation.)

These conventions permit the relevant carriers and hoteliers to limit their liability to the sums specified in the conventions. The situation could conceivably arise where the organiser was held liable under the Regulations for some fault of his supplier, say an airline, and would have to pay full compensation, whereas the supplier himself would be able to limit his liability under the Montreal Convention even though he was the one at fault. The purpose of this provision is to restore the balance between supplier and organiser. If the supplier can limit his liability then so should the organiser be able to.

The choice of words, however, is a little unfortunate. The Regulations provide that Member States may allow compensation to be limited *in accordance* with the relevant international convention. Strictly speaking, to allow an organiser to limit his liability for deficiencies with the air travel would not be *in accordance* with the Warsaw or Montreal Conventions because the Convention does not apply to tour operators. (Although there is an argument to the contrary which has not been tested. See Grant "Tour Operators, the Package Travel Regulations and the Warsaw Convention" *The Aviation Quarterly*, October 1999.) Presumably, what the Regulations mean to say is that the organiser can limit his liability under the Regulations *as if he were a carrier* under the Warsaw Convention.

A problem arises for the tour operator when a flight is not covered by the Montreal Convention but where the airline is able to limit its liability by other means. For instance, in some countries airlines can limit their liability for domestic flights and passengers can recover little by way of compensation. In such cases, a consumer could very well make a claim against the tour operator under reg.15 and recover the full amount of compensation because the tour operator would be unable to limit his liability using reg.15(3), unless he could rely on reg.15(4) if it was a non-personal injury case. The tour operator would be thrown back on any indemnity he had negotiated in his contract with the air-line—which in turn would depend on the kind of leverage that could be brought to bear during contract negotiations.

There is a great danger here for travel agents and other organisers who put tailor-made packages together involving international carriage if they are not in the habit of using standard form contracts. Unless they have a set of terms and conditions which restrict their liability in accordance with the relevant conven-tion they may find themselves first in the firing line when it comes to compen-sation. The ECJ decision in the *Club Tour* case makes this much more of an issue for travel agents, although following the cases of *ABTA v CAA* [2006] EWHC 13 (Admin) and the *Travel Republic* litigation (see Ch.2) the danger seems to have slightly diminished.

Take the example of a travel agent who organises a tailor-made package for a millionaire whose luggage, which contains thousands of pounds of valuables, is lost by the airline. The airline involved will be able to restrict its liability under the Montreal Convention to relatively modest sums, but the travel agent, without an appropriate set of terms and conditions, may be fully liable. Even when the agent does have a set of his own terms and conditions it will still probably be necessary to obtain the consumer's signature on a booking form to ensure that the terms can be *proved* to be incorporated in the contract. It follows that yet again we see the vital importance for travel companies to obtain a signed booking form or its online equivalent.

Regulation 15(3) permits the tour operator to limit the *compensation* payable in accordance with the relevant international conventions. This clearly permits the *amount* of compensation to be limited but the question of whether the *type* of compensation payable, e.g. for mental distress, is limited is more dubious. In *Reid v Ski Independence* 1999 S.L.T. (Sh Ct) 62 the court held that damages for distress and disappointment caused by aircraft delay could be recovered from the tour operator. However, the basis of the decision is that it could have been recovered anyway under the Warsaw Convention. Thus, the case does not pro-vide an answer to the question of whether, if such damages could not be recovered under the Convention, they could therefore be denied under the PTR by virtue of reg.15(3). (See now the case of *Walz v Clickair* described in Ch.13.)

Regulation 15(3) also has nothing to say on other provisions. For instance, under the Warsaw Convention there is a two year limitation period and no claims can be brought outside this period. There is nothing in reg.15(3) to suggest that the tour operator can take advantage of this shorter period. But see *Norfolk v MyTravel* described below.

One problem that may occur is that although the Montreal Convention is gradually being adopted by most countries, there are still a number of countries that have not adopted it, in which case the carriage by air could be governed by the Warsaw Convention, the Warsaw Convention as amended by the Hague Protocol, or perhaps no international convention at all. For reasons that are explained in Ch.13 on Air and Sea Travel, this will not generally impact upon travellers leaving and returning to the UK by air, as the Montreal Convention will invariably apply to such journeys. However, where the air travel is more complex, involving stopovers and internal flights, the position may be different.

In practical terms, what will this mean for tour operators faced with such a patchwork of provisions? First, the tour operator will not be able to invoke the limitation of liability if it is not contained in an international convention, so this rules out domestic licensing conditions and domestic legislation as well as voluntary agreements. This leaves the Warsaw Convention as amended by the Hague Protocol and the Montreal Convention. Secondly, it makes sense that the tour operator cannot simply choose to limit his liability according to the convention that suits him best, i.e. the unamended Warsaw Convention which imposes the lowest limits. The limitation that the operator has to abide by will be the limitation that applies to the flight (or "governs the service" as the Regulation provides) on which his clients were carried—which will vary according to the destination of the flight and the registration of the carrier—just as it does for ordinary passengers. Admittedly, this is a complicated business but no more so than for air travel as a whole.

There have been two cases which have a bearing on the ability of tour operators to limit their liability under reg.15(3). The first is *Akehurst v Thomson Holidays Ltd & Britannia Airways Ltd* Unreported May 6, 2003, Cardiff County Court. The facts of the case were that Thomson had sold package holidays to the claimants which involved a flight on a Britannia plane to Gerona airport. On arrival at Gerona the plane overshot the runway. No one was killed but several suffered minor physical injuries and a group also suffered psychological injury. Britannia admitted liability for the physical injuries because they were caused by an "accident" under the Warsaw Convention, but denied liability for the psychological injury on the basis that the Convention only covered "bodily injury". (See *Morris v KLM* [2002] 2 A.C. 628 and Ch.13 on Air and Sea Travel for an explanation of this.)

The claimants suffering psychological injury claimed for these injuries against Thomson, the tour operator, for breach of contract. Thomson's defence was that they had incorporated the Warsaw Convention into their terms and conditions with the passengers by reference and therefore they were able to exclude their liability for psychological injury. In an exhaustive examination of Thomson's "Fair Trading Charter" the judge comprehensively decided against Thomson saying that no reasonable person could have interpreted the terms and conditions as having excluded Thomson's liability for their injuries. The clause used by Thomson to achieve this object read as follows:

"16. The Conditions of your ticket:

When you travel by air or on water, the transport company's 'Conditions of Carriage' will apply to your journey. You can ask the travel agent booking your holiday to get you a copy of any conditions that apply to your journey if he/she has not already got them."

The judge held that, at best, all this managed to achieve was to make the passenger aware that the *carrier's* terms and conditions applied to the journey—a completely separate contract. It did not incorporate the Convention into the contract between Thomson and the claimants. Looked at in this way the case is not much more than yet another example of the kind of bad drafting that has bedevilled tour operators over the years. Of more interest, however, is the fact that the claimants conceded, and the judge agreed, that if the Warsaw Convention had been incorporated into the contract then Thomson would have been able to have exclude their liability for psychological injury. In other words, reg.15(3) is to be interpreted in such a way that the *kinds* of damage as well as the amounts recoverable are limited. This seems a surprising concession to make, not least because it could also be extended to the limitation period—only two years under the Convention. It is unlikely that future claimants would make such a concession. (Saggerson, 4th edn, p.376, is of the opinion that the effect of reg.15(3) is that it is only a "compensation capping provision".)

The second case involving international conventions is *Norfolk v MyTravel Group Plc* [2004] 1 Lloyd's Rep. 106. In this case, the claimant had bought a cruise from the defendants and was injured on board the ship, *The Carousel*. She sued the defendants under reg.15 of the PTR, who pleaded that the claim was time barred under the Athens Convention which provided for a two year limitation period, and the claim had been issued outside this two year period. It was held in this case that the defendants were *contracting carriers* under the provisions of the Athens Convention and could therefore take the benefit of the limitation period provided for in the Convention. It was held that there was no conflict between the Convention and the Regulations as the Regulations only provided for "damage-capping" and had nothing to say on the issue of limitation periods. Essentially, the judge was saying that where a claim could be brought under both the Regulations and the Convention the Convention took precedence—unless perhaps there were clear words in the Package Travel Directive to the contrary. (But as to the issue of liability and conflict between the two provisions, see the discussion of *Hone v Going Places* in Ch.5.)

The other thing of note about the case is that because MyTravel could bring themselves within the scope of the Convention by demonstrating that they were contracting carriers then the Convention applied to them *as a matter of law* and there was no need, as in the *Akehurst* case, to show that they had incorporated the provisions of the Convention into their contract with the claimant. For a similar decision on appeal following a claim that lost luggage resulted in a spoilt holiday, see *Warburton v JMC Holidays* Unreported 2003, Preston County Court. The same judge (H.H. Judge Appleton) also decided *Brakewell v Hotelplan Ltd (t/a Inghams)* Unreported 2011 at the same court, where on similar facts he came to the opposite conclusion, namely that Inghams were liable for the spoiling of the holiday that resulted from the loss of luggage. The difference was that in *Brakewell*, the judge felt that by a blanket reliance on art.19 of Montreal as their defence, the defendant was implicitly agreeing to the reversal of the burden of proof , and thereby lost the benefit of what was said in *Hone v Going Places* (that the Regulations apply to tour operators and that the claimant must prove negligence—see Ch.5. So, defendants need to steer a careful strategic course if they are to take the benefit of both the Montreal limits, and the *Hone* burden of proof).

Limitation in Cases of Non-personal Injury

Regulation 15(4) permits the organiser to limit his liability for non-personal injury *provided that the limitation is not unreasonable.*

It is difficult to assess what impact this is having on an organiser's liability. Conceivably, it could be of immense benefit to an organiser. Given that most breaches of contract do not give rise to personal injury, the potential for limiting liability is extensive. The problem lies in calculating when the limitation of liability is unreasonable and indeed how the organiser arrives at a figure at all.

Two situations come to mind when thinking about limitation of liability. The first is where the client on a "square-deal" holiday loses his luggage which he asserts contains designer clothes, a Rolex watch and a very expensive camera. Usually, this is an insurance problem, but occasionally the blame is laid at the door of the tour operator. In such circumstances a limit on liability would be of assistance—in much the same way that the insurance companies' liability is limited.

The second situation is where the consumer is claiming damages for distress and disappointment. In the past, tour operators have complained vociferously that such damages are often excessive and out of all proportion to the value of the holiday. Setting a limit on such damages would go some way to satisfying these complaints.

But at what level is the limit to be set? The Regulations state that the limit is not to be "unreasonable". One could argue that any limit is unreasonable if it is less than the consumer would be entitled to if the damages were assessed by a court. If one is entirely cynical then the answer depends upon whether the limit accords with what the judge assesses the damages to be. If the limit is less than his assessment then the limit is unreasonable.

Such an approach, of course, thwarts the intent of the Regulation which does permit a *limitation* on the compensation in appropriate cases. This means that in some cases the consumer will not be compensated for all his losses. Perhaps what the courts will do is set a "tariff" or "going-rate" for various kinds of damage and these will become the limits of liability accepted by both the courts and the industry. What the draftsman probably had in mind are the kind of arbitrary limits imposed under the Warsaw Convention. It might have been better, therefore, if limits had been set and it had not been left either to Member States or organisers themselves to determine what limits would not be unreasonable.

One case where a tour operator would have benefited from a limitation on liability is *Clarke & Greenwood v Airtours* [1995] C.L.Y. 1603. In that case, the clients paid £2,058 for their holiday but were awarded damages of £8,040. This included £800 for damages for distress for each member of the group of eight—including each of the three children. Admittedly, it was a disastrous holiday but the award of damages, which included nothing for personal injury, was very much out of line with other awards. In practice, what it meant is that the family could purchase four more identical holidays with the damages they were awarded for one disastrous holiday. (See Ch.10 on Remedies.)

One major operator used to have a term in its booking conditions stating that in the case of non-personal injury, damages will be limited to three times the price of the holiday. Given that even in the most extreme cases damages rarely exceed twice the price of the holiday (although Saggerson, 4th edn, p.234, regards this as an "optimistic" statement) it is difficult to see what purpose such a limit serves. It may even have the effect of encouraging larger claims than previously simply because consumers have been given such a generous yardstick by which to measure their loss. The OFT is of the opinion that a term which could leave the consumer with less than the common law or statute would allow is potentially unfair. However, they also refer to the ABTA Code of Conduct and say that they would not generally challenge a term that abided by the ABTA yardstick of limiting damages to no more than three times the price of the holiday (OFT 668, March 2004, paras 3.37, 3.38. Note, however, that this reference is to a previous version of the Code of Conduct and does not appear in the current Code, 2009).

The fact is that following *Milner v Carnival Plc (t/a Cunard)* [2010] EWCA Civ 389, discussed extensively in Ch.10, and the encouragement contained there to modesty in the awards of damages in holiday cases, these issues are likely to be less significant in the future.

At present, most operators, under the influence of the ABTA Code of Conduct, include scales of compensation covering such events as cancellation and major changes. The fact that the compensation is on a rising scale and that it is payable without proof of loss are arguments in favour of the limitation being reasonable. However, the generally low level at which the compensation is pitched would count against its reasonableness. Where the tour operator has limited the compensation to a single, low, sum, the courts have had no hesitation in rejecting it as unreasonable—see *Lathrope v Kuoni* [1999] C.L.Y. 1382 and *Jervis v Kuoni* [1998] C.L.Y. 3733 (also *Hartman v P&O Cruises Ltd* [1998] C.L.Y. 3732 which was decided under the UTCCR along similar lines).

THE UNFAIR TERMS IN CONSUMER CONTRACTS REGULATIONS

Introduction

The Unfair Terms in Consumer Contracts Regulations 1999 (SI 1999/2083) are the amended version of The Unfair Terms in Consumer Contracts Regulations 1994 (SI 1994/3159), which were passed on December 14, 1994, and came into force on July 1, 1995. The Regulations implement the EC Directive on Unfair Terms in Consumer Contracts (93/13/EEC). It should be noted that the Directive is currently the subject of a review in Brussels, as part of a wider review of Consumer Protection legislation.

The key to the Regulations lies in the title. It is a measure designed to protect *consumers* against *unfair* contract terms. We have already seen that there is a whole battery of legislation to protect consumers against exclusion clauses, but what is novel about this legislation is that it goes beyond the existing legislation in order to curb not simply exclusion clauses but any contract term which is unfair—a much broader concept than exclusion of liability.

For instance, if I say that in the event of a breach of contract by me, e.g. by not providing the swimming pool at the hotel that I promised, I will not be liable to pay compensation to you, then I am *excluding* my liability. On the other hand, if I say that if you wish to cancel your holiday you may do so but you will have to pay an exorbitant amount in cancellation charges, this is not a question of me excluding my liability, I am simply relying on a term in the contract which you may regard as *unfair*. UCTA and the PTR might catch the former but certainly not the latter, whereas the new Regulations would catch both.

Thus, the consumer has, in theory, been protected against unreasonable exclusion clauses since 1977, but as of July 1995 is also protected against a whole range of unfair terms as well. The reason why in many cases the protection has only been theoretical is that many consumers either do not know their rights or for one reason or another are not prepared to exercise those rights. One of the ways in which the Regulations seek to overcome the problem of enforcement is by empowering the OFT to restrain the use of unfair terms, in the first instance by agreement, but failing that, by applying for an injunction. As a consequence a large body of OFT "case law" had grown up around unfair terms and this has been "codified" in OFT publications. One such publication, "Unfair contract terms guidance" (OFT311, February, 2001) is of general application, but another, "Guidance on unfair terms in package holiday contracts" (OFT668, March 2004) is of specific interest to the travel industry. Although this guidance is not legally binding, it is nevertheless sufficiently authoritative for close attention to be paid to it and we shall be referring to it below wherever it supports or supplements the meagre case law in this area or indeed where there is no case law at all.

Limitations on the Applicability of the Regulations

Consumer

The Regulations only protect *consumers*. A consumer is defined as being "any natural person who, in contracts covered by these regulations, is acting for purposes which are outside his trade, business or profession." The effect of this is to place all contracts made by companies outside the scope of the Regulations as well as all business travel (reg.3(1)).

As with other consumer legislation, difficulties could arise at the margins as to what is meant by "purposes outside his business". For instance, what about the traveller who combines business and pleasure? What is the situation where his primary purpose is to go on holiday but who takes the opportunity of having a business meeting while abroad? (See *Havering LBC v Stevenson* [1970] 3 All E.R. 609 and *Davies v Sumner* [1984] 3 All E.R. 831 for a discussion of this issue in the context of the old Trade Descriptions Act 1968.)

Supplier

The protection afforded consumers under the Regulations is confined to situations where they are dealing with a seller or supplier. Seller or supplier is defined in reg.3(1) as meaning

"any natural or legal person who, in contracts covered by these Regulations, is acting for purposes relating to his trade, business or profession, whether publicly owned or privately owned".

Thus, where the travel contract is not made with a business or company, the Regulations do not apply.

Terms Not Individually Negotiated

Individually negotiated terms are not covered by the Regulations (reg.5(1)). The clear intention is to offer protection against the dangers inherent in standard form contracts. Clearly, this covers standard form contracts such as for package holidays and, therefore, most package holidaymakers will, prima facie, obtain the protection of the Regulations. In fact, the Regulations go further and say that a term will always be regarded as not being individually negotiated if it has been drafted in advance and the consumer has not been able to influence the substance of the term (reg.5(2)). Even if some terms of the contract have been individually negotiated, the Regulations will apply to the rest of it if overall it can be regarded as a "pre-formulated standard contract" (reg.5(3)). It is for the seller or supplier to show that a term was individually negotiated (reg.5(4)).

Thus, if I agree with the tour operator at the time of booking that they will provide a cot for my four-month-old child this will be an individually negotiated term and will not be subject to the Regulations. Furthermore, if the tour operator explains orally that they will not be liable if there is no cot, this too will be an individually negotiated term and will not be subject to the Regulations.

However, if the tour operator does not explain to me on an individual basis what limits it places on its liability, but simply relies upon a standard exclusion clause term, then this will not be individually negotiated and the Regulations will apply. (Note that in this example the tour operator had not merely agreed to use its best endeavours to fulfil a special request; it promised to provide the cot.)

The Main Subject Matter of the Contract

No assessment of fairness can be made about a term which relates to "the adequacy of the price or remuneration as against the services supplied" or which relates to "the definition of main subject matter of the contract" (reg.6(2)) unless it is not written in plain intelligible language (reg.6(2)).

The provision relating to price is relatively straightforward. If the tour operator sells me a full price holiday and I find myself sitting on the plane next to someone who has bought a "late bargain" at a fraction of the price I cannot complain however unfair I may regard it. The Regulations cannot be used to impose a "fair" price—unless the price was not expressed in plain intelligible language.

What amounts to "the main subject matter of the contract" is much more difficult. If I buy a package holiday to Majorca then presumably the main subject matter will be not only the destination but also the duration and the hotel. These are all "core terms" and, therefore, not subject to the unfairness test. But there will also be a myriad of other terms concerning such things as changes and amendments and cancellation and liability, all of which qualify the core terms but are not core terms in themselves, and, therefore, are subject to the unfairness test.

If we take an example of a "flight-only" package from Gatwick to Orlando then the main subject matter is a flight from Gatwick to Orlando. But what if the ticket has all kinds of restrictions attached to it—validity, duration of stay, refunds, etc. Do these form part of the main subject matter of the contract? Am I buying "a flight to Orlando" or "a flight with restrictions to Orlando"? If it is the former then the restrictions can be attacked as unfair, but if it is the latter then the Regulations do not apply.

It is our view that what the consumer buys is a "flight" and therefore any other terms and conditions relating to the flight do not "define" the main subject matter of the contract, they merely qualify it. Whether the terms are actually unfair is another question. When examining the unfairness of the term the court is entitled to take "all circumstances attending the conclusion of the contract" into account including the price (reg.4(2)). If I buy a cheap ticket do I expect to get all the benefits of a fully flexible ticket that may cost me several times more?

On the other hand, if I say to the travel company, "I don't care how you get me to Paris, by plane or boat or train or whatever, just get me there" then I probably couldn't complain if they put me on a clapped out bus and took me by road and tunnel. Here the "core" term would be to transport me by any means and that is just what they have done—by the cheapest and most uncomfortable means.

According to the OFT, the purpose of the provision is to "allow freedom of contract to prevail in relation to terms that are genuinely central to the bargain" (OFT311, para.19.13). In OFT668 they say that

"terms in package holiday contracts stating the accommodation to be provided, meals provided, transfer arrangement and the associated costs are likely to be considered core terms." (para.2.1)

In *Bairstow Eves London Central Ltd v Smith* [2004] EWHC 263 (QB) Gross J. said that core terms should be interpreted narrowly:

"Regulation 6(2) must be given a restrictive interpretation; otherwise a coach and horses could be driven through the Regulations. So, while it is not for the court to re-write the parties' bargain as to the fairness or adequacy of the price itself, Regulation 6(2) may be unlikely to shield terms as to price escalation or default provisions from scrutiny under the fairness requirement contained in Regulation 5(1)."

However, in *Office of Fair Trading v Abbey National Plc* [2009] UKSC 6, the Supreme Court held that a bank's overdraft charges were part of the "core terms" of their contract with consumers, and could not be assessed for fairness under the Regulations. The Court did comment that, under the wording of the Directive, it was open to our Parliament to have made the Regulations more stringent in this regard, but it had chosen not to do so.

Terms Which Reflect Other Statutory Provisions

According to reg.4(2), the Regulations do not apply to contractual terms which reflect:

"(a) mandatory statutory or regulatory provisions (including such provisions under the law of any Member State or in Community legislation having effect in the United Kingdom without further enactment);

(b) the provisions or principles of international conventions to which the member States or the Community are party."

The effect of this is that if the terms and conditions faithfully reflect the provisions of another enactment then the UTCCR cannot be used to oust them. Presumably, the purpose of this provision was twofold—not to duplicate existing legislation and not to upset well established rules of liability that already have domestic or international approval, such as the Montreal or Athens Conventions. The prime example here is, of course, the Package Travel Regulations. Given the comprehensive nature of the PTR it appears that if a tour operator complies with the Regulations there is very little left for the UTCCR to bite on. However, should the terms and conditions not comply, then what has happened is that the PTR, by creating a whole raft of new obligations, has created a whole range of possibilities for terms to be regarded as unfair. Prima facie, if the terms and conditions do not comply with the PTR then they will be unfair under the UTCCR—at least in so far as they provide less than what the PTR intended. So, failure to comply with the following provisions lays the tour operator open to challenge:

- liability (reg.15(1) & (2));
- exclusion of liability (reg.15(3)(4) & (5));
- surcharges (reg.11);
- changes and cancellations by the operator (regs 12, 13 &14);
- transfer of bookings (reg.10);
- insolvency and repatriation (reg.16).

Unfair Contract Terms

If a term can be brought within the Regulations then it will be subjected to an "unfairness" test. An unfair term is one which "contrary to the requirement of good faith causes a significant imbalance in the parties' rights and obligations under the contract to the detriment of the consumer." (reg.5(1)) Regulation 5(5) provides that the "indicative and non-exhaustive" list of terms in Sch.2 "*may* be regarded as unfair" (emphasis added).

Regulation 6(1) states that:

"the unfairness of a contractual term shall be assessed, taking into account the nature of the goods or services for which the contract was concluded and by referring, at the time of conclusion of the contract, to all the circumstances attending the conclusion of the contract and to all the other terms of the contract or of another contract on which it is dependent."

Thus, to establish that a term is unfair there are three requirements:

(a) a breach of the requirement of good faith; which,

(b) causes a significant imbalance in the parties' rights and obligations;

(c) to the detriment of the consumer.

These three elements will be examined in turn.

Good Faith

In determining good faith the 1994 Regulations provided that regard should be had to the following matters:

(a) the strength of the bargaining positions of the parties;

(b) whether the consumer had an inducement to agree to the term;

(c) whether the goods or services were sold or supplied to the special order of the consumer; and

(d) the extent to which the seller or supplier has dealt fairly and equitably with the consumer.

These provisions (which are almost identical to guidelines found in the Unfair Contract Terms Act (Sch.2)) have been omitted from the 1999 Regulations, but very similar words can nevertheless be found in the preamble to the Directive and, therefore, courts, when seeking guidance, may have recourse to the preamble.

Some guidance on the meaning of good faith can be derived from the House of Lords decision in *Director General of Fair Trading v First National Bank Plc* [2000] Q.B. 672. Lord Bingham said:

"The requirement of good faith in this context is one of fair and open dealing. Openness requires that the terms should be expressed fully, clearly and legibly, containing no concealed pitfalls or traps. Appropriate prominence should be given to terms which might operate disadvantageously to the customer. Fair dealing requires that a supplier should not, whether deliberately or unconsciously, take advantage of the consumer's necessity, indigence, lack of experience, unfamiliarity with the subject matter of the contract, weak bargaining position or any other factor listed in or analogous to those listed in Schedule 2 to the Regulations." (This was a decision under the 1994 Regulations)

A Significant Imbalance

It is not sufficient that the company is not acting in good faith: the lack of good faith must cause a significant imbalance in the parties' rights and obligations. Guidance on this is also to be found in Lord Bingham's judgment in the *First National Bank* case:

"The requirement of significant imbalance is met if a term is so weighted in favour of the supplier as to tilt the parties' rights and obligations under the contract significantly in his favour. This may be by the granting to the supplier of a beneficial option or discretion or power, or by the imposing on the consumer of a disadvantageous burden or risk or duty."

Clearly, if the contract is riddled with draconian exclusion clauses depriving the holidaymaker of all rights on the one hand, while on the other permitting the travel company to avoid its obligations at will, this would be an obvious example of the imbalance the Regulations are designed to curb.

To the Detriment of the Consumer

The third requirement of an unfair term is that it be to the detriment of the consumer. Unlike the other two requirements, this should not create undue difficulty. The detriment will be the delayed departure, the dirty room, the non-existent pool, etc, for which there is no compensation.

Examples of Unfair Terms

To assist in the determination of whether a term is unfair, guidance is offered in the form of Sch.2, which provides an "indicative and non-exhaustive" list of terms which may be regarded as unfair. Schedule 2 does not create a "black list", but a list of terms which *may or may not* be unfair depending on the circumstances. It has been referred to as a "grey list".

Many of the examples given are straightforward exclusion clauses that are already caught by the Unfair Contract Terms Act but there are others which may simply be unfair. For instance, examples 1(d) and 1(e) which deal with terms which may require a consumer to pay disproportionately large sums if they choose to cancel a contract. Example 1(n) concerns clauses which limit the supplier's duty to honour commitments undertaken by agents or employees—a type of clause occasionally found in travel contracts.

Plain English

There is a requirement in the Regulations that written terms must be expressed in plain, intelligible language and if there is a doubt about the meaning of the term then the interpretation most favourable to the consumer will prevail (reg.7). This amounts to no more than the *contra proferentem* rule in statutory form.

Where there is clear ambiguity there should be no problems applying this provision. Problems may arise, however, because in some cases it could be argued that there is no doubt about the meaning of the term—it only has one meaning—unfortunately it takes a lawyer to find it. Presumably, it is open to a consumer to say that he had doubts about the meaning of it because he just couldn't understand it at all. In such circumstances he could go on to say that perhaps it meant this or perhaps it meant that or perhaps it meant the other and then choose the interpretation that was most favourable to him. He might just say that as it was meaningless to all but lawyers then no meaning should be attributed to it at all.

The Effect of Finding a Term Unfair

If a term is found to be unfair then it will not be binding on the consumer but the rest of the contract will continue to be binding (reg.8). The dilemma for individual consumers is that it will often be difficult, and expensive, to contest a term which they consider to be unfair. Often, it will be a battle which they will prefer to concede rather than fight—no matter how right they may feel they are. (See "Battle with the big guns in the small claims court" *The Times*, May 10, 2006, for an account of the first author's attempt to challenge an unfair term in an airline contract.)

The Role of the Office of Fair Trading

If a complaint is made to the OFT that a term drawn up for general use is unfair, then, unless the complaint is vexatious or it is being considered by a "qualifying body" (see below), it is their duty to consider it (reg.10). After considering the complaint, and taking into account any undertakings that have been made to it, the OFT may restrain the use of the term by applying for an injunction (reg.12). Given that many consumers are either ignorant of their rights or may not be inclined to pursue them as far as court, this is clearly a very important method of curbing the use of unfair terms. If one consumer complains about a single term in a single contract then the impact of this, even if successful, is likely to be minimal. But if the OFT manages to restrain the use of such a term in all such contracts then the benefit will be felt by all consumers. It is clearly in the interests of holidaymakers to identify terms which they consider unfair and bring them to the notice of the OFT. The success of such a course of action will depend, of course, on the enthusiasm, and the resources, which the OFT decides to devote to it. There is plenty of evidence that the OFT is pursuing such terms vigorously. Regular bulletins have been published by the OFT listing the terms which have been drawn to their attention and the action they have taken. These frequently feature terms and conditions from tour operators' brochures. In October 2002 the OFT published the results of its discussions with all four major tour operators and ABTA and they all agreed to make significant changes to the terms and conditions they used or, in the case of ABTA, recommended. Much of what they agreed to has now been consolidated in OFT668.

Note, however, that although action by the OFT can be triggered by an individual complaint about an unfair term there is nothing in the Regulations empowering the OFT to take up individual cases on behalf of consumers. The powers conferred are aimed at restricting the use of unfair terms in general rather than acting on behalf of specific individuals. Nevertheless, those powers include the power to seek an injunction not only against the person actually using the unfair term, e.g. the tour operator, but also, as we have just seen in the case of ABTA, any person recommending the use of such a term.

Since the Regulations were first brought into force in 1995, a significant change in the enforcement regime has taken place. Whereas formerly it was only the OFT which could seek injunctive relief, now a whole range of "qualifying bodies" have that power. They are listed in Sch.1 and include every weights and measures authority in Great Britain (trading standards departments); the Rail

Regulator; and the Consumers' Association. These qualifying bodies must inform the OFT if they are taking up a complaint and if they are seeking an injunction.

The power of the court to award an injunction extends not only to the particular term it is being asked to consider but also "any similar term, or a term having like effect, used or recommended for use by any person" (reg.12(4)). Thus, it may be possible for the court to restrain the use of one type of clause, in, say, a TUI brochure, and at the same time to restrain the same type of clause in Thomas Cook and Kuoni brochures or on a Travel Republic website.

Schedule 2

Schedule 2 includes an "indicative and non-exhaustive" list of terms which may be regarded as unfair. Many of these terms are simply varieties of exclusion clause which would probably be caught by the PTR or UCTA already, but some are examples of unfair terms which are not simple exclusion clauses. One of these is Illustrative Term 1(n):

> "(n) limiting the seller's or supplier's obligation to respect commitments undertaken by his agents or making his commitments subject to compliance with a particular formality".

It is a fairly common problem for companies to find that employees or agents have exceeded their authority and promised clients more than they should have. It is also the case that, having placed the employee or agent in a position where either they have actual authority or apparent authority to make such promises, the company will have to honour the commitments made (*Freeman & Lockyer v Buckhurst Park Properties (Mangal) Ltd* [1964] 2 W.L.R. 618). To combat this difficulty, companies will insert a clause like this into the contract:

> "No agent, employee or representative of the Company has authority to alter, modify or waive any provision of these Conditions of Contract."

The effect of this clause is to place a restriction on the ability of employees and agents to make promises which are beyond their authority to make. The reason the restriction is printed in the terms and conditions is so that the consumer is given notice that the employee or agent has no such authority. It is thus not possible for the consumer to argue that the employee had either express or apparent authority to vary the terms and conditions of the contract (*Overbrooke Estates Ltd v Glencombe Properties Ltd* [1974] 1 W.L.R. 1335). A term like this was deleted, after intervention by the OFT, from the terms and conditions of the tour operator Voyages Jules Verne (see OFT Unfair Contract Terms Bulletin 21, June–September 2002, OFT 656, p.77, published May 2003 available at *www.oft.gov.uk*).

In Practical Terms What Does This Mean?

Perhaps I particularly wish to book a hotel where I can have adjoining rooms with other members of my party. I ask the travel agent if this is possible and he explains that although I can make a "special request" for adjoining rooms, tour operators will not guarantee such a request. This does not satisfy me so I ask the travel agent to phone the tour operator to see if something more can be done. The travel agent speaks to someone who is prepared to give such a guarantee and therefore I book the holiday. However, what the tour operator's member of staff has done is unauthorised. He should not have guaranteed me adjoining rooms. So what happens when I subsequently arrive at the hotel and find that my party is split between two floors? Can I claim breach of contract? The tour operator might endeavour to rely upon the term in their terms and conditions to the effect that special requests are not guaranteed and that any employee who promised otherwise had no authority to do so. Moreover, because I had signed the booking conditions I had had notice that the employee did not have the authority to vary the booking conditions and therefore could not argue otherwise.

This is where the Regulations come in. Is such a term unfair? We think that a good case could be made out for saying that it is—and not just in the example given above but in most cases. Apart altogether from the fact that the tour operator's bargaining position is far superior to the consumer's and that the term is buried in a long document full of legal jargon and that the consumer had no choice but to accept the term we think that most objective observers would say that the term is unfair by any standards.

Tour operators employ people in positions where it is a reasonable expectation that they have the authority that goes with that position. The employees deal with consumers who will rely upon what they say and act upon the advice that they are given. Surely it is right that if such employees make mistakes then the tour operator should be prepared to accept liability for those mistakes and not hide behind the small print in the contract—which they know full well will not be read or understood by the majority of their customers?

The OFT gives an example of such a term in a package holiday contract which the supplier deleted after OFT intervention:

"Representatives and agents are not entitled without [the supplier's] express authority to alter itineraries, cancel arrangements or tickets, make or promise refunds on our behalf or obtain loans or services or incur telecommunication expenses on your behalf." (OFT 668, para.3.6)

Schedule 2 contains other examples of unfair terms which are not exclusion clauses and therefore not entirely within the scope of this chapter. These other terms will be dealt with elsewhere in the book where appropriate. In particular, the impact of the UTCCR on cancellation charges is examined in Ch.10.

OFT 668 and OFT Action in 2002

Given that it is taking years for significant case law to develop around the UTCCR, it is worthwhile examining the approach taken in OFT668, the OFT's specific guidance on unfair terms in package holiday contracts. While this guidance does not have judicial authority it comes as near as we have today to being authoritative and it gives a clear insight into how the OFT will approach its obligations in respect of travel contracts. Specific examples of clauses that the OFT disapproved of can be found in OFT 668, but the action the OFT took in

2002 against the booking conditions of the four major tour operators and ABTA probably serves as the best practical advice available.

The guidance begins by stating that terms which do not accurately reflect the requirements of the Package Travel Regulations are potentially unfair under the UTCCR and they take a broad approach to this:

> This is not only a matter of avoiding explicit conflict with the provisions of the PTRs. Consumers will generally be unaware of their rights under the PTRs, and we consider that a term may be unfair if, by not reflecting the PTRs, it could mislead or confuse consumers (para.1.8).

When discussing the requirement for plain English they re-emphasise the duty not to mislead:

> "Transparency is also fundamental to fairness. Regulation 7 says that standard terms must use plain and intelligible language. This does not mean only that terms should be clear for legal purposes. When the OFT assesses fairness, it also has to consider what a consumer is likely to understand by the wording of a clause. Even if a clause would be clear to a lawyer, the OFT will probably conclude that it has potential for unfairness if it is likely to mislead, or be unintelligible to consumers. Those buying package holidays do not normally seek legal advice, so contracts should use language that is plain and intelligible to ordinary people." (para.2.4)

The advice goes on to explain what the OFT understands by the test of fairness and how they will apply it in practice. This is expressed in terms which echo the judgment in the *First National Bank* case:

> "The requirement of 'good faith' embodies a general principle of fair and open dealing. It means not only that terms should not be used in bad faith, but also that they should be drawn up in a way that respects consumers' legitimate interests. Therefore in assessing fairness, the OFT takes note of how a term could be used. A term is open to challenge if it is drafted so widely that it could be used in a way that harms consumers. Protest that the term is not used unfairly in practice is therefore not enough to persuade the OFT that it is immune from challenge under the Regulations. Claims like this usually show that the supplier could redraft the term more precisely both to reflect its intentions and to achieve fairness."

As indicated above, the OFT agreed significant changes to their terms and conditions with the four major tour operators in October 2002. At the same time, ABTA agreed to make changes to their recommended terms and conditions. The following types of terms were regarded as unfair and the tour operators concerned agreed to change or delete them:

- Terms which permitted tour operators to impose surcharges if costs rose but denied a reduction if they fell.

EXCLUSION OF LIABILITY AND UNFAIR CONTRACT TERMS

- Terms denying liability if complaints were received more than 28 days after the holiday.

- Terms which gave no cancellation rights after a holiday had started where there was a change to the holiday arrangements if the company offered a "suitable alternative".

- Terms which excluded payment of compensation for significant changes to a holiday before departure above a set scale, even if a consumer could prove a greater loss.

- Terms which prevented the transfer of bookings to another person where the consumer is prevented from travelling, on certain types of holiday.

- Terms which allowed the imposition of cancellation charges within eight weeks of departure where the consumer wishes to transfer a booking to another where he/she is prevented from travelling even if the cost of making the change was less than the cancellation charge.

- Terms which limited liability for lost or damaged baggage to £400 per person. Liability was increased to £1,000 per person.

- Terms which excluded liability for the non-availability of facilities outside the peak season. Compensation now offered to consumers, where appropriate, if there is a significant change to the brochure's description of the facilities.

- Terms which did not comply with the PTRs requirement that the tour operator should meet the first two per cent of any surcharge.

- Terms which did not comply with the requirement that if a significant surcharge was imposed (stated in the contract as more than a 10 per cent increase) and the consumer cancels, the tour operator should offer replacement holidays of equivalent/superior quality, if able to, as well as the option of a full refund (as required under the PTRs).

- Terms which required consumers to take out insurance but refused to refund premiums when the consumer cancelled the holiday following a significant surcharge.

- Terms which offered compensation for only certain named significant changes made to the holiday before departure.

- Terms which required the consumer to pay the difference in price on taking a more expensive substitute holiday when the original holiday was cancelled through no fault of the consumer or when the tour operator significantly altered the holiday.

- Terms which did not specify that the PTRs require that no surcharge should be made within 30 days before departure.

- Terms which failed to provide the consumer with the option of taking a replacement holiday of equivalent/superior quality, if available, or a full refund, as required by the PTRs, where building work had a significant effect on the consumer's enjoyment of the holiday.

- Terms which stated that the contract is governed exclusively by English law and granted exclusive jurisdiction to the English courts which is potentially unfair to consumers in Scotland and Northern Ireland.

- Terms which failed to make clear the options available under the PTRs when the original holiday is cancelled through no fault of the consumer.

- Terms which recommended that a 21 day notice period would be a reasonable requirement for a consumer to request a name change under reg.10 of the PTRs. This was changed so that the term now refers to what is reasonable in individual circumstances.

- Terms which excluded an insurance premium refund where a consumer cancels as a result of a significant change including an increase of more than 10 per cent of the price, contrary to the PTRs.

- Terms which stated that a name change affecting everyone on the booking will be treated as a cancellation and incur cancellation charges. This conflicts with the right under the PTRs to transfer a booking in certain circumstances.

- Terms which excluded payment of compensation for significant changes made to a holiday by the tour operator above a set scale, even if the consumer could prove a greater loss. In addition, the contract excluded compensation entirely for changes made more than 56 days before departure.

- Terms which denied liability for flight delays (contrary to PTRs requirement to be responsible for third party suppliers).

Whether the OFT could have obtained an injunction in respect of every single one of the above points may be debated. But there is no doubt that the agreement reached had an effect that will benefit over 90 per cent of package holidaymakers.

Misrepresentation

INTRODUCTION

In Ch.4 we saw how representations could be distinguished from terms of the contract and mere puffs. Once that has been done, it is necessary to distinguish between different types of misrepresentation. The reason for this is that the type of misrepresentation determines the remedies that are available to the victim. At one end of the scale the victim may end up with no remedy at all, whereas at the other end, the remedies are quite comprehensive. In this chapter we will look first at the different types of misrepresentation and then at the remedies available.

TYPES OF MISREPRESENTATION

There are three types of misrepresentation—*fraudulent* misrepresentation, *negligent* misrepresentation and *innocent* misrepresentation. Prior to 1967 there were only two types—fraudulent and innocent—but the Misrepresentation Act 1967 created a third type—negligent misrepresentation. The effect of the Act is relatively limited. Its main effect is to improve the remedies for non-fraudulent misrepresentation. It has no effect upon what amounts to a misrepresentation and what does not.

Fraudulent Misrepresentation

The accepted definition of a fraudulent misrepresentation is to be found in the case of *Derry v Peek* (1889) L.R. 14 App. Cas. 337. Lord Herschell said:

> "fraud is proved when it is shown that a false representation has been made (1) knowingly, or (2) without belief in its truth, or (3) recklessly, careless whether it be true or false".

The essence of this definition is that the representor is not guilty of fraud if he made the statement with an honest belief in its truth—no matter how ill founded that belief may be. In *Derry v Peek* itself the directors of a company had issued a prospectus in which they stated that the company had the power to operate steam driven trams rather than horse drawn trams. In fact, the company did not have this power but the directors *honestly believed* it did and were therefore not liable for fraud.

At this stage it is necessary to point out that a fraudulent misrepresentation amounts to the *tort of deceit*. In other words, when a claimant brings an action for fraudulent misrepresentation his action, technically, is not in the law of *contract* but in the law of *tort*. The reason for this is historical. Actions for deceit in the law of tort developed in such a way that they took in fraudulent statements connected to contracts as well as statements which were not related to contracts. The only practical effect this has on the law of misrepresentation is that the damages that are payable are calculated in a slightly different fashion, on a *tortious* rather that a *contractual* basis. The way this works is dealt with in the next section.

If a tour operator deliberately published statements in a brochure which he knew to be false, then he would be making fraudulent misrepresentations. So, for instance, if he published an artist's impression of a hotel and said that this hotel "will be completed" before the commencement of next season when he knows full well that it will not and he will have to move clients to another hotel, then in the words of Lord Herschell he makes a false statement "knowingly" and will be guilty of deceit. It would be different if the operator put the statement in the brochure honestly believing that it was true. Even if all the evidence pointed the other way and only somebody who was either excessively optimistic or truly stupid would have believed it, it would nevertheless not amount to fraud. It might very well be negligent but it would not be dishonest. It would always be open to the court, however, to infer from the circumstances that the statement could only have been made knowingly or recklessly because *no one* could be so optimistic or so stupid!

If a theme park operator advertised that in the forthcoming season a new ride would be open, hoping that it would be but in the full knowledge that it might not be because the construction work had started late, then this would be a reckless statement and would be treated as fraudulent misrepresentation. Likewise, if a car hire firm advertised that the latest Ford model would be available for hirers when it knew that this was unlikely because negotiations to purchase the car had broken down, this would be a reckless statement and thus amount to a fraudulent misrepresentation.

Note that allegations of fraud must be proved by a claimant on the criminal standard, i.e. beyond reasonable doubt, rather than the civil standard, on the balance of probabilities.

Negligent Misrepresentation

Prior to 1967, if a misrepresentation was not fraudulent it could only be innocent. An innocent misrepresentation therefore covered a wide spectrum of statements. It encompassed those which were very nearly fraudulent such as in *Derry v Peek* and extended to cover those which were made without any element of fault at all by the representor such as in *Oscar Chess v Williams* [1957] 1 W.L.R. 370. In that case the seller of the car had only represented that the car was younger than it really was because the log book had been very carefully forged by a previous owner and there was nothing about the model of the car or its mileage or its condition to suggest that the log book was wrong. The injustice this created was that only fraudulent misrepresentations entitled the victim to damages. Even for the most negligent of statements the victim could not be compensated with damages. There was another remedy, *rescission of the contract*, but this might not be available, in which case the victim was left without a remedy altogether.

The Misrepresentation Act 1967 was passed to remedy this situation. Section 2(1) of the Act creates an action for damages for negligent representations. Section 2(1) states:

> "Where a person has entered into a contract after a misrepresentation has been made to him by another party thereto and as a result thereof he has suffered loss, then, if the person making the misrepresentation would be liable to damages in respect thereof had the misrepresentation been made fraudulently, that person shall be so liable notwithstanding that the misrepresentation was not made fraudulently, unless he proves that he had reasonable ground to believe and did believe up to the time the contract was made that the facts represented were true."

This is phrased rather clumsily but what it comes down to is this. If a misrepresentation has been made which is not fraudulent, the representor will nevertheless be liable to pay damages *unless he can prove that he had reasonable grounds for making the statement*. Thus, the Act creates a right to damages which did not exist before, but, just as importantly, if not more so, it places the onus of proof on the representor. Once it can be shown that there is a misrepresentation, it is up to the representor to show that it was reasonable to make the statement, not for the victim to show that it was unreasonable.

The difficulties of doing this are clearly illustrated in the case of *Howard Marine & Dredging Co Ltd v Ogden & Sons Ltd* [1978] Q.B. 574. The claimants owned two barges which they hired to the defendants who wanted them to carry waste from excavation works to be dumped at sea. The capacity of the barges was crucial to the defendants. The claimant's marine manager misrepresented their capacity to the defendants. The reason for this was that he quoted them the capacity of the barges as stated in Lloyd's Register. In fact, for once, the Register was wrong. The correct capacity was contained in shipping documents which were in the claimant's possession but which the marine manager did not refer to. Once the truth was apparent the defendants, claiming misrepresentation, refused to pay any more hire charges and returned the barges. The claimants sued them for breach of contract. In a split decision the Court of Appeal decided that the claimant's marine manager did *not* have reasonable grounds for making the false statement. After reviewing all the evidence Bridge L.J. said:

> "But the question remains whether his evidence, however benevolently viewed, is sufficient to show that he had an objectively reasonable ground to disregard the figure in the ship's documents and to prefer the Lloyd's Register figure. I think it is not."

If a tour operator publishes a false statement in his brochure about the facilities at a hotel and based it upon what a very experienced resort manager told him rather than checking with the hotel owner, then a similar situation might arise. Did the tour operator have reasonable grounds for making the statement? On the one hand, the resort manager is on the spot, is very experienced, is aware of the consequences of getting such things wrong and can usually be trusted. On the other hand, it would probably be just as easy to get the information from the hotel and this would be likely to be more accurate (although in practice information from hotels tends to be rather optimistic!). What is reasonable is a question of fact and the amount of care required varies with the circumstances. If it was a matter of detail of no real importance and on which the resort manager could be expected to have a good knowledge, then relying on her might be sufficient. On the other hand, if it was a matter of some importance which the manager might not be conversant with and which was very easy to check with the hotel then this might not amount to reasonable grounds.

Innocent Misrepresentation

If the representor can prove that he did have reasonable grounds for making the statement then he will only have made an innocent misrepresentation for which the remedies are not as extensive as for negligent or fraudulent misrepresentation.

REMEDIES FOR MISREPRESENTATION

Once it has been established that not only is there a misrepresentation but what type it is, then the remedies available can be determined. Basically, there are two types of remedy: *damages* and *rescission*. Damages are financial compensation designed to compensate the victim for the harm done by the misrepresentation in so far as money can do this. Rescission of the contract is where the victim of the misrepresentation is permitted to call the contract off and the parties are treated as though the contract never existed. The availability of the remedies is determined by the type of misrepresentation and the stage the contract has reached when the victim discovers the misrepresentation. The remedies will be looked at in turn.

Rescission

To rescind a contract means to call the contract off and return the parties to the position they were in before the contract was made as if the contract had never existed (the *status quo ante*). Rescission is a remedy which is available to the victim of a misrepresentation no matter what kind of misrepresentation occurred. However, there are certain limitations on the right to rescind and if the right is lost the victim may find himself in a position where he cannot rescind and no damages are available so he is without a remedy at all.

Affirmation of the Contract

If a party knows of the misrepresentation and chooses to affirm the contract, i.e. continue with it, he cannot then turn round and rescind it or ask the courts to rescind it. So, for instance, in the case of *Long v Lloyd* [1958] 1 W.L.R. 753 the claimant purchased a lorry on the basis of a misrepresentation. After discovering the fault with the lorry he nevertheless continued to use it. It was held that this amounted to affirmation and he could not later rescind the contract when the fault proved irreparable.

If a tour operator induced clients to enter into a package holiday contract on the basis of a misrepresentation but then discovered it and sent errata to clients this would entitle the clients to rescind the contract at that stage. However, if they were not initially concerned by the misrepresentation and went on to pay the balance when it became due, they could not subsequently rescind. Paying the balance after they knew of the misrepresentation is evidence of affirmation. They had demonstrated that they wanted the contract to continue despite knowing of the misrepresentation.

Lapse of Time

Lapse of time is not in itself a reason for denying rescission, particularly if the misrepresentation has not been discovered. However, if the lapse of time is sufficiently long then it may amount to evidence of affirmation and this may give grounds for denying rescission. So, for instance, what if a client books a holiday in October to be taken in August of the following year and is informed by an errata notice in November that the brochure is inaccurate? If the client does nothing until the following June when the balance is payable and then claims the right to rescind, a court might say that such a long delay before trying to rescind amounts to affirmation and will not be permitted. In *Leaf v International Galleries* [1950] 1 All E.R. 693 a purchaser of a painting discovered after five years that it had not been painted by Constable, as had been represented to him. It was held that rescission was no longer available.

Full Restitution Impossible

The essence of rescission is that the parties can be restored to the position they were in before the contract was made. Therefore, if one party has used or damaged or consumed the subject matter of the contract before the misrepresentation is discovered it is impossible to restore the parties to their original positions, the *status quo ante*, and rescission is unavailable.

If a client only discovers the misrepresentation when in resort it will then be too late to rescind. Having already "consumed" the outward flight and perhaps some of the accommodation, the client is not in a position to restore the tour operator to his pre-contractual position.

Third Party Rights

This is a bar to rescission which normally applies in situations very different to package holiday contracts. The usual scenario arises where, for instance, Alan is induced by the fraud of Brian to sell his car to Brian in exchange for a cheque which bounces. Normally, the contract could be rescinded for fraud (that is if Brian can be found!). However, if Brian acts quickly and sells the car to Charles, an innocent buyer, before the fraud is discovered then the contract cannot be rescinded. The law will not restore Alan to his original position if an innocent third party, Charles, has acquired the subject matter of the contract in good faith before the fraud is discovered.

It is difficult to envisage circumstances where this would be relevant to package holiday contracts but conceivably it might arise in relation to transfers. Under reg.10 a consumer may transfer his contract to another in certain limited circumstances. It is possible to imagine circumstances where a tour operator, A, is induced by the fraud of B, to enter into a package holiday contract. B then transfers the holiday to C, who pays him for it, before his fraud is discovered by A. A then wishes to rescind his contract with B but because C has already acquired rights under the contract cannot do so.

Although such a situation is theoretically possible it is hard to see it arising in practice, simply because reg.10 provides that in the event of a transfer the transferee remains jointly and severally liable with the transferor for the payment of the price of the package. In other words, the tour operator has an alternative remedy to rescission which he would exercise in the circumstances.

Where Damages are Awarded in Lieu of Rescission

Section 2(2) of the Misrepresentation Act states:

> "Where a person has entered into a contract after a misrepresentation has been made to him otherwise than fraudulently, and he would be entitled, by reason of the misrepresentation, to rescind the contract, then, if it is claimed, in any proceedings arising out of the contract, that the contract ought to be or has been rescinded, the court or arbitrator may declare the contract subsisting and award damages in lieu of rescission, if of opinion that it would be equitable to do so, having regard to the nature of the misrepresentation and the loss that would be caused by it if the contract were upheld, as well as to the loss that rescission would cause to the other party."

What this means is that if the court considers that it would be fair to do so it can award damages instead of rescission. Thus, the right to rescission will be lost but damages will be available instead. It is envisaged that the courts will do this where the misrepresentation is relatively minor and can easily be compensated by a sum of money and where to rescind the contract would be out of all proportion to the damage caused by the misrepresentation. One case which examined this issue was *William Sindall Plc v Cambridgeshire CC* [1994] 3 All E.R. 932. A builder had bought land from the Council for £5 million but by the time planning permission had been obtained 18 months later there had been a slump in land prices and the land was worth only £2 million. The builder attempted to rescind the contract on the basis of a misrepresentation about the drains. The Court of Appeal held in fact that there was no misrepresentation but said that even if there had been, rescission would not have been granted. The defect with the drains could have been remedied for only £18,000 and anyway, the reason for seeking rescission was not the misrepresentation but the desire to escape from a bad bargain. If asked to do so the Court would have refused rescission and awarded damages in lieu of rescission under s.2(2) of the Act as that would have been the most equitable solution in the circumstances.

In a travel context, one can see this reasoning being applied to a couple who have booked first class long haul tickets to, say, the Maldives for their honeymoon, only for the relationship to break down before the wedding. If they sought to rescind the contract on the basis of a misrepresentation that the meals in first class were based on a menu prepared by a particular celebrity chef when in fact that was not the case one cannot imagine a court having much sympathy with them.

Damages

Damages for Fraudulent Misrepresentation

As indicated earlier, fraudulent misrepresentation amounts to the *tort of deceit*, therefore, when the damages are calculated they are measured according to *tortious* rather than *contractual* principles. What this means is that the victim of the tort will be placed, *financially*, in the position he would have been in if the statement had not been made, i.e. if the tort had not been committed. In general, this means putting him in the position he would have been in if no contract had been made. In contract the position is that the victim will be placed in the position he would have been in if the representation had been true, i.e. he will get the full benefit of the contract.

So, for example, if a client had purchased a holiday for £500 on the basis of a misrepresentation about the quality of the hotel, then the damages he would receive in tort would be the difference in value between what he actually got and the price he actually paid. In financial terms, he would then be in the same position he was in before the contract was made. So if he was supposed to be accommodated in a four star hotel and was actually accommodated in a three star hotel, then he would receive the difference between the value of a three star hotel holiday and what he actually paid. Thus, if the difference in value was assessed at £150, that is what he would get.

In contract, using the same example, the figures come out exactly the same although they are arrived at by a different route. To put the client in the position he would have been in if the representation had been true requires the tour operator to make up the difference between what the client got and what he was promised—also £150.

It would be different, however, if the client had bought a late bargain. Say he had paid £400 for a holiday which normally sold for £500. However, the hotel is substandard and what he actually gets is something worth only £350. In tort, to put him in the position he would have been in if the representation had not been made would mean giving him £50 in compensation. He is thus not out of pocket but he does not get a £500 holiday. On the other hand, in contract he will be put into the position he would have been in if the contract had been performed. In contract he would be given £150 compensation—the difference between what he actually got and what he had contracted for. He will thus receive the benefit of his bargain. (See *Hartman v P&O Cruises Ltd* [1998] C.L.Y. 3732 for this principle in operation in contract.) Note that this example depends upon the holiday being valued at £500; cf. *Milner v Carnival Plc*. There is an argument that the value of a late bargain is only what it can be sold for—in this case only £400—which means that the figures for both tortious and contractual damages would be the same again.

In addition to these damages for difference in value of the holiday itself there are also damages available for *consequential loss*. Consequential losses occur when the misrepresentation not only results in the value of the thing acquired being worth less, but the thing itself goes on to cause further loss. In holiday cases the most usual kind of consequential loss is the distress and disappointment caused by the substandard holiday—illustrated by *Jarvis v Swan Tours Ltd* [1973] Q.B. 233 (see Ch.10 on Remedies for a fuller discussion of damages for distress). This was a case of breach of contract rather than misrepresentation but it seems that emotional damage can also be claimed for misrepresentation. (See *Chesneau v Interhome*, discussed below; and *Ichard v Frangoulis* [1977] 2 All E.R. 461.)

One problem that arises with consequential losses is that in contract damages are only recoverable if they are a reasonably foreseeable consequence of the breach of contract, whereas in the tort of deceit the rule is that all the damages that flow from the fraud are recoverable whether foreseeable or not.

If a contract breaker cannot reasonably foresee that his breach will cause the damage that actually occurred then he is not liable for it. This was precisely the point that the case of *Kemp v Intasun Holidays* [1987] 2 F.T.L.R. 234 turned on. It was held that putting Mr Kemp in a dirty room would be inconvenient and upsetting but that an asthma attack was not foreseeable—in legal jargon the damage was *too remote a consequence* of the breach of contract.

The rule in the tort of deceit that all damages which flow directly from the fraudulent statement are recoverable *whether they are foreseeable or not* is illustrated by the case of *Doyle v Olby (Ironmongers) Ltd* [1969] 2 Q.B. 158.

In that case, the seller of a business had fraudulently misrepresented that the turnover of the business was entirely "over the counter", when in fact a large part of it was brought in by a travelling salesman. The accounts did not reflect this. In particular, they made no mention of wages for the travelling salesman. Lord Denning M.R. said of the claim for damages:

"In contract, the damages are limited to what may reasonably be supposed to have been in the contemplation of the parties. In fraud, they are not so limited. The defendant is bound to make reparation for all the actual damages directly flowing from the fraudulent inducement. The person who has been defrauded is entitled to say:

'I would not have entered into this bargain at all but for your representation. Owing to your fraud, I have not only lost all the money I paid you, but, what is more, I have been put to a large amount of extra expense as well and suffered this or that extra damages.'

All such damages can be recovered: it does not lie in the mouth of the fraudulent person to say that they could not reasonably have been foreseen. For instance, in this very case Mr Doyle has not only lost the money which he paid for the business, which he would never have done if there had been no fraud: he put all that money in and lost it; but also he has been put to expense and loss in trying to run a business which has turned out to be a disaster for him. He is entitled to damages for all his loss".

Thus, *if* the tour operator in the *Kemp* case had *fraudulently misrepresented* the cleanliness of the room for some reason then he would have been liable for the asthma attack whether it was foreseen not.

In *Clef Aquataine Sarl v Laporte Materials (Barrow) Ltd* [2000] 3 W.L.R. 1760 the claimant entered into long-term supply contracts with the defendant on the basis of a fraudulent representation that the goods that the defendant was making available to the claimant were being sold at the lowest price available. This was not true; the defendant sold the same goods to other purchasers at lower prices. If the claimant had been able to purchase the goods from the defendant at the lower prices it would have been able to make a larger profit when it re-sold the goods. The interesting part of the decision was that it was held that the damages recoverable for misrepresentation were not confined to *losses* incurred by the claimant but could be extended to cover *profits* as well. From a travel law perspective, however, one wonders how often a consumer is induced to enter into a contract with a travel company on the basis of similar representations. (See also the discussion of The Consumer Protection from Unfair Trading Regulations 2008 and misleading price indications in Ch.17.)

Damages for Negligent Misrepresentation

Until 1967 damages were not available for negligent misrepresentation at all. Now they are, by virtue of s.2(1) of the Misrepresentation Act 1967. It states:

> "Where a person has entered into a contract after a misrepresentation has been made to him by another party thereto and as a result thereof he has suffered loss, then, if the person making the misrepresentation would be liable to damages in respect thereof had the misrepresentation been made fraudulently, that person shall be *so liable* notwithstanding that the misrepresentation was not made fraudulently, unless he proves that he had reasonable ground to believe and did believe up to the time the contract was made that the facts represented were true." (Emphasis added)

After a period of uncertainty the courts have decided that damages for negligent misrepresentation will be calculated on the same principles as for fraudulent misrepresentation, i.e. on tortious principles. The emphasised words in the section led to this interpretation. The courts have decided that not only the basis of calculation will be tortious but that the rules relating to remoteness of damage will be tortious also.

Chesneau v Interhome, The Times, June 9, 1983 is a case involving s.2(1) of the Misrepresentation Act and the calculation of damages under it. The defendants, Interhome Ltd, had misrepresented the state of some accommodation that the claimants had hired from them. The house was not secluded as promised, there was no private pool, and the sleeping accommodation was not as described. The claimants had left the accommodation and found other accommodation but it cost them £209 more. They were suing for this amount plus a sum for distress and disappointment suffered while they searched for alternative accommodation.

In the County Court the judge had decided that as damages under s.2(1) were to be assessed on a tortious basis then he should put the parties in the position they would have been in *if the misrepresentation had not been made*. If the misrepresentation had not been made then the parties would be back in England without a contract. In such circumstances the claimants could probably have found similar accommodation at much the same price and therefore he awarded only £50 in damages for the misrepresentation. The Court of Appeal regarded this approach as entirely inappropriate in the circumstances. Given that the claimants were stuck in substandard accommodation in the middle of France by the time the misrepresentation was discovered it was somewhat artificial to assess the damages as though they were back in England. Their solution to the problem was to say that the sum of £209 represented what the claimants had to spend to *mitigate* the loss caused by the misrepresentation. In tort as in contract a victim is under a duty to mitigate his loss. The Court of Appeal thus neatly sidestepped the problem of how to assess damages in tort for a holiday which has already commenced.

It was mentioned above that where the tort of deceit has been committed the victim can claim all the losses flowing from the fraud whether they were foreseeable or not (*Doyle v Olby (Ironmongers) Ltd*). That seems fair enough if the representor has been fraudulent but what if he has not? What if the false statement had only been made negligently? In *Royscot Trust Ltd v Rogerson* [1991] 3 All E.R. 294, it was decided quite emphatically that even if the false statement is only made negligently the victim can claim all the losses he suffered even if normally they would be too remote. Basing this conclusion on s.2(1) of the Misrepresentation Act 1967, Balcombe L.J. said:

"With all respect to the various learned authors whose works I have cited above, it seems to me that to suggest that a different measure of damage applies to an action for innocent misrepresentation under the section than that which applies to an action for fraudulent misrepresentation (deceit) at common law is to ignore the plain words of the subsection and is inconsistent with the cases to which I have referred. In my judgment, therefore, the [plaintiff] is entitled to recover from the [defendant] all the losses which it suffered as a result of its entering into the agreements with the [defendant] *even if those losses were unforeseeable*". (Emphasis added) (When he refers to innocent misrepresentation this includes negligent misrepresentation)

The result of this judgment creates an anomalous situation. Someone who suffers from a negligent misrepresentation can claim damages for all the losses he suffers whether foreseeable or not (*Royscot Trust Ltd v Rogerson*) yet if the same statement amounted to a term of the contract only foreseeable losses could be recovered (*Kemp v Intasun*). The decision has come under sustained academic attack but still survives. In *Smith New Court Securities Ltd v Citibank NA* [1997] A.C. 254 the House of Lords refrained from overruling it, whilst acknowledging the criticisms.

Damages for Innocent Misrepresentation

The only situation where damages can be claimed for innocent misrepresentation is under s.2(2) of the Misrepresentation Act 1967 where the court, at its discretion, can award damages in lieu of rescission. This was discussed above in the section on the availability of rescission. However, there is some doubt as to whether a claimant can recover damages in lieu of rescission if the right to rescission has already been lost, e.g. by affirmation. In *Thomas Witter Ltd v TBP Industries Ltd* [1996] 2 All E.R. 573 the court held that the right was not lost but most cases that have considered the issue have decided otherwise (see *Floods of Queensferry Ltd v Shand Construction Ltd (No.3)* [2000] B.L.R. 81; *Zanzibar v*

British Aerospace [2000] 1 W.L.R. 2333; and *Pankhania v Hackney LBC* [2002] EWHC 2441 (Ch)).

If damages were to be awarded under s.2(2) there is no authoritative answer yet as to whether they would be calculated on tortious or contractual principles.

Misrepresentations Which Become Terms

Up to now it has been assumed that a statement can either be a term or a representation but not both. Certainly, it is the case that some statements can only be representations and some statements are only terms, but it is also possible for a statement which is originally a representation to be incorporated into the contract as a term. For instance, a brochure may contain statements about a resort that are only representations but which the client is sufficiently concerned about to ask the operator to confirm and makes it clear that the contract is only being made on that basis, i.e. the statement is being incorporated into the contract. So what was originally only a misrepresentation is a term as well.

The practical effect of this is that in some circumstances the victim can only sue for misrepresentation, in others he can only sue for breach of contract and in yet others he can sue for either breach or misrepresentation depending on which is most to his advantage.

Chesneau v Interhome appears to be the kind of case where the action could have been brought for either breach of a term of the contract or for misrepresentation. There is no indication in the report of why an action in misrepresentation was chosen. It would have seemed easier to have sued simply for breach of contract. A better example is *Mawdsley v Cosmosair* referred to in previous chapters. In that case, the statement that the hotel had a lift was found both to be an implied term, to the effect that the lift stopped at all floors, and to be a negligent misrepresentation. For good measure the court also held it to be a misleading statement under reg.4 of the Package Travel Regulations.

It used to be the case that when it came to a claim for damages claimants would prefer that a statement be classified as a term rather than a representation, because damages were then automatically available for breach of contract rather than subject to the limitations of an action in misrepresentation. However, cases such as *Royscot* that have opened up the possibility of damages for unforeseeable losses, coupled with the more favourable burden of proof established by the Misrepresentation Act, mean that actions will arise where the defendant may wish to establish that the statement was a representation rather than a term.

Relationship with the Package Travel Regulations

It is worthwhile repeating at this point that an action for misrepresentation cannot be viewed in isolation from the provisions of the Package Travel Regulations. We have already seen in Ch.5 that reg.4 creates civil liability for any misleading statements and in Ch.4 that reg.6 turns the particulars in the brochure into warranties—as just illustrated by *Mawdsley v Cosmosair* above. And it should not be forgotten that in certain circumstances misrepresentation may lead to criminal liability as well—see Chs 16 to 18.

Privity of Contract

INTRODUCTION

In English law the general rule is that only a person who is a party to a contract can sue or be sued upon it. To put it another way, if I buy a TV from an electrical shop and *give* it to you, if it does not work *you* cannot sue the shop because *you* do not have a contract with them. By the same token, if I had bought the TV for you on credit but I was not keeping up the payments the shop could not sue you because they do not have a contract with you. It would make no difference at all if I had said at the time I bought the TV that I was buying it for you—the fact that the contract was for your benefit, and you were named in it, does not make you a party to it.

This rule applies, subject to the widespread exceptions discussed below, to travel and holiday cases, just as it does to other areas of law. However, the rule has proved to be extremely inconvenient in practice and the most noticeable aspect of it is the large number of exceptions to it. The exceptions to the rule are to be found both at common law and in statute. As we shall see shortly, travel law provides one of the leading and most controversial exceptions at common law (*Jackson v Horizon Holidays Ltd* [1975] 3 All E.R. 92) and one of the newest statutory exceptions can be found in the Package Travel Regulations. In fact, we have already looked at this aspect of the Regulations in Ch.2. There we saw that reg.2 defines a "consumer" in such a way that persons who would not normally be regarded as being party to a package holiday contract are in fact treated as parties by the Regulations.

In this chapter, we will be looking first of all at the general rule at common law and how it works in practice. Then, we will look again at the common law rule specifically in relation to travel contracts. Next, we shall see how the common law rule has been overtaken and largely replaced as far as package holiday contracts (but not other travel related contracts) are concerned by the rules in the Package Travel Regulations. While looking at the rules in the Package Travel Regulations we will also examine the concept of transferring a package holiday from one consumer to another and the problems this poses. Finally, we will look at the Contracts (Rights of Third Parties) Act 1999 which may also have an effect on the rights of package holidaymakers but will certainly affect other, non-package, travellers. This Act, which is of general application, was passed following the Law Commission Report on privity of contract: *Privity of Contract: Contracts for the Benefit of Third Parties* (Cm.3329 (1996)).

Privity of Contract—The General Rule

Tweddle v Atkinson (1861) 1 B. & S. 393 is a case whose facts are far removed from the world of travel law but, nevertheless, it forms the basis of the rules on privity of contract. In that case, William Tweddle, the son of John Tweddle, was marrying the daughter of William Guy. The two fathers drew up an agreement whereby they each promised to pay a sum of money to William Tweddle. Not only was William named in the agreement, he was also expressly given the right to sue on the agreement. Unfortunately, before William Guy had paid any money to his new son-in-law he died. His estate was taken over by his executor who refused to pay the money, so William sued the estate for the money he had been promised. The court refused his claim. It was held that although he had been named in the contract he was not a party to it because he had not provided any *consideration*. We have already mentioned briefly in Ch.3 that for a valid contract to exist the parties to it have to provide consideration. In other words, you have to pay for the promises you receive from the other party. In this case, although William Tweddle had been promised £200 by his new father-in-law he had promised nothing in exchange and, therefore, could not enforce the contract.

A more straightforward example is *Dunlop Pneumatic Tyre Co Ltd v Selfridge & Co Ltd* [1915] A.C. 847 where Dunlop sold tyres to a wholesaler, Dew & Co, who in turn sold them to a retailer, Selfridge. Dunlop inserted a term in their contract with Dew & Co that when Dew & Co re-sold the tyres to retailers such as Selfridge the contract should contain a price maintenance clause, i.e. the retailer should not sell below Dunlop's list price—and if they did so they would be subject to financial penalties. Although Dew & Co followed Dunlop's instructions, Selfridge nevertheless chose to sell below list price and in consequence Dunlop sued them. The outcome was quite simple. Dunlop had a contract with Dew & Co but they did not have one with Selfridge, therefore, they could not insist on the price maintenance clause being enforced. Even though Selfridge had promised in their contract with Dew & Co not to break Dunlop's price maintenance policy, Dunlop had not given them any consideration in return.

Privity of Contract—The Impact on Travel Contracts

In *Jackson v Horizon Holidays Ltd* the claimant, Mr Jackson, had bought a package holiday to Ceylon (now Sri Lanka) for himself, his wife and his two young children. Although Mr Jackson had requested a hotel of the highest standard and was very specific about what he wanted, the hotel provided was woefully inadequate. The children's room was mildewed, there was no bath, the shower was dirty, the toilet was stained and fungus was growing on the walls. In the parents' room there was no bath and the linen was dirty. As for the facilities there was no mini-golf, no swimming pool, no beauty salon, no hairdressing salon and the food in the restaurant was unacceptable. In the County Court the defendant admitted liability and the judge awarded £1,100 damages on a holiday that cost £1,200. But the judge specifically stated that although he could award damages to Mr Jackson that included an amount for distress and disappointment under the principle established in *Jarvis v Swans Tours Ltd* [1973] 1 All E.R. 71, he could not award anything to the rest of the family for their distress and disappointment. He said:

> "the damages are the Plaintiff's; that I can consider the effect upon his mind of his wife's discomfort, vexation and the like, although I cannot award a sum which represents her vexation."

Horizon appealed to the Court of Appeal on the grounds that the damages were too high, particularly if they only represented Mr Jackson's own loss. This inevitably raised the issue of whether Mr Jackson could claim damages not only for himself but also for other members of the party.

At this point it is worthwhile quoting extensively from Lord Denning's judgment where the issues are set out:

> "[Counsel for Mr Jackson] submits that damages can be given not only for the leader of the party, in this case, Mr Jackson's own distress, discomfort and vexation, but also for that of the rest of the party.
>
> We have had an interesting discussion as to the legal position when one person makes a contract for the benefit of a party. In this case it was a husband making a contract for the benefit of himself, his wife and children. Other cases readily come to mind. A host makes a contract with a restaurant for a dinner for himself and his friends. The vicar makes a contract for a coach trip for the choir. In all these cases there is only one person who makes the contract. It is the husband, the host or the vicar, as the case may be. Sometimes he pays the whole price himself. Occasionally he may get a contribution from the others. But in any case it is he who makes the contract. It would be a fiction to say that the contract was made by all the family, or all the guests, or all the choir, and that he was only an agent for them. Take this very case. It would be absurd to say that the twins of three years old were parties to the contract or that the father was making the contract on their behalf as if they were principals No, the real truth is that in each instance, the father, the host or the vicar, was making a contract himself for the benefit of the whole party. In short, a contract by one for the benefit of third persons.
>
> What is the position when such a contract is broken? At present the law says that the only one who can sue is the one who made the contract. None of the rest of the party can sue, even though the contract was made for their benefit. But when that one does sue, what damages can he recover? Suppose the holiday firm puts the family into a hotel which is only half built and the visitors have to sleep on the floor? Or suppose the restaurant is fully booked and the guests have to go away, hungry and angry, having spent so much on fares to get there? Or suppose the coach leaves the choir stranded half-way and they have to hire cars to get home? None of them individually can sue. He can, of course, recover his own damages. But can he not recover for the others? I think he can."

Lord Denning then went on to give reasons why he thought Mr Jackson could recover which we will examine shortly, but in the meantime, it is worth looking a little more closely at the situation in the *Jackson* case. What Lord Denning is saying is that although Mrs Jackson and the twins are named on the booking form they are not parties to the contract—they are merely beneficiaries of a contract made by Mr Jackson—and as such they cannot sue in their own right. One way round problems such as this is to make a finding that the person who made the booking was doing so as agent for the others. In other words, he was authorised by the others to make a contract with Horizon on their behalf. This may be a possibility in some cases, but in this case Lord Denning rejected that idea. So we are left with a situation which is bound to arise constantly in package holiday contracts where a person for whose benefit the contract was made is unable to claim because they have no contract with the tour operator.

The reasoning Lord Denning adopted in *Jackson* to overcome the problem was suspect to say the least and has subsequently been disapproved. He referred to the judgment of Lush L.J. in the case of *Lloyd's v Harper* (1880–81) L.R. 16 Ch. D. 290 where he said:

> "I consider it to be an established rule of law that where a contract is made with A for the benefit of B, A can sue on the contract for the benefit of B, and recover all that B could have recovered if the contract had been made with B himself."

Taken at face value this appears to settle the matter in favour of Mr Jackson and this was sufficient for Lord Denning. The problem is that the statement was taken entirely out of context. In *Lloyd's v Harper*, Lush L.J. was describing a situation where A was acting as an agent or trustee for B and not simply making a contract for B's benefit. An agent or a trustee is entitled to sue on behalf of a principal or a beneficiary but an ordinary contractor is not.

A subsequent case, *Woodar Investment Development Ltd v Wimpey Construction UK Ltd* [1980] 1 W.L.R. 227, considered the *reasoning* in the *Jackson* case and strongly disapproved of it, but it is difficult to say whether they actually overturned the decision itself. Certainly, however, they indulged in some re-interpretation of what it did decide. Lord Wilberforce said:

> "I am not prepared to dissent from the actual decision in that case [*Jackson*]. *It may be supported either as a broad decision on the measure of damages* (per James LJ) or possibly as an example of a type of contract, examples of which are persons contracting for family holidays, ordering meals in restaurants for a party, hiring a taxi for a group, calling for special treatment." (Emphasis added)

He then went on to disagree with Lord Denning on the interpretation of the passage from *Lloyd's v Harper*. Lord Russell took much the same line over *Lloyd's v Harper* and also said:

> "I do not criticise the outcome of that case [*Jackson*]: the plaintiff had bought and paid for a high class family holiday; he did not get it, and therefore he was entitled to substantial damages for the failure to supply *him* with one."

And Lord Keith said:

> "That case [*Jackson*] is capable of being regarded as rightly decided on a reasonable view of the measure of damages due to the plaintiff as the original

contracting party, and not as laying down any rule of law regarding the recovery of damages for the benefit of third parties."

What is happening is that the House of Lords in the *Woodar* case is saying that although they do not agree with the way Lord Denning reached his decision in *Jackson*, nevertheless, they agree with the result and they are prepared to support the decision but on other grounds. Those grounds are that the damages that Mr Jackson received were solely for his own distress and disappointment and did not include an element for his family's distress and disappointment. This flies in the face of what was actually said in the *Jackson* case. Lord Denning expressly stated that he thought that £1,100 would be excessive if awarded only for Mr Jackson's suffering but would not be so if extended to his wife and family. Orr L.J. agreed unequivocally with him. Only James L.J. took the line adopted by the House of Lords and he certainly did not dissent from the views of Lord Denning and Orr L.J. We reproduce below what he said in full:

"In this case Mr Jackson, as found by the judge on the evidence, was in need of a holiday at the end of 1970. He was able to afford a holiday for himself and his family. According to the form which he completed, what was the form of Horizon Holidays Ltd, he booked what was a family holiday. The wording of that form might in certain circumstances give rise to a contract in which the person signing the form is acting as his own principal and as agent for others. In the circumstances of this case, as indicated by Lord Denning MR, it would be wholly unrealistic to regard this contract as other than one made by Mr Jackson for a family holiday. The judge found that he did not get a family holiday. The costs were some £1,200. When he came back he felt no benefit. He said: 'The only thing, I was pleased to be back, very pleased, but I had nothing at all from that holiday.' For my part, on the issue of damages in this matter, I am quite content to say that £1,100 awarded was the right and proper figure in those circumstances. I would dismiss the appeal."

This leaves the status of the *Jackson* case a little unclear. The only certain thing that can be said about it in the light of the House of Lords judgment in *Woodar* is that in a holiday case the person booking the holiday for a family can recover damages for his own distress—which will be that much greater because of the distress of the rest of the party. Whether the novel part of the judgment—that Mr Jackson could claim for other members of the party—has survived the body blows inflicted by *Woodar* is open to conjecture. Given that none of the law lords actually disapproved of the decision in so many words and at least one, Lord Wilberforce, expressly said that he was not prepared to dissent from it, then it may still represent the law. At least one subsequent holiday case decided by the Court of Appeal—*Kemp v Intasun Holidays* [1987] 2 F.T.L.R. 234—seems to accept the basis of *Jackson* without question. In that case, Kerr L.J. proceeded on the basis that the person making the booking could also claim on behalf of the other members of the party. He said:

"The plaintiff is a Mr Alan Kemp, but he is suing in effect, *as is accepted in these cases*, on behalf of himself and the other members of the family who

accompanied him on this holiday: Mrs Kemp and his step-daughter Susan."
(Emphasis added)

One thing is clear, however, and that is that the other members of the party
cannot sue in their own right. *Jackson* is a means of avoiding the full rigours of
the privity of contract rule but it is not a full-blown exception to it. A case in
point is *Savill and Issac v ILG Travel* [1989] C.L.Y. 2952, a pre-1992 case. The
facts of the case were that the claimant booked a holiday for himself, his wife and
two others. They complained that the holiday was substandard. Each of the four
subsequently issued a summons claiming damages limited to £500. The effect
was a total claim of £2,000 arising out of the same breach of contract, but all
brought within the small claims procedure. Before trial the defendants settled the
claim with the claimant but the other three proceeded. It was held that although
there was a breach of contract, the damages arising were less than the amount
which the defendant had already paid to the claimant. There was no basis on
which four separate actions could be grounded. Accordingly, the three remaining
summonses were dismissed. It was unreasonable for the claimants to bring four
separate actions. The basis of this decision, although it is not absolutely clear
from the brief report, is that the other three claimants were denied their claim on
the basis of the *Jackson* case.

Another point to make is that if the factual situation in *Jackson* had been a
little different then the problems of privity would not have arisen. For instance, in
Daly v General Steam Navigation Co (The Dragon) [1979] 1 Lloyd's Rep. 257;
affirmed [1980] 2 Lloyd's Rep. 415, a non-package case, it was held that where a
husband booked tickets on a cross-Channel ferry for himself and his children
there was a contract of carriage between the wife and the ferry company. The
basis on which this was decided is that the husband was regarded as the claimant's agent. Such a finding was potentially detrimental to the claimant. By
holding that she was a party to the contract she could have been bound by
exclusion clauses that would have deprived her of compensation. In the event, it
was held that the exclusion clauses were not binding on her but had they been so
she would have received no damages. In such a case she might have preferred a
finding that she was a third party beneficiary rather than a party to the contract.

A further variation can be seen in *Lockett v A&M Charles Ltd* [1938] 4 All
E.R. 170 where the court held that where a husband and wife lunched together at
a restaurant they had both made contracts with the restaurant and therefore
could both sue on their individual contracts.

The use of the rules of agency can be seen in the case of *Wilson v Pegasus
Holidays* [1988] C.L.Y. 1059. In that case, a party of children suffered a disastrous skiing holiday and each child recovered £125 damages in their own right.
It was held that the teacher who had booked the holiday had acted as agent for
each of the 31 pupils in the party.

On many booking forms it is common to find a form of words to the following
effect:

"I agree on behalf of all the clients named hereon to accept the booking
conditions overleaf." (These were the words used on the booking form in the
Jackson case itself)

In most circumstances, this has the effect of making the signatory to the booking form the agent of the others in the party. It would not overcome the problem of Mr Jackson's two twin sons who were too young to be contracting on their own behalf, no matter what the booking form said, but it would probably be sufficient to cover Mrs Jackson and other adult members of a party.

One benefit for the travel company with such a clause is that it ensures that he has a contract with all the members of the party—so that, for instance, if they do not pay, or if they cancel, the company can seek cancellation charges not only from the party leader but also the other party members if necessary. In relation to this, see the issue raised in Ch.2 relating to school party contracts and the difficulty of imposing rules of conduct on school children. But if the clause is sufficient to create a contract between the company and the other members of the party so that the company can sue them, then the converse must also apply—the other members of the party can then sue the company.

Finally, there remains the issue of whether or not the *Jackson* case and the rules of privity have any relevance any longer to package holiday cases now that the Package Travel Regulations have defined a consumer in such a way that it would include members of a family and other members of a party. The extent of this definition has already been examined in some detail in Ch.2 and will be reviewed again briefly in the next section, but the position is that although the problems raised by the *Jackson* case will not arise again in the context of package holidays as defined in the Regulations, they will continue to arise in other holiday contexts. A "fly-drive" holiday, for instance, may not be within the scope of the Regulations, and therefore there is potential for problems of privity to arise. It would be the same with booking accommodation or ferries or flights or excursions where there was no package but one person made the contract on behalf of others. So, although the Regulations may have laid some of the problems to rest, others still remain—although, these in turn may have been resolved by the Contracts (Rights of Third Parties) Act 1999.

PRIVITY OF CONTRACT—THE IMPACT OF THE REGULATIONS ON PACKAGE HOLIDAYS

In Ch.2 we explained how the definition of consumer to be found in reg.2(1) extended the protection of the Regulations, not only to the purchaser of the package, but also to other beneficiaries and transferees. For an explanation of those terms, and to save duplication, we would simply refer you back to the relevant sections of Ch.2. All that needs to be added to what we said there, as far as the other beneficiary is concerned, is that the definition would certainly cover Mrs Jackson and the two twins. There is no longer any need for Lord Denning's legal acrobatics to avoid the privity of contract rules. Mr Jackson is a principal contractor and Mrs Jackson and the twins are other beneficiaries because the package was purchased on their behalf by a principal contractor. Therefore, the whole family have full rights under the package holiday contract.

In *Henley v Cosmosair* [1995] C.L.Y. 4113, the claimant had refused to disclose holiday photographs to the defence, taken by members of her family who were not themselves claimants but who had accompanied her on holiday. The

Circuit Judge, on appeal from the District Judge, ordered that the photographs should be disclosed on the grounds that under the County Court Rules he could order her to do so if he considered they were within her "power". On the question of whether an order could have been made against members of the family because they were all co-claimants, by virtue of the definition of "consumer" in reg.2(2) of the Package Travel Regulations, the judge hesitated to do that, but there is a clear indication that he would have done so if necessary.

PRIVITY OF CONTRACT AND TRANSFEREES

A much larger breach in the privity rules, so far as package holidays are concerned, is to be found in reg.10 of the PTR. Under that Regulation, the consumer is permitted to transfer his booking to someone else, the "transferee". Thus, it is possible for someone entirely uncontemplated by the original contract to become a party to it.

Regulation 10 provides:

"10(1) In every contract there is an implied term that where the consumer is prevented from proceeding with the package the consumer may transfer his booking to a person who satisfies all the conditions applicable to the package, provided that the consumer gives reasonable notice to the other party to the contract of his intention to transfer before the date when departure is due to take place.

(2) Where a transfer is made in accordance with the implied term set out in paragraph (1) above, the transferor and the transferee shall be jointly and severally liable to the other party to the contract for payment of the price of the package (or, if part of the price has been paid, for payment of the balance) and for any additional costs incurred by that other party as a result of the transfer."

One immediate practical consequence of this, which tour operators will not find attractive, is that if the consumer can find a substitute to go in his place then that deprives the operator of the ability to levy cancellation charges in such a situation.

The right to transfer the booking to another is not unqualified. First, the right only arises if the consumer is "prevented" from proceeding with the package. Clearly, a prison sentence or a serious illness will fall into this category, but what about redundancy or a death in the family? These are occurrences which do not literally prevent a consumer from proceeding with a package but may make it highly undesirable to do so. The OFT considers that "illness, death of a close relative, jury service and so on" would qualify. (See Saggerson, 4th edn, p.106 on this point, where he argues for a liberal interpretation.) The existence of insurance to cover such eventualities may influence the interpretation of this provision. Cases where couples divorce or separate or where boyfriend and girlfriend split up could also cause difficulties of interpretation. At the other end of the scale are situations where the consumer has merely changed his mind and does not wish to proceed. The Regulation does not seem to extend the right of transfer in such circumstances. The commentary included in the original DTI Consultation Document also takes this line. It states:

"A mere change of mind is not interpreted as giving the consumer the rights in this paragraph, because in such a case he would not be *prevented* from proceeding."

Using its powers under the Unfair Terms in Consumer Contracts Regulations, the OFT required Thomas Cook (October 2002) to revise a term which required consumers to treat a booking as cancelled and to pay cancellation charges if all the names on the booking were changed. This was regarded as being in conflict with reg.10 and had to be changed so that name changes were permitted. At the same time, Airtours were also required to change a term which prevented transfers on certain types of holiday.

Secondly, the transferee must be someone who "satisfies all the conditions applicable to the package". In broad terms, this means that a pensioner would not be qualified to take the place of a person booked on a "Club 18–30" holiday and, by the same token, a 16-year-old could not take her granny's place on a Saga holiday. A married person would not satisfy the conditions for a "singles" holiday, and an inexperienced hill-climber would not be eligible for an advanced mountaineering expedition to the Andes. All these are straightforward examples and no one could take exception to a refusal by the tour operator in such circumstances, but it may be open to a tour operator to interpret the conditions applicable to the package restrictively so as to deny the right to transfer—thus benefiting from cancellation charges.

If additional costs arise from the transfer these have to be paid for, e.g. if a couple sharing a room transfer their booking to two single men who wish to have single rooms, then a single room supplement becomes payable for both of them. (There is an argument that the tour operator could refuse such a transfer anyway because this would not amount to a transfer of the booking—it would be a different booking altogether.) This supplement can be claimed by the tour operator from either the transferors or the transferees because both are "jointly and severally liable". "Additional costs" can be interpreted as also covering the administrative costs involved in making the change. As the Regulation only provides for the recovery of "costs" the question arises as to whether any administration fee can include an element of profit. On the one hand, the Regulation does not expressly rule it out. On the other hand, it would subvert the purpose of the Regulation if the transferee was faced with such large "administration" charges that it discouraged him from taking the holiday. It might be the case that if the administration charge was too great it might also fall foul of the UTCCR, although this is not mentioned by the OFT in their guidelines on unfair contract terms in package holiday contracts.

The final requirement is that the operator is informed within a reasonable time before departure. What is a reasonable time will vary according to the circumstances but it will, for instance, have to be sufficiently far in advance to satisfy airline and hotel notification requirements. In the past, DTI guidelines suggested that 21 days would be a reasonable time. We are inclined to think that in many cases this is excessively cautious. If a tour operator, with all the advantages of modern technology, can take a fresh booking within 24 hours of departure, why cannot he effect a name change in under 21 days? This view was vindicated by the OFT in October 2002 when it required ABTA to remove from its recommended terms a recommendation that 21 days would be a reasonable requirement in the case of name changes and to change it to what would be reasonable in the circumstances. When the Directive was transposed in Luxembourg the Grand Duchy also decided on a 21 day limit but, after an intervention by the Commission, agreed to change it to a period of "reasonable notice" (Report on the Implementation of Directive 90/314/EEC on Package Travel and Holiday Tours in the Domestic Legislation of EC Member States, SEC (1999) 1800 Final, para.1.1).

THE CONTRACTS (RIGHTS OF THIRD PARTIES) ACT 1999

As indicated at the beginning of the chapter, the common rule on privity of contract could be seen as depriving third parties of benefits to which they had a legitimate expectation. As far as package holidays are concerned, the decision in the *Jackson* case went a long way to redressing the balance in favour of holidaymakers, and the Package Travel Regulations seem to have filled in the blanks. By definition, of course, the Regulations do not apply to non-package travel, and therefore claimants could only look to the *Jackson* case for redress. Now, however, The Contracts (Rights of Third Parties) Act 1999 has been passed which is of general application—applying to all contracts including both package and non-package travel cases.

The most important provision of that legislation is s.1:

"S.1 Right of third party to enforce contractual term.

(1) Subject to the provisions of this Act, a person who is not a party to a contract (a 'third party') may in his own right enforce a term of the contract if—

    (a) the contract expressly provides that he may, or
    (b) subject to subsection (2), the term purports to confer a benefit on him.

(2) Subsection (1)(b) does not apply if on a proper construction of the contract it appears that the parties did not intend the term to be enforceable by the third party.

(3) The third party must be expressly identified in the contract by name, as a member of a class or as answering a particular description but need not be in existence when the contract is entered into.

(4) This section does not confer a right on a third party to enforce a term of a contract otherwise than subject to and in accordance with any other relevant terms of the contract.

(5) For the purpose of exercising his right to enforce a term of the contract, there shall be available to the third party any remedy that would have been available to him in an action for breach of contract if he had been a party to the contract (and the rules relating to damages, injunctions, specific performance and other relief shall apply accordingly)."

Very broadly, put into a travel context, what this means is that a third party, e.g. Mr Jackson's wife and children, or the claimant in *The Dragon* case, can enforce the terms of the contract against the travel company if they can show that the contract:

- expressly provides that they may, or

- purports to confer a benefit upon them, unless the parties did not intend the term(s) to be enforceable by a third party.

If we look first at package holiday contracts, while it may not be possible to find an express term which confers on the consumer the right to sue the tour operator, it is hard to envisage a situation where the contract will not purport to confer a benefit on the third party—be it transport, accommodation, meals, etc. Furthermore, in such cases, it will be equally unlikely to find an intention that the third party cannot enforce the terms—simply because this would be contrary to reg.2 of the Package Travel Regulations. But this gets us no further than what the consumer is already entitled to under the PTR; it seems to add nothing to his existing rights. Whether he enforces his rights under the PTR or the Contracts (Rights of Third Parties) Act seems immaterial.

However, there is one situation where the Act may make a difference. When tour operators contract with hotels, or other subcontractors, they often go into great detail about what the hotel has to provide for the tour operators' clients. These contracts may not confer an express right on the holidaymaker to enforce the terms of the contract, but they certainly purport to confer benefits upon the holidaymaker. If, in breach of contract, the hotelier does not provide the number or quality of meals promised, then this opens up the possibility of the holidaymaker suing the hotelier. What would make it easier would be the fact that such contracts are often made subject to English law and to the jurisdiction of the English courts.

While the tour operator remains solvent this is not necessarily the most practical way of settling the problem, but one might envisage a situation where a tour operator becomes insolvent and the hotelier, fearing he might not get paid, reduces his service to the tour operators' clients or perhaps puts them out on the street altogether. (See *Verein fur Konsumenteninformation v Osterreichische Kreditversicherungs AG* (C-364/96) for an example of the lengths hoteliers are prepared to go to protect their interests when faced with the insolvency of a tour operator.) In these circumstances, where the clients have little or no hope of recovering damages from the tour operator, a class action on behalf of all the consumers who suffered might offer a reasonable prospect of success. This prospect would be defeated, of course, if the parties to the contract—the hotelier and the tour operator—expressly provided that the third party would acquire no rights under the contract. What might be a greater bar to success would be the defence which is provided in s.3 of the Act:

"3(1) Subsections (2) to (5) apply where, in reliance on section 1, proceedings for the enforcement of a term of a contract are brought by a third party.

(2) The promisor shall have available to him by way of defence or set-off any matter that—

(a) arises from or in connection with the contract and is relevant to the term, and

(b) would have been available to him by way of defence or set-off if the proceedings had been brought by the promisee."

In other words, if the hotelier had a defence against the tour operator for failing to provide the services, then the same defence could be raised against the third parties—the holidaymakers. What better defence could the hotelier have than not having been paid by the tour operator?

There may also be some doubt as to the efficacy of such an action on the basis of the purported intention to create such a right. Professor Burrows, the Law Commissioner principally responsible for the report which led to the legislation, had this to say:

"I would anticipate that it would not normally be rebutted [the purported intention] unless there is a term in the contract expressly negating the third party's legal rights, or an express term that is otherwise inconsistent with the third party having legal rights, or *unless the parties have entered into a chain of contracts which gives the third party a contractual right against another party for breach of the promisor's obligations under the alleged 'third party' contract.*" (Emphasis added)

Given that hoteliers, tour operators and consumers enter into such a chain of contracts, it might be argued that the tour operator/hotelier contract did not confer a right on the third party to sue—for the reason that the consumer already had a perfectly good right to sue the tour operator.

Turning now to non-package contracts, there are a variety of travel services that can be purchased that do not amount to a package when bought individually: transport services, accommodation, car hire, theme park entrance tickets, etc. With transport services these are often covered by international convention, e.g. the Montreal and Athens Conventions for air and sea travel respectively, and the problems of privity are generally mitigated under these conventions by providing that they apply to "passengers" irrespective of their contractual status. You are referred to Ch.13 on Air and Sea Travel for an account of their rights.

As far as accommodation is concerned, there are no international conventions that apply and, therefore, the travellers' rights will be determined by the terms of the contract. If, and this is often the case, the contract provides for English law to apply, then by virtue of the Act all the members of a party will be able to sue the hotelkeeper for breach of contract. Again, you are referred to Ch.14 for an account of the rules that apply when booking accommodation abroad. This rather begs the question, however, of what it is that the individual member of the party can claim that the party leader could not claim anyway. If I book a room for myself and my wife and this is not provided by the hotel for some reason, then any loss I incur by having to find another hotel can be claimed by me—because it is my loss and there would be no need for my wife to claim under those circumstances. Indeed, my wife may not be able to claim at all, irrespective of whether she has a right to sue under the Act, because she did not pay for the room in the first place and she has suffered no loss. If she suffered food poisoning, however, then she would be able to claim in her own right, although she would probably have a claim in negligence anyway. The advantage the Act might give her is that the contractual obligations might be strict as opposed to fault-based.

CHAPTER NINE

Frustration of Contract and *Force Majeure*

INTRODUCTION

When terrorists attack the Twin Towers; when there is an outbreak of SARS in the Far East; when hurricanes hit Florida; when a tsunami causes devastation from Indonesia to Somalia or damages a nuclear power station in Japan; when war breaks out in the Gulf; or when a volcano erupts in Iceland it will almost certainly be the case that travel companies will have clients who will be affected. These clients may already be in their resort or they may be about to travel. In many cases, the holiday will have to be cancelled altogether: the planes cannot take off or the roads are impassable. In other cases, it may be physically possible to travel but the accommodation has been destroyed or the holiday would be so severely affected that it would not be worthwhile taking it. In yet other cases, the only practicable thing to do is abort the holiday and for clients to come home.

Such events are usually unforeseen and beyond the control of the parties to the travel contract. Neither party is at fault but difficult questions arise as to how the losses caused by the cancellation will be apportioned. If the client has already paid for the services does he lose his money? Because the travel company has not provided the services does it have to return the money? What if the client has only paid the deposit and is due to pay the balance—can he be compelled to pay it? What if the client has not paid anything yet but the company has laid out money in advance for accommodation and flights? Is the travel company compelled to bring clients home and if it does so who has to pay?

These questions are dealt with by an extremely complex mixture of the common law rules on *frustration of contract*, the rules in the Package Travel Regulations on *force majeure,* and the rules in the ABTA Code of Conduct for ABTA tour operators. Section 2 of this chapter examines the circumstances in which a court is prepared to say that a contract is frustrated. The third section takes a brief look at how the losses involved in a frustration of contract were apportioned at common law. Section 4 looks at the Law Reform (Frustrated Contracts) Act 1943 (LR(FC)A 1943) which modified and replaced the common law rules on apportionment. These rules will apply to non-package holidays. In addition, the rules to be found in the Package Travel Regulations 1992 will be examined in section 5 and, finally, section 6 looks at the rules in the ABTA Code of Conduct. (For a practical application of the rules on frustration under US law when a hurricane strikes see Barris "Hotels and Hurricanes: Legal Duties and Liabilities When Natural Disasters Strike" [2006] I.T.L.J. 212.)

Two things should be said at the outset, however. First, when it comes to accommodation-only contracts where the accommodation is supplied abroad, the English law on frustration of contract may not apply. This will depend on the application of the rules found in Ch.14 on jurisdiction and choice of law. Secondly, when it comes to transport-only contracts these will in many cases be subject to the rules in the Athens and Montreal Conventions and EC Regulations such as (EC) 261/2004 discussed in Ch.13 and again the English rules on frustration may not apply. See also the article by Barris referred to above.

WHEN IS A CONTRACT FRUSTRATED?

1. Historical Background

Historically, apart from some minor exceptions, the obligations in a contract were regarded as *absolute*, i.e. the parties to the contract were bound by its terms and if, for whatever reason, they were unable to perform their part of the bargain they would be in breach of contract. This applied even if performance was made impossible by some external intervening event over which they had no control. The logic behind this was that the parties were quite free to determine for themselves the terms of the contract and if they failed to provide for such events they would just have to accept the consequences (*Paradine v Jane* (1646) Al. 26).

This view was modified later in *Taylor v Caldwell* (1863) 3 B. & S. 826. The facts of the case were that the claimants had hired Surrey Gardens and Music Hall from the defendants for the purpose of giving four concerts. Six days before the concerts were due to be performed the hall burnt down and it was impossible to give the concerts. The claimants had not yet paid for the use of the hall but they had incurred considerable expenditure in advertising the concerts and other expenses.

It was held that the defendants were not in breach of contract for failure to provide the concert hall. Blackburn J. said:

> "Where, from the nature of the contract, it appears that the parties must from the beginning have known that it could not be fulfilled unless some particular specified thing continued to exist, so that, when entering into the contract, they must have contemplated such continuing existence as the foundation of what was to be done; there, in the absence of any express or implied warranty that the thing shall exist, the contract is not to be construed as a positive contract, but as subject to an implied condition that the parties shall be excused in case, before breach, performance becomes impossible from the perishing of the thing without the fault of the contractor."

What was decided was that once the contract became impossible to perform, the contract was *discharged* and the parties were excused from further performance. The obligations under the contract which were still to be performed were no longer enforceable.

It is generally agreed now that the basis on which a contract will be said to be frustrated is dependent upon a rule of law to the effect that if the contract becomes impossible to perform the parties will be discharged from their obligations. (See Poole, 10th edn, pp.469–470.)

Since *Taylor v Caldwell*, the courts have developed a number of categories where the contract can be said to be frustrated and the parties excused from further performance.

2. Impossibility

Apart from *Taylor v Caldwell* there are a number of cases involving impossibility. In *Asfar & Co v Blundell* [1896] 1 Q.B. 123 a contract for the sale of a cargo of dates was frustrated when the cargo was sunk and became so contaminated by water and sewage that it was effectively useless.

Contracts of *personal service* will be frustrated where the contractor dies or is incapacitated. In *Cutter v Powell* (1795) 6 Term Rep. 320 a sailor had signed on for a three month voyage but when he died half way through the contract it was held to be frustrated. In *Condor v The Barron Knights Ltd* [1966] 1 W.L.R. 87 a member of a pop group became too ill to play regularly and his contract was frustrated.

Unavailability of the subject matter of the contract can cause it to be frustrated. It has been held in numerous shipping cases that where a ship has been seized, or detained or requisitioned then this will frustrate the charterparty. Difficulties arise when the unavailability is only temporary. In *Jackson v Union Marine Insurance Co Ltd* (1874–75) L.R. 10 C.P. 125 a ship had been chartered to sail from Liverpool to Newport and then take on a cargo for San Francisco. The contract did not stipulate any time limit for completion of the task. One day out of Liverpool the ship ran aground and was out of action for eight months for repairs. It was held that the contract was frustrated. A term was implied into the contract that it would be completed within a reasonable time and that therefore the delay involved was so extensive that it served to frustrate the contract.

In such cases it is often a question of degree whether or not the delay will be sufficient to frustrate the contract or not. In *FA Tamplin Steamship Co Ltd v Anglo Mexican Petroleum Products Co Ltd* [1916] 2 A.C. 397 a ship was requisitioned during the First World War in February 1915. The charter was to last until December 1917. The House of Lords felt that the war would be over sufficiently soon to allow a substantial period of the charter to be performed as intended, and therefore held that the contract was not frustrated!

During the Falklands War, cruise ships such as the QE2 and the Canberra were requisitioned by the British Government to be used as troop carriers. As far as clients who were already booked onto the ships were concerned, this would frustrate their contracts with Cunard and P&O unless, as would be most likely, the contract provided for frustrating events.

3. Impracticability

In some circumstances, events may conspire, not to make the contract impossible to perform, but to make it particularly burdensome on one of the parties. English courts have generally taken the view that simply because the contract becomes more difficult, or expensive, or more time consuming to perform, this does not frustrate the contract. The leading case on this point is *Davis Contractors Ltd v Fareham Urban DC* [1956] A.C. 696 in which a builder agreed to build 78 houses in eight months at a fixed price. Because of shortages of materials and skilled labour the contract took 22 months to complete and cost substantially more to perform. The contractors argued that the contract had been frustrated. The House of Lords held that it was not. Lord Radcliffe said:

"it is not hardship or inconvenience or material loss itself which calls the principle of frustration into play. There must be as well such a change in the significance of the obligation that the thing undertaken would, if performed, be a different thing from that contracted for."

The same kind of problem occurred when the Suez Canal was closed during the 1956 crisis. In the case of *Ocean Tramp Tankers Corp v V/O Sovfracht (The Eugenia)* [1964] 1 All E.R. 161 a ship was chartered to sail from Genoa, via the Black Sea, to India. Both parties assumed that the ship would go via the Suez Canal but the contract did not specify. The Canal was closed after the contract was concluded and after the ship had entered it and the ship was trapped in the Canal. The Court of Appeal held that the contract was not frustrated. The journey could be completed by going via the Cape of Good Hope. This would add 30 days to a voyage that would normally take 108. Although the contract would be more burdensome and expensive it was not impossible and the impracticality was not enough to frustrate the contract. (See below for a discussion of a different aspect of the case.) The rationale behind such cases is that the courts are not willing to come to the aid of parties who are simply faced with a bad bargain. It also serves to encourage parties to expressly provide for such events rather than leaving themselves open to entirely arbitrary consequences—see below.

4. Frustration of Purpose

There are situations where the contract is not impossible to perform and neither is it impracticable in the sense that one party would have to face a much greater burden than anticipated and yet performance would be pointless and without purpose. This is what happened in the case of *Krell v Henry* [1903] 2 K.B. 740. The facts were that the defendant had hired a room from the claimant from which to watch the coronation procession of Edward VII. The King became ill and the procession was cancelled. The Court of Appeal held that the contract was frustrated. Although the room was still available for hire it would have been a fruitless exercise to make use of it.

One significant feature of that case is that it was stressed that the contract was not simply for the hire of a room but for the hire of a room from which to watch the procession. A contrasting case is *Herne Bay Steam Boat Co v Hutton* [1903] 2 K.B. 683. In that case, the contract was for the hire of a boat "for the purpose of viewing the naval review and for a day's cruise round the fleet". The naval review was in fact a royal review at Spithead by the King. The review was cancelled, again because of the illness of Edward VII. On this occasion, the Court of Appeal held that the contract was not frustrated. Although the review would not take place, nevertheless, the fleet was still there to be viewed and the harbour cruise was still possible. The distinction between the cases is fine but the difference seems to be that in the former the whole purpose of the room hire was undermined whereas in the latter one of the main purposes of the boat hire still remained. The result seems to depend upon the extent to which the recipient of the service brings home to the provider the importance of the event. (For a discussion of these cases in the context of a package holiday see Grant "Caribbean Chaos" (1998) 148 N.L.J. 190 and "It's not cricket" [1998] I.T.L.J. 51.)

5. Illegality

When war breaks out it is illegal to trade with the enemy. Any contracts affected by such illegality are frustrated. Similarly, if the government prohibits certain types of contract or requisitions goods under emergency legislation the contract is frustrated. For example, in the case of *Fibrosa Spolka Akcyjna v Fairbairn Lawson Combe Barbour Ltd* [1943] A.C. 32 a contract for the supply of machinery to a company in Poland was frustrated by the outbreak of World War II when it became illegal to trade with the enemy. In 2005, the British company E-bookers was taken over by Cendant, an American company, which proceeded to cancel all the bookings made by E-Bookers' clients to Cuba on the grounds that this would be an infringement of the American trade embargo of Cuba. On the face of it this seems to be a case of frustration of contract caused by illegality. However, given that Cendant chose to take over E-Bookers in the knowledge that they had bookings to Cuba, there may be a case for saying that this was a self-induced frustration and therefore a breach of contract rather than a frustrating event (see *Maritime National Fish Ltd v Ocean Trawlers Ltd* [1935] A.C. 524).

6. Events Provided For

The rules relating to frustration of contract are all about allocating the risk of events over which the parties have no control. If the parties have made no provision in the contract for the event then the contract will be frustrated and the risk will be allocated according to the rules in the LR(FC)A 1943. However, if the parties have expressly stated in the contract what will happen if a frustrating event occurs then the courts will give effect to their express wishes rather than impose an external solution on them. This ability to "contract out" is preserved in s.2(3) of the LR(FC)A 1943:

> "2(3) Where any contract to which this Act applies contains any provision which upon the true construction of the contract, is intended to have effect in the event of circumstances arising which operate, or would but for the said provision operate, to frustrate the contract, or is intended to have effect whether such circumstances arise or not, the court shall give effect to the said provision and shall only give effect to the foregoing section of this Act to such extent, if any, as appears to the court to be consistent with the said provision."

A number of points need to be made about this ability to contract out. First, it is often a very difficult question of interpretation to decide whether a particular clause in a contract effectively avoids a frustration of contract. For instance, in *Metropolitan Water Board v Dick Kerr & Co* [1918] A.C. 119 a company agreed in July 1914 to build a reservoir within six years, but they were to be given an extension for delays "however occasioned". In 1916, the government ordered them to stop work and sell their plant. It was held that the clause was intended to cover temporary stoppages because of labour and materials problems, not the kind of delay that actually occurred. In such circumstances the contract was frustrated. In *Jackson v Union Marine Insurance Co* a clause in the contract provided that the ship was to proceed to Newport with all possible dispatch "dangers and accidents of navigation excepted". When the ship ran aground and was out of action for eight months being repaired it was held that the contract was frustrated. The phrase "dangers and accidents of navigation excepted" was not intended to cover such a long delay.

The second point, which arises from the first, is that the contract may provide for the event in a number of ways. For instance, it may provide simply that if, say, a strike occurs the contract will not be frustrated. In such circumstances, the parties will be assumed to have contracted on the basis that if a strike occurs one or other of them will have to bear that risk. In a package holiday contract, if such a clause were inserted it might mean that the tour operator was agreeing to provide a holiday irrespective of strikes, and if one occurred and he could not provide it, then he would be in breach of contract—and would have to pay damages. Alternatively, the clause might say that the contract is not frustrated in the event of a strike and go on to say that the operator will not be liable for non-performance in such circumstances. The effect of this clause is that the strike neither frustrates the contract nor does it put the tour operator in breach. He is excused from performance but the client is still liable to pay for the holiday. The clause places the whole risk of the strike on the client. (It is unlikely that the tour operator would succeed with this because it would be prevented either by reg.15(5) of the Package Travel Regulations or s.3(2)(b)(ii) of UCTA or by the provisions of the UTCCR.)

A further variation is where the clause states that the event will frustrate the contract and then goes on to state what the consequences of the frustration will be. For instance the clause might state that the contract will be discharged by the strike and that the operator will be able to retain all the client's money. Such a consequence is different from the consequences provided for in the LR(FC)A 1943 which will be examined shortly. Such a clause will not be caught by UCTA 1977 because it is not excluding liability for *breach of contract* it is providing for the consequences of a *frustration of contract*. However, it could be caught by reg.13 or 14 of the Package Travel Regulations.

The third point to make is that tour operators who are members of ABTA do in fact expressly provide in their package holiday contracts for what they call *force majeure* events. The Code of Conduct defines what is meant by *force majeure* and requires ABTA members to expressly provide for such events in certain circumstances.

The ABTA Code of Conduct will be examined at the end of this chapter but it needs to be pointed out now that *force majeure* as defined in the Code is different from frustration of contract and different again from *force majeure* as defined in the Package Travel Regulations. Also the Code does not require a tour operator to provide comprehensively for situations which might amount to force majeure. Broadly speaking the Code applies the *force majeure* provisions to pre-departure but not post-departure events.

7. Events Foreseen

Frustrating events are usually unforeseen. The parties have made the contract without taking such eventualities into account just because they are unforeseen, and it is for that reason that the doctrine of frustration of contract has to be invoked.

The other side of the coin is that, generally, if the events were foreseen, then the parties will be taken to have contracted on that basis and will have to accept the consequences of the risk that they foresaw. For instance, take a tour operator who offered packages to Dubrovnik in the summer of 1993 without expressly providing in the contract that he would be discharged from his obligations if there was renewed fighting. It could be argued that if he could not provide the holiday he would be in breach of contract. The risk of such an event can easily be foreseen and the tour operator who contracts in such circumstances could be said to be assuming that risk.

In the case of *Walton Harvey Ltd v Walker & Homfrays Ltd* [1931] 1 Ch. 274 the claimants bought the right to display advertising on the side of the defendant's hotel for seven years. Before the period was up the hotel was demolished. The defendants were held liable for breach of contract because they knew of the risk of the building being demolished. The claimants did not know of this risk.

However, there is a big difference between events which are *foreseen* and those which are merely *foreseeable*. If we look at any of the cases on frustration of contract none of the events that occurred were totally unforeseeable. Is it completely beyond the bounds of possibility that a concert hall would burn down or a ship run aground or war break out? The issue here is that foreseeability is a flexible concept encompassing events where there is a strong likelihood that they will occur and other events where the degree of foreseeability is extremely small. Events at the latter end of the scale are regarded as being so improbable that they are capable of frustrating the contract. Those events at the other end of the scale which are readily foreseeable, as well as those which are actually foreseen, are events which will not generally frustrate the contract.

This latter statement is qualified because there are some cases where the courts have suggested that even foreseeable events may frustrate a contract in appropriate circumstances. In *WJ Tatem Ltd v Gamboa* [1939] 1 K.B. 132 the defendants chartered a ship for the purpose of evacuating civilians from Spain during the Spanish Civil War. The ship was seized by the Nationalist government and the question arose as to whether the contract was frustrated. Goddard J. held that the contract was frustrated. In the course of his judgment he said:

"I do not feel that I can hold on the evidence which I have before me that a risk of seizure of the description which took place here, and the detaining of the vessel not only for the period of her charter but for a long period thereafter, was a risk which was contemplated by the parties."

However, later in the judgment he indicated that even if the parties had contemplated that the ship would be seized the contract would still be frustrated:

"it seems to me that, if the true doctrine be that frustration depends on the absolute disappearance of the contract; or, if the true basis be 'the continued existence of a certain state of facts' it makes very little difference whether the circumstances are foreseen or not."

In the case of the *Eugenia* [1964] 2 Q.B. 226 Lord Denning M.R. made similar statements. The Eugenia had been chartered to take a cargo from the Black Sea to India. It was envisaged that the ship would go via the Suez Canal although there was no term in the contract to that effect and there was no time limit within which the voyage had to be completed. While the contract was being negotiated the Suez crisis arose. The two parties were aware of the risk and each suggested how the matter could be resolved if the Canal were to be closed but they could not agree on a solution and, therefore, the contract was silent as to the risk. The ship, in fact, entered the Canal and was caught there for several months.

The actual decision in the case was that the charterers had broken the contract by entering the Canal and had to pay damages to the owners for doing so. However, the court speculated on what the position would have been if there had been no breach. In particular, would the contract have been frustrated or not, given that the parties were aware of the risks when the contract was concluded? Lord Denning said:

"It has frequently been said that the doctrine of frustration only applies when the new situation is 'unforeseen' or 'uncontemplated', as if that were an essential feature. But it is not so. The only thing that is essential is that the parties should have made no provision for it in their contract. The only relevance of it being 'unforeseen' is this: If the parties did not foresee anything of the kind happening, you can readily infer they have made no provision for it: whereas, if they did foresee it, you would expect them to make provision for it. Such was the case in the Spanish Civil War when a ship was let on charter to the republican government. The purpose was to evacuate refugees. The parties foresaw that she might be seized by the nationalists. But they made no provision for it in their contract. Yet when it was seized, the contract was frustrated. So here the parties foresaw that the canal might become impassable: it was the very thing they feared. But they made no provision for it. So there is room for the doctrine to apply if it be a proper case for it."

Despite these comments he then went on to say that if he had been called upon to answer the question as to whether the contract was frustrated he would have said not. The closure of the canal did not bring about a "fundamentally different situation". The voyage would take longer and be more expensive but it could still be accomplished even if the Canal were closed.

8. Anticipatory Frustration

Contracts are frustrated when the frustrating event occurs and the parties' obligations cease from that moment. But what would be the situation if an event occurs which does not frustrate the contract immediately but the parties believe that it will in the near future? For instance, in the case of *Embiricos v Sydney Reid & Co* [1914] 3 K.B. 45 a Greek ship was chartered for a voyage which would take it through the Dardanelles. War broke out between Greece and

Turkey and the charterer decided to treat the contract as frustrated. In fact, the Turks unexpectedly permitted vessels to "escape" through the Dardanelles for a period of time and this meant that the voyage would have been possible. Nevertheless, the court held that the charterer's decision was justified. *At the time the decision was taken* it was a reasonable decision to take.

Sometimes, the event may not be as clear cut as the outbreak of war between Greece and Turkey and the parties will have to wait until the position is clearer. For instance, in the Iran–Iraq war a number of ships were detained in the Shatt al Arab. At first, it was believed that the war would not last long and that the ships would soon be released. At that stage the contracts for the ships would not be frustrated. Only later when it became apparent that the detention would last much longer were the contracts frustrated.

In the Gulf War of 1991 a number of tour operators had clients in India. The holidays would not be directly affected by the outbreak of war but because flights would have to be re-routed around the prospective war zone it would adversely affect the holiday, adding much more travelling time and costing substantial amounts more to the operator. Assuming that such an event could frustrate the contract (and it is not beyond doubt) the question arises as to the point at which the tour operator would be justified in saying that the holiday was frustrated. Would it be when Kuwait was initially invaded? Or when the United Nations decided to take action? Or when the allied forces started a build up of forces? Or when an outbreak of hostilities appeared imminent? Or when war actually commenced? The law seems to be that even if hostilities had never broken out, if it appeared to a reasonable person that holidays were about to be affected then a decision to treat the contract as frustrated would be justified. Foreign Office warnings would be relevant here. If they were unequivocal in their advice to avoid the area because of danger to overflying aircraft then a tour operator could rely on this to justify a decision not to perform the contract.

9. Hurricanes

In September 1998, Hurricane Georges hit the Caribbean. One of its effects was to disrupt the holidays of clients of Thomson Holidays. (*Norwegian Cruise Line Ltd v Thomson Holidays*, Q.B.D. November 29, 2000, reported on Westlaw.) Thomson had a contract for a season with Norwegian Cruise Lines for their ship, the *Norwegian Sea*, to embark and disembark Thomson clients in Santo Domingo in the Dominican Republic at seven day intervals. On September 27, because of the hurricane, it proved impossible to pick up 208 Thomson clients from Santo Domingo. The ship was, however, able to embark and disembark other Thomson clients at San Juan in Puerto Rico according to the usual schedule and to sail on an altered itinerary. Thomson claimed that the contract was frustrated because of the hurricane and wished to recover the money that had been pre-paid for the 208 passengers. The court said:

"while it may be that the contracts of individual passengers with THL were frustrated by their inability to join the vessel, the frustration of the whole cruise is a rather different concept.

FRUSTRATION OF CONTRACT AND *FORCE MAJEURE*

In *The Super Servant Two* [1990] 1 Lloyd's Rep. 1 Bingham LJ set out five truths in respect of frustration. The second and third truths as set out in Chitty at para 24-007 are that 'secondly, frustration operates to "kill the contract and discharge the parties from further liability under it" and therefore it cannot be "lightly invoked" but must be kept within "very narrow limits and ought not to be extended." Thirdly, frustration brings a contract to an end "forthwith, without more and automatically".'

Clearly the contract was not killed 'forthwith' and THL does not contend that it was.

While the concept of divisibility may be highly relevant to accrued rights of payment, I do not have the same ease of acceptance where it is sought to make two or more contracts out of one. Contracts are not like earthworms. If one is to have more than one contract, one must start with more than one contract. The contract comprised a series of obligations but it did not comprise a series of contracts. Accordingly the frustration claim fails."

Given that the contract extended for the whole season and only part of one cruise was affected, the court was essentially saying that the hurricane had not done enough to destroy the contract—it remained largely capable of performance. Interestingly, if asked, the court may have been prepared to regard the individual package holiday contracts as frustrated but that was an issue which did not arise in the case—presumably because the passengers would have had more generous treatment under the Package Travel Regulations. (For an article on Hurricane Georges see Kilbey "Of Holidays and Hurricanes" [1999] I.T.L.J. 46.)

THE CONSEQUENCES OF FRUSTRATION—THE COMMON LAW

Reasonable though it may seem at first glance to call off a contract because it has become impossible to perform, there remains the equally difficult problem of how to sort out the consequences of the frustration. In *Taylor v Caldwell*, for instance, the owner of the hall would be excused from providing the hall rather than being in breach of contract, but what about the hirer? Would he have still to pay for it, and what about the losses that he would suffer by not being able to hold the concerts?

At common law the solution to such problems was to say that from the moment the contract was frustrated both parties were excused from any further obligation—but they remained liable for any obligations that had already accrued. The loss would lie where it fell. So, for instance, in *Krell v Henry* the contract was that £25 was to be paid immediately and another £50 two days before the procession. The procession was cancelled after the £25 was paid but before the £50 became due. It was held that the first payment was made while the contract was still valid and therefore could not be recovered by the hirer. On the other hand, the second payment was not due until after the contract was frustrated and therefore need not be paid because the obligation to pay no longer existed.

If, for some reason, the hirer had not actually paid the deposit before the frustrating event even though he should have done so, the owner could have sued him for it. It was an obligation which had arisen when the contract was still valid and, therefore, it could be validly claimed. The hirer would not have been permitted to take advantage of his own breach of contract.

The way the rule worked was entirely arbitrary. If the schedule of payments had been different then the risk could have fallen entirely on one or the other of the parties depending on just when the frustrating event occurred.

In *Appleby v Myers* (1866–7) L.R. 2 C.P. 651 the claimant had agreed to install some machinery in the defendant's factory. Before the work could be completed the factory burnt down. No money was payable until the job had been completed. The claimant therefore recovered nothing.

In *Cutter v Powell* the seaman had completed over half the voyage when he died. He was only due to be paid on completion of the voyage so his widow was entitled to nothing even though a substantial benefit had been obtained by the shipowner.

In 1943 the House of Lords developed an exception to the rule that if money had been paid before the frustrating event it could not be recovered. In *Fibrosa Spolka Akcyjna v Fairbairn Lawson Combe Barbour Ltd* [1943] A.C. 32 a manufacturer agreed to sell machinery to the buyer for £4,800. The buyer paid £1,000 in advance and the remainder was to be paid on delivery. Delivery was prevented by the outbreak of war and the contract was frustrated. The buyer, having paid £1,000 received nothing in return. The House of Lords held that where there is a *total failure of consideration* by one party, i.e. the other gets nothing at all in return for his money, then the buyer could recover his money.

Although the decision would be welcomed by the buyer, it would have the opposite effect on the seller who had incurred considerable expense in building the machinery and would be paid nothing for that expense.

If these rules are applied to a package holiday context the results are quite interesting. If the client pays his deposit on booking and the contract is frustrated before the balance is due then the client will lose the deposit but will not have to pay any more. The tour operator is of course released from his obligation to provide the holiday. The position is much the same if the frustrating event occurs after the balance has been paid (or should have been paid). The client will lose his money but the tour operator will not have to provide the holiday.

But what if the contract is frustrated after the holiday has commenced? Suppose a tour operator had clients who had arrived in Russia for a two centre holiday in Moscow and Leningrad (now St Petersburg) just as the Russian government announced that the Chernobyl nuclear reactor had blown up. It would be impossible to travel to Leningrad for the second part of the holiday and to fly home from Leningrad airport as planned. Such circumstances could amount to a frustration of contract. This would mean that neither party would be under any further obligation to each other. The clients would lose their money and the tour operator could walk away from the contract saying that he was no longer under an obligation to do anything more for them! It is for this reason of course that most holiday contracts provide for what will happen in such circumstances.

In an accommodation-only contract, if the guest had paid in advance for the hotel room but the hotel had subsequently burnt down, then at common law the guest could recover the pre-payment on the basis of the decision in the *Fibrosa* case—a complete failure of consideration. This assumes that English law would apply to the contract—see Ch.14.

The Consequences of Frustration—The Law Reform (Frustrated Contracts) Act 1943

The unsatisfactory position at common law for dealing with the consequences of frustration led to the passage of The Law Reform (Frustrated Contracts) Act 1943. Broadly speaking, the Act provides means by which the risks of frustration can be apportioned between the parties. The rules are not entirely free from criticism but they are better than the old common law rules which they replace in most cases. There are contracts which are not covered by the Act but they do not include holiday contracts.

1. Money Paid or Payable

Section 1(2) provides:

"1(2) All sums paid or payable to any party in pursuance of the contract before the time when the parties were so discharged (in this Act referred to as 'the time of discharge') shall, in the case of sums so paid, be recoverable from him as money received by him for the use of the party by whom the sums were paid, and, in the case of sums so payable, cease to be so payable:
  Provided that, if the party to whom the sums were so paid or payable incurred expenses before the time of discharge in, or for the purpose of, the performance of the contract, the court may, if it considers it just to do so having regard to all the circumstances of the case, allow him to retain or, as the case may be, recover the whole or any part of the sums so paid or payable, not being an amount in excess of the expenses so incurred."

This does two things. First, it states that if one party has paid money to the other party, or was due to pay money to the other party, before the contract was frustrated then they can recover the money already paid, and keep the money they were due to pay.
  Secondly, however, it says that if the other party has already incurred expenses in the performance of the contract these expenses can be claimed out of the money already paid or payable but only if the court thinks it just to do so.
  Take, for instance, the *Fibrosa* case. In that case, £1,000 had already been paid in advance before the contract was frustrated. Under s.1(2) that money could be claimed back (as it could under the common law) but it would be subject to the court's discretion as to whether it would be just to permit the manufacturer of the machinery to retain some of the money for any expenses incurred. If the machinery had been specially built for the buyer and could not be resold elsewhere then one can imagine that a court would be tempted to make a large deduction for expenses out of the £1,000. It would be different if the machinery was in high demand and it could be sold to another buyer without loss.
  It should be noted, however, that the maximum that can be claimed for expenses is the amount paid or payable before the frustrating event. Even if the manufacturer had expended almost the whole contract price in building the machinery he would get no more than what was due when the contract was frustrated.

Applying this rule to tour operators what would be the situation if a contract was frustrated after the deposit had been paid but before the balance? First, the client is entitled to recover the amount of his deposit. Secondly, the operator is entitled to have any expenses he has incurred taken into account if the court thinks it just to do so. If the operator has already laid out money on transport and accommodation then this could be set against the deposit. Presumably, the court would enquire whether this money was recoverable by the operator from the suppliers concerned. If it could be, then it would not count as expenses. On the other hand, the Act specifically provides in s.1(4) that a reasonable sum for overhead expenses can be taken into account. However, establishing that expenses have been incurred is one thing, convincing a court that it would be just to recover them is another. It is not beyond the bounds of possibility to imagine a court saying that the operator is better placed than the client to bear the risk of the frustration and that it would be just to permit the client to recover the whole of his deposit. On the other hand, the operator might equally argue that the prepayment is a form of insurance designed specifically to protect him against such eventualities and therefore he should be able to retain all his expenses.

Frustration after departure would increase the chances of the operator having incurred expenses which he would not be able to recover. He would still have to show, however, that it would be just to recover them. Where the client has not only paid the whole of the holiday price but is stranded abroad and is facing the expense of getting himself home, would it be just to permit the operator to claim his expenses from the price of the holiday? In such circumstances it might be necessary to take into account s.1(3).

2. Benefits Received

Section 1(3) provides:

"1(3) Where any party to the contract has, by reason of anything done by any other party thereto in, or for the purpose of, the performance of the contract, obtained a valuable benefit (other than a payment of money to which the last foregoing subsection applies) before the time of discharge, there shall be recoverable from him by the said other party such sum (if any), not exceeding the value of the said benefit to the party obtaining it, as the court considers just, having regard to all the circumstances of the case and, in particular,—

(a) the amount of any expenses incurred before the time of discharge by the benefited party in, or for the purpose of, the performance of the contract, including any sums paid or payable by him to any other party in pursuance of the contract and retained or recoverable by that party under the last foregoing subsection, and
(b) the effect, in relation to the said benefit, of the circumstances giving rise to the frustration of the contract."

What this means is that in cases like *Cutter v Powell* where one party has conferred a benefit on the other party before the frustrating event occurs, the value of this benefit can be awarded by the court if it feels it would be just to do so.

Whether it would apply to cases like *Appleby v Myers* is debatable. Although a large part of the machinery had been installed by the claimants it was all destroyed in the fire. In such circumstances it could be argued that the other party obtained no benefit from the contract and therefore could not be awarded anything for it.

In package holidays where the contract is frustrated before departure this section will have little relevance, but if the contract is frustrated after departure then it may have some impact. To return to the example of the two centre holiday in Russia. If the client has been transported abroad and spent a week in Moscow before being told that the contract is frustrated, it could be said that he had obtained a valuable benefit. If so, a value has to be put on the benefit and the tour operator can make a claim for an amount which does not exceed this value. Whether this will be awarded by the court depends upon whether it is considered just to do so.

However, the court also has to take into account the fact that the client has already paid in full for the holiday and will be reclaiming all this under s.1(2) but that the tour operator will also be claiming his expenses out of this amount. Additionally, the fact that the frustrating event has left the client high and dry in Moscow has to be taken into account.

It would be open to the client to say in these circumstances that the tour operator could not claim to be paid both for his expenses under s.1(2) *and* for the part of the holiday that the client received in Moscow under s.1(3), given that the client is now having to make his own way home.

In a hotel contract where the guest had paid in advance and stayed at the hotel for several nights before the hotel was blown away by a hurricane then the court could take into account the fact that the hotel company had conferred a benefit, namely several nights accommodation, on the other party to the contract, before the contract had been frustrated.

Similarly, if a passenger with a return flight found themselves stranded at the inbound airport because the control tower had been blown away by the same hurricane, the court could take into account that the passenger had already received the benefit of the outbound flight. It should be noted, however, that such a case is highly unlikely to arise simply because airline contracts are usually sufficiently comprehensive to cover such eventualities. There is also Regulation 261/2004 to take into account. See Ch.13. Passengers stranded on the other side of the Channel by a French fishermen's blockade would be in a similar position—having benefited from the outbound ferry trip to Calais even if they couldn't return the same way.

Section 1(3)(a) might have relevance in some cases where, for instance, as a requirement of the contract the client had purchased equipment in advance of the holiday, e.g. a motor cycle touring holiday that required the client to provide his own motorbike, or a skiing holiday that required the client to provide his own skis or the trekking holiday that required hiking equipment. All these would be expenses incurred for the purpose of the performance of the contract. It might also cover situations where the client had to purchase services in advance—such as scuba diving lessons to bring him up to a minimum standard for a diving holiday.

3. Insurance

Section 1(5) provides:

> "1(5) In considering whether any sum ought to be recovered or retained under the foregoing provisions of this section by any party to the contract, the court shall not take into account any sums which have, by reason of the circumstances giving rise to the frustration of the contract become payable to that party under any contract of insurance unless there was an obligation to insure imposed by an express term of the frustrated contract or by or under any enactment."

What this means is that if one party has had the foresight to take out insurance to cover the frustrating event then this will *not* be taken into account when assessing how to apportion the losses *unless* it was an express term of the contract that insurance be taken out.

What this means is that *if* a tour operator makes it compulsory for a client to take out an insurance policy to cover frustrating events and there is a payment by the insurance company then the court may take this into account. So, for instance, if the policy provides that in the event of a strike by air traffic controllers the client can cancel and get a refund then the operator could argue that in these circumstances they should be able to reclaim their full expenses.

4. Apportionment in Practice—the *Guns 'n' Roses* Case

There is remarkably little case law on the effect of the Law Reform (Frustrated Contracts) Act but one case which illustrates its operation vividly is *Gamerco SA v ICM/Fair Warning (Agency) Ltd* [1995] E.M.L.R. 263. The facts of the case were that the rock group Guns 'n' Roses were due to perform at a football stadium in Madrid but shortly before the concert took place the stadium was found to be unsafe and use of it was prohibited. This had the effect of frustrating the contract between the promoters of the concert and the first defendants, Guns 'n' Roses. The promoters had promised to pay the group $1.1 million or 90 per cent of the gate receipts, whichever was greater. By the time the contract was frustrated the claimants had paid $412,000 on account and were due to pay another $362,000—both payments net of tax. Both parties had incurred expenses in or for the purpose of the performance of the contract. The judge held that, applying s.1(2) of the Act, the claimants were entitled to the return of the $412,000. However, he also had to consider whether the defendants could retain any money out of that pre-payment to cover their expenses under s.1(3). In deciding this question he concluded that the Act gave him a very wide discretion:

> "I see no indication in the Act, the authorities, or the relevant literature that the court is obliged to incline either towards total retention or equal division. Its task is to do justice in a situation which the parties neither contemplated nor provided for, and to mitigate the possible harshness of allowing all loss to lie where it has fallen."

After taking into account a number of matters:

- the defendants had incurred $50,000 of expenses;
- the claimant had incurred in excess of $450,000 of expenses;
- neither party had conferred a benefit on the other;
- both parties' expenditure was wasted;
- the claimant was only concerned with one contract whereas the defendants had contracts for 20 concerts; and
- although both parties were insured he was not entitled to take account of this by virtue of s.1(5) of the Act

he decided that the defendants could not retain any of the pre-payment.

THE PACKAGE TRAVEL REGULATIONS

The Package Travel Regulations do not mention frustration of contract as such, nor do they state what the relationship between the Regulations and the Law Reform (Frustrated Contracts) Act is. What they do cover are:

> "unusual and unforeseeable circumstances beyond the control of the party by whom [it] is pleaded, the consequences of which could not have been avoided even if all due care had been exercised."

These circumstances will be referred to, for the sake of convenience, as *force majeure* events. The EC Directive on which the Regulations are based specifically refers to *force majeure* but this terminology has been omitted from the Regulations. If these circumstances occur then the Regulations provide what the consequences will be. In many cases, what would be a frustrating event at common law will also be a *force majeure* event under the Regulations. The position, therefore, will be that where an event occurs which is both a frustrating event and a *force majeure* event then the Regulations will govern the matter because they were passed specifically to deal with package holidays and will therefore take precedence over the common law and the LR(FC)A 1943, which are more general provisions. If, however, an event occurs which is not a *force majeure* event, then the common law and the LR(FC)A 1943 apply.

This section will look first at what a *force majeure* event is and how it can be distinguished from a frustrating event; and secondly at how the consequences of a *force majeure* event are provided for in the Regulations.

1. Force Majeure Events

The definition of *force majeure* given above is to be found in reg.13(3)(b) and reg.15(2)(c)(i). It provides limited immunity for a tour operator who cancels a package holiday or fails to perform it properly—but only if the definition can be satisfied. To do this the operator has to show that:

- the circumstances were unusual;
- the circumstances were unforeseeable;
- the circumstances were beyond the control of the operator;
- the consequences of the circumstances could not have been avoided; even if all due care had been exercised.

The requirements are cumulative. It would not be sufficient to show that something was unusual if it was not also unforeseeable.

Many of the frustrating events already examined would probably fall within the definition. For instance, if the Suez Canal was closed preventing a cruise ship from proceeding from the Mediterranean to the Red Sea this would be a *force majeure* event which also frustrated the contract. Similarly, war breaking out in the Gulf or civil unrest in Egypt or earthquakes in Turkey would fall within both categories. But what about air traffic controllers' strikes? At common law such an event would almost certainly frustrate the contract if it went on long enough but under the much tighter definition in the Regulations it *might* fail to be classified as a *force majeure* event. The reason for this is that it might not be unusual nor even unforeseeable. Such events happen with sufficient frequency that a court might conceivably come to the conclusion that it was not a *force majeure* event. If this was the case, the rules to be applied would be the common law rules and the LR(FC)A 1943 but not the Package Travel Regulations. *Coughlan v Thomson Holidays Ltd* [2001] C.L.Y. 4276 is a case where the defendants endeavoured to establish that a flight departure delay caused by technical problems with the aircraft and the crew running out of flight hours amounted to *force majeure* but failed.

A problem might also arise in relation to civil unrest in Sri Lanka. For many years there were incidents which have affected the tourist industry. Any tour operator taking clients to Sri Lanka in such circumstances might be unable to plead *force majeure* if the situation deteriorated to such an extent that the holiday had to be cancelled. Could the operator deny that the unrest causing the cancellation was unforeseeable? (See Cons L.J. [1994] C555 for an example of how a situation such as this was treated by the German courts.)

The problem arises over the word "unforeseeable". If one uses enough imagination almost nothing is unforeseeable. Even without a lot of imagination most tour operators have experienced sufficient problems in the past to be aware of a whole range of events that could affect a typical package holiday. Does such knowledge and experience mean that any time an event which has occurred in the past occurs again then this was a "foreseeable" event and therefore does not amount to *force majeure*?

For instance, does the fact that hurricanes have happened in the past in Florida and the Caribbean mean that such events are foreseeable to a tour operator? Does the fact that a nuclear reactor once exploded near Leningrad, another almost exploded at Three Mile Island in America and one was badly damaged in Fukushima in Japan mean that it is foreseeable that holidays to Russia, America and Japan could be affected by nuclear explosions?

These events may very well be foreseeable if one thinks about it long enough but on a spectrum of foreseeability they are clearly at the bottom end. They could not be said to be "reasonably foreseeable" and certainly they would not be "foreseen" by a tour operator. Unless the definition is to lose much of its impact it would be better to interpret "foreseeable" as having a more restricted meaning such as "reasonably foreseeable". Not to do so would rob the Regulations of effect in just the kind of circumstances that it was clearly intended to cover. (This passage, which first appeared in the first edition, was noted with approval in the Argentine case—*Giambelluca, Emilia v Nabil Travel Service* L. 342247, Buenos Aires, July 11, 2002.)

The effect of a *frustrating event* is to *discharge* the contract, i.e. the contract will cease to exist as far as future obligations are concerned and the parties will be excused from further performance. This is because the whole contract has become impossible to perform. Except in very limited circumstances, there is no such thing as a partial frustration of a contract. It is all or nothing. However, when a *force majeure* event occurs, although in many circumstances it will be sufficiently serious to discharge the contract, nothing in the Regulations states that a *force majeure* event *discharges* the contract. The event may fit within the definition and not actually discharge the contract. For instance, what if during a 30-day touring holiday of Europe terrorists occupy the Louvre and clients cannot visit the museum on that day. This would amount to a *force majeure* event but it would not frustrate the contract.

In such circumstances the rules on frustration would not apply at all. Either the rules on *force majeure* in the Regulations would apply or the operator would be in breach of contract.

2. The Consequences of a *Force Majeure* Event

Pre-departure Cancellations and Withdrawals

Regulation 13 provides that where a holiday is cancelled or where the client has withdrawn because the operator has made a major change to the holiday the client will not only be entitled to a full refund or substitute holiday (see Ch.10 on Remedies) but also compensation. However, there are exceptions to this. One is that where the package has been cancelled for reasons of *force majeure*, compensation is not payable. This places a client in a much better position than he would be under the LR(FC)A 1943. Under the LR(FC)A 1943 any money already paid over would be subject to a deduction for expenses at the court's discretion. If the event was not a *force majeure* event because it was foreseeable, the Regulations would not apply and the client would have to rely on the LR(FC)A 1943 for assistance.

Post-departure Problems

Regulation 14 does not mention *force majeure* or frustration of contract at all but it will clearly have an impact in such situations. It provides that there is an *implied term in the contract* that where a tour operator is unable to provide a significant proportion of the services contracted for he shall make suitable alternative arrangements for the clients and if necessary transport the clients back to their place of departure. In "appropriate" cases compensation should also be paid.

This provision will come into operation whenever a significant proportion of the services cannot be provided—whether that is due to a frustrating event or not. If it is not a frustrating event then what the Regulation does is to provide additional remedies to the client when the operator is in breach of contract. If it is a frustrating event then the position is a considerably more complex and it depends upon the nature of the relationship between reg.14 and s.2(3) of the LR(FC)A.

You will remember that what s.2(3) states is that if there is a *term in the contract* that is intended to take effect in the event of a frustrating event occurring then that term will be enforced by the court rather than the court applying the provisions of s.1 of the LR(FC)A—but only if the term is inconsistent with the LR(FC)A.

By virtue of reg.14 there is certainly a term (albeit implied) in the contract that states that in the event of the tour operator being unable to provide a significant proportion of the services promised then he will have to make suitable alternative arrangements or bring the consumer home. It is reasonable to assume that this term is intended to take effect in the event of a frustrating event occurring. Therefore, the term implied by reg.14 will take precedence over the consequences laid down by s.1 of the LR(FC)A—but only where they are inconsistent with those consequences.

That leaves the problem of interpreting the implied term in reg.14. Is it in fact saying: "In circumstances where a contract would normally be discharged for frustration this will not happen —the contract will not be discharged. Instead the contract must be performed in a different way by the tour operator, i.e. he can fulfill his obligations under the contract by offering you a suitable alternative or by bringing you home"? Or is it saying: "If a frustrating event occurs then the contract will be discharged and the *consequences of the frustration* will be that the tour operator will have to provide a suitable alternative or take you home"? If the former interpretation is preferred then the rules in s.1 of the LR(FC)A cannot be applied at all because what the implied term is saying is that the contract is not frustrated, therefore the rules about apportioning the loss in the event of a frustration cannot be applied. If the latter interpretation is preferred then what will happen is that the courts will apply the remedies in reg.14 and also the rules in s.1 but only if those rules are not inconsistent with reg.14.

In such a complex situation it is difficult to offer any real guidance but if pushed we would prefer the former meaning. First, because reg.14 states that the tour operator must offer suitable alternative arrangements for *the continuation of the package*. These words suggest that the contract will continue in existence (although the performance of it will be varied). Secondly, the remedies in reg.14 apply not only to events which frustrate the contract but also to events which fall short of frustration, i.e. circumstances where the contract clearly does continue and therefore it would be better to adopt an interpretation of reg.14 that applied consistently to both these circumstances. Thirdly, to adopt this interpretation would be the simpler approach—it would not involve the difficulties of determining whether the provisions of reg.14 were consistent with the provisions of s.1 of the LR(FC)A.

So what does all this mean in practice? To go back to the example of the two centre holiday in Russia which is frustrated when Chernobyl blows up. If it were simply a matter of the common law and the LR(FC)A 1943 the position would be that both parties are excused from further performance. Additionally, the client is entitled to all his money back subject to deductions for expenses and for benefits already received at the discretion of the court—bearing in mind that the frustration has left the client stranded in Russia without accommodation or flights. However, if our interpretation of the Regulations is correct then the common law and the LR(FC)A become irrelevant and all a court would have to do is apply reg.14—a much more simple and straightforward situation.

The Regulation also provides that compensation is payable in "appropriate" circumstances. This will mean that the operator will have to pay compensation if the non-provision of the services was somehow due to his fault but not if the reason falls within one of the exceptions to reg.15(1) found in reg.15(2)—in particular *force majeure*. This is dealt with below.

Faced with a serious *force majeure* event, therefore, the tour operator must not abandon his customers but must at least repatriate them. Compensation however would not be appropriate.

Liability for Non-performance and Improper Performance of the Contract

Regulation 15 provides that a tour operator is liable for damage caused to the client by failure to perform the contract or the improper performance of the contract except in certain circumstances. One of those exceptions is when a *force majeure* event has occurred.

We have already seen that where a package holiday contract is cancelled before performance or where major changes have been made and the client has withdrawn under reg.13 then if this is caused by a *force majeure* event the client can have a refund but no compensation. Similarly, under reg.14 if what causes the non-provision of services is a *force majeure* event then no compensation will be payable because reg.15 states that the operator is not liable in such circumstances.

The relationship between reg.14 and reg.15 and the issue of *force majeure* was discussed in the case of *Charlson v Warner* [2000] C.L.Y. 4043. The claimants were claiming breach of contract of a skiing holiday because the holiday had to be curtailed by extreme bad weather and they had to be evacuated and flown home early. The breach alleged was that the holiday was not provided as promised. The defendants had included in their terms and conditions a *force majeure* clause very similarly drafted to reg.15(2)(c)(i). On the facts, the judge held that the adverse weather conditions could not have been predicted by the defendants and they were protected by both their standard clause and by reg.15(2)(c)(i). He went on to discuss the claimants' argument that they were also protected by reg.14:

"The claimants also rely upon paragraph 14 of the regulations which is the provision giving holidaymakers a right to suitable alternative arrangements at no extra cost if it is not possible to perform the contract. I do not find that this is of any assistance to the claimants. I accept the defendant's submissions that paragraph 14 is dependent upon paragraph 15 and has to be read conjunctively. I accept that paragraphs 14 and 15 provide different remedies but are subject to the same exclusion contained in paragraph 15(2) sub-paragraph (c)."

Although this seems to bear out the comments above, that compensation is not payable under reg.14 if it would not be available under reg.15, this is not a view which is entirely unchallenged. In *Lara Tanner v TUI UK Limited* Unreported 10–12 October, 2005, Central London County Court, this question was left open by the court. (See also M. Chapman "All at Sea: Regulation 14 of The Package Travel Regulations And 'Appropriate Compensation'" [2006] I.T.L.J. 12.)

THE ABTA CODE OF CONDUCT

The ABTA Code of Conduct (January 2009 edition) contains provisions relating to *force majeure*. The Code requires ABTA tour operators to insert terms in the contract providing for what will happen if a *force majeure* event occurs. Although the Code refers specifically to *force majeure* and defines what it means, it should be noted that it does not mean the same thing as *force majeure* in the Package Travel Regulations—although the definition comes much closer now than it has done in the past. Nor does it mean the same thing as frustration of contract at common law. For this reason, and to avoid confusion, it will be referred to as "Code of Conduct *force majeure*".

If an ABTA operator has complied with the Code, the question arises as to how the clause in the contract is affected by and relates to the LR(FC)A 1943 and the Package Travel Regulations. This will depend in part on how Code of Conduct *force majeure* is actually defined and in what circumstances the provisions will be applied.

1. Meaning of Code of Conduct *Force Majeure*

Force majeure is defined in the Code as meaning:

> "circumstances where performance and/or prompt performance of the contract is prevented by reasons of unusual and unforeseeable circumstances beyond the control of the Principal, the consequences of which could not have been avoided even if all due care had been exercised. Such circumstances include war or threat of war, riot, civil strife, industrial dispute [which is defined elsewhere], terrorist activity, natural or nuclear disaster, fire or adverse weather conditions."

This definition clearly extends further than events which would frustrate the contract at common law because it extends to events which not only prevent the whole of the performance of the contract but also to those which only prevent the prompt performance of the contract. Whereas an air traffic controllers' strike which wiped out two days of a long weekend in Paris would frustrate such a contract, it is unlikely that it would frustrate a three week holiday to Florida.

2. The Consequences of Code of Conduct *Force Majeure*

Since the Code was re-drafted in 2006 the differences between the Code and the Regulations have considerably narrowed but have not disappeared altogether.

Pre-departure Cancellation

Paragraph 3A of the Code provides that a tour operator shall not cancel a package before departure after the balance of the price has been paid unless it is for reasons of *force majeure*. If the package is cancelled for reasons of *force majeure* then according to para.3B the client should be offered either a full refund or an alternative holiday.

Pre-departure Alterations

Paragraph 3D provides that significant alteration should not be made to packages within 14 days of departure unless it is for reasons of *force majeure*. Where the alteration is made for reasons of *force majeure* then the client must be offered the choice of accepting the change or cancelling and receiving a full refund or taking alternative arrangements of a comparable standard.

Post-departure Changes

Paragraphs 4A–4C are the broad equivalent of reg.14. Tour operators are required to make suitable alternative arrangements for clients or to repatriate them if necessary. As in reg.14 there is no mention of force majeure as such although it does state that compensation is only payable where appropriate.

3. The Relationship Between Code of Conduct *Force Majeure*, Frustration of Contract and *Force Majeure* Under the Package Travel Regulations

We have already seen that where both the Package Travel Regulations and the LR(FC)A 1943 apply then the Regulations take precedence, but there are still situations where only one set of rules applies. The position with the Code of Conduct provisions is that where they are inconsistent with the Regulations the Regulations will take precedence and that where they are inconsistent with the LR(FC)A 1943 the provisions in the Code will take precedence. The reason for this is that, as already discussed earlier in this chapter, where the parties to the contract actually provide for what will happen in the event of a frustrating event occurring the wishes of the parties will prevail (s.2(3) of the LR(FC)A).

Potentially, this leaves an extremely complex situation where an event could be governed by only one set of rules or by any combination of two or three sets. In practice, however, the position is relatively simple. The following examples help to illustrate the situation.

Illustration 1

A volcano erupts unexpectedly two days before departure and the resort is destroyed by lava.

Technically, this would fall within all three categories. It would be a frustrating event, a *force majeure* event and a Code of Conduct *force majeure* event. However, because the Regulations will apply there is no need to go further. The position would be that under reg.13 the client would be entitled to be offered an alternative holiday or a full refund but would not be entitled to compensation.

Illustration 2

On arrival in resort clients cannot be accommodated in their hotel for the first two days of their 14 day holiday because there has been an unexpectedly ferocious storm which flooded the hotel.

This is not a frustrating event because it is not sufficiently serious to discharge the whole contract. Therefore, the common law rules on frustration and the LR(FC)A 1943 do not apply.

Although the definition of *force majeure* in the Code is not applicable, as such, to this post-departure situation, nevertheless, para.4A of the Code will apply—requiring the tour operator to ensure that suitable alternative arrangements are made at no extra cost to the client.

It is almost certainly a *force majeure* event and, therefore, the Regulations apply. As this is a post-departure problem it is reg.14 and 15 that apply. Regulation 14 requires the tour operator to make suitable alternative arrangements at no cost to the clients when a significant proportion of the services contracted for cannot be provided. Regulation 15 makes the operator liable for damage caused to the clients by failure to perform the contract or the improper performance of the contract. However, they are not liable to pay damages where the failure is caused by a *force majeure* event. Thus, the client is entitled to have suitable alternative arrangements made but will receive no compensation.

Illustration 3

A group of holidaymakers arrive at Luton airport to be told at check-in that there is an air traffic controllers' strike and they will be 24 hours late taking off for their two week holiday in the Caribbean. This is the third such lightning strike of the summer. The unions involved had warned that they would take industrial action if their pay claim was not settled to their satisfaction.

This is a pre-departure problem. It is probably not a frustrating event because it is not substantial enough to merit discharging the whole contract. Thus, the LR(FC)A 1943 will not apply. However, regs 12 and 13 will apply but only if the days delay can be seen as a significant alteration to an essential term—which it probably will be. An alteration of 24 hours in the time of departure would be regarded as significant by most consumers. This means that the consumer will have the option of withdrawing or being offered a suitable alternative if one is available. At that stage it is unlikely that they will withdraw and it is probably also the case that a suitable alternative cannot be found. Thus, they will take off a day late and the tour operator will be faced with a claim under reg.15 for improper performance of the contract. Can the tour operator plead *force majeure* as a defence?

It may not be regarded as a *force majeure* event because it is not "unforesee-able". On the face of it, therefore, the operator has failed to perform the contract properly and is liable under reg.15(2) to the consumer for the damage caused. However, even though the strike is not a *force majeure* event it could nevertheless be an event which could not be forestalled by the operator and, therefore, under reg.15(2)(c)(ii) the operator will not have to pay damages. (Note that under the Denied Boarding Regulations there are rules about long delays that would be applicable here—see Ch.13.)

Under the Code of Conduct it is a *force majeure* event—it is an industrial dispute which prevents the "prompt performance of the contract". As such, under paras 3B and 3E it would give the consumer the right to alternative arrangements or a full refund—essentially placing them in the same position as under the Regulations.

Illustration 4

Consumers purchase a package holiday to Rio to see the Carnival. The package is for flights, accommodation and meals but there is nothing in the contract about the Carnival. Identical packages are available from the same tour operator at other times of the year. The clients, however, specifically stated to the tour operator when booking that their sole reason for travelling was to see the Carnival. When they arrive Carnival is cancelled because of the death of the President and the whole country is in mourning. All the services the tour operator promised in the contract are still available.

Regulations 14 and 15 do not apply. Regulation 14 is only triggered if a significant proportion of *the services contracted for* are not supplied. All the services contracted for will still be supplied. Regulation 15 requires a proper performance of the *obligations under the contract*. There has been no improper performance, therefore reg.15 is inapplicable. Nevertheless, the clients are not getting what they wanted—to see the Carnival. There is an outside chance that under the principle established in *Krell v Henry* the clients may be able to claim the contract is frustrated. In practical terms, however, this may not be the best way forward. It would leave them with no rights to further accommodation or meals or return flight and subject to the rules on apportionment of loss under the LR(FC)A 1943. It might perhaps be better simply to enjoy the delights of the Copacabana and put it down to experience. (See Grant "It's not Cricket" [1998] I.T.L.J. 51.)

Just like the Regulations, the Code would not apply to this situation, and for the same reason—the cancellation of the Carnival would not be a significant alteration to a "contract for travel arrangements" (para.4A).

If the Carnival was cancelled before travel then the only difference would be that it would be reg.13 that would be inapplicable. This Regulation is only triggered by significant alterations to essential terms of the contract and if no term has been altered then the regulation cannot be invoked. From the clients' point of view they would not have any rights under the PTR and would still be faced with the problem of the LR(FC)A 1943 if they chose not to travel and wanted a refund.

Remedies

Introduction

When one of the parties to a contract breaks it, the other party, the victim of the breach, is entitled to a remedy, i.e. the law will require the contract breaker to put things right in some way. By far the most common remedy is when the court orders the contract breaker to pay damages—a sum of money to compensate the victim for the breach of contract. For really serious breaches of contract the victim also has another remedy—the right to terminate the contract—but this can only be done when there has been a breach of condition (a major term of the contract) rather than a breach of warranty. (For the difference between these two terms you should refer back to Ch.4 on Terms of the Contract.) Remember that for misrepresentation the victim has a range of remedies discussed fully in Ch.7.

There are other remedies, such as specific performance and injunctions, but these are highly unlikely to be awarded in a holiday case. Specific performance is where a court orders one party to the contract to actually perform the contract as promised. An injunction is when the court orders one party not to break the contract. Generally, they are only awarded by a court when damages would not be appropriate, where the subject matter of the contract is rare or unique and where there is no element of personal service involved. Given that damages will usually be a sufficient remedy in holiday cases that will almost inevitably rule out specific performance or an injunction. However, having said that these two remedies will not generally be available to holidaymakers, the Package Travel Regulations do provide (for package travel arrangements) remedies under regs 13 and 14 which are remarkably similar to specific performance, and there is a further remedy under reg.14 which also requires performance in kind rather than cash. Under reg.13, if a tour operator has made a significant alteration to an essential term the consumer is entitled to be offered a suitable alternative if one is available. Likewise, under reg.14, if the tour operator is unable to provide a significant proportion of the services after departure then he must make suitable alternative arrangements for the consumer at no extra cost. Also under reg.14, if the tour operator finds it impossible to make suitable arrangements he must return the consumer to his point of departure.

This is a chapter in which there has been significant change since our last edition, notably by the decision of the Court of Appeal in *Milner v Carnival Plc (t/a Cunard)* [2010] EWCA Civ 389, in which Ward L.J. starts his judgment with the words "The issue, said to be of importance to the travel industry, is this: what is the correct measure of damages for a ruined holiday?" Therefore, we will look first at the rules governing the award of damages—including the award of damages to the tour operator when the consumer breaks the contract—and then we will examine the remedies available under regs 13 and 14, the workings of which have been highlighted by the volcanic ash cloud crisis of April 2010, and other crises.

DAMAGES

Introduction

Throughout this book we have bemoaned the poor level of legal protection afforded to consumers in non-package travel situations. Happily, we can say that, at least as far as accommodation is concerned, and once the consumer of a non-package has overcome the many hurdles to establish liability, he will be awarded damages, subject to one qualification, on the same legal basis as his package-travelling brother or sister. (See, for example, *Thomson v RCI Europe* [2001] C.L.Y. 4275—a timeshare exchange case where the accommodation provided was unsuitable; and *Keppel-Palmer v Exus Travel* [2003] EWHC 3529 (QB), in which Gage J. awarded compensation after having expressly found that this was not a package.) The qualification is that in some non-package cases, e.g. transport only, there is some doubt as to whether damages for distress are recoverable (but see *Walz v Clickair* (C-63/09) discussed in Ch.13).

Damages in holiday cases are awarded under two broad headings. First, for the difference in value between what the client was promised and what he actually received. Secondly, for consequential loss, i.e. further loss caused by the breach of contract, and for the limited compensation available when a flight-plus goes wrong, see Ch.12. Under this latter heading there are a number of sub-headings. It encompasses not only out of pocket expenses such as the cost of taxis from the airport when the transfer bus is not provided, but also damages for distress, damages for physical discomfort and damages for personal injury. In *Milner*, the Court defined this as four headings: diminution in value; consequential pecuniary loss (out of pocket expenses, etc); compensation for physical inconvenience/discomfort; and, finally, mental distress.

It will become apparent that precise calculation of damages is impossible and even the most able practitioners often come unstuck in their predictions. It is an art rather than a science. The greatest difficulties arise over the award of damages for distress, which are, by their very nature, incapable of measurement in monetary terms. The difficulty of putting any figure at all on distress is compounded by the very subjective nature of the damage. Some clients are phlegmatic in the face of all difficulties, whilst others suffer extremes of disappointment when faced with the slightest problem. Often, the degree of distress suffered is not apparent to the tour operator until the client enters the witness box where the impression created, whether favourable or otherwise, is sometimes a determining factor in the level of damages awarded. This is one way perhaps of understanding the surprisingly high award made to the claimants in *Clarke & Greenwood v Airtours* [1995] C.L.Y. 1603 and the low award in *Morris v Carisma Holidays Ltd* [1997] C.L.Y. 1772.

The problems, however, are not confined to damages for distress. Even a simple calculation of difference in value can be fraught with difficulties. For instance, if the accommodation provided is so abysmal that it ruins the whole holiday how should the loss be calculated? Should the approach be to say that as the accommodation blighted the whole holiday then the whole holiday price should be refunded? Or could it be said that as the price of the accommodation amounted to, say, 30 per cent of the cost of the holiday (as is often the case when a flight is also included), then only 30 per cent should be refunded under this head? Often the answer to this question is inextricably bound up with what has been awarded by way of damages for distress and the two cannot be disentangled from each other. It is not surprising that in *Milner*, Ward L.J. counselled "I do, however, stress that judges should always be alert to ensure that there is no duplication of damages and so it is always salutary to stand back and look at the sum of the two elements in the round before arriving at the figure to award".

Basic Principles

Damages for breach of contract are intended to put the claimant "so far as money can do it in the same situation as if the contract had been performed" (*Robinson v Harman* (1848) 1 Ex. 850). It follows that damages are compensatory, not punitive. What this means in practice is that if a holiday client can establish that he was promised a room with a balcony, and his room did not have a balcony, he will be awarded a sum of money equivalent to the value of having the room upgraded. This is intended to put him in the same position, financially, as if the contract had been performed. However, to do this properly he will also need to be compensated for any distress which he suffered as a result of the breach. Only then can he be considered to be in the same position as if the contract had been performed properly.

Coupled with the rule that the client should be put in the same position as if the contract had been performed is another rule on remoteness of damage. This rule was formulated in the case of *Hadley v Baxendale* (1854) 9 Ex. 341 and will be examined in more detail later. For the present, it is sufficient to say that a travel company will have to pay damages for breaches of contract that lead to damage which is within the reasonable contemplation of the parties, but not otherwise. For instance, if a breach of contract consisted of failure to provide the promised swimming pool and as a consequence the client decided to swim in the sea and was eaten by sharks this would be regarded as too remote a consequence of the breach. On the other hand, it might not be too remote a consequence of the tour operator's failure to provide the swimming pool if it was known to the tour operator that sea water in the resort was contaminated by sewage and clients contracted a nasty disease from swimming in the polluted sea water. (See *Davey v Cosmos* [1989] C.L.Y. 2561, below.)

There is one further rule which will be examined, and that is on mitigation of loss. If a client suffers from breach of contract, he is under a duty to take reasonable steps to mitigate his loss. He cannot just sit back and wait for the damages to roll in; he must endeavour, so far as can reasonably be expected of him, to reduce his losses. So, for instance, if the holiday is defective in some way then the least that he can be expected to do is to complain. Often, a complaint to the representative is sufficient to get things sorted out. Failure to complain in such circumstances, when something could have been done, will result in a loss of compensation for the client.

Difference in Value Claims

There are numerous cases on diminution in value. One leading example is *Jackson v Horizon Holidays Ltd* [1975] 3 All E.R. 92. (For the facts see Ch.8 on

Privity of Contract.) It is very typical of holiday claims, and therefore much relied upon by County Courts—more so, in fact, than its more famous counterpart *Jarvis v Swans Tours*. The claimant was awarded £1,100 damages on a holiday that cost £1,200. The sum was initially awarded by a judge in the County Court who did not break the figure down into component parts. In the Court of Appeal Lord Denning commented upon the award and said:

> "If I were inclined myself to speculate, I think the suggestion of counsel for Mr Jackson may well be right. The judge took the cost of the holiday at £1200. The family only had about half the value of it. Divide it by two and you get £600. Then add £500 for the mental distress."

Another straightforward case is *McLeod v Hunter* [1987] C.L.Y. 1162 where £439 was awarded when the defendant substituted a cramped apartment for a luxurious villa. This was in addition to a sum for distress and disappointment.

In *Levine v Metropolitan Travel* [1980] C.L.Y. 638 the defendants argued that as the holiday was a cheap one then the damages for diminution in value should be correspondingly small. The judge rejected this argument and awarded damages for difference in value at £200 on a holiday costing £323. Two hundred pounds was also awarded for "assault on feelings". The report is brief and it is difficult to work out precisely the principles the judge was applying. However, reading between the lines, what it seems to be saying is that if you pay £300 for a late-saver bargain holiday that would normally cost, say £400, at full brochure price, then you are entitled to damages based on £400 not £300. To do otherwise would deprive you of your bargain. You bought a holiday worth £400 and therefore if what you are getting is only worth £200 you should get £200 damages because that is the difference between the value of what you purchased and what you received. On the other hand, if the holiday is only worth £300 and that is what you paid for it then damages will only be assessed on the lower figure. This point is illustrated better by *Hartman v P&O* [1998] C.L.Y. 3732 which is a case where the claimants paid a bargain price of £1,716 for a cruise that was later cancelled. The court held that they were entitled to £2,270 damages because that was the market price that they would have to pay for the cruise if they wanted to replace the one that had been cancelled. Although this "loss of bargain" approach might appear to be logical, it is fair to say that it was firmly rejected by the Court of Appeal in *Milner*. Their Lordships emphasised that diminution in value must be measured against the actual price paid— although no reasons are attached to this finding. For the facts, see below.

Most package holiday disputes that arise are connected with the accommodation. Strictly speaking, even if the accommodation is totally inadequate, the court should only award the cost of the accommodation under this head of damages. However, the cost of the accommodation doesn't necessarily bear any relation to its importance to the success of the holiday. The holiday might be totally ruined by the lack of suitable accommodation yet it may nevertheless amount to only 30 per cent of the holiday price. Refunding this to the client will not appear adequate in his eyes for accommodation which blighted the whole holiday.

There are two ways of approaching this problem. One is to view the holiday as a whole and to say that a holiday which is so blighted is worth nothing, therefore the whole holiday price should be returned. Damages for distress and disappointment would be awarded in addition to this. The other is to say that the damages for loss of accommodation should be calculated by awarding the value of the accommodation but the loss should also be reflected in the damages for distress and disappointment.

Consequential Loss—Out of Pocket Expenses

The client will be able to recover reasonable out of pocket expenses incurred because of the breach of contract by the tour operator. Obvious examples include the cost of meals taken in local restaurants where the hotel food provided as part of the package was inedible; or alternative accommodation where the original was uninhabitable. In *Harris v Torchgrove* [1985] C.L.Y. 944 the claimant received £40 for car parking fees because the promised parking at the apartment was not available and £300 was awarded for the cost of extra meals because the apartment had no oven and the fridge was "eccentric". In *Davey v Cosmos* [1989] C.L.Y. 2561 an award included a sum for ruined clothing when the claimants suffered from diarrhoea and dysentery on holiday.

Note that where, for instance, the client purchases meals from a restaurant because the hotel meals are inedible, he will not be able to claim both for the difference in value and for the out of pocket expenses. If this were permitted he would be compensated twice over.

One claim often included in this category is loss of earnings. A claimant is not entitled to claim loss of earnings for the time he was on holiday, on the alleged ground that the holiday was a waste of time and used up their holiday leave entitlement. This point was specifically addressed in *Jarvis v Swans Tours Ltd* [1973] 1 All E.R. 71 by Stephenson L.J. who said:

> "I would add that I think the judge was right in rejecting the plaintiff's ingenious claim, however it is put, for a fortnight's salary." (But see Grant "Damages for Distress" *Trading Law*, 5(7), 293; see also *Hartman v P&O* [1998] C.L.Y. 3732)

However, there is authority that where a claimant genuinely has salary deducted because a flight delay or overbooking made him late back for work he is likely to be able to recover this (*Harvey v Tracks Travel* [1984] C.L.Y. 1006; *Graham v Sunsetridge* [1989] C.L.Y. 1189; *Taylor v International Travel Services* [1984] C.L.Y. 1023).

Where a holiday has been cancelled by the tour operator before departure, and in breach of contract, the claimant will commonly have a claim for a variety of out of pocket expenses—kennel fees, locum booked to cover the claimant's business, clothes bought for the holiday, suntan lotion, etc. Provided the claimant can show that these costs were genuinely incurred, they are in principle recoverable; but note the approach of the Court of Appeal in *Milner* to the wasted expenditure claim by Mrs Milner, who had bought many very dressy clothes for the expensive cruise, which she would never get to use. The judge had allowed 50 per cent (£2,000) of their cost, but this award was removed on appeal; it is possible, though unstated, that this item instead explains why Mrs Milner was awarded £500 more for mental distress than her husband was, or that may just be because she suffered more distress.

Alternatively, the claimant may have been able to re-book a holiday; in that the claimant will have been able to use the clothes, suntan lotion, etc, but may instead have a claim for the additional cost of the substitute holiday—subject to the rules on mitigation of loss.

Consequential Loss—Mental Distress

The decision in *Milner* is again significant under this head, as we shall see. The origin of this head of damages is generally regarded as the case of *Jarvis v Swans Tours* [1973] 1 All E.R. 71 (but see *Feldman v Allways Travel Service* [1957] C.L.Y. 934). The facts were these: Mr Jarvis, a solicitor, booked a holiday with the defendants which their brochure described as a house party in Switzerland with special resident host. It promised "Welcome party on arrival. Afternoon tea and cake. Swiss dinner by candlelight. Fondue party. Yodeller evening. Farewell party". It also promised a wide variety of ski runs, the hire of ski packs, an atmosphere in the hotel of geniality, comfort and cosiness, a hotel owner who spoke English, and a bar that would be open several days a week. The brochure added "You will be in for a great time when you book this house party holiday". (Holiday companies these days rarely make the mistake of promising consumers enjoyment.) Mr. Jarvis paid £63.45 for a two week holiday over Christmas and New Year. In the first week, the house party consisted of only 13 people and for the whole of the second week, the claimant was the only person there. There was no welcome party. The ski runs were some distance away and full-length skis were only available on two days. The hotel owner did not speak English, so in the second week, the claimant had no-one to talk to at all. The cake for tea was potato crisps and dry nut cake. There was little night time entertainment. The yodeller evening consisted of a local man in his working clothes singing a few songs very quickly. The bar opened only one evening. For the second week, there was no representative at the hotel.

At the original hearing at Ilford County Court, the judge calculated the claimant's compensation only on the basis of a "difference in value claim". He felt that by means of the transport and accommodation provided, the defendants had given about half the value of the contract, and consequently awarded Mr Jarvis £31.72. He felt that he could not award anything for the disappointment or loss of enjoyment because such damages were irrecoverable in principle for breach of contract.

This last point caused the claimant to appeal to the Court of Appeal. On what was then the novel question of damages for distress Lord Denning M.R. said:

"In a proper case damages for mental distress can be recovered in contract. One such case is a contract for a holiday, or any other contract to provide entertainment and enjoyment. If the contracting party breaks his contract, damages can be given for the disappointment, the distress, the upset and frustration caused by the breach."

This view was supported by Stephenson L.J. who said:

"I agree that there may be contracts in which the parties contemplate inconvenience on breach which may be described as mental: frustration, annoyance, disappointment; and the damages for breach of it should take such wider inconvenience or discomfort into account."

The third judge, Edmund Davies L.J., also supported damages for distress. He said:

"In determining what would be proper compensation for the defendants' marked failure to fulfil their undertaking I am of the opinion that 'vexation' and 'being disappointed in a particular thing which you have set your mind upon' are relevant considerations which afford the court a guide in arriving at a proper figure.

When a man has paid for and properly expects an invigorating and amusing holiday and, through no fault of his, returns home dejected because his expectations have been largely unfulfilled, in my judgment it would be quite wrong to say that his disappointment must find no reflection in the damages to be awarded."

Since then, virtually all package holiday cases and many accommodation-only cases have included a sum to compensate for distress and disappointment (although *Morris v Carisma Holidays Ltd* mentioned above is a rare exception). Just how much will be awarded, however, remained a little of a mystery, although some guidance was offered in *Scott and Scott v Blue Sky Holidays* [1985] C.L.Y. 943 where it was presciently said (but for many years largely ignored) that damages for distress and disappointment should not be related to the price of the holiday. The intangible nature of the damage makes accurate prediction almost impossible. This has been recognised in a number of cases including *Jarvis v Swans Tours* itself where Lord Denning said:

"I know that it [distress] is difficult to assess in terms of money, but it is no more difficult than the assessment which the courts have to make every day in personal injury cases for loss of amenities." (An almost identical statement was made in *Stedman v Swan's Tours* (1951) 95 S.J. 727 by Singleton L.J.)

In *Adcock v Blue Sky Holidays* Unreported May 13, 1980, Bridge L.J. also likened the process to awarding damages in personal damages cases. He said:

"The assessment of damages in a case of this nature is not a mathematical exercise. It is not dissimilar from the assessment of damages in personal injuries cases, although perhaps it can be said in this kind of case it is even more difficult than in a personal injuries case to arrive at the appropriate figure with any degree of precision."

And Ward L.J. said in *Milner*:

"Doing the best one can is hardly the most enlightening guidance for those who have to perform the task, but I am not sure I can improve upon it."

The difficulty is such that the issue was often fudged, quite explicitly. Eveleigh L.J. in *Adcock v Blue Sky Holidays* said:

"I would not in the present case find it necessary to assess in detail the effect of these conditions upon each of the people concerned. I would prefer to take the broader approach and say: What is the kind of holiday they were entitled to expect, what is the kind of holiday they got, and what do I think that that is worth in damages and I for myself would award the sum of £500."

It is against this background of uncertainty that the *Milner* case has provided greater clarity in the criteria for assessing this head of damage. The facts of the *Milner* were these. Mr and Mrs Milner bought a cruise for themselves on the maiden round the world cruise of Cunard's Queen Victoria. It was priced at £65,558, but the Milners managed to negotiate a discount and actually paid £59,052. The cruise lasted 102 nights. It would take many pages of this book to set out the lavish promises and descriptions of the cruise made by Cunard— readers are referred to the law report at [2010] EWCA Civ 389 for more—so here is just a flavour: "When Samuel Cunard set out to deliver mail across the Atlantic 167 years ago, he little realised he was taking the first step towards a new standard of luxury travel. Since then Cunard has become a byword for comfort, style, and the ultimate in effortless exploration generation after generation. Today the legendary Cunard experience continues to exceed your expectations—with all its accomplished hallmarks—from the very first moment you step aboard ... Wouldn't you long to savour the star treatment like screen idols and noble royals of yesteryear? Don't you deserve a taste of the high life? Welcome then to some of the most spacious and sumptuous suites at sea". And so on.

The Milners booked long in advance to secure the cabin they wanted, amidships; they turned down a free upgrade to an even more superior suite, because it was not amidships. They were greatly looking forward to the event.

The Milners only stayed on board for 28 of the 102 nights. The reason is that, as the judge put it, they had been promised the experience of a lifetime, and "this is what they got, but not in the way they had bargained for". The ship was having serious teething problems, and the grinding and banging sounds of the metal plates flexing and vibrating and reverberating in the area of their cabin, made sleep impossible. They became ill from the resulting stress. They were eventually moved several times, but never able to settle properly or fully unpack. Most of the substitutes provided were not as good as the suite booked, but for several days they did enjoy a suitable suite, but always with the knowledge that their stay was temporary as the suite may be needed for new customers at the next port of call. Mr Milner kept a diary of the days on board, which is set out extensively in the judgment. There were some good moments for the couple, but mostly stress and disappointment. After 28 nights, they were offered a cabin which was not amidships, had a shower instead of a bath, inadequate wardrobe/storage space, and was intended for disabled passengers. It is important to the understanding of the decision in this case to realise that the trial judge found that they could have accepted this alternative suite, and that their departure from the ship was in effect by a voluntary agreement, as part of which Cunard agreed to refund the unused portion of the price (£48,270), which they eventually did, after proceedings had been commenced. See more on this point under reg.14 below.

CHAPTER TEN

Ward L.J. offered the following suggestions for making the assessment of these types of damages (mental distress/disappointment, etc) more consistent:

- The award should be in the nature of a conventional figure, or range of figures (Judgment para.36). In arriving at this, use should be made of "comparables".

- The first comparable, though not the most compelling, were the decisions in large numbers of first instance decisions culled from Current Law (para.37). Fifty-six such cases were put before the Court, plus the High Court decision in *Keppel-Palmer v Exus Travel*, see below. These showed modest awards. Ruined foreign weddings got the highest, just over £4,000; ruined honeymoons £321 to £1,890; other special holidays £264 to £1,161; ordinary holidays £83 to £1,876.

- The next comparable was the awards suggested by the Judicial Studies Board (JSB) in their Guidelines, for psychiatric injuries, and for post-traumatic stress disorder. At the bottom end, modest four figure sums were considered the benchmark by the Judicial Studies Board (para.38).

- Another comparable is discrimination cases in which awards had been made for injury to feelings. Guidelines had been issued by the Court in *Vento v Chief Constable of West Yorkshire* [2002] EWCA 1871. Again, at the lowest end, these were modest four figure, or even, sometimes, three figure, sums (para.39).

- Then there are bereavement claims. Ward L.J. said (para.40) "Perhaps the most acute form of distress is that which is suffered by a parent who has lost a child. Here damages are limited by statute and the present figure is no more than £10,000."

- Ward L.J. at para.41 also quoted from the House of Lords decision in *Farley v Skinner* (below): "I consider that awards in this area should be restrained and modest. It is important that logical and beneficial developments in this corner of the law should not contribute to the creation of a society bent on litigation."

- Set against these comparables, Ward L.J. considered holiday damages. He said (para.58) "Physical inconvenience and discomfort is necessarily ephemeral. Disappointment, distress, annoyance and frustration are likewise the feelings one experiences at the time and which last painfully for some time thereafter. But one is not disabled, the psyche is not injured, and one gets on with life. Every time one thinks back, one relives the horror but the reliving of it is transitory".

He then considered the award in this case. The judge has awarded £2,500 each for diminution in value, £7,500 each for mental distress, etc, and £2,000 for Mrs Milner's dresses. Ward L.J. felt that the approach to diminution was about right, but was based on the actual price instead of the discounted price; he therefore reduced that to a total of £3,500. He disallowed the claim in respect of the dresses. As to mental distress, he felt that the judge had gone wrong (possibly, he said, because the judge was seduced by being addressed by an advocate who is one of the co-authors of this august tome, described as a "well known text-book"). In particular, it was "wrong to use the price of the holiday as a bench-mark for damages". He reduced these awards to £4,000 for Mr Milner and £4,500 for Mrs Milner, describing these figures as "exceptional" to cater for the ruination of an exceptional event. Normal awards would be considerably lower.

Although the award of damages for mental distress/disappointment is now beyond question as far as *package* holiday cases are concerned, the precise ambit of damages for distress in general have been reviewed in a number of cases. In *Hayes v James & Charles Dodd* [1990] 2 All E.R. 815 the Court of Appeal was concerned to confine damages for distress within fairly narrow limits. It held that such damages were available only if the object of the contract was to provide peace of mind or freedom from distress and were not recoverable for anguish and vexation arising out of the breach of a purely commercial contract. On the face of it, this merely re-affirms the existing position as far as holidays are concerned. A package holiday contract is one designed to provide peace of mind and, therefore, clearly falls within *Hayes v Dodd*.

Some extension of the principle is to be found in *Ruxley Electronics & Construction Ltd v Forsyth* [1996] A.C. 344 in which a swimming pool constructed at a house turned out to be not quite as pleasing as contracted for and the House of Lords felt that damages for loss of amenity was more appropriate than the disproportionate cost of rebuilding the pool. In another important House of Lords case, *Farley v Skinner (No.2)* [2001] UKHL 49, a surveyor who had been asked to advise on whether a house was affected by aircraft noise negligently gave it the "all clear". The House of Lords felt that this was an appropriate case to award damages for distress—even though only one of the purposes of the contract had been to provide pleasure, relaxation or peace of mind. However, problems arise with "flight-only" holidays. Is a flight a contract to provide peace of mind or freedom from distress? There are those who might suggest quite the opposite! On the other hand, the context in which such contracts are made may need to be taken into account. Clients buying such flights usually do so as part of a holiday and if the contract is broken then they will suffer just the same distress as a client who books the flight as part of a package—in fact they could be sitting next to them on the plane (or delayed with them in the departure lounge as the case may be). The client who buys the flight-only simply to get from A to B, as with the businessman who buys a scheduled flight ticket, may be regarded as making a purely commercial contract and on that reasoning would not be eligible for damages for distress. This was certainly the view of one court—see *Lucas v AVRO* [1994] C.L.Y. 1444. A similar decision was in *Noble v Leger Holidays Ltd* [2000] C.L.Y. 4029 about a coach trip to Disneyland Paris. Only the coaching was unsatisfactory, so the court awarded the diminution in value, but, surprisingly, not claims for distress/disappointment. Support for these two county court decisions can be found in the High Court case of *Wiseman v Virgin Atlantic Airways Ltd* [2006] EWHC 1566 (QB). Here, a claimant was denied boarding on a flight from Nigeria unless he paid a bribe, and when he refused, he was continually denied boarding each day for 12 days. He recovered his hotel, restaurant, taxi, etc, expenses, but nothing for "hurt feelings" or for the break-down of his engagement, because English law restricts tightly the circumstances in which such damages are recoverable. Damages for mental distress, as a general rule, are still not recoverable for breach of contract, and *Jarvis* (as extended in

Ruxley and *Farley*) must be seen as an exception, albeit a now well established one, to the general rule. However, maverick cases do emerge from time to time. See *Graham v Sunsetridge* [1989] C.L.Y. 1189 where damages for distress were awarded for what appears to be a delay in a "flight-only" contract; and of course the Denied Boarding Regulation (reg.261/2004) gives rights of compensation in favour of the consumer against the carrier in cases of cancellation and denied boarding. These are awarded on a statutory basis, but the Regulation makes clear that its purpose is to reduce the "serious trouble and inconvenience to passengers" (Preamble, para.2)—see Ch.13. (See also *Amoabeng v El-Sawy Travel Ltd* [2000] C.L.Y. 4047; *Brunton v Cosmosair Plc* [2003] C.L.Y. 232; and "Case Note: *Marshall & Dixon v KLM*" [2002] I.T.L.J. 63 for other County Court cases involving damages for distress in non-package cases.) Further support for such damages can be found in the recent ECJ case, *Walz v Clickair SA* (C-63/09) where the court held that damages could be awarded for "non-material" loss under the Montreal Convention for loss of baggage.

As indicated earlier, most complaints concern accommodation. Damages for distress will be awarded where substandard accommodation is provided, but the level of award may vary according to the kind of accommodation and the type of holiday (see the *Keppel-Palmer* case below). For example, in a summer holiday where the accommodation is in a complex with swimming pools, sports facilities, entertainment, etc, all on site, it may be expected that the client will spend a great deal of time in or near the accommodation, so that poor accommodation will severely spoil the holiday. On the other hand, on a skiing holiday the party may scarcely see their rooms except when sleeping, so the damages for an identical breach of contract should be the same when assessing difference in value claims but different when assessing damages for distress.

By contrast, it will be noticed that in the *Jarvis* case, the defendants had promised to keep the claimant entertained all day, by means of the skiing during the day time and the house party at night. Since the claimant was hardly provided with any of this, this may help to explain why a total award of twice the holiday price was considered appropriate. By contrast, the *Jackson* case was a more typical summer holiday case, in which the defective accommodation caused serious disappointment but did not undermine the entire purpose of the holiday. In that case a total award of £1,100 was made as against a price of £1,200 (the award broken down as £600 for difference in value, and £500 for disappointment). *Jackson* is, as has been stated, more typical of the run of the mill holiday claim, and has often been found helpful by county court judges as a benchmark against which to measure the facts of any particular case which the judge has to decide, but *Milner* will probably be the authority of choice henceforth. It has not been uncommon in cases of truly disastrous holidays in the past for the court to award damages of twice the price of the holiday—representing a full refund and damages for distress and disappointment of another 100 per cent. As already mentioned, *Clarke & Greenwood v Airtours* is an extreme example of such awards, which strays from compensation of claimants to improper punishment of defendants (see the judicial attention it received in "Benchmarks" L.S.G. June 17, 1998, Judge Geoffrey Martin). These types of awards are unlikely to be seen again following *Milner*. However, "special" holidays such as honeymoons and anniversaries, etc, will still merit higher awards.

Even before *Milner*, criticism had been levelled at the seemingly high awards for distress and disappointment in some cases. Tomlinson and Wardell ("Damages in Holiday Cases" (1988) 85 L.S.Gaz. 28) make what now seems a prescient comparison with personal injury cases:

> "We submit that, in awarding distress damages, the courts should bear in mind the well established conventional scale of figures to cover matters such as pain and suffering in personal injury cases. A person who suffers an agonising and debilitating injury from which he recovers completely after a period of two weeks would be unlikely to recover more than £500 pain and suffering damages. It would be inconsistent for courts to award substantially greater damages for the pain and suffering caused by a ruined holiday for a similar period." (Inflation impacts on these figures.)

This may, of course, be more of a reflection on the low awards for personal injury than high awards for distress. Simply because one group of claimants are poorly compensated is not a reason to drag everyone down to that level. Note also that personal injury awards for pain and suffering are to be raised soon by 10 per cent.

It is therefore interesting that in a rare High Court case of a straightforward defective holiday villa, the damages awarded were relatively modest—*Keppel-Palmer v Exus Travel* [2003] EWHC 3529 (QB). £88,000 had been paid for a luxury Caribbean villa for a month over the millennium; there was a depressingly familiar list of complaints of low standards, leaking roof, lack of heating, etc; plus a complaint that the butler was "a buffoon who could not even mix a decent cocktail". Gage J. awarded the sum of £25,000. Ward L.J. in *Milner* pointed out with approval that only £3,000 of this sum was for mental distress, etc; although he did query the assertion of Gage J. that this head of damage may be more modest for the wealthy (who can afford more holidays) than for the poor.

Regulation 15(4) of the Package Travel Regulations provides that organisers can limit damages for non-personal injury to a sum which is "not unreasonable". Given the unpopularity of damages for distress amongst tour operators it is not surprising that some at least attempt to limit this head of liability—perhaps by saying that total damages cannot exceed a conventional sum such as the price of the holiday or twice the price. (See discussion of the OFT Guidance on unfair contract terms in Ch.6.) However, again, following *Milner*, there may not be such need to rely on this type of limitation.

In *Lathrope v Kuoni Travel Ltd* [1999] C.L.Y. 1382 Kuoni had fixed a sum of £50 per day of holiday lost through flight delay regardless of the cost of the (quite expensive) holiday. The Court held that such an inflexible limit was never likely to be a "not unreasonable" limit. See also *Jervis v Kuoni* [1998] C.L.Y. 3733, a similar decision where the breach of contract was defective accommodation.

Consequential Loss—Physical Discomfort

Prior to *Jarvis v Swans Tours* it was well established that damages could be claimed for a breach of contract resulting in physical discomfort. Lord Denning referred to a number of these cases in *Jarvis*. He said:

"The courts in those days only allowed the claimant to recover damages if he suffered physical inconvenience, such as having to walk five miles home, as in *Hobbs v London & South Western Railway Co* (1875) LR 10 QB 111; or to live in an overcrowded house: see *Bailey v Bullock* [1950] 2 All E.R. 1167." (See also *Stedman v Swan's Tours* and *Farley v Skinner* on this issue.)

In *Cook v Spanish Holiday Tours* (1959) 103 S.J. 873 the claimants were awarded £25 damages for disappointment which included a sum to compensate them for the inconvenience of having to spend the first night of their honeymoon on a park bench! Perhaps not as distressing but more common would be the physical inconvenience of being stuck at an overcrowded Gatwick or Luton airport for many hours.

More recently, the issue of discomfort in long haul flights in economy class has resulted in an award of £500 to the Claimant in the case of *Horan v JMC Holidays* Unreported 2002, Chester County Court—regardless of the fact that the seat pitch and layout had been approved by the CAA; it was held still not to be of a "reasonable standard". But other Courts have refused identical claims, see *Watt v First Choice Holidays* Unreported February 20, 2002, Liverpool County Court. See also *Grahame v JMC Holidays Ltd* [2002] C.L.Y. 2324, for a case in which CAA approval was discussed as the vital criterion.

In *Wiseman v Virgin* [2006] EWHC 1566 (QB), the court confirmed that had Mr Wiseman suffered physical discomfort an award would have been made for it; but staying in a pleasant hotel, even if you are only there because the airline is wrongly denying you boarding, cannot be classed as physical discomfort.

This head of damage was confirmed as still appropriate for holiday cases in *Milner*; and the Milners did suffer it; but the award for general damages is not broken down between mental distress and this head.

Consequential Loss—Physical Injury

There is nothing exceptional about claiming damages for personal injury, including psychiatric/stress injuries (see *Griggs v Olympic Holidays Ltd (No.1)* [1996] C.L.Y. 2184) in breach of contract cases. It is a recognised and well established head of damages. Fortunately, it is a category which arises in only a minority of cases. Many of the case authorities which have arisen are to be found in Ch.5.

As an example, one case where the claimants succeeded is *Davey v Cosmos* [1989] C.L.Y. 2561. In that case the claimants suffered from dysentery and diarrhoea because of the negligence of the defendants. Damages were awarded which included a sum for the pain and suffering of the illness.

The assessment of damages for personal injuries is a major topic in its own right and readers are referred to the standard texts or Current Law. A huge volume of case law exists, as well as the Judicial Studies Board Guidelines for assessing such damages (10th edn, 2010), making it easier for the parties to calculate the court's likely award in advance, and so settle the case. It further assists defendants that a claimant must file a medical report with any court action. This contrasts sharply with the position already described in relation to claims for disappointment and distress, which are so subjective and impressionistic.

Remoteness of Damage

As explained above, a claimant can only recover damages which are not too remote a consequence of the breach of contract. The rule in *Hadley v Baxendale* was formulated by Alderson B:

"Where two parties have made a contract which one of them has broken, the damages which the other party ought to receive in respect of such breach of contract should be such as may fairly and reasonably be considered either arising naturally *i.e.* according to the usual course of things, from such breach of contract itself, or such as may reasonably be supposed to have been in the contemplation of both parties at the time they made the contract, as the probable result of the breach of it." (See also the difficult case of *Transfield Shipping Inc v Mercator Shipping Inc (The Achilleas)* [2008] UKHL 48.)

The test lays down that any damage which results from the breach of contract which is not in the reasonable contemplation of the parties at the time they made the contract is not recoverable. The test in fact has two limbs or branches. This was explained by Asquith L.J. in a later case, *Victoria Laundry (Windsor) v Newman Industries* [1949] 2 K.B. 528. He said:

"In cases of breach of contract, the aggrieved party is only entitled to recover such part of the loss actually resulting as was at the time of the contract reasonably foreseeable as liable to result from the breach."

What was at that time reasonably foreseeable depends on the knowledge then possessed by the parties or, at all events, by the party who later commits the breach.

For this purpose, knowledge "possessed" is of two kinds; one imputed, the other actual. Everyone, as a reasonable person, is taken to know the "ordinary course of things" and consequently what loss is liable to result from a breach of contract in that ordinary course. This is the subject-matter of the "first rule" in *Hadley v Baxendale*. But to this knowledge, which a contract-breaker is assumed to possess whether he actually possesses it or not, there may have to be added in a particular case knowledge which he actually possesses of special circumstances outside the "ordinary course of things", of such a kind that a breach in those special circumstances would be liable to cause more loss. Such a case attracts the operation of the "second rule" so as to make additional loss also recoverable. (See *Kemp v Intasun* below on what is meant by natural consequences.)

So, for instance, if a tour operator places clients in a 14-storey hotel and the lift breaks down, the damage that flows from that "in the ordinary course of things" is that many clients will suffer physical inconvenience from having to climb the stairs. The effects will be short lived, however, for most of the population. Once they have recovered their breath they will be alright. There should be no problems fitting this within the first rule or limb of *Hadley v Baxendale*. If, however, the clients are elderly or disabled then it may not simply be discomfort they suffer if they attempt to climb the stairs. They may suffer further physical injury or exacerbate their disabilities in the attempt. If they are known to be elderly or disabled then the second rule in *Hadley v Baxendale* applies. In this case there are special circumstances actually known to the tour operator which put the effects of the breach within his contemplation. (See *Causby v Portland Holidays* [1995] C.L.Y. 1604.)

In the *Victoria Laundry* case, Asquith L.J. talked about the damage being reasonably foreseeable as liable to result. However, later cases, in particular the House of Lords case, *Koufos v C Czarnikow Ltd (The Heron II)* [1969] 1 A.C. 350, have narrowed the scope of the test. Now it can be said that the test is not one of reasonable foresight but one of reasonable contemplation. The practical effect of the difference in terminology is that a claimant must prove a higher likelihood of the damage occurring under a reasonable contemplation test than under a reasonable foresight test. In *The Heron II* the judges used phrases such as "not unlikely" and "quite likely" and "a real danger" or "a serious possibility" to describe the degree of foresight required of the defendant before he was liable for the damage.

This was an issue which the courts had to face in *Kemp v Intasun Holidays* [1987] 2 F.T.L.R. 234. The facts were that Intasun, in breach of contract, placed Mr Kemp, an asthmatic, in a dirty, dusty room. He was moved out of the room after the first night but the whole of the first week of his holiday was blighted by an asthma attack brought on by the dirty room. It was held that the family were entitled to damages for the breach of contract for being placed in a disgustingly filthy room for 30 hours, but these damages were for difference in value and for distress and disappointment not for the asthma attack. On the question of damages for the asthma the Court of Appeal held that it did not occur in the ordinary course of things for a person placed in a dusty room to have an asthma attack. Asthma was a sufficiently rare illness for it not to be regarded as the natural consequence of sleeping in a dusty environment. Thus, Mr Kemp failed to recover damages under the first rule in *Hadley v Baxendale*. (See *Waters v Thomson* [2000] C.L.Y. 879 for a case on asthma where remoteness was not an issue.)

This is what the court had to say on what would amount to the ordinary course of things in a package holiday case:

"[The tour operator] must also accept liability for any other consequences which should have been in the reasonable contemplation of the parties if these flowed naturally from his breach and caused additional foreseeable loss or damage. Such liability would be equally within the rule expressed in the passage from the headnote which I have read and which is often referred to as the first rule in *Hadley v Baxendale* (1854) 9 Exch 347, [1843–60] All E.R. Rep. 461. For instance, if the consequence of not providing the contractual accommodation is not merely the loss of its enjoyment and so forth, but also the fact that the claimants has to sleep out on the beach, with the result that their health suffered in a natural and ordinarily foreseeable way because they caught colds or even pneumonia, then that would be a natural and foreseeable additional consequence which would equally flow from the tour operator's breach. In such circumstances his liability would not be limited to the basic damages on account of disappointment and loss of enjoyment to which I have referred." (Kerr L.J.)

The question then arose as to whether Intasun had any special knowledge that put the asthma attack within their reasonable contemplation. There was evidence that prior to making the booking Mrs Kemp had made a preliminary visit to the travel agency and while she was choosing the holiday she explained to the travel clerk that her husband was not with her because he was suffering from an asthma attack. It was not until a month later that the holiday was booked. If it could be shown that the knowledge of the travel agency could be attributed to Intasun there were grounds for arguing that Intasun had the knowledge that made the asthma attack an event which could be reasonably contemplated. The court avoided this difficult problem by saying first that the travel agents were not the agents of Intasun at the time the conversation took place. Secondly, that a casual conversation such as took place between Mrs Kemp and the travel clerk could not give rise to contractual obligations on the part of Intasun. In other words, the special knowledge has to be "brought home" more forcibly than in a passing conversation. This is a view which was endorsed by Treitel in *The Law of Contract*, 11th edn, p.969, but which has disappeared from the 12th edn.

Contrast, however, the position where at least *some* personal injury is foreseeable; the full amount of injury can then be recovered even though the tour operator could not have anticipated that full extent without special knowledge being brought home—see the somewhat controversial case of *Brown v Thomson Tour Operations Ltd* [1999] C.L.Y. 1412 and also Ward "Case Commentary: Brown v Thomson Tour Operations" [1999] I.T.L.J. 170.

It is worth mentioning again at this point that in cases of misrepresentation as opposed to breach of contract the rule on remoteness is that damages are recoverable even where the loss was not foreseeable (*Royscot Trust Ltd v Rogerson* [1991] 3 All E.R. 294); but see Ch.7 for a fuller discussion of this case, and the criticisms there have been of it.

Mitigation of Loss

A disappointed client who suffers from breach of contract cannot just sit back and let the damages roll in. He is under a duty to mitigate his loss, i.e. take reasonable steps to reduce his loss. The rule is an aspect of the rules on remoteness—the defendant can foresee that the reasonable claimant will act reasonably to minimise his loss. The two most common practical applications in travel law involve first, the choice faced by a consumer who is offered some alternative to his booked arrangements; and, secondly, the duty to complain when things go wrong.

The rule has three aspects. First, the claimant cannot recover for loss which he could have avoided by taking reasonable steps to do so. Secondly, the claimant can recover for expenses incurred in taking reasonable steps to avoid loss. Thirdly, the claimant cannot recover for loss which he has succeeded in avoiding.

The first principle was explained in *British Westinghouse Electric & Manufacturing Co Ltd v Underground Electric Railways Co of London Ltd (No.2)* [1912] A.C. 673. Lord Haldane L.C. said:

"The fundamental principle is thus compensation for pecuniary damage naturally flowing from the breach; but this first principle is qualified by a second which imposes on the plaintiff the duty of taking reasonable steps to mitigate the loss consequent on the breach, and debars him from claiming any part of the damage which is due to his neglect in taking such steps."

In *Payzu Ltd v Saunders* [1919] 2 K.B. 581 a seller of goods had contracted to provide the goods on credit but broke the contract and refused to supply them except for cash. The buyer refused to pay cash and sued for breach of contract. It was held that he should have mitigated his loss by taking the goods for cash:

"in commercial contracts it is generally reasonable to accept an offer from the party in default."

There are a number of reported cases on just this point. In *Tucker v OTA Travel* [1986] C.L.Y. 383 a flight was overbooked but when an alternative was offered it was held that the client had refused it on reasonable grounds. Similarly in *Rhodes v Sunspot Tours* [1983] C.L.Y. 984 the claimant was held to have acted reasonably in refusing an alternative apartment because of the atmosphere of distrust that existed between the parties by that stage. Other examples of reasonable grounds for refusing an offer of alternative accommodation are: smaller villa offered with shared pool and no compensation offered—*Buhus-Orwin v Costa Smerelda Holidays Ltd* [2001] C.L.Y. 4279; hotel over 10km away and holidaymakers to bear own expenses—*Currie v Magic Travel Group* [2001] C.L.Y. 4278. (See also *Askew v Intasun North* [1980] C.L.Y. 637; *Abbatt v Sunquest Holidays* [1984] C.L.Y. 1025; *Corbett v Top Hat Tours* [1989] C.L.Y. 1194.)

On the other hand, in *Toubi v Intasun Holidays* [1988] C.L.Y. 1060 it was held unreasonable for a claimant to refuse the offer of an alternative hotel when the original one was overbooked. He preferred to cancel his holiday. He did receive a full refund of the holiday price but he was refused damages for distress and disappointment.

It is difficult to draw any general conclusions from any of these cases other than the fact that they illustrate the general principle. This is simply because what amounts to a reasonable refusal depends upon the facts of the particular case.

The second principle is illustrated by the case of *Banco de Portugal v Waterlow & Sons Ltd* [1932] A.C. 452. The defendants printed banknotes for the claimants. In breach of contract they delivered them to a criminal who put them into circulation. The claimants withdrew the issue from circulation and undertook to exchange all the old notes for new ones. It was held that the defendants were liable not only for the cost of printing the original notes but also for the cost of exchanging the notes when they were withdrawn from circulation. This was expenditure incurred in reasonable mitigation of their loss, having regard to the bank's commercial obligation to the public.

In *Chesneau v Interhome* The Times, June 9, 1983, the defendants provided the claimants with inferior accommodation. The claimants incurred further expenditure by finding more suitable accommodation. This was regarded as a reasonable mitigation of loss in the circumstances. Similarly, in *Trackman v New Vistas, The Times*, November 24, 1959, it was held that the claimant was entitled to mitigate his loss by booking into a hotel which would provide the standard of accommodation he had been promised. However, the case of *Ruxley Electronics* referred to above is authority for the proposition that the cost of reinstatement must not be wholly disproportionate to the damage which it is sought to mitigate.

The *British Westinghouse* case also illustrates the third principle that the claimant cannot claim for loss that he has succeeded in avoiding. The facts of the case were that the claimants had bought a turbine that was less efficient than promised. As a result of the breach they later bought new turbines which were so efficient that the savings in running costs compared to the original machines exceeded the cost of replacing them. On that basis the claimants could not claim the cost of replacing the turbines because that loss was more than offset by the efficiency savings on the new turbines.

So if, by booking themselves into an acceptable hotel, consumers have therefore enjoyed their holiday they cannot claim for distress and disappointment for that period as well as the cost of the new hotel. This is the most common type of holiday case where damages for disappointment are inappropriate. (See *Hartman v P&O* above.)

Most tour operators are aware of the client's duty to mitigate his loss and specifically provide for this in the terms and conditions. They expressly state that in the event of problems arising the client should inform the representative so as to give the tour operator the opportunity to put things right. An example of this policy operating to the benefit of the tour operator is the case of *Czyzewski v Intasun* Unreported 1990, County Court. Intasun had provided the claimant with a room with an "offensive" toilet. He complained, and after unsuccessful attempts were made to repair the toilet he was offered an alternative room—which he refused. It was held that this was an unreasonable refusal to mitigate his loss and he was awarded only £50 damages—based on the limited time he would have suffered had he accepted the alternative.

Another case where damages were reduced because of a failure to mitigate by the client is *Scott and Scott v Blue Sky Holidays* [1985] C.L.Y. 943. The claimants had not complained to the tour operator's representative about the food and this failure operated to reduce what would otherwise have been substantial damages. It is not enough for a travel company merely to say that the claimant failed to complain at the time; they must have some evidence that, had a complaint been made, a better alternative would have been available—*Robinson v MyTravel* Unreported October 1, 2004, Kettering County Court.

The rule on mitigation is enshrined in reg.15(9) which provides:

"(9) The contract must clearly and explicitly oblige the consumer to communicate at the earliest opportunity, in writing or any other appropriate form, to the supplier of the services concerned and to the other party to the contract any failure which he perceives at the place where the services concerned are supplied."

This Regulation should be read in conjunction with reg.8(2) which obliges the operator to provide the client with contact names and addresses, and with Sch.2, para.12 which requires the operator to incorporate into the contract the periods within which the client must complain (presumably, although not expressed, this means the follow up letter of complaint on return home).

Thus, the organiser is under a contractual duty to inform the consumer that he in turn is under a contractual duty to complain. It also seems that the consumer must complain to both the operator and the supplier in writing or other appropriate form—presumably an oral complaint would be appropriate in some circumstances, e.g. if the transfer bus was being driven recklessly an oral complaint might have more impact than a written one—especially if delivered with appropriate emphasis! If he does not complain at the earliest opportunity or does not complain to both then he will be in breach of contract. In practical terms, this means that the consumer is under a contractual duty to mitigate his loss and if he fails to do so in the manner provided in the Regulations he will have to suffer the consequences—loss of compensation for those defects in the holiday which could have been remedied if the consumer had complained promptly.

There will be no loss of compensation where failure to complain would have made no difference or where it was sufficient to complain to just the organiser or supplier—on the grounds that the breach of contract does not cause the organiser any loss.

Given that there is already a common law duty to mitigate loss it is difficult to see what this provision adds to the law except perhaps to drive home to the consumer more forcefully that he should complain. Where it might make a difference is where a complaint is made some weeks or months after the consumer has returned home and the organiser has no record of what happened and is unable to assemble the evidence to combat the complaint. It might be the kind of problem that could not have been mitigated at the time, e.g. food poisoning, but if the organiser has notice of it at the time he may be able to defend himself more ably at a later date.

If the organiser does not inform the consumer of his obligation to complain then the immediate effect of this (at least in theory) is to permit the consumer to repudiate the contract. Regulation 9 states that all the terms of the contract must be set out in writing or other appropriate form before the contract is made. Failure to do so is a breach of condition which entitles the consumer to cancel the contract.

But what is the effect if the statement is not included but the consumer does not repudiate, takes the holiday and does not complain promptly? Can the consumer argue that he has no obligation to complain promptly because the organiser has failed to inform him of this? On the one hand, the consumer is in breach of the term imposed by reg.15(9), whereas on the other, the organiser is in breach of reg.9. If the two obligations are regarded as being linked—that the obligation to complain promptly is dependent upon being informed of this duty then the consumer is excused his failure and will suffer no penalty for it. On the other hand, if the two are regarded as separate obligations the consumer cannot hide behind the organiser's failure—he must complain promptly regardless of the organiser's breach. This latter view is the one to be preferred if only because it should be a matter of common sense to complain promptly. Also, because the common law duty to mitigate probably exists independently of the Regulations and the consumer will have to comply with this independent duty regardless of the Regulations.

One other minor point about making complaints is the interpretation of the phrase "at the place" in reg.15(9). Does this mean that the consumer must complain promptly at the place where he is on holiday or does it mean that if there is a problem at the place where he is on holiday then he must complain but it does not necessarily have to be there, and then so long as it is done promptly? In most circumstances it will come down to the same thing. There will be a complaint about the holiday and it will be possible to complain there and then but in some cases that may not be practicable. For instance, what if the consumer is on a gite holiday in deepest provincial France and the local owner is either not known or not contactable or speaks only French? How is the consumer to complain "at the place" where the services are supplied. The answer probably lies in reg.8(2)(b) which makes it a criminal offence for the organiser not to provide the consumer with, at the very least, a contact number where the organiser can be reached during the stay.

See also Ch.6 on the subject of failure by the consumer to write in after the holiday within the time limit set out in the contract for making complaints and the OFT's views on the 28-day time limit recommended by some travel companies.

Eviction Cases

There are a group of cases in which the consumer is bringing an action against the tour operator for damages where the hotelier has evicted the consumer from the hotel for misconduct. Although it is the tour operator who is being sued for breach of contract the essence of the action is whether the consumer's conduct was sufficient to justify an eviction. If so then the tour operator is not in breach of contract.

It has been held by the Court of Appeal that provided the tour operator can prove the consumer is guilty of serious misconduct justifying eviction, the consumer cannot claim compensation for the fact that accommodation was not provided for the full period of the holiday. However, the burden of proof is on the tour operator (*Spencer v Cosmos, The Times*, December 6, 1989). It is not sufficient for the tour operator to rely on the judgment of the hotelier alone. Other evidence will usually be required but often this is difficult to acquire. Incidents justifying eviction frequently take place late at night when only a night porter or a sub-contracted security guard is on duty and it is often impossible to bring them to the UK to act as witnesses at a trial.

An interesting variation on this theme came in the case of *Hickman v CIT Ltd* Unreported 1991, Willesden County Court. In that case, the claimants were evicted for misconduct. The judge found their conduct was "boorish" but not serious enough to warrant their eviction from the hotel. He, therefore, awarded them damages for loss of part of their holiday but felt he was entitled to reduce the damages because of the contribution they made to their own problems. It is difficult to fit this decision precisely into legal principle but it is a form of rough justice.

Conclusions

As a rule of thumb for the assessment of damages in practice a good starting point is the guidance offered by District Judge Geoffrey Martin, a judge who had particular interest in Holiday Law issues, who suggested in the *Law Society's Gazette*, June 17, 1998:

"As a rough guide and ignoring the extremes, total damages for an inordinately bad holiday tend to hover around two to two and a half times the total cost.

Damages for a holiday when a few things go wrong range from half up to the total cost. A series of petty complaints can justify a small award for diminution but nothing for distress and disappointment".

These figures now look high in the aftermath of *Milner*. However, over the last few years the assessment of damages in holiday cases has settled down, and it is indeed very notable that there has been a steep decline in the number of holiday cases reported in Current Law; this suggests either that the decisions made are hardly worthy of report (i.e. predictable), or perhaps that this predictability is at last facilitating the parties to reach an amicable settlement before trial. The decision in *Milner* may only accelerate this trend.

CANCELLATION BY THE CLIENT

Introduction

Most tour operators include a clause in their booking conditions stating that if the client cancels the holiday then he must pay compensation to the operator according to a scale of charges. Usually the charges are on a sliding scale commencing with just the deposit and getting larger as the date of departure draws near and ending up with a charge of 100 per cent on or about the actual date of departure. The charges are designed to cover the operator against the risk of not being able to resell the holiday. If this is all they do then they are unexceptionable but in some cases the scale is particularly steep, rising quickly to a peak long before the departure date. In such circumstances the suspicion is that the scale is not simply designed to compensate the operator for the loss he will suffer but there may also be an element of profiteering in the scale. If this is the case the question arises as to whether or not the client has to pay the full scale charge or can get away with paying less?

The answer to this question is that it depends upon which of two quite distinct categories the clause falls into.

A cancellation clause will be placed in the first category if the cancellation is regarded as a breach of contract by the client. In such cases the cancellation charges represent what are called agreed or liquidated damages. These will be enforced unless they amount to a penalty. Cancellation clauses are placed in the second category if they are seen as giving the client an option to terminate the contract. If the client chooses to exercise this option then the contract provides that he must pay a price for doing so—the cancellation charges. In such circumstances the client is not breaking the contract he is merely exercising his rights under it and the sum he pays in these circumstances does not amount to damages for breach and does not attract the rules about penalties.

These two categories will be examined in turn and the consequences of categorising a cancellation clause one way or the other will be considered. The impact of the Unfair Terms in Consumer Contracts Regulations 1999 will also be considered.

Liquidated Damages

This section will proceed on the assumption that cancellation charges amount to agreed damages which are payable because the client breaks the contract when he cancels.

Generally speaking, the courts are favourably disposed to the parties to a contract agreeing between themselves what the consequences of a breach of contract will be. There are numerous reasons for this. First, it means that the parties have a clear idea of what their liabilities will be in the event of a breach because they have assessed them in advance. It means they go into the contract with their eyes open as to the risks they run if they do break the contract. It is simply an aspect of good contract planning. Secondly, because the sum is fixed in advance difficult problems of quantification and remoteness do not arise. Thirdly, the payment of the damages is not complicated by having to prove actual loss; agreed damages are payable automatically on proof of breach. Finally, it avoids litigation. Going to court is an expensive, wasteful, time-consuming, unsatisfactory business and anything which eliminates or reduces this possibility is welcomed—even by the courts.

Therefore, if the cancellation charges can be classified as agreed damages the courts will uphold the clause. On the other hand, if it amounts to a penalty clause the cancellation charges are not payable and only the actual losses incurred by the tour operator are payable. (Note that if greater damages are incurred than are provided for in the liquidated damages clause the victim of the breach is still bound by the clause and cannot claim the higher amount—*Diestal v Stevenson* [1906] 2 K.B. 345. Note also, however, that where the agreed damages clause is imposed on the consumer by the tour operator to cover breaches by the tour operator then this may be treated as an exclusion clause or an unfair contract term—see Ch.6.) So what distinguishes an agreed damages clause from a penalty?

An agreed damages clause exists when the sums involved amount to a genuine pre-estimate of the losses that might flow from the breach of contract. On the other hand a penalty clause exists when the sum is greater than any genuine pre-estimate of loss and is inserted into the contract to punish the other party for breach rather than simply compensate the victim. One phrase commonly used is that a penalty clause is inserted "in terrorem", to frighten the other party into performing, although the phrase has been criticised by Lord Radcliffe, who said in the case of *Bridge v Campbell Discount Co Ltd* [1962] 1 All E.R. 385:

> "I do not think that that description adds anything of substance to the idea conveyed by the word 'penalty' itself, and it obscures the fact that penalties may quite readily be undertaken by parties who are not in the least terrorised by the prospect of having to pay them and yet are, as I understand it, entitled to claim the protection of the court when they are called on to make good their promises."

There have been a number of cases where the distinction has been discussed and the most important of these is *Dunlop Pneumatic Tyre Co Ltd v New Garage & Motor Co Ltd* [1915] A.C. 79 where Lord Dunedin stated the principles by which penalty clauses can be distinguished from agreed damages clauses:

"(a) It will be held to be a penalty if the sum stipulated for is extravagant and unconscionable in amount in comparison with the greatest loss that could conceivably be proved to have followed from the breach.

(b) It will be held to be a penalty if the breach consists only in not paying a sum of money, and the sum stipulated is a sum greater than the sum which ought to have been paid.

(c) There is a presumption (but no more) that it is a penalty when a single sum is made payable by way of compensation, on the occurrence of one or more or all of several events, some of which may occasion serious and others but trifling damage.

(d) It is no obstacle to the sum stipulated being a genuine pre-estimate of damage, that the consequences of the breach are such as to make precise pre-estimation almost an impossibility. On the contrary, that is just the situation when it is probable that pre-estimated damage was the true bargain between the parties."

The facts of the case itself were that Dunlop had contracted to sell tyres to the defendants who had agreed not to tamper with the marks on the goods, not to sell or offer the goods to any private customers or to any co-operative society at less than the claimant's current list prices, not to supply to persons whose supplies the claimants had decided to suspend, not to exhibit or export without the consent of the claimants, and to pay the sum of £5 by way of agreed damages for every tyre sold in breach of the agreement. The purpose of the agreement was to maintain prices. Although illegal now this practice was not so in 1915.

The court accepted that any of the practices outlawed by the contract would contribute to undermining the price maintenance agreement and would damage the claimant's business. Lord Dunedin, in holding that the clause was not a penalty said:

"But though damage as a whole from such a practice [selling below list price] would be certain, yet damage from any one sale would be impossible to forecast. It is just, therefore, one of those cases where it seems quite reasonable for parties to contract that they should estimate that damage at a certain figure, and provided that figure is not extravagant there would seem no reason to suspect that it is not truly a bargain to assess damages, but rather a penalty to be held in terrorem."

A more recent case, *Alfred McAlpine Capital Projects Ltd v Tilebox Ltd* [2005] EWHC 281 (TCC), held that a pre-estimate of damages did not have to be correct to be reasonable, and there had to be a substantial discrepancy between the level of damages stipulated in the contract and the level of damages likely to be suffered before the agreed pre-estimate could be said to be unreasonable.

If we apply these principles to cancellation charges the question to be answered is whether or not the tour operator, in setting the charges, has made a genuine pre-estimate of the loss that would flow from the cancellation? On the face of it the type of scale usually employed, which imposes a higher charge the nearer the departure date, seems to take into account the greater risk that the operator runs of not reselling the holiday the nearer to departure the cancellation is. But what evidence is there for such a scale? Are the figures plucked out of the air at random or are they based on exhaustive research? Are they just a guess based on incomplete information or are they simply adopted because everybody else uses just about the same figures therefore they must be OK? Clearly, if they are based on actual booking and cancellation patterns and losses have been calculated precisely and the scale accurately reflects the average loss that the operator would incur for cancellations at particular times before departure then the scale would be unimpeachable. On the other hand, the operator might be in real difficulties if the scale was merely guesswork.

Prior to the restrictive practices case that was brought by the Office of Fair Trading against them, ABTA recommended a scale of cancellation charges that was adopted by most tour operators. The scale was as follows:

Period before departure within which cancellation received by company	Charge
More than 42 days	Deposit
29–42 days	30 per cent of holiday price
15–28 days	45 per cent of holiday price
1–14 days	60 per cent of holiday price
On or after day of departure	100 per cent of holiday price

No one quite knows how this scale came to be adopted by ABTA and it was, in fact, abandoned by them as a result of the pending action. The current Code (2009) says very little about such charges. However, Alan Milner, former Dean of Trinity College, Oxford and former legal correspondent of the *Travel Trade Gazette*, did some empirical research at a leading tour operator to test the accuracy of the scale, and although his findings are a little tentative because of the relatively small sample size he employed the good news for tour operators is that the money recouped in cancellation charges almost exactly equalled the actual losses suffered by the tour operator. (See Milner "Liquidated Damages: An empirical study in the Travel Industry" (1979) 42 M.L.R. 508). In other words, it could be demonstrated that the scale was not imposing a penalty for breach that was "extravagant and unconscionable" in relation to the actual losses. Moreover, it could also be argued that the imposition of a scale like this was appropriate in an industry where precise calculation of actual loss might be very difficult.

Unfortunately, as Milner concedes, the findings do not necessarily hold true in all cases because they were specific to a particular company for a particular season, a particular resort and for a particular scale of charges. Given the volatility and complexity of the package holiday market there is no guarantee that the scale could be applied by other companies with destinations in other countries. Simply adopting the scale would not necessarily protect the operator against a charge that he was not making a genuine pre-estimate of his losses. Something more might be required. But given that precise calculation of the losses in advance is almost impossible and that losses could vary from season to season then probably the tour operator would not have to do more than show he had taken an intelligent stab at the scale based upon the information available to him.

The Milner article, however, contains much more good news for the operator.

He identifies a number of reasons why tour operators are unlikely to be seriously challenged over cancellation clauses. First, the money involved is usually in the hands of the tour operator and any client who wishes to recover it must sue to do so. Most clients are not prepared to do this, either because they believe that the charges are legally enforceable anyway, or because they are simply not prepared to embark upon legal proceedings and all the trouble that that involves. Secondly, when the money has not been paid, tour operators are in fact quite prepared to issue proceedings, which are usually undefended. Thirdly, there is the role of insurance. Where clients are insured for cancellation they will claim against their insurance company, thereby deflecting any desire they may have to challenge the scale of charges. The insurance companies themselves could challenge the scale but Milner found no evidence of this at the time he wrote the article. He believed this was because the level of claims for cancellation was so low that it was not a significant problem for them.

Finally, even if the matter does come to court it is not for the tour operator to prove his scale is a genuine pre-estimate of loss but for the client to show that it is not; that it is in fact extravagant and unconscionable. Moreover, the law is such that the tour operator can hide behind the fact that it is impossible to calculate his losses precisely and need not show therefore that his calculations are accurate!

Thus, it would appear that only in the most extreme of cases is the tour operator not going to be able to defend his cancellation charges. Indeed, the trend of recent case law shows a desire by courts not to find penalty clauses except in extreme cases—see, for example, *Azimut-Benetti SpA v Healey* [2010] EWHC 2234. See also the bank charges litigation (*Office of Fair Trading v Abbey National Plc* [2009] UKSC 6 and also the Court of Appeal and High Court cases) which discussed the issue of whether bank charges could be regarded as penalties.

On the other hand, if the charges are shown to be a penalty the operator will then have to be able to prove his actual loss and this might, in fact, be difficult to do. It is for this very reason, of course, that agreed damages clauses attract the approval of the law in the first place. No one who could possibly avoid it would want to embark upon difficult questions of quantification and remoteness.

Options to Terminate

The alternative approach to cancellation charges is to regard the clause as giving the client the option to terminate the contract early if he chooses to do so. In which case, he is not breaking the contract, he is abiding by it and exercising one of his rights under it—the right to escape from it short of completion—but having to pay a price to do so.

The context in which this problem has usually arisen is in cases of hire purchase. In a typical hire purchase contract the owner of the goods lets it out on hire to the hirer on the terms that if a certain number of hire payments are made the hirer can then purchase the goods for a further small payment. Invariably, the contract also provides that if the hirer wishes to terminate the agreement before he has made all the payments he may do so provided he makes up the payments to a certain minimum. This minimum payment clause often amounted to two-thirds of the value of the goods and was intended to cover "depreciation". In fact, these minimum payments often far exceeded any conceivable depreciation and merely amounted to profit for the owner. As such, they closely resembled penalty clauses—they were extravagant and unconscionable and were imposed in situations very similar to breach.

The argument came to a head in the Court of Appeal in the case of *Bridge v Campbell Discount Co Ltd* [1961] 2 All E.R. 97. Mr Bridge had acquired a car from the Campbell Discount Company on hire purchase. He paid £105 deposit and agreed to make monthly payments of approximately £10 until he had made up the total payments to £482. After making only one monthly payment he found he could not keep up the payments and wrote to the company saying:

> "I am very sorry but I will not be able to pay any more payments on the Bedford Dormobile. Will you please let me know when and where I will have to return the car? I am very sorry regarding this but I have no other alternative."

He later returned the car to the garage where he had first acquired it. The company then invoked cl.6 of the hire purchase contract which provided:

> "The hirer may at any time terminate the hiring by giving notice in writing to the owners, and thereupon the provisions of clause 9 hereof apply."

Clause 9 stated that upon exercising the option to terminate the hirer had to make up the payments to two-thirds of the total hire purchase price.

Holroyd Pearce L.J. said:

> "The hirer exercised his option under clause 6 by giving notice. Clause 9 then applied. Under clause 9 he has to pay such sum as will make up the rentals to two third of the purchase, viz., the sum here claimed. No breach of contract or damages are in question for the hirer is simply exercising his right to return the car with all the incidents set out under clause 9. Therefore the doctrine of penalties does not apply."

Stated like this the law is quite straightforward. If the hirer is exercising an option to terminate this does not amount to breach and therefore the court will not investigate the question of whether the minimum payments clause is extravagant or unconscionable. Put another way, the owner can put whatever amount he likes into the minimum payments clause and get away with it. (Note that such clauses in hire purchase contracts are now heavily regulated by the Consumer Credit Act 1974 and the courts have a wide discretion to disallow them in consumer credit contracts.)

However, the matter did not end there. The case was appealed to the House of Lords under the name *Bridge v Campbell Discount Co Ltd* [1962] 1 All E.R. 385. There, the court proceeded on a completely different basis. They said that the circumstances showed that Mr Bridge was not exercising his right to terminate, he was actually breaking the contract. Lord Morton said:

> "I am of opinion, however, that the appellant [Bridge] never had the slightest intention of exercising the option contained in clause 6, and the terms of his letter show that he did not have clause 6 in mind. He frankly and simply

informs the respondents that 'I will not be able to pay any more payments on the Bedford Dormobile.' There is no reference to any option, and I cannot reconcile the statement just quoted with the view that he intended to exercise an option, the terms whereof put him under an immediate obligation to pay a further large sum to the respondents. To my mind, the letter means that the writer feels reluctantly compelled to break his agreement, and the apologetic terms of the letter confirm me in this view. Why should the hirer apologise so humbly, twice, if he thought that he was merely exercising an option given to him by the agreement?"

If it was a breach then cll.7 and 8 applied. By virtue of these clauses the company could retake possession of the vehicle, terminate the agreement because of the hirer's breach and claim the payments due under cl.9. In these circumstances, the doctrine of penalties applied. The court went on to decide that the payments under cl.9 in the event of a breach did amount to a penalty and Mr Bridge only had to pay the company's actual losses as opposed to the charges laid down in cl.9.

Thus, the case turned on the interpretation placed upon Mr Bridge's actions. The Court of Appeal interpreted what he was doing as an option to terminate, therefore, the doctrine of penalties did not apply. The House of Lords put a different interpretation on his actions and said he was in breach and, therefore, the doctrine did apply.

As Lord Denning pointed out in the House of Lords, this leads to a paradox. The conscientious hirer who has difficulties making the payments and who does the right thing under the contract and exercises his option to terminate has to make up the payments as laid down in the minimum payments clause, whereas the unconscientious hirer who falls behind with his payments but does nothing until the owner comes along and repossesses the car and then sues only has to pay the actual losses for his breach.

Although the court was not actually called upon to solve this paradox it did not stop four of their lordships expressing an opinion on the matter. What they said, however, was not helpful because two of them said that if the option had been exercised then the minimum payment clause was valid, whereas the other two expressed the opinion that they would have applied the doctrine of penalties to an option clause. In effect, this meant that on this point the Court of Appeal judgment was still valid because it had not been overruled.

A later House of Lords case, however, *Export Credits Guarantee Department v Universal Oil Products Co* [1983] 2 All E.R. 205 has confirmed that the doctrine of penalties does not apply to sums which are payable on the occurrence of an event which is not a breach.

What this means in practice for travel companies' cancellation clauses is that *if* operators want to ensure that the clauses are enforceable without having to prove that the sums involved are a penalty, then they should be drafted in such a way that they can only be interpreted as conferring an option to terminate, not as imposing damages for breach. Wordings should be tightened up. Instead of using a clause such as this:

"If you cancel your booking [w]e will ask you to pay cancellation charges on the scale shown below. These charges reflect our estimated loss as a result of dealing with your booking to the point of cancellation and any other losses we may have to pay." (Airtours, 2002)

or one like this:

"Because we start to incur costs in relation to your arrangements from the time we confirm your booking, if you cancel we have to make a charge, and the nearer to your departure date you cancel, the more the charge will be." (Olympic, 2002)

an operator should choose a much more explicit form of words to make it clear that the cancellation is the exercise of an option not a breach, e.g:

"You have an option to cancel your holiday which must be exercised in writing. The fees for the exercise of this option are ..." (Balkan Holidays, 1992)

The first two clauses leave open the possibility that a court could interpret a cancellation as either a breach or an option to terminate. The third can only reasonably be interpreted as an option. If a court accepted it it would mean that the operator could put what figures he liked in the scale of charges and it could not be questioned by the courts. (Subject to the application of the UTCCR.)

But getting the drafting right is only half the answer. The client must actually exercise the option. If, as in the *Bridge* case, his actions could be interpreted as a breach of contract, then the clause will not apply at all because it doesn't cover breach. In which case, the operator is back to proving his actual loss—or also having an agreed damages clause in the contract on a scale which is less fierce than the option to terminate clause. This, of course, would look very peculiar in the brochure—having two different scales for essentially the same thing.

Anyone advising a client who is having difficulties making the payments and who is considering cancelling would be well advised to look carefully at the cancellation clause and determine whether it is an agreed damages clause or an option to terminate clause. If it was the latter, and the charges seemed excessive, the advice to the client should be to make it clear that he is not exercising an option but is repudiating the contract altogether and simply refusing to pay any more, and if the tour operator wants his money he will have to sue for it. If it is the former, then again the adviser should carefully consider whether the scale of payments is excessive or extravagant, and if it is, advise the client not to pay. It would then be up to the travel company to sue.

At the end of the day, unless the company succeeds in getting the client to exercise a genuine option to terminate, the client will not have to pay an amount which is extravagant or unconscionable so long as he is prepared to exercise his legal rights. On the one hand, faced with an option to terminate clause with extravagant payments attached to it the client should just ignore it and inform the company he is in breach. On the other hand, faced with an agreed damages clause which is in reality a penalty he should be prepared to challenge it.

From the operator's point of view, if he wants to avoid difficulties he would be well advised not to rely upon a scale which is excessive. Additionally, he should provide for both breach and an option to terminate so that all possibilities are covered and the likelihood of litigation is minimised.

There are several travel cases which involve the issue of cancellation charges. The first is *Global of London (Tours and Travel) Ltd v Tait* 1977 S.L.T. (Sh. Ct.) 96. Having made her booking and paid her deposit in January the client did nothing further. On August 4, only five days before she was due to depart, the tour operator wrote to her and said: "Your attitude to the whole matter has now entailed your booking's complete cancellation", and claimed cancellation charges. The court held that cl.4 of the contract permitted the client to cancel in writing—but she had not done this and the court would not imply a cancellation when the clause clearly required written cancellation. Alternatively, cl.2 permitted the tour operator to cancel if the balance was not paid within 56 days of travel. In this latter case, however, they would be restricted to retaining the deposit but no more. The lesson here for the tour operator was either to act more quickly when faced with default or to draft a clause which imposed a sliding scale of charges—which most tour operators now do.

The second travel case which deals specifically with cancellation charges is *Thomson Travel Ltd v Hall* Unreported 1981, County Court. Mr Hall had booked his holiday on July 19, and then cancelled it on July 21, because his employers wanted him to go abroad on business during his holiday. Mr Hall refused to pay the 60 per cent cancellation charges due under the contract. The judge held, relying on the Court of Appeal judgment in the *Bridge* case, that the cancellation clause was an option to terminate clause and that therefore the doctrine of penalties did not apply. As Mr Hall had exercised his option and was not in breach he was therefore liable to pay the whole sum. The judge said:

"The first important matter to emphasise is that there was no breach of contract here. Under the contract which Mr Hall signed he was entitled if he wished to do so to cancel and he exercised that option, and that option it is stated in the contract is to be exercised at a price."

If Mr Hall had not followed the procedure under the contract but had simply intimated that he was not going to pay any more then he might have been regarded as being in breach in which case the clause would not have applied.

The third case shows what might happen where the consumer has not read the booking conditions (including the cancellation charge clause) and they were therefore not incorporated into the contract. In *Russell v Thomson Holidays* Unreported April 14, 2005, Bristol County Court, the actual booking conditions provided for 90 per cent cancellation charges at the date of cancellation by the consumer. But the consumer successfully argued that she had never been told about the conditions. What was the common law position? The judge held that, on a balance of probabilities, Thomson would have been able to mitigate its loss by re-selling the holiday at half price. Therefore he allowed only a 50 per cent cancellation charge by way of damages.

Finally, in *Clark v Travelsphere* Unreported October 22, 2004, Leeds County Court, mentioned below, Travelsphere successfully enforced a 100 per cent cancellation charge when the Claimants were no-shows at the departure airport.

The Unfair Terms in Consumer Contracts Regulations

We referred in Ch.6 on exclusion clauses to the Unfair Terms in Consumer Contracts Regulations 1999. These regulations cover not simply exclusion clauses but any kind of unfair terms in contracts which have not been individually negotiated and which contravene the requirement of good faith. As has been seen, Sch.3 lists terms which may be regarded as unfair. The list includes terms:

> "(d) permitting the seller or supplier to retain sums paid by the consumer where the latter decides not to conclude or perform the contract, without providing for the consumer to receive compensation of an equivalent amount from the seller or supplier where the latter is the party cancelling the contract.
>
> (e) Requiring any consumer who fails to fulfil his obligation to pay a disproportionately high sum in compensation."

Both these provisions appear targeted at cancellation charges. Consumer groups believe that both these provisions apply to some of the higher levels of cancellation charges required by tour operators. They also suggest a more promising line of argument for insurance companies than those explored above. One answer given by tour operators is this: that in the event that they cancel a holiday, they refund a sum which is more than 100 per cent of the price, i.e. a full refund plus compensation calculated on a scale which varies according to the time before departure the holiday was cancelled; whereas if the consumer cancels, he or she must forfeit a sum which is a maximum of 100 per cent, and usually less.

The problem with taking this approach, however, is that the sums are not necessarily comparable. The sum payable by the tour operator is a full refund—because the consumer didn't get a holiday at all—*plus* a sum for distress and disappointment and any out of pocket expenses—which is why it adds up to more than 100 per cent. On the other hand, when the consumer cancels the tour operator has to be compensated for the lost sale. This should only be 100 per cent if he fails to sell the holiday again. In many cases the loss will be substantially less because of the operator's ability to make late sales—which suggests that compensation should be payable on much gentler scales than presently employed.

One case, referred to earlier, *Hartman v P&O Cruises*, looked at the issue of cancellation charges in the light of a decision by P&O to cancel the claimants' cruise and to refund the money plus £40 per head compensation. According to the brief report the court held:

> "that the 1992 Regulations could not be considered in isolation, because they did not deal with unfair contract terms which were governed by the 1994 Regulations [now the 1999 Regulations], in particular Reg. 4(1) and Reg. 4(2) and Sch. 3 para. 1(d). If the terms relied upon by P were reasonable then H entered into a binding contract to restrict their damages to GBP 40 each. P were clearly in the stronger bargaining position and the restriction of compensation to GBP 40 per person was unfair, particularly when compared with the sum that P would have kept had it been H who had cancelled the cruise the day before departure. Therefore, there was no limit on the award of damages."

Following disquiet about rising levels of cancellation charges, the OFT carried out a two year review of cancellation charges, from 2002, but in the end decided that no action needed to be taken by them under their powers; their March 2004 Guidance on Unfair Terms in Package Holiday Contracts OFT 668 (equally applicable, in our view, to non-packages) says at para.3.24:

"3.24 The OFT does not object in principle to the use of such sliding scales since they provide consumers with the certainty of knowing precisely how much they are liable to lose by cancelling at any given point.

3.25 However, fairness must not be sacrificed to simplicity ... [a]t the time the contract is made, [the scales] should represent a genuine pre-estimate of the supplier's loss from cancellations."

Annexe C to the Guidance sets out a fairly uncontroversial list of criteria for assessing the likely costs of cancellation.

REMEDIES UNDER REGULATION 13

Regulation 13 provides (for packages only, of course) that in certain circumstances, when the organiser is unable to provide the promised package, the consumer is entitled to be offered an alternative package—as well as or instead of damages. On the face of it, this was a radical departure from the remedies traditionally available from the law but, in reality, it is a practice which had become quite commonplace in the travel industry long before the advent of the Regulations. Tour operators, faced with the inevitable fact that a service designed and marketed many months, if not years, in advance of performance, could not always be delivered as promised, would often offer an alternative holiday to clients rather than cancel the holiday altogether and have to pay substantial damages. Clients, on the other hand, were often grateful to be offered a substitute package if the alternative was not to go abroad at all.

In recent times, these Regulations have been significant in protecting consumers unable to depart on a package holiday as a result of various emergencies—volcanic ash, snow at Heathrow and civil unrest in Egypt were just three such examples in 2010–11.

The right to be offered an alternative package is to be found in reg.13, but it is dependent not only on the provisions in reg.13 but also the provisions of reg.12. Regulation 12 gives the consumer a right to withdraw from the contract if there are significant alterations to essential terms. If the consumer does withdraw under reg.12 then under reg.13 he has the right to be offered an alternative holiday. This right exists not only if the consumer withdraws under reg.12 but also, under reg.13, if the tour operator cancels the package for other reasons.

Regulation 12 provides:

"12 In every contract there are implied terms to the effect that—

(a) where the organiser is constrained before the departure to alter significantly an essential term of the contract, such as the price, he will inform the consumer as quickly as possible in order to enable him to take appropriate decisions and in particular to withdraw from the contract without penalty or to accept a rider to the contract specifying the alterations made and their impact on the price; and

(b) the consumer will inform the organiser or the retailer of his decision as soon as possible."

A number of difficulties present themselves here regarding the interpretation of this Regulation. First, what is meant by "essential terms"? Are they the terms found in Sch.2 of the Regulations which are compulsory terms of the contract? They seem to be regarded as essential by the drafters of the Directive otherwise they would not feature as compulsory terms of the contract. But are these the only terms that are essential? For instance, the operator might have advertised the package as suitable for singles only but then at the last minute decided to throw it open to married persons as well. It could very well be an essential term of the contract that the package is only open to singles, but it doesn't feature in the Annex—in which case it might not be governed by reg.12.

Are the terms in the Schedule to be regarded as essential simply because they are in the Schedule? Are they all to be regarded as sufficiently important as to give rise to the right to withdraw from the contract if significantly altered? On balance the answer seems to be the latter.

This raises a second problem. What is meant by "significant"? At present, tour operators tend to classify changes into major and minor changes in their terms and conditions and in some cases permit the consumer to cancel in the event of major changes. Changes in the day of departure, resort, hotel and airport frequently feature in such lists and there is no reason to believe that under the Regulations the situation will be different. There may be other changes, however, which may appear insignificant initially but when viewed from the perspective of the consumer are much more important. For instance, if the brochure promises that water sports are available in resort this may not be a vital element of many clients' holidays but in individual cases they may have built their whole holiday around it. It may, in those circumstances, amount to an "essential" term of the contract.

The OFT in its 2004 Guidance referred to above deals with this problem by suggesting that it is an unfair contract term to declare that only a specified list of items can be regarded as major or significant changes.

Some idea of what amounts to a significant term can be gleaned from *Golby v Nelson's Theatre & Travel Agency* (1967) 111 S.J. 470, a case which pre-dates the Package Travel Regulations by some years. In that case the Court of Appeal had to decide whether a flight change gave rise to the right to cancel a holiday to Israel. A booking had been made on a non-stop scheduled BOAC flight, BA 316, to Tel Aviv. A day before travel the claimant was informed that the flight number had been changed to BA 924 and the flight would be leaving 75 minutes later. In the mistaken belief that this was not a non-stop flight, and without listening to the travel agent, the claimant repudiated the contract and claimed the return of his deposit. The court held that this did not amount to a breach of condition, nor even to a breach of contract at all, and denied him the return of his deposit.

Regulation 12 applies where the operator is *constrained* to alter the essential terms of the contract. The term originally used in the draft Regulations was *compelled*—a term which is more restrictive than constrained. Compelled suggests that alterations can only be made for events beyond the control of the operator and where he has no choice in the matter, but the use of constrained implies that changes can be made on financial grounds alone. This broadens the range of situations where the operator can "legitimately" make alterations but it also broadens the circumstances where the consumer is entitled to additional remedies. *Hayes v Airtours* [2001] C.L.Y. 4283, a case arising out of Hurricane Georges which devastated parts of the Dominican Republic, held that the tour operator was not in breach of reg.12. Although the hurricane hit the resort only two days after the claimants arrived, the nature of hurricanes is so uncertain that even with only two days to go its path was unpredictable and the best estimate was that it would have avoided the island. (See Kilbey "Of Holidays and Hurricanes" [1999] I.T.L.J. 46 for a discussion of this issue.)

Considerable help in interpreting the word "constrained" is given by the cases of *Lambert v Travelsphere* [2005] C.L.Y. 1977 and *Clark v Travelsphere* (above). Both cases arose out of the outbreak of the SARS disease in various parts of the world, in this case, Hong Kong. In the *Lambert* case, the consumers cancelled the holiday at a time when the FCO/Department of Health were advising against travel to Hong Kong, but there was still a chance that warning would be lifted. In *Clark*, there was a tour of mainland China first, to which Hong Kong was an add-on at the end of the tour, and the hope was that the warning would be lifted while the China tour was in progress, but the claimants did not turn up at the airport for the tour at all. In the event, Hong Kong remained off-limits, and more patient customers received appropriate refunds; but both these claims failed. In *Lambert* H.H. Judge Darroch said that a tour operator was not constrained within reg.12 while there remained a "flicker of hope" that the holiday could continue; and this test was adopted in *Clark*. (See Saggerson and Prager "A Flicker of Hope" [2004] I.T.L.J. 183.)

Note that the operator is under a duty to inform the consumer as quickly as possible of the changes in essential terms. This means that the operator cannot keep the information to himself and only divulge it to the client at the last moment—when the client will have no choice but to accept. Two cases involving First Choice Holidays illustrate the consequences for tour operators for failing to comply with this requirement. In *Graham v First Choice Holiday & Flights Ltd* [1997] C.L.Y. 1771 the tour operator knew two days prior to departure that the claimants' accommodation was not available (two weeks at the most expensive hotel offered to them) but failed to inform them. As a consequence the claimants were accommodated for part of the time in a business hotel with few tourist facilities 80km from where they wanted to be. They asked to be returned home but that was not possible. On their return First Choice returned the whole of the holiday price to them and the court awarded them a further £500 for distress and disappointment. The report is a brief one and reg.12 is not mentioned, nor is reg.15, but the case seems a straightforward application of the two.

In *Hook v First Choice Holiday & Flights Ltd* [1998] C.L.Y. 1426 the tour operator knew four days before the claimants departed on holiday that their hotel was not available and did inform them of this. They were told that the alternative being offered to them was in the same resort and of equivalent quality. They were further told that if they chose to cancel they would only receive a 10 per cent refund. The claimants reluctantly agreed to the change. The hotel, although of the same star rating, was of inferior quality. It was decided that the claimants' holiday had not been entirely ruined and they were entitled to a 20 per cent discount on the price for diminution of value (£200) and £250 for distress and disappointment. Of more significance, however, is that the judge said that the claimants had not been "properly informed" of their full rights under reg.12, including the right to withdraw without penalty, and that in such circumstances tour operators should inform consumers in writing of the options available to them. In this case he felt that there had been "an element of H being duped into believing he had no right to cancel". (See also *Crump v Inspiration East Ltd* [1998] C.L.Y. 1427 for a case where the tour operator failed to inform the consumer of significant problems in resort which they knew about before departure.) Indeed, there have been cases where, on similar facts to *Hook*, a full refund has been awarded where a claimant has been deprived of the right to his reg.13 options by non-notification.

It is not just the operator who is under an obligation in reg.12. It is also an implied term that the consumer notifies the operator or agent as soon as possible of his decision. It is not specified what the penalty will be but it could very well be that the consumer would lose his right to withdraw if he did not act quickly enough. But note that the client is under no obligation to take the decision quickly—merely to inform the operator as quickly as possible once the decision has been made.

If the consumer does withdraw from the contract under reg.12 his rights will be governed by reg.13. This offers the consumer the choice of either an alternative package or a full refund and, in most circumstances, compensation. Regulation 13 provides:

"13(1) The terms set out in paragraphs (2) and (3) below are implied in every contract and apply where the consumer withdraws from the contract pursuant to the term in it implied by virtue of regulation 12(a), or where the organiser, for any reason other than the fault of the consumer, cancels the package before the date when it is due to start.

(2) the consumer is entitled—

(a) to take a substitute package of equivalent or superior quality if the other party to the contract is able to offer him such a substitute; or

(b) to take a substitute package of lower quality if the other party to the contract is able to offer him one and to recover from the organiser the difference in price between the price of the package purchased and that of the substitute package; or

(c) to have repaid to him as soon as possible all the moneys paid by him under the contract.

(3) The consumer is entitled, if appropriate, to be compensated by the organiser for non-performance of the contract except where—

(a) the package is cancelled because the number of persons who agree to take it is less than the minimum number required and the consumer is informed of the cancellation, in writing, within the period indicated in the description of the package; or

(b) the package is cancelled by reason of unusual and unforeseeable circumstances beyond the control of the party by whom this exception is pleaded, the consequences of which could not have been avoided even if all due care had been exercised, provided that it is not open to that party to rely on this exception in cases of overbooking."

As already indicated, the obligation to offer a substitute package if available corresponds with existing practice and, for ABTA members, had long been formalised in the ABTA Code. It appears that the duty to offer an alternative if available is not optional—the consumer is entitled to the offer if the organiser is able to offer it. The organiser does not appear to have the choice of simply refunding the consumer's money rather than offering an alternative. In practice, this is unlikely to happen because in most circumstances the operator would prefer to hold on to the booking, but it may be that with a particularly "difficult" client who is already unhappy with the alteration the operator may not wish to offer an alternative even if one was available. Regulation 13(2)(a) seems to preclude this possibility.

One problem that arises under reg.13(2)(a) is what is meant by a substitute package of equivalent or superior quality? Put at its simplest, this means that if the tour operator is unable to offer two weeks in the chosen resort at the four star Grand Hotel then he could offer the same two weeks at the four star Excelsior Hotel just a couple of hundred yards down the beach. This would clearly be a package of equivalent quality. Likewise, if the operator couldn't offer a four star alternative but was able to upgrade the consumer to a five star hotel in the same resort this would be a substitute of superior quality.

But difficulties could arise if, for instance, the operator was unable to offer an equivalent or near equivalent package to the consumer but, nevertheless, was able to offer a far superior one to a different destination. Let's say that the consumer had booked a two night city break in Paris at a two star hotel at the height of the season and at the last minute the tour operator was unable to provide this. Not only that but there was no further availability in Paris at all—but the operator still has four night breaks available in Vienna in a four star hotel—or, if we push this example to the limits—a 14 day package to a deluxe hotel in Rio.

The problem from the tour operator's point of view is that the consumer is entitled to take a substitute package of equivalent or superior quality if the tour operator is able to offer him such a substitute. Clearly the operator is able to offer the alternatives in Vienna and Rio and clearly the Regulations envisage that the consumer will get a superior holiday in some circumstances. So why should the consumer not be entitled to the packages in Vienna or Rio?

One answer which has a certain superficial attraction is that of course the consumer can have the package to Vienna or Rio just so long as he is prepared to pay the difference in price. This is certainly a solution which some tour operators have successfully adopted but it may not be sanctioned by the Regulations. The Regulations are, in fact, silent as to whether or not the operator can charge extra for a superior substitute, but there is one indication that they cannot. Regulation 13(2)(b), which deals with the right to an inferior package, does actually say that the consumer is entitled to the difference in price when offered an inferior quality package. The inference that can be drawn from this is that if the Regulations do provide for a financial adjustment in reg.13(2)(b) but do not in reg.13(2)(a) then this must be for a reason—and the reason is that the operator is not allowed to charge extra for the superior package. If it had been intended that the tour operator could charge extra then this would have been provided for in the Regulation—as it was in reg.13(2)(b).

On the other hand, an opposing argument can be constructed. As we shall see, under reg.14, where alternative arrangements are made for a consumer after departure, it is expressly stated that these shall be at no extra charge to the consumer. If it is expressly stated there, why not in reg.13? One answer is that, after departure, the consumer can almost be likened to a prisoner of the tour operator who must be protected from being ripped off with extra charges; whilst before departure, the consumer is in a much stronger position to decide whether or not to pay any proposed extra charges.

Consumers who felt compelled to pay the extra might be able to recover it in some circumstances if it could be seen as a payment made in order to mitigate loss in the face of a breach of contract.

The OFT, in its 2004 Guidance referred to above, says that it is an unfair term, in its opinion, to require a consumer to pay extra for a superior substitute package. But as the OFT say, it is for a court, not the OFT, to decide whether in fact a term is unfair, and this may be an area where a court challenge to the OFT view is feasible

If the tour operator is able to offer an equivalent or slightly superior holiday, as they will be able to do in most cases, then this remains an academic problem, but it is nevertheless the case that on occasion the operator will be faced with a dilemma like this and will have to solve it. One way is to argue that the words should be interpreted in context. If the operator is required to provide a substitute for a city break holiday to Paris then the substitute must also be a city break holiday to Paris. To require the operator to offer holidays to Vienna or Rio—at no extra cost—would be so different from the original package that it could not be a reasonable interpretation of the Regulations.

The OFT's views whether the tour operator is obliged to offer a significantly better holiday is that:

"At the same time the supplier is not expected to offer a holiday which is so far superior as not to be a genuine substitute. Nor is the supplier required to offer a superior substitute if it is able to offer one of equivalent quality. If the supplier offers a substitute of genuinely equivalent quality, it may offer a substitute of superior quality at additional cost." (para.3.15)

Failing that, the only recourse for the operator would simply be to refuse to supply the alternative. This would place the operator in breach of the implied term but it would probably not increase the damages. Ultimately, it would be a financial decision for the operator—will it cost me more to upgrade the client from Paris to Vienna or Rio than to cancel the holiday altogether and pay damages for distress and disappointment? There will also be the loss of goodwill to take into account.

If the operator is unable to offer an alternative package, or the consumer rejects it and decides to withdraw from the contract anyway, then the operator is required to repay "all the moneys paid by him under the contract". Whether this includes insurance premiums will depend upon whether the insurance was paid as part of the package or whether it was purchased separately. The OFT

Guidance indicates that it is unfair to withhold insurance premiums paid as part of a package.

The modern reality is that many consumers now have the sophistication and courage to negotiate a deal which suits them, when these situations arise.

Whether or not the consumer withdraws or takes an alternative package he is entitled to damages for the non-performance of the contract (reg.13(3)). Nothing is said about the manner in which the damages are to be calculated (although reg.15(4) does permit tour operators, if they are so minded, to provide that damages can be limited to an extent that is not unreasonable), therefore, the principles established in *Jarvis v Swans Tours* and *Milner v Carnival Plc* will still be applicable. So, too, will the rules on mitigation of damage. Thus, if the operator does offer a suitable alternative and the consumer, for no good reason, refuses it, then the consumer will get little or nothing by way of damages. Most tour operators provide a table of compensation in their booking conditions. There is, of course, nothing wrong with this practice, but the sums concerned are only legally enforceable if they are not unreasonable.

Where a substitute package has been provided the damages are likely to be relatively small and in many cases the consumer may not receive any damages at all—simply because the substitute would be adequate compensation. It will be noted that compensation is payable "if appropriate" and one example where it may not be appropriate is if the substitute package is superior, but no additional charge has been made.

Damages are not recoverable in two circumstances. The first is where the operator cancels for lack of numbers. In such cases, as long as this is expressly provided for in the contract and the operator complies with the time limits, the consumer is limited to recovering the price of the holiday (or substitute arrangements). Note that ABTA operators cannot cancel for lack of minimum numbers after the balance of the price has been paid (para.3A of the Code.)

The second situation where the consumer is denied compensation is where the contract is cancelled by reason of unusual and unforeseeable circumstances beyond the control of the party by whom it is pleaded, the consequences of which could not have been avoided even if all due care had been exercised. This is the *force majeure* defence and for a more detailed examination of the *force majeure* provisions you should refer back to Ch.9.

The workings of regs 12 and 13 were illustrated during the volcanic ash crisis of April 2010. Those consumers who were unable to depart because flights were grounded were able to obtain full refunds but no additional compensation. Package tour operators had to bear the loss of these refunds, and often of paying for unused services in destinations, e.g. hotels or cruises. Contrast this with the independent traveller who may get back the cost of his flights, but not of any pre-booked ground arrangements, which the supplier (e.g. hotel) remained ready and willing to supply.

In *Josephs v Sunworld Ltd* [1998] C.L.Y. 3734, in a muddled report where the remedies under regs 12, 13 and 14 seem to have been confused, it was held that there had been a breach of both reg.12 and reg.13 and that the tour operator had failed to offer the consumer the alternative of continuing with the holiday and claiming compensation or returning home. (*Westerman v Travel Promotions Ltd* [2000] C.L.Y. 4042 is another case where there seems to be some confusion over the remedies under regs 12 and 13 and those under reg.14.)

REMEDIES UNDER REGULATION 14

Regulation 14 covers the situation where major changes to the package occur after departure. It provides:

"14(1) The terms set out in paragraphs (2) and (3) below are implied in every contract and apply where, after departure, a significant proportion of the services contracted for is not provided, or the organiser becomes aware that he will be unable to procure a significant proportion of the services to be provided.

(2) The organiser will make suitable alternative arrangements, at no extra cost to the consumer, for the continuation of the package and will, where appropriate, compensate the consumer for the difference between the services to be supplied under the contract and those supplied.

(3) If it is impossible to make arrangements as described in paragraph (2), or these are not accepted by the consumer for good reasons, the organiser will, where appropriate, provide the consumer with equivalent transport back to the place of departure or to another place to which the consumer has agreed and will, where appropriate, compensate the consumer."

This Regulation appears to cover the non-provision of service, whereas reg.15, which also has a bearing on this Regulation, covers the improper provision of the services as well as the non-provision of the services. In some cases, this may be a difficult distinction to make. For instance, if the brochure states that rooms are air-conditioned and the air-conditioning system is not working is that a case of non-provision or improper provision? The same argument could be applied where the hotel does provide the advertised meals but they are inedible. In reality, there are large areas of overlap between the two regulations. *Charlson v Mark Warner*, below, is one of few cases to consider this overlap.

As with reg.12 the requirement in reg.14 is that a "significant" proportion of the services not be provided before the consumer is entitled to the benefit of the Regulation. How large a proportion amounts to significant will be a question of fact in each case. If, for instance, the consumer finds that the hotel he booked is not available then, prima facie, this would amount to a significant proportion of the services. It would be the same if in a package consisting of transport to London, overnight accommodation and tickets to "Les Miserables", the tour operator found that he could not provide the tickets to the theatre. It would not be regarded as "significant" if on a 10 day package to Paris the bottle of champagne was not in the bedroom as promised.

If the failure is significant then the organiser is first obliged to make "suitable" alternative arrangements. This could mean booking the consumer into an alternative hotel, arranging for meals to be taken elsewhere, arranging for the promised boat trip on the Seine to be taken on the second day of the holiday rather than the first. Even if the alternative is "suitable" it is provided that the consumer is entitled to compensation for the difference between the service offered and the service actually supplied "where appropriate". Presumably this means that if the service supplied is cheaper than that offered then the consumer is entitled to a refund of the difference in price. It is not entirely clear whether the compensation is only to cover difference in value or whether it also encompasses compensation for the distress and disappointment suffered because of the difference. Even if it does cover the latter, the amounts involved are not likely to be large, simply because the alternative could not be called suitable if it caused a significant amount of distress (Saggerson, 4th edn, suggests that only "difference in value" compensation is payable under reg.14).

The obligation placed on the organiser is that he "will" make suitable alternative arrangements and only if it is "impossible" to do so will he be able to offer transport home. Suppose, for instance, the consumer has contracted for a two star hotel in Paris on July 14 and the tour operator cannot offer this but there is a suite available in the most expensive hotel in Paris. Is this a suitable alternative? Certainly, it is suitable to the consumer. Is it impossible to arrange? Certainly not, all it takes is a phone call. Is the operator obliged to book it? Nothing in the Regulation seems to give him any alternative, no matter what the cost to him. This is similar to the dilemma facing the operator under reg.13, already discussed, where there are alternative packages available but at much greater cost. *Thompson v Airtours Holidays Ltd (No.1)* [1999] C.L.Y. 3819 is authority for the proposition that the onus is on the tour operator to make an offer to find alternative accommodation. Airtours knew what was available but an offer was not made.

When considering the cost of upgrading, it should be borne in mind that the alternative could be much more costly. The Regulations provide that if the organiser does find it impossible to make alternative arrangements or they are not accepted by the consumer for good reasons, the organiser is under an obligation to return the consumer to his starting point, where appropriate. At common law, the consumer was able to mitigate his loss by returning home under his own steam and could reclaim the cost as part of his damages, but there was no obligation on the tour operator to assist him. This is a major departure from the common law and from the ABTA Code. Cases such as *Booth and Ingram v Best Travel Ltd* [1990] C.L.Y. 1542, *Abbatt v Sunquest* [1984] C.L.Y. 1025 and *Bragg v Yugotours* [1982] C.L.Y. 777 are all pre-1992 cases which would now fall to be decided under reg.14, and where the tour operator, having failed to provide suitable alternative arrangements, would be under an obligation to repatriate the consumers. In *Dixon v Direct Holidays*, above, the court found breaches of reg.14 in the failures both to find suitable alternatives, and the failure to repatriate. *Marsh v Thomson Tour Operators* [2000] C.L.Y. 4044 is a case where the tour operator went beyond what is required in reg.14. The brochure promised that if consumers were not satisfied with the holiday then they could ask to be repatriated and would be given a full refund. After failing to satisfy the expectations of the claimant Thomson reluctantly agreed to fly him home but did not offer the promised refund on the grounds that his request was not reasonable. The court held:

"that the guarantee did not specify that a customer's dissatisfaction had to be 'reasonable', and such a term could not be implied. The guarantee was included by Thomson as a sales gimmick, to provide something extra to set it apart from the competition. If the operation of the guarantee was limited to situations where it was reasonable for a customer to request to be flown home, it would be worth little."

The obligation to repatriate is only imposed where it is "appropriate" to do so. If the failure to provide the services occurred with only two days of a 21 day holiday to Australia remaining then it might be deemed inappropriate for the organiser to have to book the consumer on to an expensive scheduled flight home. Perhaps the organiser might not have been able to provide the two day trip to the Great Barrier Reef which was regarded as the highlight of the package. Even though this might be regarded as significant and the organiser might not have been able to make suitable alternative arrangements, nevertheless, the remedy might be out of all proportion to the fault of the organiser. Slightly different considerations would apply on Majorca where there is a wide choice of cheap flights back to the UK on most days.

The consumer is not entitled to reject the alternative arrangements without good reason. If he has no good reason then the organiser is not obliged to transport him home. Presumably, if he then chooses to go home at his own expense the tour operator would not be obliged to compensate him in such circumstances. Having offered a suitable alternative and the consumer having rejected it for no good reason then the organiser could argue that the alternative should have been accepted as a reasonable mitigation of loss and the decision to go home was not a reasonable decision in the circumstances. In *Milner v Carnival* discussed extensively above, the Milners, after disembarking in Hawaii, had to pay for their own passage home. They claimed this cost under reg.14, but the claim was disallowed because the Milners were found not to have had good reasons for rejecting the final cabin offered to them; their disembarkation was treated as consensual.

There is a suggestion that even if the alternative is suitable the consumer may yet have good reasons for rejecting it. It is hard to envisage such a case but they might arise in circumstances such as occurred in *Harvey v Tracks Travel* [1984] C.L.Y. 1006. In that case, the claimant had suffered such privations already that no matter what alternative she was offered it might have been reasonable for her to say: "Enough is enough. I want to go home now. I no longer have any confidence in your ability to provide me with the rest of the holiday. Nor do I have any confidence that the alternative you are offering me will be any better than what you have already provided—no matter what assurances you give me." A similar situation arose in *Rhodes v Sunspot Tours* [1983] C.L.Y. 984 where the consumer was offered a succession of substandard apartments.

Where the consumer has been transported home the organiser "shall, where appropriate, compensate the consumer". Thus, a consumer would receive compensation on a pro rata basis for the truncation of his holiday and also damages for distress. In most cases, compensation would be appropriate under reg.14; indeed, a consumer who returns home almost as soon as the holiday has begun will expect a full refund of the holiday price plus damages for disappointment, etc, of an equivalent amount. An exception would be where the disruption of the holiday arrangements has been caused by *force majeure*, e.g. the outbreak of war or circumstance falling within reg.15(2)(b)(ii). It will be noted, that unlike reg.13, there is no exception under reg.14 for *force majeure*. Thus, at the very least the tour operator remains under an obligation to transport the consumer home; but alternative arrangements or compensation may not be appropriate. (This does of course raise a further question about the overlap between regs 14 and 15, where *force majeure* is permitted as an exception. On this point see *Charlson v Mark*

Warner, referred to in Ch.9, where it was decided that *force majeure* was a defence under reg.14 also.). In *Lara Tanner v TUI UK Ltd* Unreported October 18, 2005, Central London County Court—see Chapman "All at sea" [2006] I.T.L.J. 7—a cruise was badly affected by bad weather and three out of five scheduled ports of call had to be omitted. The judge held that TUI could not contract out of their obligations under reg.14 by trying to define a limit to the ambit of the services it was providing (i.e. by saying they were not contractual "services" if they could not be provided as a result of *force majeure*); but it was not "appropriate" to order compensation in such circumstances. The claim was dismissed.

What is the position where, for example, at the end of a holiday the return flight cannot operate for *force majeure* reasons, e.g. volcanic ash, snow at Heathrow, etc? All the services contracted for have been provided, except the flight home. The answer is that the tour operator has an irreducible obligation to get the consumer home by the best available means (including, e.g. rail). As we have also seen in Ch.5 there is also a duty to give practical assistance as required by reg.15(7), but this particular provision carries no further obligation, e.g. to pay for additional hotel nights or meals. The harshness of this for consumers is ameliorated because the airline does have such obligations to them—see the section on reg.261/2004 in Ch.13. Whether there is any further obligation under reg.14 is debatable. On the one hand, tour operators can point to para.8 of Sch.1 to the PTR which states that if a brochure is published it must contain certain information, including,

> "The arrangements (*if any*) which apply if consumers are delayed at the outward or homeward points of departure." (Emphasis added)

This seems to suggest that tour operators have a choice as to whether they provide assistance to consumers delayed at an airport and therefore they can choose not to give assistance. The problem with this provision is that it does not appear in the Directive itself and is therefore of doubtful authority. On the other hand, given that the PTR are a consumer protection measure and given the current pro-consumer stance of the ECJ it is certainly arguable that making suitable alternative arrangements "for the continuation of the package" could be interpreted as requiring the tour operator to pay for the extra meals and accommodation. It remains the fact, however, that the consumer has unambiguous statutory rights to such assistance under reg.261/2004 against EU carriers and other non-EU carriers departing from an EU airport. One remedy would be for the tour operator to provide the assistance in the first instance and then to claim an indemnity from the carrier—perhaps by seeking an assignment of their rights from the consumer. However, the reluctance of airlines to accept their responsibilities under reg.261/2004 might make this approach less than practical.

The need for consumers to act reasonably under reg.14 is shown by *Martin v Travel Promotions Ltd (t/a Voyage Jules Verne)* [1999] C.L.Y. 3821. In that case, the delay of an internal flight in India meant that the claimants missed a connecting international flight to Heathrow. The court held that the tour operator was under a duty under reg.14 to make suitable alternative arrangements. Their solution was to book the claimants on a flight the next day. In the meantime, the claimants had gone out and purchased first class airfares on the same flight. It was held that the defendants were in breach of contract but that the loss to the claimants was not caused by that breach but by the claimants' hasty and disproportionate actions in purchasing the first class fares. Another case is *Hibbs v Thomas Cook Group Ltd* [1999] C.L.Y. 3829. After 10 days of a 15 day trip around the Rocky Mountains the tour operator found that a ferry had been suddenly withdrawn from service because of "entirely unforeseen" mechanical problems and the tourists in the group has to be re-routed. They complained about the new itinerary but the court held that the ferry breakdown amounted to *force majeure* which would have excused the tour operator from its obligation to perform the entire contract and they could simply have flown the claimant back to the UK. The decision is suspect for a number of reasons. First, there is the question of whether mechanical problems amount to *force majeure*. Secondly, *force majeure* does not necessarily release the tour operator from its obligation to perform the contract. Thirdly, there is a clear duty to make suitable alternative arrangements unless it is impossible to do so.

An interesting illustration of the problems arose early in 1998 when tour operators took a number of British tourists on a package which included tickets for a test match between the West Indies and England. The match was abandoned on the first day because the pitch had been prepared so poorly. The law has long made clear that a consumer has no remedy where a cricket match is rained off, but here the situation was different—incompetence was involved. For those consumers unable to extend their holiday in order to view the next match, no suitable alternative arrangements could be made and, harsh as this is for the tour operator, it appears that compensation may be appropriate—although this was denied in a case that was decided under the ABTA arbitration scheme, where the terms of the contract showed that the match itself was not a "service" for which the travel company was liable (see Grant "Caribbean Chaos" (1998) 148 N.L.J. 190 and "It's not Cricket" [1998] I.T.L.J. 51).

A Gap in the Regulations?

Regulation 13 provides that where the tour operator cancels the holiday "before the agreed *date* of departure" the consumer is entitled to the remedies in that Regulation, i.e. an offer of alternative packages or a full refund. Regulation 14 on the other hand provides for remedies if a significant proportion of the services contracted for cannot be provided "after departure". It is possible to envisage a consumer caught between these two provisions and being denied a remedy. What if, for example, a consumer turns up at the airport on the agreed date but because of industrial action is prevented from departing. The next day, after clients have been hanging around the airport for 24 hours, the tour operator decides to cancel the package because he believes it will be impossible to perform the contract. An example was provided in 2005 by the ship *Aurora* which was boarded by passengers, but was unable to commence its cruise. This cancellation happened *after* the agreed date of departure but *before* any actual departure. The consumer, therefore, is not entitled to the benefits he would otherwise have under regs 13 or 14. Regulation 15 is of no immediate assistance either because in cases of *force majeure* or events which cannot be forestalled by the operator there is no right to compensation. However, the ABTA Code of Conduct does provide that if a tour operator cancels a tour for reasons of *force majeure* "after the balance due date" then an alternative holiday or a refund must be offered (paras 3A and 3B). If the ABTA Code did not apply then, arguably, the common law rules on frustration could be invoked. For a discussion of these points see Kilbey "Delayed Departure, Cancellation and the Package Travel Regulations" [1998] I.T.L.J. 110 and Saggerson "Delayed Departure and Cancellation. Hope for Consumers this Side of Midnight" [1999] I.T.L.J. 6.

RECTIFICATION

This section applies equally to packages and non-packages.

Rectification is a remedy available to the parties to a contract when they have reached agreement but by mistake they have failed to express the agreement correctly in writing. For instance, a tour operator may have agreed with a client that the price for a particular holiday will be £1,000 but when the confirmation invoice arrives it states £100. In these circumstances, the tour operator can apply to have the document rectified to reflect the true position. The basis of this principle is that if there has been a mistake then the other party cannot take advantage of it if the mistake is obvious. In *Craddock Bros Ltd v Hunt* [1923] 2 Ch. 136 the owner of property agreed to sell it exclusive of its adjoining yard. Unfortunately, the document in which this oral agreement was expressed stated that the yard was included in the sale. In these circumstances, the court ordered that the contract should be rectified to express the true agreement between the parties. It is, of course, necessary to be able to prove that the written document did not represent what the parties had truly agreed which may not always be easy.

The situation described above needs to be distinguished from a slightly different situation, also involving mistake but which proceeds on a different basis. What if a tour operator, by mistake, indicates that the price of a holiday is only £100 when it is really £1,000, e.g. if the viewdata or website information has been corrupted? If this can be interpreted as an offer by the operator to sell at that price and the client accepts this offer does the client have a contract at the lower price? The operator would argue that the holiday at £100 was not on offer at all and, therefore, was not open for acceptance by the client. The distinction between the two situations is that in the former there is a common mistake which has resulted in an acknowledged agreement being incorrectly expressed but in the latter there is a unilateral mistake by the operator resulting in a dispute as to whether a contract exists at all. (See Ch.3 on this point and the case of *Chwee Kin Keong v Digilandmall.com* [2004] 2 S.L.R. 594 (affirmed [2005] SGCA 2) discussed there.)

In *Hartog v Colin & Shields* [1939] 3 All E.R. 566 the two parties had been negotiating for the sale of some hareskins and throughout the negotiations the price had been expressed as so much per piece—which was customary in the trade. The seller then, by mistake, quoted a price per pound which in the circumstances was absurdly low. The buyer purported to accept this offer but the seller refused to sell. When it came to court Singleton L.J. said:

> "The plaintiff could not reasonably have supposed that the offer contained the offerors' real intention."

Note that the test is not whether the seller had made a genuine mistake but whether the buyer should have known this.

The problem facing travel companies is of course that such absurdly low offers are not unknown in the industry and the problem would be to convince a court that the client did not really suspect that the offer was just too good to be true; this is not such a problem in practice because the problem frequently arises in the following form: travel agents surf through Viewdata looking for unlikely low prices and then make bookings for themselves or their friends. In such a case it would be easier for the travel company to demonstrate that the buyer should have known that the offer did not contain their real intention.

TERMINATION FOR BREACH OF CONDITION IN NON-PACKAGE CASES

As we have just seen, package holiday makers have a range of specific remedies under the PTR for serious breaches of contract which are not available to non-package holiday makers. Such consumers would have to look to their common law rights in the event of a serious breach of contract. As we have seen already in Ch.4, their rights depend upon whether the breach amounts to a breach of condition, entitling the victim to repudiate the contract, or a breach of warranty only giving rise to an action for damages.

CHAPTER ELEVEN
Travel Agents

INTRODUCTION

We have already seen in Ch.1 how travel agents fit into the structure of the industry. Because they are by name "agents", it is tempting to think that they can never be liable for anything. However, as we have already seen in Ch.2 and Ch.5, this is very far from the case; furthermore, we will see in Chs 16 and 17 how travel agents can fall foul of the criminal law.

However, the topic of agency has become of much greater relevance over recent years than merely to the high street travel agent. The trends we have frequently commented on in the travel industry have led to increasing numbers of travel providers claiming agency status; indeed, quite a lot of recent case law can be classified as disputes over agency status, despite coming from very varied and unrelated backgrounds, e.g.:

1. The criminal prosecution of Travel Republic by the CAA.

2. The personal injury excursion cases, especially *Moore v Hotelplan* (see Ch.5).

3. The TOMS VAT cases, *International Life Leisure*, and particularly the *Medhotels* case (see below).

For ease of reference, we set out here the various ways in which a travel agent may be liable in civil law for any problems which might arise from a package (or, indeed, more widely for any travel services), with cross references where necessary to places in the book where this topic is more fully explored.

Let us start with a summary:

A travel agent might be sued:

- As a travel agent, having allowed itself to be held out as a tour operator or principal, or with principal undisclosed.

- As, in effect, a tour operator under a "split contract" or "dynamic packaging" arrangement or similar, but only if the combined deal is sold at an inclusive price.

- As a travel agent, for negligence or negligent mis-statement.

- Under reg.4 of the PTR which expressly provides that a travel agent can be liable for supplying misleading descriptive matter concerning a package—see Ch.5.

- As a "flight-plus" arranger under the new ATOL Regulations. See Ch.12 on Insolvency.

320

Held Out as an Organiser

If the consumer is reasonably led to believe that the travel agent is, in fact, the organiser of a package, the agent will have the liability of an organiser for the package. To escape this risk, the travel agent must make it clear to the consumer, before the contract is entered into, that they are "only an agent".

An alternative analysis of this type of situation would be to say that the law holds an agent liable where the existence of a principal is undisclosed. Indeed, the basic law is that a trader *is* a principal unless and until he has successfully established that he is "only" an agent.

In looking at all these situations regarding agents, it should be borne in mind that as well as the traditional travel agent, the term also includes newspapers and magazines offering "reader's offers" type holidays.

Many references have been made in this book to the Court of Appeal decision in *Hone v Going Places* [2001] EWCA Civ 947—see especially Ch.5. In the High Court (Unreported November 16, 2000, QBD) an important issue had been the potential liability of Going Places, a well known travel agent, as organiser. This issue was not the subject of any appeal, and, therefore, the decision of Douglas Brown J. on this issue remains good law.

He set out the facts as follows:

"The defendant is a very well known travel agent with many high street shops and also invites business through advertisements on the ITV Teletext service. This branch of the defendant's enterprise is called 'Late Escapes' and specialises in late or last minute holiday bookings. It is now agreed that the defendant acts as a retail agent for tour operators but there was an issue as to whether the defendant had made it known to, or clear, to the claimant or his brother who actually made the holiday booking, that they were acting as retail agents for a tour operator.

On 22 September 1996 the claimant saw a holiday advertised on a Teletext message for 14 nights at a hotel at Gumbet in Turkey on a date convenient for him and at an acceptable price. Mr Iredale, the Sales and Operations Manager for Late Escapes, thought it unlikely that the advertisements would identify a resort and would have been more likely to name a country or general area as shown in the sample Teletext message put in evidence. I accept the claimant's evidence that the area and the identity of the location was important to him and the probability is he saw that on screen.

The following day his brother, Mr Duncan Hone, booked the holiday by telephone. Mr Hone himself looked at the Teletext message and then telephoned the number shown. He did not remember the details save that the holiday was through Going Places. He knew that his brother, then a serving police officer, was particularly anxious about booking a holiday through a reputable and well known concern. A telephone sales representative now known only as Gillian, dealt with Mr Hone. He asked if the holiday advertised was still available and it was. He gave the Visa number of the joint card held by himself and his wife and booked for four persons, that is, himself and his wife, his brother and his then fiancée. He is certain, and although pressed on this in cross examination, remained certain that there was no mention of Suntours or Sunways during the conversation. Gillian told him that a confirmation of the booking would be sent by post and the tickets were to be collected at the airport.

There is no challenge on behalf of the defendant that Suntours or Sunways had not been mentioned before the holiday was booked and paid for. It is a little surprising that Mr Iredale confirmed the contents of his witness statement namely, that the fact the holiday is provided by a tour operator, in this case Suntours, would not be made known to the customer until after the deal had been concluded and the credit card payment made. Although the precise Teletext message which the claimant and his brother would have seen was not in evidence, specimens showing details of the resorts and prices at page 80 and 81 in the Core bundle are agreed to be representative of the screen text that would have been seen by them. There is a page which contains no details of holidays but which is a general advert for Going Places although they are not mentioned by name. There, in large letters 'GO DIRECT AND SAVE £££££££s' and at the bottom it says in small print 'We act as retail agents for ATOL holders'. ATOL stands for Air Travel Organiser's Licence. Neither the claimant nor his brother has any recollection of seeing that and indeed if they had, there is nothing to connect that advertisement with Going Places. All the sample pages contain the words 'Retail Agt ATOL Hldr' "

We have set out this passage at some length because there is nothing unusual about the transaction. Many holidays or travel arrangements are booked this way. The judge held Going Places liable as the organiser under reg.15, although, as we have seen elsewhere, in the end they escaped liability on the facts of this particular accident. The case emphasises that in the courts, agency is a question of fact, not law. And that is further emphasised by the following.

It is not just in the field of packages that questions of agency are relevant. There is a significant difference between the liability of principals and agents for VAT under the Tour Operators Margin Scheme (TOMS). It is (happily) not the function of this book to delve into tax law, and we deal with this subject therefore purely in the context of agency; but it will suffice to say in simple terms that a principal is liable for VAT on sales (on the margin), but an agent is not. Therefore, there are large tax advantages—as well as much else in terms of bonding, liability, etc—to being an agent.

The case law demonstrates the importance of looking at the reality of the transaction. In *International Life Leisure Ltd v Revenue and Customs Commissioners* Unreported March, 2006, Manchester Tribunal Centre, the appellant ("ILL") contended that they were mere agents when selling hotels and apartments. But it was held that the contract terms meant that the consumer was buying from ILL as principals; the accommodation owner was not identified as the principal on the contract documentation, and there was no obligation on the consumer to pay the owner; further, ILL accepted responsibility for the quality of the accommodation and was entitled to make changes to the accommodation booked. There were other provisions too, e.g. cancellation charges by ILL, and the right for ILL to mark up the owner's price. In the circumstances, although the word agency was used, the plain facts were found to be that ILL acted as principal.

Although there were some common features in the contractual documents, a radically different result was achieved in the case of *Secret Hotels2 Ltd (formerly*

Med Hotels Limited) v Revenue and Customs Commissioners [2011] UKUT 308 (TCC) (usually called the *Med Hotels* case).

The First-tier Tribunal (Tax Chamber) ("FTT") in 2010 had found that in its sale of accommodation, Med Hotels ("Med") was acting as principal; and it relied amongst other things on the following points:

- The contract with the hotel imposed many duties on the hotel, but Med were only required to deal accurately with bookings and relay money.

- Med imposed cancellation charges on consumers where their contracts with hotels had no such requirements.

- If the hotel could not provide the accommodation, Med agreed to try to find alternatives.

- Med provided "reps" in resort to look after consumers, there being no obligation imposed by the hotel to do so. The contract between Med and ground handlers for these services referred to consumers as Med customers.

- Med dealt with customer complaints, sometimes paid compensation and recharged the hotel for it, despite the hotel contract having no provisions which permitted this. Sometimes Med gave out discount vouchers, redeemable against *any* hotel which they featured.

- Above all, Med defined their commission as being the difference between the hotel's price to them and their price to consumers. This was held to be inconsistent with agency, especially as it was said that the hotel would not even know how much Med charged, and therefore how much the hotel should declare (if it were the principal) for VAT purposes.

On appeal there was a very different result indeed. Morgan J. held:

- In construing a contract, whilst one looks at all of its provisions and the relevant background, "The court cannot be influenced, when construing a written agreement, by material which would not have been available to the parties when they entered into that agreement" (para.88).

- This means that in construing the contract with consumers, it is immaterial what the contract with hotels or ground handlers, etc, may say, as consumers would not have seen these.

- The contract with consumers said: "Medhotels.com act as booking agents on behalf of all the hotels, apartments and villas featured on this website ... Once the contract is made, the accommodation provider is responsible to you to provide what you have booked and you are responsible to pay for it". There were other terms reinforcing this.

- "In the absence of an allegation that the written agreements were shams ... I do not see that I am able to disregard the effect of the written agreements" (para.128).

- Whilst there is a difference between supplying as agent, and supplying by resale, none of the surrounding circumstances in this case were inconsistent with agency. The judge analysed previous cases in which the calculation of a commission by way of a mark-up was held to be a permissible feature of agency. Providing reps, and paying compensation, were held to be entirely consistent with Med's "protecting its own economic interest in the arrangements" (para.128).

- The hotels could see what price Med was charging by looking at Med's website, where the prices were available to be viewed by them (para.18).

- The correct approach is ordinary English common law construction; nothing in VAT law is relevant or requires a different result (para.114). There was nothing economically unreal about agency in this case (para.112).

- "Finally, it [The FTT] seems to have regarded anything which could be argued to be inconsistent with an agency relationship as far more weighty than the many matters which pointed unambiguously towards an agency relationship." (para.133)

This decision provides a salutary reminder on how to interpret contracts, and also on agency being a question of fact. But it liberates in a remarkable way agents who wish to offer a kind of "agency-plus" product to consumers, looking after their interests; who wish to charge by mark-up rather than a more traditional approach to commission; and who wish still to be able to avoid VAT, and (as the judge was at pains to say that his approach was a common law one) liability for the product. But, of course, the paperwork and system needs to be carefully prepared, as it seems was successfully done by Med.

It will be interesting to see whether this decision fuels a drive towards agents adopting the flight-plus model, by which they can retain their status as agents whilst offering (as well as say reps/compensation, etc, in the Med manner) security for consumers' money by way of an ATOL. A sort of super-agency-plus, perhaps?

At the time of writing, HMRC's appeal is pending.

Split Contract Arrangements/Dynamic Packaging

We have already seen in Ch.2 how the European Court of Justice, in *Club Tour v Garrido*, held a Portuguese travel agent liable as organiser under the Package Travel Directive. Club Tour had put together a "package" of flights and a Club Med Holiday in Greece at the request of the consumer. The Club Med Resort was overrun by wasps. Club Tour argued that the holiday sold was outside the scope of the Package Travel Directive. But the European Court of Justice held:

"The term 'package' must be interpreted so as to include holidays organised by travel agents at the request of and in accordance with the specifications of the consumer. The term 'pre-arranged combination' must be interpreted so as to include combinations of tourist services put together at the time when the contract is concluded between the travel agents and the consumer".

Despite this ruling, many English travel agents will continue to argue that the different way in which the English travel industry is set up means that this Judgment does not apply to them.

In this context note:

- because of the defect with the holiday, the consumer had refused to pay for it. It was Club Tour who were suing the consumer for non-payment. In those circumstances, it is hardly surprising that the question of whether a contract existed between the parties seems to have been taken as read. After all, in English conceptual terms, Club Tour must have been suing for breach of contract.

- Hence, the judgment is framed in terms of "the contract concluded between the travel agent and the consumer".

An English agent would traditionally say that even if they put together a combination of flights and accommodation for a holiday or a business trip, they clearly do so in each case as agent for the airline/ATOL holder and as agent for the accommodation company. Therefore, there never is any contract between the travel agent and the consumer; and therefore the *Club Tour* case is completely irrelevant.

This analysis, however, needs to be reviewed in the light of the Court of Appeal decision in *ABTA v CAA* [2006] EWHC 13 (Admin) and the *Travel Republic* litigation. These cases have been fully discussed in Ch.2, so for present purposes it is sufficient to say that the above argument by travel agents remains open to them, but only if they are *not* selling a "pre-arranged combination at an inclusive price", as defined by the Court. If, however, they are selling such a combination, they will be liable as the organiser, notwithstanding any claims of agency. This means not only potential liability under reg.15 PTR (see Ch.5), but also subjection to all the other requirements of the PTR, including providing security (see Ch.12), and the criminal provisions described in Chs 16 and 17. So it is perfectly possible to be an agent vis-a-vis the suppliers, but an organiser vis-a-vis the consumer, in the case of a package. In the case of a flight-plus, it should be possible, given appropriate documentary wording, to retain agency status throughout; the only extra obligation is to provide the financial security of an ATOL, and protect against financial failure as we see below in Ch.12.

Other Party to the Contract

The possibility that the agent might be "the other party to the contract", and indeed the definition of "contract", have been fully dealt with in Ch.2. In the High Court decision of *ABTA v CAA* [2006] EWHC 13 (Admin), Goldring J. made it clear that the courts should interpret the words in a pure common law way in terms of the ordinary law of contract and agency (para.161). This would make it easier for an agent to be just that, and not, therefore, the other party to the contract. However, the Court of Appeal left the position less clear (see, for example, the judgment at para.15, where Chadwick L.J. coins the phrase "counter-party" as a substitute for "other party to the contract"). Probably, as no one suggests Goldring J. was wrong on the point, his view prevails. But the issue remains open for argument; after all, if a travel agent sells, as agent for an airline and as agent for a hotel, something to a consumer which he combines at an inclusive price, then he *is* the organiser and liable, regardless of his agency status. But the question then is not "can an agent be the other party to the contract?", because the agent is not an agent (or, to be technically correct, a "retailer") if he is an organiser. (See also *Minhas v Imperial Travel* [2003] I.T.L.J. 69.)

Liability as an Agent

What is an Agent?

Several learned works have been written on this subject, and our readers are referred to them for a detailed examination of the law (e.g. Fridman *The Law of Agency; Bowstead and Reynolds on Agency*) For our purposes, it suffices to say that an agent is someone authorised to do certain acts on behalf of his principal. When he has carried out those acts, the effect will be that his principal is legally bound by the acts. For example, if a tour operator authorises a travel agent to sell certain holidays, then if the agent sells those holidays, the tour operator must fulfil the agreement with the customers. (But see Grant "An Agent but not a Retailer" [1996] T.L.J. 29.)

In return, an agent in the commercial world will be entitled to be paid, usually by way of commission, by his principal.

Even if the agent oversteps his authority, but this was not obvious to a third party, the principal will still be bound. For example, an airline authorises a travel agent to sell flight tickets. After a while the airline tells the agent that the flight is fully booked, but the agent carries on selling the tickets. The agent is in possession of tickets and appears to a validly appointed agent for the airline. The airline will be bound to honour the contract with the innocent member of the public, by performing it or paying compensation for breach of it.

Whose Agent is a Travel Agent? Can an Agent be Agent for the Consumer?

It is one of the most extraordinary features of holiday law that there is no authoritative answer to this question. Is the travel agent the customer's agent or the tour operator's agent? If the travel agent is the customer's agent, he will owe duties to the customer and if he fails in those duties, the customer will be able to sue him. If the travel agent is agent of the tour operator, then he does not owe any duty to the customer (certainly not in contract, but we will look at the position in negligence later)—and the customer will have to sue the tour operator, and not the travel agent, if things go wrong.

However, piecing together all the evidence, we now feel confident enough to offer this rule of thumb: the travel agent is agent for the consumer up until the time that a contract is made between the consumer and the tour operator; and from that time on the agent is agent for the tour operator. We emphasise that this is a rule of thumb; the courts will look at each situation and make their own judgment based on all the circumstances.

Indeed, the opposite result happened in the case of *Holland v First Choice* Unreported October 8, 2003, Reigate County Court. The travel agent was Travelchoice, part of the same group of companies as First Choice, and had promised far more about the honeymoon than First Choice ever did, in inducing the claimants to contract. After hearing that the booking clerk wore a First Choice livery, and had a quota of First Choice holidays to sell, the judge held that the agent was agent for the tour operator at the booking stage and therefore First Choice was liable for the over-lavish promises made. This case has clear implications for the so-called "vertically integrated" groups of travel companies.

So what is the evidence for our rule of thumb?

The Nature of the Transaction

Useful guidance can be obtained from the world of insurance. It is settled law that an insurance agent, who is hired to recommend one particular company, is agent for the company; whilst an insurance broker is for most purposes the agent of the proposer (see *Chitty on Contracts*).

Unlike an insurance agent, but more akin to a broker, a travel agent will stock the brochures of a large number of different tour operators. How can it then be said that he is agent for any one of them? His first duty, upon the customer entering the shop, may be to guide the customer towards some brochures and positively to discourage the customer from other brochures. The next customer who walks in might be given a totally opposite recommendation. The answer appears to be that in this stage of the transaction, the agent is certainly not the agent of the tour operator; although the *Holland* case above shows that where the Travel Agent is closely tied to a sister company tour operator and its products, that may produce a different result.

Some guidance on this is given in the Court of Appeal decision of *Kemp v Intasun Holidays* [1987] 2 F.T.L.R. 234. In that case, Mrs Kemp went into her local Thomas Cook to book a holiday. Before she had homed in on Intasun as the holiday she would definitely book, she informed the Thomas Cook staff that her husband was ill with asthma. Subsequently, she booked the Intasun holiday. If Thomas Cook were acting as agents for Intasun, then the knowledge they had about Mr Kemp's medical condition would, in law, be treated as knowledge that Intasun had. Intasun would then be aware that they were carrying a passenger with a health problem and could be liable for additional compensation if, as happened, Mr Kemp was put in a dusty bedroom. Kerr L.J. put it this way:

"Special circumstances must be brought home to a tour operator before damages in respect of injury to health are also to be recoverable. The only possible basis for the latter conclusion is the casual conversation which Mrs Kemp had with one or more of the ladies at Thomas Cook before this holiday was booked. In my view there can be no doubt at all, with all due respect to the Judge, that he was in error in attributing any contractual consequences, at any rate so far as Intasun are concerned, to that conversation. One can put the matter in many different ways, but there is none whereby this casual conversation can possibly have any contractual consequences for these defendants.

At the time of that conversation, Thomas Cook *were not the agents of the defendants,* let alone for the purpose of receiving or passing on the contents of the conversation. Whether they became their agent at a later stage and, if so, for what purpose, it is unnecessary to decide". (Emphasis added)

Mr Kemp's Barrister had pointed out that the Thomas Cook witness had said at court that while she could not remember the conversation, if it had occurred she would have made a note of it. Kerr L.J. went on:

"I cannot see that he derives any benefit from that. ... Either, as the Judge appears to have thought, the conversation was too casual to make any impact on Miss Hodge's mind, or it may be—though I express no view about it—that some note should have been made of it by her. But in any event that would have no bearing on any liability of Intasun".

The Judge in the original court in Worcester had said that Thomas Cook had been given the information about Mr Kemp's health, and he had held that this knowledge was attributable to Intasun. He had said:

"The fact that it is not given for practical purposes, or to make special arrangements, is neither here nor there. If I go into a travel agent in a wheelchair, I am entitled to rely on that agent's knowledge".

Kerr L.J. in the Court of Appeal commented on this view saying:

"Without expressing any view about a point which was not argued, it may be that a client going into a travel agent's in a wheelchair is for certain purposes entitled to rely on that agent's knowledge of his condition. But that would be a matter between the travel agent and the customer, and Thomas Cook are not parties to this action".

The other Judge in the Court of Appeal, Parker L.J., commented, somewhat testily, about this argument:

"It may be that it is part of what appears to occur in this industry—that the customer finds that everybody he turns to says 'It's not my fault—it's somebody else's' ".

A later case goes right to the point. *Brewer v Best Travel Ltd* [1993] C.L.Y. 76 is a decision of Swansea County Court and therefore of persuasive and not binding authority. On the other hand, the decision was by the Circuit Judge on an appeal on a point of law from the District Judge, with a Reserved Judgment, so that it can be said that the matter was very carefully considered.

Mr Brewer had told the Court that he wanted to stay on holiday in some particular apartments. It was common ground that what the travel agents actually booked, for him, with Best Travel Limited, was a "late availability" type of package where the accommodation is allocated on arrival in resort by the tour operator. Needless to say, Mr Brewer did not get his chosen apartment. He sued the tour operator, Best Travel. The travel agents gave evidence that they had booked what Mr Brewer had requested, but the District Judge ruled that this was not correct, and Mr Brewer had made his wishes quite clear. He held Best Travel Limited liable for not providing the correct accommodation. Best Travel appealed on the ground that the travel agents were acting as agents for the customer at the time the booking (and the mistake) were made and that, therefore, they as the tour operator were not to blame and their appeal succeeded. Best Travel had not broken their agreement, because there never had been a proper agreement between them and Mr Brewer, thanks to the failure of Mr Brewer's travel agent.

Similarly, in *Williams v Cosmos* Unreported 1995, Newport County Court, before booking a holiday the claimant told his travel agent that he was a keen marksman and was taking two shotguns with him on holiday. The tour operator was never told this, nor was the sub-contracted airline, and at check-in the claimant was told the guns could not be carried. He refused to travel, and sued Cosmos for his lost holiday. It was held that the travel agent was his agent and any failure to take necessary steps to ensure carriage of the guns was their responsibility, not that of Cosmos. (It was, by the way, also held that the airline was entitled to refuse to carry the guns and ammunition under the Air Navigation Order 1985 and Cosmos were not in breach of contract by reason of this refusal.)

But does this mean that the consumer can sue the travel agent for breach of contract?

Payment

For there to be a contract to be breached, there must be some consideration passing from the consumer to the travel agent. Well, who does pay the travel agent? The most obvious answer is the tour operator, who will pay the agent a fixed commission. But some customers, who wish to hold the travel agent liable, would argue differently. They would say that in effect they pay the travel agent, because they hand their money to the travel agent who keeps some of it and passes the balance on to the tour operator. But surely the truth is that the customer pays the price demanded by the tour operator, and it is the tour operator who arranges for some of that price to be paid/retained by the travel agent by way of commission. If that is right, no consideration passes from the consumer and there is no contract between consumer and travel agent—and, logically, no possible breach of contract. The consumer will have to rely on his rights in the law of negligence, which we will look at shortly. (But see also the analysis by Wohlmuth referred to below.)

An agent, by definition, cannot make a secret profit at the expense of his principal. It is clear that an agent who feels free to set his own price, and does not merely rely upon commission, is generally not acting as an agent at all, but is acting as a principal in his own right—*Re Neville* (1871) L.R. 6 Ch. App. 397. (But note how this case was distinguished in the *Med Hotels* case, above). It is common to find in practice that, if an agent has hiked up the price himself, he does not send to the customer a copy of the tour operator's confirmation invoice in order to hide his own covert charges. This is further evidence that they are not acting as an agent, particularly as the ABTA Code of Conduct requires that such documentation be sent on (and where the ATOL Regulations apply, they and the Code require that such document is sent by the next working day after receipt. Similar requirements exist for flight-plus—see Ch.12).

It is interesting to note that airlines have been cutting the amount of commission received by travel agents with sporadic similar moves by tour operators and other principals. There is an increasing trend among travel agents to charge their customers a service charge. Such a move certainly clarifies the legal relationships, as plainly then there would be a contract between the customer and travel agent, at least leading up to the completion of a booking between the customer and the tour operator.

Can One be Agent for the Consumer Throughout a Transaction?

The increasing trend towards (and expense of) regulation, and in particular the advent of flight-plus, has led to the assumption that there is only one escape route from all this—to be agent for the consumer throughout. But is it as simple as the agent merely asserting that status on the paperwork? Regrettably or not, we believe that it is not that simple. As we have seen, agency is a question of fact, not law, and despite the apparent liberalisation of what agency can mean, and include, in the *Med Hotels* case, there are still some basic pitfalls to avoid.

In June 2011 ABTA published a Guidance Note on "Agent for the Consumer", and included the following points, addressed to its members:

1. You are unlikely to be agent for the consumer if you set the terms of the purchase by the consumer of the travel services ... your role is to find travel services for the consumer on terms that suit the consumer, not to decide the price or terms.

2. Acting with reasonable care and skill for the consumer means making the consumer aware of all suitable choices, including those at lowest cost, and not operating from just preferred travel suppliers (unless agreed by the consumer).

3. Any commission earned from the supplier must be disclosed. [This is the "no secret profit" point—see above.]

4. Suppliers need to be made aware of your "agent for the consumer" status.

5. You should have a written agency agreement with the consumer.

6. Monies collected from the consumer are held on his behalf, so in effect the consumer has not paid for the travel services until you pass the money on. The consumer should be made aware of this.

The Department for Transport, in its consultation on flight-plus, suggested that the offence of a misleading omission, under the Consumer Protection etc Regulations 2008 (see Ch.17) could be invoked if consumers are not made fully aware of the relationships and their implications for the consumer, where an agent claims "agent for the consumer" status and the Civil Aviation Bill 2012 contains powers to bring "agent for the consumer" arrangements within the ATOL scheme.

It is interesting to speculate what difference, if any, the Med Hotels case would make to the above ABTA Guidance, which immediately preceded it. It may be the case that there is enough material here to allow a judge to make findings in whichever direction he prefers! But on a strict interpretation of the law, we believe the ABTA Guidance is to be commended and in 2012 the Government included the power to outlaw sales of flights as "agent for the consumer" in its Civil Aviation Bill.

When, If At All, Does the Agency Switch?

As we have seen, the various contractual documents may be clear on this. But if not, and in any event, the standard ATOL terms provide some assistance on this issue. The significance of ATOLs is explained in Chs 1 and 12. Where holiday or travel arrangements are protected by an ATOL, then the contract between consumer and tour operator is subject to the standard ATOL terms, which have legal force through a statutory instrument.

Standard Term 1.11 reads:

"The licence holder shall not enter into a licensable transaction through an agent unless the licence holder has made it clear in writing to the agent and to the end user through their booking terms and conditions that any money paid by the end user to the agent under or in contemplation of the contract is held by the agent on behalf of the licence holder until the date on which the agent pays the money to the licence holder".

This term was last revised in 2008, but the major revision had taken place in 1997, prior to which such money (commonly called "pipeline monies") was held as agent for the license holder once a confirmation of the booking was issued, but the parties were free to contract as to the position before the confirmation. So far as the holding of money is concerned, the position is now clear; but during the consultation period which led to the revised rule, all parties were at pains to express that the position of the travel agent in all regards except as the holding of money was to be unaffected by the changed rule (for "flight-plus" see Ch.12). See Ch.12 which explains that from April 2012 "pipeline monies" will be held on trust for the Air Travel Trustees.

When Can an Agent be Sued?

By the Consumer

We have seen that the courts will be reluctant to construe a contract between the consumer and the travel agent where his position as agent for the supplier is clear. Despite this, the writers have seen innumerable examples whereby the consumer sues the travel agent, usually as co-defendant with the tour operator. The writers have never known any such claim to succeed (but see *Blumer v Gold Medal Travel Group Plc* [2008] C.L.Y. 650, mentioned in Ch.3, on a different point where the supplier was an insolvent airline). An exhaustive test took place in the unreported case of *Edwards v Intasun and Lunn Poly* Unreported 1991, Guildford County Court. In a trial that lasted no less than four days, the claimants tried to claim that Lunn Poly were in breach of contract for the alleged shortcomings of Intasun Holidays. However, by the fourth day, Counsel for the claimants had to concede, under pressure from the Judge, that in fact there was no contract at all between the customers and Lunn Poly.

However, in one very, important, though limited, way, the Package Travel Regulations do impose civil liability on the retailer. This is under reg.4, where the consumer has suffered loss as a result of relying on any misleading descriptive matter concerning the package supplied by the retailer. This has been dealt with in detail in Ch.5. The result is that a retailer will be liable to the consumer if, for example, the swimming pool promised in the tour operator's brochure was not actually there; but will not be liable if the pool did exist, but was (say) unusable because the filter pump had broken. The loss of enjoyment suffered by the holidaymaker will, however, be the same in both cases!

This right of action against retailers is of particular importance to consumers in two circumstances:

- Where the tour operator has become insolvent shortly after the holiday—none of the bonding schemes in operation currently offer any security for claims for compensation made after a holiday has taken place. This will change, however, in respect only of the supplier's insolvency, under the new flight-plus arrangements.

- Where the tour operator takes a hard line in opposing the claim, the retailer may, for various commercial reasons, prove to be more of a "soft touch".

By the Supplier

High & Wild v Travel Counsellors Plc Unreported June 2, 2008, Bolton County Court, is an interesting case. A Mr Smith and his fiancée had approached the defendant agents to source a honeymoon in Africa. Part of the trip included days spent at the Ngorongoro Crater in Tanzania. The defendant put the business the way of the claimant, who sent out a confirmation that everything was booked together with an invoice; Travel Counsellors therefore collected the money from Mr Smith, and the arrangement was to hold it in a Trust Account until the trip was completed.

Then it emerged that the holiday should not have been confirmed, because the hotel at the crater was never booked. It was indeed full. When the claimant eventually disclosed that, Mr Smith was very angry and cancelled; High & Wild then said that they could book the hotel, apparently by "bumping" other booked customers, but this left Mr Smith so unimpressed and without faith in the arrangements that he refused to withdraw his cancellation. So Travel Counsellors refunded the money they held for him.

The claimant argued that the commercial agreement between the parties meant that the defendant were agents who must follow the instructions of their principal, High & Wild, and held the money as agent for them. They should not have returned the money to Mr Smith.

But the judge held that the situation was not as simple as that. Normally, an agent could not be liable for a default by the principal; but reg.4 of the PTR's (which applied because the confirmation of the crater hotel was "misleading descriptive matter"—see Ch.5) left the agent potentially liable as well as the principal; and they might also be liable as "the other party to the contract", because of its wide definition (see Ch.2) under reg.15. In any event the Smiths had been entitled to a refund from High & Wild under regs 12 and 13 (a significant pre-departure change), and so even if the defendant were in breach of their duty as agent, it had caused no loss as High & Wild would have had to return the money to the customers anyway.

To an extent there is a pre-echo here of the *Med Hotels* decision and a recognition of the fact that an agent has both his own economic interests in the transaction and those of its customers to look after.

AN ALTERNATIVE VIEW

As can be seen from all the above, the precise legal position and responsibilities of a travel agent have been surprisingly resistant to analysis. Could this be because the wrong questions are being asked? Is the whole question "whose agent is the travel agent?" a red herring? Certainly there has been thinking in America to that effect. Paul Wohlmuth in his article "The Liability of Travel Agents: a study in the selection of appropriate legal principles" [1966] Temple Law Quarterly, 29 has argued that in reality there is a contract between consumer and travel agent. He concludes:

"the question of travel agents' liability is very much an open one. The few available decisions on the subject are not very informative, [my approach] has led to the following conclusions:—

(1) The travel agent resembles more closely an independent middleman than an agent.
(2) The interaction between the travel agent, client and hotel or carrier is best viewed as an interweaving of contractual relations.
(3) Even if the travel agent could be considered an agent, it merely clouds the issue to treat him as such for the purpose of liability. The issue is: should the travel agent be held liable to the client under various circumstances? This question, aside from the problem of negligence, can best be answered by treating the travel agent as one who contracts with his client and then, by determining what the travel agent expressly impliedly and as a matter of legal imposition, undertakes to do in his relations with the client".

Wohlmuth identifies three contracts in the client/tour operator/travel agent relationship. First, a contract between client and tour operator for the provision of the holiday. Secondly, a contract between tour operator and travel agent whereby the tour operator agrees to pay the travel agent commission for each of the tour operator's holidays the travel agent sells. Thirdly, a contract between client and travel agent whereby the travel agent agrees to exercise reasonable care and skill on the client's behalf to secure the reservations and handle the documentation, etc, and in return the client agrees to abide by his contract with the tour operator—thus permitting the agent to earn his commission.

There is no doubt that the American courts have been prepared to adopt this analysis—see the case of *Pellegrini v Landmark Travel* reported in [1998] I.T.L.J. 22. However, it must be said that there is no English case which supports this approach. The English courts continue to analyse the position of the travel agent by reference to the law of agency, or by reference to negligence, the subject to which we now turn.

LIABILITY IN NEGLIGENCE

The law of negligence can offer a more helpful route to enforcing rights against the travel agent. It is worth remembering here that travel agents conduct a much wider range of business than just package holidays including flights; rail tickets, hotels, business travel, etc. Many problems arise in those areas also (e.g. mistakes in ticketing). Where the agent charges a booking fee for his services, he can be sued in breach of contract if he makes such a mistake—breach of an implied term for reasonable care and skill. But if no fee is charged (i.e. there is no consideration), recourse must be had to a claim in negligence.

Negligence—the Duty of Care

The concept that negligence which causes damage should result in a right of legal action is surprisingly young in English law—indeed it does not pre-date the package holiday by so many years. It was properly established in the famous "Snail in the Ginger Beer Bottle" case of *Donoghue v Stevenson* [1932] A.C. 562. One of the best known passages from an English judgment is the following from Lord Atkin:

> "The rule that you are to love your neighbour becomes in law you must not injure your neighbour; and the lawyers question, who is my neighbour? receives a restricted reply. You must take reasonable care to avoid acts or omissions which you can reasonably foresee would be likely to injure your neighbour. Who, then, in law is my neighbour? The answer seems to be—the persons who are so closely and directly affected by my act that I ought reasonably to have them in my contemplation as being so affected when I am directing my mind to act or omissions which are causing question".

This case established the test to discover whether a duty of care exists in law which, if broken, gives rise to a claim for compensation. However, a normal travel agent's business would still not have been subject to legal action. Why not? Because the type of damage which was recoverable was physical, e.g. damage to property or injury to a person. Mere loss of money, economic loss, was not recoverable in 1932 for negligence. However, substantial inroads have been made into that proposition since the case of *Hedley Byrne & Co Ltd v Heller & Partners Ltd* [1964] A.C. 465. The defendants were bankers who negligently gave a good reference about a worthless company, one of their customers. The claimants lost a lot of money by relying on the reference and sued the defendant Bank. In the House of Lords, Lord Morris said:

> "It should now be regarded as settled law that if someone possessed of a special skill undertakes, quite irrespective of the contract, to apply that skill for the assistance of another person who relies upon such skill, a duty of care will

arise. The fact that the service is to be given by the means of or by the instrumentality of words can make no difference. Furthermore if in a sphere in which a person is so placed that others could reasonably rely upon his Judgment or skill or upon his ability to make careful enquiry, the person takes it upon himself to give information or advice to, or allows his information or advice to be passed on to another person who, as he knows or should know, will place reliance upon it, then a duty of care will arise".

Figuratively, Lord Morris could almost have had travel agents and their customers in mind. If, therefore, a travel agent's advice is careless and the person who relies on it suffers an economic loss, then he will be liable in negligence.

Furthermore, as other cases show, all the staff of a travel agency will be expected to show the requisite skill—so young trainees had better be kept under close supervision! (See the discussion of *Parker v TUI* in Ch.5 for other potential travel law uses of a claim in negligence.)

COMMON PROBLEMS IN PRACTICE

Passports and Visas

Where package travel is involved, we have already seen in Ch.5 that the Package Travel Regulations put specific legal obligations on "The Other Party to the Contract", normally the organiser. In practice, many tour operators expect travel agents to give this advice, and of course the duty falls on travel agents when they are selling non-packages, e.g. flight tickets. Also, as we have seen, the legal requirement only applies to information required for British Citizens. What if a travel agent sells a package to a country, for which a Visa is not required by British nationals—but fails to establish that one of the party is, for example, an Irish Citizen who may still need a Visa? There could well be liability here. See the section on reg.7 in Ch.16 in the light of amendments to that Regulation. (See also *Bagley v Intourist Moscow* [1984] C.L.Y. 1024.) But note that the 2009 ABTA Code obliges both principals and agents to give this information if it is reasonably practical to obtain. The ABTA requirement applies to all travel arrangements, and not just packages; so a flight-plus would be covered too.

Health Requirements

The same comments apply here. An interesting point arises in this way: the 1992 Regulations require information to be given accurately in the brochure and in the contract—but what if things change after the contract is made—e.g. an outbreak of illness—in the resort. The tour operator may have some liability (see *Davey v Cosmos* [1989] C.L.Y. 2561), but does the travel agent have liability too? The answer is "probably not" as this extends too far the concept of "careless misstatement" in the *Hedley Byrne* case. In *Spencer v Lotus* Unreported 2000, Manchester County Court, a travel agent stated that he did not know whether vaccinations were recommended for the Dominican Republic. In fact they were. A Circuit Judge on appeal held Lotus not liable where the customer took a risk and booked the holiday anyway. The answer "I do not know" cannot ground an action for negligent misstatement.

Again, note that the 2009 ABTA Code requires both principals and agents to give information on compulsory health requirements to consumers, and, as above, the requirement extends beyond packages.

Outbreaks of Violence

If a holiday area is affected by violence, whether political or criminal, whether aimed at tourists or not, does the travel agent have a duty to advise? The current stand taken by the travel industry is that the British Foreign Office is in the best position to make judgments about these matters, and that a small high street travel agency cannot be expected to have greater knowledge and insight into the situation. Therefore, advice is given purely on the basis of current Foreign Office warnings. See also in this context: Dickerson "The Liability of Tour Operators and Suppliers for Physical Injuries sustained by Travellers on Tour" [1995] T.L.J. 44.

The 2009 ABTA Code requires principals and agents to advise consumers of the availability of Foreign Office advice, and of the existence of the website *www.fco.gov.uk/knowbeforeyougo*.

Mistakes on Ticketing or Timing

Clearly the travel agent can be liable for writing the wrong times in airline tickets, or for giving customers wrong timings for flight departures (especially where, in a late booking, tickets are to be collected on departure at the airport).

Other Regular Problems

Overselling holidays by making promises beyond what the tour operator has promised, advising that a holiday is suitable for the disabled where it is not, making mistakes in the booking by pressing the wrong button, selling inadequate holiday insurance, failing to advise as to the best prices available for flight seats; in all these cases, there is potential liability for the travel agent.

It sometimes happens that travel agents fail to pass on to their customers a change to holiday arrangements notified to the travel agent by the tour operator. As we have seen, however, by this time the travel agent will almost certainly have become the agent of the tour operator, and therefore it will be possible for the customer to sue the tour operator, who may, however, join in the travel agent as a third party. This leads us conveniently on to the relationship between travel agent and tour operator.

TRAVEL AGENT AND TOUR OPERATOR

As travel agents and tour operators are both commercial entities, the law is much less ready to jump in with implied terms to assist one or the other. The relationship between the two is therefore generally governed in two ways: by a written agency agreement, or by ABTA's Code of Conduct (but see Ch.1 and the The Foreign Package Holidays (Tour Operators and Travel Agents) Orders 2000 (SI 2000/2110), which requires clear disclosure of links between "linked" tour operators and travel agents where either have over five per cent of their respective markets in packages; and 2001 (SI 2001/2581), which outlaws "most favoured customer" clauses in agency agreements, see below). Despite the long ago abolition of the rule known as "stabiliser" by ABTA (which used to have the effect of creating what was largely a closed shop in the travel industry), it remains the case (at least at the time of writing—there are constant rumours of defections from ABTA membership!) that most high street travel agencies are ABTA Members and therefore bound by its Code. Furthermore, the Code is often expressly incorporated into agency agreements. In the past, there were separate Travel Agents and Tour Operators Codes of Conduct. However, recognising the blurred distinction between these in the modern marketplace, ABTA now issue one Code imposing largely identical duties on all members. The Code as issued in January 2009 is set out in Appendix 3 to this book.

Of course, the Code will not apply to non-members, which include a number of online entities such as Expedia, and several bedbanks.

Agency Agreements

Agency agreements between travel agent and tour operator have become increasingly complicated. As it is a commercial agreement between commercial entities, courts generally will enforce the agreement without reference to the Unfair Contract Terms Act. In 1997 the Office of Fair Trading investigated the relationships between tour operators and travel agents in a market where many of the leading travel agencies are owned by, or under common ownership with, leading tour operators, causing possible market distortion (so called "vertical integration" which also involves airlines). The potential for market abuse can clearly be seen and was declared to be a "complex monopoly" by the OFT (see Ch.1). The result was the Foreign Package Holidays (Tour Operators and Travel Agents) Orders 2000 and 2001 which outlawed (a) the tying of travel insurance policy sales to the purchase of discounted holidays and (b) "most favoured customer" clauses whereby a tour operator won't sell through or discriminates against an agent who does not match for his holidays any offers he makes for other tour operator holidays. Greater transparency in the common ownership of the constituent parts of vertically integrated groups was also required; hence we now have, e.g. "World of TUI" common branding for tour operator, travel agent and airline, etc.

In previous editions we have set out common terms to be found in agency agreements such as:

- for the agent to promote and sell the tour operator's products and display its brochures prominently;

- for the agent to ensure that the tour operator's booking conditions are brought to the attention of the consumer;

- for the agent to obtain the deposit and send on the tour operator's confirmation and invoice, and to recover the balance due from the customer and collect any cancellation or amendment charges;

- for the operator to pay the agent's commission;

- for both parties to comply with the Rules and Code of Conduct of ABTA;

- for the agent to notify all customers who have booked or enquire about booking in respect of any corrections or alterations made by the tour operator to brochures or literature. Some agreements recite that the agent is responsible for giving health, passport and visa requirements to consumers;

- for the agent not to oversell the holiday by making representations about it beyond those appearing in the tour operator's brochure or other literature;

- for either party to indemnify the other where appropriate. This usually states that the travel agent indemnifies the tour operator in respect of any claims which the tour operator faces as a result of the breach of the agreement by a travel agent, as we have discussed; and the tour operator indemnifies the travel agent vice versa, this latter provision being particularly important in view of reg.4;

- for the operator to comply with certain quality standards.

The fact is, however, that whilst these terms are still to be found in more traditional relationships, many agency agreements these days, reflecting that booking is likely to be online, are more about access to websites and content, and read more like technology agreements than traditional travel industry documents. And, indeed, it is often said that the modern online agent has more in common with a search engine than with a travel agent. But agency agreements are to be compulsory in connection with all flight sales under the ATOL Regulations 2012 (see Ch.12), and on the back of that, ABTA amended their Code of Conduct in February 2012 to make it compulsory for all members that sell through agents to have a written agency agreement in place, for *all* types of sales.

Incorporation of terms into consumer contracts is rarely an issue with online booking (as the consumer is required to "tick" the relevant box). And "errata" now tend to be notified by electronic means. Nonetheless, indemnities, and terms as to quality assurance, are still commonly to be found nestling among the terms about distribution channels, intellectual property rights and the like.

Chapter Twelve
Insolvency and Security

Introduction

For the average consumer, there are not many transactions in a lifetime for which he is required to hand over large sums of money so far in advance of receiving the goods or services as he does with a holiday. The dangers are obvious and the holiday industry, which enjoys a high media profile, has often found itself the centre of attention when a holiday company collapses. The media coverage generally focuses upon:

- The large numbers of consumers who have not yet taken their holidays but have paid over their hard-earned savings to the now insolvent company.

- Other consumers who are stranded overseas at the time of the insolvency, with unpaid hotels threatening to eject them onto the street, and airlines threatening not to carry them home.

Until recently, and within limits, the industry has responded very well to this challenge. Driven partly by the self-interest of wishing to restore public faith in the industry, and partly by a genuine concern for consumers, a mixture of statutory and voluntary schemes to protect holidaymakers against a tour operator's insolvency has grown up during the last three decades, and these remain important today, within the more comprehensive framework established by the Package Travel Regulations 1992.

The trouble with this, as the name suggests, is that it only applies to packages. As has been explored elsewhere in this book, notably in Chs 1 and 2, the market has dramatically changed as a result of the likes of low-cost airlines, internet-based accommodation-only suppliers, etc. Following the clarification given as to what is a "package" by the case of *ABTA v CAA* [2006] EWHC 13 (Admin), and the Travel Republic litigation (see Ch.2), there remains a vast array of arrangements which do not come within the definition of package, in respect of which any prepayment made by a customer will be lost in the event of insolvency; and there will be no repatriation for those stranded overseas at the time, either (except at doubtless great expense by other companies sensing a chance for a quick profit). Once again, the rift between packages and non-packages is a true chasm, in terms of the different protection offered to consumers. Hence, the development of the "flight-plus" concept, of which more below.

One ray of hope which has long existed is provided by s.75 Consumer Credit Act 1974, which makes a credit card company (whose card has been used to make the relevant payment) jointly liable with the trader in such circumstances. In a helpful development, the Court of Appeal held in *Office of Fair Trading v Lloyds TSB Bank Plc* [2006] EWCA Civ 268, that the section also covered transactions entered into overseas, as long as the consumer can demonstrate that he has a claim against the trader.

Despite this welcome clarification, the protection given by s.75 is bound to be patchy and often rather random, depending on when a card was used as the method of payment. There is a limited amount of ATOL protection for "flight-only"—see below.

In the case of packages however, the picture is much more friendly to consumers. The statutory scheme is the ATOL scheme operated by the Civil Aviation Authority, which covers (in effect) any package holiday or package arrangements which includes a flight as one of its elements. A package covered by the scheme is known as a "Licensable Activity". (Certain "flight-only" arrangements are also covered by the scheme—namely tickets for charter flights; and for scheduled flights—not bought direct from the carrier—where a confirmed ticket is not given to the consumer immediately on booking.)

The voluntary schemes have arisen piecemeal for members of certain organisations. We have already discussed the structure of the industry in Ch.1, and the various bodies in it. The best known scheme is operated by ABTA for its members, and it is the proud boast of ABTA that no customer who has booked with an ABTA operator has ever lost their money or been stranded. However, the dilution, however slight, of the ABTA protection in 2006 may result in this boast becoming sadly out of date. The Federation of Tour Operators runs a similar scheme for its large tour operator members, and AITO also runs a scheme for its generally smaller independent operators. Lesser known but important schemes were also set up for members of the Passenger Shipping Association (PSA), and the Confederation of Passenger Transport Bonded Coach Holiday Scheme (BCH).

All the above schemes impose strict quality controls. All require that its members be, or be run by, fit persons, persons who have not had a history of company failures, personal insolvencies or dishonest behaviour. A fairly rigorous examination of the Company accounts is also carried out. The CAA imposes its "ATOL Standard Terms" on ATOL Holders (including personal guarantees by directors in many cases), whilst ABTA imposes its strict Codes of Conduct.

The advantage of these schemes is that they have worked extremely well. Nonetheless, the way the Regulations are drafted and enforced leaves plenty of opportunity for abuse. They are enforced by overworked and underfunded Trading Standards Departments who have little training or experience to help them understand what is and what is not adequate protection—e.g. in spotting "creative accountancy" in company accounts. Of course, where a breach of ATOL Regulations is involved, the CAA also have an enforcement role.

FLIGHT-PLUS

Into the yawning gap between well-protected packages and the increasing number of unprotected arrangements there has now been inserted the new concept of flight-plus, introduced by the Civil Aviation (Air Travel Organisers Licensing) Regulations 2012, and due to come into force on April 30, 2012. Note that the flight-plus concept is all about protecting consumers in the event of insolvency, it is not about liability for poor quality or dangerous holidays or the like; hence, we deal with it substantively in this chapter.

It should be added that, as well as improving consumer protection, flight-plus is also driven by the need to reduce the deficit in the Air Travel Trust Fund. One new provision which will further assist that, and reduce disputes, in the event of failures is that pipeline monies will be held for the benefit of the ATT.

By reg.22, a flight-plus exists when:

"(a) Flight accommodation is made available which includes a minimum—
   i. A flight out of the United Kingdom; or
   ii. A flight into the United Kingdom where the consumer has commenced the journey in the United Kingdom and departed the United kingdom using another means of transport; and
(b) living accommodation outside the United Kingdom or self-drive car hire outside the United Kingdom or both is supplied by any person under or in connection with the contract for such flight accommodation; and
(c) the arrangement covers a period of more than 24 hours or includes overnight accommodation."

It is further provided that:

- If a flight-plus exists, then any other tourist service (not ancillary to living accommodation or car hire) and accounting for a significant proportion of the flight-plus is also included in the flight-plus scheme.

- A package is not a flight-plus.

- A flight which begins and ends in the UK is not part of any flight-plus.

- Note that the Regulation also goes on to explain that in determining whether a flight-plus exists, there must be disregarded any living accommodation, self-drive car hire or other tourist service which is requested to be booked by the consumer other than on the same day as the consumer requests to book the flight accommodation or on the previous day or the next day.

Points to Note

- Unlike packages, a flight-plus cannot apply to a holiday in the UK.

- Also unlike packages, business travel is excluded; to be more precise, sales of flight-plus and flight-only to limited companies and limited liability partnerships are excluded, but not sales to individuals who are travelling for business purposes.

- However, like packages, the arrangement must last 24 hours or include overnight accommodation, so, for example, a day trip to see Father Christmas in Lapland is neither a package nor a flight-plus.

- If, for example, there was an arrangement which meant flying from Leeds to Gatwick, and then a flight overseas plus accommodation or car hire, making a flight-plus, then the flight-plus would be protected but the domestic flight would not benefit from that protection.

- Once a flight-plus exists, then if the trader also sells other services (e.g. a transfer, or ski pack, or whatever), they will be protected as part of the flight-plus too.

- It has also been confirmed that all this means that if a principal sells a flight-plus (paying the appropriate protection levy on it), and then a travel agent adds a car hire (for example), the agent will sell a new flight-plus and have to pay another levy, so that the basic parts of the flight-plus are protected twice, in effect. (Similarly, where an agent adds a hire car to an existing (flight-inclusive) package, he creates a flight-plus on top of the package. But if the package provider fails, the ATT will reimburse to the flight-plus arranger the full cost of the package.)

- Unlike the provisions for packages about "pre-arranged combinations" and "inclusive price" (see Ch.2), a flight-plus encompasses arrangements which can cover customer requests over a maximum three day period. Online travel agents have pointed out the practical difficulties they will be caused in a scenario where the consumer books a flight on day one, then the next day returns to the website and books (as a new transaction) car hire. This will be a flight-plus, but the agent will be quite unaware that a flight-plus has been created. The solution proposed by the Department for Transport is that such websites should ask consumers at an early point whether the product is for use with any other holiday product purchased the same or the previous day. This is better than nothing, but leaves plenty of room for error, we would suggest.

- Where there is no flight-plus, but merely a "flight-only", the consumer rights (which were originally proposed to be reduced) are maintained; unless the flight was purchased from an agent acting as "agent for the consumer", in which case, there is now no right to reimbursement in the event of financial failure of the ATOL holder, just repatriation..

- Note the words "requests to book"; it is the request, not the booking/contract, which triggers the creation of a flight-plus. Thus, as long as the consumer's request to book the accommodation, etc, is made within the requisite time frame, there will be a flight-plus even if the request is not confirmed (or the booking made) until after that period. The request need not be for a specific hotel to qualify. We can imagine some litigation will follow as to what amounts to a "request to book", even though this is clearer than the original wording proposed, which was just "requests".

- Further note that if, say, the consumer later cancels the accommodation element, leaving just the flight, then the flight-plus and its liabilities will cease to exist.

Flight-plus Arranger

This term is defined by reg.23, to mean a person (or company, of course) who:

(a) As principal or agent, makes available flight accommodation in response to a request which has been made directly to them by a consumer; and

(b) has taken or takes any step which is intended to include, facilitate or enable or has the effect of including, facilitating or enabling the inclusion of that flight accommodation as a component of a flight-plus.

Points to Note

- It makes no difference whether the arranger acts as principal, or as agent for the supplier. (Note: it is proposed that "agent for the consumer" transactions will also come within the ATOL scheme once the Civil Aviation Bill 2012 becomes law.)

- Of course, if you are a flight-plus provider, you must have an ATOL either yourself or via the cover of an "approved body" (such as a travel agency consortium). This will protect consumer pre-payments in the event of the insolvency of the arranger, and repatriation where needed.

- Speaking of "Accredited Bodies", the burden placed upon them is quite heavy. They are responsible for ensuring that members pass the CAA's "fit and proper person" test for ATOL holders. Members must not hold their own ATOL's, nor can they be members of another Accredited Body. In fact the Accredited Body is required to fulfil its members' flight-plus obligations to consumers in the event of financial failure—onerous indeed!

- Only traders who deal direct with consumers are covered. Business-to-business transactions are excluded.

- The wording of (b) above is extremely wide. At the risk of stating the obvious, the word "facilitate" only means "to make easier". The Consultation paper from the Department for Transport explains that the DfT intends this definition to be "interpreted widely". It could cover a range of steps including:

  - Procuring the various flight-plus elements through contracts with one or more suppliers.
  - Entering into arrangements with another unrelated supplier to pass the customer's details to them, including by electronic means, so that the consumer does not have to re-enter details such as, for example, the holiday dates and destinations, when searching for a hotel on the other supplier's website.
  - Setting up separate companies (under common ownership or control) to provide the different elements of a flight-plus.

It is clear from this that so-called "click throughs" are intended to be covered by the legislation, although not of course those operated by airlines—see below.

Liabilities of a Flight-plus Arranger

At first blush, the liabilities imposed on a flight-plus arranger have a familiar ring about them. There is liability to provide the flight (reg.24). There is liability to make suitable alternative arrangements at no extra cost to the consumer (or give a full refund) if any of the elements cannot be provided before departure (reg.25).

For non-provision of any of the elements after departure, there is a requirement again to make suitable arrangements at no extra cost to the consumer, or if impossible, or the alternatives are rejected by the consumer for good reason, a refund must be given for the unused services (including additional tourist services booked and forming part of the flight-plus) (regs 26 and 28).

These echo provisions (e.g. regs 12 to 15) in the Package Travel Regulations, but there are two major differences:

1. reg.29 makes clear that liability only arises in the event of failure (i.e. financial failure) of the supplier of one of the elements, or of an ATOL holder providing the flight. There is no liability for non-performance otherwise (e.g. overbooking by the hotel), and certainly none for improper performance (e.g. injury being caused by the negligence of the hotel); and

2. the compensation payable is limited by reg.27 to the difference in value between what was paid for and what was delivered, plus reasonably incurred out of pocket expenses. So there is no provision for compensation for loss of enjoyment, distress, disappointment, etc, as would exist for a package.

Exemptions From Flight-plus ATOL Requirements

Unless you are an ATOL holder, there are only three (normal) ways in which you can sell flight accommodation; by virtue of reg.9, the three exemptions are the actual operator of the airline, an agent for an ATOL holder, and an airline ticket agent. Note:

- The exemption of airlines is considered very controversial by the travel/holiday industry, as it creates an unlevel playing field. (Suggestions those airlines had indeed been brought into the Scheme by inept drafting of the original draft Regulations led to a hasty redraft! See Stewart "Flight-Plus—Marks Out of 10?" [2011] T.L.Q. 158.) However, the Government is taking powers to bring airlines ultimately within the ATOL system in the Civil Aviation Bill 2012.

- Agents can only qualify for the exemption by having in place a written agency agreement with their ATOL holding principals which complies with reg.30, by containing specified terms, provides for the issue of ATOL certificates, and authorises the transaction. Note that *all* flight sales via agents, including packages, will require an agency agreement to be in place; and not just flight-plus.

- An "airline ticket agent" is an agent for an aircraft operator who sells directly to the consumer where a confirmed ticket is issued immediately. "Confirmed ticket" includes any documentation which provides the consumer with access to the flight without the need for further payment.

Flight-plus—Comments

The proof of the pudding for flight-plus will be seen if consumers are better informed and protected. A few thoughts on this:

- The DfT watchwords for these proposals are "clarity for consumers". That is to be encouraged. The new ATOL Certificate, to be used from October 2012, is designed with this in mind. It must be supplied to the consumer, either by the principal or by the agent (but if by the agent, it can be created by the principal for that purpose). But consumers will need to understand the difference in protection offered by packages, by a flight-plus, and by a flight-only or other arrangement. For example, when there is entitlement to repatriation only; when there are refunds (or the provisions of alternatives) available; and when there is full protection, e.g. if injury is sustained on holiday through supplier negligence. The prescribed ATOL Certificate will, in our view, only go some way to create that clarity, as it concentrates on financial protection, and not on quality or health and safety guarantees. Where no ATOL Certificate is supplied (e.g. because the sale is by an airline ticket agent), the CAA is working with airlines to establish a means by which consumers can verify the status of the agent, and that no further payment will be required. But this does not seem to be a wholly satisfactory arrangement for achieving the desired clarity.

- Flight-plus may prove to be more attractive to traders than packaging. They offer consumers a "badge" of protection, but avoid the cost of liability, public liability insurance, etc. So some may change their business models to sell the new product instead of packages; and overall consumer protection would thereby be reduced.

- There remains the possible escape route of traders selling as "agent for the consumer", acknowledged to be outside the scheme. In practice, it is very hard, and certainly very different, to be agent for the consumer instead of the trader, so this may be an option that is more attractive to traders in theory than in practice, and in any event is likely to be brought within the ATOL system by the Civil Aviation Bill 2012, when enacted (see Ch.11 on Travel Agents).

THE RULES UNDER THE PACKAGE TRAVEL REGULATIONS

Regulation 16(1) provides that:

"The other party to the contract shall at all times be able to provide sufficient evidence of security for the refund of money paid over and for the repatriation of the consumer in the event of insolvency."

Note that:

- The words "shall at all times be able to provide" suggests that Trading Standards Officers have a right to demand the evidence at any time; but the effect of Sch.3, para.3 is that a Trading Standards Officer can only demand to see the evidence of adequate security if he has reasonable grounds for suspecting that an offence has been committed.

- The security has to cover two things, the refund of money paid over and the repatriation of the consumer. The remainder of regs 16 to 21 provide a set of rules, in some detail, as to how security for the refund of money paid over is to be provided; but are (surprisingly) completely silent as to how security for the repatriation of the consumer is to be organised. Most repatriations are organised by the CAA who have got it down to a fine art as far as air package holidays covered by an ATOL are concerned—known as "licensable activity". However, for non-licensable activity where, for instance, security is provided by a trust account under regs 20 or 21, one wonders how the trustee, who may be a local accountant or banker, can ever have the expertise to persuade hotels and airlines far away overseas to continue services for the customers of the failed company.

Note also that by reg.16(5) the security is required until the contract has been fully performed. This means "until the holiday or travel is over", and it expressly does not require the organiser to provide security in respect of claims for improper performance of the contract under reg.15. Therefore, as has always been the case, consumers who have already travelled on a holiday which turned out to be disastrous because of the insolvency of the tour operator will only be unsecured creditors against their failed holiday company. There is no security for such claims.

There are various methods set down whereby the necessary security can be provided.

Other European Jurisdictions

Security will be sufficient if the package is covered by measures adopted by another member state of the EU under art.7 of the Directive—see reg.16(2)(a). Experience suggests that there is not always reciprocity, in cases where a tour operator is bonded by some permitted method in the UK, but wants to sell in other jurisdictions.

ATOL

Where the arrangement is one in respect of which an ATOL is required to be held under the new Civil Aviation (Air Travel Organisers' Licensing) Regulations 2012—including the new flight-plus arrangements—no further security needs to be provided. It remains to be seen whether the new rules on flight-plus will generate the same litigation as in the *ABTA v CAA* cases where companies try and avoid the new rules.

Bonding—Regulations 17 and 18

Two methods of bonding are provided whereby a bond is entered into by an authorised institution under which the institution binds itself to pay an approved body (of which the organiser is a member) a particular sum in the event of the insolvency of the organiser. Bonds have to be renewed at least every 18 months.

The difference between reg.17 and reg.18 turns on whether the approved body does or does not have a reserve fund or insurance cover to cover prepayments by consumers. The approval of the Secretary of State is required for all approved bodies and/or the reserve fund itself.

Where no reserve fund or insurance exists, then reg.17 provides that the sum which the bonding institution must pay shall be such sum as may reasonably be expected to enable all the monies paid over by consumers under or in contemplation of the contracts for relevant packages which have not been fully performed to be repaid and in any event not less than 25 per cent of all the payments which the organiser estimates he will receive under or in contemplation of contracts for packages in the 12 months from the start date of the bond, or the maximum amount of all payments which the organiser expects to hold at any one time in respect of contracts which have not been fully performed, whichever sum is the smaller. Because of the seasonal nature of the holiday industry, the first of these two calculations may produce the smaller sum. For example, a traditional summer holiday package company will hold maximum prepayments in about June or early July, just before the peak season, and these indeed may well exceed 25 per cent of all payments it will receive in a year; but on the other hand, it is also the time of year when in normal trading circumstances that company is least likely to become insolvent, because its cash flow will be very good. Having said that, events in summer 2010 (e.g. the failure of Goldtrail), and in 2011 show that even the summer peak can be a time of failure in a bad economic climate.

Where the approved body does have a reserve fund or insurance, then reg.18 provides the method of calculating the size of the bond required; in effect it is the same calculation which we have just described under reg.17, except that the percentage of all payments which the organiser estimates he will receive during the 12 month period is reduced from 25 per cent to 10 per cent, making it even more likely that this is the lesser of the two sums. A number of well established bodies including ABTA, FTO and AITO together with the PSA and the BCH have acquired approved body status for the purposes of these regulations.

In practice, bonding, by whatever method, is extremely expensive for tour operators, a major part of their overheads. Furthermore, the bonding authorities, for good reasons, insist on seeing a healthy balance sheet with large capital resources, often to be provided in hard cash (and personal guarantees from the directors). This can be backbreaking for a tour operator after a difficult year's trading, but of course the object of all these rules is consumer protection. But the opposite may be achieved inadvertently; the burden is so great, and the advantages of not carrying that burden (as their competitors, the low-cost airlines and non-package operators, do not) so tempting (not to mention the cost of liability insurance and TOMS VAT), that many tour operators flee from package sales. As we have seen, flight-plus aims to bridge that gap.

However, it is also the case that since the CAA introduced the ATOL Protection Contribution (APC) in 2008 whereby all tour operators (and now flight-plus) arrangers have to pay a £2.50 contribution to the Air Travel Trust Fund to cover tour operator failures the prevalence of bonding has much diminished. Ironically, because the market for such a product has also diminished, those tour operators who are required by the CAA to have a bond have to pay more for it.

In a test case ABTA's famous "consumer promise" has been held by the Court of Appeal to create a right in the consumer to sue ABTA for reimbursement following the insolvency of an ABTA member, see *Bowerman v ABTA* [1996] C.L.C. 451. (ABTA subsequently altered the wording of its promise slightly, but probably not to the extent of altering the principle. See Ch.3 for a fuller discussion of this case. Note the ABTA Consumer Promise's significance is now much reduced by the watering down of their protection, e.g. for accommodation-only, since 2006.)

Insurance

Regulation 19 permits security to be provided under one or more appropriate policies of insurance under which the insurer agrees to indemnify consumers, who shall be the insured persons under the policy, against the loss of money paid over by them under or in contemplation of contracts for packages, in the event of the organiser becoming insolvent. It is required that the organiser makes it a term of every contract with the consumer that the consumer acquires the benefit of such an insurance policy in the event of the insolvency. There are further provisions to prevent the insurance policy being avoided by the insurer on technical grounds.

The availability of insurance to meet this market has proved to be variable. And problems can occur even when an insurance product is available. AITO found, in mid 2011, that an insurer was refusing to pay out consumers, following the failure of one of its insured tour operators, Skiing Europe (an AITO member), because, it alleged, the insured had been less than fully truthful in completing the application form for cover. Can such a potential situation comply with reg.19 at all? (See Josephides "Insurance as a Means of Arranging Financial Protection to Consumers" [2011] T.L.Q. 251; see also *Blodel-Pawlik v HanseMerkur Reise-versicherung AG* ECJ Case 134/11.)

Further problems are highlighted by two Austrian cases before the European Court. In *Verein fur Konsumenteninformation v Osterreichische* (C-364/96) [1999] All E.R. (EC) 183, the Austrian Tour Operator Karthago went bust, and hoteliers in Crete insisted that consumers pay again or they would not be allowed to leave their hotels! The insurers refused to reimburse the consumers on the grounds that they had not been legally obliged to pay the hotelier a second time. However, the court held that consumers must be compensated under art.7, which protects the "money paid over and the repatriation of the consumer in the event of insolvency".

In the other case, *Rechberger v Austria* (C-140/97) [1999] E.C.R. I-3499, insurance was based on five per cent of turnover over three months. This proved insufficient to reimburse consumers. The Court held that Austria had not sufficiently implemented art.7, and it was not a defence for Austria to say that the losses only happened because of unexpected and unwise trading by the tour operator. (It is interesting to note that the holidays in this case were offered as a prize by a newspaper, and that the only payment made by consumers was either for airport taxes only, or in some cases for a single room supplement as well. Austria argued this was not a package; the Court said that the services sold were a package, and it made no difference that payment was only required for part.)

Trust Accounts

If there was one provision in the Package Travel Regulations 1992 which drew universal cries of "rubbish!" it was reg.20 which allowed package organisers to provide security by placing money in a trust account. As we shall see, anyone can be a trustee, there is no effective checking procedure, there is no means by which a consumer can tell whether a trust account is being properly operated and, in short, the system was wide open to abuse by unscrupulous operators. On

December 31, 1992, when the Regulations came into effect, it was widely expected that reg.20 had so little credibility that it would fall into instant disuse.

In fact, despite the obvious hazards, and continuing misgivings, trust accounts are alive and flourishing. The reasons are that they provide the only legal method of compliance with reg.16 for many companies. Small tour operators, people running coach tours, hotels offering bargain break weekends and the like are excluded from other methods of providing security by the prohibitive costs or the unwillingness of bonding and insurance companies to take them on. Some credibility has been added by the emergence of the Travel Trust Association ("TTA"), which currently claims about 370 members, and by the likes of Travlaw Trust.

So what are the rules? All monies paid by a consumer must be held by a person as trustee for the consumer until the contract has been fully performed (or money forfeited as cancellation charges). There are no rules as to who should be the trustee, and theoretically it could be the managing director's wife or husband, or the office junior. A reputable company will appoint a bank, accountant or solicitor. It could not, of course, be the company's own solicitors—the solicitor holds the money as trustee for consumers—and this would create a conflict of interest with the company.

The cost of administering the trust is to be paid by the organiser. Any interest earned on the monies held by the trustee accrue to the organiser.

Regulation 20(4) provides that the trustee shall release to the organiser the appropriate sum of money from the trust account when he receives a statement signed by the organiser to the effect that:

- a contract for a package, the price of which is specified in the statement, has been fully performed; or

- the organiser has repaid to the consumer a sum of money specified in the statement which the consumer had paid in respect of the package; or

- the consumer has, on cancellation of the package, forfeited a sum of money specified in the statement.

Paragraph 5 permits the trustee to require the organiser to provide further information or evidence before releasing any sum mentioned in the statement.

In the event of the insolvency of the organiser, the monies held in trust by the trustee are to be applied to meet the claims of consumers who are creditors of the organiser in respect of contracts for packages for which the arrangements were established and which have not been fully performed and, in the unlikely event that there is a surplus after those claims have been met, it shall form part of the estate of the insolvent organiser. (It will be noticed that nothing is said about the need to repatriate consumers.)

In the more likely event that the money in trust is insufficient to meet the claims of consumers, payments to those consumers are to be made by the trustee on a *pari passu* basis.

Such has been the popularity of this method that organisations such as the TTA have become an established part of the scene. They aim to bring legitimacy and credibility to organisers using this method of providing security on payment of a fee, and on submitting accounts and brochures. The tour organiser can claim to be a member of the Association which, they hope, will bring comfort to consumers. The Association does not act as trustee itself, but has a strict Code of Conduct for members about Trust Accounts. The trustee must be a banker, accountant or solicitor. Credit card companies have agreed to make payments received for the merchant directly into the trust account. In addition, TTA guarantee (via insurance) a repayment of (as at 2011) up to £11,000 per passenger to cover any shortfall in the trust account, on insolvency. Further, TTA have negotiated with the CAA to make ATOL available in a more affordable form for TTA members (a discounted small business ATOL).

The most obvious normal disadvantage for an organiser using the trust account method of bonding is a cash flow problem; they cannot touch the customer's money until the holiday is over, and yet may well have to pay suppliers such as airlines "up front". Despite all the potential pitfalls, trust accounts look set to grow yet further in popularity, fuelled by the advent of flight-plus (not of course directly regulated by regs 20 and 21, but likely to be similar in effect); and a number of different organisations are offering trust accounts schemes, from travel agency consortia to a law firm.

This cash flow implication does not apply under reg.21, another method of providing security by way of a trust account—but in this case only available to organisers acting "otherwise than in the course of business". A small number of voluntary organisations (and perhaps a large number of schools—see Ch.2 on the definition of organiser) may be able to take advantage of these rules, which are similar to those already set out except that:

- The costs of administering the trust can be paid for out of the monies held in trust.

- The statement signed by the organiser and produced for the trustee can require money to be paid over to the organiser because a sum is required for the purpose of paying for a component or part of a component of a package.

See also Brown "Trust Me—I'm a Tour Operator" [1994] 3 T.L.J. 11 and Sheen "Is consumers' money really safe in a trust?" [1998] I.T.L.J. 57.

Offences

An organiser who fails to provide sufficient evidence of security as required by reg.16 is guilty of an offence and liable on summary conviction to a fine not exceeding level five (£5,000 at the current time); or the matter can be dealt with in the Crown Court where an unlimited fine can be imposed. Further identical penalties are imposed by reg.22 for any organiser who makes a false "statement" to a trustee under regs 20 or 21 requiring the release of monies. The defence of due diligence is available to defendants under regs 16 and 22. (The due diligence defence is discussed at length in Ch.18.)

The first prosecution under reg.16, in Humberside, resulted in a fine of £250 which was condemned as too low by industry and consumer groups. Several further cases have seen higher fines imposed but the feeling persists that enforcement is too sporadic to be really effective—especially for package holidays within the UK. Breaches of the ATOL Regulations can also result in criminal prosecution by the CAA, see, e.g. the *Travel Republic* case in Ch.2.

Trains and Boats and Planes

INTRODUCTION

Although this book started life as an examination of package holiday law and a consumer's rights in relation to tour operators and travel agents, it has now been extended, as the pattern of taking holidays has changed, to cover the rights of independent travellers, including those who travel to their destinations by sea or air.

With this in mind, it is our intention in the first section of this chapter to examine two major areas of air law that are relevant to holidaymakers. These are the Montreal Convention (which has largely superseded the Warsaw Convention) and EC Regulation 261/2004 on denied boarding, cancellation and long delays. The Montreal Convention sets out a passenger's rights against a carrier in respect of death or injury, delay to passengers or baggage and loss, damage or delay to baggage. Regulation 261/2004 does as its name suggests—provide enhanced rights to passengers suffering from denied boarding (i.e. those passengers who are "bumped" when their plane is overbooked), flight cancellations and long delays. This is a controversial piece of legislation which has been referred for interpretation to the ECJ on a number of occasions and as we write there are a number of outstanding cases awaiting decision. The second part of the chapter deals with the rights of consumers who are covered by the Athens Convention on carriage of passengers by sea. We also touch briefly on the rights of travellers by rail and coach.

AIR LAW

Introduction

In 2010, UK residents made 55.6 million visits abroad, of which 43.2 million were by air (Travel Trends 2010, Office for National Statistics—*www.-statistics.gov.uk*). Since 1929, when the Warsaw Convention was first concluded, air passengers such as these have been protected by a series of international conventions culminating in the Montreal Convention 1999 (Convention for the Unification of Certain Rules for International Carriage by Air done at Montreal on May 28, 1999) which first entered into force in the UK on June 28, 2004.

Subject to what is said below most international air travel from the UK is now covered by the Montreal Convention which has now (October 2011) been ratified by 102 nations who between them are responsible for the overwhelming number of international flights (a list is available at *www.icao.int*). A residual category still exists which is covered by its predecessor, the Warsaw Convention, but even in those cases EU carriers are covered by EC Regulation 889/2002 which imposes the same liabilities as the Montreal Convention.

The Montreal Convention covers:

- Death or injury of passengers.

- Delay of passengers or baggage.

- Damage or loss of baggage.

In Europe, and to a lesser extent outside Europe, UK passengers have also acquired rights under EC Regulation 261/2004 which protects consumers against:

- Denied boarding.

- Long delays.

- Cancellations.

Both these sets of provisions will be examined in detail.

The Montreal Convention

The Montreal Convention became part of UK law in June 2004. Currently, 102 states, including the US, China and all the members of the EU have signed up to it. Note that where the Convention applies it provides exclusive remedies and there are no other common law remedies—see *Sidhu v British Airways* [1997] A.C. 430. This principle has been extended to deny liability in cases of disability discrimination (*Hook v British Airways Plc* [2012] EWCA Civ 66), racial discrimination (*Nobre v American Airlines*, 2009 WL 5125976 (SD Fla 2009) and defamation (*McCauley v Aer Lingus* [2011] IEHC 89).

International Carriage

The Convention only applies to international carriage, which is defined in the following fashion:

"*Article 1*

2. For the purposes of this Convention, the expression *international carriage* means any carriage in which, according to the agreement between the parties, the place of departure and the place of destination, whether or not there be a break in the carriage or a transhipment, are situated either within the territories of two States Parties, or within the territory of a single State Party if there is an agreed stopping place within the territory of another State, even if that State is not a State Party. Carriage between two points within the territory of a single State Party without an agreed stopping place within the territory of another State is not international carriage for the purposes of this Convention.

3. Carriage to be performed by several successive carriers is deemed, for the purposes of this Convention, to be one undivided carriage if it has been regarded by the parties as a single operation, whether it had been agreed upon under the form of a single contract or of a series of contracts, and it does not lose its international character merely because one contract or a series of contracts is to be performed entirely within the territory of the same State."

Thus, a flight from England to France would be covered by the Convention because both parties are signatories to the Convention—or High Contracting Parties, to use the terminology of the Convention. Likewise, flights from England to Spain, Greece, Turkey, Italy and the US, all popular holiday destinations, would be covered by the Convention. However, Thailand, another popular destination for British holidaymakers, is not a signatory to the Convention. One's immediate reaction to that might be to conclude that it is not covered by the Convention. This would be the case if it was just a one-way flight. However if it was a round-trip, as most holiday flights are, then it would be covered. This is because the definition of international carriage encompasses those flights where the place of departure and the place of destination are within the territory of a High Contracting Party so long as there is an agreed stopping place outside the territory of that state—even if the agreed stopping place is not within the territory of a High Contracting Party.

Similarly, if the flight to Thailand was just one leg of a journey from London to Sydney return then the flight would be international carriage covered by the Convention because the definition of successive carriage in art.1(3) would cover it. Equally, so long as the parties agreed that it was a single operation, the feeder legs of the London–Sydney journey would also be international carriage—for instance, the connecting flights from Newcastle upon Tyne to Heathrow and Sydney to Newcastle NSW. For a discussion of the meaning of "international carriage" in an English court see *Grein v Imperial Airways Ltd* [1937] 1 K.B. 50 where it was held that a return flight from Croydon to Brussels via Antwerp was international carriage even though at the time Belgium was not a party to the Warsaw Convention (the forerunner of the Montreal Convention).

Purely domestic carriage and one-way international carriage to a state which is not a High Contracting Party is not covered by the Convention. However, as far as Community carriers are concerned, their liability is determined by Regulation (EC) No 889/2002 on Air Carrier Liability in the Event of Accidents. Essentially, what this does is apply the Montreal Convention to non-Montreal Convention travel carried on by Community carriers. To all intents and purposes this means domestic flights within the various EU states.

Main Provisions of the Montreal Convention

The carrier's liability to passengers, the limitations on that liability and the defences available are set out in Ch.III of the Convention.

CHAPTER THIRTEEN

(i) Death and injury

Liability

Article 17.1 provides:

> "The carrier is liable for damage sustained in case of death or bodily injury of a passenger upon condition only that the accident which caused the death or injury took place on board the aircraft or in the course of any of the operations of embarking or disembarking."

Note that this is a strict liability, subject to the available defences and the limitation on liability provisions.

To establish liability on the carrier's part to the passenger it has to be established that:

- death, wounding or other bodily injury was caused;

- by an accident;

- on board the aircraft or in the course of embarking or disembarking.

The meaning of death and wounding are relatively straightforward but "other bodily injury" has caused problems. The particular problem arises in cases where passengers have suffered mental injury unaccompanied by any physical injury—where there has been an emergency landing or inflight incident, etc. International authorities are now predominantly in favour of the view that psychiatric harm or mental injury is not covered by art.17. In the American case *Eastern Airlines v Floyd* 499 US 530 (1991) it was held by the Supreme Court that there was no liability for purely mental injury. In that case, all three engines on an aircraft had simultaneously failed and passengers had been told that the aircraft would have to ditch. In the event, the pilot regained control and no one was injured. *Floyd* was followed by *El Al Israel Airlines v Tseng* 119 S Ct 662 (1999) in which the Supreme Court confirmed the decision in *Floyd*. More recently, the House of Lords has also come to the same conclusion in two appeals heard at the same time, *King v Bristow Helicopters Ltd* and *Morris v KLM Royal Dutch Airlines* [2002] UKHL 7. (See Goh "The Meaning Of 'Bodily Injury' In International Carriage By Air" [2002] I.T.L.J. 139 for a discussion of these cases.) In the *King* case the claimant suffered mental injury when he was involved in a helicopter crash. The helicopter took off from a floating platform in the North Sea in poor weather. The helicopter ascended and hovered for a short period, at which point its two engines failed. It descended and landed on the helideck. Smoke engulfed the helicopter; there was panic on board; and passengers feared that the helicopter was about to crash into the sea. The door was opened and the passengers disembarked. The claimant developed post-traumatic stress disorder. As a result of the stress he suffered an onset of peptic ulcer disease. He could not recover for his mental injury but as this had caused a physical injury he was allowed to claim for that. However, the case does suggest that if the mental injury can be shown to be as a result of physical damage to the brain then this is recoverable as a physical injury. (See *Weaver v Delta Airlines Inc* 56 F Supp 2d 1190 (1999).)

"Accident" is another word that has caused problems. It clearly covers crashes and collisions, but will also cover extreme turbulence, sudden unexpected depressurisation, and violent touchdowns. It will not cover light or moderate turbulence, routine depressurisation during landing or a merely bumpy or hard landing. Articles falling from overhead lockers, hot drinks being spilled, or the collapse of a seat would all be accidents. The authorities are split on cases of food poisoning.

What would not be an accident is where the passenger faints or suffers a heart attack or an asthmatic attack during the flight where this is not triggered by some external unexpected event. Although in popular terms these might be regarded as accidents they are not classified as accidents under the Convention because they are not caused by something external to the passenger. In *Chaudhari v British Airways Plc, The Times,* May 7, 1997, the plaintiff was a passenger on board one of the defendant's flights. He was a disabled person who already suffered from paralysis to the left side of his body. He sustained further injury when attempting to leave his seat. The court held that the injury was not caused by any unexpected or unusual event external to him, but by his own personal, particular or peculiar reaction to the normal operation of the aircraft. He fell as a result of his pre-existing medical condition and therefore his injury was not caused by an accident within the meaning of art.17.

Morris v KLM, discussed above in the context of mental injury, also raised the issue of what amounts to an accident. The claimant, a girl of 15, had travelled unaccompanied on a KLM flight from Kuala Lumpur to Amsterdam and had been indecently assaulted during the flight by a male passenger in the adjoining seat. She suffered clinical depression as a result of the assault and brought an action for damages against the defendant airline claiming that the assault was an "accident" within the ambit of art.17. Referring to the US case of *Air France v Saks* 470 US 392 (1985), in which a similar incident had occurred, the Court of Appeal in *Morris* held that the incident was an accident and this decision was not appealed in the House of Lords.

There were a spate of cases a few years ago in which claims were made against airlines for causing DVT. As far as the UK is concerned the matter has been conclusively decided by the decision in *Re Deep Vein Thrombosis and Air Travel Group Litigation* [2005] UKHL 72 in which the House of Lords decided that DVT is not an "accident" within the meaning of the Warsaw Convention. (The same reasoning would apply under the Montreal Convention.) (See S. Gates and G. Leloudas "DVT Litigation—The End of the Runway?" [2005] I.T.L.J. 119 and S. Liddy "Recent DVT Litigation in Australia" [2005] I.T.L.J. 124 for a discussion of the DVT litigation.)

Lord Scott stated that:

'... an event or happening which is no more than the normal operation of the aircraft in normal conditions cannot constitute an art 17 accident and, second, that the event or happening that has caused the damage of which complaint is made must be something external to the passenger."

Whether or not the airline had been negligent by not warning passengers of the risk of DVT the claimants could not show that DVT constituted an accident.

A recent Court of Appeal case *Barclay v British Airways Plc* [2008] EWCA Civ 1419 re-affirmed the meaning of "accident" as defined in *Saks* and applied in *Chaudhari*. The facts of the case were that as the claimant lowered herself into her seat, with her body weight towards the right, her right foot suddenly slipped on a strip embedded in the floor of the aircraft and went to the left. She heard and felt her knee "pop" and as it gave way it struck the armrest and she was injured. Laws L.J. said:

> "There was no accident here that was external to the appellant, no event which happened independently of anything done or omitted by her. All that happened was that the appellant's foot came into contact with the inert strip and she fell. It was an instance, to use Leggatt LJ's words in *Chaudhari*, of 'the passenger's particular, personal or peculiar reaction to the normal operation of the aircraft'."

What amounts to the operations of embarking or disembarking and at what stage they begin and end is not as simple as it appears at first glance. The problem is summed up by Leland:

> "Despite a substantial volume of litigation on the interpretation of Article 17 in both common and civil law jurisdictions, the question has remained clouded in some complexity. One of the greatest impediments to a clear vista has been the strategy of airlines in dealing with actions for compensation for injuries incurred by clients. Essentially the terms of Article 17 have proved to be a chameleon, providing both shield and sword to potential defendants. If for example an airline thinks it has a very strong defence to a claim of negligence against it then it is in their interest to prove that the Convention does not apply, thus placing an onus on the plaintiff to prove negligence. If, on the other hand, the defendant airline's case is a weak one, they will argue that the Convention does apply, thus limiting the amount of compensation recoverable by the passenger." ([1997] I.T.L.J. 162)

Now that liability is essentially unlimited under the Convention, the limitation of damages is not an issue, but another reason for using the Convention is that the limitation period is only two years under the Convention, whereas for personal injury at common law it is three years. Thus, a plaintiff commencing an action after two years but before three would need to bring his case at common law rather than within the Convention.

An Irish case, cited by Leland, contains a statement of the law as it is commonly understood to be at present:

> "To make a prima facie case that a particular claim is within Article 17 it must be established (i) that the accident to the passenger is related to a specific flight and (ii) that it happened while the latter was actually entering or about to enter the aircraft, or (iii) if it happened in the terminal building, or otherwise on the airport premises, that the location of the accident is a place where the injured party was obliged to be while in the process of embarkation. Whether or not the location as so defined is within the ambit of Article 17 will depend upon the circumstances of each individual case. The location of the accident is just one

of the factors for consideration in determining the scope of the phrase 'any of the operations of embarking' within the meaning of the article." (Barr J. in *Galvin v Aer Rianta*, Irish High Court, October 13, 1993)

The same issue arose in *Phillips v Air New Zealand Ltd* [2002] EWHC 800 (Comm) where the judge applied the same tests as in the *Galvin* case. (See Saggerson "Case Comment: Susan Phillips v Air New Zealand" [2002] I.T.L.J. 144 for a discussion of this case.) Morrison J., relying upon *Galvin*, said:

"The Judge applied the three criteria test in this way, in the context of an embarkation case:

'As to embarkation, I am satisfied that to make a prima facie case that a particular claim is within Art 17 it must be established

(1) that the accident to the passenger is related to a specific flight; and
(2) that it happened while the latter was actually entering or about to enter the aircraft; or
(3) if it happened in the terminal building or otherwise on the airport premises, that the location of the accident is a place where the injured party was obliged to be in the process of embarkation.' "

A recent US case which illustrates the fact-based approach to the issue is *Walsh v Koninklijke Luchtvaart Maatschappij N.V.* S.D.N.Y. September 12, 2011; *www.nvflyer.com*. The plaintiff tripped over a metal bar and fell in a departure gate seating area while walking to join a line of persons waiting to board a flight from Amsterdam to New York. The court made a preliminary ruling that a reasonable jury could conclude the plaintiff was injured while "embarking" because the incident occurred while the airline was "exercising control" over the plaintiff. The court reasoned that the airline had control over the plaintiff because the trip and fall took place in the departure gate seating area and while the plaintiff was walking to join a line in response to the airline's boarding announcements.

Defences

A defence is provided in art.20:

"Article 20 Exoneration

If the carrier proves that the damage was caused or contributed to by the negligence or other wrongful act or omission of the person claiming compensation, or the person from whom he or she derives his or her rights, the carrier shall be wholly or partly exonerated from its liability to the claimant to the extent that such negligence or wrongful act or omission caused or contributed to the damage. When by reason of death or injury of a passenger compensation is claimed by a person other than the passenger, the carrier shall likewise be wholly or partly exonerated from its liability to the extent that it proves that the damage was caused or contributed to by the negligence or other wrongful act or omission of that passenger. This Article applies to all the liability provisions in this Convention, including paragraph 1 of Article 21."

Failure to wear a seatbelt after having been warned to do so would fall within this defence if the passenger was then injured during turbulence. Blackshaw gives the example of a passenger burnt in a fire in the lavatory caused by lighting a cigarette, despite being prohibited from doing so, being caught by this defence. Passengers who are injured by falling luggage when removing the luggage from the overhead bins against the instructions of the cabin crew would also have no claim.

Exclusion of Liability

Article 26 contains a blanket prohibition on the use of exclusion clauses. It provides:

"Article 26 Invalidity of Contractual Provisions

Any provision tending to relieve the carrier of liability or to fix a lower limit than that which is laid down in this Convention shall be null and void, but the nullity of any such provision does not involve the nullity of the whole contract, which shall remain subject to the provisions of this Convention."

This would be effective to combat most varieties of exclusion clause including those that set short time limits or impose onerous conditions. Shawcross and Beaumont draw attention to the practice of some airlines which require disabled passengers to sign a waiver and suggest that they would be of doubtful effectiveness.

Limitation of Liability

As far as death or bodily injury is concerned there are now effectively no limits to liability.

Article 21 provides:

"Compensation in Case of Death or Injury of Passengers

1. For damages arising under paragraph 1 of Article 17 not exceeding 100,000 Special Drawing Rights for each passenger, the carrier shall not be able to exclude or limit its liability.
2. The carrier shall not be liable for damages arising under paragraph 1 of Article 17 to the extent that they exceed for each passenger 100,000 Special Drawing Rights if the carrier proves that:

   (a) such damage was not due to the negligence or other wrongful act or omission of the carrier or its servants or agents; or
   (b) such damage was solely due to the negligence or other wrongful act or omission of a third party."

A Special Drawing Right (SDR) is a unit of currency created by the International Monetary Fund in 1989 (*www.imf.org*) and is based upon the value of a basket of currencies. The Convention provided for the raising of the limit in line with inflation and this was done in 2009 and the limit is now 113,100 SDRs which comes to almost exactly £113,100 at today's values (October 2011).

When the Limitations do not Apply

It used to be the case under the Warsaw Convention that the airline would lose its limitation of liability protection if it did not issue a ticket that contained the right information. The position under the Montreal Convention is that a ticket must still be issued but failure to do so does not affect the limitation of liability:

"Article 3 Passengers and Baggage

1. In respect of carriage of passengers, an individual or collective document of carriage shall be delivered containing:

   (a) an indication of the places of departure and destination;
   (b) if the places of departure and destination are within the territory of a single State Party, one or more agreed stopping places being within the territory of another State, an indication of at least one such stopping place.

2. Any other means which preserves the information indicated in paragraph 1 may be substituted for the delivery of the document referred to in that paragraph. If any such other means is used, the carrier shall offer to deliver to the passenger a written statement of the information so preserved.

3. The carrier shall deliver to the passenger a baggage identification tag for each piece of checked baggage.

4. The passenger shall be given written notice to the effect that where this Convention is applicable it governs and may limit the liability of carriers in respect of death or injury and for destruction or loss of, or damage to, baggage, and for delay.

5. Non-compliance with the provisions of the foregoing paragraphs shall not affect the existence or the validity of the contract of carriage, which shall, nonetheless, be subject to the rules of this Convention including those relating to limitation of liability."

(ii) Loss and Destruction of Baggage

Liability for Checked Baggage

Article 17 provides:

"...

2. The carrier is liable for damage sustained in case of destruction or loss of, or of damage to, checked baggage upon condition only that the event which caused the destruction, loss or damage took place on board the aircraft or during any period within which the checked baggage was in the charge of the carrier. However, the carrier is not liable if and to the extent that the damage resulted from the inherent defect, quality or vice

of the baggage. In the case of unchecked baggage, including personal items, the carrier is liable if the damage resulted from its fault or that of its servants or agents.

3. If the carrier admits the loss of the checked baggage, or if the checked baggage has not arrived at the expiration of twenty-one days after the date on which it ought to have arrived. the passenger is entitled to enforce against the carrier the rights which flow from the contract of carriage.

4. Unless otherwise specified, in this Convention the term "baggage" means both checked baggage and unchecked baggage."

Note again that, subject to the defences and limitations, this is a strict liability. The elements of the liability are that the carrier is liable if:

- damage or destruction is caused;

- to checked baggage;

- during the carriage by air.

There must be damage or destruction of the baggage if an action is to fall within this article. Delay to baggage is covered by separate provisions in art.19.

Checked baggage needs to be distinguished from cargo and from unchecked baggage. As far as holidaymakers are concerned, the distinction between baggage and cargo will rarely, if ever, concern them. In practice, where the distinction does arise, the matter is usually conclusively decided by reference to the documentation provided by the carrier. If a baggage check is issued it is baggage. If an airway bill is issued then it will be cargo. The need to make the distinction arises because different limitations of liability apply and there are different periods of notice for making a complaint.

The distinction between checked baggage and unchecked baggage is between that baggage for which the passenger receives a baggage check and hands over control of it to the carrier, and that baggage which he retains control of himself and takes onto the aircraft—usually referred to as hand luggage. It used to be the case that there were different liability limits but this is not so under the Montreal Convention. The distinction now is that for unchecked baggage the carrier is only liable if fault can be proved.

The period during which the liability will arise is defined as the period where the baggage is in the charge of the carrier. Usually, this will be the period between handing over the baggage at check-in and then recovering it from the carousel at the destination airport. It clearly covers those periods during which the baggage is being dealt with by ground handlers and for whom the carrier is responsible.

Claiming for Damage to Baggage

In order to recover compensation for damage to baggage the passenger must comply with certain formalities and time limits. Article 31 provides:

"1. Receipt by the person entitled to delivery of checked baggage or cargo without complaint is prima facie evidence that the same has been delivered in good condition and in accordance with the document of carriage or with the record preserved by the other means referred to in paragraph 2 of Article 3 and paragraph 2 of Article 4.

2. In the case of damage, the person entitled to delivery must complain to the carrier forthwith after the discovery of the damage, and, at the latest, within seven days from the date of receipt in the case of checked baggage and fourteen days from the date of receipt in the case of cargo. In the case of delay, the complaint must be made at the latest within twenty-one days from the date on which the baggage or cargo have been placed at his or her disposal.

3. Every complaint must be made in writing and given or dispatched within the times aforesaid.

4. If no complaint is made within the times aforesaid, no action shall lie against the carrier, save in the case of fraud on its part."

One important point to note is that in the case of destruction of baggage, as opposed to damage, no notice is required. In other cases, the passenger must adhere to strict requirements:

- the complaint must be made in writing;

- to the carrier;

- within seven days, or in the case of delayed baggage, within 21 days of receipt.

It is important, therefore, for holidaymakers to make prompt complaint about any damage or risk losing their rights altogether. These conditions will apply to both checked and unchecked baggage as the Convention makes no distinction between the two.

One trap for the unwary is that art.31(2) covers partial loss as well as damage. In *Fothergill v Monarch Airlines Ltd* [1980] 2 All E.R. 696 the plaintiff complained within the time limit about damage to his suitcase but did not complain about the loss of contents which he only discovered later. It was held that he could not recover for the contents.

Defences

The Montreal Convention provides the new art.20 defence of contributory negligence, and also the defence in art.17.2 (quoted above) based upon any inherent defect, quality or vice of the baggage.

Exclusion of Liability

Article 26 applies to the exclusion of liability for baggage as it does to liability for personal injury or death, i.e. there is a blanket prohibition.

Limitation of Liability for Baggage

Article 22 provides:

CHAPTER THIRTEEN

"2. In the carriage of baggage, the liability of the carrier in the case of destruction, loss, damage or delay is limited to 1000 Special Drawing Rights for each passenger unless the passenger has made, at the time when the checked baggage was handed over to the carrier, a special declaration of interest in delivery at destination and has paid a supplementary sum if the case so requires. In that case the carrier will be liable to pay a sum not exceeding the declared sum, unless it proves that the sum is greater than the passenger's actual interest in delivery at destination."

A Special Drawing Right (SDR) is a unit of currency created by the in 1989 (*www.imf.org*) and is based upon the value of a basket of currencies. The Convention provided for the raising of the limit in line with inflation and this was done in 2009 and the limit is now 1,131 SDRs which comes to almost exactly £1,130 at today's values (October 2011). This is a relatively modest sum by modern standards and ought to be supplemented by insurance cover whenever possible. Note, however, that it is not unknown for insurers to include a clause in their policies excluding liability while the baggage is in the care of a carrier. Passengers have the alternative of declaring a higher value and paying extra in which case they will be able to claim the higher sum.

Despite these limitations on liability these sums are not paid automatically. The passenger must still prove the value of the contents in order to recover up to the limit—which, in most cases, will probably not be difficult. The CAA warn that airlines often deduct a sum for depreciation. In situations when suitcases suffer considerable delay but are ultimately recovered intact it is a source of constant amazement for airlines and insurance companies the disparity between the contents declared by the passenger and the contents the case actually contained.

A recent referral to the ECJ, *Sanchez v Iberia* (C-410/11) has thrown up an interesting question on the limitation of liability. The court is being asked to decide what the limit of liability is when passengers have mixed their belongings in one bag: is each passenger entitled to claim the full limit or can only one person claim the limit? The authors venture to suggest that it is the former.

When the Limitations do not Apply

As with liability under art.17, the passenger must be given notice of the limitations on liability, but if the carrier fails to do so he will not lose the benefit of the limits. The relevant provisions are to be found in art.3:

"...

3. The carrier shall deliver to the passenger a baggage identification tag for each piece of checked baggage.
4. The passenger shall be given written notice to the effect that where this Convention is applicable it governs and may limit the liability of carriers in respect of death or injury and for destruction or loss of, or damage to, baggage, and for delay.
5. Non-compliance with the provisions of the foregoing paragraphs shall not affect the existence or the validity of the contract of carriage, which

shall, nonetheless, be subject to the rules of this Convention including those relating to limitation of liability."

Under art.22(5), recklessness or intent to cause damage will also deprive the carrier of the limitations on liability. In *Newell v Canadian Pacific Airlines Ltd* 74 DLR 3d 574 (1976) the carrier placed the passengers' two pet dogs in the hold—this despite an offer by the passengers to purchase all the seats in first class to accommodate themselves and their pets! One dog was killed and the other became severely ill when carbon dioxide was given off by a consignment of dry ice carried in the same hold. The carrier was held to have been reckless in the circumstances; they knew that harm would result from their actions. Note that this case is interesting for the fact that damages were also awarded for distress and disappointment. (See below the case of *Walz v Clickair*, relatively speaking a much more important case on damages for distress and disappointment.)

Kinds of Damage

A much more recent case, *Walz v Clickair SA* (C-63/09) also decided that damages were available for distress and disappointment, or in the language of the ECJ—non-material damage. In that case, the claimant, Mr Walz, brought an action against Clickair claiming damages for the loss of checked baggage on a flight from Barcelona (Spain) to Oporto (Portugal) operated by that company. He claimed total damages of €3,200: €2,700 for the value of the lost baggage and €500 for non-material damage resulting from that loss. Clickair denied the claim on the basis that this exceeded the 1,000 SDRs provided for by the Montreal Convention. As Harding remarks ("A Sting in the Tail—The Recent Decision of the European Court Of Justice in Walz v Clickair" [2010] T.L.Q. 151) the ECJ "seemingly without difficulty" interpreted "damage" in arts 17(2) and 22(2) to include both material and non-material damage. He points out two issues which make the decision a little problematic. First, it flies in the face of a number of English first instance decisions (summarised in the case of *Cowden v British Airways Plc* [2009] 2 Lloyd's Rep. 653) and other decisions from the US; secondly, it creates an anomaly between claims for accidents which do not permit recovery even for mental injury and claims for loss or destruction of baggage which now, according to *Walz*, permit recovery for mere distress and disappointment. However, it is consistent with the ECJ decision in *Leitner v TUI Deutschland* (C-168/00) [2002] All E.R. (EC) 561which held that damages for distress could be recovered in package travel cases. Imagine two couples on the same international flight, both of whom lose their luggage. If one couple were on a package holiday there is no doubt that they could claim for the distress and disappointment caused by the loss of the luggage (*Glover v Kuoni Travel* [1987] C.L.Y. 1151) but if the other couple were "flight-only" passengers then according to the authorities quoted in *Cowden* they would not be able to recover for the distress.

In arriving at its decision this is what the ECJ had to say on their approach on how to interpret the term damage in the Convention:

"21 Since the Montreal Convention does not contain any definition of the term 'damage', it must be emphasised at the outset that, in the light of the aim of that convention, which is to unify the rules for international carriage by air, that term must be given a uniform and autonomous interpretation, notwithstanding the different meanings given to that concept in the domestic laws of the States Parties to that convention."

This seems a laudable objective but when contrasted with the decision in the US Supreme Court case *Zicherman v Korean Airlines* 516 US 217 (1996) we can see a different approach:

"We conclude that Articles 17 and 24(2) of the Warsaw Convention permit compensation only for legally cognizable harm, but leave the specification of what harm is legally cognizable to the domestic law applicable under the forum's choice-of-law rules." (Scalia J.)

The inconsistency with the claims for psychiatric harm under art.17(1) following an accident and the claims for distress and disappointment under art.17(2) following loss of baggage can be reconciled in this way: if you are claiming for damages following an accident you first have to show that bodily harm has occurred and if you cannot do that then you have no claim at all—either for personal injury damages or psychiatric harm—whereas under art.17(2) you have to show loss or destruction of baggage and if you can show that then you are entitled to damages flowing from that, which, according to the ECJ, will include non-material damage. In other words, the provisions are drafted differently and as a consequence produce different results in relation to mental distress.

It might also be unwise to rely too much on cases such as *Cowden*—not least because it seems to have been overtaken by the *Walz* decision. *Cowden* was only a County Court case where the claimant represented himself but the defendant was represented by a firm of solicitors who practice at the cutting edge of air law. Readers can draw their own conclusions from that.

(iii) Delay of Passengers or Baggage

Liability for Delay

Article 19 provides:

"The carrier is liable for damage occasioned by delay in the carriage by air of passengers, baggage or cargo. Nevertheless, the carrier shall not be liable for damage occasioned by delay if it proves that it and its servants and agents took all measures that could reasonably be required to avoid the damage or that it was impossible for it or them to take such measures."

There were some difficulties about the definition of delay in the Warsaw Convention which apply equally to the Montreal Convention. For instance, does it cover the situation where the delay occurs before the passenger has checked in or before he has boarded the plane or does it just cover delays while the aircraft is airborne? Different views have been expressed on these matters and none seems to prevail but it seems reasonable to measure the delay in terms of arrival time. If the airline timetable states a particular arrival time then the flight is delayed if it arrives later than the time scheduled in the timetable. This was the perspective taken by two leading aviation lawyers at a conference in London in 1987. Professor Bin Cheng and Peter Martin suggested the following definition of delay:

"Delay occurs when passengers and their belongings of which they themselves have charge have not been carried to their immediate or final destination or when checked baggage or cargo has not been delivered within the time expressly agreed upon or, in the absence of such agreement, within the time which it would be reasonable to require of a diligent carrier, having regard to the circumstances of the case." (The "Alvor Draft" Lloyd's of London 4th International Aviation Law Seminar, London, 1987)

English case law suggests that so long as the delay is not unreasonable then there will be no breach of art.19. What is reasonable is of course a question of fact and this will have to be measured in terms of the scheduled time of arrival, the length of the flight and the fact that passengers choose to fly primarily because of its speed—and they are prepared to pay substantial sums for this.

Note that if the flight is cancelled altogether this is not a delay and therefore not dealt with by the Convention. In such cases the liability is dealt with the provisions of EC Regulation 261/2004 on Denied Boarding, Cancellations and Long Delays which is discussed in detail below.

Measuring whether baggage has been delayed will, in most cases, be relatively straightforward. If it was intended to be carried on the same aircraft as the passenger but fails to arrive at the same time then prima facie it will be have been delayed. However, this may not be the case where the passenger has excess baggage and it is carried on a later aircraft.

Damages Recoverable for Delay

According to Giemulla, Schmid and Ehlers:

"Damage in this context could be, for example, the costs of accommodation and transportation if the passenger missed his only connecting flight because the arrival of his flight was delayed, or additional expenses (e.g. additional fee for a first-class ticket) in order to reach the destination in time by a different flight." ("Warsaw Convention" WC art.19. II Liability for Delay. 1. The Damage)

For delay to baggage it is common practice for airlines to offer a sum of money to replace essential items of clothing until the baggage arrives. The limitations on damages in these cases means that there may be little difference in compensation between baggage merely delayed or totally destroyed. Because of this, courts sometimes feel it right to scale down delay damages.

Whether damages for distress and disappointment can be recovered for delay is a moot point. There is no authoritative decision to guide us. For a view that such damages are not recoverable see Clarke, *Contracts of Carriage by Air*, p.120. For a small claims arbitration where these issues were discussed see "Case Note: Marshall & Dixon v KLM" [2002] I.T.L.J. 63. and there is also the Scottish case *Reid v Ski Independence* 1999 S.L.T. (Sh Ct) 62. The approach in *Walz* may also be of relevance here. If the ECJ is prepared to award damages for distress for the loss of baggage it is only a small step to awarding it for delay to the baggage. It would also be consistent with the decision in *Leitner* to award damages for distress in package holiday cases.

Defences

The defence available to carriers in the event of delay is contained within art.19 which provides:

> "The carrier is liable for damage occasioned by delay in the carriage by air of passengers, baggage or cargo. Nevertheless, the carrier shall not be liable for damage occasioned by delay if it proves that it and its servants and agents took all measures that could reasonably be required to avoid the damage or that it was impossible for it or them to take such measures."

Delays can occur for many reasons—weather, air traffic control problems, mechanical problems, industrial action, etc. If the airport is completely snow-bound or the ATC computer system has crashed and aircraft simply cannot take off, then on the face of it the airline has a defence. However, this is not as simple as it appears. The requirement in art.19 is to avoid *damage*. If the flight is, say, a Heathrow–Paris flight, then the airline might be able to re-route its passengers on Eurostar. This is an option that can be found in the General Conditions of Contract issued by IATA, and, until recently, was adopted by most scheduled carriers. Under the General Conditions, airlines can, at their option, re-route passengers on the flights of other carriers or even by surface transportation (GCC art.10.2). This would not be possible, of course, on long-haul routes, but it should be considered for short-haul domestic routes in cases where it appears the delay will be at all significant. Many carriers are modifying their terms and conditions to confine re-rerouting to their own aircraft and routes. Whether this would be reasonable, given that they used to do it, is debatable.

Even in cases where re-routing cannot be undertaken the requirement is still to avoid the damage—which could mean providing meals and even overnight accommodation.

Note that there is an overlap here with Regulation 261/2004 which requires airlines to provide assistance in the form of refreshments, meals and overnight accommodation in the event of long delays regardless of the reason for the delay. In such circumstances it would be difficult to argue that it would not be reasonable to offer such assistance to avoid the damage under the Montreal Convention.

Where the problem is mechanical three issues arise. First, can the airline argue that the delay could not have been avoided because mechanical problems are not predictable? The answer to this may lie in the purchasing and maintenance policies of the airline concerned. If the airline buys or leases second-hand aircraft, only maintains them to the minimum standard required and has no back-up aircraft standing by in case of difficulties, then one could argue forcibly that the delay was preventable. Compared to the best practice of other airlines, such a policy is simply courting disaster. The decision in the European Court of Justice case *Wallentin-Hermann v Alitalia* (C-549/07) [2009] Bus. L.R. 1016, which is discussed in some detail below in relation to delays under Regulation 261/2004, may also be relevant here in relation to what is avoidable when it comes to technical problems.

Secondly, if other airlines have departures to the passengers' destination, then why cannot these passengers be re-routed on the flights of others? This may not be possible in small provincial airports but in major international airports there will often be seats available on alternative flights—subject, of course, to price—which may be the real stumbling block when it comes to re-routing.

Thirdly, is it possible to hire in an alternative aircraft? This may not be a realistic alternative, i.e. it goes beyond what is reasonably necessary in circumstances where the delay is likely to be short-term, but where the delay is likely to be longer, or where perhaps there is a history of mechanical failures, then this may be an option the airline should consider—and if it does not, then it is failing to take all necessary measures to prevent the damage.

The view of the Department of Transportation in the US on the question of delays can be seen in this extract from a letter written to the chief executives of 59 US airlines by Secretary of Transportation, Federico Pena, in December 1994:

"Carriers with few backup aircraft or crews should be conservative in scheduling their flights in order to limit inconvenience to consumers. Routine lengthy flight delays or frequent flight cancellations that result from unavailability of aircraft or crew will be considered unrealistic scheduling, which is actionable under [the Federal Aviation Act]. Also, to the extent that such airlines have a limited ability to accommodate overbooked passengers, they must be especially cautious in applying their overbooking procedures."

As in the UK, the DoT maintains records of flight delays. The yardstick in the US for determining whether a flight is late is whether it lands within 15 minutes of its scheduled arrival time.

All this seems to suggest that delays for mechanical problems do not necessarily give the carrier an automatic defence—either because the problems can be attributed to the carrier in the first place, or because other means can be found to get the passengers to their destination—and, in any case, steps should be taken to alleviate the damage to passengers by the provision of appropriate refreshments and accommodation. According to Clarke (p.131) the airline must, at the very least, have a contingency plan for when mechanical failures occur.

For an interesting comparison of how charter (as opposed to scheduled) airlines compare in terms of delay see the league table issued by the Air Transport Users Council in April 1997 (and subsequently) and discussed in [1997] I.T.L.J. 117. The significant feature of this table is that external factors such as weather and air traffic control are neutral, they do not affect the rankings. What the table demonstrates is that some airlines are just better than others at reducing delays. In other words, the airlines at the bottom of the table would probably not be able to demonstrate that they had taken all necessary measures to avoid the delay.

Contributory negligence is also a defence under art.20. The usual example cited is of the passenger who turns up so late at check-in that he misses his flight. In such cases, any delay would be caused solely by the passenger's own negligence and would afford a complete defence.

CHAPTER THIRTEEN

Exclusion of Liability for Delay

On the face of it, art.26 of the Montreal Convention precludes exclusion of liability for delay. However, passengers may still be faced with a term like this in their contract of carriage based upon IATA's General Conditions of Carriage:

> "Carrier undertakes to use its best efforts to carry the passenger and his or her baggage with reasonable dispatch and to adhere to published schedules in effect on the date of travel."

According to Miller:

> "The object of such clauses is to deny to the passenger/shipper the right to expect the performance of the carriage at a particular time. Since there is nothing with which the actual time of performance can be compared, no delay can appear.
>
> ... the actual conditions of carriage do not openly contradict the terms of Article 19, but they deprive the article of any real meaning. The principle of liability for delay is respected, but the condition precedent to the application of the text i.e. the existence of delay, is made unattainable." (Kluwer (1978) *Liability in International Air Transport*, pp.154–56)

However, later, after a review of case law, she concludes:

> "... the only effect produced by the provision of the Conditions of Carriage dealing with delay is to exonerate the carrier for cases of slight delay."

Limits of Liability for Delay

Liability for delay of passengers is limited by art.22(1) and for the delay of baggage by art.22(2) which provide:

> "1. In the case of damage caused by delay as specified in Article 19 in the carriage of persons, the liability of the carrier for each passenger is limited to 4,150 [4,694] Special Drawing Rights.
> 2. In the carriage of baggage, the liability of the carrier in the case of destruction, loss, damage or delay is limited to 1,000 [1,131] Special Drawing Rights for each passenger unless the passenger has made, at the time when the checked baggage was handed over to the carrier, a special declaration of interest in delivery at destination and has paid a supplementary sum if the case so requires. In that case the carrier will be liable to pay a sum not exceeding the declared sum, unless it proves that the sum is greater than the passenger's actual interest in delivery at destination."

The figures in square brackets represent the increases in the limits introduced by ICAO in 2010.

When the Limitations Do Not Apply

The art.22(5) provisions on intent and recklessness also apply to delay of passengers and baggage.

(iv) Jurisdiction Under the Montreal Convention

If an English consumer wants to sue an airline under the Montreal Convention can they do so in an English court? This will depend upon art.33 which provides for a variety of jurisdictions:

"Article 33—Jurisdiction

1. An action for damages must be brought, at the option of the plaintiff, in the territory of one of the States Parties, either before the court of the domicile of the carrier or of its principal place of business, or where it has a place of business through which the contract has been made or before the court at the place of destination.

2. In respect of damage resulting from the death or injury of a passenger, an action may be brought before one of the courts mentioned in paragraph 1 of this Article, or in the territory of a State Party in which at the time of the accident the passenger has his or her principal and permanent residence and to or from which the carrier operates services for the carriage of passengers by air, either on its own aircraft, or on another carrier's aircraft pursuant to a commercial agreement, and in which that carrier conducts its business of carriage of passengers by air from premises leased or owned by the carrier itself or by another carrier with which it has a commercial agreement.

3. For the purposes of paragraph 2,

    (a) 'commercial agreement' means an agreement, other than an agency agreement, made between carriers and relating to the provision of their joint services for carriage of passengers by air;

    (b) 'principal and permanent residence' means the one fixed and permanent abode of the passenger at the time of the accident. The nationality of the passenger shall not be the determining factor in this regard."

This gives the claimant the right to sue, in cases other than death or personal injury:

- before the court of the domicile of the carrier or of its principal place of business; or

- where it has a place of business through which the contract has been made; or

- before the court at the place of destination.

In addition, if the claimant has suffered death or personal injury the claimant can also sue:

- in the territory of a State Party in which at the time of the accident the passenger has his or her principal and permanent residence and, broadly speaking, the carrier does business there.

In practice, this means that English consumers flying on UK airlines will be able to sue them in this country but complications arise with an airline like Ryanair which is domiciled in Ireland and where it is dubious whether they have a place of business in the UK through which the contract has been made. In such cases, the consumer would have to establish that England was the "place of destination". With round-trip flights this would not be too difficult to establish but where single tickets have been bought the consumer might find themselves having to sue in Ireland—unless it was a personal injury case.

Regulation 261/2004 on Denied Boarding, Cancellation and Long Delays

Thanks to the chaos caused by the eruption of the Icelandic volcano Eyjafjallajokull in April 2010, and recent decisions of the ECJ, this regulation has become the focus of probably the most contentious area of travel law. There has been denied boarding legislation since 1991 when EC Regulation 295/91 was passed and became part of English law. This was introduced to combat the problem of deliberate overbooking by airlines, which, when it went wrong, resulted in passengers being "bumped". (See *British Airways Board v Taylor* [1976] 1 All E.R. 65 for an example of this in practice which reached the House of Lords on a Trade Descriptions Act issue.) This legislation has now been updated and the compensation limits raised. The opportunity was also taken to introduce compensation for flight cancellations and to require airlines to offer assistance to passengers affected by long delays. Note that a recent, controversial, decision of the European Court of Justice in the joined cases, *Sturgeon v Condor* (C-402/07) and *Bock v Air France* (C-432/07), now provides for compensation in the event of delay as well as cancellation. It was formerly believed that compensation for delay was not available under Regulation 261/2004 because that might conflict with the Montreal Convention. (See *R. (on the application of International Air Transport Association (IATA)) v Department of Transport* (C-344/04) [2006] E.C.R. I-403 for a discussion of these issues.)

The rationale for the legislation is set out in the preamble to the Regulation:

"(1) Action by the Community in the field of air transport should aim, among other things, at ensuring a high level of protection for passengers. Moreover, full account should be taken of the requirements of consumer protection in general.

(2) Denied boarding and cancellation or long delay of flights cause serious trouble and inconvenience to passengers.

(3) While Council Regulation (EEC) No 295/91 of 4 February 1991 establishing common rules for a denied boarding compensation system in scheduled air transport created basic protection for passengers, the number of passengers denied boarding against their will remains too high, as does that affected by cancellations without prior warning and that affected by long delays.

(4) The Community should therefore raise the standards of protection set by that Regulation both to strengthen the rights of passengers and to ensure that air carriers operate under harmonised conditions in a liberalised market."

Rules Applicable Generally to Denied Boarding, Cancellations and Delays

Whether it is a case of denied boarding, cancellation or delay a passenger must show they come within the scope of the Regulation. To qualify, they have to satisfy the requirements of art.3. They must show that they:

- departed from an airport in a Member State; or

- departed from an airport in another state en route to a Member State (unless compensation or assistance was received in that other state) on a Community carrier;

- had a confirmed reservation on the flight concerned; or

- were transferred to another flight from the one on which they held a reservation, irrespective of the reason; and

- except in the case of flight cancellation, checked-in at the time stipulated in advance, in writing, by the air carrier or tour operator; or, if no time was indicated,

- checked in no later than 45 minutes before the published departure time; and

- were not travelling free of charge or on reduced fares not available directly to the public (but frequent flyer passengers will qualify).

Emirates Airlines Direktion für Deutschland v Schenkel (C-173/07) [2009] All E.R. (EC) 436 decided that when a passenger is returning from outside the EU on a non-EU carrier the Regulation does not apply even though the passenger had a return ticket from an airport within the EU. Passengers in this situation would have to rely upon the denied boarding regulations of other states, on the airline's contract of carriage or upon the goodwill of the carrier. Clearly, however, passengers travelling to the EU on an EU carrier would be protected—as evidence by a class action commenced in the US (*Gurevich v Alitalia*, March 2011; www.courthousenews.com/2011/03/21/Alitalia.pdf).

Denied Boarding

Denied boarding is defined in art.2 in this fashion:

"(j) 'denied boarding' means a refusal to carry passengers on a flight, although they have presented themselves for boarding under the conditions laid down in Article 3(2), except where there are reasonable grounds to deny them boarding, such as reasons of health, safety or security, or inadequate travel documentation;"

Where the criteria in art.3 can be established and the carrier expects to have to deny boarding to passengers, art.4 requires the carrier to first of all call for volunteers who would be willing to surrender their reservations in return for "benefits" to be agreed between them. Even where enough volunteers can be found, the carrier is still required to offer passengers assistance under art.8, i.e. reimbursement or re-routing.

Where enough volunteers cannot be found the carrier can then deny boarding to passengers against their will, in which case the passengers will be entitled to the remedies set out in arts 7, 8 and 9.

Compensation and Assistance for Denied Boarding

Under art.4, if a passenger is denied boarding against his will he must be *immediately* compensated under art.7. Article 7 provides compensation on a sliding scale depending on the length of the flight and the length of the delay caused.

The following table (taken from the website of the AUC) summarises the position:

Length of flight	Delay to destination	Compensation
Up to 1,500km	Up to 2 hours	€125
Up to 1,500km	Over 2 hours	€250
1,500km to 3,500km	Up to 3 hours	€200
1,500km to 3,500km	Over 3 hours	€400
Over 3,500km	Up to 4 hours	€300
Over 3,500km	Over 4 hours	€600

In addition to compensation, the passenger also has the right to reimbursement or re-routing under art.8. According to art.8 the passenger must be offered the choice between the two.

Reimbursement must be made within seven days and must cover:

- the full cost of the ticket for parts of the journey already made;

- the cost of any further parts of the journey not yet made if they serve no further purpose; and

- a return flight to the first point of departure at the earliest opportunity if relevant.

Re-routing should be made under comparable transport conditions to the final destination at the earliest opportunity, or under comparable transport conditions at a later date at the customer's convenience (subject to availability of seats).

The airline must also provide assistance under reg.9. This consists of:

- meals and refreshment in a reasonable relation to the waiting time;

- hotel accommodation where necessary;

- transport between the airport and the accommodation;

- two telephone, fax, telex or email messages.

Note that there are no defences in the Regulation for denied boarding—unlike for cancellation. The rationale being that denied boarding is due to airlines deliberately adopting overbooking policies.

Two situations have given rise to concern on the part of airlines. What if, for the sake of argument, a door on an aircraft fails with the result that the aircraft does not have enough functioning exits to comply with safety regulations. The aircraft is fit to fly but the number of passengers has to be reduced and so some are disembarked. Clearly they are "denied boarding", not for reason of deliberate overbooking but for safety reasons. This may not be a defence under the Regulations.

A second scenario is where an aircraft is grounded for safety or technical reasons and most of the passengers can be put on another, smaller aircraft, but some are left behind. Does this amount to "denied boarding"?

One clue can be found in art.3(2)(b) which envisages that the Regulations apply where the passenger has:

"(b) ... been transferred by an air carrier or tour operator from the flight for which they held a reservation to another flight, irrespective of the reason."

This suggests, but no more, that this second scenario has been contemplated by the legislator and it gives rise to denied boarding rights.

There have been two recent referrals to the ECJ (*Finnair Oyj v Timy Lassooy* (C-22/11); *Germán Rodríguez Cachafeiro and Maria Reyes Martínez-Reboredo Varela-Villamayor v Iberia Líneas Aéreas de España S* (C-321/11)) which may answer some of these questions.

Re-routing is also a term that has the potential to cause difficulty. In the past, many airlines offered in their terms and conditions to re-route passengers on their own aircraft or on the aircraft of other airlines but this remedy is being removed from many sets of terms and conditions. Does this mean that when the airline comes to offer re-routing they can confine it to flights on their own aircraft, as this would amount to re-routing "under comparable transport conditions"?

Cancellation

Cancellation is defined in the following way in art.2:

"(l) 'cancellation' means the non-operation of a flight which was previously planned and on which at least one place was reserved."

At the margins there are difficulties distinguishing between a cancellation and a delay but there is now high level guidance from the ECJ, in the joined cases *Sturgeon v Condor* (C-402/07) and *Böck v Air France* (C-432/07), as to the difference. The real significance of the case, however, is that it decided that compensation is now payable for long delays in much the same way as for cancellations. This was a controversial aspect of the decision which is discussed later, but suffice it to say that it was a hugely unpopular decision with the airline industry who are challenging it in the ECJ on a broad front (*TUI Travel v Civil*

CHAPTER THIRTEEN

Aviation Authority (C-629/10); *Germanwings GmbH v Amend* (C-413/11); *João Nuno Esteves Coelho dos Santos v TAP Portugal* (C-365/11); *Van de Ven & Van de Ven-Janssen v KLM* (C-315/11); *Nadine Büsch and Björn Siever v Ryanair Ltd* (C-255/11).

In the *Sturgeon* case, the facts were that the Sturgeons booked return tickets with Condor from Frankfurt am Main to Toronto. The return flight from Toronto to Frankfurt was due to depart at 16.20 on July 9, 2005. Following check-in, passengers on that flight were informed that the flight was cancelled, as was indicated on the airport departures board. Their luggage was returned to them and they were then driven to a hotel where they spent the night. The following day, the passengers were checked-in at another airline's counter for a flight with the same number as that on their booking. Condor did not schedule another flight with the same number for the day concerned. The passengers were given different seats from those they had been allocated on the previous day. The booking was not converted into a booking for a flight scheduled by another airline. The flight concerned arrived in Frankfurt at around 07.00 on July 11, 2005, some 25 hours after its scheduled arrival time. The Sturgeons took the view that, in light of all the circumstances, in particular the delay of more than 25 hours, the flight had been not delayed but cancelled. They claimed €600 per person plus damages, since, in their view, the damage sustained was the result not of a flight delay but of a cancellation. Condor contended that the action should be dismissed on the ground that the flight in question was delayed and not cancelled. Prior to the proceedings before the national court, Condor claimed that the flight had been delayed as the result of a hurricane in the Caribbean but during the proceedings it attributed the delay to technical faults on the plane and illness among the crew.

The facts of the *Böck* case were that Mr Böck and Ms Lepuschitz booked return tickets with Air France from Vienna to Mexico City via Paris. The Mexico City–Paris flight which Mr Böck and Ms Lepuschitz were due to take was scheduled to depart at 21.30 on March 7, 2005. When they came to check-in, they were immediately informed, without the check-in taking place, that their flight was cancelled. The cancellation resulted from a change in the flight planning between Mexico City and Paris, which arose because of a technical breakdown on the aircraft due to fly from Paris to Mexico City and on account of the need to observe the rest period prescribed by law for the crew. In order to get back earlier, Mr Böck and Ms Lepuschitz accepted Air France's offer of seats on a flight operated by Continental Airlines, which was scheduled to leave the following day, March 8, 2005 at 12.20. Their tickets were cancelled and then new tickets were issued to them at the Continental Airlines counter. The other passengers on the Mexico City–Paris flight, who did not take the Continental Airlines flight, left Mexico City, with a number of additional passengers, on March 8, 2005 at 19.35. That flight, whose original number was followed by the letter "A", was operated in addition to the regular flight scheduled by Air France on the same day. Mr Böck and Ms Lepuschitz arrived in Vienna almost 22 hours after the scheduled arrival time. They brought an action against Air France claiming €600 compensation per person for cancellation of their flight, on the basis of arts 5 and 7(1)(c) of Regulation 261/2004.

When the two cases were referred to the ECJ the court was asked the following three questions:

374

- whether a flight delay must be regarded as a flight cancellation for the purposes of arts 2(l) and 5 of Regulation 261/2004 where the delay is long;

- whether arts 5, 6 and 7 of Regulation 261/2004 must be interpreted as meaning that passengers whose flights are delayed may, for the purpose of the application of the right to compensation laid down in art.7 of that regulation, be treated as passengers whose flights are cancelled, and

- whether a technical problem in an aircraft is covered by the concept of "extraordinary circumstances" within the meaning of art.5(3) of Regulation 261/2004.

The First Question

The court held that so long as a flight is operated in accordance with its original flight plan then it is not cancelled, even if the delay is substantial. The difference between a delayed flight and a cancelled flight is that the latter involves the non-operation of a flight which was previously planned. If delayed passengers are carried on a flight where the original planning was different from the delayed flight, i.e. a completely different flight, then it can be said that the delayed flight was cancelled. Even if passengers are told that the flight is cancelled or their baggage is returned to them this does not necessarily mean that their flight is cancelled—this could simply be down to a misclassification of the situation.

The meaning of "cancellation" was also the subject of a more recent case. In *Rodríguez v Air France* (C-83/10) the facts were that the claimants had a contract to fly from Paris to Vigo. The applicants in the main proceedings entered into an air transport contract with Air France to carry them from Paris to Vigo. The plane took off as planned but because of a technical problem it returned to Paris. The claimants were re-routed on other aircraft. There was no evidence to show that the original aircraft took off later and belatedly reached its destination. The ECJ was asked whether this amounted to a cancellation of the flight and the answer they gave was that Regulation 261/2004 must be interpreted as meaning that in such a situation cancellation does not refer only to the situation in which the aeroplane in question fails to take off at all, but also covers the case in which that aeroplane took off but, for whatever reason, was subsequently forced to return to the airport of departure where the passengers on that aeroplane were transferred to other flights.

The Second Question—Compensation for Delay as well as Cancellation?

The second question will be answered later.

The Third Question—the Meaning of "Extraordinary Circumstances"

The Court held that this question had already been answered in the *Wallentin-Hermann* case, discussed below.

If a flight is cancelled the passenger is entitled to the same remedies as for denied boarding and has to qualify for them in the same way, i.e. by satisfying the requirements in art.3 relating to travelling from an airport in a Member State or on a Community carrier and having satisfied the check-in requirements, etc.

However, limitations are placed on the remedies available. The right to compensation is lost if:

- the passenger is informed of the cancellation between two weeks and seven days before the scheduled departure time and they are offered re-routing permitting them to depart no more than two hours before the scheduled departure and arrive at their final destination no more than four hours after the scheduled arrival time; or

- the passenger is informed less than seven days before the departure and is offered re-routing allowing them to depart no more than one hour before the scheduled time of departure and arrive no later than two hours after the scheduled arrival time.

Furthermore, under art.5(3), compensation is not payable if the airline can prove that the cancellation is caused by extraordinary circumstances which could not have been avoided even if all reasonable measures had been taken. This imposes a double burden on the airline (on whom the burden of proof lies). First, they have to establish that what occurred was caused by "extraordinary circumstances". Secondly, they have to show that they took "all reasonable measures" to prevent the cancellation.

Guidance on what amounts to "extraordinary circumstances" is given in *Wallentin-Hermann v Alitalia* (C-549/07). The facts of the case were that Mrs Wallentin-Hermann booked three seats on a flight with Alitalia from Vienna to Brindisi via Rome for herself, her husband and her daughter. The flight was scheduled to depart from Vienna on June 28, 2005 at 06.45 and to arrive at Brindisi on the same day at 10.35. After checking-in, the three passengers were informed, five minutes before the scheduled departure time, that their flight had been cancelled. They were subsequently transferred to an Austrian Airlines flight to Rome, where they arrived at 09.40, that is, 20 minutes after the time of departure of their connecting flight to Brindisi, which they therefore missed. Mrs Wallentin-Hermann and her family arrived at Brindisi at 14.15. The cancellation of the Alitalia flight from Vienna resulted from a complex engine defect in the turbine which had been discovered the day before during a check. Alitalia had been informed of the defect during the night preceding that flight, at 01.00. The repair of the aircraft, which necessitated the dispatch of spare parts and engineers, was completed on July 8, 2005. Mrs Wallentin-Hermann requested that Alitalia pay her €250 compensation pursuant to arts 5(1)(c) and 7(1) of Regulation 261/2004 due to the cancellation of her flight and also €10 for telephone charges. Alitalia rejected that request.

When the case came to the ECJ for a preliminary ruling it had to decide whether a technical problem could amount to "extraordinary circumstances" and whether the airline had taken all reasonable measures to prevent the cancellation if it had maintained the aircraft to minimum legal standards.

On the issue of "extraordinary circumstances" the court referred to Recital 14 of the Preamble to the Regulation which stated:

"(14) As under the Montreal Convention, obligations on operating air carriers should be limited or excluded in cases where an event has been caused by extraordinary circumstances which could not have been avoided even if all reasonable measures had been taken. Such circumstances may, in particular, occur in cases of political instability, meteorological conditions incompatible with the operation of the flight concerned, security risks, unexpected flight safety shortcomings and strikes that affect the operation of an operating air carrier."

The court said that a technical defect could amount to a flight safety shortcoming and, therefore, could be "extraordinary circumstances", but the list was only indicative of what *may* amount to "extraordinary circumstances". It would only be "extraordinary circumstances" if it was not inherent in the normal exercise of the activity of the air carrier concerned and was beyond the actual control of that carrier on account of its nature or origin. Given the stringent safety regime under which aircraft operated, which was part and parcel of the standard operating conditions, the resolution of a technical problem caused by failure to maintain an aircraft must be regarded as inherent in the normal exercise of an air carrier's activity. Therefore, the court said, " ... technical problems which come to light during maintenance of aircraft or on account of failure to carry out such maintenance cannot constitute, *in themselves*, 'extraordinary circumstances' under Article 5(3) of Regulation No 261/2004." (Emphasis added)

But if the technical problems stemmed from events which were not inherent in the normal operation of the aircraft, such as latent defects identified by the manufacturer or by sabotage or terrorism then "extraordinary circumstances" might exist.

On the issue of whether the carrier had taken all reasonable measures to avoid the cancellation, the court took a hard line:

"39. It must be observed that the Community legislature intended to confer exemption from the obligation to pay compensation to passengers in the event of cancellation of flights not in respect of all extraordinary circumstances, but only in respect of those which could not have been avoided even if all reasonable measures had been taken.

40. It follows that, since not all extraordinary circumstances confer exemption, the onus is on the party seeking to rely on them to establish, in addition, that they could not on any view have been avoided by measures appropriate to the situation, that is to say by measures which, at the time those extraordinary circumstances arise, meet, inter alia, conditions which are technically and economically viable for the air carrier concerned.

41. That party must establish that, *even if it had deployed all its resources in terms of staff or equipment and the financial means at its disposal, it would clearly not have been able—unless it had made intolerable sacrifices in the light of the capacities of its undertaking at the relevant time—to prevent the extraordinary circumstances with which it was confronted from leading to the cancellation of the flight.*

42. It is for the referring court to ascertain whether, in the circumstances of the case in the main proceedings, the air carrier concerned took measures appropriate to the situation, that is to say measures which, at the time of the extraordinary circumstances whose existence the air carrier is to establish, met, inter alia, conditions which were technically and economically viable for that carrier." (Emphasis added)

The upshot of this seems to be that routine maintenance problems will not excuse an airline from paying compensation for cancellations and even if the problem is extraordinary it will have to deploy all its resources to avoid the cancellation unless that would impose an *intolerable* burden on the airline.

If the passenger accepts reimbursement following a cancelled flight then the right to assistance and re-routing are extinguished from that point. This was an issue that arose in the case of *Marshall v Iberia Lineas Aereas de Espana SA* Unreported December 13, 2010, Mayor & City of London Court. The claimants had travelled from Ecuador as far as Madrid on a return flight to Heathrow. They were stranded at Madrid Airport by the volcanic ash cloud. They then made their own arrangements to travel home. The decision on the facts was that the airline had not refused to re-route them when it became possible nor had it refused assistance. The basis of the decision seems to be that the claimants exercised the choice available to them under art.8 to take reimbursement rather than re-routing. The case is only a small claims case and, therefore, of limited value and there may be grounds for doubting its authority (although the claimant in the case was a QC and a Recorder—on which the judge had some interesting comments—and the defendants were represented by solicitors). For instance, art.14.2 of the Regulation requires that carriers "shall provide each passenger affected with a written notice setting out the rules for compensation and assistance in line with this Regulation". It is not clear that the airline did this but if they did not it prompts the question as to whether the "choice" made by the Marshalls was a properly informed one made in the full knowledge of the consequences of that choice.

Delay

The *Böck* and *Sturgeon* cases not only discussed the difference between cancellation and delay they also decided that, contrary to received wisdom, compensation could be claimed for delay. The reasoning goes like this:

- Article 5(1) of Regulation 261/2004 provides for compensation for passengers whose flight is *cancelled.*

- Passengers do not have an *express* right to compensation if their flight is only delayed.

- Community law must not only be interpreted according to the wording of the legislation but also according to its purpose and the context in which it appears.

- The concept of "extraordinary circumstances" permits a carrier to deny compensation to a passenger in the event of a cancellation.

- Recital 15 of the preamble, however, states that "extraordinary circumstances" exist when an air traffic control decision leads to a cancellation *or a long delay*.

- This linking of the notion of long delays to "extraordinary circumstances" by the legislature must also mean that the notion is linked to compensation.

- This is implicitly borne out by Recitals 1–4 of the Regulation which provide that the Regulations seek to ensure a high level of consumer protection for air passengers irrespective of whether they are denied boarding, their flight is cancelled or they suffer a long delay.

- This is reinforced by the *Wallentin-Hermann* case, discussed above, which provides that the provisions conferring rights on air passengers must be interpreted broadly.

- For these reasons it cannot be automatically presumed that passengers whose flights have been delayed have no right to compensation.

- Community legislation must be interpreted (a) in such a manner so as not to affect its validity, and (b) where it is open to more than one interpretation, to give effect to that interpretation which ensures that it retains its effectiveness.

- Community legislation must also be interpreted in accordance with the principle of equal treatment so comparable situations must not be treated differently and different situations must not be treated in the same way unless such treatment is objectively justified.

- The objective of Regulation 261/2004 is to protect air passengers by redressing damage suffered by them. In the light of this objective situations covered by the Regulation must be compared by reference to the type and extent of the various types of inconvenience and damage suffered.

- In this instance, passengers who are delayed must be compared with passengers whose flights are cancelled.

- There is no objective difference between the type of damage suffered—loss of time; and no objective reason for treating them differently.

As a consequence of this reasoning the Court held that passengers whose flights are delayed may rely on the right to compensation laid down in art.7 of Regulation 261/2004 where they suffer, on account of such flights, a loss of time equal to or in excess of three hours, that is to say when they reach their final destination three hours or more after the arrival time originally scheduled by the air carrier.

In addition, as with the provisions on denied boarding and cancellation, the "care and assistance" remedies are available on a sliding scale depending upon how long the delay lasted. The table below (taken from the AUC website) summarises the care and assistance position for passengers who have been delayed.

Distance of flight	Length of delay	Assistance
All flights	Overnight and more than 5 hours	• Meals and refreshments in relation to waiting time • Two free telephone calls, emails, telexes or faxes • Hotel accommodation and transfers • Reimbursement of ticket (if passenger decides not to travel)
All flights	More than 5 hours	• Meals and refreshments in relation to waiting time • Two free telephone calls, emails, telexes or faxes • Reimbursement of ticket (if passenger decides not to travel)
Over 3,500kms	More than 4 hours	• Meals and refreshments in relation to waiting time • Two free telephone calls, emails, telexes or faxes
1,500 to 3,500kms	More than 3 hours	• Meals and refreshments in relation to waiting time • Two free telephone calls, emails, telexes or faxes
Up to 1,500kms	More than two hours	• Meals and refreshments in relation to waiting time • Two free telephone calls, emails, telexes or faxes

Another issue is that re-routing is not one of the options available for delay. One can imagine that a passenger is delayed for long periods at some remote airport and wishes to come home using other aircraft or other airlines. This is not an option that the passenger is entitled to. They could, of course, claim their right to reimbursement but if they are travelling on a low-cost airline then the refund may not take them very far—maybe only a taxi ride to the next airport from which scheduled flights can be taken. They will of course receive refreshments, meals and accommodation but that may not be what they want.

One issue that has arisen is what happens if the passenger is not offered what s/he is entitled to under the Regulation? Can they sue for damages? One school of thought is that the Regulations do not, and cannot, provide for compensation because in doing so this would trespass on the scope of the Montreal Convention and this would be an infringement of our international obligations. The only way of enforcing the Regulations as they apply to delay is for the enforcing authority, the CAA, to bring a prosecution. (See McDonald "European Court of Justice

Denies IATA's Case" [2006] I.T.L.J. 24). As far as individual redress is concerned this leaves the passenger only with his rights under the Montreal Convention. However, Barham argues that, notwithstanding some English County Court cases to the contrary (*Parker v TUI Ltd (t/a Austravel)* [2007] C.L.Y. 297 and *Rigby v Iberia* Unreported April 17, 2009, CC), compensation is available for passengers denied their right to care and assistance under the Regulation ("Volcanic Ash—An Assessment of EC Regulation 261/2004 As The Dust Settles" [2010] T.L.Q. 146). This view seems to be vindicated and the matter put beyond doubt by the *Rodriguez* decision (see also the *Rehder* decision) where the ECJ said quite categorically:

> "44. However, when a carrier fails to fulfil its obligations under Article 8 and Article 9 of Regulation No 261/2004, air passengers are justified in claiming a right to compensation on the basis of the factors set out in those articles."

Of course, how much the passenger can claim is a moot point. Following the volcanic ash cloud incident passengers made claims for accommodation from airlines with varying degrees of success. As one might expect, on the one hand, airlines accused passengers of exploiting the position by paying for five star accommodation, while passengers accused the airlines of refusing to pay for even basic accommodation. The advice issued by the European Commission, which is available on the DG TREN website (interestingly headed "Non Paper"!) has this to say on the matter:

> "The intention of the Regulation is that **adequate** care of the needs of passengers waiting for re-routing under Article 8(1)(b) is to be provided. This should be provided without imposing a disproportionate and unfair burden on the air carrier concerned."

It goes on to provide more specific advice:

> "When assessing whether the carrier's offer to compensate a passenger's expenses linked to assistance/rerouting may be considered as 'adequate', [National Enforcement Boards] may take into account a set of criteria, amongst which: a) whether passengers were actually in need of assistance or not (depending on how far from their place of residence they were); b) the distance between the accommodation and the airport (in order to not to delay the rerouting as soon as it becomes possible); c) the availability, average conditions and prices practiced for rooms and hotels in the relevant area, region or State concerned; d) the treatment of other passengers in a comparable situation; e) balancing adequate assistance for the passenger with unnecessary expense for the airlines; f) average conditions and prices practiced in the place, region or State concerned. NEBs may use public index available [sic] on average hotel costs to help their assessment of what can be considered as 'adequate' cost of the accommodation.
>
> 15. This would also mean that g) accommodation does not necessarily imply in all events the continuation of the stay of the passenger in the same hotel where

he was previously lodged, h) nor the automatic right for the passengers to decide himself where and at what condition he is to be accommodated. In the case of passengers making their own alternative travel arrangements (by whatever mode) and subsequently seeking reimbursement from the carrier, NEBs should take account of efforts made by the carrier to finding alternative transportation, particularly where a carrier made no effort at all. In all circumstances relating to alternative travel and other assistance, NEBs may accept that air carriers reimburse passengers' expenses against receipts up to a certain 'reasonable' level in line with the above mentioned criteria. In any event passengers who feel that they are entitled to have more of their expenses reimbursed retain the right to pursue the air carrier through a national Court procedure."

Jurisdiction and Time Limits

As we have seen earlier in this chapter, if a claimant wishes to sue an airline under the Montreal Convention the case can only be brought before a limited number of courts. In the case of *Rehder v Air Baltic Corporation* (C-204/08) [2010] Bus. L.R. 549 the ECJ had to decide which courts had jurisdiction under Regulation 261/2004. The facts of the case were that the claimant, Mr Rehder, who lived in Munich, booked a flight from Munich to Vilnius with Air Baltic, the registered office of which was in Latvia. The flight was cancelled and Mr Rehder eventually arrived more than six hours late. He sued Air Baltic for compensation under Regulation 261/2004 in his local court in Munich. Air Baltic contended that they should be sued in Latvia and the Munich court had no jurisdiction.

The ECJ held that the case should be decided according to the rules in Regulation 44/2001, on jurisdiction and the recognition and enforcement of judgments in civil and commercial matters, the Brussels Regulation. According to that Regulation the airline could be sued in "the place in a Member State where, under the contract, the services were provided or should have been provided" (art.5(1)(b). It then went on to hold that at the claimant's choice, the airline could be sued in the court which had territorial jurisdiction over the place of departure or place of arrival of the aircraft, as agreed in the contract. This was because the services were provided at both the airport of departure and the airport of arrival—and not at the headquarters of the airline.

What is not immediately clear from Regulation 261/2004 is the time limit within which claims must be brought. Is it the two year limit found in the Montreal Convention, or some other limit? This is yet another question which has been referred to the ECJ (*Joan Cuadrench More v KLM* (C-139/11)).

CARRIAGE BY SEA

The increasing popularity of cruising as a form of holiday makes it more relevant than formerly to consider the law on international carriage by sea. As we shall see, the basic scheme is similar, but not identical, to the position in carriage by air.

The Athens Convention 1974 governs the position. It has been in force in the UK since 1996 by virtue of the Merchant Shipping Act 1995.

Who is the Carrier?

Article 1 of the Convention distinguishes "carrier" from "performing carrier". The carrier means a person by or on behalf of whom a Contract of carriage has been concluded, whether the carriage is actually performed by him or by a performing carrier. A performing carrier means a person other than the carrier, being the owner, charterer or operator of the ship, who actually performs the whole or a part of the carriage.

As we have seen, there is much debate as to whether, in the context of carriage by air, a tour operator can be a carrier. It is much clearer that the tour operator could take the risk (and benefit) of being a carrier under the Athens Convention, even though not a performing carrier.

Limitation Period

By art.16, any action for death, personal injury or loss or damage of luggage must be issued within two years of the date of disembarkation (as it was contracted to be). In very limited circumstances this can be extended to three years (and not at all thereafter) if domestic rules allow for suspension or interruption of the limitation period. (Note that this is not the same as the discretion to disapply the limitation period contained in s.33 of our own Limitation Act 1980.) In *Higham v Stena Sealink Ltd* [1996] 2 Lloyd's Rep. 26 the claimant, while a passenger on the defendants' ferry *Stena Cambria* sailing between Holyhead and Dunlaoghaire in the Republic of Ireland, suffered injury when she slipped on some broken glass on the deck and fell. She disembarked later the same day but failed to issue proceedings within the two year period and thus failed in her action.

Note that for claims for lost or damaged luggage there are additional requirements for written notice to be given at or immediately after the occurrence.

International Carriage

The Athens Convention applies to any international carriage by sea where the ship is flying the flag of a Convention country, or the Contract was made in a Convention country. The "International" element of the carriage is defined in accordance with common sense and includes carriage which starts and ends in the same place, as many cruises do, but has least one port of call in another country. However, popular river cruises—such as on the Rhine—are of course excluded, even if more than one country is visited.

Liability

This is defined by art.3(1) of the Athens Convention which says:—

> "The Carrier shall be liable for the damage suffered as a result of the death of or personal injury to a passenger and the loss of or damage to luggage if the incident which caused the damage so suffered occurred in the course of

Carriage and was due to the fault or neglect of the Carrier or of his servants or agents acting within the scope of their employment".

There are three points to note from this definition:

- Note the reference to personal injury as distinct from "bodily injury" in the Montreal Convention. It is clear that psychiatric damage *is* included under the Athens Convention. This may be important to passengers affected by the sinking of the Costa Concordia in January 2012.

- Note the word "incident" as distinct from the words "accident" which appears in the Montreal Convention. Incident is, of course, a much wider word. Having said that, it is not clear that in practice there is going to be much difference. One can speculate whether DVT is any more the result of an "incident" than it is of an "accident"; but in the real world DVT appears to be an unlikely result of a cruise anyway!

- At first blush it looks as though the definition requires the claimant to prove fault; however, art.3 goes on to presume fault in cases of injury or damage to cabin luggage which arise from or in connection with shipwreck, collision, stranding, explosion, fire or defect in the ship. This appears to cover all the most serious situations likely to arise. In any other situation—perhaps, for example, food poisoning—the claimant will have to prove fault (note, however, that in case of stored luggage, fault is presumed in every case).

Limits on Damage

Limits on damage are somewhat less generous than under the Montreal Convention. The limits for personal injury and death are defined in units of account; approximate value in sterling is £46,204. (For cabin luggage it is £825, for other luggage about £1,188.) (The value for injury, etc, is expressed as 46,666 Special Drawing Rights, the daily value of which can be discovered at *www.imf.org*.)

A trap for consumers is that valuables (e.g. jewellery) are not covered unless deposited with the carrier for the agreed purpose of safekeeping.

For consumers there are two pieces of good news:

- For British registered carriers/ships, the limit on damages for personal injuries is raised to approximately £297,030.

- There are proposals (the 2002 protocol) to substantially increase the limitations in the Athens Convention. However, these proposals appear to be a considerable distance from enactment; as at September 2010, only 4 of the 10 states needed to approve the measure, in order to activate it, had done so. See, however, the section on EU Regulation below, especially regarding Regualtion 392/2009. The effect should be that these provisions come into force within the EU by the end of 2012.

Practical Examples

Many issues arose in the case of *Lee v Airtours Holidays Ltd* [2004] 1 Lloyd's Rep. 683 (see Saggerson "Case Comment: That Sinking Feeling—Psychiatric Injury, Lost Valuables And The Demise Of The Cruise Ship 'Sun Vista'. *Lee & Lee v Airtours Holidays Limited*" [2002] I.T.L.J. 198).

The claimants suffered psychiatric damage and the loss of valuables when their cruise ship caused fire and sank. The points to be noted in this case are:

- Airtours were held to be a carrier within the definition set out above.

- Psychiatric injury is recoverable.

- The valuables were in their cabin safe, not deposited with the carrier for safekeeping.

- The Airtours Booking Conditions provided for damages to be limited in accordance with International Conventions. However, the claimants had booked on the telephone and had never seen the conditions, therefore, the Judge held them to be irrelevant to this case.

- Article 14 of the Athens Convention stipulates that the Convention provides exclusive remedies against the carrier—the position is, therefore, similar to that seen under the Warsaw Convention in *Sidhu v British Airways* [1997] A.C. 430.

- Surprisingly, in view of the exclusivity of the Convention (and surely wrongly?), the Judge held that there was a parallel remedy under reg.15 of the Package Travel Regulations against Airtours as tour operator, as distinct from Airtours as a carrier. Financial limits for injury or lost property, therefore, did not apply (presumably it would follow that the two year limitation period also did not apply).

In any event, held the Judge, financial limits on the lost valuables did not apply because the claimants had asked the ship to look after the valuables, but this request was declined.

Contrast this case with the decision in *Norfolk v Mytravel* [2004] 1 Lloyd's rep. 106 in which the Circuit Judge held that the Athens Convention "overrode" the PTR's, and, therefore, where, as here, a claimant is injured on a cruise, the two year limitation period from the Convention will apply, even in a claim against a tour operator.

Neither of these decisions appears to contain the complete answer—certainly, as we have seen in Ch.5, the Court of Appeal in *Hone v Going Places* drew a clear distinction between fault liability under the PTR's, and strict liability under the (then) Warsaw Convention. A higher level of authority than *Lee* or *Norfolk* appears to be needed.

EU Regulation

The EU has legislated in this area also. Regulation (EC) 1177/2010 concerning the rights of passengers when travelling by sea and inland waterway is to apply from December 18, 2012. Meanwhile, Regulation (EC) 392/2009 on the liability of carriers of passengers by sea in the event of accidents, is likely to apply from December 31, 2012.

The former of these reflects Regulation 261/2004 on denied boarding, long delays and cancellation of flights which we discussed above. It contains provisions, for, among other things:

- Non-discrimination between passengers of different nationalities—art.4.

- Non-discrimination against, and assistance for, Persons of Reduced Mobility ("PRMs")—arts 7 to 15, which cover many topics; no extra charges to be made to PRMs (art.7); very limited exceptions to non-discrimination, e.g. on health and safety grounds (art.8); a right to assistance in ports and on board ship (art.10); need for training of staff (art.14); compensation for loss of or damage to mobility equipment (art.15).

- Rights of passengers in the event of cancellation or delay.

- Reimbursement or re-routing where the delay exceeds 90 minutes.

- Assistance (including food/drink/accommodation, where needed, although these can be limited to €80 per night and for a maximum of three nights (art.17).

- Compensation based on a percentage of the ticket price, with a minimum threshold—25 per cent if delay exceeds 25 per cent of scheduled journey time, 50 per cent for longer delays (art.19, however, note the exceptions in art.20, especially where weather conditions endangering the ship cause the delay).

- Rules concerning complaint handling, e.g. a two month time limit on replies to complaints (art.24).

Note that only ships/boats with a capacity of less than 12 passengers are exempted from the Regulation. Note also that (unlike Athens, as we have seen), the Regulation applies to inland waterways as well as sea trips and, therefore, a Rhine cruise would be within its scope. Embarkation or disembarkation must be within the EU. A cruise is covered, but not including the rights to reimbursement/ rerouting/compensation contained in arts 18 and 19. However, the Package Travel Regulations are likely to afford a remedy in those cases.

By contrast, Regulation 392/2009 reflects but goes further than the 2002 Protocol to the Athens Convention, see above. It applies where that Protocol applies and where the ship flies a Member State flag, departs from or arrives in a Member State or the contract for carriage is made in a Member State (art.2); and, therefore, not just to international carriage. The effect is that a carrier is liable for up to 250,000 Special Drawing Rights per passenger for injury (but subject to deduction for contributory negligence), unless the carrier proves that the incident was caused by war or a similar *force majeure* event, including an act of terrorism; and if the extent of damage warrants this, up to a ceiling of 400,000 SDR's, unless the carrier proves the (slightly less onerous burden) that the loss happened through no fault of the carrier's (art.7).

Furthermore, art.7 requires advance payments to be made, proportionate to any injury or death, and to be paid within 15 days of the accident; in the event of death, that payment must be not less than €21,000.

There are limits for baggage too, 2,250 SDRs for cabin luggage, €12,700 for other luggage; and there are provisions allowing the deduction of small excesses for each claim (art.8).

The basic two year limitation period is maintained (art.16), but this can be extended up to five years if the period is interrupted (as per the three years for Athens, see above).

Other Modes of Transport

To complete the picture, the EU has also legislated in the area of rail transport, and bus and coach transport.

Rail

As we saw briefly in Ch.6 on exclusion of liability, the Berne Convention of 1980 exists in respect of international carriage by rail but it is limited in scope. Now the EU has legislated in this area. The Rail Passenger Rights Regulation (EC 1371/2007) entered into force in December 2009. The undoubtedly excellent boost that this gives to passenger rights is somewhat spoilt by the number of exemptions which Member States are allowed to grant, by virtue of art.2. Urban, suburban and regional services may be exempted for five years, and then two further periods of five years. And then there is a renewable exemption for international services for which a substantial part of the journey takes place outside the EU. The UK has taken maximum advantage of this first exemption, whereas, for example, it is believed that Germany has not opted to exempt at all. The result is a rather patchwork and opaque implementation.

Nonetheless, the Regulation enhances passenger rights on long distance and international rail journeys (e.g. Eurostar). The areas it covers include: a requirement to sell through tickets wherever possible (art.9); a list of information that must be provided to passengers before the journey (e.g. connections involved, facilities for PRMs, services on board, complaint procedures, timings and availability of cheapest and fastest journeys, etc (note that this applies to tour operators too)), and during the journey (next stop, facilities on board, delays, etc); rules on reimbursement and re-routing (art.16); there is the anticipated strict liability for injury or death caused by an accident, subject to the railway undertaking showing lack of fault (e.g. the act of third party, etc (art.11)); in the event of death at least €21,000 must be paid within 15 days (art.12); liability for missed connections (art.15); and rules requiring assistance for and non-discrimination against PRMs.

Bus and Coach

In February 2011, the EU adopted Regulation EU 181/2011 on passenger rights in bus and coach travel. It will—once in force on March 1, 2013—cover journeys over 250kms, and again there are exemptions available for domestic journeys and some international journeys outside the EU. Any ceiling set on compensation for accidents must not be lower than €220,000 per person and €1,200 for each item of luggage. Liability will be dealt with in accordance with national law. There will also be rights in respect of assistance, accommodation, compensation, etc, which are similar to the provisions in the train/sea/air regulations.

Comparisons Between the European Regulations on Passenger Rights

The four Regulations share several similar features. There are requirements for assistance and accessibility for PRMs. In cases of long delay, all passengers get information, a choice between rerouting and reimbursement, meals, etc, and compensation.

On the other hand, there are major differences between the four. The following are examples: the scope (and exemptions, especially in the case of rail) vary considerably; so, inevitably in context, do the periods of delay required to trigger rights. As we have seen, assistance in the form of meals, accommodation, etc, are limited in the case of sea carriage, but not, to the chagrin of airlines at the time of volcanic ash, in the case of air. Ceilings and minima for compensation also differ.

Despite the fact that much of this legislation is very recent, the Commission began consultation in 2012 on making the Regulations more convergent.

Foreign Affairs

INTRODUCTION

In the course of this book we have seen that the "old-style" tour operator is potentially responsible for injury or illness caused to a consumer during the course of the package holiday in a wide variety of situations ranging from the flight, the coach, the hotel and increasingly, in some cases, an excursion.

In such circumstances, the claim can be brought by the consumer in the courts of England and Wales (or Scotland or Northern Ireland if appropriate to the consumer). Unfortunately, as we have also seen many times in this book, not all accidents or problems abroad fit into this easy category; and that is increasingly the fact. In other cases, the first question arises; where can any court action be brought, in the UK or overseas? What law applies? And how can a foreign action be funded? In this chapter we aim to explore these topics. Before doing so it is worth remembering that s.75 of the Consumer Credit Act 1974 should give to a consumer a legal claim in the UK against his credit card company for the defaults of foreign suppliers—see the case of *Office of Fair Trading v Lloyds TSB Bank Plc* [2007] UKHL 48 mentioned in Ch.12.

JURISDICTION

It is unfortunately the fact that there are a wide variety of circumstances in which a consumer may become ill or be injured whilst overseas, but no claim is possible against a tour operator. Here are a few examples:

- Whilst crossing the road in resort, a consumer is knocked down and injured by a speeding motorist.

- A consumer decides to visit a local restaurant and suffers food poisoning as a result.

- A consumer purchases an excursion locally (e.g. jeep safari, water park, banana boat) and is injured while on the excursion.

- A consumer is injured whilst participating in arrangements which turn out not to be a "package" under the Regulations, e.g. a split contract which is successful from the trader's standpoint; or perhaps the rental of accommodation-only, e.g. a French villa with dangerous steps; or simply renting a hire car which is defective and causes injury.

- Arrangements are made by a consumer directly, either by telephone or over the internet, with a foreign supplier such as a French villa owner, hotel or transport provider, and the consumer is injured by the service.

Of course, the damage suffered by the consumer may not be injury or illness; a French villa contracted direct with its French owner may have turned out to be dirty and disappointing and the consumer wishes to bring a claim. It used to be the case that the hurdles which lie in the path of such actions made the typical "small claim" uneconomic, but as we shall see, this problem has been, to some extent, eased by the advent of the European Small Claims Procedure, in effect since January 2009; but even so, it is often only going to be a larger sort of claim, e.g. injury/illness, which justifies action against an overseas defendant.

This chapter will concentrate upon accidents, etc, suffered within the European Union, or contracts made with suppliers in the EU. As we shall see, these situations are quite difficult enough. We will indicate where the remarks we make are of international application, rather than merely European.

Even within Europe, one must be careful of the precise position. All the EU countries are now governed by EU Council Regulation 44/2001 ("the Judgment Regulation"), which came into force on March 1, 2002; whilst Norway, Switzerland and Iceland are governed by the Lugano Convention 2007, in force since various dates in 2010 and 2011. Regulation 44/2001 is currently the subject of a consultation and updating process in Brussels, but it is not thought that the changes are likely to touch on the areas described below.

The good news is that the general principles in the Judgment Regulation, and the Lugano Convention, are the same; where the differences of detail are significant, we will note them below.

The Basic Rule

It has to be realised that the basic rule, whether under the Judgment Regulation, or Lugano—or even the Hague Convention 1965 which deals with service of international proceedings outside the EU—is this; that defendants are entitled to be sued in their own jurisdiction.

Thus, in our above example of the villa rented direct from the French owner, the basic rule is that the French owner is entitled to be sued in the courts of France. The Spanish restaurant which has poisoned a consumer is entitled to be sued in the courts of Spain; and so on (and of course, as a daunting non-EU example, if that illness is caused by a restaurant in Peru or Zaire, then those are the courts where any claim must be pursued).

It follows that, if a consumer is searching for an opportunity to commence proceedings in his own home court, say the courts of England and Wales, it is always the case that he will have to uncover and establish one of the exceptions to the basic rule. There are a number of exceptions, of which the most relevant are set out below. Some are more helpful than others. It should be added that generally, within the EU, one simply applies these rules without need to consider which forum is the most convenient ("forum non conveniens" principle). When suing a party outside the EU, that principle becomes very significant, however. It should also be noted that in cases of international carriage by air covered by the Montreal Convention there are separate rules on jurisdiction.

Exceptions to Basic Rule—Possible UK Jurisdiction

Contract Claims

In a case of breach of contracts, art.5 of the Judgment Regulation provides an exception to the basic rule, namely that action may be commenced in the courts where the place of performance of the obligations in question is. Unfortunately, this rule (replicated in Lugano) is not much help. The place of performance will generally be the same country as the defendant's home court. Thus, the rental of the French Villa was to take place in France, and the poisonous meal was served in Spain.

Claims in Tort

The same problem arises here; the exception to the basic rule is that proceedings may be commended in "the courts of the place where the harmful event occurred". If the Italian driver has run over the consumer in Italy, then again this is the same court. (If, of course, the driver who knocks you down in Italy, or anywhere else, is in fact British—which happens more often than one might imagine—then you can sue the defendant in his home court in the appropriate part of the UK, although interesting questions of applicable law, the measure of damages, etc, can arise).

Consumer Contracts

This may be more useful in some circumstances. Article 15 of the Judgment Regulation permits the consumer to bring an action in his own jurisdiction if it concerns a contract for the supply of goods or the supply of services, and the contract was "concluded with a person who pursues commercial and professional activities in the Member State of the consumer's domicile or, by any means, directs such activities to that member state or to several countries including the Member State, and the contract falls within the scope of such activities". Any contract for the supply of transport only is excluded; but included is a contract which "for an inclusive price, provides for a combination of travel and accommodation". So the traditional package holiday, including transport and accommodation, and purchased from a supplier in a foreign EU country, is covered, and the consumer can commence a claim in his own court. In fact, basically, any consumer contract which fulfils the rules and is not just for transport, is covered. One need not, therefore, be too exercised by the omission of "other tourist services" from this pared down definition of a "package".

Indeed, the wording of art.15 has clearly taken into account the ever-increasing use by consumers of the internet as a means of ordering goods and services from overseas suppliers. A website that accepts bookings from UK residents (whether a hotel's own website or a non-package "accommodation-only" supplier) is clearly pursuing activities in the UK, and (especially if in English) directing its activities to our member state, i.e. the UK. Indeed, the ECJ gave this factor among a checklist of other factors (the international nature of the service, the provision of an international telephone number, use of domain name such as ending .co.uk, and use of a language or currency not normal in the defendant's home state), to be weighed up in deciding whether services are "directed to" the consumer's country—*Pammer v Karl Schluter* (C-585/08) and *Hotel Alpenhof v Heller* (C-144/09) decided on December 7, 2010.

Non-internet contacts are of course covered too. A French villa owner who advertises in the *Sunday Times*, resulting in an English consumer making a booking, will therefore find himself subject to English jurisdiction under art.15.

Where Lugano applies, the good news is that the "new" Lugano, in force since 2010–11, is brought into line, and no longer excludes internet transactions.

Of course, contracts for a meal in a restaurant in Spain could not possibly come within this exception, or any other contract entered into *whilst overseas*.

Choice of Jurisdiction Clauses

A significant exception to the basic rule is that where the parties have agreed exclusive jurisdiction to the courts of a particular country, such agreement overrides any other provisions of the Regulation (or Conventions). Article 23 of the Regulation states that,

> "if the parties, one or more of whom is domiciled in a Member State, have agreed that a court or the courts of a Member State are to have jurisdiction to settle any disputes which have arisen or which may arise in connection with a particular legal relationship, that court or those courts shall have jurisdiction. Such jurisdiction shall be exclusive unless the parties have agreed otherwise".

There is a requirement that such agreement be in writing or evidenced in writing. Writing includes email.

This provision can benefit both consumers and travel companies. The difficulty for consumers is that they are unlikely, at the time of making any contract for any travel or holiday service, to write a term into the Contract for English jurisdiction—and still less so when, for example, buying tickets to enter a waterpark ("Two adults and two children please, and this contract is subject to the exclusive jurisdiction of the courts of England and Wales"—perhaps not!). There is certainly a case for greater education of consumers on these matters! All may not be lost, however, if a consumer enters into a contract with an exclusive foreign jurisdiction clause; the European Court case of *Oceano Grupo Editorial SA v Quintero* (C-240–244/98) shows that the court retains power under the Unfair Terms in Consumer Contracts legislation to declare such a term unfair in the appropriate case (for unfair terms, see Ch.6). It should be noted, however, that this case was confined to choice of jurisdiction *within* Spain.

Where a tour operator is sued over, for example, an accident in a hotel, then as we shall shortly see, it is possible for the tour operator to join the hotel as a Third Party (Pt 20 defendant) into the proceedings—but not if, for example, the hotel contract provides for exclusive Spanish jurisdiction. In the latter event, the tour operator will have to defend the English proceedings as best it can. If he loses, or reaches a compromise settlement, he will then have to start new proceedings in Spain against the hotel to effect recovery.

Third Party or Additional Defendant

Following on from the above, art.6 of the Regulation says that a defendant in an EU State may be sued:

"1. Where he is one of a number of defendants, in the Courts for the place where any one of them is domiciled, provided the claims are so closely connected that it is expedient to hear and determine them together to avoid the risk of irreconcilable judgments resulting from separate proceedings.

2. As a Third Party in an action under warranty or guarantee or in any other Third Party proceedings, in the Court seized of the original proceedings, unless these were instituted solely with the object of removing him from the jurisdiction of the Court which would be competent in his case."

We have already seen how the Third Party provision can assist a tour operator, with a properly drawn supplier contract, to effect recovery/indemnity from a hotel or other supplier as part of English proceedings started against the tour operator by a consumer.

In addition, however, this provision can benefit the consumer. If he can find one sensible and meaningful defendant in England and Wales to sue, then he can join a defendant from any other part of the EU (or the other Convention Countries) as a second defendant in the English proceedings, under this provision. For example, in our water-park example, the consumer may discover that the defective water slide which injured him was manufactured in Sheffield. Thus, he could sue the English manufacturer as first defendant, and add the Spanish water-park as second defendant. The overriding criteria of the courts is to try to avoid at all costs the possibility that, on the same set of facts, a court in one country might reach one decision, whilst the court in another country reaches a different decision.

There has been recent case law as to whether a claim in contract and a claim in tort can be said to be "so closely connected" that they can be joined together under this provision. See *Watson v First Choice* [2001] EWCA Civ 972. Fortunately, there has been clarification from the European Court, in *Freeport Plc v Arnoldsson* (C-98/06), that different legal bases does not preclude joinder.

But there is no doubt that where, for example, a consumer is injured in a road accident which is the fault of two different vehicles, one driven by an English driver (or a driver employed by an English corporation) and the other from, say, Spain, that both can be made co-defendants in English proceedings.

EU Fourth and Fifth Motor Insurance Directives

This exception may assist those injured in a road traffic accident overseas. The European Fourth Motor Insurance Directive 2000/26/EC dated May 16, 2000, came into effect on January 19, 2003. It will assist a British consumer injured in a road traffic accident elsewhere within the EU in two ways:

1. It introduces a streamlined system for dealing with claims. Within each EU country there is required to be an information centre, enabling victims to discover details of insurance of the foreign vehicle/driver. In the UK, that centre is the MIIC, the Motor Insurers Information Centre, a subsidiary of the Motor Insurers Bureau (*www.mib.org.uk*). Secondly, each motor insurer within the EU is required to appoint a claims representative in each

EU country empowered to negotiate settlements; thirdly, within each EU country a compensation body is set up to pay compensation (recoverable from the compensation body in the country of the driver/vehicle) where a Third Party driver is uninsured or unidentified.

2. Even more dramatically, art.3 of the Directive states that; "each Member State shall ensure that injured parties in accidents enjoy a direct right of action against the insurance undertaking covering the responsible person against civil liability".

Within the UK, this was brought into force by the European Communities (Rights against Insurers) Regulations 2002. Other EU countries have similar provisions, and, indeed, many already allowed direct actions against insurers, unlike the UK.

One then has to turn to arts 9 and 11 of the Judgment Regulation (44/2001)—the same Regulation has already been discussed in this chapter in other contexts. The effect of arts 9 and 11 is that where an insurer can be sued direct, the insurer can be sued either in the insurer's home court, or in the claimant's home court. If an English consumer is injured in a road accident in France or Spain, he can sue the insurer of the French or Spanish driver in the English Court.

At one stage there was controversy as to whether the above correctly stated the legal position in the UK. Fortunately, this has been put beyond doubt by the Fifth Motor Insurance Directive, which came into force in 2007.

Jurisdiction Based on an Agent, Branch or Place of Business in England

It is often possible to serve proceedings in England, and thereby give the English court jurisdiction, by virtue of the existence of an agent of the foreign company, or a branch of a foreign company, or the foreign company having a place of business in England. For example, the foreign hotel (whether in the EU or maybe even in say Egypt) may be part of an international chain, with a branch, place of business or even headquarters in England. In that case, there may be no need to serve outside the jurisdiction, or to be concerned as to whether English courts have jurisdiction at all (absent a contractual term giving another country exclusive jurisdiction, of course).

In the case of agencies and branches, there needs to be a connection between the agent or branch and the contract or dispute; but that requirement does not apply where there is an English place of business. The rules—which require a reading of CPR Pt 6, the Companies Act and the Judgment Regulation—are complex, and readers are referred to a specialist work such as *Litigation with a Foreign Aspect* (2009) by Michael James for a fuller treatment; but it is important to realise that these valuable options exist.

Enforcement

Getting an English judgment is one thing; enforcing it overseas, if the foreign defendant does not pay voluntarily, is quite another. The reader is referred to the notes in the White Book in CPR6 regarding jurisdiction and service; and CPR 74 regarding enforcement and the required procedures.

Foreign Limitation Periods

It is worth pointing out, that just because English jurisdiction is possible against an overseas defendant, it does not necessarily follow that English law will apply. Foreign law may well apply, either because the contract says so, or because foreign law is the most applicable law following the rules in Rome I—see below. Of most relevance to consumers is the risk that foreign limitation periods might apply to a claim. These vary widely from country to country, even within the EU. Any consumer bringing a claim of this nature must urgently, therefore, check the appropriate limitation period. Particularly short ones include Switzerland (one year from date of knowledge) and California (one year). By contrast, Denmark, Greece and the Netherlands allow five years (but only two for direct actions against insurers).

In 2007, the European Parliament adopted a proposal for a standard four year limitation period, subject to exceptions, for all cross-border claims within the EU, but this has not been followed up as yet.

IF OVERSEAS PROCEEDINGS ARE NECESSARY

It may well be that a particular claim cannot be brought within one of the exceptions listed above to the basic rule. In such circumstances there may be no alternative but to commence action in the defendant's home court (even where an English judgment can be obtained, it may still need to be pursued by way of enforcement through the foreign court, if the defendant does not pay up voluntarily).

For example, the second author has a friend who, whilst on holiday in Corfu, went to the beach and booked to go on a "banana boat" ride. She was injured through the negligence of the driver/owner of the banana boat. This does not come within any of the above listed exceptions, and there was, therefore, no alternative but to pursue the claim in Greece.

In these circumstances the very first point to look out for, as already stated, is the foreign limitation period, which will certainly apply. The second point to note is that no such action will be simple to pursue. Much work remains to be done within the EU (let alone the wider international community), to ease the burden on consumers/victims in cross border cases.

Funding

The logistics and finance of such a case dictate that no small claim is likely to be worth pursuing in a foreign court (but see the note on the European Small Claims procedure below). If one books an excursion whilst overseas, and it fails to live up to its description, then frankly the trader is likely to get away with it.

The services of a foreign lawyer in the appropriate country are likely to be needed. How can a lawyer be chosen, and how can he/she be funded? As to a choice of lawyer, it is possible to consult the Law Society, or a directory such as Chambers Global Directory (2011). APIL (the Association of Personal Injury Lawyers, *www.apil.org.uk*) keep a list. If the consumer has travelled with a tour operator, but it is not the tour operator whom he wishes to sue, then the tour operator may be able to provide details of their own legal contacts in the country in question. Finally, the International Bar Association (IBA) has a Leisure Industries section.

Possible sources of funding include:

- Possible availability of some type of legal aid or conditional/contingency fee arrangement in the country in question.

- If a consumer travelled with the tour operator but it is not the tour operator who is to be sued, then up until September 2006 ABTA members were at least required in their reasonable discretion to lend up to £5,000 by way of legal expenses in such cases. It is worth checking the booking conditions—they may still contain this provision despite ABTA's requirement now being withdrawn.

- Many travel insurance policies contain legal expenses cover.

- Some credit cards bring, with their use, insurance of this nature.

- Household insurance may include this cover.

Failing the above possibilities, private funding of the foreign lawyer may be necessary. A clear statement of hourly rates, likely costs, etc, together with regular budget reports, should be required.

It should be remembered that few countries adopt as clear a model of fee shifting or "loser pays" as exists in the UK. The resulting economics of pursuing a claim therefore also need investigation.

The EU Small Claims Procedure

A helpful development for the smaller claims is the European Small Claims Procedure (Regulation 861/2007) which came into force in January 2009. This provides, for cross-border claims only, a procedure standard across the EU, for resolving Small Claims not exceeding €2,000 plus interest and expenses. The ability to recover any legal costs (and any available appeal procedure) depends on the rules of the country having jurisdiction. So, for example, if an English consumer is able to start a claim in an English court (e.g. under the consumer contracts exception above) the procedure in the small claims track in CPR Pt 27 will apply (see Ch.15) but not the usual "no costs" rule (see CPR 78.14(2)). The procedure (which involves the completion of a standard form of claim, and of defence, and judgment being given very rapidly thereafter, within 30 days) is intended to be a written one only, unless the judge considers a hearing necessary; any hearing can be held via electronic media, but of course language may create some problems here. Speaking of language, a major drawback of the procedure, as with all cross-border litigation, can be the high cost of translation of all documents which are to be served on the defendant in his own language. Whilst art.6 permits the claim to be in the language of the court, a defendant can refuse service if it is not in his language, and if he does so, the court can require the claimant to provide a translation. Despite its limitations, the procedure does genuinely enfranchise those who have a cross-border claim for an amount not otherwise worth pursuing. But the feeling persists that the procedure will not fulfil its potential until (a) the financial limit is increased and (b) the EU finally realises its e-justice dream that the whole procedure (and much else besides) can be transacted online. At present, the online element is restricted to the forms (and information) being available for download. But there is no doubt that a major advantage of the procedure is that judgments are automatically and directly enforceable in the defendant's member state. The procedure and forms can be accessed via the Europa website.

European Order for Payment (Regulation 1896/2006)

It is worth remembering that, where there is an undisputed (debt) claim, this procedure can be used cross-border, and that whilst it bears many similarities to the Small Claims Procedure in the look and style of the forms and procedures, it does not have the constraint of the €2,000 (or indeed any) financial limit.

CHOICE OF LAW: ROME I

Once it has been decided which court can hear the dispute it has to be decided which law will apply. The answer to this can be found in the Rome I Regulation (593/2008), which applies to all Member States of the EU. It came into force on December 17, 2009, and applies to all contracts entered into after that date. (Tortious claims are dealt with under Rome II.)

The general rule, to be found in art.3, is that the parties have freedom of choice to decide which law applies so long as they have expressed that choice or that choice can be demonstrated with reasonable certainty by reference to the terms of the contract or the circumstances of the case. Article 4 goes on to say that in the absence of a choice the contract will be governed by a set of rules; for example, in the case of the sale of services (e.g. holidays), it is the law of the place where the service provider has his habitual residence. In the case of a contract of carriage, art.5 says that the law will be that of the passenger's residence, provided transport started or ended there. However, both these provisions are subject, in the case of consumers, to art.6 which provides:

"Consumer contracts

1. Without prejudice to Articles 5 and 7, a contract concluded by a natural person for a purpose which can be regarded as being outside his trade or profession (the consumer) with another person acting in the exercise of his trade or profession (the professional) shall be governed by the law of the country where the consumer has his habitual residence, provided that the professional:

(a) pursues his commercial or professional activities in the country where the consumer has his habitual residence, or

(b) by any means, directs such activities to that country or to several countries including that country,

and the contract falls within the scope of such activities.

2. Notwithstanding paragraph 1, the parties may choose the law applicable to a contract which fulfils the requirements of paragraph 1, in accordance with Article 3. Such a choice may not, however, have the result of depriving the consumer of the protection afforded to him by provisions that cannot be derogated from by agreement by virtue of the law which, in the absence of choice, would have been applicable on the basis of paragraph 1.

3. If the requirements in points (a) or (b) of paragraph 1 are not fulfilled, the law applicable to a contract between a consumer and a professional shall be determined pursuant to Articles 3 and 4.

4. Paragraphs 1 and 2 shall not apply to:

(a) a contract for the supply of services where the services are to be supplied to the consumer exclusively in a country other than that in which he has his habitual residence;

(b) a contract of carriage other than a contract relating to package travel within the meaning of Council Directive 90/314/EEC of 13 June 1990 on package travel, package holidays and package tours."

The broad effect of this article is to provide that the law of the consumer's place of residence will apply to the contract, in our case English law, so long as the defendant "directed services to" the consumer in his own country (see the *Pammer* case referred to above). However, this does not apply where the services are supplied exclusively in another country. For instance, with hotel services which are supplied in another country the consumer would be thrown back on arts 3 and 4, i.e. was there an express choice of law, or failing that, which country's laws are indicated by the rules in those Articles?

The chances are that the result of such an investigation would be that it would be the foreign law that applied, either because the hotel had inserted a choice of law clause in the contract, or it could be said that the contract was to be performed there, the service provider being resident there.

CHAPTER FIFTEEN
Practical Litigation

INTRODUCTION

This chapter is addressed to consumers and their advisers who may wish to pursue a claim against a travel company; and also to travel companies (package or non-package), travel agents and their advisers who receive such a claim. First, we will examine what can be expected from the court system; and then we will pass on some practical tips on conducting the litigation.

The civil court procedures are governed by the Civil Procedure Rules 1998 ("CPR"). April 1999 was the date when these rules took effect, and there have been no less than 58 sets of amendments to them since then, at the time of writing (January 2012). Despite these many changes, and the 12 years or more that they have been in force, and the complete review of the Rules as they impact on costs conducted by Jackson L.J. published in January 2010, the rules start at Pt 1 by saying they are a "new procedural code". They revolutionised the way in which the Civil Courts operate. All cases must be dealt with in a way which is just and proportionate to their importance. They have been recognised as generally very successful, though concerns are often expressed that they have increased costs, rather than reducing them as desired, by requiring everything to be prepared much earlier ("front loading").

At the same time, legal aid has been withdrawn from almost all civil proceedings. Therefore legal aid is rarely available to consumers wishing to sue a holiday company whether for breach of contract or for personal injury. Instead, lawyers are able to conduct all litigation on a "no win no fee" basis (known as conditional fee arrangements, or CFA's). If the case is lost, the lawyer receives nothing; but if it is won, the lawyer will normally expect an enhanced fee. An insurance policy ("after the event" or ATE) is, available at (in theory) a reasonable price to guard against the risk of having to pay the defendant's costs in the event of losing. Bearing in mind the likelihood that the vast majority of package holidays are purchased by people in the middle-income bracket who would not normally have qualified for legal aid, the changes to these rules are likely to have found favour among holidaymakers as increasing access to justice. However, as part of the Legal Aid, Sentencing and Punishment of Offenders Bill 2011, and proposed changes to the rules, the Ministry of Justice proposes to adopt the Jackson report as far as personal injury claims (inter alia) are concerned. The effect is that in cases of personal injury, success fees and ATE premiums will generally no longer be recoverable from defendants, and instead success fees will be recoverable, subject to maximum limits, out of damages awarded/agreed and paid to the claimant; general damages for pain and suffering will be increased by 10 per cent to compensate for any costs deduction; and ATE rendered largely redundant because, generally, a successful defendant will no longer recover costs from the claimant ("QOCS" or Qualified One-way Costs Shifting). Contingency fees may well be legalised too.

As an alternative, a consumer who wishes to avoid recourse to lawyers at all can do so by limiting the size of his claim within the limits of the ABTA Arbitration Scheme or the small claims track of the County Court.

COURT OR ARBITRATION?

The consumer is faced with a choice—to start a court action or to submit his claim to arbitration. Arbitration in this context means arbitration that exists outside the ordinary court system.

There are several arbitration schemes administered by CEDR (Centre for Effective Dispute Resolution), of which one of the best known is the ABTA scheme. Indeed, it is by far the most heavily used consumer arbitration scheme in the UK. This allows claims of up to £5,000 per person or £25,000 per booking form to be referred to arbitration, to which ABTA members have to agree. Small personal injury claims of up to £1,000 can be handled under this scheme, as part of a general quality complaint. (ABTA operates a mediation scheme also run by the respected CEDR Solve for personal injury claims over £1,000 in value.)

The CEDR arbitration scheme has several advantages:

- It is cheap. Fees are cheaper than going to court.

- It is relatively quick.

- As the arbitrator decides the case merely by reading the papers, there is none of the ordeal of giving live evidence in Court; about 80 per cent of claims result in an award to the consumer.

- An appeal (a review by a senior arbitrator) can be made by either party but only on the grounds that no reasonable arbitrator should have made the decision under challenge. (In the courts, appeals need permission and can only be on the grounds (in effect) of error of law or serious procedural error.)

There are, however, two disadvantages for a claimant:

- Merely reading the papers will almost certainly not have the same emotional impact upon the arbitrator as seeing and hearing the holidaymaker live in court will have for the judge. Also, many people have difficulty expressing themselves cogently in writing.

- *Holiday Which?* magazine conducted a survey which showed that if there is a good claim, judges will generally award higher compensation on average than arbitrators (September 1996, pp.184–187).

Travel companies, of course, do not get a choice—they must deal with whichever procedure the consumer has elected to pursue. Perhaps surprisingly, many travel companies prefer the court system feeling that, if they have a valid defence, it is easier to persuade a judge who is sitting in front of them. The judge will invariably draw attention to any particular points that concern him, and these can then be addressed. By contrast, one never knows what points impress or upset an arbitrator.

If the consumer chooses arbitration, he or she must write out a full account of all their complaints and submit this together with copies of all supporting documents. The respondent travel company then writes out its full defence, again with any relevant documents, and submits these. The claimant is allowed to respond to any points arising out of the defence. Then, all the papers are placed in front of the arbitrator, who issues a written decision. Any award made can be enforced, if necessary, through the courts. (See [1994] T.L.J. 35–42 for three separate accounts of the arbitration process—allowance should be made for the now increased ambit of the scheme as set out above. See also Munro "Arbitration Review Procedure: Fear of the Unknown" [2002] I.T.L.J. 195 for an account of the review.)

As an alternative to taking action themselves some consumers will complain to their trading standards department. Should the case be suitable for a criminal prosecution, and the travel company is found guilty, the prosecution can ask the magistrates to order the defendant to pay compensation. Whether the court does this, and if so, in what amount, is something of a lottery.

THE ROAD TO COURT

The days when parties could simply rush off to court are gone. The procedure laid down by the Pre-Action Protocols must be followed before proceedings are issued. The purpose of the Protocols is, by early exchange of information, to encourage settlement; but if settlement proves impossible, then at least the parties are better prepared for the speed of the timetable which a court will fix in proceedings.

The most relevant Protocols for our purposes are the personal injury Pre-Action Protocol, and the Disease and Illness Protocol. As a generality, where there is no relevant Pre-Action Protocol, parties should follow the Practice Direction on Pre-Action Conduct introduced in 2009. Although work was once done on the preparation of a dedicated holiday claims Pre-Action Protocol, that work has not been completed and there is no current sign of development on this front.

The Protocols encourage:

- The claimant to set out the reasons for his claim (and particulars of his loss or injury) in detail.

- The defendant to admit liability where appropriate. If denying liability, the defendant must state why and also disclose all relevant documents in his possession at that stage.

- The defendant to formally admit/deny liability within three months. Where, however, the incident complained of took place overseas, that period is extended to a maximum of six months.

- The joint selection of experts wherever possible. Parties who fail to find common ground in the choice of expert are likely to have to explain their reasons to a court at a later date, if the case does not settle.

There is a County Court in almost every town of substance (although fewer than there were, following a round of court closures in 2011–12). There are somewhat fewer offices (Registries) of the High Court. Every personal injury action where the claim is valued at £50,000 or less must be started in the County Court and not the High Court. If a claim for personal injuries is issued in the High Court, it must contain a statement that the claim is worth £50,000 or more. There are penalties laid down for abusing this system. In practice, claims well into six figures are routinely started in the County Court. The unified rules of the CPR make the difference between courts negligible anyway.

It follows that almost every claim against holiday companies will proceed in the County Court.

Currently, the claim must be started in the Salford Business Centre but may indicate any preferred County Court, and this is usually the one most convenient for the claimant's home or work. Holiday claims are generally what is called "unliquidated", i.e. not a claim for a fixed sum of money, but for compensation which the court must assess. The action should, therefore, continue in the claimant's home court.

On receipt of a Claim Form, the defendant has 14 days in which to lodge at court his Defence—28 days if he lodges at court the Acknowledgement of Service form received with the Claim Form within 14 days. The Defence (and indeed the Particulars of Claim before it) must be verified by a "Statement of Truth". This makes the parties accountable for the truth of their claim or Defence. Signing (or authorising the signature of) a Statement of Truth without an honest belief in the facts stated is a contempt of court punishable by imprisonment.

Once a Defence is served, he court will then send out an Allocation Questionnaire to each party, with a strict time limit for completion and return. This is a vital document. On the basis of the answers given, the District Judge will decide, often without a hearing, what steps are to be taken in the action. These will include:

(a) Allocation to one of the three tracks. This is usually done on the basis of the true value of the claim as assessed by the District Judge, although there are other criteria. The small claims track is the normal track for claims valued at £5,000 or less. This includes personal injury claims, but on a more limited basis—they can only be referred to the small claims track if the amount of compensation (general damages) for pain and suffering will not exceed £1,000 as part of an overall claim not exceeding £5,000. At the time of writing there are proposals to increase the financial ambit of the small claims track to £10,000. The small claims ceiling for personal injury claims remains at £1,000.

Claims which exceed the small claims limit but have a value of less than £25,000 are normally allocated to the fast-track. This figure may increase soon. Claims too large or complex for the fast-track will be allocated to the multi-track.

(b) A standard form of directions no longer exists for holiday claims (previously set out in the CPR—Practice Direction 27) brought within the small claims track; but normal directions will provide for disclosure of documents including photographs and videos, and the exchange of signed witness statements.

On other tracks, orders will be made for disclosure by each party to the other of relevant documents, and a mutual exchange of witness statements; and for limits on the number of expert witnesses, indeed frequently directing that any expert evidence should be given by a jointly selected or instructed expert. Expert evidence is rare on the small claims track; on the fast-track any expert evidence at trial will normally be in the form of a written report, and, therefore, it is important for the parties to take advantage of the right to challenge written expert evidence by asking the expert questions in writing. In the multi-track it is still quite common for experts to attend Court and be cross examined, and it is more common for each party to be allowed their own choice of expert. In ordinary cases, the most common type of experts needed are medical experts to deal with injury/illness claims, and also engineering or other liability expert evidence as to whether the hotel complied with local standards, or whether, e.g. a lift, or a swimming pool filter, were operating properly. (Please see Ch.5 for discussion of the need for expert evidence where breach of local standards is an issue—e.g. *Wilson v Best Travel, Holden v First Choice*, and *Hilton v Mytravel*. The most commonly contentious issue here is whether the more appropriate expert is an engineer who can inspect and measure the accident site by reference to local standards, or a local lawyer who can authoritatively state what the relevant local standard is, but is unlikely to be able to assess/measure the site).

(c) A hearing date (with a time limit given by the Court) will normally be fixed in the small claims track; in the other tracks a "trial window", usually a period of three weeks, will be fixed (which in the fast-track will be not more than 30 weeks away) and, at a later date, the parties must indicate any days within the trial window which are inconvenient for the trial to take place. Fast-track trials will not exceed one day.

A claimant must, in practice, decide whether to limit the claim to a figure within the small claims procedure. Sometimes the decision is easy—for example, a minor complaint about a cheap package. Often it is not so clear cut.

The major advantage of using the small claims system is that, unlike the usual case in English law, the loser does not have to pay the legal costs of the winner. The maximum which the losing party can be ordered to pay is a sum up to £90 of the loss of earnings of the opposite party or a witness, plus the actual travel and subsistence expenses of the opposite party or witness. In addition, if the defendant loses, he can be ordered to pay a court fee or other costs which are marked on the claim form (there are some rare exceptions to these rules—see CPR, Pt 27.14).

The system means that in most small cases the consumer can safely launch proceedings for up to £5,000 without having to fear the fact that he or she is taking on a large corporation which can afford lawyers. On the other hand, if the case turns out to be quite difficult, the claimant will still have to soldier on without legal assistance, or pay for it out of his own pocket. On balance, however, the advantages outweigh the disadvantages providing the claim is not worth substantially more than £5,000. (But note what is said above about the proposed introduction of QOCS, which will alter this dynamic substantially.)

It is not possible for a defendant in a small claims case to make a formal so-called "Part 36 offer"; but the court will still take into account any "without prejudice" written offer of settlement made by the defendant in deciding what orders for witnesses expenses, and possibly even legal cost, to make at the end of the hearing.

The hearing itself is generally very informal but there is an enormous variety in approach from court to court, and indeed from District Judge to District Judge within the courts. Some judges conduct a matter in a fairly formal way, so that the only difference from a full trial is that it takes place in a private room and without fancy legal robes (but note: the public can attend if there is room). Other judges take the case by the scruff of the neck and virtually say to one party or the other, "Well I've read the papers and you are going to have a job to persuade me that you are in the right—what have you got to say?" Most judges come somewhere between these two extremes. It is a fairly rough and ready form of justice, and litigants should not arrive expecting a really thorough examination of the issues. Many courts list a number of hearings to take place at the same time, and the District Judge is under enormous pressure to complete the hearings quickly. At the very least, the judge must allow cross-examination of the other party and his witnesses (*Chilton v Saga Holidays* [1986] 1 All E.R. 841) although this can be limited. Furthermore, the judge must give reasons for his decision. As we have already seen there are limited rights to appeal to the Circuit Judge, the only grounds being that the District Judge made an error of law or fact or serious error of procedure. Permission to appeal is needed, and should be sought in the first instance from the District Judge at the end of the hearing.

PREPARING FOR TRIAL

Fast or multi-track trials are a much more formal business. Unlike in small claims witnesses give evidence on oath. They will be cross-examined, and there are likely to be full opening and closing speeches (though with time limits), legal submissions, etc. Subject to obtaining permission, there are the same limited rights of appeal as we saw above, from the District Judge to the Circuit Judge and from the Circuit Judge to a High Court Judge (in fast-track) or to the Court of Appeal.

The loser can expect to be ordered to pay the legal costs of the winner (subject to the new QOCS proposal—see above). The costs are often likely to be at least a four figure sum in fast-track, or five in multi-track. Accurate costs estimates must be filed in advance. Costs, therefore, become a significant consideration in deciding the tactics of the case. Most defendants will, if they feel there is weakness in their case, make a Part 36 Offer and the claimant will recover legal costs only up to the date of the Offer if the judge ultimately awards less than the Offer; and thereafter the claimant will be ordered to pay the defendant's costs. As these latter costs include the costs of trial, by far the most expensive part of any litigation, the claimant ends up substantially out of pocket. A carefully calculated Part 36 Offer is, therefore, the greatest weapon in the hands of the defendant travel company, as it is only a brave or foolhardy claimant who presses on in the face of it. If, of course, the claimant is awarded more than the payment into court, the defendant will have to pay all his legal costs throughout. The precise interplay between Part 36 CPR, and the new proposed QOCS rule, is still the subject of discussion as we write this. Please note that although we use the phrase "all his legal costs", in fact, the costs you can recover from the other party rarely exceed 75 to 80 per cent of the bill the claimant may receive from his own lawyers. There are several reasons for this, some more worthy than others, but they tend to underline the wise words of a court of Appeal judge who commented "litigation is not an activity which has contributed markedly to the happiness of mankind". (For advice on how to calculate or judge a payment into court see Ch.10 on remedies which deals in some detail with damages.)

In cases run under the current system of Conditional Fee Agreements (see above), the amount of percentage uplift allowed to a successful claimant's lawyer, and of the insurance premium, fall to be argued about. A body of case law has grown up to assist with such judgments.

ADDITIONAL POINTS

Specific rules (CPR Part 19) deal with class or group actions, which the courts used to struggle to fit within their existing rules. This is of particular interest in holiday law, where there is an increasing trend towards class actions where, for example, a large number of people have been affected by a bad hotel, or given food poisoning or injured in a coach accident. However, in practice, it is extremely rare for a Group Litigation Order to be made in holiday cases, largely because the names of all the potential members of the class of claimants are readily ascertainable. GLO's are used more in cases such as product liability claims, where the identity and size of the class of claimants is unknown.

A defendant travel company can usually join in a supplier, e.g. a foreign hotel (or, say, the parents of a child claimant, cf. *R. (A Child) v Iberotravel Ltd* (2001) dealt with in Ch.5), as an additional party (Part 20 defendant) and thereby obtain an indemnity or a contribution to the claim. But such claims must be made while the original action by the claimant is still live, otherwise they will be an abuse of process. See *Barton v Golden Sun Holidays Ltd* [2007] EWHC 3455 (QB).

There is an ever-growing emphasis on encouraging parties to refer their dispute to alternative dispute resolution (ADR), cf. *Dunnett v Railtrack Plc* [2002] EWCA Civ 303 where a successful party in the Court of Appeal was refused costs because it had declined to participate in a mediation. Parties can, however, refuse mediation for good reason, e.g. expense, or desire to set a legal precedent (*Halsey v Milton Keynes General NHS Trust* [2004] EWCA Civ 576). At the time of writing, there were still suggestions that mediation might be made compulsory, either in small claims, or even across the board.

PRACTICAL TIPS TO HELP YOU WIN YOUR CASE

(i) Photographs

Judges frequently joke in holiday cases that it would be advisable to take a "judicial view" of the site—in other words, the whole court travel out to see the location being complained of. Mercifully for the purses of those funding the litigation, this rarely actually happens (but see *Osborne v Malta Sun Holidays*

Unreported August 18, 1998, Birmingham County Court, where the parties and the judge and their advisors all visited the hotel in Malta at the centre of the dispute. For comment see Mason "Consumer Claims—The Worm Turns" [1998] I.T.L.J. 106). The next best evidence available to the judge is photographs (or videos and DVDs)—indeed they are often the most compelling evidence available.

Many consumers are already aware of how important it is to take photographs of their complaints. This is so if they wish to demonstrate a dirty room, or intrusive building works, or a scruffy beach; it is doubly so if the claim concerns injuries sustained in an accident. Photographs should be taken immediately before the scene changes. Take, for example, an accident or near drowning in the deep end of the swimming pool. There may be no notices up with depth markings, or sudden hidden changes of depth. After the accident has happened, hotel management may well move quickly to put these things right—so immediate photographs are essential. Now that mobile phones routinely feature cameras, most people are able to take a visual record at a moment's notice.

Of course the same applies for a defending tour operator. Perhaps there are notices up with depth markings, or notices warning parents that children should not swim without supervision. Consumers may deny that they ever saw any such signs. If photographs are taken well after the event, it gives the claimants (and some willing judges) an opportunity to suggest that things were altered after the accident.

DVD or video evidence is frequently used by both sides too, in particular if it is important to show perspective, or to pan round a wide area, or of course if any moving parts were involved in an accident, e.g. a chairlift to the beach which malfunctioned in one case. Because DVDs and videos (and mobile phones) have a sound facility too, consumers often use them to demonstrate building work or traffic noise. In addition, modern cameras, both video and still, may have the valuable feature that they automatically put the date on the film.

Ironically, the claimant's photographs can be a useful weapon for the defendants, particularly in quality complaints. It is all too easy for the claimant to stand in the witness box complaining bitterly about what a miserable time they had on holiday. Their holiday of a lifetime was ruined by some trivial defects in their bedroom. It is all too difficult for the travel company to contradict this in evidence, and the judge is left with not much option but to accept the claimant's evidence. However, if the defendant insists upon the claimants disclosing all their holiday photographs, and not just the one or two showing the bare wires in the bedroom, they may show a very different story of happy faces, sun drenched beaches, excursions, nightclubs, etc, giving the judge a true picture of what the holiday was like. (The second author once asked for all the claimant's photographs to be disclosed only to receive an extremely abusive response for wanting to view snaps of the claimant's wife topless on the beach!)

(ii) Physical Evidence

It may be important to preserve physical evidence, possibly for an eventual trial. In the case of *Hoffman v Intasun Holidays Limited* Unreported 1990, High Court, the claimant was a young woman who badly injured her leg on what she claimed to be defective swimming pool steps. The steps themselves mysteriously disappeared shortly afterwards. Fortunately for Intasun, this case was decided before the extended liability in the 1990 ABTA Code of Conduct and the PTR, and they won the case. Nowadays, the absence of the steps might have made all the difference between winning and losing.

In one case also attended by the second author, a claimant giving evidence was complaining that the window in her bedroom had been too small to let in decent light. To emphasise her point she delved into the bag she had with her in the witness box and suddenly pulled from it, with a flourish, the window itself, which she had removed from the hotel! This may be going to extremes.

(iii) Witnesses

Many consumers are very organised. If a major quality problem (e.g. damp or cold) affects a holiday hotel, mass meetings of guests are held, committees are formed, petitions written out and names and addresses exchanged for future mutual aid as witnesses. Such evidence can be very telling at trial, although evidence by Mr Smith that his own bedroom was defective is not really evidence in support of a breach of contract as alleged by Mrs Jones about her bedroom—it is better if Mr Smith has first hand experience of the claimant's bedroom himself. As has already been said, there is an increasing trend towards class actions by groups of dissatisfied or injured holidaymakers. This trend is facilitated by the advent of social networking sites such as Facebook and Twitter. And increasingly courts are asked to consider as evidence the reviews and postings about a hotel found on Tripadvisor and similar sites.

Holiday companies, by contrast, face a number of difficulties in this area. If an accident occurs in a factory in front of a group of workers, most of that group may still be together months or even years later. It is in the nature of holidays that witnesses are together for only a short time. In one case, a young man told the representative in front of a number of other clients that he injured his ankle while dancing in a disco. Subsequently, he claimed in court that he sustained the injury because of a rocky flagstone around the swimming pool. By the time the action commenced, the representative could not remember who the other clients were. For the judge, it would be simply one person's word against another.

Another problem travel companies face is the expense and difficulty of bringing overseas witnesses to trial in England—hoteliers, swimming pool maintenance staff, even the defendant's own representatives. Technology, allowing video-link evidence from overseas, is an answer, although not cheap. A particular difficulty surrounds the eviction of holidaymakers from their hotel for misbehaviour. The burden of proof lies on the tour operator to prove that the eviction was justified—*Spencer v Cosmos, The Times*, December 6, 1989 (see also Ch.10). Inevitably, the incident giving rise to the eviction has happened in the middle of the night when the only person on duty was a seasonal night porter whose entire name (to the best of anyone's recollection) was Jose. Fortunately, for them, the traditional travel companies are becoming more aware of the need to plan for litigation. Training courses for overseas representatives explain the need to obtain statements immediately from the people concerned, without waiting several months to see if a claim is issued by the consumer. By contrast, bedbanks and dynamic packagers are often left struggling for such evidence. Of course, travel companies can now often also rely on Tripadvisor and the like, if these give a hotel the thumbs up. Computer print-outs from the travel company showing that the low or non-existent number of other complaints about a hotel are also sometimes used. They may influence a judge who is not sure what to make of the claimant's evidence

In travel cases, as in any litigation, favourable evidence you can obtain from "the other side" is worth ten times as much as evidence from your natural supporters. Look at it this way: when a judge looks at his list for the day and sees a holiday case on it he knows even before the case starts what he is in for. He is going to hear a claimant whingeing on about what a miserable time he had, and then he is going to hear a holiday representative say how absolutely fantastic everything was. He knows he is probably going to find for the claimant unless the claimant is intrinsically unbelievable, but he will probably reduce the damages to allow for probable exaggeration by the claimant. All this the judge knows before he starts. What, however, is really going to wake the judge up is the unexpected—for example, a statement put in evidence by the claimant and signed by the defendant's representative confirming that everything was truly awful—or by an official of the local Tourist Board; or on the other side, if the defendant calls another consumer who was there at the time who will say that they had a fantastic holiday, spoilt only the endless whingeing of Mr and Mrs Claimant. Such evidence is gold dust to the tour operator.

It is, of course, possible to serve in written form the evidence of any witness who is overseas, under the provisions of the Civil Evidence Act 1995. The relevant procedure for doing this is set out at CPR Part 33. Indeed, the rule against hearsay in civil proceedings was virtually abolished when this Act came into force for actions commenced after January 1997. This can be useful for filling in one or two fringe details. As the major defence evidence, it is generally useless. The weight to be placed on such evidence is a matter for the judge; so imagine: there in the court room are the claimants shedding tears in the witness box about what a terrible time they had, and the only thing the defendants have to put against this is a piece of paper! Which way is the judge going to decide the case? Come to that, which way would you decide the case? One should never underestimate the extent to which holiday cases are an emotional experience for all concerned.

(iv) Expert Witnesses

In ordinary holiday cases, these are almost unknown—after all we are all experts on holidays. In an illness or injury claim, medical evidence is required. This point is sometimes missed by a claimant where there are a large number of allegations, one of which is that they suffered sickness and diarrhoea, or an attack of asthma, as a consequence of some problem with the holiday; or suffered depression afterwards (as distinct from mere disappointment). Engineers or other experts or foreign lawyers may be required to explain the reasons for an accident, or the appropriate local standards.

(v) Witness Statements

It will be remembered that for County Court (and High Court) trials, the exchange of witness statements is compulsory. No party is allowed to call a witness unless the substance of what that witness is to say is contained in an exchanged witness statement (CPR Part 32.10). This rule applies equally to fast-track and multi-track cases. This puts a very high premium on early preparation of witness statements which should also be thorough. In theory, the statements should be prepared by lawyers. This will generally be possible for the claimants, but may often not be practicable for the defendants where witnesses live or work overseas. This is why holiday representatives are sometimes trained in writing statements themselves. The defendant statements must deal positively with each of the complaints of the consumer. There is a tendency to respond in detail to the first four or five complaints, at which point the witness appears to get bored and ignore the remaining 12 complaints. This is not good enough. It is a mistake to assume that the claimant's complaints appear in decreasing order of seriousness. The judge will look at each complaint separately, and will also look at the effect on the holiday of the totality of the complaints.

In practice it can be difficult to persuade a court to allow new witness statements to be served after the formal exchange has taken place. This entails making an application and attending court, a considerable extra expense. "Difficult" becomes "impossible" if a trial date would have to be adjourned as a result of the new evidence.

It is normal for the judge to order that witness statements shall stand as the witness' evidence in chief, thereby shortening the trial. In practice, a few supplementary questions are asked, to deal with the other side's case—or at least to allow the witness to find his/her voice in the witness box prior to the ordeal of cross-examination.

(vi) Documents

The booking form invoice and brochure will generally be available, if relevant. Other types of document commonly relevant to holiday claims are menus, sketch plans and vouchers for out of pocket expenses (e.g. restaurant bills or at least credit card statements for meals eaten out where the allegation is that the hotel restaurant was abysmal). An accident might happen during a risky excursion (jeep safari, midnight tobogganing, etc.) In that case, a leaflet which did (or did not) mention the risks involved or indeed the identity of the excursion promoter would be relevant (see the discussion on *Moore v Hotelplan* in Ch.5. Such documents were also gold dust for the claimant in the Dominican quad bike excursion case of *Moran v First Choice* [2005] EWHC 2478 (QB) discussed there. Such documents are in circulation for a very short time and need to be preserved immediately. The travel companies, by contrast, may have prepared a health and safety report on a hotel which is relevant to prove or disprove allegations. (See *Patrick v Cosmosair* Unreported March 5, 2001, Manchester CC, as discussed in Chapman "Excursions: Tour Operators and the Negligence of Local Suppliers" [2002] I.T.L.J. 123.) And it is likely that the hotel will have its own audit documentation, if this can be obtained.

CHAPTER FIFTEEN

Finally, many travel companies, from an excess of caution or a fear of the law's trickeries, mark every single letter which they send out "without prejudice". If, in fact, the letter does not consist of an attempt to resolve the dispute outside the court it can still be referred to in court by the claimant at the hearing.

Criminal Offences Under the Package Travel Regulations

INTRODUCTION

The travel industry is not immune from the criminal law. There are those members of the industry, admittedly a small minority, who have, deliberately or inadvertently, contravened the regulatory regime. It could be by indicating that a hotel is air conditioned when it is not (*Wings v Ellis* [1984] 1 All E.R. 1046) or by giving the impression that a hotel was built when it was not (*R. v Clarksons Holidays Ltd* (1973) 57 Cr. App. R. 38) or by wrongly classifying a hotel as three "keys" when it was only one "key" (*Direct Holidays Plc v Wirral MBC* Unreported April 28, 1998, Divisional Court) or by indicating that a resort had a beach when it didn't (*Thomson Travel v Roberts* (1984) 148 J.P. 666) or by misleading passengers about the price they would have to pay for flights (*Essex CC v Ryanair* Unreported 2005, Chelmsford Crown Court). On this point see also the comments of the court in *Association of British Travel Agents Ltd v British Airways Plc* [2000] 1 Lloyd's Rep. 169; affirmed [2000] 2 Lloyd's Rep. 209 where airlines were taken to task for the manner in which the calculated their fares.

Until 2008, travel companies could be prosecuted under the Trade Descriptions Act 1968 (TDA) or the pricing provisions of the Consumer Protection Act 1987 (CPA) or, as we shall see in this chapter, the criminal offences created by the Package Travel Regulations. However, in 2008 the TDA and the CPA were swept away and repealed by the Consumer Protection from Unfair Trading Regulations 2007 (SI 2008/1277) ("Consumer Protection Regulations" or "CPR" for ease of reference).

In this chapter we will examine the criminal offences in the PTR, in Ch.17 we will look at the offences in the CPR and then, finally, we will discuss the "due diligence" offence which is available to defendants under both sets of regulations. Bear in mind that, as throughout the book, the PTR only apply to package holidays, but the CPR create general offences under which any company, not just travel companies, can be prosecuted.

The criminal offences in the PTR can be found in regs 5, 7 and 8. One significant feature of these regulations is that they provide that certain important information *must be given* to the consumer at various points in the contracting process *and* must be accurate.

BROCHURES—REGULATION 5

The Regulations do *not* require a brochure to be made available to consumers, but where a brochure *is* made available it lays down stringent requirements as to what must be included.

Regulation 5 provides:

"(1) Subject to paragraph (4) below, no organiser shall make available a brochure to a possible consumer unless it indicates in a legible, comprehensible and accurate manner the price and adequate information about the matters specified in Schedule 1 to these Regulations in respect of the packages offered for sale in the brochure to the extent that those matters are relevant to the packages so offered.

(2) Subject to paragraph (4) below, no retailer shall make available to a possible consumer a brochure which he knows or has reasonable cause to believe does not comply with the requirements of paragraph (1).

(3) An organiser who contravenes paragraph (1) of this regulation and a retailer who contravenes paragraph (2) thereof shall be guilty of an offence and liable:—Criminal Offences under the PTR

    (a) on summary conviction, to a fine not exceeding level 5 on the standard scale; and

    (b) on conviction on indictment, to a fine."

The effect of this Regulation is to ensure that certain information goes into the brochure—on pain of incurring a criminal penalty. As to the defences available and other general provisions, see Ch.18 below.

Thus, the elements of the offence are that:

- if a brochure;
- is made available;
- to a possible consumer;
- by an organiser;
- it must contain certain information;
- which must be legible, comprehensible, accurate and adequate.

Therefore, the offence is committed if either the brochure does not contain the information required, or it is not legible, comprehensible, accurate and adequate. For tour operators, as with the CPA, this is a strict liability offence but for travel agents is an additional requirement that they must know or have reasonable cause to believe that the requirements of para.1 have not been complied with.

A Brochure

Regulation 5 is concerned with the information provided in a *brochure*. We all know a brochure when we see one but at the margins there are some forms of advertising that may or may not be brochures. Some brochures are little more than leaflets or pamphlets and others amount to only a single sheet or two. Do all these amount to brochures? The Regulations are no help at all. Brochures are defined in reg.2(1) in the following manner:

" 'brochure' means any brochure in which packages are offered for sale".

A dictionary definition is not much more help:

"Booklet, pamphlet, esp. giving information about place". (The Concise Oxford Dictionary)

The dictionary does state that the word is derived from the French word "brocher" meaning a stitch and that brochure literally means "stitching". This suggests that to be a brochure it must be substantial enough or contain enough pages to require stitching, or, given that most brochures are not now stitched but stapled or thermal bound, to have required stitching in the past. This would raise difficulties with those smaller "brochures" consisting simply of a single sheet of paper folded in concertina fashion. It would be hard to dispute that such things are brochures even though they might not fit within a conventional definition of one.

Even more difficult would be newspaper advertisements; for example, Readers Travel Clubs and other similar features found in many local and national newspapers and magazines. Frequently, they contain considerable amounts of information, including booking conditions, itineraries and booking forms and are intended to fulfil the function of brochures, yet one would be hard pressed to call it a brochure. However, the European approach to statutory interpretation is to take a much broader, purposive approach and it may be that even newspaper advertisements would be caught by the term brochure.

Another pitfall for the operator in relation to brochures is when a supplement to a main brochure is published which may not contain all the relevant information. To avoid being caught by reg.5, the quickest solution is to ensure that the supplement does contain the required information. Another possible solution is to state clearly that this is only "part" of the brochure and if the consumer wishes to obtain all the relevant information he must read it in conjunction with the main brochure.

A photocopy of a page of a brochure handed to a consumer by a travel agent is probably not, on its own, a brochure.

Since May 2001 ABTA's Code of Conduct has provided its own definition of a brochure:

"**Brochure:** a communication in any printed, viewable, audible or other form which specifies the contents of Travel Arrangements offered by a Member in sufficient detail to allow a Client to reliably book the Travel Arrangements without obtaining additional information from the Member."

Clearly, this is intended to cover more than the conventional printed brochure. In particular, the definition would encompass internet travel sites so long as the information provided was sufficiently detailed. Whether a court would accept that the Regulations went so far is a moot point but the fact that the industry itself is prepared to admit that this is a brochure would probably go a long way to convincing them. It is worthwhile noting that when the EU Commission gets round to revising the Package Travel Directive the likelihood is that the position will be much clearer.

The emphasis in reg.5 on brochures inevitably means that, as technology develops, the Regulation becomes less and less relevant to what is going on in the real world. Not only is ABTA's definition more helpful and realistic, but ABTA, in its Code of Conduct, lays down its "Standards on Websites and Online Trading" (latest version February 2008), to ensure that its members provide honest, truthful and comprehensive websites; and also has, in the Guidance issued with the Code, a list of recommended steps for travel agents to take to ensure that Window Cards are as up to date and accurate as possible.

Is Made Available

Under the now repealed TDA, it was an offence to *make* a false statement and in the leading case of *Wings v Ellis* [1985] A.C. 272 the House of Lords held that a statement was made every time it reached the next link in the chain of distribution and every time a consumer read it. Although reg.5 does not employ the same words, the ones it does use are sufficiently similar to give rise to the same interpretation. It could be said that the operator was making the brochure available to a consumer if he sends him one direct or if he distributes it to agents to make available to consumers. So long as a brochure was intended for public consumption it would not matter how it came into the hands of a consumer—it would all count as being made available to the consumer. Strictly speaking, the offence could be committed even where a consumer had not read the brochure. It could even be argued that the offence is committed where the consumer had not yet acquired one; it would still be available to him when sitting on the travel agent's shelf. In the real world, however, the prosecution need a complainant of some sort to give evidence in court. It must be remembered also that criminal statutes must be strictly construed in favour of the defendant.

If the brochure was not legible, comprehensible or accurate when first made available then an offence will be committed. But what if it subsequently becomes inaccurate? For instance, what if it states that UK nationals do not need visas to visit the USA but after publication the rules are changed and visas are required. If the brochure is still being racked by travel agents then, unless the operator has told the agents not to display it, the brochure is still being made available *by the operator* and it is inaccurate and, therefore, the operator is committing an offence. This was a difficulty that tour operators faced under both the Trade Descriptions Act 1968 in relation to false statements and the Consumer Protection Act 1987 in relation to misleading prices. The problem is that the brochure has a life of several months and yet the information in it can change from day to day (see Ch.18, the section concerned with whether errata are effective, for guidance on this point).

To a Possible Consumer

One departure that the Regulation makes from the Directive is to make it an offence to make the brochure available to a *possible consumer* whereas the Directive only refers to *the consumer*. The practical effect of this is to considerably widen the potential scope of the offence. A consumer is defined in the Directive and the Regulations as a person "who takes or agrees to take the package". Thus, a consumer is only someone who has a contract with the operator or who actually goes on the package. But a *possible consumer* could be anyone who might wish to go on the package. Whether this will make any real difference is debatable. Although it is foreseeable that there will be possible consumers who discover brochures which may not be legible, comprehensible and accurate it is unlikely that they will complain. Even if they do so, will a prosecution be brought? It is likely that only those consumers who suffer from a breach of the Regulation will complain and only serious breaches will give rise to a prosecution. However, Trading Standards sometimes make enquiries posing as "possible consumers" in order to bolster their evidence; the Court has approved such tactics, at least under the different wording of the Consumer Protection Act 1987 *(Toys R Us v Gloucestershire CC* (1994) 158 J.P. 338).

By an Organiser

The term "organiser" will cover conventional tour operators but following the *Club Tour* case will also encompass travel agents who put ad hoc packages together—but only so long as they publish a brochure. See Ch.2 for a discussion of this case and the implications of the *ABTA v CAA* litigation.

Which Contains Certain Information

The first thing to say about reg.5 is that many tour operators already provide the required level of information as a matter of routine in their brochures, therefore, this requirement should not impose any additional burdens on them. The only difficulties which should arise will be over matters of detail, in particular, the itinerary. Health and visa requirements may also be a problem. However, the need to give passport and visa information applies to UK nationals only when the brochure is made available in the UK. The requirement to advise on health formalities applies to everyone.

The information which must be included in the brochure is set out in Sch.1 to the PTR. Most of the items in the schedule are self-explanatory. However, we will deal with a few points from the Schedule, and most importantly, the issue of the price of the package.

(i) The Price

In the early days after the Package Travel Regulations came into force, no one got very excited about the fact that the "price of the package" was one of the items required by reg.5 to be stated in a legible, comprehensible and accurate manner.

This simple requirement appeared to add nothing to the much more complex and sophisticated requirements of the Consumer Protection Act.

As time has gone on, however, reg.5 has been revealed as having real teeth. The way in which it has been interpreted by Trading Standards Departments has certainly irritated the package holiday industry, distorted the market and put tour operators at a serious disadvantage to the likes of low-cost airlines, who vary their prices minute by minute; not to mention the non-package providers, and those who sell via the internet and can alter prices whenever the market dictates.

The reason is this: as we have already seen, an offence is committed under reg.5 if information is given but in a way which is, say, inaccurate (or incomprehensible); it is also committed if the information is not given at all.

The requirement is for the price to be indicated. The industry has tried to argue that "indicate" merely means that a vague clue is given as to what the price might be. For details ask elsewhere. However, Trading Standards Officers, not unreasonably, interpret the words as meaning simply "to state the price".

Therefore, the price must be given and it must be given accurately. Thus, for the life of the brochure, the price stated in the brochure must be the actual price. It cannot be changed (or at least it cannot be increased—Trading Standards Officers, as a concession, say they will not prosecute where the price is reduced). There is no Code of Practice, as existed under the CPA, permitting changes to brochure prices to be made in certain circumstances (although the Code of Practice continues to exist in a non-statutory form and may be relevant as part of a "due diligence" defence to a reg.5 offence—see Ch.18 on defences).

Furthermore, tour operators cannot get round the Regulation by omitting prices altogether from the brochure, but merely suggesting that the consumer enquires at the travel agency desk, or on the internet, or wherever. The reason is, as we have seen, that it is equally an offence to omit the price from the brochure.

Brochures are extremely expensive to produce and cannot be replaced to reflect ever-changing market conditions. Thus, this requirement of reg.5 imposes a straightjacket on the normal workings of the market—another factor driving the demise of the traditional brochure.

An interesting argument has been run that regs 5 and 6 should be read together as they emanate from one article of the Directive, namely art.3.2. That permits changes in certain circumstances as we have seen under reg.6 (see Ch.4). In English law, art.3 has been transposed as two different things, the civil section (reg.6) and the criminal section (reg.5). The response of Trading Standards to this argument is that there is nothing to prevent the UK Government legislating in a way which is more tough than the directive; and that the words in reg.5 are clear.

The requirement for prices to be stated comprehensively probably adds nothing to the requirement under the CPR that traders should not engage in commercial practices that amount to misleading omissions (see Ch.17).

At the time of writing, it appears that some of the heat has gone out of the debate about the iniquities of reg.5. Trading Standards Departments, feeling that consumers are now more sophisticated and used to ever-varying prices, e.g. on the web, and that they are stampeding towards unprotected non-packages anyway, seem to be turning a blind eye to minor breaches of reg.5, e.g. where a brochure has been in circulation for some time, and prices honoured, but then the tour operator effects a price increase. But, of course, it will only take one prosecution to revive the argument.

(ii) The Means, Characteristics and Categories of Transport

The DTI published guidelines and indicated that in their view these words are to be taken in the general sense and that it is not necessary to specify, for example, the type of aircraft in a package involving air travel; although perhaps a holidaymaker of a nervous disposition going to one of the smaller Caribbean islands for a holiday might prefer to be told in advance that the second leg of the journey from Barbados to St Vincent was not by wide-bodied jet but a much smaller propellor-driven aircraft. This problem is now addressed by a different means, namely Regulation 2111/2005 which requires that (as from July 16, 2006) tour operators and travel agents tell consumers the identity of the airline with whom they will be flying, at the time of reservation or, if not yet known, as soon as possible thereafter.

(iii) The Type of Accommodation, etc

Again, the DTI indicates its view that the tourist classification under the Rules of an EU Member State can only be given where such rules exist. Where a classification system exists but is not mandatory (as is the case in the UK) then the organiser is free to use it or not as he pleases; but the category or degree of comfort must be indicated by one means or another. The "main features" of accommodation is a rather vague concept—does the hotel have en suite bathroom facilities, a bar, a restaurant, a swimming pool? A consumer, however, might feel that many other smaller facilities were main features as far as he was concerned. To whom are the features main? The organiser, the bulk of consumers or the individual consumer? This is particularly important bearing in mind that the offence is not confined simply to inaccuracy; but to omission of the "main features" as well. In *Inspirations East Ltd v Dudley MBC* (1998) 162 J.P. 800 (see also [1998] I.T.L.J. 16) the Divisional Court failed to make an express finding that an offence of stating matters in a brochure inaccurately could only be committed if it would also have been an offence to omit the same information; however, they proceeded on the assumption that this was correct. In the early pages of their brochure, Inspirations had indicated that the standard wheelchair/disabled logo against a hotel meant that the hotel was most suitable for those with walking difficulties or who use a wheelchair and that the lift, room and bathroom doors had been measured and there were ramps to every public area. This was under a heading in large bold type saying "Holidays for the Elderly and Disabled". The complainant booked a holiday at a hotel in the brochure which exhibited the logo, because she wished to take her wheelchair-bound daughter. They found that, while the swimming pool area was accessible from the hotel via a ramp and across a patio, there were five steps down to the pool itself from the patio and no ramps. Pill L.J. and Garland J. made the point that the "main features" of a hotel might vary from case to case. The information must be stated accurately where relevant to the packages on offer; and that, by virtue of the use of the logo and the bold paragraph on the introductory pages "Holidays for the Elderly and Disabled", "the brochure was plainly intended, it seems to me, to encourage disabled people to go on holidays offered in the brochure. That is made relevant by the presence of the disabled logo".

Inspirations, it seems, had made "suitability for the disabled" into a main feature by the boldness of their claims. It remains to be seen in future cases where a line might be drawn. It may be that some guidance can be drawn from the changes to accommodation that would be regarded as significant under reg.12, and the OFT's Guidance on Unfair Contract Terms—see Chs 6 and 10.

Note that all this information needs to be given only "where relevant to the package". There will be no need to name a hotel, for example, for the type of economy holiday sold on the basis that the hotels are allocated by the tour operator on arrival—but the main features expected must still be named. The DTI feels this may apply also to the type of package which is an extended tour of a number of cities.

(iv) Passport/Visa/Health Formalities

After the 1998 amendments the requirement applies to "general information about passport and visa requirements which apply to nationals of the Member State of States in which the brochure is made available." For most British tour operators this will be British nationals. But some tour operators distribute brochures in Eire and this will have to be taken into account too. Note also the different criteria under reg.7 below. The January 2011 Guidance to the ABTA Code requires members to give reasonable assistance to clients in obtaining this information in cases where the information is not readily available—presumably this is for non-British clients.

(v) Cancellation for Minimum Numbers

The number need not be stated, but the deadline date for cancellation must be stated and adhered to. Organisers bound by ABTA's rules, however, are unable to stipulate any date for cancellation after the date when payment of the balance of the price is due.

(vi) Arrangements in Event of Delay

It appears that complete silence on this point will not suffice. The organiser must either state the arrangements (e.g. refreshments, meals, hotel) or must specify that no arrangements apply in the event of delay—the idea being that the consumer will know what he is getting for his money and can make an informed choice. ABTA operators are already under such an obligation. The Denied Boarding Regulation will be relevant here too—see Ch.13.

Which is Legible, Comprehensible, Adequate and Accurate

Legible and comprehensible should cause no real problem to a tour operator. Presumably "legible" refers to the type size in the brochure. If the print is so small it cannot be read even by someone with good eyesight it would fail this requirement. As far as "comprehensible" is concerned this test will presumably be similar: could the text be readily understood by a person of average intelligence? (In this context the requirement in reg.3 of the Unfair Terms in Consumer Contracts Regulations 1999 that contracts be written in intelligible language might be of relevance.) For instance, it is a requirement that information about the price be comprehensible and this will include information about surcharges. If a tour operator tried to explain his surcharge policy in the kind of language found in reg.11 he would surely fail the test! The real meat is in the word "accurate". This appears to put a premium on precise and express information, and is harder to satisfy than a mere requirement that the words be "not misleading". Although the information will have to be "accurate" it will probably be subject to a *de minimis* test. If the inaccuracy is not material it will probably not constitute an offence. It is not possible to be dogmatic on this point because, unlike the CPR, the Regulations do not actually say that the offence is only committed if the inaccuracy is material. Even if courts were to take a strict line it is unlikely that minor inaccuracies would be prosecuted—either because consumers would not complain or because Trading Standards Officers have better things to do with their time.

There has been a view that the words "legible, comprehensible and accurate" are requirements only as the price of the package; whilst only "adequate information" is required as to the matters in Sch.1. However, in the case of *Inspirations East Limited v Dudley MBC*, the court rejected that view. Pill L.J. agreed that the wording was "clumsy" but said, "it is clear to me that the words legible, comprehensible and accurate are intended to govern not only the price but the information; and the word adequate is included as a means of strengthening the protection which the Regulations provide". In light of the words used in art.3 of the Directive this must be the correct interpretation.

Packages Offered for Sale

A technical point that arises from the wording of the Regulation is that it speaks of "packages *offered for sale* in the brochure". On the face of it an operator could escape liability simply by saying that he was not *offering for sale* the packages in the brochure. A tour operator's brochure does not usually constitute an offer for sale. The brochure is merely an invitation to treat and it is for the consumer to make an offer to buy. However, this eventuality is covered by reg.2(1) which provides:

> " 'an offer' includes an invitation to treat whether by means of advertising or otherwise, and cognate expressions shall be construed accordingly."

Similar provisions existed in the Trade Descriptions Act and they are aimed at preventing the tour operator escaping criminal liability on the basis of a technicality of the law of contract such as occurred in the case of *Fisher v Bell* [1961] 1 Q.B. 394. In that case a shopkeeper who displayed a flick knife in his window escaped conviction for *offering* a dangerous weapon for sale as the display was only an invitation to treat not an offer. The effect of reg.2(1) will be to deprive tour operators of a similar defence.

Travel Agents

Regulation 5(2) creates criminal liability for travel agents but, in a change from the original consultation document, only if the agent "knows or has reasonable cause to believe" that the brochure does not comply with reg.5(1), i.e. it is an offence, like reg.8 of the CPR, that requires *mens rea*. For corporate defendants

CHAPTER SIXTEEN

this will mean that the prosecution will have to show that a "directing mind" of the company had the requisite knowledge. (See Ch.17 on the CPR for this.) As long as the agent does not know or have reasonable cause to believe then he escapes liability but once he does then he can be convicted. On the face of it this seems eminently fair but on reflection the practicalities of complying with the Regulation are immense.

Given the amount of information that must be provided in the brochure it will not be long before some of it is found to be inaccurate and the agent informed of this. At this stage he will know that the information is inaccurate and he will be committing an offence if he *makes available* the brochure. The only escape then is either to take the drastic step of taking the brochures off display or ensuring a fail-safe errata system in the brochures themselves. The alternative is to avail themselves of the due diligence defence in reg.24 (see Ch.18). Whether this would work depends upon whether a court would accept the argument that even though an inaccurate or deficient brochure was made available it amounted to the taking of all reasonable care to prevent the commission of the offence if, say, the travel agent drew the consumer's attention to it before a booking was made. Although that may be the only practicable way to deal with brochures that rapidly become out of date it, nevertheless, means that agents will be racking brochures that they know are inaccurate and will be allowing consumers to walk out of the agency with bundles of such brochures. (See Nardi "Due Diligence: the Travel Agent's Perspective" [1994] T.L.J. 13 on this issue.)

Multiple travel agencies have the added problem that once the company knows from one branch that a brochure is inaccurate then they will know that the same brochure in all its branches is inaccurate and they will have to take company-wide steps to address the problem. Knowledge of the inaccuracy might typically come from the tour operator himself, but might also come from information supplied by a client, or even by a different tour operator who features the same hotel and notifies the travel agent that, for example, the hotel swimming pool has closed. However, so long as the knowledge is confined to branch level the company can escape conviction by invoking the principle in *Tesco v Nattrass* [1972] A.C. 153, that no "directing mind" of the company knew of the inaccuracy. But once the branch manager has informed senior personnel at head office then the company will have the requisite knowledge. The way the offence is framed it is not unlikely that a factual situation, similar to the *Wings* case, under the TDA could arise: a consumer returns from an early season holiday and complains to his travel agent that the brochure he booked his holiday from was inaccurate. At this stage no offence has been committed by the travel agent as the agent did not know or have reasonable cause to believe the brochure was inaccurate (the tour operator's position is different, of course). Once the manager informs head office then the company faces potential prosecution unless it removes all the brochures from the racks or puts errata stickers on the offending passage. If, however, an offending brochure, despite the best efforts of the travel agent, is made available to a consumer, then the travel agent has probably committed a prima facie offence. He knows that the brochure is inaccurate and he has made it available. The mental element, as under *Wings*, relates to the inaccuracy not to the making available. The agent can, of course, still raise the due diligence defence and escape conviction (see Ch.18 on defences).

To assist travel agents and, indeed, tour operators in this situation, ABTA used to recommend that all its travel agent members display the following notice prominently and close to the brochure racks:

"Important notice: the prices or details contained within brochures displayed in this shop may have changed since the brochures were printed. Please ask our staff for details. You will be informed about any changes that we are aware of before you book as part of our commitment to quality customer service".

This so-called "shelf talker" could, with other measures, form part of a due diligence defence—see Ch.18.

PRE-CONTRACT—REGULATION 7

Although information about health formalities and visa requirements must be provided in the brochure, if a brochure is made available, there is an independent requirement in reg.7 that the tour operator provide the same kind of information before the contract is concluded. The wording is almost identical to the wording in Sch.1 and there is no reason to believe that they impose different obligations. The rationale for having two identical requirements is presumably to cover the situation where the consumer books a holiday without the assistance of a brochure.

Regulation 7 provides:

"7(1) Before a contract is concluded, the other party to the contract shall provide the intending consumer with the information specified in paragraph (2) below in writing or in some other appropriate form.
    (2) The information referred to in paragraph (1) is:—

   (a) general information about passport and visa requirements which apply to Nationals of the Member State or States concerned who purchase the package in question, including information about the length of time it is likely to take to obtain the appropriate passports and visas;
   (b) information about health formalities required for the journey and the stay; and
   (c) the arrangements for security for the money paid over and (where applicable) for the repatriation of the consumer in the event of insolvency.

    (3) If the other party to the contract contravenes paragraph (1) of this regulation he shall be guilty of an offence and liable:—

   (a) on summary conviction, to a fine not exceeding level 5 on the standard scale
   (b) on conviction on indictment, to a fine."

One difference between reg.7 and Sch.1 is that not only must information be given about passport and visa requirements, but also the length of time it is likely to take to obtain them.

Much of what is required in reg.7 is also required by reg.5, thus, if a tour operator does provide a brochure which complies with reg.5 he will also be complying with reg.7 except for the time limits for passports and visas.

One problem that arises is for tour operators who do not publish brochures and who use telesales to sell their holidays. How are they to comply with reg.7? The requirement is to provide this information *in writing or in other appropriate form before the contract is made.* Generally, in such a situation the contract is concluded over the phone, so unless the contract is to be postponed until after the information is received, putting the information in the post will slow things down considerably. It could be argued that the only practicable way to comply is to give the information orally. This could be justified on the ground that this would be an *appropriate* method of providing the information in the circumstances. If the consumer is prepared to contract over the phone in the first place then it would be difficult to argue that the information was not given in an appropriate form. It would be wise to ensure that in any subsequent written confirmation the information about health and visas is confirmed in writing. This will deflect later complaints that the information was not provided.

If it were just the health and visa requirements that were to be given over the phone this would probably not prove too burdensome. However, under reg.9, there is a requirement (albeit with civil not criminal sanctions) that *all* the terms of the contract are reduced to writing or other appropriate form *before* the contract is made. This obligation is one which telesales operators without brochures will have great difficulty complying with.

The penalty for not complying with reg.7 will be criminal and will be imposed on *the other party to the contract.* Usually this will be the operator but in some circumstances could be the agent (see the discussion on "other party to the contract" in Ch.2). Indeed, it has been common practice in the industry, regardless of the precise combined effect of the 1998 amendments to regs 5 and 7, to impose the visa and passport requirements on travel agents, especially where the consumers are not British nationals—see the note on the ABTA Guidance to its Code, above. However, it may be, that for the present at least, reg.7(2)(b) is largely redundant. Although in certain cases it is highly advisable to take health precautions, there are very few countries where there is a *requirement* to do so.

Technically, reg.7 also applies to domestic as well as foreign packages. This means that domestic tour operators and hoteliers selling packages ought to go through the motions of telling clients that they do not need passports or visas, nor are there any health formalities for the journey or the stay. Again, for defence and other provisions, see Ch.18.

IN GOOD TIME BEFORE DEPARTURE—REGULATION 8

In addition to all the contractual information to be provided and information on health and visa requirements there are certain other details which must be provided before travel.

Regulation 8 provides:

"8(1) The other party to the contract shall in good time before the start of the journey provide the consumer with the information specified in paragraph (2) below in writing or in some other appropriate form.

(2) The information referred to in paragraph (1) is the following:—

(a) the times and places of intermediate stops and transport connections and particulars of the place to be occupied by the traveller (for example, cabin or berth on ship, sleeper compartment on train);

(b) the name, address and telephone number—

    (i) of the representative or other party to the contract in the locality where the consumer is to stay,
or, if there is no such representative,

    (ii) of any agency in that locality on whose assistance a consumer in difficulty would be able to call,
or, if there is no such representative or agency, a telephone number or other information which will enable the consumer to contact the other party to the contract during the stay; and

(c) in the case of a journey or stay outside the United Kingdom by a child under the age of 16 on the day when the journey or stay is due to start, information enabling direct contact to be made with the child or the person responsible at the place where he is to stay; and

(d) except where the consumer is required as a term of the contract to take out an insurance policy in order to cover the cost of cancellation by the consumer or the cost of assistance, including repatriation, in the event of accident or illness, information about an insurance policy which the consumer may if he wishes, take out in respect of the risk of those costs being incurred.

(3) If the other party to the contract contravenes paragraph (1) of this regulation he shall be guilty of an offence and liable:—

(a) on summary conviction, to a fine not exceeding level 5 on the standard scale; and

(b) on conviction on indictment, to a fine".

Again, for defence provisions see Ch.18.

There is no definition of the words "in good time". The DTI recommended a minimum of seven days and ABTA urges on its members the minimum of 14 days. Obviously, shorter periods will be appropriate in the case of last minute bookings.

Intermediate Stops and Transport Connections

This may cause problems. The DTI considered that intermediate stops are those which significantly affect the nature of the package, and do not include meal or refreshment breaks. If travel is by a train, and it stops at intermediate stations, this would surely not be covered. What, however, of flights which stop to pick up or re-fuel en route? It could possibly make a difference if the passengers have to troop off the plane during this procedure, and then re-embark, although this seems rather a random test. Many passengers would argue that an extra landing and take-off makes a flight a more daunting proposition and is therefore significant; but what, in fact, is the difference in principle from the Eurostar train that stops at Lille on its way to Brussels?

Representative

It will be seen that this is a three-step procedure. If there is a representative, his or her contact details must be supplied; if not, contact details for a local agency; and if there is no representative and no agency, a telephone contact number to enable the consumer contact with the organiser.

It is a matter of some astonishment to tour operators that it is considered a matter worthy of criminal penalty if they fail to give the name, etc, of their representative. In the nature of things, representatives come and go—does the law really require them to say to consumers: "your representative is Tracy and her telephone number is ... "?

In practice, the larger tour operators give the name and address of their local office. This does not strictly comply with the law, but the hope must be that Trading Standards Officers will consider the purpose of this regulation—that a consumer in difficulty will have somewhere to turn.

In the absence of these, there must be a telephone contact number, perhaps the operator's own office number. It does not say that the number must be manned. While this must be implied, the question is—between what hours must it be manned? Normal working hours or 24 hours? What about weekends? In practice, the major tour operators maintain a 24-hour emergency contact service; the small operators do not (the very wide definition of an organiser must also be borne in mind here).

Insurance

The requirement to give insurance details will not create problems in practice—tour operators and travel agents make considerable commission out of the sale of holiday insurance and will be keen to draw its existence to the attention of consumers much earlier than is required by reg.8. But a substantial percentage of holiday insurance is, in fact, now sold by banks and the like as annual policies.

In contrast to reg.5, the writers are unaware of any actual prosecutions which have been launched under reg.8.

CHAPTER SEVENTEEN

The Consumer Protection From Unfair Trading Regulations

INTRODUCTION

As explained in the previous chapter, the Trade Descriptions Act 1968 (TDA) and the pricing provisions of the Consumer Protection Act 1987 (CPA) have been repealed and replaced by The Consumer Protection from Unfair Trading Regulations 2008 (SI 2008/1277) (CPR). The new regulations have been brought into force to comply with our obligations to the EU. Their origin lies in the Unfair Commercial Practices Directive (2005/29/EC). These new regulations replace the relatively detailed and specific offences of the old legislation with a more general duty to trade fairly, or rather, not to trade unfairly by indulging in "unfair commercial practices". Although it must be said that there are prohibitions against some quite specific unfair practices.

Interestingly, the Directive is a "maximum harmonisation" measure, i.e. Member States of the EU, unlike with previous directives, cannot provide for greater, or lesser, protection than the Directive sets out. Article 4 provides:

"Member States shall neither restrict the freedom to provide services nor restrict the free movement of goods for reasons falling within the field approximated by this Directive."

This is unlike, for instance, the Package Travel Directive which permits Member States to bring in measures which go beyond the initial protection the Directive provides (1990/314/EC, art.9: "Member States may adopt or return more stringent provisions in the field covered by this Directive to protect the consumer"). The reason behind this is to ensure that there is a "level playing field" throughout the EU—reducing costs to traders and improving consumer confidence. This rationale can be found in paras 3 and 4 of the Preamble to the Directive:

"(3) The laws of the Member States relating to unfair commercial practices show marked differences which can generate appreciable distortions of competition and obstacles to the smooth functioning of the internal market. In the field of advertising, Council Directive 84/450/EEC of 10 September 1984 concerning misleading and comparative advertising establishes minimum criteria for harmonizing legislation on misleading advertising, but does not prevent the Member States from retaining or adopting measures which provide more extensive protection for consumers. As a result, Member States' provisions on misleading advertising diverge significantly.

(4) These disparities cause uncertainty as to which national rules apply to unfair commercial practices harming consumers' economic interests and create many barriers affecting business and consumers. These barriers increase the cost to business of exercising internal market freedoms, in particular when businesses wish to engage in cross border marketing, advertising campaigns and sales promotions. Such barriers also make consumers uncertain of their rights and undermine their confidence in the internal market."

It should be recognised from the outset that, as the name suggests, this is a consumer protection measure. Should confirmation of this be required, authority for this can be found in para.1 of the Preamble to the Directive:

"Article 153(1) and (3)(a) of the Treaty provides that the Community is to contribute to the attainment of a high level of consumer protection by the measures it adopts pursuant to Article 95 thereof".

As with many consumer protection measures it will, of course, benefit those reputable traders who already comply with the standards set out in the Regulations because their less reputable rivals will face prosecution if they fail to comply—just the kind of levelling effect the Directive aims to achieve.

INTERPRETATION

In looking at this area of law it is tempting to look at, and apply, the extensive case law we have inherited from the TDA and the CPA which covers much the same ground as the CPR. However, it is wise to bear in mind guidance provided by Briggs J. in the recent case of *Office of Fair Trading v Purely Creative Ltd* [2011] EWHC 106 (Ch), involving companies charged with breaching the CPRs, where he describes the approach courts should take to the interpretation of UK legislation which is derived from Europe:

"Domestic regulations designed to implement EU directives, and in particular maximum harmonisation directives, must be construed as far as possible so as to implement the purposes and provisions of the directive. The interpretation of words and phrases is neither a matter of grammars nor dictionaries, nor even a matter of the use of those phrases (or of the underlying concepts) in national law. If similar words and phrases are used in the directive itself, then they must be interpreted both in the directive and in the implementing regulations by means of a process of interpretation which is independent of the member state's national law and, for that matter, independent of any other member state's national law. For that purpose the primary recourse of the national court is to the jurisprudence of the ECJ. The national court may also obtain assistance from, but is not bound by, guidance issued by the Commission, and by the decisions of other national courts as to the meaning of the relevant directive."

So when we use previous case law for illustrative purposes the commentary should be read in the light of the guidance provided by Briggs J.

The Scheme of the Regulations

For our purposes the relevant parts of the Regulations are Parts 1, 2 and 3. Part 1 is the interpretation section where many of the terms used in the latter part of the Regulations are defined. It is here that we are introduced to many of the terms that are of pivotal importance in defining the offences made illegal by the Regulations. Terms such as "the average consumer", "materially distort the economic behaviour", "transactional decision" and "commercial practice" are introduced here—many of them very technical in nature and unfamiliar to UK practitioners.

Part 2 prohibits "unfair commercial practices". It then goes into more detail about what amounts to such a practice. A commercial practice is unfair if:

- it contravenes the requirements of professional diligence; and it materially distorts or is likely to materially distort the economic behaviour of the average consumer with regard to the product (reg.3);

- it is a misleading action (reg.5);

- it is a misleading omission (reg.6);

- it is aggressive (reg.7); or

- it is listed in Sch.1 to the Regulations.

In addition, it is also an unfair commercial practice for a "code owner" to promote unfair commercial practices in a code of conduct. This would apply to bodies such as ABTA which have formulated codes of conduct for their members. However, despite the fact that this is designated as an unfair commercial practice, the Regulations do not make it a criminal offence. As the Guidance published jointly by the Office of Fair Trading and BERR (the Department for Business Enterprise and Regulatory Reform, now BIS, the Department for Business Innovation and Skills) comments, "Any enforcement action, if needed, will be taken through the civil route via part 8 of the Enterprise Act 2002" (OFT 1008, p.45).

Part 3 creates the offences which relate to the prohibited commercial practices. A trader commits an offence if:

- he knowingly or recklessly engages in a commercial practice which contravenes the requirements of professional diligence and the practice materially distorts or is likely to materially distort the economic behaviour of the average consumer with regard to the product (reg.8);

- he engages in a commercial practice which is a misleading action (reg.9);

- he engages in a commercial practice which is a misleading omission (reg.10);

- he engages in a commercial practice which is aggressive (reg.11);

- he engages in a commercial practice set out in certain paragraphs of Sch.1 (reg.12).

CHAPTER SEVENTEEN

All these offences will be examined in some detail in due course.

Note that apart from the first, which requires the defendant knowingly or recklessly to have committed the offence, these are strict liability offences, requiring no *mens rea* on the part of the defendant. This strictness, however, is mitigated by the inclusion of the "due diligence" offence in Pt 3 at reg.17—in a form familiar to anyone dealing with regulatory offences, and in particular the old Trade Descriptions Act and the Consumer Protection Act.

The Impact on the Travel Industry

The big question for the travel industry is whether the regulatory burden will be greater or smaller than under the previous regime. We will have answered this question in some detail by the end of this chapter, but for the moment we will confine ourselves to some general observations. First, for those traders who operate their businesses honestly and diligently there should be no fear of prosecution. This was always the case and it should be no different under the new regime. There may be concern that the majority of the offences are "strict liability" offences rather than ones requiring *mens rea* as under the old Trade Descriptions Act. However, the effect of the due diligence defence mitigates the strictness of the new regime, as it did where it could be invoked under the TDA. And of course the pricing offences under the old Consumer Protection Act were strict liability offences anyway.

If we look briefly at some of the old case law in the light of the new law this will give us an indication of how things may have changed, or not, as the case may be.

British Airways Board v Taylor [1976] 1 All E.R. 65 was a prosecution that went to the House of Lords on the issue of whether or not BOAC had made a false statement about whether a passenger had a confirmed seat on a plane. He had been issued with a confirmed reservation but on checking-in he had been "bumped" because the plane was overbooked. The case turned, not on whether BOAC *knew* that the statement was false, but whether it was false at all. Was it a false statement of fact or a promise as to the future—which could not be true or false—and, therefore, not contrary to s.14 of the TDA? The House of Lords held it was the former and the airline was convicted. Today, the prosecution would be brought under reg.9, which makes it an offence to engage in a misleading action as defined in reg.5. On the face of it, to issue a confirmed reservation that a passenger has a seat on a plane when this was not necessarily the case, because a denied boarding policy was in place, would be a misleading action under reg.5. It is a misleading action if the statement is false (the issue in the *BOAC* case) *or* if its overall presentation deceives or is likely to deceive the average consumer about "the availability of the product" (reg.5(2)(a) and reg.5(5)(a)). Unless the defendant could raise the due diligence defence, they would be convicted of an offence under reg.9. Therefore, the outcome of a similar case under the new regime is likely to be the same—either because the statement would be regarded as false or because it could be regarded as deceptive. The legislation seems to give the prosecutor more options. And, unlike the TDA, the offence could be committed without *mens rea*.

Wings v Ellis [1984] 1 All E.R. 1046 was a prosecution under s.14 of the TDA.

The facts of the case were that the defendant tour operator, Wings, published a brochure in early 1981 advertising holidays for the 1981–82 season. Unfortunately, there was a mistake in the brochure. It stated that a particular hotel had air-conditioning when in fact it did not. Wings did not discover this until May 1981. At that point they issued errata to all existing clients and instructed all telephone sales staff to inform travel agents and prospective clients of the error before bookings were made. At least one client, however, was not told of the lack of air-conditioning before travelling. On return he complained to his local trading standards department who subsequently brought a prosecution under s.14(1)(a). Under that section it is an offence for a person "to make a statement which he knows to be false". The problem was that Wings knew the statement was false but they didn't know they were making it. Ultimately, the case made its way to the House of Lords on the difficult issue of whether Wings could be convicted when, in reality, they had no *mens rea*. In convicting Wings, the House of Lords conceded that although this was a case normally requiring *mens rea*, a literal interpretation of the offence turned it into one of "semi-strict liability" (Lord Scarman).

On the face of it, a prosecution may be easier under the new regime. Such a statement would be a misleading action under reg.5 giving rise to an offence under reg.9 and no knowledge or recklessness would have to be proved by the prosecution to establish a prima facie offence had been committed. However, if the defendant had acted with all due diligence then they would have a workable defence under reg.17—as Wings would have had if they had chosen to raise it. That they didn't choose to raise it was probably because it wouldn't have worked—their "due diligence system" would not have survived scrutiny.

On this brief initial review it appears that framing the offence may be easier and that a trader, having made a misleading statement, would have to fall back on the due diligence defence to escape prosecution.

Concurrent Liability

It should not be forgotten that large parts of the travel industry are subject to both the Package Travel Regulations 1992 and to the ATOL Regulations 2012 which create other criminal offences and which are both in the process of being reviewed. The ATOL Regulations, in particular, have attracted recent judicial attention and provided the incentive for their review (See *ABTA v CAA* [2006] EWHC 13 (Admin) and *CAA v Travel Republic Ltd* Unreported November 10, 2009, Westminster Magistrates' Court).

And, of course, there is still the possibility of civil liability. False or misleading statements which can be prosecuted under the criminal law are also likely to amount to misrepresentation or breach of contract in the civil law giving rise to compensation for the victim.

Definitions

We will now examine some of the crucial definitions and terminology used in the CPR. The definitions comprise the "building blocks" of the criminal offences created by the Regulations and are fundamental to an understanding of the law.

CHAPTER SEVENTEEN

Consumer

A "consumer" is defined in the CPR as:

"any individual who in relation to a commercial practice is acting for purposes which are outside his business".

The definition in the Directive is:

" 'consumer' means any natural person who, in commercial practices covered by this Directive, is acting for purposes which are outside his trade, business, craft or profession".

This means that, for the purposes of these Regulations, a consumer is a person or persons acting in a private capacity. A consumer cannot be a business or someone acting on behalf of a business, trade, craft or profession. At Recital 8 to the Unfair Commercial Practices Directive it is stated:

"This Directive directly protects consumer economic interests from unfair business-to-consumer commercial practices."

In the travel industry this means that the consumer is the typical holidaymaker booking a package holiday or cruise for their summer break, someone purchasing a ticket on a flight or ferry to visit family abroad, a booking for a hotel room or other accommodation, even bookings for ancillaries such as car hire and attraction tickets. A business person booking a flight to attend a meeting in the course of their business or employment would not fall within the definition of a "consumer" and, therefore, the CPR does not apply to this (rather large) category of travel industry customer.

"Consumer" is also defined in the Package Travel, Package Holidays and Package Tours Regulations 1992 (PTR), the Unfair Contract Terms Act 1977 (UCTA) and in that part of the Consumer Protection Act 1987 (CPA) relating to misleading prices which has now been repealed. What is important to note is that the new definition under the CPR is different to those under the CPA, the PTR and UCTA. Under the CPA, for instance, the definition of a consumer was "any person who might wish to be supplied for his own private use and consumption". At first glance this appears to protect only private consumers, but it was interpreted to mean that no actual supply needed to be made—which meant that a trading standards officer could qualify as a "consumer" under those provisions (see *Toys R Us v Gloucestershire CC* (1994) 158 JP 338). In the CPR the words "might be" do not appear in the definition of consumer. In the CPR the consumer "is acting for purposes which are outside his business" which suggests a narrower scope. However, the important point here is that whilst the term "consumer" is not a new one to the travel industry, none of these previous definitions have any bearing in relation to the CPR. Only the defined meaning of "consumer" set out in reg.2 of the CPR can be considered when interpreting who is a consumer, and, by extension, the "average consumer".

Average Consumer

One of the most important definitions is that of the "average consumer" which is set out in reg.2(2)–(6) of the CPR. Distinction is made between the "average consumer" (reg.2(2)) and the average consumer who is a member of a "particular group of consumers" (reg.2(3)) and the average consumer who is a member of a group of consumers who are "particularly vulnerable" (reg.2(4) and (5)).

Reference to the average consumer can be found in all of the prohibitions (regs 3–7). In reg.3(3)(b) it is stated a commercial practice is unfair if:

"it materially distorts or is likely to materially distort the economic behaviour of the average consumer with regard to the product."

Under reg.5 a misleading action is one which:

"deceives or is likely to deceive the average consumer"

or it causes the average consumer to take a:

"transactional decision he would not have taken otherwise".

The latter wording also appears in reg.6 for what constitutes a misleading omission.

Aggressive commercial practices are defined in reg.7 and one exists if:

"(a) it significantly impairs or is likely to impair the average consumer's freedom of choice in relation to the product concerned through the use of harassment, coercion or undue influence; and

(b) it thereby causes or is likely to cause him to take a transactional decision he would not have taken otherwise."

In defining the average consumer reg.2(2) states:

"In determining the effect of a commercial practice on the average consumer where the practice reaches or is addressed to a consumer or consumers account shall be taken of the material characteristics of such an average consumer including his being reasonably well informed, reasonably observant and circumspect."

Interestingly, the definition of an average consumer appears in the CPR but it does not appear in the Directive itself. The basis of the definition contained in the CPR does, however, derive its origin from the Directive. Recital 18 of the Directive does state:

" ... this Directive takes as a benchmark the average consumer, who is reasonably well-informed and reasonably observant and circumspect, taking into account social, cultural and linguistic factors as interpreted by the Court of Justice."

The latter part of this wording—"taking into account social cultural and linguistic factors"—has been omitted from the definition in the CPR but at para.14.32 of the Guidance published by BERR the omitted wording is emphasised to expand upon what is meant by the "notional average consumer". This may indicate that whilst the wording does not appear in the CPR it will be taken into consideration when considering the application of the average consumer measure—in accordance with the principles of interpretation when considering European legislation.

The test for the average consumer is an objective one. It is not necessary to show that actual consumers have in reality been affected by an unfair commercial practice, simply that they are likely or it is/was foreseeable that they may be. The average consumer is the representative for the whole population of consumers, the Joe Bloggs or "man on the Clapham omnibus" who represents the average person in our society who is a consumer and not acting for commercial purposes. If the average consumer's "material characteristics" include being "reasonably well informed, reasonably observant and circumspect" (reg.2(2) CPR) then what does this mean? This will be considered later.

The "Average Targeted Consumer" and the "Vulnerable Consumer"

Two distinctions are made in the CPR to the average consumer generally. These are contained in reg.2 paras (4) and (5) CPR. Regulation 2(4) CPR states:

"In determining the effect of a commercial practice on the average consumer where the practice is directed to a particular group of consumers, reference to the average consumer shall be read as referring to the average member of that group."

The average consumer who is an average member of a particular group of consumers is referred to as the "average targeted consumer" in the Guidance (and hereafter for ease of reference). It is the characteristics and perspective of the average targeted consumer that is relevant where a commercial practice is targeted or directed at a particular group of consumers. This could include, for instance, PGL holidays for children or Saga holidays for more mature holidaymakers. It could also include religious tourism, for example the Hajj pilgrimage.

Regulation 2(5) goes on to state:

"In determining the effect of a commercial practice on the average consumer—

a) Where a clearly identifiable group of consumers is particularly vulnerable to the practice or the underlying product because of their mental or physical infirmity, age or credulity in a way which the trader could reasonably be expected to foresee, and

b) Where the practice is likely to materially distort the economic behaviour only of that group,

A reference to the average consumer shall be read as referring to the average member of that group."

Here the test is that the vulnerability of that particular group could have been reasonably foreseen by a trader. This is again an objective test and it is not necessary for the trader to actually foresee the effect only that the trader could or should have reasonably foreseen it.

At para.14.37 of the Guidance the meaning of "vulnerable" is considered. Mental or physical infirmity would include those suffering from impairment such as blindness or deafness, those confined to wheelchairs and other disabilities. The age can be either of the young or old, the categories no doubt particularly meant by these criteria are children and the elderly who can be particularly vulnerable for different but obvious reasons. Credulity covers:

" ... groups of consumers who may readily believe specific claims. The term is neutral, so the effect is to protect members of a group who are for any reason open to be influenced by certain claims" (para.14.37 of the Guidance).

Only vulnerability on the basis of infirmity, age or credulity is referred to in the Regulations so it appears no other vulnerability may be taken into consideration.

The result of this "tiered" approach to identifying an average consumer is stated clearly in the Guidance (para.14.31):

"This means that different practices, and even the same practices in different circumstances, may be found to have different effects depending on the type of consumer they reach or affect. However, this concept is intended to help the courts decide if a practice is prohibited due to the impact or potential impact it has on the relevant consumers. The provisions concerning vulnerable consumers are there to ensure that traders do not unfairly exploit vulnerable people where their practices might not change non-vulnerable consumers' decisions."

Who is the Average Consumer?

At para.14.32 of the Guidance it is stated:

" 'Average' does not mean a statistically average consumer."

Therefore, if the statistics show that the most typical consumer at an up-market hotel chain such as Four Seasons is aged between 30–50, has a high net worth income, is well travelled and is generally an experienced travel industry consumer, this will not equate to the "average consumer". The standard of the typical consumer at a Four Seasons hotel cannot be applied to ascertain who the average consumer is.

So if the average consumer is not an actual consumer, who is the average consumer? As emphasised earlier, the average consumer is one that is "reasonably well informed, reasonably observant and circumspect" but no further guidance is given on how to interpret this definition. These words have been considered before, most notably as a result of litigation in relation to trademarks and the issue of confusion (as to this see *Lloyd Schufabrik Meyer & Co GmbH v Klijsen Handel BV* (C-342/97) [1999] E.C.R. I-3819 at [26] and *Gut*

Springenheide GmbH v Oberkreisdirektor des Kreises Steinfurt (C-210/96) [1998] E.C.R. I-4657 at [31]), but it is new terminology in the consumer protection field.

In considering the terms "reasonably well informed", is a consumer who falls into that category experienced at booking and going on holidays or flights? Or are they simply expected to know things that are within the general knowledge of private consumers of the travel industry? The case of *R. v Clarksons Holidays Ltd* (1973) 57 Cr. App. R. 38 dealt with an "artist's impression" in a tour operator's brochure and whether it amounted to a "false trade description" that the hotel and its facilities actually existed. A jury (of average consumers perhaps?) convicted the company. However, almost 40 years have elapsed since that case was decided and in that time there has been a huge expansion of the whole travel industry market with more affordable options making travel much more commonplace than in the 1970s. As a consequence, the travelling public is generally more sophisticated today, and this, coupled with a good dose of consumer scepticism, could very well lead to a different result. Would a reasonably well informed travel consumer expect that where only an artist's impression is shown that the actual accommodation may actually look different, or have different or incomplete facilities? Particularly if that reasonably well informed consumer has been reasonably observant and circumspect and has read the terms and conditions highlighted at the back of the brochure? These questions have no straightforward answer at this stage, as without any authorities on the CPR the authors can only speculate that the answers may be different under these new Regulations. If "social, cultural and linguistic factors" are also to be taken into account it is fair to say that it is likely the outcome of litigation would turn on its own facts, each being determined by the particular factors taken into consideration. See the case of *Southwark LBC v Time Computer Systems Ltd*, *Independent*, July 14, 1997 for a TDA case on what can be expected of a consumer of computer equipment—bearing in mind Briggs J.'s warning about the interpretation of European legislation.

If a commercial practice is aimed at a sector of a market rather than the whole market, the "average targeted consumer" then the average consumer is considered within the context of that smaller grouping. For instance: a package holiday is put together with the theme of photography, for example a trip to Lake Garda with a tour itinerary particularly designed to maximise photographic opportunity of points of interest in the region perhaps with a tour guide. The package is then advertised in a magazine or other publication whose target audience/market sector is photography professionals rather than in the tour operator's mainstream brochure. This would be when the test for an average targeted consumer would be relevant. The average person, whilst still being reasonably well informed, reasonably observant and circumspect, would have the perspective of being an average member of the group targeted—in this example that would be photography professionals. So, being professionals, would it be reasonable to expect that they would know what natural lighting would be needed to obtain the type of photos they are expecting to achieve from the trip and that natural lighting changes depending upon the weather and seasons? Would it therefore seem reasonable to expect that when a professional photographer books a package holiday of this nature during the off peak season he can anticipate the kind of weather that can be expected during that off peak season, which will inevitably reduce his opportunities for taking a picture of the lake with still waters, blue skies and a clear vista of the horizon? If so, it may not be necessary for the package tour operator to give explicit warnings with regard to the weather and natural lighting—the average targeted consumer, in this case professional photographers, cannot complain about being misled about the suitability of the weather; they are a sufficiently sophisticated group to know otherwise.

To take another scenario; a cheap skiing trip is advertised in a magazine or other publication aimed at professional, keen and experienced skiers for dates at the beginning and end of the skiing season. By virtue of the fact that the commercial practice targeted professional, keen and experienced skiers, the average targeted consumer test would apply. So if, as has happened in the past, there is insufficient snow in either or both of these "shoulder" parts of the season would the average targeted consumer, in this instance, be able to complain about the lack of snow? Or at least, the lack of warning of the risk of no snow in the advertisement or brochure? Being an average member of the average targeted group who are professionals and experienced skiers and being reasonably well informed, observant and circumspect would they not be better informed and therefore be expected to know that the beginning and end of the season is risky, particularly as that is reflected in the cheap price?

If a "Pilgrimage to Mecca" package tour was put together and aimed at those wanting to undertake the Hajj this would be another example where the average targeted consumer test would apply, but this is also an example of when the "social, cultural and linguistic factors" may be very relevant. If the package has been put together and aimed at Muslims wanting to undertake the pilgrimage would the average member of the group expect, without explicit mention of the fact, for meals only to contain Halal meat? For their tour timetable to include appropriate breaks for prayer? That an Imam would be arranged to accompany them and a guide experienced in performing the Hajj? Again, there are no answers to these questions but it is food for thought.

The third and final distinction of "type" of average consumer is one that is the average member of a vulnerable group. The example given in the guidance describes what might be a "vulnerable group":

"Consumers who need to use wheelchairs might be a vulnerable group in relation to advertising claims about ease of access to a holiday destination".

Unlike with the averaged targeted consumer, there appears to be no necessity to show that the vulnerable consumer has been targeted, so the advertisement may be contained in a tour operator's seasonal brochure for general consumption. The fact that claims or statements are made within the brochure which are only relevant to those in particular need of those provisions, such as access for wheelchairs, means that the claim is only applicable to the smaller group of the population to whom they are relevant. This definition is aimed at protecting those who, due to their vulnerability, may be in more need of protection than the average consumer who is not vulnerable.

To take an unlikely example: a group of aged, and ailing, nuns book a pilgrimage tour to Lourdes having considered literature in the tour operator's brochure which emphasised the miraculous healings that have taken place there, and giving the impression that modern pilgrims might also benefit from a visit. On their return, none of them had experienced or even witnessed a miraculous healing and they are deeply dissatisfied by this. This could be an instance when the nuns may be considered "vulnerable" as a result of their credulity—as devout Roman Catholic nuns, they were not worldly, they were innocents abroad and they trusted and relied on the marketing material as truth. It is unlikely that the average consumer would be affected in the same way but the average member of a vulnerable group would be affected differently. In order to establish that the average consumer in this circumstance was one that was the average member of the vulnerable group, it would need to be shown that the nuns were members of a "clearly identifiable group of consumers" and that their vulnerability (in this case credulity) was reasonably foreseeable by the tour operator and that the commercial practice was "likely to distort the economic behaviour only of that group". If successful, the question of whether the tour operator had breached any prohibitions or committed any offences would be considered from the perspective of the average consumer who is vulnerable.

Transactional Decision

A "transactional decision" is defined in the CPR at reg.(2)(1) as:

" ... any decision taken by a consumer, whether it is to act or to refrain from action, concerning

a) Whether, how and on what terms to purchase, make payment in whole or in part for, retain or dispose of a product; or
b) Whether, how and on what terms to exercise a contractual right in relation to a product."

The words in the CPRs derive from those found in the Directive itself. In the Guidance the phrase "take a different decision" is used as shorthand for transactional decision which perhaps better describes what is meant by the definition of "transactional decision". At para.14.23 of the Guidance a transactional decision is described as:

" ... an important concept covering a wide range of decisions that have been or may be taken by consumers in relation to products. This is wide in chronological scope, covering decisions taken before, during or after a contract is formed."

General examples included in the Guidance are whether to buy goods or a service, to exercise a cancellation right, a right to a refund or replacement or a right in relation to an after-sales service.

So, if a consumer when booking a flight direct with the airline is informed that there are no seats in economy remaining and only first class seats are available, when this is in fact not the case, then this may be a misleading action, in breach of reg.5 "if it causes or is likely to cause the average consumer to take a transactional decision he would not have taken otherwise". The transactional decision in this example may be that the misleading action causes the average consumer to purchase the first class tickets at the higher price. Similarly, when booking a hotel room either direct or as part of a package holiday, if a consumer is informed that only executive rooms remain available at the chosen accommodation (when in fact this is not the case) and these come at an added supplement, then this too would be a breach of reg.5 if the consumer booked the executive room.

It may very well be the case that airlines who inform passengers, in breach of EC Regulation 261/2004, that they cannot recover expenses for food and accommodation while stranded at foreign airports by the recent cloud of ash emanating from an Icelandic volcano, are committing a criminal offence if it causes those passengers not to pursue their rights.

Materially Distort

The general prohibition of unfair commercial practices is contained in reg.3. The second part of the two part test (contained in reg.3(3)(b)) for ascertaining if a commercial practice is unfair is to consider if it:

" ... materially distorts or is likely to distort the economic behaviour of the average consumer with regard to the product".

The "product" can be goods or a service. "Materially distort the economic behavior" is defined in the CPR at reg.(2)(1) as:

" ... in relation to an average consumer appreciably to impair the average consumer's ability to make an informed decision thereby causing him to take a transactional decision that he would not have taken otherwise."

This definition is imported from the Directive without amendment. The "materially distort" test is concerned with whether the practice has actually or is likely to have the effect on the average consumer's actions or decisions. The Guidance (para.10.9) stipulates that:

"The impairment must be significant enough to change the decisions the average consumer makes."

To use the earlier example of the purchase of a flight, this may also demonstrate material distortion. As part of the reservation process the consumer is told that the flights to the desired destination are limited and due to their popularity are selling very quickly. If such a statement could cause or is likely to cause the average consumer to purchase perhaps at a time before they would do so if emphasis had not been put on the fact that the flights were soon likely to become unavailable, and the statements are not true, then this would materially distort the economic behaviour of the average consumer. The consumer, who contacted reservations to buy two economy seats on a flight, has in fact purchased two first class seats on a flight on an impulse due to relying on the statements made by the reservations team.

For example, an airline (Airline A) advertises flights to Rome for 99p and this makes Airline A the cheapest, at face value, compared to other airlines. As a result of the advertised price a consumer opts to book their flights to Rome with Airline A. But after 10 or so pages of the internet booking process and having invested 50 minutes of time the consumer is presented with a final price of £79. The consumer thinks that this may not be the most competitive price available but having reached this stage in the booking process decides they don't have time to go through the same process with each airline and commits to purchase with Airline A. The authors think that it is very possible that if challenged, such an advertising practice could be deemed to materially distort the economic behaviour of the average consumer, by "impair[ing] the average consumer's ability to make an informed decision" and causing them to make a transactional decision that they would not otherwise have taken. The counter-argument would no doubt be that such a practice of low lead-in prices not equating to the actual final price is widely known and that the average consumer would be aware of this. But would the average targeted consumer or the average consumer who is vulnerable be similarly aware?

Business and Trader

These two definitions are closely related to each other so we will examine them together rather than separately before moving on to look at what is meant by a "commercial practice" with which there is also a strong relationship. Put simply, "a commercial practice" is a practice carried on by a "trader" and a trader is someone who, in relation to a commercial practice, is acting for purposes relating to his "business". This explanation does some injustice to the detail of the definitions but it demonstrates just how the three are linked to each other.

Business is defined in the following way:

"Business includes a trade, craft or profession" (reg.2(1)).

Trader is defined as meaning:

" ... any person who in relation to a commercial practice is acting for purposes relating to his business, and anyone acting in the name of or on behalf of a trader" (reg.2(1)).

This brevity is not particularly surprising. Previous consumer protection legislation has been no more illuminating, presumably because we are supposed to know a business when we see one—rather like we know an elephant when we see one. Interestingly, the Guidance prepared by BERR in conjunction with the Office of Fair Trading does not examine the meaning of "business" in its glossary of terms.

As far as the travel industry is concerned this lack of explanation should not really be an issue; tour operators, travel agents, airlines, cruiselines, etc, can all be seen as businesses and therefore fall fairly and squarely within the scope of the Regulations. At the margins, however, it may be difficult to say what constitutes a trade or business. For instance, if a lecturer in tourism organised a foreign holiday for staff and students on an occasional basis, say once a year, and on which he made a modest profit, would this amount to a "trade or business" and would he be a trader? Or the bridge club organiser who takes players abroad once a year, out of season, to a hotel on the Costa del Sol, and again, makes a modest profit?

The guidance offered by the OFT and BERR states:

"Whether or not a person is a trader in any particular circumstance must be assessed on a case by case basis. When determining whether or not a person is acting as a trader, the courts are likely to take a number of factors into account, such as whether there is a profit-seeking motive, the number and frequency of transactions, and the time between the purchase and sale of products" (para.14.22).

The leading English case is *Davies v Sumner* [1984] 3 All E.R. 831, a House of Lords case which decided that a self-employed courier for a television company who had bought himself a car in order to carry out his business was not acting in the course of a business when he sold it. The defendant merely sold the car as a piece of equipment used in his business rather than as stock in trade. There was no regular disposal of such assets nor a disposal of a single asset for profit. In the circumstances, the sale of the car did not form an integral part of D's business. The decision has been criticised as "narrow" by Howells and Weatherill (p.166).

In *Davies v Sumner,* in support of his decision, Lord Keith said:

" ... the occasional sale of some worn out piece of shop equipment would not fall within the enactment."

However, he qualified this in one respect. He said:

"The need for some degree of regularity does not, however, involve that a one-off adventure in the nature of trade, carried through with a view to profit, would not fall within s.1(1) because such a transaction would itself constitute a trade."

If we examine *Davies v Sumner* closely we can see that it was actually looking at two questions. First, was the defendant's sale of the car related to his business as a courier? Secondly, could the selling of the car amount to a business in itself? Both questions were answered in the negative. Looking at mainstream travel industry activities, unlike our tourism lecturer or bridge club organiser, it is difficult to see how these more difficult issues would arise.

The rider to the definition: " ... anyone acting in the name of or on behalf of a trader" is intended to catch the actions of employees and agents of the trader. It makes the company vicariously liable for the statements and actions of its employees. For instance, if a guest was misled by reservation staff at a hotel about the possibility of a late check-out this provision would make the hotel company responsible for the statement.

CHAPTER SEVENTEEN

Commercial Practice

Commercial practice is defined as meaning:

" ... any act, omission, course of conduct, representation or commercial communication (including advertising and marketing) by a trader, which is directly connected with the promotion, sale or supply of a product to or from consumers, whether occurring before, during or after a commercial transaction (if any) in relation to a product" (reg.2(1)).

The definition is sufficiently comprehensive to cover most things a trader in the travel industry is likely to do. If we borrow from the existing case law on trading standards we see that it would certainly cover the brochure descriptions that figured in cases such as *Wings v Ellis* [1984] 3 All E.R. 577 (a false statement in the brochure that hotel rooms were air-conditioned when they were not); *Yugotours v Wadsley* [1988] Crim. L.R. 623 (a brochure photograph depicting a three-masted schooner rather than the two-masted schooner that was actually provided); *R. v Clarksons Holidays Ltd* (1973) 57 Cr. App. R. 38 (an artist's impression of an hotel which showed the hotel as complete when it was not); *Direct Holidays Plc v Wirral MBC* Unreported April 28, 1998, Divisional Court (a brochure wrongly classified a hotel as having three "keys" rather than one).

It would also cover the oral representation made in *Herron v Lunn Poly (Scotland) Ltd* 1972 S.L.T. (Sh. Ct.) 2 to the effect that a hotel was complete when it was not. The statement in a letter in the case of *British Airways Board v Taylor* [1976] 1 All E.R. 65 to the effect that a passenger had a "confirmed" reservation when he did not would also be caught by this provision.

On the wider issue of the airline practice of overbooking and then "bumping" passengers when the calculation goes wrong, this would certainly amount to a commercial practice within the definition because it would amount to a "course of conduct". The question of its unfairness is another matter, which may have to take account of the existence of EC Regulation 261/2004 which regulates denied boarding.

Statements about the price of travel products clearly fall within the definition of commercial practices. Whether it is a one-off statement of the price in a brochure, or the complex calculation of prices on the internet sites of "no frills" airlines or car hire companies, the prices stated would amount to "representations". The pricing strategy on internet sites would also amount to a "course of conduct" which may also involve an "omission" if crucial details such as taxes, insurance and credit card charges are omitted from the "final price". Again, the issue here is not the unfairness of such practices but the prior question of whether they fall within the definition of a "commercial practice".

Advertising on television, radio, over the internet, in newspapers, on billboards, in social media and on flyers would all be caught by the definition. This would include paid for "advertorial" content where it is not immediately obvious to the consumer that this is objective reporting. It would be a "commercial communication" which includes "advertising and marketing".

The commercial practice must be "directly connected with the promotion, sale or supply of a product to or from consumers". Most of the examples given above satisfy this criterion in that they concern statements aimed directly at consumers.

A more tenuous relationship may nevertheless also fall within the scope of the Regulations. The OFT/BERR guidance provides this example:

"A trader makes and sells processed cheese slices to supermarkets. Although the trader does not sell directly to consumers, any labels he produces must be compliant with the CPRs as they are directly connected with the promotion and sale of the cheese slices to consumers."

Granted, this is far removed from the travel industry, but an analogy may be drawn from the accommodation sector. Many hotels will contract with accommodation wholesalers or bedbanks on a principal to principal basis but in doing so they will provide information about their hotels that is intended to be provided by the bedbanks to the consumer. Rather like the cheesemaker, this information is directly connected with the promotion of the sale of the product. Note that the relationship of consumer, bedbank and hotel is fraught with legal difficulties and it may very well be the case that the hotel does have a direct contract with the consumer—in which case the relationship is much more direct. (See, for instance, the cases of *Secret Hotels2 Ltd (formerly Med Hotels Ltd) v Revenue and Customs Commissioners* [2011] UKUT 308 (TCC) and *International Life Leisure Limited v The Commissioners for Her Majesty's Revenue and Customs* Unreported 13 and 14 March, 2006, Manchester Tribunal Centre.) Note also that the hotel is potentially liable under the Regulations for the information it provides irrespective of whether it actually has a contract with the consumer.

A further feature of the definition is that it covers not only pre-contractual information but also any representations made "during" and "after" the transaction. This has serious implications for the handling of complaints during the currency of a holiday and after the consumer has returned home. For instance, if a travel company adopted an across the board policy of not responding at all to complaints from consumers this would be an "omission" or a "course of conduct" directly connected with the sale of the product "*after* a commercial transaction" in relation to that product. Similarly, if a travel company responded to complaints by asserting, falsely, that the consumer had no legal rights in relation to the complaint this would be an "act" or "representation" or a "commercial communication" occurring after the transaction in relation to the product.

One important aspect of the definition to note is that it not only applies to a course of conduct but also to single acts or omissions so a trader only has to perform a single act or omit to do a single thing before falling foul of the regulations.

Invitation to Purchase

An invitation to purchase means:

" ... a commercial communication which indicates characteristics of the product and the price in a way appropriate to the means of that commercial communication and thereby enables the consumer to make a purchase".

The essence of this definition is that *if* a commercial communication does indicate the characteristics and price of a product in such a way that it *enables the consumer to make a purchase* then it amounts to an invitation to purchase. Presumably this means that sufficient information is provided upon which a valid contract can be made. As such it may be co-terminous with an "invitation to treat" in that both may provide enough information on which to make a contract, but in many cases an invitation to purchase will be more detailed. For example, an airline may advertise "Flights to Alicante for £5. Visit our website at www.zootair.co.uk for further details." This may be an invitation to treat but it would not be an invitation to purchase because it would not enable the consumer to make a purchase. However, if the consumer visited the website and got to the stage where full details of the flight were displayed, e.g. price, airport, departure and arrival times, this would be both an invitation to treat and an invitation to purchase. (Although in contractual terms it might be argued that the details on the screen went beyond a mere invitation to treat and amounted to a contractual "offer". See, for instance, *Carlill v Carbolic Smoke Ball Co* [1893] 1 Q.B. 256 and *Bowerman v Association of British Travel Agents Ltd* [1996] C.L.C. 451 and other standard offer and acceptance cases on this point.)

The significance of the definition is that reg.6 defines what is meant by a misleading omission (which forms the basis of the offence in reg.10). Regulation 6 makes a commercial practice a misleading omission if it omits or hides "material information". In relation to invitations to purchase what is material is further defined in reg.6(4) as follows:

"(4) Where a commercial practice is an invitation to purchase, the following information will be material if not already apparent from the context in addition to any other information which is material information under paragraph (3)—

    (a) the main characteristics of the product, to the extent appropriate to the medium by which the invitation to purchase is communicated and the product;

    (b) the identity of the trader, such as his trading name, and the identity of any other trader on whose behalf the trader is acting;

    (c) the geographical address of the trader and the geographical address of any other trader on whose behalf the trader is acting;

    (d) either—

        (i) the price, including any taxes; or

        (ii) where the nature of the product is such that the price cannot reasonably be calculated in advance, the manner in which the price is calculated;

    (e) where appropriate, either—

        (i) all additional freight, delivery or postal charges; or

        (ii) where such charges cannot reasonably be calculated in advance, the fact that such charges may be payable;

    (f) the following matters where they depart from the requirements of professional diligence—

(i)   arrangements for payment,
(ii) arrangements for delivery,
(iii) arrangements for performance,
(iv) complaint handling policy;

(g) for products and transactions involving a right of withdrawal or cancellation, the existence of such a right."

The effect of this is to ensure that once a commercial communication can be
regarded as an invitation to purchase it must contain the information listed in
reg.6(4) and if it does not then an offence is committed. For instance, to return to
the Zootair example: the website may indeed contain enough information to
enable the consumer to make a purchase but it may not contain some of the
information, such as the trader's geographical address, that is required by
reg.6(4). If so, an offence has been committed. The trader has to tread the line
between being vague enough so as to ensure it is not an invitation to purchase or
detailed enough to ensure that nothing material is omitted from the communication so as to avoid prosecution. (See *Konsumentombudsmannen v Ving
Sverige AB* (C-122/10) for a detailed discussion of this issue.)

An invitation to purchase is also relevant to the offences contained in reg.12
and Sch.1. Paragraph 6 of Sch.1 makes it an offence to make an invitation to
purchase a product at a specified price and then refuse to show the consumer the
product or refuse to take orders for it with the intention of promoting a different
product—bait and switch.

The definition makes clear that the information must be read in context. The
communication must be made "in a way appropriate to the means of that
commercial communication".

Professional Diligence

Professional diligence means:

" ... the standard of special skill and care which a trader may reasonably be
expected to exercise towards consumers which is commensurate with either—

(a) honest market practice in the trader's field of activity, or
(b) the general principle of good faith in the trader's field of activity"

This definition is important because it constitutes part of the definition of an
unfair commercial practice found in reg.3 which in turn forms the basis of the
general offence under reg.8.

The OFT/BERR Guidance gives us a shorthand version of what is meant by
professional diligence:

"A simple way of understanding professional diligence would be to ask: 'Is the
trader acting to a standard that a reasonable person would expect?'"
(para.14.19)

So the question arises as to what amounts to honest market practice or the general principle of good faith *in the travel industry*? Judging by the practice of some no frills airlines one might suggest, cynically, that standards in the industry are not very high. Seeking to add hidden charges to the overall price at every possible opportunity or to keep you on a website until you have lost the will to live and simply give in and pay rather than start again with another airline on another site are not practices generally to be applauded. But that would be to tar the whole industry with the actions of a few. The travel industry is no worse than many others and a good deal better than some—second hand car dealers and estate agents or even bankers come to mind in this regard!

Interestingly, the definition seems to suggest that different industries have different standards of honesty and good faith; and that the standard, although objective, varies according to whether one is a car dealer or a travel agent or a lawyer. Be that as it may, this book is concerned with the travel industry so we have to examine what amounts to professional diligence in that industry.

Perhaps we can illustrate what we mean with an example. Let us say that a hotel is concerned about the feedback that it is getting on Tripadvisor or similar sites and it decides to counter what it regards as unfair, or even malicious, comment by asking its own staff to post favourable reviews on Tripadvisor as if they were guests of the hotel. Is this "honest" or "in good faith"? If the reviews are, in fact, entirely fictitious and paint an unduly complimentary view of the hotel then it would be hard to say that they were honest or posted in good faith. However, what if they were objectively correct and entirely balanced in their comment, designed merely to counteract the unfair criticism? The problem for the hotel is that if the comments are posted anonymously or without revealing that they were posted by staff it would be difficult to overcome the suspicion that they are acting in bad faith. If they are so sure of the quality of their hotel why do they need to resort to the subterfuge of anonymous comments? If they want to refute what they regard as unjustifiable criticism why not counter it directly and openly on Tripadvisor?

To apply the OFT/BERR test, would the hotel be acting to a standard that a reasonable person would expect? The answer is almost certainly no—however sympathetic one might be to the hotel's plight one would feel deceived by the favourable postings. Such a finding would lead almost inevitably to a breach of the general offence in reg.8.

To further exemplify the issue, would it amount to bad faith or dishonesty if a travel agent failed to disclose the commission rates they obtained from their suppliers, thereby obscuring the fact that they encouraged consumers to take product X rather than product Y because they earned a higher commission from X rather than Y? This practice is not unknown in the travel industry and is regarded as ordinary practice, if not good practice, and is certainly not regarded as dishonest. However, if travel agents can actually be classified as agents of the consumer (rather than independent contractors) then this conflict of interest would be contrary to their fiduciary duty and would almost inevitably contravene the due diligence standard.

Product

Product means:

" ... any goods or service and includes immovable property, rights and obligations" (reg.2(1))

The important point about this definition is that it includes services as well as tangible products. This would bring just about everything the travel industry sells within the scope of the Regulations—flights, hotels, cruises, excursions, timeshare, rail and bus travel and so on. Car and bike rental would be covered but probably as "goods" rather than services.

THE OFFENCES

We now move on to examine the five offences created by Pt 3 of the CPR.

Regulation 8—Engaging in a Commercial Practice which Contravenes the Requirements of Professional Diligence

Regulation 8 provides:

"**Offences relating to unfair commercial practices**

8. (1) A trader is guilty of an offence if—

(a) he knowingly or recklessly engages in a commercial practice which contravenes the requirements of professional diligence under regulation 3(3)(a); and

(b) the practice materially distorts or is likely to materially distort the economic behaviour of the average consumer with regard to the product under regulation 3(3)(b).

(2) For the purposes of paragraph (1)(a) a trader who engages in a commercial practice without regard to whether the practice contravenes the requirements of professional diligence shall be deemed recklessly to engage in the practice, whether or not the trader has reason for believing that the practice, might contravene those requirements."

The wording of reg.8 means that to be guilty of the offence of engaging in unfair commercial practices under the general prohibition set out in reg.3 a trader must satisfy both (1)(a) and (b) and therefore a prosecution will only succeed if it can be shown that a trader:

- knowingly or recklessly
- engaged in a commercial practice
- which contravened the requirement of professional diligence, and

- the practice distorted or was likely to have materially distorted the economic behaviour of the average consumer with regard to the product.

We have already discussed the meaning of "commercial practice", "professional diligence" and distortion of economic behaviour so we will be confining ourselves to a discussion of "knowingly or recklessly" here.

Knowingly and Recklessly

This offence is the only offence in the Regulations which is not strict liability. Regulation 8 is a *mens rea* offence. To be guilty of an offence a "guilty mind" would need to be established by the prosecution. At para.12.5 of the Guidance published by the OFT and BERR it states:

"For a person to be convicted of a contravention of the general prohibition, which is a mens rea offence, it must also be shown that he had a specified state of mind. The specified state of mind will be knowledge or recklessness ... "

The Guidance goes on to further clarify this at para.12.6:

"In the case of a prosecution for contravening the general prohibition, the mental element ('knowing or recklessly') only needs to be shown in relation to contravention of 'the requirements of professional diligence'. It does not need to be shown in relation to the effect on the average consumer, assessed against the material distortion and transactional decision concepts."

Accordingly, only reg.8(1)(a) is subject to the requirement to prove a guilty mind. Regulation 8(1)(b) is a simple objective test as to whether or not the behaviour of the consumer has been affected.

The words "knowingly and recklessly" are not new to consumer protection legislation. They were used in s.14(1) of the Trade Descriptions Act 1968 and were extensively examined in a series of cases, sometimes with controversial results.

The wording in s.14 diverges in a small but significant manner from reg.8 and, therefore, it would be dangerous to assume that the caselaw is applicable to reg.8, but it is nevertheless instructive to look at the caselaw to see how cases under reg.8 might be decided.

Section 14(1) Trade Descriptions Act 1968 stated:

"It shall be an offence for any person in the course of any trade or business—

(a) To make a statement which he knows to be false; or
(b) Recklessly to make a statement which is false; ... "

Knowingly

On the issue of "knowingly", the leading TDA case is a House of Lords case, *Wings v Ellis* [1984] 1 All E.R. 1046, which was discussed earlier in this chapter and where the facts are set out in some detail.

If a prosecution were to be brought today on the same facts, but under reg.8 of the CPR, would it succeed? The prosecution would have to show that Wings "knowingly" engaged in a commercial practice which contravened the requirements of due diligence. Put more broadly: did they know they were doing something which was not commensurate with them exercising the degree of honesty or good faith expected from a trader in that field?

They certainly knew that the brochure contained an error but they did not know that the error was being disseminated because they had taken steps to prevent this. On that basis they would not be guilty of the offence today if prosecuted under reg.8. This is not to say, however, that they would not be guilty under any of the other provisions. Indeed, a prosecution under reg.8 would probably not be seriously considered today given the other, strict liability, offences that exist.

But if we return to one of the examples used above, that of the hotel that posted favourable reviews on Tripadvisor written by its own staff, would that contravene reg.8? If we ask the same question as above would we get the same answer? Did they know they were doing something which was not commensurate with them exercising the degree of honesty or good faith expected from a trader in that field? According to the Guidance (para.10.5), professional diligence is an objective standard and, therefore, if it could be said objectively that what they were doing was not commensurate with being honest or acting in good faith, then so long as they knew they were doing it they would be guilty. As already indicated, it is the authors' view that this would fail the professional diligence test—and, therefore, it follows from this that the hotel would be guilty of a reg.8 offence. The danger here for the hotel is that although they do not *believe* that what they are doing is wrong, they certainly *know* that they are doing it—but their belief in the righteousness of their conduct will not do them any good.

The same principles would apply to one of the other examples used, that of the websites operated by no frills air carriers. *If* it could be established that the complexity and ambiguity of the website amounted to a breach of professional diligence because it was not commensurate with "the general principle of good faith in the trader's field of activity" then a conviction could very easily follow, given that the airline would *know* that it was engaging in that practice.

What of the cruise line that advertises a headline price on its website but does not give any indication that port charges are not included until a very late stage in the booking process? This is just the kind of practice that the no frills airlines have been vilified for, and if it amounts to a failure of professional diligence, would also lead to a conviction.

Recklessly

"Recklessly" in the CPR will certainly have the meaning given to it in other areas of the criminal law where it connotes dishonesty on the part of the defendant, but what is significant in the CPR, as with the TDA, is that the word is given an extended meaning. Regulation 8(2) provides:

> "(2) For the purposes of paragraph (1)(a) a trader who engages in a commercial practice without regard to whether the practice contravenes the requirements of professional diligence shall be deemed recklessly to engage in

the practice, whether or not the trader has reason for believing that the practice, might contravene those requirements."

Under the TDA, recklessness was defined in much the same way. Section 14(2)(b) provided:

"(b) a statement made regardless of whether it is true or false shall be deemed to be made recklessly, whether or not the person making it had reasons for believing that it might be false."

If we make the assumption that "without regard" under reg.8 will be interpreted in the same way as "regardless" under s.14 then the caselaw on recklessness under s.14 will be equally relevant to reg.8.

Two cases under s.14 of the TDA are particularly instructive in this regard. Neither is a travel industry case but both illustrate vividly the impact of this extended definition. The first is *MFI Warehouses v Nattrass* [1973] 1 All E.R. 762. In this case, the defendants had published an advertisement in which the price and delivery terms on which some furniture was available were ambiguous. On one interpretation the advertisement could be understood to mean that the furniture was available on certain terms when in fact it was not. MFI were prosecuted under s.14(1)(b) as having recklessly made a false statement as to the provision of a facility. The advertisement had been drafted by a director of the company and approved by the chairman. The latter had considered the advertisement for five to ten minutes but had not directed his mind as to whether the advertisement contained statements which were false. The magistrates convicted and the defendants appealed to the Divisional Court. The issue on appeal was whether the actions of MFI could be regarded as reckless within the meaning of the Act.

Lord Widgery C.J. said that normally recklessness involved dishonesty and that according to the usual meaning attached to the word MFI would not be guilty. Despite existing case law on the meaning of recklessness in other contexts Lord Widgery felt constrained to ignore it and base his decision on the definition in the Act. Taken literally it meant that recklessness amounted to no more than *not having regard to* the truth or falsity of the statement. Seen in this light the actions of the chairman who considered the advertisement for five to ten minutes but did not think about whether it was true or false amounted to recklessness and the company had been properly convicted. As with the *Wings* case the judge justified his decision by saying that this was a consumer protection statute and that it was not unreasonable to impose on the advertiser a positive obligation to have regard to whether his advertisement was true or false.

Dixons Ltd v Roberts 82 L.G.R. 689 took this development a stage further. In that case, an advertisement had been prepared which contained a false statement. This advertisement had been amended by the company secretary. Unfortunately, the amended advertisement also contained a false statement but the company secretary had not considered the possibility that the amended advertisement could be false. Upholding the justices on this point Forbes J. said:

"The justices finding of fact indicates quite clearly that they considered that it was this amended statement which he [the company secretary] did not sufficiently think through. [T]he explanation of their decision is thus that they considered that the company secretary did not have regard to the falsity or otherwise of the amended statement. In my view the justices were right to conclude that the defendants had recklessly made a statement which was false."

It is clear that in neither of these two cases were the defendants reckless in the normal sense of the word. They were, in fact, no more than negligent or careless. The implications of this for brochure preparation are patent. A tour operator cannot afford any form of sloppy practice to creep in to the process unless he wishes to invite a prosecution.

A straightforward tour operating case under the TDA which illustrates the requirement of recklessness is *Best Travel Company Ltd v Patterson* Unreported, 1986. This was an unsuccessful appeal from a decision of the magistrates to convict. The facts were that Best Travel, trading under the name of Grecian Holidays, published a brochure in November 1983 featuring the Palace Hotel, Malia, Crete. The brochure stated that the hotel facilities included a bar, lounge and breakfast room. In January 1984 two clients booked a holiday at the hotel for September 1984. Just before they departed they were told that no bar, lounge or breakfast room existed at the hotel. On arrival they discovered that the ground floor of the hotel was no more than a building site.

Best had contracted with the hotel in July 1982 and the contract provided that the facilities would be completed by March 1983. By July 1983 the facilities had not been completed and Best knew this. Best had no further contact with the hotel until April 1984 when they were told that the facilities *would* be ready, i.e. they were not ready yet. Thus, between July 1983 and January 1984, when the clients booked, Best had no contact with the hotel and did not investigate whether the facilities had been completed. Yet they went ahead and published the brochure in November 1983 stating that the facilities existed, and the statements in the brochure were still being made, uncorrected, in January 1984.

The Divisional Court had little hesitation in agreeing with the magistrates that the circumstances in which the statement about the facilities was made amounted to recklessness by Best. If they had not investigated then they could not know whether the facilities existed and therefore they were making a statement "regardless" of its truth or falsity. We are drawn inevitably to the conclusion that the case would be decided in the same way under reg.8. Not investigating the facilities before making the statement would be engaging in a commercial practice "without regard" to whether it contravened the requirements of professional diligence.

One major aspect of this offence which we have not yet discussed is "who" must have acted knowingly or recklessly. This issue will be discussed later but one of the leading cases on this point is *Airtours v Shipley* (1994) 158 J.P.N. 319 which can usefully be discussed now on the issue of what amounts to recklessness. The facts were that Airtours had featured a hotel in one of their brochures that was said to have an indoor swimming pool. This was not the case. The hotel did not have and never had had an indoor swimming pool. Airtours conceded that the false statement had somehow crept into the brochure because of a mistake at head office—which they could not explain. This was despite an errata policy which the court described as an "excellent system". For reasons which will be discussed more fully below, Airtours were found not guilty because their "excellent" errata system demonstrated that they had not acted recklessly.

However, it is interesting to speculate on what might have been the outcome of the case if the errata system had not been so good. What if the company had merely issued a general instruction to staff that the brochure was "not to contain inaccuracies" and then left them to get on with it? Have they engaged in a commercial practice without regard to whether it contravened the requirements of professional diligence? Have they thought about whether what they are doing meets the standard of skill and care which could reasonably be expected of them if they are acting in accord with honest market practice or general principles of good faith in their industry? At one level "yes"; they have given consideration to the fact that the brochure should not contain inaccuracies and they have given instructions to that effect. But is that enough? Such a general exhortation would come nowhere near the kind of errata systems employed by leading tour operators as exemplified by the *Airtours* case itself. If they had properly had regard to what amounted to professional diligence, could they have ended up with such an amateurish system? It is certainly not beyond doubt that such a crudely devised system could give rise to a finding of recklessness as defined in the Regulations.

The State of Mind of the Defendant

To say that the defendant must knowingly or recklessly make a false statement requires that he have a particular state of mind. With most CPR prosecutions the defendants will be limited companies which do not, of course, have either minds or bodies. In these circumstances, the rule is that a "directing mind" of the company has to have the requisite state of mind. A directing mind means someone in the company of such seniority that he can be regarded as acting as the "brains" of the company. Managing directors, directors, company secretaries, etc, fall into this category. In a leading TDA case, *Tesco Supermarkets Ltd v Nattrass* [1972] A.C. 153, Lord Reid said that a company would only be criminally liable for the acts of:

" ... the board of directors, the managing director and perhaps other supervisor officers of [the] company [who] carry out the functions of management and speak and act as the company."

Lord Diplock, in his speech, said the Articles of Association of a Company define who is the directing mind: frequently the directors of the company.

This point is made quite simply by the judge in the *Best* case discussed above. He said:

"The state of the mind of the company, it is trite law to say, must be the state of mind of a person or persons who were sufficiently in control of the company to act as its mind for this purpose. It is agreed that the human person who filled that role is a gentleman named Mr. Shacalis. [The managing director] For all effective purposes, Mr. Shacalis was the appellant company for the purposes of ascertaining its state of mind."

A case going the other way is *Wings v Ellis* [1984] 1 All E.R. 1046. On a charge of recklessly making a false statement under s.14(1)(b) of the TDA it was said by Mann J. in the Divisional Court in a decision which was not appealed:

> "In particular, we reject the respondent's suggestion that Michael Stephen-Jones, who approved the photograph and who variously called himself a 'long haul development manager' and 'the contracts manager', could be inferred to be a member of the relevant class. [i.e. the directing minds of the company]"

Thus, if no one sufficiently senior in the company acted knowingly or recklessly then the company cannot be convicted. That at least is the theory. However, case law has made inroads into this principle. In *Wings v Ellis* when it came to the House of Lords it was decided that so long as the [directing mind of the] company knows the statement is false there is no requirement that there be knowledge of it being *made*. Lord Scarman said:

> "The day-to-day business activities of large enterprises, whatever their legal structure, are necessarily conducted by their employees, and particularly by their sales staff. It follows that many of the acts prohibited by the Act will be the acts of employees done in the course of the trade or business and without the knowledge at the time of those who direct the business. It will become clear that the Act does cover such acts."

In *Yugotours Ltd v Wadsley* [1988] Crim. L.R. 623, a case involving a prosecution under s.14(1)(b) for recklessly making a false statement, the court came close to dispensing with the requirement of *mens rea* altogether (see the first edition of *Holiday Law*, pp.287–289 for a full discussion of the case) but in *Airtours v Shipley* (1994) 158 J.P.N. 319 this view was rejected. The facts were that Airtours had featured a hotel in one of their brochures that was said to have an indoor swimming pool. This was not the case. The hotel did not have and never had had an indoor swimming pool. Airtours conceded that the false statement had somehow crept into the brochure because of a mistake at head office—which they could not explain. This was despite an errata policy which the court described as an "excellent system". (See Cooper "Due Diligence—The Tour Operator's View" [1994] T.L.J. 11 for a discussion of errata systems.) The errata policy, although devised by the directing minds of Airtours, was operated by middle management who were directly responsible to the directors.

A prosecution under s.14(1)(b) for recklessly making a false statement succeeded in the magistrates' court. The magistrates said that although Mrs Bryan, the Overseas Operations Controller at Airtours responsible for the brochure, was not one of the directing minds of the company, nevertheless the company could be convicted because the directors had "delegated" their functions to her. In other words, she became the directing mind of the company for this purpose.

However, on appeal to the Divisional Court, the decision was overturned. The court said that the justices' reliance on a theory of delegation was based upon a selective reading of the judgments in *Tesco v Nattrass* [1971] 2 All E.R. 127. Although it is perfectly possible for a board of directors to delegate its functions to others, and *Tesco v Nattrass* confirms this, the case actually decided that on the facts no delegation had taken place. The Divisional Court preferred to adopt

451

CHAPTER SEVENTEEN

the reasoning from the *Tesco* case that concluded there was no delegation. McCowan L.J. in the Divisional Court quoted the following passage by Lord Morris from the *Tesco* case:

"My Lords, with respect, I do not think that there was any feature of delegation in the present case. The company had its responsibilities in regard to taking all reasonable precautions and exercising all due diligence. The careful and effective discharge of those responsibilities required the directing mind and will of the company. A system had to be created which could rationally be said to be so designed that the commission of offences would be avoided. There was no such delegation to the manager of a particular store. He did not function as the directing mind or will of the company. His duties as the manager of one store did not involve managing the company. He was one who was being directed. He was one who was employed but he was not a delegate to whom the company passed on its responsibilities. He had certain duties which were the result of the taking by the company of all reasonable precautions and of the exercising by the company of all due diligence. He was a person under the control of the company. He was, so to speak, a cog in the machine which was devised: it was not left to him to devise it."

He also adopted the skeleton argument put up by counsel for Airtours:

"It is contended by the appellant that Mrs Bryan only had a discretion to produce the holiday brochure in question and that such a discretion was limited by the errata policy of checking for mistakes set up by the directors. The directors of the appellant company had, therefore, not delegated their authority to run and manage the appellant company but had simply employed Mrs Bryan to produce a holiday brochure within set guidelines and procedures. Mrs Bryan had not been given full discretion to act independently of instruction from the directors but had been given a measure of discretion to produce the holiday brochure in question within the framework of instructions embraced by the errata policy document. The directors of the appellant company simply, therefore, employed Mrs Bryan to work within a system that had been created and designed so that the commission of offences would be avoided. Her duties did not involve managing the company but preparing a company brochure. She was, so to speak, a cog in the machine which was devised and it was not left to her to devise it."

Thus, Airtours were not guilty on the grounds that any recklessness that occurred was not that of the directing minds of the company or anyone to whom they had delegated any authority to manage the company. The company itself was not reckless because by setting up a proper errata system and ensuring that it operated effectively they were having regard to the truth or falsity of the statements in the brochure (s.14(2)(b)).

On the question of the *Yugotours* case, although the court was unable to overrule that decision, it went out of its way to cast doubt on its authority. It suggested that the reasoning was a "radical departure from principle and authority". It also said that insofar as it cast doubt on the decision of Mann J. on the issue of recklessness in the *Wings* case it was also wrong. (See Bragg

452

"Recklessness and Authority" [1996] T.L.J. 97 for a discussion of the *Airtours* case.)

Looking beyond the narrow confines of travel law and the TDA for assistance on this question of attributing the knowledge of senior managers to their companies, the problem was examined in *Meridian Global Funds Management Asia Ltd v Securities Commission* [1995] 2 A.C. 500 by the Privy Council. They said that whether there could be such attribution depended upon the interpretation to be placed upon the statute imposing liability and the policy it sought to achieve, and that different statutes might treat the actions of employees differently. However, on the issue of the TDA they seemed content with the approach adopted by the House of Lords in the *Tesco* case.

If we apply this case law to the CPR what would be the outcome? Would there be a conviction in *Airtours v Shipley* under reg.8 if the facts were to re-occur today? Could the directing minds of the company be said to be "recklessly" engaging in a commercial practice which contravened the requirements of professional diligence? If, as in the *Airtours* case, the directors had devised an "excellent" errata system, designed to eliminate brochure errors if operated properly, and a lowly employee, a mere "cog in the machine", had failed to follow the system correctly then it is difficult to see how the company could be convicted. Put another way, the directors *would* have had regard to whether the company was engaging in a commercial practice which contravened the requirements of professional diligence.

Of course, if the directors had not devised an errata system at all, then the company would be guilty of an offence because then there would have been no regard to whether the company was engaging in a commercial practice which contravened the requirements of professional diligence.

Continuing Statements

The problem for many travel companies is that the statements they make are of a lasting nature—in brochures, on websites, in flyers, on posters and in advertorials. With the TDA, the offence was committed when the false statement was "made" and this could be when it was first made, or when a consumer read the statement weeks or months later in an uncorrected brochure. The same question arises with the CPR: can the defendant be prosecuted under reg.8 for a mistake in a brochure that a consumer reads weeks after it was published, and after the travel company knows it is false? Were they engaging in a commercial practice they *knew* contravened the requirements of due diligence? If, as in the *Wings* case, strenuous efforts were made to recall the brochures and/or correct the mistake then it could be argued that they were not engaging in such a practice, then it is arguable that an offence was not being committed.

Regulation 9—Engaging in a Commercial Practice which is a Misleading Action

This is the first of the strict liability offences in the CPR. Note that although no state of mind needs to be proved by the prosecution, the severity of this is mitigated by the due diligence defence to be found in reg.17. The defence is discussed in the next chapter.

Regulation 9 provides:

"A trader is guilty of an offence if he engages in a commercial practice which is a misleading action under regulation 5 otherwise than by reason of the commercial practice satisfying the condition in regulation 5(3)(b)."

Regulation 5 provides an extensive definition of what amounts to a misleading action:

"5.—(1) A commercial practice is a misleading action if it satisfies the conditions in either paragraph (2) or paragraph (3).

(2) A commercial practice satisfies the conditions of this paragraph—

(a) if it contains false information and is therefore untruthful in relation to any of the matters in paragraph (4) or if it or its overall presentation in any way deceives or is likely to deceive the average consumer in relation to any of the matters in that paragraph, even if the information is factually correct; and

(b) it causes or is likely to cause the average consumer to take a transactional decision he would not have taken otherwise.

(3) A commercial practice satisfies the conditions of this paragraph if—

(a) it concerns any marketing of a product (including comparative advertising) which creates confusion with any products, trade marks, trade names or other distinguishing marks of a competitor; or

(b) it concerns any failure by a trader to comply with a commitment contained in a code of conduct which the trader has undertaken to comply with, if—

(i) the trader indicates in a commercial practice that he is bound by that code of conduct, and

(ii) the commitment is firm and capable of being verified and is not aspirational, and it causes or is likely to cause the average consumer to take a transactional decision he would not have taken otherwise, taking account of its factual context and of all its features and circumstances.

(4) The matters referred to in paragraph (2)(a) are—

(a) the existence or nature of the product;

(b) the main characteristics of the product (as defined in paragraph 5);

(c) the extent of the trader's commitments;

(d) the motives for the commercial practice;

(e) the nature of the sales process;

(f) any statement or symbol relating to direct or indirect sponsorship or approval of the trader or the product;

(g) the price or the manner in which the price is calculated;

(h) the existence of a specific price advantage;

(i) the need for a service, part, replacement or repair;

(j)   the nature, attributes and rights of the trader (as defined in paragraph 6);

(k)   the consumer's rights or the risks he may face.

(5) In paragraph (4)(b), the "main characteristics of the product" include—

(a)   availability of the product;

(b)   benefits of the product;

(c)   risks of the product;

(d)   execution of the product;

(e)   composition of the product;

(f)   accessories of the product;

(g)   after-sale customer assistance concerning the product;

(h)   the handling of complaints about the product;

(i)   the method and date of manufacture of the product;

(j)   the method and date of provision of the product;

(k)   delivery of the product;

(l)   fitness for purpose of the product;

(m) usage of the product;

(n)   quantity of the product;

(o)   specification of the product;

(p)   geographical or commercial origin of the product;

(q)   results to be expected from use of the product; and

(r)   results and material features of tests or checks carried out on the product.

(6) In paragraph (4)(j), the "nature, attributes and rights" as far as concern the trader include the trader's—

(a)   identity;

(b)   assets;

(c)   qualifications;

(d)   status;

(e)   approval;

(f)   affiliations or connections;

(g)   ownership of industrial, commercial or intellectual property rights; and

(h)   awards and distinctions.

(7) In paragraph (4)(k) "consumer's rights" include rights the consumer may have under Part 5A of the Sale of Goods Act 1979 or Part 1B of the Supply of Goods and Services Act 1982."

False or Deceptive Actions

A trader is guilty of an offence if:

- he engages in a commercial practice

- which contains false or deceptive information,

- relating to one of the categories in reg.5(4), and

- it causes the average consumer to take a transactional decision he would not otherwise have taken.

We have already looked at what is meant by a commercial practice and trans-actional decision so for the moment we will concentrate on the meat of this offence—false or deceptive information in relation to the long list of categories in reg.5(4).

False Information

False information is information which is untruthful in relation to the matters listed in reg.5(4)—which in turn is expanded upon in regs 5(5)(6) and (7). As we have already seen, there is a considerable body of case law under the TDA dealing with false statements and it is informative to examine these cases in the light of the new legislation.

Direct Holidays Plc v Wirral MBC Unreported April 28, 1998, Divisional Court was a prosecution under s.14(1)(b) for falsely describing the official clas-sification of some holiday apartments. They were described as "three keys" rather than "one key". Although this was false, to succeed in a prosecution it must be false in relation to the categories listed in reg.5(4). The nearest category is reg.5(4)(b), "the main characteristics of the product", which is further defined in reg.5(5)(o) to include the "specification of the product". It might also fall under reg.5(5)(r), the "results and material features of tests or checks carried out on the product", given that the classification of the hotel would probably be as a result of checks carried out by some kind of tourist authority. There is also the possibility of it being false in relation to the "nature" of the product (reg.5(4)(a)).

Yugotours v Wadsley [1988] Crim. L.R. 623, was a prosecution for publishing a picture of a three-masted schooner when, in fact, it was a two-masted schooner and had no sails. Under the CPR this would be false in relation to the "nature" of the product (reg.5(4)(a)) or the "main characteristics of the product" (reg.5(4)(b), in conjunction with reg.5(5)(o)—"specification of the product").

These are very straightforward cases, as is *Wings v Ellis* [1984] 3 All E.R. 577, which we have looked at already on a number of occasions where an hotel was described as having air-conditioning when it didn't. This, too, would fall under reg.5(4)(a)—false as to the "nature of the product"—or reg.5(4)(b), in conjunc-tion with reg.5(5)(o)—false as to the "specification of the product".

Deceptive Information

Under the TDA there was only one question: was the statement false? However, under the CPR the question is wider: was the information false *or deceptive*? And deceptive will cover situations where the information is factually correct but the consumer is nevertheless deceived by it or its overall presentation. The facts of *R. v Clarksons Holidays Ltd* (1972) 57 Cr. App. R. 38 are a useful vehicle for exploring this issue. In that case, a brochure featured a hotel which was not yet built. On the page giving the holiday details the hotel was depicted by an artist's impression. Nothing else on that page suggested that the hotel was incomplete but at the end of the brochure, a further 160 pages on, it stated:

"Artist's Impressions

In the case of most hotels which are in the course of construction we are unable to provide photographs which will help our clients see what the new hotel will be like. To give our clients this information we therefore print 'artists' impressions,' which are based on the architect's plans and drawings and other information available at the time this brochure is published. Such 'impressions' are clearly shown on the appropriate pages and are published in good faith and to help our clients with their choice. If some details of construction, surroundings and background are later found to differ, we only accept responsibility to our clients if such differences, if any, are fairly judged to have materially marred our clients' holiday. We constantly seek to improve both the range and standards of hotel accommodation and consequently inaugurate a number of brand new hotels each season. Every effort is made to ensure that new hotels are 100 per cent ready but clients will appreciate that some delay in the completion of some facilities is possible. In such rare instances we will, of course, make an appropriate refund to the client or provide extra facilities, entertainment etc. in lieu."

The case turned on whether the statement was actually false. Could the artist's impression be interpreted as meaning that the hotel actually existed, in which case the statement was false; or was this merely a statement that the hotel would be like this when the consumers arrived—which was not a statement which was false when it was made. The jury convicted Clarksons and the Divisional Court upheld the conviction. Under the CPR, the prosecution would probably find a conviction easier to secure because they would be able to argue that even though the information about the hotel was technically correct, it nevertheless deceived consumers—subject, of course, to the "average consumer" test already discussed.

There are similarities between the offence in reg.9 which is based upon the consumer being *deceived*, and reg.4 of the Package Travel Regulations 1992 which make it a civil offence to *mislead* a consumer. The leading case on reg.4 is *Mawdsley v Cosmosair Plc* [2002] EWCA Civ 587. The facts of the case can be found in Ch.5 and the court decided that the claimants had been misled about the lift in the hotel. The question that arises under the CPR is which category in reg.5 does this relate to, and would the statement about the lift amount to deceptive information in relation to this category?

The category the statement falls most closely into is reg.5(4)(b)—"the main characteristics of the product", which is further defined in reg.5(5)(o) to include the "specification of the product". It is hard to imagine a court denying that a lift in a hotel was a "main characteristic".

Assuming a lift is a "main characteristic", would the statement in the brochure "lift (in main building)", although "factually correct", deceive the "average consumer"? Given the decision by the Court of Appeal in a civil context, that the words were misleading, it is difficult to see a criminal court coming to a decision that they were not deceptive. To escape conviction, the defendant would have to fall back on the due diligence defence.

The Categories in Regulation 5(4)

The information must not only be false or deceptive it must also relate to one of the categories in reg.5(4). We do not pretend to be able to provide an exhaustive examination of all these categories and the various ways in which a travel company could infringe the law but we will give some examples of the kind of false or deceptive information a defendant might provide in relation to some of those categories.

The Existence or Nature of the Product (reg.5(4)(a))

The *Clarksons* case is a good example of this category. The tour operator deceived the consumers into believing that the hotel existed when it didn't. The TDA also had a category of making a false statement about the *nature* of services and as the hotel was not complete and also a number of advertised facilities were not available, Clarksons were also prosecuted under that provision.

In *Buckinghamshire CC v Crystal Holidays Ltd* Unreported January 26, 1993, Divisional Court, the defendant tour operator had advertised that the resort had an 18-hole golf course. The brochure said: "The pride of the village *is* the new 18-hole Bernhard Langer golf course." (Emphasis added) When holidaymakers arrived, they found that the course had not been built yet. Another example of false information about the existence of a product.

The Main Characteristics of the Product (reg.5(4)(b))

This category has to be read in conjunction with reg.5(5).

Availability of the Product (reg.5(5)(a))

If a hotel advertised that rooms were available for occupation from 14.00 on the day of arrival and this was not so, this would be a misleading action in relation to the availability of the product. Likewise, if an airline advertised that an executive lounge was available for business class passengers and it wasn't, this would also be misleading as to the availability of the product. Simply advertising that holidays were available when they weren't would also contravene this provision.

Benefits (reg.5(5)(b))

If a hotel advertised that it had a spa and that a particular treatment at the spa would "remove wrinkles" and this turned out to be false, this would be a misleading action relating to the benefits of the product.

Risks of the Product (reg.5(5)(c))

If a hotel advertised that its swimming pool was supervised and it wasn't, this would be misleading as to the risks of the product. That would be a straightforward *false* statement. If it published a photograph of the pool with a lifeguard on duty but it turned out that a lifeguard was on duty for only limited periods of the season, it might be easier to say that this was deceptive rather than false. Adventure tour operators need to be mindful of this provision.

Handling of Complaints (reg.5(5)(h))

If a tour operator stated in its brochure that it responded to consumer complaints within 28 days and this was untrue, this would amount to a breach of reg.5(5)(h). It would be similar if it advertised that complaints could be referred to an independent arbitration service but it turned out that this was a body appointed solely by, and responsible only to, the travel industry.

Fitness for Purpose (reg.5(5)(l))

If a tour operator advertised that its holidays at a particular hotel were "suitable for children" but it turned out that the hotel was largely patronised by elderly clients and there were few children's facilities, this would infringe this "fitness for purpose" requirement. Claims about suitability for the disabled would also come under this category. See *Inspirations East Ltd v Dudley MBC* (1998) 162 J.P. 800 for a PTR case on this issue.

Quantity (reg.5(5)(n))

If an airline advertised "Flights for 50p—Stansted to Tralee", and it turned out that it was not possible to buy a flight at that price, this would be false and therefore, prima facie, in contravention of reg.9. The big question, however, is whether this "causes or is likely to cause the average consumer to take a transactional decision he would not otherwise have taken". (For an interesting variation on this theme go to YouTube and type in "Fascinating Aida Cheap Flights")

More difficult would be the case where the airline did have such seats available but only one per flight. Although only of persuasive authority the Advertising Standards Authority regularly investigates such claims and finds against advertisers if they have not demonstrated that they have made a reasonable estimate of the likely response and that they were capable of meeting that response (CAP Code, s.8.9) or they have not made a reasonable estimate of the demand for the product (CAP Code, s.3.27). The BERR Pricing Practices Guide, May 2008, URN 08/918, referred to more extensively in Ch.18 has this to say on availability:

> "1.9.3 General notices saying, for example 'half price sale' or 'up to 50% off' should not be used unless the maximum reduction quoted applies to at least 10% of the range of products on offer at the commencement of the sale."

Specification (reg.5(5)(o))

If an airline advertised that it had a fleet of modern jet aircraft but passengers found themselves being flown to a remote Caribbean island on an ageing turbo prop this would be false in relation to the specification of the product.

The Price or the Manner in Which the Price is Calculated (reg.5(4)(g))

This category and the next one, the existence of a specific price advantage, are probably the most important of the categories in reg.5(4) and now that the part of the CPA 1987 dealing with misleading prices has been repealed, it is the first line of defence against misleading prices. Interestingly, the CPA took several full sections to control misleading prices, whereas the CPR takes only two lines. It will be interesting to see whether this broad brush European approach is any more or less successful in curbing misleading price claims than the more detailed UK legislation.

One feature of the CPA was that it was accompanied by a statutory code of practice which set out what amounted to good practice in relation to pricing policies. With the advent of the CPR this code no longer has any legal effect but, nevertheless, BERR has published a non-statutory "Pricing Practices Guide" (BERR/Pub 8727/15k/06/08/NP.URN 08/918; *http://www.bis.gov.uk/files/file46254.pdf*) which contains much of the same information as the former statutory guidance. This guidance contains much good advice and is certainly a "first aid" guide as to what not to do to avoid prosecution under the CPR. Breach of the code does not amount to the commission of an offence *per se* under the Regulations but it would be a foolish trader who ignored the advice.

The advice covers price comparisons, actual prices to the consumer and prices which become misleading after they have been published—much the same kind of advice as the previous guidance.

Just above we looked at "Flights for 50p—Stansted to Tralee" and argued that if no flights were available at that price at all then this would be false in relation to the *quantity* of the product. Would it also be false or deceptive in relation to the *price* of the product? Again, one could make out a prima facie case that it was indeed false or deceptive—but would it satisfy the condition that it would cause the average consumer to take a transactional decision he would not otherwise have taken? Don't we all know that these headline prices are not what they seem and we expect to pay far more in the way of "optional extras"? The problem is that the airlines have "educated" us into such a suspicion of these low headline prices that we don't believe them anyway!

If we look at some of the cases decided under the CPA this might provide some guidance as to the type of case that might arise. However, as indicated at the outset, a successful prosecution under the CPA does not necessarily mean a similar result under the CPR.

One travel industry case involving misleading prices was *Berkshire CC v Olympic Holidays Ltd* (1994) 158 J.P. 421 in which a confirmed booking was made between a client and a tour operator on the basis of a computer print out which displayed a price which was £182 lower than the actual price. In other words, there had been an error on the screen so that a price was displayed which was £182 lower than the brochure price—which Olympic asserted was the actual price. Olympic were charged with a breach of s.20(1) of the CPA for advertising a price which was less than in fact it was. Ultimately, they were found not guilty by the Divisional Court on the grounds that they had exercised all due diligence to prevent the offence occurring, however, the magistrates believed that a prima facie offence had occurred. If these facts were to re-occur today what might the outcome be under the CPR?

It is likely that there would be a similar outcome. It could be said that the information was false and/or likely to deceive the consumer under reg.5(2)(a). However, if the defendant could make out a due diligence defence they would escape conviction.

The *Olympic* case is an example of a price simply being false but reg.5(4)(g) also covers the manner in which a price is *calculated*—which leads us into the murky waters of airline, hotel and car hire pricing.

One case under the CPA which addressed this kind of issue in passing was *Association of British Travel Agents Ltd v British Airways Plc* [2000] 1 Lloyd's Rep. 169; affirmed [2000] 2 Lloyd's Rep. 209. In January 1999, IATA airlines changed the basis on which their fares were calculated in such a way that travel agents received less commission. What they did was to ask travel agents to represent the Passenger Service Charge (PSC) on tickets as a tax. The PSC is a charge levied on airlines by airports for the provision of certain airport services and is calculated according to the volume of passengers the airline puts through the airport. It is important to note that the PSC is *not* a tax and it is *not* a charge on passengers, it is merely one of the overheads of airline operation. However, by calling it a tax the airlines would not then have to pay commission on that element of the fare!

One of the issues that arose out of the case was whether there was an implied term in the standard contract between IATA airlines and ABTA tour operators to the effect that the airlines would not require travel agents to commit an illegal act—i.e. give a misleading price indication as to the method of calculating the price of an airline ticket. On the point the judge in the High Court had this to say:

> "Under s. 20(1) of the 1987 Act, it is an offence to give to 'any consumers an indication which is misleading as to the price at which any services are available'. Since the definition of 'misleading' in s.21(2) encompasses an indication which is misleading as to a 'method' of determining a price, it seems clear enough that a document which states that the total price includes an ingredient for tax when it does not, conveys an indication that the method of determining the price 'is not what in fact it is' within s. 21(2)(a)."

If these facts were to occur today and an airline advertised prices to consumers as being "£50 plus taxes of £25" would this contravene the CPR? The answer would almost certainly be yes if that charge of £25 for taxes included the PSC. The way many airlines get around this problem is to say that the £25 covers "taxes, charges and fees"—a phrase calculated to be wide enough to encompass the PSC. But is it wide enough not to be deceptive? It gives the impression that these are mandatory sums which are imposed by others rather than being the normal overheads of the business—like wages and fuel costs.

In 1997, controversy arose over the way in which Air Passenger Duty (APD) is shown in brochures. Following the ABTA Code of Practice, most tour operators correctly included it in the basic price. For some time at least one major operator refused to do so, arguing that airlines always showed taxes separately and thereby gained an apparent price advantage. However, following a complaint to the Advertising Standards Authority by the Air Transport Users Council in 1997, the ASA required airlines to consolidate their prices and most airlines complied immediately. (See ASA Monthly Report for December 1997.) Some airlines, however, continued to drag their heels and the Office of Fair Trading was still trying to bring them into line as recently as June 2011 when it warned them about "drip pricing" and about the surcharges they imposed for using a credit card.

In the 2005 case of *Essex CC v Ryanair* Unreported, Chelmsford Crown Court, the airline was convicted of offences when it made no mention, on its website front pages, of additional taxes fees or other charges, which were then a nasty shock for consumers who came across them later. However, Ryanair were acquitted in those cases where they initially mentioned the existence of charges as being extra, even though the amounts were not specified (nor, of course, included in the basic price). This part of the decision has surprised many, but being a jury decision, it is not capable of further analytical penetration. Perhaps, as indicated previously, it is just that the average consumer is becoming more sophisticated in these matters.

A non-travel case involving misleading prices is *Toyota (GB) Ltd v North Yorkshire CC* (1998) 162 J.P. 794. In that case, which was decided under the CPA, the defendants published an advertisement for a car which gave a headline price of £11,655 but included in very small print at the bottom of the advertisement further obligatory charges of £445 for taxes and delivery charges, etc. It was confirmed on appeal that despite the qualifying words the advertisement amounted to a misleading price indication under s.20(1) because it conveyed that the car was available for £11,655 when it was not. The test would be different under the CPR—was it likely to deceive the average consumer (reg.5) and cause them to take a different transactional decision? Case law under the TDA, *Southwark LBC v Time Computer Systems Ltd, Independent*, July 14, 1997 and *Northamptonshire CC v Purity Soft Drinks Ltd* [2004] EWHC 3119 (Admin) suggest that the position is not clear cut. In the former case, an advertisement for a computer was in a 20-page brochure contained in a specialist computer magazine. The computer was represented in a photograph surrounded by boxes of software. The prosecution contended that the advertisement constituted a false trade description on the basis that although the software had been pre-installed on the machine it was not supplied with either the software disks or manuals. Although on the page in the brochure where the photograph appeared there was no specific reference to the fact that no disks or manuals were supplied there were a number of such references in other parts of the brochure. Both the magistrates and the Divisional Court found that it was reasonable to expect the reasonable customer to consider the brochure as a whole and that taken as a whole the brochure did not contain a false trade description. In the latter case, on food labelling, it was held that the "statement" is the whole statement, not just a part removed from its context.

When it comes to hotel pricing, one of the most pernicious charges is the "resort fee" charged by hotels that offer the use of a swimming pool or beach access, attendants and towels. If a guest books an hotel online, at a "fully inclusive price" and then finds on arrival that they have to pay an extra, mandatory, resort fee is this false or deceptive? If the pool is described as one of the features of the hotel and the resort fee is not mentioned during the booking process one is drawn to the conclusion that this would be a contravention of the Regulations as the "overall presentation" is likely to deceive the guest that the pool facilities are available at no extra cost. As always, however, the devil is in the detail. Often the resort charge and other "taxes collected locally" are mentioned on the website but buried in the detail of the booking and not included in the "total price" that the guest pays. This permits the travel company to plead that the charges were not deceptive because they were expressly mentioned. Whether they would get away with this if the evidence was that consumers were regularly surprised by the resort fee is a moot point. By way of anecdotal evidence the first author, to his great chagrin, believing himself to be a "savvy traveller" and knowledgeable about internet travel sites, has been caught out by such practices on more than one occasion and had to argue the point on arrival at the hotel reception—with only limited success.

Car hire charges are at least as byzantine as airline and hotel charges, if not more so: a myriad of confusing insurance options; one-way drop off fees; extra driver charges; local taxes; airport concession recovery fees; energy surcharges; and various fuelling options. As with the "resort charges", the car hire charges are likely to have been mentioned during the booking process but often in such a way as to confuse or obfuscate. One example the authors have come across is a car hire company that charges an airport concession recovery fee—which is made clear in the initial booking. However, the same company does not permit the hirer to pay for an extra driver when booking online, this must be done at the counter when collecting the car. No indication is given on the website of how much the extra driver will cost, nor that when this extra service is purchased the airport concession recovery fee is increased pro rata. Given that there is only one car involved and one airport and no indication that the fee varies according to the number of drivers this would give grounds for saying that the information is likely to deceive the average consumer as to how the price is calculated.

One problem that tour operators in particular are faced with is what to do if they have published a brochure with prices included, but then wish to raise those prices. Under the old legislation, specific provision was made for prices which were accurate when published but subsequently became misleading. Essentially, the tour operator would escape liability if it took all reasonable steps to prevent consumers relying upon the old price. However, under the CPR there is no such provision, it simply provides that the commercial practice is a misleading action if the price is false. So if a consumer sees a holiday advertised in a brochure and then tries to book it at the brochure price only to be told that the price had been increased this would amount to a prima facie offence. The tour operator would have to turn to the due diligence defence if they wished to escape conviction. In this respect the advice given in the "Pricing Practices Guide" might be of assistance:

"**3.3.1** The price indication should apply for a reasonable period: what is reasonable will depend on the circumstances. Should a price indication become misleading, you should make sure the correct price indication is given to anyone who orders the product to which it relates. You should do so before the consumer is committed to buying the product.

3.4.2 Should a price indication become misleading while your brochure is still current, you should make this clear to the travel agents to whom you distributed the brochure"

The Existence of a Specific Price Advantage (reg.5(4)(b))

The Pricing Practices Guide has this to say about price comparisons:

"**1.1.1** The CPRs prohibit traders from giving false or misleading information, or omitting material information, about price or the manner of calculation of the price for a product, where this causes or is likely to cause the average consumer to take a transactional decision he would not otherwise have taken. If you choose to make price comparisons, you should therefore be able to justify them, and to show that any claims you make are accurate and valid – in particular, that any price advantage claimed is real.

1.1.2 In general you should compare like with like. This implies that the products compared should be the same, or very similar; and should have been on offer in the same outlet. Also, the basis of the price comparison should be reasonable in terms of time. What is reasonable will depend on the circumstances.

1.1.3 If your comparison is made on a basis which differs on any point from the practice recommended in this Part of the Guide, you should make the basis of the comparison explicit, so far as it differs. Any such explanation should be clear, and easily accessible to the consumer: it should be unambiguous, easily identifiable and (except where this is impractical, for instance, in distance contracts that are concluded orally), easily legible by the consumer. It should set out positively what comparison is being made, rather than vague negative disclaimers (e.g., 'price compared may not have been on offer for 28 consecutive days')."

So if a travel company advertises that certain of its products are "on sale" or "discounted" or "cheaper than our competitors" and this turns out not to be true, then this would be a breach of reg.5(4)(h)—the advertisement contained false information which was likely to cause the consumer to take a different decision, i.e. to buy the product. More difficult would be the case where say an airline advertises flights from Gatwick to Malaga for "Only £50!"—which in fact represents a £10 increase in price over the normal price. Does the use of the word "only" coupled with the exclamation mark signify a "specific price advantage"? Is the average consumer deceived into believing that they are getting a price advantage? To put it another way: do they think they are getting a bargain? The advertisement is factually true, the flights only cost £50, but is its presentation likely to deceive?

If the wording was "Special Offer. Flights to Malaga £50" this would tend toward a finding that the advertisement was deceptive. It suggests much more strongly that this is a bargain, cheaper than the regular price. The Pricing Practices Guide suggests that such an approach might be an infringement:

"1.1.4 You should make the meaning of any price comparison clear to the consumer. You should not leave consumers to guess whether or not a price comparison is being made. If no price comparison is intended, you should avoid words or phrases which, in their normal everyday use and in the context in which they are used, are likely to give consumers the impression that a price comparison is being made."

Despite being passed in 2008, very few cases have been brought under the CPR and, to our knowledge, none against travel industry companies for infringing the pricing provisions, so it may yet be some time before we have authoritative decisions on what amounts to an offence.

The Nature, Attributes and Rights of the Trader (reg.5(4)(j))

This is further defined in reg.5(6) to include the trader's:

(a) identity;

(b) assets;

(c) qualifications;

(d) status;

(e) approval;

(f) affiliations or connections;

(g) ownership of industrial, commercial or intellectual property rights; and

(h) awards and distinctions.

Thus, if a hotel indicated that it had the *approval* of the AA or the RAC and this was not the case, an offence would be committed. It would be the same if an airline suggested it was a member of IATA, or a tour operator that it was a member of ABTA or AITO, as this would relate to its *status* or *affiliations*. If a tour operator were to say that its holidays were protected by the ATOL scheme when they were not would be false as to its *status* as an ATOL licensed operator. If a cruiseline were to say that it was "Cruiseline of the year 2011" and this was not so this would be false as to its *awards* or *distinctions*.

The Consumer's Rights or the Risks He May Face (reg.5(4)(k))

If a tour operator stated in its terms and conditions that if a *force majeure* event occurred while the consumer was on a package holiday the operator would have no further responsibility for the consumer, this would be a misleading action as to the consumer's rights under reg.14 of the Package Travel Regulations, which require the operator to make suitable alternative arrangements under such circumstances.

If an EU registered airline stated that it was under no obligation to provide assistance to passengers who were subject to a long delay, this would be a contravention of EU Regulation 261/2004 which requires airlines to provide assistance in those circumstances—and, therefore, a breach of reg.9.

If an adventure tour operator included a clause in its terms and conditions that it would not be liable for any injuries sustained by consumers arising out of the activities they undertook on the tour "under any circumstances", this would be a breach of the Unfair Contract Terms Act 1977, the Package Travel Regulations 1992 and the Unfair Terms in Consumer Contracts 1999 which all outlaw the exclusion of liability for negligence. Inevitably, therefore, it would be a breach of reg.9 because it misled consumers about their rights.

Regulation 10—Engaging in a Commercial Practice Which is a Misleading Omission

Regulation 10 provides:

"A trader is guilty of an offence if he engages in a commercial practice which is a misleading omission under regulation 6."

Regulation 6 provides:

"6.—(1) A commercial practice is a misleading omission if, in its factual context, taking account of the matters in paragraph (2)—

(a) the commercial practice omits material information,
(b) the commercial practice hides material information,
(c) the commercial practice provides material information in a manner which is unclear, unintelligible, ambiguous or untimely, or
(d) the commercial practice fails to identify its commercial intent, unless this is already apparent from the context,

and as a result it causes or is likely to cause the average consumer to take a transactional decision he would not have taken otherwise.
(2) The matters referred to in paragraph (1) are—

(a) all the features and circumstances of the commercial practice;
(b) the limitations of the medium used to communicate the commercial practice (including limitations of space or time); and
(c) where the medium used to communicate the commercial practice imposes limitations of space or time, any measures taken by the trader to make the information available to consumers by other means.

(3) In paragraph (1) "material information" means—

(a) the information which the average consumer needs, according to the context, to take an informed transactional decision; and
(b) any information requirement which applies in relation to a commercial communication as a result of a Community obligation."

There are also special rules in reg.6 relating to invitations to treat:

"(4) Where a commercial practice is an invitation to purchase, the following information will be material if not already apparent from the context in addition to any other information which is material information under paragraph (3)—

(a) the main characteristics of the product, to the extent appropriate to the medium by which the invitation to purchase is communicated and the product;
(b) the identity of the trader, such as his trading name, and the identity of any other trader on whose behalf the trader is acting;
(c) the geographical address of the trader and the geographical address of any other trader on whose behalf the trader is acting;
(d) either—

(i) the price, including any taxes; or
(ii) where the nature of the product is such that the price cannot reasonably be calculated in advance, the manner in which the price is calculated;

(e) where appropriate, either—

(i) all additional freight, delivery or postal charges; or

(ii) where such charges cannot reasonably be calculated in advance, the fact that such charges may be payable;

(f) the following matters where they depart from the requirements of professional diligence—

(i)   arrangements for payment,
(ii) arrangements for delivery,
(iii) arrangements for performance,
(iv) complaint handling policy;

(g) for products and transactions involving a right of withdrawal or cancellation, the existence of such a right."

Misleading Omissions

If we break the offence down into its component parts we can see that a trader is guilty if:

- he engages in a commercial practice

- which, in context,

  — omits or hides material information, or
  — provides material information in an unclear, unintelligible, ambiguous or untimely manner, or
  — fails to identify its commercial intent

- and as a consequence causes the average consumer to take a transactional decision he would not otherwise have taken.

As with previous offences, we will not dwell on the first and third components of the offence, having discussed them earlier.

The key principle in reg.6 is that the omission must be "material" which, broadly speaking, means the information which a consumer needs to take an "informed" transactional decision.

If we go back to some of the previous case law and look at *Mawdsley v Cosmosair Plc* [2002] EWCA Civ 587 it could be said that in that case there was an omission to inform consumers that the lift did not stop at the mezzanine floor where the restaurant was located. Was this omission material? Did the Mawdsley family need this information to make an informed decision? Almost certainly. Without this information the Mawdsleys made a transactional decision which they probably would not have taken if they had known that they could not take the lift to the restaurant floor.

When it comes to selling hotel rooms, particularly in a holiday context, is it an omission of "material information" not to reveal that the hotel lies under an airport flight path or next to a noisy road or in the centre of a "party" resort? We would venture to say yes. While some consumers might positively want to book such an hotel for reasons of convenience, there would be many others who would want to know such information because what they are looking for on holiday is rest and relaxation away from the noise and bustle of everyday life. More difficult to decide would be an omission of any statement about the fire safety precautions at the hotel—particularly if they did not attain the kind of standard applicable in Western Europe or the US. Are hoteliers and tour operators supposed to declare that hotels are firetraps? Or what about the tour operator who declares that a hotel "complies fully with all local fire safety standards" but fails to explain that there are no local standards? This information would probably be regarded as unclear or ambiguous and therefore in breach of reg.6(1)(c).

Now that many consumers make decisions about hotels based on reviews on such sites as Tripadvisor, is it an omission of material information not to reveal the reviews posted on Tripadvisor—including the bad ones? Given the popularity of such sites it would be hard to deny that this information was "material" but reg.6(2)(a) requires "all the features and circumstances of the commercial practice" to be taken into account. It might be argued that if such review sites are so well known there is no need for the hotel to re-publish the reviews. Consumers can find this information for themselves quite easily. It would be different if the hotel published the reviews it had received, but only those which were favourable. This would be the omission or hiding of material information or providing the information in an "ambiguous" or "unclear" manner.

Regulation 6(3)(b) refers to information requirements which apply in relation to a "Community obligation". Of particular relevance in this respect are the Package Travel Regulations 1992 (PTR) which are part of UK law by virtue of the Package Travel Directive 1990. The PTR set out stringent information requirements as to information to be provided in advance and also in the contract (see Schs 1and 2 to the Regulations). The information covers such things as the type of transport; details about the accommodation including classification, degree of comfort and location; the itinerary; the meal plan; the price; name and address of the organiser and retailer; and the financial security arrangements for the package.

Thus, if a tour operator omitted to disclose the hotel rating or that not all meals were part of the package this would infringe not only the PTR but also the CPR, because this would be material information which the consumer would need to make an informed decision and failure to provide it might cause the consumer to take a different transactional decision.

Another, less well known piece of legislation, also of European origin are the Electronic Commerce (EC Directive) Regulations 2002 (SI 2002/2013). These require, amongst other things, that companies doing business over the internet must provide " ... the details of the service provider, including his electronic mail address, which allow him to be contacted rapidly and communicated with in a direct and effective manner" (reg.6(1)(c)). Failure to do so would be both a breach of the E-Commerce Regulations and the CPR—for omitting information required by a "Community obligation". But would the average consumer take a transactional decision that he would not otherwise have taken if, for instance, an airline did not provide an email address which would enable them to communicate directly and effectively with the airline? It would probably not deter the consumer from making the contract in the first place but it is important to note that the transactional decision need not relate to the initial making of the contract, it can relate to deciding "whether, how and on what terms to exercise a contractual right in relation to a product" (see the definitions in reg.2). So if a consumer wished to complain to the airline about a breach of contract but could only do so in writing, perhaps to a foreign jurisdiction, because no email address was provided, this might cause them to abandon their claim. This would be a transactional decision they would not otherwise have made because the omission of the address made it too inconvenient to pursue their claim.

Providing "material information in a manner which is unclear, unintelligible, ambiguous or untimely" also amounts to an offence. This brings us back, yet again, to the no frills airline pricing practices when booking over the internet where non-optional fees and charges are added to the price on a drip feed basis until the final price exceeds the initial headline price by significant amounts. To the uninitiated, such a booking process could very well be "unclear" and "unintelligible" but would such a person be "an average consumer"—a person who is "reasonably well informed, reasonably observant and circumspect" (reg.2)? Such is the proliferation of such sites and the number of bookings made over them, so numerous, that it could be argued that the average consumer could be expected to have a reasonable grasp of how to navigate such sites despite their complexity.

In relation to such sites, however, the key word may be "untimely". If some of the pricing information is withheld until towards the end of the booking process, credit card charges for instance, by which time the consumer has expended so much emotional capital in getting to that page that they are unlikely to start again with another provider, then it could be argued that the information has been provided in an untimely manner—causing the consumer to take a trans-actional decision they might not otherwise have taken.

Invitations to Purchase

Invitations to purchase were discussed above. There we saw that an invitation to purchase means:

> " ... a commercial communication which indicates characteristics of the pro-duct and the price in a way appropriate to the means of that commercial communication and thereby enables the consumer to make a purchase".

If the commercial communication satisfies these conditions then reg.6(4)(a)–(g) lists certain information which is regarded as material to the making of an informed decision which, if omitted, could amount to an offence—if it causes, or is likely to cause, the consumer to take a different transactional decision. These categories are listed above.

One of the categories listed is "the main characteristics of the product" (reg.6(4)(a)). If an airline website failed to mention that flights it was selling were on ageing propeller-driven aeroplanes rather than modern jets this could very well be a failure to provide information about the main characteristics of the product. If a car hire firm omitted to say that their cars operated on LPG rather than petrol or diesel this too would be a failure to provide information about the main characteristics of the product.

Another of the categories is the "geographical address of the trader" (reg.6(4)(c)). Despite attempts by the EU to create a single European market, consumers are still more likely to purchase products within their own jurisdiction rather than from somewhere else in Europe. The language barrier (particularly for UK citizens) is one of the reasons contributing to this, but there is also the issue of dealing with a company within the consumer's own jurisdiction—a business which is easily accessible and which, if necessary, can be sued within the consumer's jurisdiction. This is the rationale for defining such information as "material" and it is a small step to say that a failure to reveal where the business is based, particularly if it is outside the consumer's domestic jurisdiction, could cause the consumer to take a transactional decision he might not otherwise have taken.

One final category to mention in passing is that found in reg.6(4)(d)(i) and (ii). This provision makes the price, including taxes, and the manner in which a price is calculated, information which is material and which must be included in an invitation to purchase. Much of what needs to be said about this has already been discussed in relation to the offence in reg.9.

Regulation 11—Engaging in a Commercial Practice Which is Aggressive

Regulation 11 provides:

"A trader is guilty of an offence if he engages in a commercial practice which is aggressive under regulation 7."

Regulation 7 provides:

"(1) A commercial practice is aggressive if, in its factual context, taking account of all of its features and circumstances—

(a) it significantly impairs or is likely significantly to impair the average consumer's freedom of choice or conduct in relation to the product concerned through the use of harassment, coercion or undue influence; and

(b) it thereby causes or is likely to cause him to take a transactional decision he would not have taken otherwise.

(2) In determining whether a commercial practice uses harassment, coercion or undue influence account shall be taken of—

(a) its timing, location, nature or persistence;

(b) the use of threatening or abusive language or behaviour;

(c) the exploitation by the trader of any specific misfortune or circumstance of such gravity as to impair the consumer's judgment, of which the trader is aware, to influence the consumer's decision with regard to the product;

(d) any onerous or disproportionate non-contractual barrier imposed by the trader where a consumer wishes to exercise rights under the contract, including rights to terminate a contract or to switch to another product or another trader; and

(e) any threat to take any action which cannot legally be taken.

(3) In this regulation—

(a) "coercion" includes the use of physical force; and
(b) "undue influence" means exploiting a position of power in relation to the consumer so as to apply pressure, even without using or threatening to use physical force, in a way which significantly limits the consumer's ability to make an informed decision."

If we break the offence down into its component parts we can see that a trader is guilty of an offence if:

• he engages in a commercial practice which is aggressive, such that it

• significantly impairs or is likely significantly to impair the average consumer's freedom of choice or conduct in relation to the product concerned

• through the use of harassment, coercion or undue influence and

• it thereby causes or is likely to cause him to take a transactional decision he would not have taken otherwise.

The first thing that needs to be said about the offence in reg.11 is that the travel industry, with perhaps one exception, does not generally indulge in such practices. That exception is the timeshare industry which over the years has attracted a reputation for its high pressure sales techniques. Indeed, apart from the timeshare industry it is difficult to find examples of commercial practices by travel companies which come anywhere near aggressive.

If we take the facts of *Dixon v Direct Holidays Plc* [2006] C.L.Y. 1991 as a starting point we might be able to embellish the facts in such a way that they would satisfy reg.12. In that case, the claimants were accommodated in an appallingly filthy damp apartment with raw sewage bubbling up in the bath and had to deal with hostile staff amongst other things. The party wanted to go home early but they were refused. No suitable alternatives were offered and the family had to endure substandard accommodation for the rest of the holiday. Under these circumstances they had a good claim under reg.14 of the Package Travel Regulations to be repatriated. One can imagine the claimants asking to be taken home but the defendants refusing to do so and coercing them into staying by saying, falsely, that the claimants had no rights in these circumstances and if they chose to fly home at their own expense they would lose not only their holiday but also the costs of the flight. As a consequence, the family decided not to take the risk of losing their money and remain behind in the substandard accommodation. This could be viewed as the defendant exercising "undue influence" over the claimants, i.e. they were exploiting a position of power in relation to the claimants so as to apply pressure, even without using or threatening to use physical force, in a way which significantly limited the claimants' ability to make an informed decision.

Regulation 12—Commercial Practices Unfair in All Circumstances

Regulation 12 provides that:

CHAPTER SEVENTEEN

"A trader is guilty of an offence if he engages in a commercial practice set out in any of paragraphs 1 to 10, 12 to 27 and 29 to 31 of Schedule 1."

The list of practices found in Sch.1 are as follows:

"1. Claiming to be a signatory to a code of conduct when the trader is not.

2. Displaying a trust mark, quality mark or equivalent without having obtained the necessary authorisation.

3. Claiming that a code of conduct has an endorsement from a public or other body which it does not have.

4. Claiming that a trader (including his commercial practices) or a product has been approved, endorsed or authorised by a public or private body when the trader, the commercial practices or the product have not or making such a claim without complying with the terms of the approval, endorsement or authorisation.

5. Making an invitation to purchase products at a specified price without disclosing the existence of any reasonable grounds the trader may have for believing that he will not be able to offer for supply, or to procure another trader to supply, those products or equivalent products at that price for a period that is, and in quantities that are, reasonable having regard to the product, the scale of advertising of the product and the price offered (bait advertising).

6. Making an invitation to purchase products at a specified price and then—

(a) refusing to show the advertised item to consumers,
(b) refusing to take orders for it or deliver it within a reasonable time, or
(c) demonstrating a defective sample of it,

with the intention of promoting a different product (bait and switch).

7. Falsely stating that a product will only be available for a very limited time, or that it will only be available on particular terms for a very limited time, in order to elicit an immediate decision and deprive consumers of sufficient opportunity or time to make an informed choice.

8. Undertaking to provide after-sales service to consumers with whom the trader has communicated prior to a transaction in a language which is not an official language of the EEA State where the trader is located and then making such service available only in another language without clearly disclosing this to the consumer before the consumer is committed to the transaction.

9. Stating or otherwise creating the impression that a product can legally be sold when it cannot.

10. Presenting rights given to consumers in law as a distinctive feature of the trader's offer.

11. Using editorial content in the media to promote a product where a trader has paid for the promotion without making that clear in the content or by images or sounds clearly identifiable by the consumer (advertorial).

12. Making a materially inaccurate claim concerning the nature and extent of the risk to the personal security of the consumer or his family if the consumer does not purchase the product.

13. Promoting a product similar to a product made by a particular manufacturer in such a manner as deliberately to mislead the consumer into believing that the product is made by that same manufacturer when it is not.

14. Establishing, operating or promoting a pyramid promotional scheme where a consumer gives consideration for the opportunity to receive compensation that is derived primarily from the products.

15. Claiming that the trader is about to cease trading or move premises when he is not.

16. Claiming that products are able to facilitate winning in games of chance.

17. Falsely claiming that a product is able to cure illnesses, dysfunction or malformations.

18. Passing on materially inaccurate information on market conditions or on the possibility of finding the product with the intention of inducing the consumer to acquire the product at conditions less favourable than normal market conditions.

19. Claiming in a commercial practice to offer a competition or prize promotion without awarding the prizes described or a reasonable equivalent.

20. Describing a product as 'gratis', 'free', 'without charge' or similar if the consumer has to pay anything other than the unavoidable cost of responding to the commercial practice and collecting or paying for delivery of the item.

21. Including in marketing material an invoice or similar document seeking payment which gives the consumer the impression that he has already ordered the marketed product when he has not.

22. Falsely claiming or creating the impression that the trader is not acting for purposes relating to his trade, business, craft or profession, or falsely representing oneself as a consumer.

23. Creating the false impression that after-sales service in relation to a product is available in an EEA State other than the one in which the product is sold.

24. Creating the impression that the consumer cannot leave the premises until a contract is formed.

25. Conducting personal visits to the consumer's home ignoring the consumer's request to leave or not to return, except in circumstances and to the extent justified to enforce a contractual obligation.

26. Making persistent and unwanted solicitations by telephone, fax, e-mail or other remote media except in circumstances and to the extent justified to enforce a contractual obligation.

27. Requiring a consumer who wishes to claim on an insurance policy to produce documents which could not reasonably be considered relevant as to whether the claim was valid, or failing systematically to respond to pertinent correspondence, in order to dissuade a consumer from exercising his contractual rights.

28. Including in an advertisement a direct exhortation to children to buy advertised products or persuade their parents or other adults to buy advertised products for them.

29. Demanding immediate or deferred payment for or the return or safe-keeping of products supplied by the trader, but not solicited by the consumer, except where the product is a substitute supplied in accordance with regulation 19(7) of the Consumer Protection (Distance Selling) Regulations 2000 (inertia selling).

30. Explicitly informing a consumer that if he does not buy the product or service, the trader's job or livelihood will be in jeopardy.

31. Creating the false impression that the consumer has already won, will win, or will on doing a particular act win, a prize or other equivalent benefit, when in fact either—

(a) there is no prize or other equivalent benefit, or
(b) taking any action in relation to claiming the prize or other equivalent benefit is subject to the consumer paying money or incurring a cost."

If, as with the other offences, we break the reg.12 offence down into its component parts, we see that a trader commits an offence if:

• he engages in a commercial practice listed in Sch.12.

The important thing to note about the reg.12 offence is that it does not require the prosecution to prove that it caused consumers to take a different transactional decision. The offence is complete once the trader has engaged in the practice—subject, of course, to the due diligence defence.

Although the list is long, much of it can be ignored as far as the travel industry is concerned either because the practices are not relevant to the industry or not the kind of practice the industry indulges in on a widespread scale. Category 17, for example, falsely claiming that the product is able to cure illnesses, dysfunction or malformations, is not the kind of claim that has any real relevance to the industry—although perhaps tour operators taking pilgrims to Lourdes might wish to be careful about this provision. And category 24, "creating the impression that the consumer cannot leave the premises until a contract is formed" is not a practice found in the travel industry outside of the less reputable parts of the timeshare industry.

Category 1, "claiming to be a signatory to a code of conduct" when that is not the case, may be relevant if a non-member of ABTA claims to be a member and category 4, claiming that a trader has been approved by a public or private body, would be relevant to hotels which falsely claimed to have been graded by the AA, the RAC or Visit Britain. Categories 5 and 7 might also catch some travel companies.

Failing to respond to consumer complaints is a practice caught by category 27 but there is a degree of ambiguity in the provision. Does it only apply to insurance claims or does it apply more generally? The latter seems to be an interpretation more in line with the general tenor of the legislation and there seems no legitimate reason for limiting it to insurance claims. Even if this is so the offence consists of "systematically" failing to respond to complaints which is a relatively high threshold to cross. And would it cover those companies that did respond but only by a blanket denial of liability that did not meet the specific complaints?

Defences

INTRODUCTION

The two statutory provisions which impose criminal liability on travel companies which we have examined—The Package Travel Regulations 1992 (the PTR) and the Consumer Protection from Unfair Trading Regulations 2008 (the CPR)—contain similar, though not identical, defence provisions—known for convenience as the "due diligence" defence.

We will now examine the rules in detail, and explain why, in fact, they are sometimes of very little help to travel companies in practice.

THE PTR

Regulation 24 of the Regulations provides a defence to offences under regs 5, 7 and 8 (which require certain information to be given to consumers) and also to regs 16 and 22 (information relating to security of monies, and bonding) in the following terms:

"24(1) Subject to the following provisions of this regulation, in proceedings against any person for an offence under regulation 5, 7, 8, 16 or 22 of these Regulations, it shall be a defence for that person to show that he took all reasonable steps and exercised all due diligence to avoid committing the offence.

(2) Where in any proceedings against any person for such an offence the defence provided by paragraph (1) above involves an allegation that the commission of the offence was due-

(a) to the act or default of another; or
(b) to reliance on information given by another,

that person shall not, without the leave of the court, be entitled to rely on the defence unless, not less than seven clear days before the hearing of the proceedings, or, in Scotland, the trial diet, he has served a notice under paragraph (3) below on the person bringing the proceedings.

(3) A notice under this paragraph shall give such information identifying or assisting in the identification of the person who committed the act or default or gave the information as is in the possession of the person serving the notice at the time he serves it.

(4) It is hereby declared that a person shall not be entitled to rely on the defence provided by paragraph (1) above by reason of his reliance on information supplied by another, unless he shows that it was reasonable in all the

475

circumstances for him to have relied on the information, having regard in particular-

    (a) to the steps which he took, and those which might reasonably have been taken, for the purpose of verifying the information; and

    (b) to whether he had any reason to disbelieve the information."

THE CPR

The equivalent defence is found in reg.17 of the CPR:

"17.—(1) In any proceedings against a person for an offence under regulation 9, 10, 11 or 12 it is a defence for that person to prove—

    (a) that the commission of the offence was due to—

        (i) a mistake;

        (ii) reliance on information supplied to him by another person;

        (iii) the act or default of another person;

        (iv) an accident; or

        (v) another cause beyond his control; and

    (b) that he took all reasonable precautions and exercised all due diligence to avoid the commission of such an offence by himself or any person under his control.

(2) A person shall not be entitled to rely on the defence provided by paragraph (1) by reason of the matters referred to in paragraph (ii) or (iii) of paragraph (1)(a) without leave of the court unless—

    (a) he has served on the prosecutor a notice in writing giving such information identifying or assisting in the identification of that other person as was in his possession; and

    (b) the notice is served on the prosecutor at least seven clear days before the date of the hearing."

IN GENERAL

It will be seen that under the CPR, the burden is on the defendant to prove (on the balance of probabilities) that the commission of the offence was due to one of the specific factors namely:

- a mistake, or
- reliance on some information supplied to him, or
- the act or default of another person, or
- an accident, or
- some other cause beyond his control.

But it is a two stage test. *In addition*, the defendant has to show that he took all reasonable precautions and exercised all due diligence to avoid the commission of the offence.

The PTR differ in that they do not give a list of specific defences that can be pleaded, but merely provide a general defence of due diligence. There is no reason to believe that the five specific defences cannot be raised under the PTR, however. In fact, there is clear recognition of this because they provide that if the defendant attempts to show the commission of the offence was due to the act or default of another or due to reliance on information provided by another, then notice must be given to the prosecution.

The leading case on the statutory defence is *Tesco v Nattrass* [1972] A.C. 153. It was a case under the now repealed Trade Descriptions Act (TDA) for making a false claim about prices. However, the case remains relevant on the issue of the defence. The facts were that Tesco displayed a poster in one of their supermarket windows stating that packets of soap powder were available inside the store for 2/11d each. In fact, the packets inside cost 3/11d each. Tesco's defence was that the commission of the offence by them was due to "the act or default of another" namely their store manager. The House of Lords agreed that the store manager was sufficiently junior for him not to be regarded as the company:

> "The acts or omissions of shop managers were not the acts of the company itself." (Lord Reid)

Thus, a Company can, in many instances, cast the blame on their employees. Likewise, it may be relatively easy to show that a mistake was made or that the defendant relied on information supplied to him. To do this is only to satisfy half of the defence. The defendant has to go on to show that he took all reasonable precautions and exercised all due diligence. Lord Diplock said that the law would not penalise:

> "an employer or principal who has done everything that he can reasonably to be expected to do by supervision or inspection, by improvement of his business methods or by exhorting those whom he may be expected to control or influence to prevent the commission of the offence".

In the same case, Lord Reid said that a "paper system" operated in a "perfunctory" fashion would not be good enough. A system has to be more than just a pious expression of policy without any substance to it.

One case decided under the misleading price provisions of the Consumer Protection Act 1987 (now also repealed) already mentioned—*Berkshire CC v Olympic Holidays* (1994) 158 J.P. 421 (see Ch.13)—was decided in the tour operator's favour on the basis of the due diligence defence. The magistrates decided that the software which caused the wrong price to be displayed on the screen had been substantially tested before going live and that its accuracy could not have been checked further. The error was due to an unexplained fault unconnected to the software. They held that Olympic had taken all reasonable steps and exercised all due diligence, i.e. they had a proper system. The Divisional Court confirmed this decision. It is interesting to note, however, that they did so less than enthusiastically. Essentially, they said that the magistrates' decision was a decision on the facts that they could not disturb unless it was patently wrong. As the decision fell within a spectrum of what a reasonable bench could decide then the decision would stand but they hinted that they might have come to a different decision themselves.

For travel companies who are prosecuted under reg.8 of the CPR (but not Regs 9, 10, 11 or 12) this is academic because the "due diligence" defence is not available to them. This makes sense because the offence requires the prosecution to show that the defendant acted *knowingly* or *recklessly* when engaging in a commercial practice that contravened the requirements of professional diligence. Once this has been established it would be a contradiction in terms to say that the defendant took all reasonable precautions and exercised all due diligence to avoid the commission of the offence. Under the TDA, which did allow the defence, this reasoning was accepted in *Coupe v Guyett* [1973] 2 All E.R. 1058 (a non-travel case) where Lord Widgery C.J. said:

> "the defence under Section 24 will *rarely*, if ever, be appropriate to a charge under Section 14. I say that because, if I am right, in order to establish the charge under Section 14 you have to show knowing falsity or recklessness, which themselves are inconsistent with the statutory defence." (Emphasis added)

Note, however, that the defence was actually a possibility on the facts in the House of Lords case of *Wings v Ellis* [1984] 1 All E.R. 1046.

In Ch.17 we looked at the case of *Airtours v Shipley* (1994) 158 J.P. 835 where the tour operator escaped liability on the basis of the system they employed to detect misdescriptions in their brochures. It is important to note that this was *not* an example of the due diligence defence being used. The importance of having a proper system was not that it established due diligence *defence* on Airtours' part but that it enabled them to demonstrate that they had not been reckless in the first place, i.e. there had been no breach of the Act because the elements of the *offence* could not be established by the prosecution.

The position under the CPA and the Regulations is, however, different. In these cases (with one exception for travel agents under reg.5(2) of the PTR where it must be shown that the travel agent *knew* or *had reasonable cause to believe* that the brochure did not comply with the Regulations and another under reg.8 of the CPR), it is not necessary for the prosecution to show that the defendants committed the offences knowingly or recklessly. Therefore, it is more logically consistent for the defendants to set up the statutory defence of due diligence.

In practice, the same type of evidence will have to be put before the Court by the defendant whether under the PTR or the CPR.

The difference is where the burden of proof lies. Whereas under reg.8 of the CPR and reg.5(2) of the PTR the prosecution must prove knowledge or recklessness beyond a reasonable doubt, the defendant theoretically needs to prove nothing; whereas under the other provisions of the PTR and the CPR the burden is on the defendant to prove all due diligence on a balance of probabilities.

Under reg.9 of the CPR, which deals with misleading actions, a travel agent may have more success than their principals, given that most prices they quote and much information they provide are not their own but those of others. If they do plead that it was the act or default of the travel principal or reliance upon information supplied by the principal, they will still have to show that they took all reasonable precautions and exercised all due diligence.

Previously, under s.39(4) of the CPA, it was provided that in deciding whether the due diligence defence will apply, a court can take into account what steps were taken or could reasonably have been taken to verify information supplied by another (e.g. a tour operator, an airline or a hotel) and whether the defendant, e.g. a travel agent, had reasons for disbelieving the information. This suggests that it would be dangerous for a travel agent just to sit back and say there was nothing he could do apart from rely on the prices printed on the brochure or displayed on the screen. Furthermore, with the typical modern "travel agent" being a web-based accommodation-only provider, allegedly acting merely as agent for the hotels, etc, featured, it seems unlikely that a court would conclude that it was safe for the agent to publish information sourced entirely from the hotel, without at least some checking system in place, if only on a random sampling basis. This provision has been repealed but the authors venture to suggest that verifying information provided by another would still form part of the test of whether the travel agent had taken all reasonable care and had exercised all due diligence.

This does, however, present a dilemma for the travel agent. It is not practicable to check all holiday prices and all brochure or website information. What then should he do? He will of course deal diligently with notified errata, but what about all the other thousands of prices in the brochure? One way may be to set up a system of random sampling as other major retailers do. If so, the information should be recorded and could be used as evidence that steps are taken to prevent the commission of an offence. At any rate it would certainly look better that saying nothing had been done. (See Nardi "Due Diligence—The Travel Agent's Perspective" [1994] T.L.J. 13 for an excellent discussion of this problem.)

In the case of cards in travel agency windows, a stricter checking regime will be needed because these are the travel agent's own documents. In the past, Trading Standards Officers in many parts of the UK have "blitzed" travel agencies searching for cards which were out of date or misleading. The January 2011 ABTA Code of Conduct Guidance contains suggestions of what steps may be necessary for a due diligence window card system. (See "The Bulletin" [2003] I.T.L.J. vii for an example of "blitzing" being done by the OFT in relation to travel websites.)

All Reasonable Steps?

It will be noticed that all the defences require proof by the defendant, on a balance of probabilities, not just that diligence was used and reasonable steps taken, but that *all* due diligence and *all* reasonable steps were used. In practice, this has proved a very heavy burden for travel companies to discharge. The operator will find his system subjected to minute examination in court. If the prosecution can think of one idea, which is reasonable, which the defendant could have used but did not, the defence will fail. Even under the CPR and the PTR, it remains a conundrum. If the system the defendant describes is good, how come the offence was committed in the first place? Of course, the law does not require perfection, only that all *due* diligence and all *reasonable* steps are used.

Travel companies, however, often feel that the burden in court in reality is a great deal higher than that.

This was illustrated by the case of *Buckinghamshire CC v Crystal Holidays Limited* Unreported January 26, 1993, Divisional Court, in which Kennedy L.J. said:

> "it seems to me that once one is able to identify a precaution which can properly be described as a reasonable precaution which was not taken, such as the different wording being put in the brochure in this case, then that really is the end of the case so far as reliance upon Section 24 (1)(b) is concerned."

In that case, the defendants had advertised that the resort had an 18-hole golf course. The brochure said: "The pride of the village *is* the new 18 hole Bernhard Langer golf course." (Emphasis added) When holidaymakers arrived they found that the course had not been built yet. Bulldozers were still on the site. Extreme weather conditions had caused the site to become waterlogged and delayed the completion of the course. The court accepted the prosecution's contention that it would have been a reasonable precaution to have altered the wording. The words suggested by the prosecution were: "The pride of the village *will be* a new golf course which is scheduled to be open." (Emphasis added)

However, the larger tour operators, in particular, now have very sophisticated systems, often highly computerised, and have found it easier recently to establish due diligence. In *Airtours PLC v Shipley* (1994) 158 J.P.N. 319 the Airtours system was praised as "excellent" by the court.

A number of non-travel cases have illustrated the point that merely relying upon a supplier, however reputable, is not due diligence. For instance, in *Sherratt v Geralds the American Jewellers* (1970) 114 S.J. 147 waterproof watches sold by the defendants had been purchased from an impeccable source but were not waterproof. It was held that the shop should have carried out its own tests. In *Garratt v Boots the Chemists Limited* Unreported 1980, Boots sold pencils with an illegal level of lead. They had informed their supplier of the relevant law and made compliance with the law a term of the contract. But Lane L.C.J. said:

> "All reasonable precautions are strong words. One obvious and reasonable precaution which could have been taken in the present case was to take random samples of the various batches of pencils ... of course I scarcely need to say that every case will vary in its facts; but what might be reasonable for a large retailer might not be reasonable for a village shop. One does not know whether the random sample would have in fact produced detection of the errant pencils. It might have, it might not have. But to say that it was not a precaution which had reasonably to be taken does not seem to me to accord with good sense."

It follows that relying on hotel descriptions supplied by the hotelier, or a local agent, with little attempt to check the truth, will not be due diligence—and the bigger the operator the greater the responsibility to check. In *Carmarthenshire CC v Med Hotels Ltd* Unreported September, 2006, Llanelli Magistrates Court, the accommodation-only supplier Med Hotels Ltd pleaded guilty to a s.14(1)(b) TDA offence where they described a hotel, on their website, as three star, when it was in fact two star. The fact that the hotelier had confirmed, in the contract, that the hotel was three star, was not sufficient checking. The facts are reminiscent of *Garratt*, above.

Sunworld Ltd v Hammersmith & Fulham LBC [2000] 1 W.L.R. 2102 is a case where the tour operator escaped conviction under s.14 of the TDA on a technicality, but where the court had some harsh words to say on their brochure checking system. Sunworld had a system which, on the face of it, was quite sophisticated and which they described to the court as working "extremely well". It consisted of a four-part process for ensuring the accuracy of the information in the brochure. An area manager was sent a Product Information Form (PIF) on which he had to enter the details of any property which went into the brochure. This had to be certified as correct by him and also by the property manager. When these details were ready to go into the brochure galley proofs were sent to the resort manager which again had to be certified as correct by him and the property manager. The process was repeated twice more—when the brochure was published and at the commencement of the season. However, despite all this, errors crept into the brochure due to the fault of an employee, Ms Mittroyani. This is what Simon Brown L.J. had to say about the system:

"Mr James said in his evidence that 'the system works extremely well'; nobody apparently asked him even whether the errors here were the only ones ever to have been made. No one asked whether Ms Mittroyanni had proved to be an unusually unreliable area manager. No one asked what instructions were given to the copywriters. No one asked what if any sanctions attended were visited upon copywriters who departed from the PIF, or area managers who failed to correct such departures."

THE PRICING PRACTICES GUIDE

The now repealed CPA provided another line of defence. Section 25 provided for the publication of a Code of Practice for the guidance of traders. The Code was published by the DTI and its purpose was to indicate what amounts to good and bad practice. It was open to both the prosecution and the defence to make use of the Code in appropriate circumstances—either to assist in proving the commission of an offence or to show that an offence has not been committed. Section 25(2) provided:

"A contravention of a Code of Practice approved under this section shall not of itself give rise to any criminal or civil liability, but in any proceedings against any person for any offence under Section 20(1) or (2) above—

(a) any contravention by that person of such a Code may be relied on in relation to any matter for the purpose of establishing that that person committed the offence or of negativing any defence; and

(b) compliance by that person with such a Code may be relied on in relation to any matter for the purpose of showing that the commission of the offence by that person has not been established or that that person has a defence".

Although this provision no longer exists, the Code has been reissued in a revised form ("Pricing Practices Guide" (BERR/Pub 8727/15k/06/08/NP.URN 08/918; *http://www.bis.gov.uk/files/file46254.pdf*)) and contains a great deal of sensible and clear advice in relation to such matters as sale prices, special offers, introductory offers and comparison with other companies' prices. The question, therefore, arises as to what impact the new Guidance has now that its statutory role has been removed. The answer must be that its effect is probably much the same as previously—if a trader complies with its provisions then it will go a long way to satisfying the due diligence defence and if the trader has not complied then it will help to establish the offence. It is worthwhile, therefore, examining some of its provisions as they relate to the travel industry.

There is a general theme that prices must remain valid for 28 days before any change in the price can be compared to the previous price (para.1.2.3). As to the use of the terms "value" or "worth" these should not be used in price comparisons (para.1.8.1). The Guidance makes it clear that the CPR outlaw the use of the word "free" when the consumer has to pay anything other than the unavoidable cost of responding to the commercial practice (para.1.10.1). The Code also advises that traders must make clear to consumers at the time of the offer for sale exactly what they will have to do to get the "free offer". If there are any conditions attached to the "free offer", at least the main points must be given with the price indication and consumers must be made clearly aware where they can get the full details. In one case, under the CPA Code, a tour operator offered "free car hire" with a holiday. The consumer asked whether he could get the holiday cheaper if he did not take up the car hire, and was told that this was possible. Thus, the tour operator unwittingly fell foul of the Code, and, therefore, the CPA.

Offers of the type "from £99" or "up to 60% off" are required by the Guidance to offer at the cheapest price at least 10 per cent of the range of product on offer at the start of the sale (para.1.9.3). In the holiday and travel context, this does beg the question of what is the "range of product" in a brochure or on a website; just the May departures to Majorca, or every departure on offer? In practice, travel companies try to comply by offering a reasonable number of holidays at the lowest price. The Advertising Standards Authority also contains provisions along the same lines (CAP Code para.8.9) and failure to comply might suggest a failure of due diligence.

The Guidance has specific advice for travel companies. They are told:

"2.2.16 Brochures for package holidays are required to indicate the price of each package in a legible, comprehensive and accurate manner. All price indications, including those on websites, etc., should make clear the basis for the price shown, e.g., departure date or standard of accommodation. You should include any non-optional extra charges in the basic price and should not show them as additions, unless they are only payable by some consumers, e.g., single room supplements.

2.2.17 Any charges which are not included in the basic price, because they are not paid by all customers or are optional, should be clearly described. The amounts and the circumstances in which they are payable should be stated near the basic price, or the consumer should be directed to where in the brochure or website the information is available.

2.2.18 If the price displayed is not a fixed offer but liable to change before the consumer makes a booking, this should be made clear wherever it applies, e.g., by a box or annotation on each page of the brochure or webpage. The way in which the price will be calculated must be clearly explained, and the consumer directed to where in the brochure or website the information is available. If you reserve the right to increase prices after consumers have made their booking, this should likewise be consistently brought to the consumer's attention and the consumer directed to where in the brochure or website the information is available. There are specific rules in the Package Travel, Package Holidays and Package Tours Regulations 1992 which limit your rights to increase package holiday prices once a booking has been made."

As a result of this provision, the price panels in brochures commonly contain a battery of cross references to the pages where flight supplements, child offers, etc, are set out in detail. This has the paradoxical effect of increasing the complexity of the price panels.

As we have seen previously, websites often do not disclose the full price until the booking process is nearly completed and we have also seen there is a possibility that this might give rise to an offence under the CPR. The offence in question would be under reg.8—knowingly or recklessly engaging in an unfair commercial practice which contravenes the requirements of due diligence. The problem for defendants is that the due diligence defence is not available for this offence. The answer to this problem is for defendants not to engage in the practice to start with.

The Guidance also has interesting advice on errata which is dealt with in the next section.

ARE ERRATA EFFECTIVE?

One of the most hotly debated issues in the travel industry in the past, although the heat seems to have gone out of the debate more recently, was this.

A tour operator issues a brochure. He may send over a million copies of it out to several thousand travel agents. Immediately, the public will come and remove some of those brochures from the travel agency racks, often without asking the travel agency staff any questions about holidays. The tour operator discovers a completely innocent mistake which has crept in, perhaps, say, a half board supplement, or the official classification of a hotel. Is the tour operator bound to be guilty of an offence (subject to proving one of the defences), or is there anything at all that he can do at this stage to render himself not guilty?

The problem for the tour operator is that the due diligence defence requires that the defendant do all that he reasonably can to *avoid* committing the offence, i.e. he must take action *before* the offence is committed. Bragg makes this clear:

"This presupposes that the precautions have to be taken before the commission of the offence, so that actions taken after the offence has been committed to try to negative it, are irrelevant for anything other than mitigation." (p.176)

So if the offence crystallises, as in the case of reg.5 of the PTR, when the brochure is *made available*, then it is difficult to see how the defence can apply to errata issued after the brochure has been made available. If it is to apply it must be applied to actions the tour operator has taken *before* the brochure has been made available to prevent errors being made.

With reg.9 of the CPR the offence is committed when the trader makes a representation which is false and thereby causes, or is likely to cause, the consumer to take a transactional decision which he would not otherwise have taken. So if a consumer takes the brochure from the travel agent's shelves, reads it, and is misled by a false statement, e.g. that a hotel has a children's club when it hasn't, and as a consequence returns to the travel agency in order to book a package holiday at that hotel for himself and his young family, then an offence has been committed—he was caused to take a transactional decision that he would not otherwise have taken. Assuming that the tour operator's due diligence system was not good enough—as in the 1993 *Thomson* case quoted above—would an errata that is drawn to the consumer's attention at the time of booking make any difference? Again, it is unlikely—the offence has already been committed.

This is the line that was taken in an interesting case that took place before the stipendiary magistrate at Liverpool on July 26, 1993, involving Thomson Tour Operators Limited. Thomson had innocently misstated the amount of a supplement. As soon as they discovered it, and before the complainant booked the holiday, they placed the correct information on the viewdata system. Therefore, the travel agent was able to advise the complainant of the correct price before he booked the holiday. Nonetheless, it was held that the company was still guilty of an offence. The court held that correcting an error by viewdata was the best possible means available, and that it showed that the company had used all due diligence *after* it discovered the mistake. That alone was not enough. It still had to demonstrate that the original mistake was caused despite all due diligence and all reasonable steps. The company was unable to do this. There was, however, the strongest possible mitigation and a fine of only £100 was imposed. By contrast, another stipendiary magistrate sitting at Oldham in 1996 found First Choice Holidays guilty of an offence purely because (as she found) viewdata correction on its own was not enough (*R. v First Choice* Unreported February 27, 1996, Oldham Magistrates' Court).

This tour operator, wishing to escape liability, would have to establish the kind of due diligence system that the defendant had put in place in the case of *Airtours v Shipley* (1994) 158 J.P.N. 319, discussed earlier. The system prevented a finding of "recklessness" against Airtours—which would go a long way to satisfying a court that they had taken all reasonable precautions and exercised all due diligence.

A further straw in the wind was the case of *Marshall v Airtours* (1994), an unreported Magistrates' Court decision. On similar facts to the *Thomson* case, and after hearing expert evidence from ABTA, the magistrates had acquitted Airtours. The prosecution appealed, raising two essential points, (i) was a viewdata correction too late to correct an offence which had been committed when the brochure was read? (ii) is due diligence relevant *after* an offence is committed? However, shortly before the Divisional Court hearing the prosecution dropped the appeal.

Needless to say, tour operators were not very happy with this situation under the CPA, which can be characterised as a conflict at the interface of the old print technology and the newer internet or viewdata technology. And this is exacerbated by reg.5 of the PTR which appears on one view to disallow any change to the brochure price.

One attempt to marry legality with commercial sense was so-called (but misnamed) "fluid pricing", first introduced into the UK in late 1995. The price in the brochure is the highest price that can be charged but the tour operator reserves the right to move prices up and down up to that ceiling.

The DTI 1995 Guidelines on the PTR placed a responsibility on travel agents, saying that they would be culpable if they failed to use "shelf talkers" to draw the attention of potential clients to the fact that there were errors or changes in the brochure. Clients could then ask at the desk where the viewdata screen could be used to show them. Subsequently, ABTA drafted a Notice which they strongly urged all agents to display prominently. It read:

"The prices or details contained within brochures displayed in this shop may have changed since the brochures were printed. Please ask our staff for details. You will be informed of any changes that we are aware of before you book as part of our commitment to quality customer service".

The purpose is for it to be used as part of a due diligence defence by agent or operator. We would still commend it, but it no longer appears to be an ABTA requirement. (Note that LACORS also published guidance on fluid pricing.)

A different way of looking at this argument is to say that the errata notification is a "disclaimer". The defence of a disclaimer is not to be found in the statutes, but has been created by the courts (mostly to deal with second-hand car dealers disclaiming mileage reading on cars). The principle is that the disclaimer nullifies the effect of any misleading statement by overriding it. To achieve this, the disclaimer must be as "bold, precise and compelling" as the original mis-statement (*Norman v Bennett* [1974] 3 All E.R. 351). The disclaimer must also be brought to the attention of the consumer before he is committed to the contract. The difficulty for tour operators is that the consumer may well have read the uncorrected brochure at home before learning of any viewdata errata. If there was also a "shelf talker", as described above, it may well be argued that this would be an effective disclaimer. In the *First Choice* case referred to earlier, one of the defences raised before the magistrate was that the brochure contained a disclaimer. It was held, however, that this was ineffective on the grounds that it did not satisfy the criteria in *Norman v Bennett*—it did not refer to prices at all and was badly sited in the brochure. It did not do enough to "flag up" the possibility of price inaccuracies.

The BERR Pricing Practices Guide has advice for the travel industry on the problem of prices which become misleading after they have been published:

"**3.4** Selling through agents

Holiday brochures and travel agents
3.4.1 ... Should a price indication become misleading for any other reason, tour operators who sell direct to consumers should have regard to paragraph 3.3.1

[see below], and tour operators who sell through travel agents should have regard to paragraphs 3.4.2 and 3.4.3 below.

3.4.2 Should a price indication become misleading while your brochure is still current, you should make this clear to the travel agents to whom you distributed the brochure.

3.4.3 Where you promote last minute price offers by advertisements/cards in window displays or on websites, you should keep the information up to date. When an offer is no longer available, you should remove it from the display or website.

3.4.4 In all circumstances, travel agents should ensure that the correct price indication is made clear to consumers before they make a booking.

3.3 Mail order advertisements, catalogues, leaflets, websites and similar advertising

3.3.1 The price indication should apply for a reasonable period: what is reasonable will depend on the circumstances. Should a price indication become misleading, you should make sure the correct price indication is given to anyone who orders the product to which it relates. You should do so before the consumer is committed to buying the product."

Clearly, this is good practice and in most cases it will head off any complaints but it should not be taken as a suggestion that it will prevent the commission of an offence. The text seems to hark back to s.20(2) of the CPA where defendants could escape liability for prices which subsequently became misleading if they took reasonable steps to correct the price. There is no equivalent provision in the PTR or the CPR.

Travel companies that sell their products exclusively over the internet have an advantage over those companies who publish brochures in that they can correct false or misleading information on the web almost instantly. But will such corrections avail them? Let us return to the example of the consumer who sees a holiday which features a hotel with a children's club. If, instead of acquiring a brochure, let us suppose, she surfs the web and finds this holiday and prints off the details on Day 1. She then consults with her partner on Day 2 and they decide to book the holiday. She returns to the website on Day 3, only to find that a correction has been made and the hotel no longer features a children's club. If, as previously, the travel company cannot show that it has exercised due diligence *before* it loaded the false information onto the website, then the correction will not prevent an offence being committed.

A DUE DILIGENCE SYSTEM

Each company must devise its own system appropriate to its size and operations but we offer the following as common features of the better "due diligence" systems we have encountered.

(a) All the company's quality control systems should operate according to written guidelines. Ideally there should also be a manual, especially for brochure and website content production and the accuracy of brochure and website information.

(b) Compliance with the manual should be regularly monitored and documented.

(c) No accommodation or transport should be sold to clients unless the company first has a contract with the supplier.

(d) All accommodation should be personally inspected by a company employee who completes a detailed questionnaire about the hotel.

(e) Brochure and website copy should be approved by the hotelier who should be required to sign an approval form.

(f) The brochure and website proofs should be carefully checked including all price information. The checking process should be documented.

(g) There should be regular updates from resorts throughout the season.

(h) There should be an effective website/viewdata errata system to catch new customers before they book and to notify existing customers without delay. The system should be activated by consumer comment as well as by resort reports.

(i) All personnel should be properly trained in their tasks, particularly as to the impact of the law on their work; the attendance at training should be documented.

This system would include the features that were described as excellent in the *Airtours v Shipley* case. It can be seen, had step (e) been followed, Direct Holidays would probably have been acquitted in the *Wirral* case (see Ch.17) but they failed to take steps to check the "key rating" of the accommodation.

A system such as this creates a problem for accommodation-only providers on the internet; even if they present themselves as "only agents" they are still responsible in the criminal law for the accuracy of their website, etc, but they rarely have the facilities, or the overseas staff, to make effective checks, and often accept the hotel's own description at face value. Such a strategy is understandable, but carries a risk of prosecution if information is inaccurate.

The specific topic of travel agency window cards is addressed in the Guidance issued by ABTA in 2011 with its revised Code of Conduct, which suggests, among other steps, daily checking that cards remain accurate as to price and availability.

Finally, there is the prospect that repeated offending against any of the provisions in the PTR or the CPR can result in action being taken by the Office of Fair Trading and a number of other bodies, including Trading Standards departments and the CAA, under their Enforcement Order powers. These orders can be used to restrain further breaches and if not complied with can lead to further penalties. (See below.)

CHAPTER EIGHTEEN

THE POSITION OF EMPLOYEES

It can been seen from the *Tesco* case that it is possible for companies to use that aspect of the statutory defence involving placing the blame on "the act or default of another", if the other is an employee of the company, provided that the employee is sufficiently junior so as to render him not part of the "directing mind" of the Company. (In the *Wings* case, this argument was used successfully to negative the *recklessness* of the company, rather than as part of the statutory defence. For the company to be reckless the "directing mind" of the Company must be shown to be reckless.)

Under the TDA there was a reluctance by companies to blame their employees. This was because under s.23 of that Act, where it was shown that the commission of an offence was due to the act or default of some other person, that other person shall also be guilty of the offence. The CPR takes much the same position. Regulation 16 provides:

"16.—(1) This regulation applies where a person "X"—

(a) commits an offence under regulation 9, 10, 11 or 12, or
(b) would have committed an offence under those regulations but for a defence under regulation 17 or 18,

and the commission of the offence, or of what would have been an offence but for X being able to rely on a defence under regulation 17 or 18, is due to the act or default of some other person "Y".

(2) Where this regulation applies Y is guilty of the offence, subject to regulations 17 and 18, whether or not Y is a trader and whether or not Y's act or default is a commercial practice.

(3) Y may be charged with and convicted of the offence by virtue of paragraph (2) whether or not proceedings are taken against X."

Thus it would be open to the prosecuting authorities to prosecute an individual employee if it could be shown that the commission of the offence was due to their act or default. However they would in turn be able to rely on the due diligence defence.

However, the position for employees is rather brighter under the PTR. Regulation 25(1) provides:

"25(1) Where the commission by any person of an offence under regulation 5, 7, 8, 16 or 22 of these Regulations is due to an act or default committed by some other person in the course of any business of *his*, the other person shall be guilty of the offence and may be proceeded against and punished by virtue of this paragraph whether or not proceedings are taken against the first-mentioned person." (Emphasis added)

An employee of a Company, in the ordinary sense, is not guilty of any act or default in the course of any business of *his*, and therefore cannot be prosecuted in addition to or instead of the Company itself. This point has been confirmed by the House of Lords in the case of *R. v Warwickshire CC Ex p. Johnson* (1993).

Directors and senior staff are, however, not so happily placed. There are virtually identical provisions under reg.25(2) of the PTR and reg.15 of the CPR. Regulation 15 of the CPR provides:

"15.—(1) Where an offence under these Regulations committed by a body corporate is proved—

- (a) to have been committed with the consent or connivance of an officer of the body, or
- (b) to be attributable to any neglect on his part,

the officer as well as the body corporate is guilty of the offence and liable to be proceeded against and punished accordingly."

In practice, what happens is that if a Trading Standards department takes the view that offences are being committed by the deliberate policy of the board of the company (for example, a deliberate policy of over-booking hotels), the directors as well as the company may be prosecuted. Where, however, the offence is committed by a company "doing its incompetent but obvious best", and in spite of the desire of the management to obey the law, then it is extremely rare for any director to be prosecuted. Prosecutions of employees below the rank of director are rarer still, though not unheard of.

PROCEDURE

All the offences we have been discussing are to be prosecuted by Trading Standards departments, attached to the local authority. Many of these are under-resourced, and they have many responsibilities beyond holidays. Enforcement of the law is, therefore, patchy at best, although from time to time there are flurries of prosecutions. Each of the offences we have discussed can be dealt with in the Magistrates' Court where there is a maximum fine of £5,000 for each offence. Compensation can also be ordered. Each of the matters can also be dealt with in the Crown Court where there is the possibility of an unlimited fine. However, courts must always have regard to the means of a defendant in fixing the level of a fine.

In the case of each offence, the prosecution must commence proceedings no later than three years from the commission of the offence, or one year from its discovery by the prosecutor, whichever is the earlier. In each case a wide variety of powers is given to Trading Standards Officers to investigate the offence, and it is a separate offence to obstruct a Trading Standards Officer in the course of his duty. Some travel companies have, over the years, discovered to their horror that, in a serious case, Trading Standards officers will use their power to seize some or all of their working documents to take away, by the lorryload if necessary, to examine them at their own offices for evidence of offences. Full details of all these powers are set out in the Schedules of the relevant statutes, e.g. Sch.3 of the PTR which is set out in Appendix 2 to this book. The powers are not, however, limitless, and are subject to the Police and Criminal Evidence Act 1984 and its Codes, so far as relevant, including the provisions on powers of search, and tape recording of interviews. (See Kerrigan "Trading Standards Officers must comply with Search Code" [1996] T.L.J. 91, but beware that the Codes have been revised since this article was written.)

ENFORCEMENT ORDERS

This powerful tool in the hands of the enforcement authorities has been the subject of rapid progress in recent times. It enables the authorities to put a stop to traders whose conduct in the sale of goods or services to consumers harms the collective interest of consumers in the UK(and indeed there is provision for EU wide enforcement in respect of some misconduct).

Although there were limited powers given to the OFT under the Fair Trading Act 1973, a major enhancement of the powers of the authorities was made by way of the Stop Now Orders (EC Directive) Regulations 2001, which came into force on June 1, 2001. These regulations were shortly overtaken by the powers conferred by the Enterprise Act 2002 which permits the imposition of Enforcement Orders to stop traders committing breaches of a specified list of legislation (both domestic and European) if their actions are causing harm to the collective interests of consumers.

The list of legislation is long and includes, for example, the Malicious Communications Act 1988 and the Intoxicating Substances (Supply) Act 1985. As far as we are concerned, however, it includes the CPR and the PTR as well as the Unfair Contract Terms Act 1977 and the Misrepresentation Act 1968. A recent addition to the list is EC Regulation 261/2004 on Denied Boarding, Long Delays and Cancellations.

The enforcement authorities are divided into three categories—general enforcers, designated enforcers and community enforcers. The general enforcers are the OFT and the Trading Standards Services. Designated enforcers include:

- The Civil Aviation Authority;
- The Director General of Electricity Supply for Northern Ireland;
- The Director General of Gas for Northern Ireland;
- The Director General of Telecommunications;
- The Director General of Water Services;
- The Gas and Electricity Markets Authority;
- The Information Commissioner;
- The Office of the Rail Regulator;
- The Consumers' Association (Which?).

A Community enforcer is a qualified entity for the purposes of the Injunctions Directive (98/27/EC) which is a body listed in the Official Journal of the European Communities, but which is not a general or a designated enforcer; thus, it will apply only to enforcers from other EU states.

The type of infringement which might lead to an Enforcement Order includes:

- a fluid pricing policy which may infringe reg.5 of the PTR;

- excessive cancellation charges;

- repeated failure to give consumers the requisite holiday information, or giving misleading information;

- repeated failure to warn consumers in advance of changes to holiday arrangements;

- repeated failure to perform the holiday properly;

- repeated failure to allow transfers of packages;

- repeated failure to observe the surcharge rules;

- a system of window cards which is not kept up to date or omits compulsory charges;

- continuing to sell holidays without proper bonding/security arrangements in place.

Guidance issued by the OFT in 2003 (OFT 512) states that the following principles will be applied to enforcement policy:

- action is necessary and proportionate, as set out in the Enforcement Concordat, where there is evidence of a breach of the relevant consumer protection law and of consumer harm stemming from the breach;

- business will normally be given reasonable opportunity to put matters right;

- wherever possible court action will only be taken after undertakings have been sought;

- proceedings will be brought by the most appropriate body:

    — with proper regard for other statutory regulatory means and for non statutory mechanisms, and
    — with regard to the application of the Home Authority Principle;

- the OFT will ensure that any action is coordinated so that the business concerned is not subjected to unnecessary multiple approaches; and

- in line with the OFT's general approach to putting information into the public domain, publicity on Pt 8 cases will be accurate, balanced and fair.

The Regulations provide for interim orders to be made. Thus, for example, the travel company whose brochures or website were thought by the authorities to be harming the interest of consumers by an unfair pricing policy could be forced to withdraw its brochures from sale, or even have its website closed, pending the final hearing by the High Court or County Court of the Application for an Enforcement Order. It is not clear whether the authorities could be ordered by the Court, as a condition of granting an interim order, to give an undertaking to be responsible for any losses suffered by the trader as a result of an interim order, in circumstances where ultimately the authorities failed to get an Enforcement Order.

It can now be seen that the authorities have wide powers to prevent travel companies abusing consumers, whether by misleading descriptions, misleading price campaigns whether in a brochure or website or by any other means and even breaches of contract. Thus, an airline which repeatedly abandons its passengers at some foreign location, because of technical difficulties and an insufficiently large fleet of planes to respond to the problem, could find itself the subject of an enforcement order procedure to stop this happening; and one can think of many other examples besides.

Enforcement orders are seen as a weapon of last resort, where individual prosecution by trading standards is inadequate, and the trader will not undertake voluntarily to "mend his ways". It should be noted that where the infringer is a company, enforcement action can also be taken against a director, manager, secretary or other similar officer or a person who is a controller of the company, where any such persons have consented to or connived in the infringement. An order made against one company in a group can be extended to cover all companies within that group.

It perhaps goes without saying that failure to comply with an enforcement order, or breach of an undertaking, is a contempt of court punishable by imprisonment or unlimited fines.

Council Directive on Package Travel, Package Holidays and Package Tours

COUNCIL DIRECTIVE

of 13 June 1990

on package travel, package holidays and package tours

(90/314/EEC)

THE COUNCIL OF THE EUROPEAN COMMUNITIES, Having regard to the Treaty establishing the European Economic Community, and in particular Article 100a thereof,

Having regard to the proposal from the Commission,[1]

In cooperation with the European Parliament,[2]

Having regard to the opinion of the Economic and Social Committee,[3]

Whereas one of the main objectives of the Community is to complete the internal market, of which the tourist sector is an essential part;

Whereas the national laws of Member States concerning package travel, package holidays and package tours hereinafter referred to as 'packages', show many disparities and national practices in this field are markedly different, which gives rise to obstacles to the freedom to provide services in respect of packages and distortions of competition amongst operators established in different Member States;

Whereas the establishment of common rules on packages will contribute to the elimination of these obstacles and thereby to the achievement of a common market in services, thus enabling operators established in one Member State to offer their services in other Member States and Community consumers to benefit from comparable conditions when buying a package in a Member State;

Whereas paragraph 36(b) of the Annex to the Council resolution of 19 May 1981 on a second programme of the European Economic Community for a consumer protection and information policy[4] invites the Commission to study, *inter alia*, tourism and, if appropriate, to put forward suitable proposals, with due regard for their significance for con-

---

[1] O.J. No. C 96, 12. 4. 1988, p. 5.
[2] O.J. No. C 69, 20. 3. 1989, p. 102 and O.J. No. C 149, 18. 6. 1990.
[3] O.J. No. C 102. 24. 4. 1989, p. 27.
[4] O.J. No. C 165, 23. 6. 1981, p. 24.

sumer protection and the effects of differences in Member States' legislation on the proper functioning of the common market;

Whereas in the resolution on a Community policy on tourism on 10 April 1984[5] the Council welcomed the Commission's initiative in drawing attention to the importance of tourism and took note of the Commission's initial guidelines for a Community policy on tourism;

Whereas the Commission communication to the Council entitled 'A New Impetus for Consumer Protection Policy', which was approved by resolution of the Council on 6 May 1986,[6] lists in paragraph 37, among the measures proposed by the Commission, the harmonization of legislation on packages;

Whereas tourism plays an increasingly important role in the economies of the Member States; whereas the package system is a fundamental part of tourism; whereas the package travel industry in Member State would be stimulated to greater growth and productivity if at least a minimum of common rules were adopted in order to give it a Community dimension; whereas this would not only produce benefits for Community citizens buying packages organized on the basis of those rules, but would attract tourists from outside the Community seeking the advantages of guaranteed standards in packages;

Whereas disparities in the rules protecting consumers in different Member States are a disincentive to consumers in one Member State from buying packages in another Member State;

Whereas this disincentive is particularly effective in deterring consumers from buying packages outside their own Member State, and more effective than it would be in relation to the acquisition of other services, having regard to the special nature of the services supplied in a package which generally involve the expenditure of substantial amounts of money in advance and the supply of the services in a State other than that in which the consumer is resident;

Whereas the consumer should have the benefit of the protection introduced by this Directive irrespective of whether he is a direct contracting party, a transferee or a member of a group on whose behalf another person has concluded a contract in respect of a package;

Whereas the organizer of the package and/or the retailer of it should be under obligation to ensure that in descriptive matter relating to packages which they respectively organize and sell, the information which is given is not misleading and brochures made available to consumers contain information which is comprehensible and accurate;

Whereas the consumer needs to have a record of the terms of contract applicable to the package; whereas this can conveniently be achieved by requiring that all the terms of the contract be stated in writing or such other documentary form as shall be comprehensible and accessible to him, and that he be given a copy thereof;

Whereas the consumer should be at liberty in certain circumstances to transfer to a willing third person a booking made by him for a package;

Whereas the price established under the contract should not in principle be subject to

[5] O.J. No. C 115, 30. 4. 1984, p. 1.
[6] O.J. No. C 118, 7. 3. 1986, p. 28.

revision except where the possibility of upward or downward revision is expressly provided for in the contract; whereas that possibility should nonetheless be subject to certain conditions;

Whereas the consumer should in certain circumstances be free to withdraw before departure from a package travel contract;

Whereas there should be a clear definition of the rights available to the consumer in circumstances where the organizer of the package cancels it before the agreed date of departure;

Whereas if, after the consumer has departed, there occurs a significant failure of performance of the services for which he has contracted or the organizer perceives that he will be unable to procure a significant part of the services to be provided; the organizer should have certain obligations towards the consumer;

Whereas the organizer and/or retailer party to the contract should be liable to the consumer for the proper performance of the obligations arising from the contract; whereas, moreover, the organizer and/or retailer should be liable for the damage resulting for the consumer from failure to perform or improper performance of the contract unless the defects in the performance of the contract are attributable neither to any fault of theirs nor to that of another supplier of services;

Whereas in the cases where the organizer and/or retailer is liable for failure to perform or improper performance of the services involved in the package, such liability should be limited in accordance with the international conventions governing such services, in particular the Warsaw Convention of 1929 in International Carriage by Air, the Berne Convention of 1961 on Carriage by Rail, the Athens Convention of 1974 on Carriage by Sea and the Paris Convention of 1962 on the Liability of Hotel-keepers; whereas, moreover, with regard to damage other than personal injury, it should be possible for liability also to be limited under the package contract provided, however, that such limits are not unreasonable;

Whereas certain arrangements should be made for the information of consumers and the handling of complaints;

Whereas both the consumer and the package travel industry would benefit if organizers and/or retailers were placed under an obligation to provide sufficient evidence of security in the event of insolvency;

Whereas Member State should be at a liberty to adopt, or retain, more stringent provisions relating to package travel for the purpose of protecting the consumer,

HAS ADOPTED THIS DIRECTIVE:

Article 1

The purpose of this Directive is to approximate the laws, regulations and administrative provisions of the Member States relating to packages sold or offered for sale in the territory of the Community.

Article 2

For the purposes of this Directive:

APPENDIX ONE

1. 'package' means the pre-arranged combination of not fewer than two of the following when sold or offered for sale at an inclusive price and when the service covers a period of more than twenty-four hours or includes overnight accommodation:

(a) transport;

(b) accommodation;

(c) other tourist services not ancillary to transport or accommodation and accounting for a significant proportion of the package.

The separate billing of various components of the same package shall not absolve the organizer or retailer from the obligations under this Directive;

2. 'organizer' means the person who, other than occasionally, organizes packages and sells or offers them for sale, whether directly or through a retailer;

3. 'retailer' means the person who sells or offers for sale the package put together by the organizer;

4. 'consumer' means the person who takes or agrees to take the package ('the principal contractor'), or any person on whose behalf the principal contractor agrees to purchase the package ('the other beneficiaries') or any person to whom the principal contractor or any of the other beneficiaries transfers the package ('the transferee');

5. 'contract' means the agreement linking the consumer to the organizer and/or the retailer.

Article 3

1. Any descriptive matter concerning a package and supplied by the organizer or the retailer to the consumer, the price of the package and any other conditions applying to the contract must not contain any misleading information.

2. When a brochure is made available to the consumer, it shall indicate in a legible, comprehensible and accurate manner both the price and adequate information concerning:

(a) the destination and the means, characteristics and categories of transport used;

(b) the type of accommodation, its location, category or degree of comfort and its main features, its approval and tourist classification under the rules of the host Member State concerned;

(c) the meal plan;

(d) the itinerary;

(e) general information on passport and visa requirements for nationals of the Member State or States concerned and health formalities required for the journey and the stay;

(f) either the monetary amount or the percentage of the price which is to be paid on account, and the time-table for payment of the balance;

(g) whether a minimum number of persons is required for the package to take place and, if so, the deadline for informing the consumer in the event of cancellation.

The particulars contained in the brochure are binding on the organizer or retailer, unless:

— changes in such particulars have been clearly communicated to the consumer before conclusion of the contract, in which case the brochure shall expressly state so,

— changes are made later following an agreement between the parties to the contract.

Article 4

1. (a) The organizer and/or the retailer shall provide the consumer, in writing or any other appropriate form, before the contract is concluded, with general information on passport and visa requirements applicable to nationals of the Member State or States concerned and in particular on the periods for obtaining them, as well as with information on the health formalities required for the journey and the stay;

(b) The organizer and/or retailer shall also provide the consumer, in writing or any other appropriate form, with the following information in good time before the start of the journey;

(i) the times and places of intermediate stops and transport connections as well as details of the place to be occupied by the traveller, *e.g.* cabin or berth on ship, sleeper compartment on train;

(ii) the name, address and telephone number of the organizer's and/or retailer's local representative or, failing that, of local agencies on whose assistance a consumer in difficulty could call.
Where no such representatives or agencies exist, the consumer must in any case be provided with an emergency telephone number or any other information that will enable him to contract the organizer and/or the retailer;

(iii) in the case of journeys or stays abroad by minors, information enabling direct contact to be established with the child or the person responsible at the child's place of stay;

(iv) information on the optional conclusion of an insurance policy to cover the cost of cancellation by the consumer or the cost of assistance, including repatriation, in the event of accident or illness.

2. Member States shall ensure that in relation to the contract the following principles apply:

(a) depending on the particular package, the contract shall contain at least the elements listed in the Annex;

(b) all the terms of the contract are set out in writing or such other form as is comprehensible and accessible to the consumer and must be communicated to him before the conclusion of the contract; the consumer is given a copy of these terms;

(c) the provision under (b) shall not preclude the belated conclusion of last-minute reservations or contracts.

3. Where the consumer is prevented from proceeding with the package, he may transfer his booking, having first given the organizer or the retailer reasonable notice of his intention before departure, to a person who satisfies all the conditions applicable to the package. The transferor of the package and the transferee shall be jointly and severally liable to the organizer or retailer party to the contract for payment of the balance due and for any additional costs arising from such transfer.

4. (a) The prices laid down in the contract shall not be subject to revision unless the

contract expressly provides for the possibility of upward or downward revision and states precisely how the revised price is to be calculated, and solely to allow for variations in:

— transportation costs, including the cost of fuel,
— dues, taxes or fees chargeable for certain services, such as landing taxes or embarkation or disembarkation fees at ports and airports,
— the exchange rates applied to the particular package.

(b) During the twenty days prior to the departure date stipulated, the price stated in the contract shall not be increased.

5. If the organizer finds that before the departure he is constrained to alter significantly any of the essential terms, such as the price, he shall notify the consumer as quickly as possible in order to enable him to take appropriate decisions and in particular:

— either to withdraw from the contract without penalty,

— or to accept a rider to the contract specifying the alterations made and their impact on the price.

The consumer shall inform the organizer or the retailer of his decision as soon as possible.

6. If the consumer withdraws from the contract pursuant to paragraph 5, or if, for whatever cause, other than the fault of the consumer, the organizer cancels the package before the agreed date of departure, the consume shall be entitled:

(a) either to take a substitute package of equivalent or higher quality where the organizer and/or retailer is able to offer him such a substitute. If the replacement package offered is of lower quality, the organizer shall refund the difference in price to the consumer;

(b) or to be repaid as soon as possible all sums paid by him under the contract.

In such a case, he shall be entitled, if appropriate, to be compensated by either the organizer or the retailer, whichever the relevant Member State's law requires, for non-performance of the contract, except where:

(i) cancellation is on the grounds that the number of persons enrolled for the package is less than the minimum number required and the consumer is informed of the cancellation, in writing, within the period indicated in the package description; or

(ii) cancellation, excluding overbooking, is for reasons of *force majeure*, *i.e.* unusual and unforeseeable circumstances beyond the control of the party by whom it is pleaded, the consequences of which could have not have been avoided even if all due care had been exercised.

7. Where, after departure, a significant proportion of the services contracted for is not provided or the organizer perceives that he will be unable to procure a significant proportion of the services to be provided, the organizer shall make suitable alternative arrangements, at no extra cost to the consumer, for the continuation of the package, and where appropriate compensate the consumer for the difference between the services offered and those supplied.

If it is impossible to make such arrangements or these are not accepted by the consumer for good reasons the organizer shall, where appropriate, provide the consumer, at no extra costs, with equivalent transport back to the place of departure, or to another return-point to which the consumer has agreed and shall, where appropriate, compensate the consumer.

Article 5

1. Member States shall take the necessary steps to ensure that the organizer and/or retailer party to the contract is liable to the consumer for the proper performance of the obligations arising from the contract, irrespective of whether such obligations are to be performed by that organizer and/or retailer or by other suppliers of services without prejudice to the right of the organizer and/or retailer to pursue those other suppliers of services.

2. With regard to the damage resulting for the consumer from the failure to perform or the improper performance of the contract, Member States shall take the necessary steps to ensure that the organizer and/or retailer is/are liable unless such failure to perform or improper performance is attributable neither to any fault of theirs nor to that of another supplier of services, because:

— the failures which occur in the performance of the contract are attributable to the consumer,

— such failures are attributable to a third party unconnected with the provision of the services contracted for, and are unforeseeable or unavoidable,

— such failures are due to a case of *force majeure* such as that defined in Article 4(6), second subparagraph (ii), or to an event which the organizer and/or retailer or the supplier of services, even with all due care, could not foresee or forestall.

In the cases referred to in the second and third indents, the organizer and/or retailer party to the contract shall be required to give prompt assistance to a consumer in difficulty.

In the matter of damages arising from the non-performance or improper performance of the services involved in the package, the Member States may allow compensation to be limited in accordance with the international conventions governing such services.

In the matter of damage other than personal injury resulting from the non-performance of improper performance of the services involved in the package, the Member States may allow compensation to be limited under the contract. Such limitation shall not be unreasonable.

3. Without prejudice to the fourth subparagraph of paragraph 2, there may be no exclusion by means of a contractual clause from the provisions of paragraphs 1 and 2.

4. The consumer must communicate any failure in the performance of a contract which he perceives on the spot to the supplier of the services concerned and to the organizer and/or retailer in writing or any other appropriate form at the earliest opportunity.

This obligation must be stated clearly and explicitly in the contract.

Article 6

In cases of complaint, the organizer and/or retailer or his local representative, if there is one, must make prompt efforts to find appropriate solutions.

APPENDIX ONE

Article 7

The organizer and/or retailer party to the contract shall provide sufficient evidence of security for the refund of money paid over and for the repatriation of the consumer in the event of insolvency.

Article 8

Member States may adopt or return more stringent provisions in the field covered by this Directive to protect the consumer.

Article 9

1. Member States shall bring into force the measures necessary to comply with this Directive before 31 December 1992. They shall forthwith inform the Commission thereof.

2. Member States shall communicate to the Commission the texts of the main provisions of national law which they adopt in the field governed by this Directive. The Commission shall inform the other Member States thereof.

Article 10

This Directive is addressed to the Member States.

Done at Luxembourg, 13 June 1990.

For the Council

The President

D. J. O'MALLEY

The Package Travel, Package Holidays and Package Tours Regulations 1992

1992 No. 3228

Amendments in square brackets inserted by SI 1995/1648 and SI 1998/1208

CONSUMER PROTECTION

The Package Travel, Package Holidays and Package Tours
Regulations 1992

Whereas the Secretary of State is a Minister designated for the purposes of section 2(2) of the European Communities Act 1972 in relation to measures relating to consumer protection as regards package travel, package holidays and package tours;

And whereas a draft of these Regulations has been approved by a resolution of each House of Parliament pursuant to section 2(2) of and paragraph 2(2) of Schedule 2 to that Act;

Now, therefore the Secretary of State in exercise of the powers conferred on him by section 2(2) of that Act hereby makes the following Regulations:

Citation and commencement

1. These Regulations may be cited as the Package Travel, Package Holidays and Package Tours Regulations 1992 and shall come into force on the day after the day on which they are made.

Interpretation

2.—(1) In these Regulations—

"brochure" means any brochure in which packages are offered for sale; "contract" means the agreement linking the consumer to the organiser or to the retailer, or to both, as the case may be:
"the Directive" means Council Directive 90/314/EEC on package travel, package holidays and package tours; ["member State" means a member State of the European Community or another State in the European Economic Area;]
"offer" includes an invitation to treat whether by means of advertising or otherwise, and cognate expressions shall be construed accordingly;
"organiser" means the person who, otherwise than occasionally, organises packages and sells or offers them for sale, whether directly or through a retailer;
a "the other party to the contract" means the party, other than the consumer, to the contract, that is, the organiser or the retailer, or both, as the case may be;
"package" means the pre-arranged combination of at least two of the following

components when sold or offered for sale at an inclusive price and when the service covers a period of time more than twenty-four hours or includes overnight accommodation:—

(a) transport;

(b) accommodation;

(c) other tourist services not ancillary to transport or accommodation and accounting for a significant proportion of the package,

and

(i) the submission of separate accounts for different components shall not cause the arrangements to be other than a package:

(ii) the fact that a combination is arranged at the request of the consumer and in accordance with his specific instructions (whether modified or not) shall not of itself cause it to be treated as other than pre-arranged:

and

"retailer" means the person who sells or offers for sale the package put together by the organiser.

(2) In the definition of "contract" in paragraph (1) above, "consumer" means the person who takes or agrees to take the package ("the principal contractor") and elsewhere in these Regulations "consumer" means as the context requires, the principal contractor, any person on whose behalf the principal contractor agrees to purchase the package ("the other beneficiaries") or any person to whom the principal contractor or any of the other beneficiaries transfers the package ("the transferee").

Application of Regulations

3.—(1) These regulations apply to packages sold or offered for sale in the territory of the United Kingdom.

(2) Regulations 4 to 15 apply to packages sold or offered for sale on or after 31st December 1992.

(3) Regulations 16 to 22 apply to contracts which, in whole or part, remain to be performed on 31st December 1992.

Descriptive matter relating to packages must not be misleading

4.—(1) No organiser or retailer shall supply to a consumer any descriptive matter concerning a package, the price of a package or any other conditions applying to the contract which contains any misleading information.

(2) If an organiser or retailer is in breach of paragraph (1) he shall be liable to compensate the consumer for any loss which the consumer suffers in consequence.

Requirements as to brochures

5.—(1) Subject to paragraph (4) below, no organiser shall make available a brochure to a possible consumer unless it indicates in legible, comprehensible and accurate manner the price and adequate information about the matters specified in Schedule 1 to these

Regulations in respect of the packages offered for sale in the brochure to the extent that those matters are relevant to the packages so offered.

(2) Subject to paragraph (4) below, no retailer shall make available to a possible consumer a brochure which he knows or has reasonable cause to believe does not comply with the requirements of paragraph (1).

(3) An organiser who contravenes paragraph (1) of this regulation and a retailer who contravenes paragraph (2) thereof shall be guilty of an offence and liable:

(a)   on summary conviction, to a fine not exceeding level 5 on the standard scale;

    and

(b)   on conviction on indictment, to a fine.

(4) Where a brochure was first made available to consumers generally before 31st December 1992 no liability shall arise under this regulation in respect of an identical brochure being made available to a consumer at any time.

Circumstances in which particulars in brochure are to be binding

6.—(1) Subject to paragraphs (2) and (3) of this regulation, the particulars in the brochure (whether or not they are required by regulation 5(1) above to be included in the brochure) shall constitute implied warranties (or, as regards Scotland, implied terms) for the purposes of any contract to which the particulars relate.

(2) Paragraph (1) of this regulation does not apply:

(a)   in relation to information required to be included by virtue of paragraph 9 of Schedule 1 to these Regulations: or

(b)   where the brochure contains an express statement that changes may be made in the particulars contained in it before a contract is concluded and changes in the particulars so contained are clearly communicated to the customer before a contract is concluded.

(3) Paragraph (1) of this regulation does not apply when the consumer and the other party to the contract agree after the contract has been made that the particulars in the brochure, or some of those particulars, should not form part of the contract.

Information to be provided before contract is concluded

7.—(1) Before a contract is concluded, the other party to the contract shall provide the intending consumer with the information specified in paragraph (2) below in writing or in some other appropriate form.

(2) The information referred to in paragraph (1) is:

(a)   general information about passport and visa requirements which apply to [nationals of the member States or States Concerned] who purchase the package in question, including information about the length of time it is likely to take to obtain the appropriate passports and visas;

(b)   information about health formalities required for the journey and the stay; and

(c) the arrangements for security for the money paid over and (where applicable) for the repatriation of the consumer in the event of insolvency.

(3) If the intending consumer is not provided with the information required by paragraph (1) in accordance with that paragraph the other party to the contract shall be guilty of an offence and liable:

(a) on summary conviction, to a fine not exceeding level 5 on the standard scale:

and

(b) on conviction on indictment, to a fine.

Information to be provided in good time

8.—(1) The other party to the contract shall in good time before the start of the journey provide the consumer with the information specified in paragraph (2) below in writing or in some other appropriate form.

(2) The information referred to in paragraph (1) is the following:

(a) the times and places of intermediate stops and transport connections and particulars of the place to be occupied by the traveller (for example, cabin or berth on a ship, sleeper compartment on train);

(b) the name, address and telephone number—

(i) of the representative of the other party to the contract in the locality where the consumer is to stay,
or, if there is no such representative,

(ii) of an agency in that locality on whose assistance a consumer in difficulty would be able to call,
or, if there is no such representative or agency, a telephone number or other information which will enable the consumer to contract the other party to the contract during the stay;

and

(c) in the case of a journey or stay abroad by a child under the age of 16 on the day when the journey or stay is due to start, information enabling direct contact to be made with the child or the person responsible at the place where he is to stay;

and

(d) except where the consumer is required as a term of the contract to take out an insurance policy in order to cover the cost of cancellation by the consumer or the cost of assistance, including repatriation, in the event of accident or illness, information about an insurance policy which the consumer may, if he wishes, take out in respect of the risk of those costs being incurred.

(3) If the consumer is not provided with the information required by paragraph (1) in accordance with that paragraph the other party to the contract shall be guilty of an offence an liable:

(a) on summary conviction, to a fine not exceeding level 5 on the standard scale; and

(b) on conviction on indictment, to a fine.

Contents and form of contract

9.—(1) The other party to the contract shall ensure that—

(a) depending on the nature of the package being purchased, the contract contains at least the elements specified in Schedule 2 to these regulations;

(b) subject to paragraph (2) below, all the terms of the contract are set out in writing or such other form as is comprehensible and accessible to the consumer and are communicated to the consumer before the contract is made; and

(c) a written copy of these terms is supplied to the consumer.

(2) Paragraph (1)(b) above does not apply when the interval between the time when the consumer approaches the other party to the contract with a view to entering into a contract and the time of departure under the proposed contract is so short that it is impracticable to comply with the sub-paragraph.

(3) It is an implied condition (or, as regards Scotland, an implied term) of the contract that the other party to the contract complies with the provisions of paragraph (1).

(4) In Scotland, any breach of the condition implied by paragraph (3) above shall be deemed to be a material breach justifying rescission of the contract.

Transfer of bookings

10.—(1) In every contract there is an implied term that where the consumer is prevented from proceeding with the package the consumer may transfer his booking to a person who satisfies all the conditions applicable to the package, provided that the consumer gives reasonable notice to the other party to the contract of his intention to transfer before the date when departure is due to take place.

(2) Where a transfer is made in accordance with the implied term set out in paragraph (1) above, the transferor and the transferee shall be jointly and severally liable to the other party to the contract for payment of the price of the package (or, if part of the price has been paid, for payment of the balance) and for any additional costs arising from such transfer.

Price revision

11.—(1) Any term in a contract to the effect that the prices laid down in the contract may be revised shall be void and of no effect unless the contract provides for the possibility of upward or downward revision and satisfies the conditions laid down in paragraph (2) below.

(2) The conditions mentioned in paragraph (1) are that—

(a) the contract states precisely how the revised price is to be calculated;

(b) the contract provides that price revisions are to be made solely to allow for variations in:

  (i) transportation costs, including the cost of fuel,
  (ii) dues, taxes or fees chargeable for services such as landing taxes or embarkation or disembarkation fees at ports and airports, or
  (iii) the exchange rates applied to the particular package; and

(3) Notwithstanding any terms of a contract.

(i)   no price increase may be made in a specified period which may not be less that 30 days before the departure date stipulated; and

(ii) as against an individual consumer liable under the contract, no price increase may be made in respect of variations which would produce an increase of less than 2%, or such greater percentage as the contract may specify, ("non-eligible variations") and that the non-eligible variations shall be left out of account in the calculation.

Significant alterations to essential terms

12. In every contract there are implied terms to the effect that—

(a)   where the organiser is constrained before the departure to alter significantly an essential term of the contract, such as the price (so far as regulation 11 permits him to do so), he will notify the consumer as quickly as possible in order to enable him to take appropriate decisions and in particular to withdraw from the contract without penalty or to accept a rider to the contract specifying the alterations made and their impact on the price; and

(b)   the consumer will inform the organiser or the retailer of his decision as soon as possible.

Withdrawal by consumer pursuant to regulation 12 and cancellation by organiser

13.—(1) The terms set out in paragraphs (2) and (3) below are implied in every contract and apply where the consumer withdraws from the contract pursuant to the term in it implied by virtue of regulation 12(a), or where the organiser, for any reason other than the fault of the consumer, cancels the package before the agreed date of departure.

(2) The consumer is entitled—

(a)   to take a substitute package of equivalent or superior quality if the other party to the contract is able to offer such a substitute; or

(b)   to take a substitute package of lower quality if the other party to the contract is able to offer him one and to recover from the organiser the difference in price between the price of the package purchased and that of the substitute package; or

(c)   to have repaid to him as soon as possible all the monies paid by him under the contract.

(3) The consumer is entitled, if appropriate, to be compensated by the organiser for non-performance of the contract except where—

(a)   the package is cancelled because the number of persons who agree to take it is less than the minimum number required and the consumer is informed of the cancellation, in writing, within the period indicated in the description of the package; or

(b)   the package is cancelled by reason of unusual and unforeseeable circumstances beyond the control of the party by whom this exception is pleaded, the consequences of which could not have been avoided even if all due care had been exercised.

(4) Overbooking shall not be regarded as a circumstance falling within the provisions of sub-paragraph (b) of paragraph (3) above.

Significant proportion of services not provided

14.—(1) The terms set out in paragraphs (2) and (3) below are implied in every contract and apply where after departure, a significant proportion of the services contracted for is not provided or the organiser becomes aware that he will be unable to procure a significant proportion of the services to be provided.

(2) The organiser will make suitable alternative arrangements, at no extra cost to the consumer, for the continuation of the package and will, where appropriate, compensate the consumer for the difference between the services to be supplied under the contract and those supplied.

(3) If it is impossible to make arrangements as described in paragraph (2), or these are not accepted by the consumer for good reasons, the organiser will, where appropriate, provide the consumer with equivalent transport back to the place of departure or to another place to which the consumer has agreed and will, where appropriate, compensate the consumer.

Liability of other party to the contract for poor performance of obligations under contract

15.—(1) The other party is liable to the consumer for the proper performance of the obligations under the contract, irrespective of whether such obligations are to be performed by that other party or by other suppliers of services but this shall not affect any remedy or right of action which that other party may have against those other suppliers of services.

(2) The other party to the contract is liable to the consumer for any damage caused to him by the failure to perform the contract or the improper performance of the contract unless the failure or the improper performance is due neither to any fault of that other party nor to that of another supplier of services, because—

(a) the failures which occur in the performance of the contract are attributable to the consumer;

(b) such failures are attributable to a third party unconnected with the provision of the services contracted for, and are unforeseeable or unavoidable; or

(c) such failures are due to—

   (i) unusual and unforeseeable circumstances beyond the control of the party by whom this exception is pleaded, the consequences of which could not have been avoided even if all due care had been exercised; or

   (ii) an event which the other party to the contract or the supplier of services, even with all due care, could not foresee or forestall.

(3) In the case of damage arising from the non-performance or improper performance of the services involved in the package, the contract may provide for compensation to be limited in accordance with the international conventions which govern such services.

(4) In the case of damage other than personal injury resulting from the non-performance or improper performance of the services involved in the package, the contract may include a term limiting the amount of compensation which will be paid to the consumer, provided that the limitation is not unreasonable.

(5) Without prejudice to paragraph (3) and paragraph (4) above, liability under paragraphs (1) and (2) above cannot be excluded by any contractual term.

(6) The terms set out in paragraphs (7) and (8) below are implied in every contract.

(7) In the circumstances described in paragraph (2)(b) and (c) of this regulation, the other party to the contract will give prompt assistance to a consumer in difficulty.

(8) If the consumer complains about a defect in the performance of the contract, the other party to the contract, or his local representative, if there is one, will make prompt efforts to find appropriate solutions.

(9) The contract must clearly and explicitly oblige the consumer to communicate at the earliest opportunity, in writing or any other appropriate form, to the supplier of the services concerned and to the other party to the contract any failure which he perceives at the place where the services concerned are supplied.

Security in event of insolvency—requirements and offences

16.—(1) The other party to the contract shall at all times be able to provide sufficient evidence of security for the refund of money paid over and for the repatriation of the consumer in the event of insolvency.

(2) Without prejudice to paragraph (1) above, and subject to paragraph (4) below, save to the extent that—

(a) the package is covered by measures adopted or retained by the member State where he is established for the purpose of implementing Article 7 of the Directive; or

(b) the package is one in respect of which he is required to hold a licence under the Civil Aviation (Air Travel Organiser's Licensing) Regulations 1972 or the package is one that is covered by the arrangements he has entered into for the purposes of those Regulations.

The other party to the contract shall at least ensure that there are in force arrangements as described in regulations 17, 18, 19 or 20 or, if that party is acting otherwise than in the course of business, as described in any of those regulations or in regulation 21.

(3) Any person who contravenes paragraph (1) or (2) of this regulation shall be guilty of an offence and liable:

(a) on summary conviction to a fine not exceeding level 5 on the standard scale; and

(b) on conviction on indictment, to a fine.

(4) A person shall not be guilty of an offence under paragraph (3) above by reason only of the fact that arrangements such as are mentioned in paragraph (2) above are not in force in respect to any period before 1 April 1993 unless money paid over is not refunded when it is due or the consumer is not repatriated in the event of insolvency.

(5) For the purposes of regulations 17 to 21 below a contract shall be treated as having been fully performed if the package or, as the case may be, the part of the package has been completed irrespective of whether the obligations under the contract have been properly performed for the purposes of regulation 15.

Bonding

17.—(1) The other party to the contract shall ensure that a bond is entered into by an authorised institution under which the institution binds itself of pay an approved body of which that other party is a member a sum calculated in accordance with paragraph (3) below in the event of the insolvency of that other party.

(2) Any bond entered into pursuant to paragraph (1) above shall not be expressed to be in force for a period exceeding eighteen months.

(3) The sum referred to in paragraph (1) above shall be such as may reasonably be expected to enable all monies paid over by consumers under or in contemplation of contracts for relevant packages which have not been fully performed to be repaid and shall not in any event be a sum which is less than the minimum sum calculated in accordance with paragraph (4) below.

(4) The minimum sum for the purposes of paragraph (3) above shall be a sum which represents:

(a) not less than 25% of all the payments which the other party to the contract estimates that he will receive under or in contemplation of contracts for relevant packages in the twelve month period from the data of entry into force of the bond refereed to in paragraph (1) above; or

(b) the maximum amount of all the payments which the other party to the contract expects to hold at any one time, in respect of contracts which have not been fully performed.

whichever sum is the smaller.

(5) Before a bond is entered into pursuant to paragraph (1) above, the other party to the contract shall inform the approved body of which he is a member of the minimum sum which he proposes for the purposes of paragraph (3) and (4) above and it shall be the duty of the approved body to consider whether such sum is sufficient for the purpose mentioned in paragraph (3) and, if it does not consider that this is the case, it shall be the duty of the approved body so to inform the other party to the contract and to inform him of the sum which, in the opinion of the approved body is sufficient for that purpose.

(6) Where an approved body has informed the other party to the contract of a sum pursuant to paragraph (5) above, the minimum sum for the purposes of paragraphs (3) and (4) above shall be that sum.

(7) In this regulation—

"approved body" means a body which is for the time being approved by the Secretary of State for the purposes of this regulation;
"authorised institution" means a person authorised under the law of a member State [, of the Channel Islands or of the Isle of Man] to carry on the business of entering into bonds of the kind required by this regulation.

Bonding where approved body has reserve fund or insurance

18.—(1) The other party to the contract shall ensure that a bond is entered into by an authorised institution, under which the institution agrees to pay to an approved body of which that other party is a member a sum calculated in accordance with paragraph (3) below in the event of the insolvency of that other party.

(2) Any bond entered into pursuant to paragraph (1) above shall to be expressed to be in force for a period exceeding eighteen moths.

(3) The sum refereed to in paragraph (1) above shall be such sum as may be specified by the approved body as representing the lesser of—

(a) the maximum amount of all the payments which the other party to the contract expects to hold at any one time in respect of contracts which have not been fully performed; or

(b) the minimum sum calculated in accordance with paragraph (4) below.

(4) The minimum sum for the purposes of paragraph (3) above shall be a sum which represents not less than 10% of all the payments which the other party to the contract estimates that he will receive under or in contemplation of contracts for relevant packages in the twelve month period from the date of entry referred to in paragraph (1) above.

(5) In this regulation "approved body" means a body which is for the time being approved by the Secretary of State for the purposes of this regulation and no such approval shall be given unless the conditions mentioned in paragraph (6) below are satisfied in relation to it.

(6) A body may not be approved for the purposes of this regulation unless—

(a) it has a reserve fund or insurance cover with an insurer authorised in respect of such business in a member state [, the Channel Islands or of the Isle of Man] of an amount in each case which is designed to enable all monies paid over to a member of the body of consumers under or in contemplation of contracts for relevant packages which have not been fully performed to be repaid to those consumers in the event of insolvency of the member; and

(b) where it has a reserve fund, it agrees that the fund will be held by persons and in a manner approved by the Secretary of State.

(7) In this regulation, authorised institution has the meaning given to that expression by paragraph (7) of regulation 17.

Insurance

19.—(1) The other party to the contract shall have insurance under one or more appropriate policies with an insurer authorised in respect of such business in a member State under which the insurer agrees to indemnify consumer's who shall be insured persons under the policy, against the loss of money paid over by them under or in contemplation of contracts for packages in the event of insolvency of the contractor.

(2) The other party to the contract shall ensure that it is a term of every contract with a consumer that the consumer acquires the benefit of a policy of a kind mentioned in paragraph (1) above in the event of the insolvency of the other party to the contract.

(3) In this regulation:

"appropriate policy" means one which does not contain a condition which provides (in whatever terms) that no liability shall arise under the policy, or that any liability so arising shall cease:

(i)   in the event of some specified thing being done or omitted to be done after the happening of the even giving rise to a claim under the policy;

(ii) in the event of the policy holder no making payments under or in connection with other policies; or

(iii) unless the policy holder keeps specified records or provides the insurer with or makes available to him information therefrom.

Monies in trust

20.—(1) The other party to the contract shall ensure that all monies paid over by a consumer under or in contemplation of a contract for a relevant package are held in the United Kingdom by a person as trustee for the consumer until the contract has been fully performed or any sum of money paid by the consumer in respect of the contract has been repaid to him or has been forfeited on cancellation by the consumer.

(2) The costs of administering the trust mentioned in paragraph (1) above shall be paid for by the other party to the contract.

(3) Any interest which is earned in the monies held by the trustee pursuant to paragraph (1) shall be held for the other party to the contract and shall be payable to him on demand.

(4) Where there is produced to the trustee a statement signed by the other party to the contract to the effect that—

(a)   a contract for a package the price of which is specified in that statement has been fully performed;

(b)   the other party to the contract has repaid the consumer a sum of money specified in that statement which the consumer had paid in respect of a contract or a package; or

(c)   the consumer has on cancellation forfeited a sum of money specified in that statement which he had paid in respect of a contract for a relevant package,

the trustee shall (subject to paragraph (5) below) release to the other party to the contract the sum specified in the statement.

(5) Where the trustee considers it appropriate to do so, he may require the other party to the contract to provide further information or evidence of the matters mentioned in sub-paragraph (a), (b) or (c) of paragraph (4) above before he releases any sum to that other party pursuant to that paragraph.

(6) Subject to paragraph (7) below, in the event of the insolvency of the other party to the contract the monies held in trust by the trustee pursuant to paragraph (1) of this regulation shall be applied to meet the claims of consumers who are creditors of that other party in respect of contracts for packages in respect of which the arrangements were established and which have not been fully performed and, if there is a surplus after those claims have been met, it shall form part of the estate of that insolvent other party for the purposes of insolvency law.

(7) If the monies held in trust by the trustee pursuant to paragraph (1) of this regulation are insufficient to meet the claims of consumers as described in paragraph (6), payments to those consumers shall be made by the trustee on a pari passu basis.

Monies in trust where other party to contract is acting otherwise than in the course of business

21.—(1) The other party to the contract shall ensure that all monies paid over by a consumer under or in contemplation of a contract for a relevant package are held in the United Kingdom by a person as trustee for the consumer for the purpose of paying for the consumer's package.

(2) The costs of administering the trust mentioned in paragraph (1) shall be paid for out of the monies held in trust and the interest earned on the monies.

(3) Where there is produced to the trustee a statement signed by the other party to the contract to the effect that—

(a) the consumer has previously paid over a sum of money specified in that statement in respect of a contract for a package and that sum is required for the purpose of paying for a component (or part of a component) of the package;

(b) the consumer has previously paid over a sum of money specified in that statement in respect of a contract for a package and the other party to the contract has paid that sum in respect of a component (or part of a component) of the package;

(c) the consumer requires the repayment to him of a sum of money specified in that statement which was previously paid over by the consumer in respect of a contract for a package; or

(d) the consumer has on cancellation forfeited a sum of money specified in that statement which he had paid in respect of a contract for a package,

the trustee shall (subject to paragraph (4) below) release to the other party to the contract the sum specified in the statement.

(4) Where the trustee considers it appropriate to do so, he may require the other party to the contract to provide further information or evidence of the matters mentioned in sub-paragraph (a), (b), (c) or (d) of paragraph (3) above before the releases to that other party any sum from the monies held in trust for the consumer.

(5) Subject to paragraph (6) below, in the event of the insolvency of the other party to the contract and of contracts for packages not being fully performed (whether before or after the insolvency) the monies held in trust by the trustee pursuant to paragraph (1) of this regulation shall be applied to meet the claims of consumers who are creditors of that other party in respect of amounts paid over by them and remaining in the trust fund after deductions have been made in respect of amounts released to that other party pursuant to paragraph (3) and, if there is a surplus after those claims have been met, it shall be divided amongst those consumers pro rata.

(6) If the monies held in trust by the trustee pursuant to paragraph (1) of this regulation are insufficient to meet the claims of consumers as described in paragraph (5) above, payments to those consumers shall be made by the trustee on a pari passu basis.

(7) Any sums remaining after all the packages in respect of which the arrangements were

established have been fully performed shall be dealt with as provided in the arrangements or in default of such provision, may be paid to the other party to the contract.

Offences arising from breach of regulations 20 and 21

22.—(1) If the other party to the contract makes a false statement under paragraph (4) of regulation 20 or paragraph (3) of regulation 21 he shall be guilty of an offence.

(2) If the other party to the contract applies monies released to him on the basis of a statement made by him under regulation 21(3)(a) or (c) for a purpose other than that mentioned in the statement he shall be guilty of an offence.

(3) If the other party to the contract is guilty of an offence under paragraph (1) or (2) of this regulation shall be liable—

    (a) on summary conviction to a fine not exceeding level 5 on the standard scale; and

    (b) on conviction on indictment, to a fine.

Enforcement

23. Schedule 3 to these Regulations (which makes provision about the enforcement of regulations 5, 7, 8, 16 and 22 of these Regulations) shall have effect.

Due diligence defence

24.—(1) Subject to the following provisions of this regulation, in proceedings against any person for an offence under regulations 5, 7, 8, 16 or 22 of these Regulations, it shall be a defence for that person to show that he took all reasonable steps exercised all due diligence to avoid committing the offence.

(2) Where in any proceedings against any person for such an offence the defence provided by paragraph (1) above involves an allegation that the commission of the offence was due—

    (a) to the act or default of another; or

    (b) to reliance on information given by another.

that person shall not, without the leave of the court, be entitled to rely on the defence unless, not less than seven clear days before the hearing of the proceedings, or, in Scotland, the trial diet, he has served a notice under paragraph (3) below on the person bringing the proceedings.

(3) A notice under this paragraph shall given such information identifying or assisting in the identification of the person who committed the act or default or gave the information as is in the possession of the person serving the notice at the time he serves it.

(4) It is hereby declared that a person shall not be entitled to rely on the defence provided by paragraph (1) above by reason of his reliance on information supplied by another, unless he shows that it was reasonable in all circumstances for him to have relied on the information, having regard in particular—

    (a) to the steps which he took, and those which might reasonably have been taken, for the purpose of verifying the information; and

(b) to whether he had any reason to disbelieve the information.

Liability of persons other than principal offender

25.—(1) Where the commission by any person of an offence under regulations 5, 7, 8, 16 or 22 of these Regulations is due to an act or default committed by some other person in the course of any business of his, the other person shall be guilty of the offence and may be proceeded against and punished by virtue of this paragraph whether or not proceedings are taken against the first-mentioned person.

(2) Where a body corporate is guilty of an offence under any of the provisions mentioned in paragraph (1) above (including where it is so guilty by virtue of the said paragraph (1) in respect of any act or default which is shown to have been committed with the consent or connivance of, or to be attributable to any neglect on the part of any director, manager, secretary or other similar officer of the body corporate or any person who was purporting to act in any such capacity he, as well as the body corporate, shall be guilty of that offence and shall be liable to be proceeded against and punished accordingly.

(3) Where the affairs of a body corporate are managed by its members, paragraph (2) above shall apply in relation to the acts and defaults of a member in connection with this functions of management as if he were a director of the body corporate.

(4) Where an offence under any of the provisions mentioned in paragraph (1) above committed in Scotland by a Scottish partnership is proved to have been committed with the consent or connivance of, or to be attributable to neglect on the part of, a partner, he (as well as the partnership) is guilty of the offence and liable to be proceeded against and punished accordingly.

(5) On proceedings for an offence under regulation 5 by virtue of paragraph (1) above committed by the making available of a brochure it shall be a defence for the person charged to prove that he is a person whose business it is to publish or arrange for the publication of brochures and that the received the brochure for publication in the ordinary course of business and did not know and had no reason to suspect that its publication would amount to an offence under these Regulations.

Prosecution time limit

26.—(1) No proceedings for an offence under regulation 5, 7, 8, 16 or 22 or these Regulations or under paragraphs 5(3), 6 or 7 of Schedule 3 thereto shall be commenced after—

(a) the end of the period of three years beginning within the date of the commission of the offence; or

(b) the end of the period of one year beginning with the date of the discovery of the offence by the prosecutor,

whichever is the earlier.

(2) For the purposes of this regulation a certificate signed by or on behalf of the prosecutor and stating the date on which the offence was discovered by him shall be conclusive evidence of that fact; and a certificate stating that matter and purporting to be so signed shall be treated as so signed unless the contrary is proved.

(3) In relation to proceedings in Scotland, subsection (3) of section 31 of the Criminal

Procedure (Scotland) Act 1975 (date of commencement of proceedings) shall apply for the purposes of this regulation as it applied for the purposes of that section.

Saving for civil consequences

27. No contract shall be void or unenforceable, and no right of action in civil proceedings in respect of any loss shall arise, by reason only of the commission of an offence under regulations 5, 7, 8, 16 or 22 of these Regulations.

Terms implied in contract

28. Where it is provided in these Regulations that a term (whether so described or whether described as a condition or warranty) is implied in the contract it is so implied irrespective of the law which governs the contract.

Denton of Wakefield
Parliamentary Under-Secretary of State,
Department of Trade and Industry

22 December 1992

SCHEDULE 1   Regulation 5

Information to be included (in addition to the price) in brochures where relevant to packages offered

1. The destination and the means, characteristics and categories of transport used.

2. The type of accommodation its location, category or degree of comfort and its main features and, where the accommodation is to be provided in a member State, its approval or tourist classification under the rules of that member State.

3. The meals which are included in the package.

4. The itinerary.

5. General information about passport and visa requirements which apply for [nationals of the member State or State in which the brochure is made available] and health formalities required for the journey and the stay.

6. Either the monetary amount or the percentage of the price which is to be paid on account and the timetable for payment of the balance.

7. Whether a minimum number of persons is required for the package to take place and, if so, the deadline for informing the consumer in the event of cancellation.

8. The arrangements (if any) which apply if consumers are delayed at the outward or homeward points of departure.

9. The arrangements for security for money paid over and for the repatriation of the consumer in the event of insolvency.

APPENDIX TWO

Elements to be included in the contract if relevant to the particular package

1. The travel destination(s) and, where periods of stay are involved, the relevant periods, with dates.

2. The means, characteristics and categories of transport to be used and the dates, times and points of departure and return.

3. Where the package includes accommodation, its location, its tourist category or degree of comfort, its main features and, where the accommodation is to be provided in a member State, its compliance with the rules of that member States.

4. The meals which are included in the package.

5. Whether a minimum number of persons is required for the package to take place and, if so, the deadline for informing the consumer in the event of cancellation.

6. The itinerary.

7. Visits, excursions or other services which are included in the total price agreed for the package.

8. The name and address of the organiser, the retailer and, where appropriate, the insurer.

9. The price of the package, if the price may be revised in accordance with the term which may be included in the contract under regulation 11, an indication of the possibility of such price revisions, and an indication of any dues, taxes or fees chargeable for certain services (landing, embarkation or disembarkation fees at ports and airports and tourist taxes) where such costs are not included in the package.

10. The payment schedule and method of payment.

11. Special requirements which the consumer has communicated to the organiser or retailer when making the booking and which both have accepted.

12. The periods within which the consumer must make any complaint about the failure to perform or the inadequate performance of the contract.

SCHEDULE 3 Regulation 23

ENFORCEMENT

Enforcement authority

1.—(1) Every local weights and measures authority in Great Britain shall be an enforcement authority for the purposes of regulations 5, 7, 8, 16 and 22 of these Regulations ("the relevant regulations"), and it shall be the duty of each such authority to enforce those provisions within their area.

(2) The Department of Economics Development in Northern Ireland shall be an enforcement authority for the purposes of the relevant regulations, and it shall be the duty of the Department to enforce those provisions within Northern Ireland.

Prosecutions

2.—(1) Where an enforcement authority in England or Wales proposes to institute proceedings for an offence under any of the relevant regulations it shall be as between the enforcement authority and the Director General of Fair Tradings be the duty of the enforcement authority to give to the Director General of Fair Trading notice of the intended proceedings, together with a summary of the facts on which the charges are to be founded, and to postpone institution of the proceedings until either—

(a) twenty-eight days have elapsed since the giving of that notice; or

(b) the Director General of Fair Trading has notified the enforcement authority that he has received the notice and the summary of the facts.

(2) Nothing in paragraph 1 above shall authorise a local weights and measures authority to bring proceedings in Scotland for an offence.

Powers of offices of enforcement authority

3.—(1) If a duty authorised officer of an enforcement authority has reasonable grounds for suspecting that an offence has been committed under any of the relevant regulations, he may—

(a) require a person whom he believes on reasonable grounds to be engaged in the organisation or retailing of packages to produce any book or document relating to the activity and take copies of it or any entry in it, or

(b) require such a person to produce in a visible and legible documentary form any information so relating which is contained in a computer, and take copies of it,

for the purpose of ascertaining whether such an offence has been committed.

(2) Such an officer may inspect any goods for the purpose of ascertaining whether such an offence has been committed.

(3) If such an officer has reasonable grounds for believing that any documents or goods may be required as evidence in proceedings for such an offence, he may seize and detain them.

(4) An officer seizing any documents or goods in the exercise of his power under subparagraph (3) above shall inform the person from whom they are seized.

(5) The powers of an officer under this paragraph may be exercised by him only at a reasonable hour and on production (if required) of his credentials.

(6) Nothing in this paragraph—

(a) requires a person to produce a document if he would be entitled to refuse to produce it in proceedings in a court on the grounds that it is the subject of legal professional privilege or, in Scotland, that it contains a confidential communication made by or to an advocate or a solicitor in that capacity; or

(b) authorises the taking possession of a document which is in the possession of a person who would be so entitled.

4.—(1) A duly authorised officer of an enforcement authority may, at a reasonable hour and on production (if required) of his credentials, enter any premises for the purpose of ascertaining whether an offence under any of the relevant regulations has been committed.

(2) If a justice of the peace, or in Scotland a justice of the peace or a sheriff, is satisfied—

(a) that any relevant books, documents or goods are on, or that any relevant information contained in a computer is available from, any premises, and that production or inspection is likely to disclose the commission of an offence under the relevant regulations; or

(b) that any such offence has been, is being or is about to be committed on any premises,

and that any of the conditions specified in sub-paragraph (3) below is met he may by warrant under his hand authorise an officer of an enforcement authority to enter the premises, if need be by force.

(3) The conditions referred to in sub-paragraph (2) above are—

(a) that admission to the premises has been or is likely to be refused and that notice of intention to apply for a warrant under that subparagraph has been given to the occupier;

(b) that an application for admission, or the giving of such a notice, would defeat the object of the entry.

(c) that the premises are unoccupied; and

(d) that the occupier is temporarily absent and it might defeat the object of the entry to await his return.

(4) In sub-paragraph (2) above "relevant", in relation to books, documents, goods or information, means books, documents, goods or information which, under paragraph 3 above, a duly authorised officer may require to be produced or may inspect.

(5) A warrant under sub-paragraph (2) above may be issued only if—

(a) in England and Wales, the justice of the peace is satisfied as required by that sub-paragraph by written information on oath;

(b) in Scotland, the justice of the peace of sheriff is so satisfied by evidence on oath; or

(c) in Northern Ireland, the justice of the peace is so satisfied by compliant on oath.

(6) A warrant under sub-paragraph (2) above shall continue in force for a period of one month.

(7) An officer entering any premises by virtue of this paragraph may take with him such other persons as may appear to him necessary.

(8) On leaving premises which he has entered by virtue of a warrant under sub-para-

graph (2) above, an officer shall, if the premises are unoccupied or the occupier is temporarily absent, leave the premises as effectively secured against trespassers as he found them.

(9) In this paragraph "premises" includes any place (including any vehicle, ship or aircraft) except premises used only as a dwelling.

Obstruction of officers

5.—(1) A person who—

(a) intentionally obstructs an officer of an enforcement authority acting in pursuance of this schedule;

(b) without reasonable excuse fails to comply with a requirement made of him by such an officer under paragraph 3(1) above; or

(c) without reasonable excuse fails to give an officer of an enforcement authority acting in pursuance of this Schedule any other assistance or information which the officer may reasonably require of him for the purpose of the performance of the officer's functions under this Schedule,

shall be guilty of an offence.

(2) A person guilty of an offence under sub-paragraph (1) above shall be liable on summary conviction to a fine not exceeding level 5 on the standard scale.

(3) If a person, in giving any such information as is mentioned in subparagraph (1)(c) above,—

(a) makes a statement which he knows is false in a material particular; or

(b) recklessly makes a statement which is false in a material particular,

he shall be guilty of an offence.

(4) A person guilty of an offence under sub-paragraph (3) above shall be liable—

(a) on summary conviction, to a fine not exceeding level 5 on the standard scale; and

(c) on conviction on indictment, to a fine.

Impersonation of officers

6.—(1) If a person who is not a duly authorised officer of an enforcement authority purports to act as such under this Schedule he shall be guilty of an offence.

(2) A person guilty of an offence under sub-paragraph (1) above shall be liable—

(a) on summary conviction, to a fine not exceeding level 5 on the standard scale; and

(b) on conviction on indictment, to a fine.

Disclosure of information

7.—(1) If a person discloses to another any information obtained by him by virtue of this Schedule he shall be guilty of an offence unless the disclosure was made—

APPENDIX TWO

(a) in or for the purpose of the performance by him or any person of any function under the relevant regulations; or

(b) for a purpose specified in section 38(2)(a), (b) or (c) of the Consumer Protection Act 1987.

(2) a person guilty of an offence under sub-paragraph (1) above shall be liable—

(a) on summary conviction, to a fine not exceeding level 5 of the standards scale; and

(b) on conviction on indictment, to a fine.

Privilege against self-incrimination

8. Nothing in this Schedule requires a person to answer any question or give an information if to do so might incriminate him.

Code of Conduct of the Association of British Travel Agents

CODE OF CONDUCT

The Travel Association

ABTA Ltd	*Issued:* 20 January 2009

THIS CODE, WHICH IS BINDING UPON ALL ABTA MEMBERS, HAS BEEN APPROVED BY THE BOARD OF DIRECTORS

The primary aims of this Code of Conduct are:

- To ensure that the public receives the best possible service from Members
- To maintain and enhance the reputation, standing and good name of ABTA and its Members

This Code of Conduct becomes effective from 20 January 2009 and supersedes the previous issue dated 28 February 2008.

CONTENTS

1. Before booking
2. Making the booking
3. Between booking and travel
4. After departure
5. Communications between Members and consumers and ABTA
6. General conduct
7. Compliance with this Code of Conduct
8. Definitions of terms used in this Code of Conduct
   &
   Liability Insurance Notification Form

This Code of Conduct should be read in conjunction with the following documents, which form an integral part of the Code:

- *ABTA's Standards on Brochures and Booking Conditions*
- *ABTA's Standards on Websites and Online Trading*
- *Guidance on the Application of the Code of Conduct*

Further guidance on the application of this Code of Conduct can be obtained from ABTA.

CODE OF CONDUCT

1. BEFORE A BOOKING IS MADE

What is this section about?	Who does it apply to?
It contains the rules relating to Advertising, Brochures and Websites and ensures that all Clients have adequate information to make the right choice of Travel Arrangements.	Agents and Principals

ABTA MEMBERS SHALL:

Accurate Information

1A) Make every effort to ensure that accurate information is provided to enable Clients to exercise an informed judgement in making their choice of Travel Arrangements.

Brochures and Booking Conditions

1B) Ensure that their Brochures and booking conditions comply with ABTA's Standards on Brochures and Booking Conditions. See *Guidance on the Application of the Code of Conduct*.

Websites and Online Trading

1C) Ensure that their websites and online booking procedures comply with ABTA's Standards on Websites and Online Trading.

Advertising

1D) Ensure that no Advertising or Promotion or any other publication, whether in writing or otherwise, shall contain anything that is likely to mislead the public. See *Guidance on the Application of the Code of Conduct*.

ABTA Logo and Number

1E) Show the ABTA logo and their ABTA number in all Advertising for Travel Arrangements, unless this is impracticable, e.g. on Teletext or where press advertising is in classified run-on form. In these cases the ABTA number must be shown.

Unfair Advertising

1F) Not encourage consumers to make use of travel agents, for example to pick up brochures, without also encouraging them to make a booking with the Agent.

Accessibility

1G) Ensure that, in accordance with the Equality Act 2010, they
   * make reasonable adjustments to the way they deliver their services so that disabled people can use them, and
   * take reasonable steps to tackle physical features of premises that prevent, or make it unreasonably difficult for, disabled people to access their services. See *Guidance on the Application of the Code of Conduct*.

APPENDIX THREE

2. MAKING THE BOOKING

What is this section about?	Who does it apply to?
It's about the booking process and it ensures that all Clients are given the correct information relevant to their particular booking.	Agents and Principals

ABTA MEMBERS SHALL:

Suitable Arrangements

2A) Make every effort to ensure that the Travel Arrangements sold to their Clients are compatible with their Clients' individual requirements.

Booking Procedures

2B) Ensure that satisfactory booking and documentation procedures are followed and, where appropriate, that such procedures are in accordance with the procedures laid down by the Principal. See *Guidance on the Application of the Code of Conduct.*

Financial Protection

2C) Inform Clients about any arrangements that apply to their booking for the protection of their money.

Data Protection

2D) Comply with relevant data protection requirements and ensure that they have in place an effective policy for protecting the privacy of Clients, which shall be available to Clients. See *Guidance on the Application of the Code of Conduct.*

Booking Conditions

2E) Ensure that their Clients are aware of booking and other published conditions, including Agents' terms of business, applicable to their Travel Arrangements before any contract is made and that all Clients have access to a set of booking conditions in written or other appropriate form. See *Guidance on the Application of the Code of Conduct.*

Health Requirements

2F) Before a contract is made, inform their Clients of health requirements that are compulsory for the journeys to be undertaken. Members must also advise Clients travelling abroad to check recommended practice with their GP, practice nurse or travel health clinic. See *Guidance on the Application of the Code of Conduct.*

Passport and Visa Information

2G) Before a contract is made, advise their Clients of passport, visa and other entry and transit requirements for the journeys to be undertaken where it is reasonably practicable for the Members to obtain this information. In other cases, Members shall offer Clients reasonable assistance in obtaining such information. See *Guidance on the Application of the Code of Conduct.*

FCO Advice

2H) Before a contract is made, advise their Clients of the availability of any advice issued by the Foreign & Commonwealth Office. This can be viewed at www.fco.gov.uk/knowbeforeyougo. See *Guidance on the Application of the Code of Conduct.*

CODE OF CONDUCT

Building Works

2I) Ensure that all prospective Clients are alerted to any building works which may reasonably be considered to seriously impair the enjoyment of Travel Arrangements and provide them with accurate information about the extent of the building works. See *Guidance on the Application of the Code of Conduct*.

Insurance - Availability

2J) Before a contract is made, draw their Clients' attention to the advisability of obtaining travel insurance. See *Guidance on the Application of the Code of Conduct*.

Insurance - Suitability

2K) Ensure that any insurance policy issued to a Client is appropriate for the Client's requirements in relation to the nature of travel booked and any hazardous activities that may be undertaken that are known to the Member. See *Guidance on the Application of the Code of Conduct*.

Insurance - Disclosure

2L) Ensure that Clients are aware of the need to comply with the insurance company's requirements and of their duty to disclose to the insurance company all relevant information, e.g. pre-existing illness.

Insurance - Documentation

2M) Ensure that Clients are given, without delay, a document showing the effective start date of cover, the premium paid and the insurance company's name, address and reference number. Principals should provide full written details of cover with the confirmation invoice, or where there is insufficient time to issue a confirmation, provide this to Clients with tickets and documentation provided at the point of departure. See *Guidance on the Application of the Code of Conduct*.

Insurance - Terms of Business

2N) Ensure that they make prompt sales and other financial returns to the insurance provider as required under any agreement with them.

Ticket on Departure

2O) Not impose a charge for the provision of a ticket on departure more than 14 days before the date of departure unless they can show that other means of distribution were not practicable.

Statement for Receipts and Invoices

2P) Ensure that they include the following statement in a prominent position on all receipts and confirmations issued by them:

> *Important Notice. This is an important document. You should retain this as you will need it if your travel arrangements are protected under a scheme of financial protection and you need to make a claim.*

Dispatch of Documents

2Q) Issue and pass on the correct receipts, confirmations, tickets and other relevant documents relating to the Travel Arrangements booked as soon as reasonably practicable. Tickets, unless required to be sent out immediately, must be with Clients a reasonable time before departure. See *Guidance on the Application of the Code of Conduct*.

3. BETWEEN BOOKING AND TRAVEL

What is this section about?	Who does it apply to?
It deals with the conduct of ABTA Members in the period before departure and ensures that changes in this period are correctly dealt with.	The obligations are on Principals but Agents should be aware of their Clients' rights and of the requirements in 3C to inform Clients of alterations.

ABTA MEMBERS SHALL:

Cancellation by Principals

See *Guidance on the Application of the Code of Conduct.*

3A) Not cancel Travel Arrangements after the balance due date unless it is necessary to do so as a result of Force Majeure, or unless the Client defaults in payment of the balance.

Clients' Options on Cancellation

3B) If they are Principals who cancel previously confirmed Travel Arrangements, inform Agents and direct Clients without delay and offer Clients the choice of:

   i) alternative Travel Arrangements if available; or

   ii) a full refund of all monies paid. Such refunds shall be sent to Agents and direct Clients without delay.

Notification of Alterations

3C) Inform their Clients without delay when they are advised of any alterations to Travel Arrangements and Agents shall act as intermediaries between their Principals and Clients in any subsequent negotiations.

Significant Alterations by Principals

See *Guidance on the Application of the Code of Conduct.*

3D) Not make a significant alteration to Travel Arrangements less than 14 days before the departure date of the Travel Arrangements unless it is necessary to do so as a result of Force Majeure.

Clients' Options on Significant Alterations

3E) If they are Principals who make a significant alteration to previously confirmed Travel Arrangements, inform Agents and direct Clients without delay and offer Clients the choice of:

   i) accepting the alteration; or

   ii) cancelling the Travel Arrangements and receiving a full refund of all monies paid. Such refund shall be sent to Agents and direct Clients without delay; or

   iii) alternative Travel Arrangements of comparable standard, if available.

Compensation for Cancellation or Alterations

3F) If they are Principals who cancel or make a significant alteration to previously confirmed Travel Arrangements for reasons other than Force Majeure on or after the balance due date, offer Clients reasonable compensation, in addition to the requirements in 3B or 3E. Such compensation may be offered in accordance with a rising scale of payments calculated so that the nearer to the time of departure that the alteration occurs, the higher the level of compensation to be paid.

Cancellation or Amendment Invoices

3G)   Issue any cancellation or amendment invoice as soon as reasonably practicable.

Overbooking

3H)   Take all reasonable steps to ensure that Travel Arrangements are not cancelled or altered as a result of overbooking. See *Guidance on the Application of the Code of Conduct*.

Building Works

3I)   If they are Principals who become aware or ought reasonably to have become aware of building works which may reasonably be considered to seriously impair the enjoyment of Travel Arrangements, notify Clients of the situation without undue delay, provide them with accurate information about the extent of the building works and offer them the opportunity to transfer to alternative Travel Arrangements. Where the alternative constitutes a significant alteration to the Travel Arrangements in line with 3E above, the provisions of that clause are to be followed.

Surcharges

3J)   When selling Packages, comply with the Package Travel Regulations 1992, including the rule against surcharging inside 30 days of departure and the obligation to absorb an amount equal to 2% of the holiday cost. Information for Members can be found in the *Business Support Manual*, including the procedure for notifying ABTA of proposed surcharges.

APPENDIX THREE

4. AFTER DEPARTURE

What is this section about?	Who does it apply to?
This section deals with the conduct of ABTA Members once Travel Arrangements have commenced. It contains the rules relating to changes to Travel Arrangements and contact details and assistance if something goes wrong.	Principals

ABTA PRINCIPALS SHALL:

Alterations or Cancellations

4A) Where they make a significant alteration to or cancel a contract for Travel Arrangements after departure, ensure that suitable alternative arrangements are made at no extra cost to Clients. See *Guidance on the Application of the Code of Conduct*.

Package Arrangements

4B) With regard to Packages, where it is impossible to make suitable alternative arrangements or where these are not accepted by Clients for good reason, provide Clients, where appropriate, with equivalent transport back to the place of departure or to another place to which Clients have agreed.

Compensation

4C) Where appropriate, compensate Clients. See *Guidance on the Application of the Code of Conduct*.

Contact Numbers

4D) Provide contact details so that Clients can contact them during their stay. This should be the name, address and phone number of their representative in the area, or, if there is no representative, of an agency on whom Clients in difficulty can call, or, if there is none, a phone number or other information to contact the Principal.

Additional Assistance

4E) Where appropriate and subject to their reasonable discretion, provide prompt assistance to Clients in difficulty.

5. COMMUNICATIONS BETWEEN MEMBERS AND CONSUMERS AND ABTA

What is this section about?	Who does it apply to?
It contains the rules relating to the timescales for responding to correspondence as well as dispute handling and the ABTA Arbitration Scheme and ensures that complaints are well handled.	Agents and Principals

ABTA MEMBERS SHALL:

Confidentiality

5A) Treat all transactions and communications with Clients as confidential.

Correspondence with Clients

5B) Deal with all correspondence with Clients as promptly as possible and, in any event, within the following time limits:

   i) an acknowledgement shall be sent not later than 14 days from the date of receipt of correspondence and

   ii) detailed reply, or a reply containing a detailed explanation for any delay, shall be sent not later than 28 days from the date of receipt of correspondence. See *Guidance on the Application of the Code of Conduct.*

Correspondence with ABTA

5C) Ensure that, where ABTA requires a response to correspondence within a specified period, such response is sent within that period. See *Guidance on the Application of the Code of Conduct.*

Dealing with Disputes

5D) Make every reasonable effort to reach a speedy solution in the event of a dispute with a Client. Members must also deal with a Client's formally appointed representative in the same way.

Agents' Responsibilities

5E) If they are an Agent, make every reasonable effort to deal with complaints of a minor and general character with a view to avoiding recourse to Principals. When complaints are of such a nature that reference to the Principal is necessary, they shall use their best endeavours acting as an intermediary to bring about a satisfactory conclusion.

ABTA Arbitration

5F) Allow any dispute arising out of an alleged breach of contract or negligence by them to be referred to the arbitration scheme arranged by the Board of Directors. It shall be subject to such time, financial and other restrictions as from time to time shall apply. See *Guidance on the Application of the Code of Conduct.*

Rules of ABTA Arbitration

5G) Comply with the terms, rules and regulations of the Arbitration Scheme referred to in clause F above..

6. GENERAL CONDUCT

What is this section about?	Who does it apply to?
The general conduct of ABTA Members in areas that are not covered more specifically elsewhere in this Code of Conduct.	Principals in respect of all but 6G and 6J. Agents in respect of all but 6K.

ABTA MEMBERS SHALL:

Standard of Service

6A) Maintain a high standard of service to Clients.

Disrepute

6B) Not bring ABTA or its membership into disrepute.

Compliance with the Law

6C) Comply with all relevant statutory and regulatory requirements.

Awareness of this Code

6D) Ensure that they and their staff are familiar with the provisions of this Code of Conduct.

Misrepresentation of ABTA Membership

6E) Not, directly or indirectly, represent a non-ABTA member as a Member in any way. Members must also not permit or assist in any way a non-ABTA member to represent itself as a Member.

Trading Names

6F) Notify ABTA in writing of their trading names, before they start using them. For the purposes of this paragraph, trading name means a name that is not the formal legal name under which ABTA membership is registered.

Public Notices

6G) If they are Agents, display in a prominent position at each of their offices which is open to the public, their certificate of membership currently in force and an ABTA information notice in such form as the Board of Directors may from time to time approve but which shall include the words: *We act as agent only for selected operators*. The current form of notice can be seen on the ABTA website.

Payment of Debts

6H) Settle all debts due without delay or within any period agreed with the creditor. A continued failure to do so shall constitute prima facie evidence of an inability to meet liabilities under Article 12(1) of the Articles of Association.

CODE OF CONDUCT

Client Refunds

6I) Apply for and forward to clients any applicable refund without delay. See *Guidance on the Application of the Code of Conduct*.

Contact Details

6J) If they are Agents, supply on request to ABTA a telephone number where they may be contacted outside office hours to facilitate emergency contact by Principals.

Liability Insurance

6K) If they are Principals, ensure that they obtain liability insurance to cover claims made by clients. They shall ensure that evidence that liability insurance has been obtained is supplied to ABTA within 28 days of the commencement of such insurance policy by either completing the Liability Insurance Notification form or by confirmation from their insurance broker. Acceptance by ABTA of such evidence is not an acceptance by ABTA of the adequacy of such insurance. See *Guidance on the Application of the Code of Conduct*.

Representations about Financial Status

6L) Not make any representations about the financial status of any other Member.

Business Support

6M) Accurately complete and return the checklists contained in the *Business Support Manual* as requested and comply with requests made by ABTA in connection with the checklists.

APPENDIX THREE

7. COMPLIANCE WITH THIS CODE OF CONDUCT

What is this section about?	Who does it apply to?
This section deals with how compliance with this Code of Conduct is enforced.	Agents and Principals

ABTA MEMBERS SHALL:

Investigation and Enforcement

7A)   Co-operate in any investigation undertaken by ABTA into an alleged breach of this Code of Conduct and follow the following procedures for investigation and enforcement:

Allegations of Infringement

7B)   If any infringement of this Code is alleged against a Member, the facts shall be reported to ABTA for preliminary investigation.

Provision of Information

7C)   The Member against whom the allegation has been made shall provide, at the request of ABTA, such further information or documents as may be required within such a period as may be specified.

Fixed Penalty Offences

7D)   Where ABTA, after due investigation, has reason to believe that a Member has committed a fixed penalty offence as set out below, ABTA may issue the Member with a fixed penalty notice in respect of the offences.

The following breaches of this Code by a Member constitute a fixed penalty offence and attract a fine of £400, which may be varied by the Board of Directors from time to time:

1 B, C, E
2 O, Q
3 G, J
5 B, C
6 F, G, H, I

Apparent breaches of the remaining Clauses of this Code are not fixed penalty offences and therefore shall be referred to the Code of Conduct Committee. ABTA has at all times the discretion to refer directly to the Code of Conduct Committee all alleged breaches of this Code including breaches of this Code which would normally constitute a fixed penalty offence.

Dealing with Fixed Penalty Notices

7E) Where ABTA issues a fixed penalty notice the Member may:

(a) pay the fine within 14 days as set out in the fixed penalty notice; or

(b) request in writing to ABTA that the matter be referred to the Code of Conduct Committee.

Reference to the Code of Conduct Committee

7F) Where the Member fails to pay the fine within the specified period, or requests the matter be referred to the Code of Conduct Committee, or fails to respond to the fixed penalty notice, ABTA shall refer the matter to the Code of Conduct Committee. ABTA shall not refer the matter to the Code of Conduct Committee until the period specified in the fixed penalty notice has expired. The Code of Conduct Committee has the powers granted in paragraph J below and may impose a penalty higher than the £400 imposed by the fixed penalty notice.

Undertakings

7G) Where ABTA, after due investigation, has reason to believe that the facts alleged against the Member constitute infringement of this Code, ABTA may, at its discretion, require the Member to give to ABTA undertakings as to its future conduct. Where the Member refuses to give such undertakings the Secretariat shall refer the matter to the Code of Conduct Committee.

Breach of Undertakings

7H) Where ABTA, after due investigation, has reason to believe that the facts alleged against the Member constitute a breach of an undertaking given by a Member in accordance with Clause 7G above ABTA shall refer the matter to the Code of Conduct Committee.

Procedure for Reference to the Code of Conduct Committee

7I) Where ABTA, after due investigation, has reason to believe that the facts alleged against the Member constitute infringement of this Code, the facts may be submitted to the Code of Conduct Committee who shall give the Member at least 14 days' notice in writing of the time and place of hearing of the complaint. The Member shall be entitled to make representations at the hearing either personally (with or without legal representation) or in writing.

Decisions of the Code of Conduct Committee

7J) The Code of Conduct Committee shall have the power to impose a reprimand or a fine or to suspend or terminate membership of ABTA or to require the Member to provide an undertaking in a form determined by the Code of Conduct Committee. The decision of the Code of Conduct Committee shall be notified to the Member, who shall have the right, exercisable within 14 days after the service of the notice upon him, to appeal to the Appeal Board against such decision.

If the Member does not appeal, then at the expiration of the 14 day period, he shall be liable to sustain the reprimand or pay the fine or his membership of ABTA shall be suspended or terminated.

Appeals

7K) The Appeal Board shall be constituted in accordance with Article 13 of the Articles of Association. A member wishing to appeal shall complete the Notice of Appeal and send this to ABTA along with the required appeal fee.

APPENDIX THREE

If the decision appealed against is a fine, the Member shall also enclose payment of the fine. If the appeal is successful the Association shall repay the fine, or any part thereof deemed refundable by the Appeal Board, to the Member together with interest thereon at a rate to be decided from time to time by the Board of Directors.

If the decision appealed against is a reprimand, suspension or termination of membership, the decision shall not take effect unless and to the extent that it is confirmed or varied by the Appeal Board.

The Member will be give at least 14 days' notice of the date of the appeal hearing. The Appeal Board shall determine the appeal as it sees fit. The decision will be notified to the appellant in writing and will then be communicated to the Board of Directors.

Publication of Decisions

7L) The Board of Directors shall arrange for decisions of the Code of Conduct Committee and the reasons therefore to be published.

8. DEFINITIONS

For the purposes of this Code of Conduct, definitions are as follows:

ABTA: ABTA Ltd.

Advertising: a means of promoting Travel Arrangements by any printed, viewable, audible or other form.

Agent: a Member or other person, company or firm when carrying on business as an agent for a Principal.

Appeal Board: A body established by the Board of Directors, under Article 13 of the Articles of Association, to determine appeals and comprising at least one person from the following categories: a solicitor or barrister of not less than 10 years' standing; a person having no financial interest in, or business connection with, the travel industry; and a Member unconnected with the case under appeal.

Articles of Association: ABTA's Articles of Association.

ATOL Regulations: The Civil Aviation (Air Travel Organisers' Licensing) Regulations 1995.

Board of Directors: ABTA's Board of Directors.

Brochure: a communication in any printed, viewable, audible or other form which specifies the contents of Travel Arrangements offered by a Member in sufficient detail to allow a Client to reliably book the Travel Arrangements without obtaining additional information from the Member.

Client: a person, company or firm acting in a personal or business capacity who is a consumer or prospective consumer of the Travel Arrangements offered by a Member.

Code of Conduct Committee: A Committee, established by the Board of Directors under Article 11 of the Articles of Association, to exercise its powers of administering or enforcing this Code of Conduct.

Force Majeure: circumstances where performance and/or prompt performance of the contract is prevented by reasons of unusual and unforeseeable circumstances beyond the control of the Principal, the consequences of which could not have been avoided even if all due care had been exercised. Such circumstances include war or threat of war, riot, civil strife, industrial dispute (as defined below), terrorist activity, natural or nuclear disaster, fire or adverse weather conditions.

Industrial Dispute: a dispute which affects the services to be provided under a Package which the Principal cannot reasonably be expected to overcome by substituting comparable alternative arrangements other than a dispute between the Principal and his employees.

Member: a Member of ABTA.

On-line: websites (which term shall include individual web pages) and electronic or digital media accessible by consumers, including software, whether or not a live communication link is established.

APPENDIX THREE

Package: a pre-arranged combination of at least two of the following three components when sold or offered for sale at an inclusive price and when the service covers a period of more than 24 hours or includes overnight accommodation:

    a) transport;

    b) accommodation;

    c) other services not ancillary to transport or accommodation and forming a significant part of the package.

Principal: a Member or other person, company or firm who enters into a contract with, or who holds himself out as being able to enter into a contract with, the Client under which he agrees to supply Travel Arrangements, or a Member or other person, company or firm who supplies Travel Arrangements, or who holds himself out as being able to supply Travel Arrangements, under the terms of an ATOL.

Promotions: activities designed to stimulate the sale or purchase of Travel Arrangements offered by a Member by means other than Advertising as defined above.

Travel Arrangements: all services sold by or on behalf of Members including, but not exclusively, transport services, accommodation services, other travel services and Packages as defined above.

CODE OF CONDUCT

PRINCIPAL'S LIABILITY INSURANCE NOTIFICATION FORM

FOR ALL MEMBERS WITH RELEVANT PRINCIPAL/TOUR OPERATOR BUSINESS

NAME OF MEMBER: .... ABTA NO: ....

ADDRESS: ....

THIS FORM MUST BE COMPLETED AND SENT TO ABTA ON AN ANNUAL BASIS, AS EVIDENCE OF COMPLIANCE WITH CLAUSE 6K OF THE CODE OF CONDUCT.

PLEASE NOTE THAT EMPLOYER'S LIABILITY INSURANCE COVER IS <u>NOT</u> SUFFICIENT FOR THIS PURPOSE.

✓ complete section A then

✓ provide a copy of your policy and certificate of insurance OR

✓ ask your insurer/broker to complete section B and return the form to ABTA

SECTION A THE MAIN POLICY DETAILS   **To be completed by ABTA Member**

Name of Insurer: ....

Policy Number: ....

Period of Cover: From ....   To: ....

Name of Insurance Broker (if applicable): ....

I hereby certify that the insurance policy detailed above, indemnifies me/us in respect of legal liability arising from my/our business as a Tour Operator/Principal, including liability as an Organiser as defined in The Package Travel, Package Tours and Package Holidays Regulations 1992.

☐   NB Standard policies may contain exclusions, which mean that they do not fully cover your liability as an Organiser; for example, an exclusion of liability arising from the use of motor vehicles, ships and aircraft. Please tick this box to confirm that you are fully covered. This can be done by ensuring that your policy contains an adjustment for this exclusion or by purchasing an additional policy.

Name: ....

Email: ....

Contact No: ....

Signature: .... Date: ....

Continued....

APPENDIX THREE

We (full name of Insurer/Insurance Broker)..

of (address) ....

....

hereby certify that the insurance policy detailed in Section A indemnifies

....….................. (name of ABTA Member)

in respect of legal liability arising from their business as a Tour Operator/Principal, including liability arising as an Organiser as defined in The Package Travel, Package Tours and Package Holidays Regulations 1992.

This is in respect of the ABTA Member's obligation under Clause 6K of the ABTA Code of Conduct which states that ABTA Members shall, "If they are Principals, ensure that they obtain liability insurance to cover claims made by clients. They shall ensure that evidence that liability insurance has been obtained is supplied to ABTA within 28 days of the commencement of such insurance policy by either completing the Liability Insurance Notification form or by confirmation from their insurance broker. Acceptance by ABTA of such evidence is not an acceptance by ABTA of the adequacy of such insurance."

Name: ....

Email: ....

Contact No: ....

Signature: ....   Date: ....

PLEASE SEND TO:
LEGAL DEPARTMENT, ABTA, 30 PARK STREET, LONDON SE1 9EQ. FAX: 020 3117 0581, EMAIL: businesssupport@abta.co.uk

538

Bibliography

The following sources are referred to in the text or were used in the preparation of the book.

Blackshaw, C., *Aviation Law and Regulation* (Pitman, 1992).

Bragg, Richard, *Trade Descriptions* (Oxford: Clarendon Press, 1991).

Butterworths Trading and Consumer Law (1993–).

Cheshire, Fifoot & Furmstons Law of Contract, edited by M.P. Furmston, 15th edn (Butterworths, 2006).

Chitty on Contracts, edited by H. Beale et al., 30th edn (2011)

Clarke, Malcolm A., *Contracts of Carriage by Air* (LLP, 2002).

Cordato, A., *Australian Travel and Tourism Law*, 4th edn (Australia: Butterworths, 2006).

Dickerson, T., *Travel Law* (New York: Law Journals Seminars Press, 1981–2011).

Diederiks-Verschoor, I.H.Ph., *An Introduction to Air Law*, 8th edn (Kluwer Law International, 2006).

Giemulla, E. et al. (eds), *Montreal Convention* (Wolters Kluwer, 2006).

International Travel Law Journal (I.T.L.J.) (formerly *Travel Law Journal*), Travel Law Centre, University of Northumbria (1997–2006) (*http://tlc.unn.ac.uk*).

McKendrick, Ewan, *Contract Law*, 9th edn (Palgrave, 2011).

Poole, Jill, *Textbook on Contract*, 10th edn (Oxford University Press, 2009).

Saggerson, Alan, *Travel Law and Litigation*, 4th edn (xpl, 2008).

Shawcross and Beaumont on Air Law, edited by D. McLean et al., (LexisNexis, 1991–).

Travel Law Journal (T.L.J.) (now *International Travel Law Journal*), Travel Law Centre, University of Northumbria (1994–1996).

Travel Law Quarterly (T.L.Q.) (Oakhurst Academic Press, 2009–2012) (www.tlq.travel).

Treitel on the Law of Contract, edited by E. Peel, 13th edn (2011).

Vrancken, Patrick et al., *Tourism and the Law* (Butterworths, 2002).

Yates, D., *Exclusion Clauses in Contracts*, 2nd edn (Sweet & Maxwell, 1982).

Index

LEGAL TAXONOMY
FROM SWEET & MAXWELL

This index has been prepared using Sweet and Maxwell's Legal Taxonomy. Main index entries conform to keywords provided by the Legal Taxonomy except where references to specific documents or non-standard terms (denoted by quotation marks) have been included. These keywords provide a means of identifying similar concepts in other Sweet & Maxwell publications and online services to which keywords from the Legal Taxonomy have been applied. Readers may find some minor differences between terms used in the text and those which appear in the index. Suggestions to *sweetandmaxwell.taxonomy @thomson.com*.

(all references are to page number)

INDEX

INDEX

INDEX

INDEX

INDEX

INDEX

555

INDEX

INDEX

INDEX

INDEX

INDEX

INDEX